Clement of Alexandria

The Stromata or Miscellanies

Clement of Alexandria
The Stromata or Miscellanies

Clement of Alexandria
The Stromata or Miscellanies

© Lighthouse Publishing 2018

All rights reserved. Without limiting the rights under copyright reserved above, no part of this publication may be reproduced, stored in a retrieval system, or transmitted, in any form or by any means (electronic, mechanical, photocopying, recording or otherwise), without the prior written permission of the copyright owner of this book.

Published by
Lighthouse Christian Publishing
SAN 257-4330
5531 Dufferin Drive
Savage, Minnesota, 55378
United States of America

www.lighthousechristianpublishing.com

THE STROMATA, OR MISCELLANIES

Book I

CHAPTER I.—PREFACE—THE AUTHOR'S OBJECT—THE UTILITY OF WRITTEN COMPOSITIONS.

[*Wants the beginning*] .... that you may read them under your hand, and may be able to preserve them. Whether written compositions are not to be left behind at all; or if they are, by whom? And if the former, what need there is for written compositions? and if the latter, is the composition of them to be assigned to earnest men, or the opposite? It were certainly ridiculous for one to disapprove of the writing of earnest men, and approve of those, who are not such, engaging in the work of composition. Theopompus and Timæus, who composed fables and slanders, and Epicurus the leader of atheism, and Hipponax and Archilochus, are to be allowed to write in their own shameful manner. But he who proclaims the truth is to be prevented from leaving behind him what is to benefit posterity. It is a good thing, I reckon, to leave to posterity good children. This is the case with children of our bodies. But words are the progeny of the soul. Hence we call those who have instructed us, fathers. Wisdom is a communicative and philanthropic thing. Accordingly, Solomon says, "My son, if thou receive the saying of my commandment, and hide it with thee, thine ear shall hear wisdom." He points out that the word that is sown is hidden in the soul of the learner, as in the earth, and this is spiritual planting. Wherefore also he adds, "And thou shalt apply thine heart to understanding, and apply it for the admonition of thy son." For soul, methinks, joined with soul, and spirit with spirit, in the sowing of the word, will make that which is sown grow and germinate. And every one who is instructed, is in respect of subjection the son of his instructor. "Son," says he, "forget not my laws."

And if knowledge belong not to all (set an ass to the lyre, as the proverb goes), yet written compositions are for the many. "Swine, for instance, delight in dirt more than in clean water." "Wherefore," says the Lord, "I speak to them in parables: because seeing, they see not; and hearing, they hear not, and do not understand;" not as if the Lord caused the ignorance: for it were impious to think so. But He prophetically exposed this ignorance, that existed in them, and intimated that they would not understand the things spoken. And now the Savior shows Himself, out of His abundance, dispensing goods to His servants according to the ability of the recipient, that they may augment them by exercising activity, and then returning to reckon with them; when, approving of those that had increased His money, those faithful in little, and commanding them to have the charge over many things,
He bade them enter into the joy of the Lord. But to him who had hid the money, entrusted to him to be given out at interest, and had given it back as he had received it, without increase,
He said, "Thou wicked and slothful servant, thou ought to have given my money to the bankers, and at my coming I should have received mine own." Wherefore the useless servant "shall be cast into outer darkness." "Thou, therefore, be strong," says Paul, "in the grace that is in Christ Jesus. And the things which thou hast heard of me among many witnesses, the same commit thou to faithful men, who shall be able to teach others also." And again: "Study to show thyself approved unto God, a workman that needed not to be ashamed, rightly dividing the word of truth."

If, then, both proclaim the Word—the one by writing, the other by speech—are not both then to be approved, making, as they do, faith active by love? It is by one's own fault that he does not choose what is best; God is free of blame. As to the point in hand, it is the business of some to lay out the word at interest, and of others to test it, and either choose it or not. And the judgment is determined within themselves. But there is that species of knowledge which is characteristic of the herald, and that which is, as it were, characteristic of a messenger, and it is serviceable in whatever way it operates, both by the hand and tongue. "For he that sowed to the Spirit, shall of the Spirit reap life everlasting. And let us not be weary in well-doing." On him who by Divine Providence meets in with it, it confers the very highest advantages,—the beginning of faith, readiness for adopting a right mode of life, the impulse towards the truth, a movement of inquiry, a trace of knowledge; in a word, it gives the means of salvation. And those who have been rightly reared in the words of truth, and received provision for eternal life, wing their way to heaven. Most admirably, therefore, the apostle says, "In everything approving ourselves as the servants of God; as poor, and yet making many rich; as having nothing, yet possessing all things. Our mouth is opened to you." "I charge thee," he says, writing to Timothy, "before God, and Christ Jesus, and the elect angels, that thou observe these things, without preferring one before another, doing nothing by partiality."

Both must therefore test themselves: the one, if he is qualified to speak and leave behind him written records; the other, if he is in a right state to hear and read: as also some in the dispensation of the Eucharist, according to custom enjoin that each one of the people individually should take his part. One's own conscience is best for choosing accurately or shunning. And its firm foundation is a right life, with suitable instruction. But the imitation of those who have already been proved, and who have led correct lives, is most excellent for the understanding and practice of the commandments. "So that whosoever shall eat the bread and drink the cup of the Lord unworthily, shall be guilty of the body and blood of the

Lord. But let a man examine himself, and so let him eat of the bread and drink of the cup." It therefore follows, that every one of those who undertake to promote the good of their neighbors, ought to consider whether he has betaken himself to teaching rashly and out of rivalry to any; if his communication of the word is out of vainglory; if the only reward he reaps is the salvation of those who hear, and if he speaks not in order to win favor: if so, he who speaks by writings escapes the reproach of mercenary motives. "For neither at any time used we flattering words, as ye know," says the apostle, "nor a cloak of covetousness. God is witness. Nor of men sought we glory, neither of you, nor yet of others, when we might have been burdensome as the apostles of Christ. But we were gentle among you, even as a nurse cherishes her children."

In the same way, therefore, those who take part in the divine words, ought to guard against betaking themselves to this, as they would to the building of cities, to examine them out of curiosity; that they do not come to the task for the sake of receiving worldly things, having ascertained that they who are consecrated to Christ are given to communicate the necessaries of life. But let such be dismissed as hypocrites. But if any one wishes not to seem, but to be righteous, to him it belongs to know the things which are best. If, then, "the harvest is plenteous, but the laborers few," it is incumbent on us "to pray" that there may be as great abundance of laborers as possible.

But the husbandry is twofold,—the one unwritten, and the other written. And in whatever way the Lord's laborer sow the good wheat, and grow and reap the ears, he shall appear a truly divine husbandman. "Labor," says the Lord, "not for the meat which perishes, but for that which endures to everlasting life." And nutriment is received both by bread and by words. And truly "blessed are the peace-makers," who instructing those who are at war in their life and errors here, lead them back to the peace which is in the Word, and nourish for the life which is according to God, by the distribution of the bread, those "that hunger after righteousness." For each soul has its own proper nutriment; some growing by knowledge and science, and others feeding on the Hellenic philosophy, the whole of which, like nuts, is not eatable. "And he that planted and he that watered," "being ministers" of Him "that gives the increase, are one" in the ministry. "But every one shall receive his own reward, according to his own work. For we are God's husbandmen, God's husbandry. Ye are God's building," according to the apostle. Wherefore the hearers are not permitted to apply the test of comparison. Nor is the word, given for investigation, to be committed to those who have been reared in the arts of all kinds of words, and in the power of inflated attempts at proof; whose minds are already pre-occupied, and have not been previously emptied. But whoever chooses to banquet on faith, is steadfast for the reception of the divine words, having acquired already faith as a power of judging, according to reason. Hence ensues to him persuasion in abundance. And this was the meaning of that saying of prophecy, "If ye believe not, neither shall ye understand." "As, then, we have opportunity, let us do good to all, especially to the household of faith." And let each of these, according to the

blessed David, sing, giving thanks. "Thou shalt sprinkle me with hyssop, and I shall be cleansed. Thou shalt wash me, and I shall be whiter than the snow. Thou shalt make me to hear gladness and joy, and the bones which have been humbled shall rejoice. Turn Thy face from my sins. Blot out mine iniquities. Create in me a clean heart, O God, and renew a right spirit in my inward parts. Cast me not away from Thy face, and take not Thy Holy Spirit from me. Restore to me the joy of Thy salvation, and establish me with Thy princely spirit."

He who addresses those who are present before him, both tests them by time, and judges by his judgment, and from the others distinguishes him who can hear; watching the words, the manners, the habits, the life, the motions, the attitudes, the look, the voice; the road, the rock, the beaten path, the fruitful land, the wooded region, the fertile and fair and cultivated spot, that is able to multiply the seed. But he that speaks through books, consecrates himself before God, crying in writing thus: Not for gain, not for vainglory, not to be vanquished by partiality, nor enslaved by fear nor elated by pleasure; but only to reap the salvation of those who read, which he does, not at present participate in, but awaiting in expectation the recompense which will certainly be rendered by Him, who has promised to bestow on the laborers the reward that is meet. But he who is enrolled in the number of men ought not to desire recompense. For he that vaunts his good services, receives glory as his reward. And he who does any duty for the sake of recompense, is he not held fast in the custom of the world, either as one who has done well, hastening to receive a reward, or as an evil-doer avoiding retribution? We must, as far as we can, imitate the Lord. And he will do so, who complies with the will of God, receiving freely, giving freely, and receiving as a worthy reward the citizenship itself. "The hire of a harlot shall not come into the sanctuary," it is said: accordingly it was forbidden to bring to the altar the price of a dog. And in whomsoever the eye of the soul has been blinded by ill-nurture and teaching, let him advance to the true light, to the truth, which shows by writing the things that are unwritten. "Ye that thirst, go to the waters," says Esaias. And "drink water from thine own vessels," Solomon exhorts. Accordingly in "The Laws," the philosopher who learned from the Hebrews, Plato, commands husbandmen not to irrigate or take water from others, until they have first dug down in their own ground to what is called the virgin soil, and found it dry. For it is right to supply want, but it is not well to support laziness. For Pythagoras said that, "although it be agreeable to reason to take a share of a burden, it is not a duty to take it away."

Now the Scripture kindles the living spark of the soul, and directs the eye suitably for contemplation; perchance inserting something, as the husbandman when he engrafts, but, according to the opinion of the divine apostle, exciting what is in the soul. "For there are certainly among us many weak and sickly, and many sleep. But if we judge ourselves, we shall not be judged." Now this work of mine in writing is not artfully constructed for display; but my memoranda are stored up against old age, as a remedy against forgetfulness, truly an image and outline of those vigorous and animated discourses which I was privileged to hear, and of blessed and truly remarkable men.

Of these the one, in Greece, an Ionic; the other in Magna Græcia: the first of these from Coele-Syria, the second from Egypt, and others in the East. The one was born in the land of Assyria, and the other a Hebrew in Palestine.

When I came upon the last (he was the first in power), having tracked him out concealed in Egypt, I found rest. He, the true, the Sicilian bee, gathering the spoil of the flowers of the prophetic and apostolic meadow, engendered in the souls of his hearers a deathless element of knowledge.

Well, they preserving the tradition of the blessed doctrine derived directly from the holy apostles, Peter, James, John, and Paul, the sons receiving it from the father (but few were like the fathers), came by God's will to us also to deposit those ancestral and apostolic seeds. And well I know that they will exult; I do not mean delighted with this tribute, but solely on account of the preservation of the truth, according as they delivered it. For such a sketch as this, will, I think, be agreeable to a soul desirous of preserving from escape the blessed tradition. "In a man who loves wisdom the father will be glad." Wells, when pumped out, yield purer water; and that of which no one partakes, turns to putrefaction. Use keeps steel brighter, but disuse produces rust in it. For, in a word, exercise produces a healthy condition both in souls and bodies. "No one lighted a candle, and put it under a bushel, but upon a candlestick, that it may give light to those who are regarded worthy of the feast." For what is the use of wisdom, if it makes not him who can hear it wise? For still the Savior saves, "and always works, as He sees the Father." For by teaching, one learns more; and in speaking, one is often a hearer along with his audience. For the teacher of him who speaks and of him who hears is one—who waters both the mind and the word. Thus the Lord did not hinder from doing good while keeping the Sabbath; but allowed us to communicate of those divine mysteries, and of that holy light, to those who are able to receive them. He did not certainly disclose to the many what did not belong to the many; but to the few to whom He knew that they belonged, who were capable of receiving and being molded according to them. But secret things are entrusted to speech, not to writing, as is the case with God.

And if one say that it is written, "There is nothing secret which shall not be revealed, nor hidden which shall not be disclosed," let him also hear from us, that to him who hears secretly, even what is secret shall be manifested. This is what was predicted by this oracle. And to him who is able secretly to observe what is delivered to him, that which is veiled shall be disclosed as truth; and what is hidden to the many, shall appear manifest to the few. For why do not all know the truth? why is not righteousness loved, if righteousness belongs to all? But the mysteries are delivered mystically, that what is spoken may be in the mouth of the speaker; rather not in his voice, but in his understanding. "God gave to the Church, some apostles, and some prophets, and some evangelists, and some pastors and teachers, for the perfecting of the saints, for the work of the ministry, for the edifying of the body of Christ."

The writing of these memoranda of mine, I well know, is weak when compared with that spirit, full of grace, which I was privileged to hear. But it will be an image to recall the archetype to him who was struck with the thyrsus. For "speak," it is said, "to a wise man, and he will grow wiser; and to him that hath, and there shall be added to him." And we profess not to explain secret things sufficiently—far from it—but only to recall them to memory, whether we have forgot aught, or whether for the purpose of not forgetting. Many things, I well know, have escaped us, through length of time, that have dropped away unwritten. Whence, to aid the weakness of my memory, and provide for myself a salutary help to my recollection in a systematic arrangement of chapters, I necessarily make use of this form. There are then some things of which we have no recollection; for the power that was in the blessed men was great. There are also some things which remained unnoted long, which have now escaped; and others which are effaced, having faded away in the mind itself, since such a task is not easy to those not experienced; these I revive in my commentaries. Some things I purposely omit, in the exercise of a wise selection, afraid to write what I guarded against speaking: not grudging—for that were wrong—but fearing for my readers, lest they should stumble by taking them in a wrong sense; and, as the proverb says, we should be found "reaching a sword to a child." For it is impossible that what has been written should not escape, although remaining unpublished by me. But being always revolved, using the one only voice, that of writing, they answer nothing to him that makes inquiries beyond what is written; for they require of necessity the aid of someone, either of him who wrote, or of someone else who has walked in his footsteps. Some things my treatise will hint; on some it will linger; some it will merely mention. It will try to speak imperceptibly, to exhibit secretly, and to demonstrate silently. The dogmas taught by remarkable sects will be adduced; and to these will be opposed all that ought to be premised in accordance with the profoundest contemplation of the knowledge, which, as we proceed to the renowned and venerable canon of tradition, from the creation of the world, will advance to our view; setting before us what according to natural contemplation necessarily has to be treated of beforehand, and clearing off what stands in the way of this arrangement. So that we may have our ears ready for the reception of the tradition of true knowledge; the soil being previously cleared of the thorns and of every weed by the husbandman, in order to the planting of the vine. For there is a contest, and the prelude to the contest; and there are some mysteries before other mysteries.

Our book will not shrink from making use of what is best in philosophy and other preparatory instruction. "For not only for the Hebrews and those that are under the law," according to the apostle, "is it right to become a Jew, but also a Greek for the sake of the Greeks, that we may gain all." Also in the Epistle to the Colossians he writes, "Admonishing every man, and teaching every man in all wisdom, that we may present every man perfect in Christ." The nicety of speculation, too, suits the sketch presented in my commentaries.

In this respect the resources of learning are like a relish mixed with the food of an athlete, who is not indulging in luxury, but entertains a noble desire for distinction.

By music we harmoniously relax the excessive tension of gravity. And as those who wish to address the people, do so often by the herald, that what is said may be better heard; so also in this case. For we have the word, that was spoken to many, before the common tradition. Wherefore we must set forth the opinions and utterances which cried individually to them, by which those who hear shall more readily turn.

And, in truth, to speak briefly: Among many small pearls there is the one; and in a great take of fish there is the beauty-fish; and by time and toil truth will gleam forth, if a good helper is at hand. For most benefits are supplied, from God, through men. All of us who make use of our eyes see what is presented before them. But some look at objects for one reason, others for another. For instance, the cook and the shepherd do not survey the sheep similarly: for the one examines it if it be fat; the other watches to see if it be of good breed. Let a man milk the sheep's milk if he need sustenance: let him shear the wool if he need clothing. And in this way let me produce the fruit of the Greek erudition.

For I do not imagine that any composition can be so fortunate as that no one will speak against it. But that is to be regarded as in accordance with reason, which nobody speaks against, with reason. And that course of action and choice is to be approved, not which is faultless, but which no one rationally finds fault with. For it does not follow, that if a man accomplishes anything not purposely, he does it through force of circumstances. But he will do it, managing it by wisdom divinely given, and in accommodation to circumstances. For it is not he who has virtue that needs the way to virtue, any more than he, that is strong, needs recovery. For, like farmers who irrigate the land beforehand, so we also water with the liquid stream of Greek learning what in it is earthy; so that it may receive the spiritual seed cast into it, and may be capable of easily nourishing it. The *Stromata* will contain the truth mixed up in the dogmas of philosophy, or rather covered over and hidden, as the edible part of the nut in the shell. For, in my opinion, it is fitting that the seeds of truth be kept for the husbandmen of faith, and no others. I am not oblivious of what is babbled by some, who in their ignorance are frightened at every noise, and say that we ought to occupy ourselves with what is most necessary, and which contains the faith; and that we should pass over what is beyond and superfluous, which wears out and detains us to no purpose, in things which conduce nothing to the great end. Others think that philosophy was introduced into life by an evil influence, for the ruin of men, by an evil inventor. But I shall show, throughout the whole of these *Stromata*, that evil has an evil nature, and can never turn out the producer of aught that is good; indicating that philosophy is in a sense a work of Divine Providence.

CHAPTER II.—OBJECTION TO THE NUMBER OF EXTRACTS FROM PHILOSOPHICAL WRITINGS IN THESE BOOKS ANTICIPATED AND ANSWERED.

In reference to these commentaries, which contain as the exigencies of the case demand, the Hellenic opinions, I say thus much to those who are fond of finding fault. First, even if philosophy were useless, if the demonstration of its uselessness does good, it is yet useful. Then those cannot condemn the Greeks, who have only a mere hearsay knowledge of their opinions, and have not entered into a minute investigation in each department, in order to acquaintance with them. For the refutation, which is based on experience, is entirely trustworthy. For the knowledge of what is condemned is found the most complete demonstration. Many things, then, though not contributing to the final result, equip the artist. And otherwise erudition commends him, who sets forth the most essential doctrines so as to produce persuasion in his hearers, engendering admiration in those who are taught, and leads them to the truth. And such persuasion is convincing, by which those that love learning admit the truth; so that philosophy does not ruin life by being the originator of false practices and base deeds, although some have calumniated it, though it be the clear image of truth, a divine gift to the Greeks; nor does it drag us away from the faith, as if we were bewitched by some delusive art, but rather, so to speak, by the use of an ampler circuit, obtains a common exercise demonstrative of the faith. Further, the juxtaposition of doctrines, by comparison, saves the truth, from which follows knowledge.

Philosophy came into existence, not on its own account, but for the advantages reaped by us from knowledge, we receiving a firm persuasion of true perception, through the knowledge of things comprehended by the mind. For I do not mention that the *Stromata*, forming a body of varied erudition, wish artfully to conceal the seeds of knowledge. As, then, he who is fond of hunting captures the game after seeking, tracking, scenting, hunting it down with dogs; so truth, when sought and got with toil, appears a delicious thing. Why, then, you will ask, did you think it fit that such an arrangement should be adopted in your memoranda? Because there is great danger in divulging the secret of the true philosophy to those, whose delight it is unsparingly to speak against everything, not justly; and who shout forth all kinds of names and words indecorously, deceiving themselves and beguiling those who adhere to them. "For the Hebrews seek signs," as the apostle says, "and the Greeks seek after wisdom."

CHAPTER III.—AGAINST THE SOPHISTS.

There is a great crowd of this description: some of them, enslaved to pleasures and willing to disbelieve, laugh at the truth which is worthy of all reverence, making sport of its barbarousness. Some others, exalting themselves, endeavor to discover calumnious objections to our words, furnishing captious questions, hunters out of paltry sayings, practicers of miserable artifices, wranglers, dealers in knotty points, as that Abderite says:—

"For mortals' tongues are glib, and on them are many speeches;
And a wide range for words of all sorts in this place and that."

And—

"Of whatever sort the word you have spoken; of the same sort you must hear."

Inflated with this art of theirs, the wretched Sophists, babbling away in their own jargon; toiling their whole life about the division of names and the nature of the composition and conjunction of sentences, show themselves greater chatterers than turtle-doves; scratching and tickling, not in a manly way, in my opinion, the ears of those who wish to be tickled.

"A river of silly words—not a dropping;"

just as in old shoes, when all the rest is worn and is falling to pieces, and the tongue alone remains. The Athenian Solon most excellently enlarges, and writes:—

"Look to the tongue, and to the words of the glozing man,
But you look on no work that has been done;
But each one of you walks in the steps of a fox,
And in all of you is an empty mind."

This, I think, is signified by the utterance of the Savior, "The foxes have holes, but the Son of man hath not where to lay His head." For on the believer alone, who is separated entirely from the rest, who by the Scripture are called wild beasts, rests the head of the universe, the kind and gentle Word, "who taketh the wise in their own craftiness. For the Lord knows the thoughts of the wise, that they are vain;" the Scripture calling those the wise (σοφούς) who are skilled in words and arts, sophists (σοφιστάς). Whence the Greeks also applied the denominative appellation of wise and sophists (σοφοί, σοφισταί) to those who were versed in anything Cratinus accordingly, having in the *Archilochii* enumerated the poets, said:—

"Such a hive of sophists have ye examined."

And similarly Iophon, the comic poet, in *Flute-playing Satyrs*, says:—

"For there entered
A band of sophists, all equipped."

Of these and the like, who devote their attention to empty words, the divine Scripture most excellently says, "I will destroy the wisdom of the wise, and bring to nothing the understanding of the prudent."

CHAPTER IV.—HUMAN ARTS AS WELL AS DIVINE KNOWLEDGE PROCEED FROM GOD.

Homer calls an artificer wise; and of Margites, if that is his work, he thus writes:—

"Him, then, the Gods made neither a delver nor a ploughman,
Nor in any other respect wise; but he missed every art."

Hesiod further said the musician Linus was "skilled in all manner of wisdom;" and does not hesitate to call a mariner wise, seeing he writes:—

"Having no wisdom in navigation."
And Daniel the prophet says, "The mystery which the king asks, it is not in the power of the wise, the Magi, the diviners, the Gazarenes, to tell the king; but it is God in heaven who revealed it."

Here he terms the Babylonians wise. And that Scripture calls every secular science or art by the one name wisdom (there are other arts and sciences invented over and above by human reason), and that artistic and skilful invention is from God, will be clear if we adduce the following statement: "And the Lord spoke to Moses, See, I have called Bezaleel, the son of Uri, the son of Or, of the tribe of Judah; and I have filled him with the divine spirit of wisdom, and understanding, and knowledge, to devise and to execute in all manner of work, to work gold, and silver, and brass, and blue, and purple, and scarlet, and in working stone work, and in the art of working wood," and even to "all works." And then He adds the general reason, "And to every understanding heart I have given understanding;" that is, to everyone capable of acquiring it by pains and exercise. And again, it is written expressly in the name of the Lord: "And speak thou to all that are wise in mind, whom I have filled with the spirit of perception."

Those who are wise in mind have a certain attribute of nature peculiar to themselves; and they who have shown themselves capable, receive from the Supreme Wisdom a spirit of perception in double measure. For those who practice the common arts, are in what pertains to the senses highly gifted: in hearing, he who is commonly called a musician; in touch, he who moulds clay; in voice the singer, in smell the perfumer, in sight the engraver of devices on seals. Those also that are occupied in instruction, train the sensibility according to which the poets are susceptible to the influence of measure; the sophists apprehend expression; the dialecticians, syllogisms; and the philosophers are capable of the contemplation of which themselves are the objects. For sensibility finds and invents; since it persuasively exhorts to application. And practice will increase the application which has knowledge for its end. With reason, therefore, the apostle has called the wisdom of God "manifold," and which has manifested its power "in many departments and in many modes"—by art, by knowledge, by faith, by prophecy—for our benefit. "For all wisdom is from the Lord, and is with Him forever," as says the wisdom of Jesus.

For if thou call on wisdom and knowledge with a loud voice, and seek it as treasures of silver, and eagerly track it out, thou shalt understand godliness and find divine knowledge." The prophet says this in contradiction to the knowledge according to philosophy, which teaches us to investigate in a magnanimous and noble manner, for our progress in piety. He opposes, therefore, to it the knowledge which is occupied with piety, when referring to knowledge, when he speaks as follows: "For God gives wisdom out of His own mouth, and knowledge along with understanding, and treasures up help for the righteous." For to those who have been justified by philosophy, the knowledge which leads to piety is laid up as a help.

CHAPTER V.—PHILOSOPHY THE HANDMAID OF THEOLOGY.

Accordingly, before the advent of the Lord, philosophy was necessary to the Greeks for righteousness. And now it becomes conducive to piety; being a kind of preparatory training to those who attain to faith through demonstration. "For thy foot," it is said, "will not stumble, if thou refer what is good, whether belonging to the Greeks or to us, to Providence." For God is the cause of all good things; but of some primarily, as of the Old and the New Testament; and of others by consequence, as philosophy. Perchance, too, philosophy was given to the Greeks directly and primarily, till the Lord should call the Greeks. For this was a schoolmaster to bring "the Hellenic mind," as the law, the Hebrews, "to Christ." Philosophy, therefore, was a preparation, paving the way for him who is perfected in Christ.

"Now," says Solomon, "defend wisdom, and it will exalt thee, and it will shield thee with a crown of pleasure." For when thou hast strengthened wisdom with a cope by philosophy, and with right expenditure, thou wilt preserve it unassailable by sophists. The way of truth is therefore one. But into it, as into a perennial river, streams flow from all sides. It has been therefore said by inspiration: "Hear, my son, and receive my words; that thine may be the many ways of life. For I teach thee the ways of wisdom; that the fountains fail thee not," which gush forth from the earth itself. Not only did He enumerate several ways of salvation for any one righteous man, but He added many other ways of many righteous, speaking thus: "The paths of the righteous shine like the light." The commandments and the modes of preparatory training are to be regarded as the ways and appliances of life.

"Jerusalem, Jerusalem, how often would I have gathered thy children, as a hen her chickens!" And Jerusalem is, when interpreted, "a vision of peace." He therefore shows prophetically, that those who peacefully contemplate sacred things are in manifold ways trained to their calling. What then? He "would," and could not. How often, and where? Twice; by the prophets, and by the advent. The expression, then, "How often," shows wisdom to be manifold; every mode of quantity and quality, it by all means saves some, both in time and in eternity. "For the Spirit of the Lord fills the earth." And if any should violently say that the reference is to the Hellenic culture, when it is said, "Give not heed to an evil woman; for honey drops from the lips of a harlot," let him hear what follows: "who lubricates thy throat for the time." But philosophy does not flatter. Who, then, does He allude to as having committed fornication? He adds expressly, "For the feet of folly lead those who use her, after death, to Hades. But her steps are not supported." Therefore remove thy way far from silly pleasure. "Stand not at the doors of her house, that thou yield not thy life to others." And He testifies, "Then shall thou repent in old age, when the flesh of thy body is consumed." For this is the end of foolish pleasure. Such, indeed, is the case. And when He says, "Be not much with a strange woman," He admonishes us to use indeed, but not to linger and spend time with, secular culture. For what was bestowed on each generation advantageously, and at seasonable times, is a preliminary training for the word of the Lord. "For already some men, ensnared by the charms of handmaidens, have despised their consort philosophy, and have grown old, some of them in music, some in geometry, others in grammar, the most in rhetoric." "But as the encyclical branches of study contribute to philosophy, which is their mistress; so also philosophy itself co-operates for the acquisition of wisdom. For philosophy is the study of wisdom, and wisdom is the knowledge of things divine and human; and their causes." Wisdom is therefore queen of philosophy, as philosophy is of preparatory culture. For if philosophy "professes control of the tongue, and the belly, and the parts below the belly, it is to be chosen on its own account. But it appears more worthy of respect and preeminence, if cultivated for the honor and knowledge of God." And Scripture will afford a testimony to what has been said in what follows. Sarah was at one time barren, being Abraham's wife. Sarah having no child, assigned her maid, by name Hagar, the Egyptian, to Abraham, in order to get children. Wisdom, therefore, who dwells with the man of faith (and Abraham was reckoned faithful and righteous), was still barren and without child in that generation, not having brought forth to Abraham aught allied to virtue. And she, as was proper, thought that he, being now in the time of progress, should have intercourse with secular culture first (by Egyptian the world is designated figuratively); and afterwards should approach to her according to divine providence, and beget Isaac."

And Philo interprets Hagar to mean "sojourning." For it is said in connection with this, "Be not much with a strange woman." Sarah he interprets to mean "my princedom." He, then, who has received previous training is at liberty to approach to wisdom, which is supreme, from which grows up the race of Israel. These things show that that wisdom can be acquired through instruction, to which Abraham attained, passing from the contemplation of heavenly things to the faith and righteousness which are according to God. And Isaac is shown to mean "self-taught;" wherefore also he is discovered to be a type of Christ. He was the husband of one wife Rebecca, which they translate "Patience." And Jacob is said to have consorted with several, his name being interpreted "Exerciser." And exercises are engaged in by means of many and various dogmas. Whence, also, he who is really "endowed with the power of seeing" is called Israel, having much experience, and being fit for exercise.

Something else may also have been shown by the three patriarchs, namely, that the sure seal of knowledge is composed of nature, of education, and exercise.

You may have also another image of what has been said, in Thamar sitting by the way, and presenting the appearance of a harlot, on whom the studious Judas (whose name is interpreted "powerful"), who left nothing unexamined and uninvestigated, looked; and turned aside to her, preserving his profession towards God. Wherefore also, when Sarah was jealous at Hagar being preferred to her, Abraham, as choosing only what was profitable in secular philosophy, said, "Behold, thy maid is in thine hands: deal with her as it pleases thee;" manifestly meaning, "I embrace secular culture as youthful, and a handmaid; but thy knowledge I honor and reverence as true wife." And Sarah afflicted her; which is equivalent to corrected and admonished her. It has therefore been well said, "My son, despise not thou the correction of God; nor faint when thou art rebuked of Him. For whom the Lord loves He chastens, and scourges every son whom He receives." And the foresaid Scriptures, when examined in other places, will be seen to exhibit other mysteries. We merely therefore assert here, that philosophy is characterized by investigation into truth and the nature of things (this is the truth of which the Lord Himself said, "I am the truth"); and that, again, the preparatory training for rest in Christ exercises the mind, rouses the intelligence, and begets an inquiring shrewdness, by means of the true philosophy, which the initiated possess, having found it, or rather received it, from the truth itself.

CHAPTER VI.—THE BENEFIT OF CULTURE.

The readiness acquired by previous training conduces much to the perception of such things as are requisite; but those things which can be perceived only by mind are the special exercise for the mind. And their nature is triple according as we consider their quantity, their magnitude, and what can be predicated of them. For the discourse which consists of demonstrations, implants in the spirit of him who follows it, clear faith; so that he cannot conceive of that which is demonstrated being different; and so it does not allow us to succumb to those who assail us by fraud. In such studies, therefore, the soul is purged from sensible things, and is excited, so as to be able to see truth distinctly. For nutriment, and the training which is maintained gentle, make noble natures; and noble natures, when they have received such training, become still better than before both in other respects, but especially in productiveness, as is the case with the other creatures. Wherefore it is said, "Go to the ant, thou sluggard, and become wiser than it, which provides much and, varied food in the harvest against the inclemency of winter." Or go to the bee, and learn how laborious she is; for she, feeding on the whole meadow, produces one honey-comb. And if "thou prays in the closet," as the Lord taught, "to worship in spirit," thy management will no longer be solely occupied about the house, but also about the soul, what must be bestowed on it, and how, and how much; and what must be laid aside and treasured up in it; and when it ought to be produced, and to whom. For it is not by nature, but by learning, that people become noble and good, as people also become physicians and pilots. We all in common, for example, see the vine and the horse. But the husbandman will know if the vine be good or bad at fruit bearing; and the horseman will easily distinguish between the spiritless and the swift animal. But that some are naturally predisposed to virtue above others, certain pursuits of those, who are so naturally predisposed above others, show. But that perfection in virtue is not the exclusive property of those, whose natures are better, is proved, since also those who by nature are ill-disposed towards virtue, in obtaining suitable training, for the most part attain to excellence; and, on the other hand, those whose natural dispositions are apt, become evil through neglect.

Again, God has created us naturally social and just; whence justice must not be said to take its rise from implantation alone. But the good imparted by creation is to be conceived of as excited by the commandment; the soul being trained to be willing to select what is noblest.

But as we say that a man can be a believer without learning, so also we assert that it is impossible for a man without learning to comprehend the things which are declared in the faith. But to adopt what is well said, and not to adopt the reverse, is caused not simply by faith, but by faith combined with knowledge. But if ignorance is want of training and of instruction, then teaching produces knowledge of divine and human things. But just as it is possible to live rightly in penury of this world's good things, so also in abundance. And we avow, that at once with more ease and more speed will one attain to virtue through previous training. But it is not such as to be unattainable without it; but it is attainable only when they have learned, and have had their senses exercised. "For hatred," says Solomon, "raises strife, but instruction guarded the ways of life;" in such a way that we are not deceived nor deluded by those who are practiced in base arts for the injury of

those who hear. "But instruction wanders reproachless," it is said. We must be conversant with the art of reasoning, for the purpose of confuting the deceitful opinions of the sophists. Well and felicitously, therefore, does Anaxarchus write in his book respecting "kingly rule:"
"Erudition benefits greatly and hurts greatly him who possesses it; it helps him who is worthy, and injures him who utters readily every word, and before the whole people. It is necessary to know the measure of time. For this is the end of wisdom. And those who sing at the doors, even if they sing skillfully, are not reckoned wise, but have the reputation of folly." And Hesiod:—

"Of the Muses, who make a man loquacious, divine, vocal."

For him who is fluent in words he calls loquacious; and him who is clever, vocal; and "divine," him who is skilled, a philosopher, and acquainted with the truth.

CHAPTER VII.—THE ECLECTIC PHILOSOPHY PAVES THE WAY FOR DIVINE VIRTUE.

The Greek preparatory culture, therefore, with philosophy itself, is shown to have come down from God to men, not with a definite direction but in the way in which showers fall down on the good land, and on the dunghill, and on the houses. And similarly both the grass and the wheat sprout; and the figs and any other reckless trees grow on sepulchers. And things that grow, appear as a type of truths. For they enjoy the same influence of the rain. But they have not the same grace as those which spring up in rich soil, inasmuch as they are withered or plucked up. And here we are aided by the parable of the sower, which the Lord interpreted. For the husbandman of the soil which is among men is one; He who from the beginning, from the foundation of the world, sowed nutritious seeds; He who in each age rained down the Lord, the Word. But the times and places which received [such gifts], created the differences which exist. Further, the husbandman sows not only wheat (of which there are many varieties), but also other seeds—barley, and beans, and peas, and vetches, and vegetable and flower seeds. And to the same husbandry belongs both planting and the operations necessary in the nurseries, and gardens, and orchards, and the planning and rearing of all sorts of trees.

In like manner, not only the care of sheep, but the care of herds, and breeding of horses, and dogs, and bee-craft, all arts, and to speak comprehensively, the care of flocks and the rearing of animals, differ from each other more or less, but are all useful for life. And philosophy—I do not mean the Stoic, or the Platonic, or the Epicurean, or the Aristotelian, but whatever has been well said by each of those sects, which teach righteousness along with a science pervaded by piety,—this eclectic whole I call philosophy. But such conclusions of human reasoning, as men have cut away and falsified, I would never call divine.

And now we must look also at this, that if ever those who know not how to do well, live well; for they have lighted on well-doing. Some, too, have aimed well at the word of truth through understanding. "But Abraham was not justified by works, but by faith." It is therefore of no advantage to them after the end of life, even if they do good works now, if they have not faith. Wherefore also the Scriptures were translated into the language of the Greeks, in order that they might never be able to allege the excuse of ignorance, inasmuch as they are able to hear also what we have in our hands, if they only wish. One speaks in one way of the truth, in another way the truth interprets itself. The guessing at truth is one thing, and truth itself is another. Resemblance is one thing, the thing itself is another. And the one results from learning and practice, the other from power and faith. For the teaching of piety is a gift, but faith is grace. "For by doing the will of God we know the will of God." "Open, then," says the Scripture, "the gates of righteousness; and I will enter in, and confess to the Lord." But the paths to righteousness (since God saves in many ways, for He is good) are many and various, and lead to the Lord's way and gate. And if you ask the royal and true entrance, you will hear, "This is the gate of the Lord, the righteous shall enter in by it." While there are many gates open, that in righteousness is in Christ, by which all the blessed enter, and direct their steps in the sanctity of knowledge. Now Clemens, in his Epistle to the Corinthians, while expounding the differences of those who are approved according to the Church, says expressly, "One may be a believer; one may be powerful in uttering knowledge; one may be wise in discriminating between words; one may be terrible in deeds."

CHAPTER VIII.—THE SOPHISTICAL ARTS USELESS.

But the art of sophistry, which the Greeks cultivated, is a fantastic power, which makes false opinions like true by means of words. For it produces rhetoric in order to persuasion, and disputation for wrangling. These arts, therefore, if not conjoined with philosophy, will be injurious to everyone. For Plato openly called sophistry "an evil art." And Aristotle, following him, demonstrates it to be a dishonest art, which abstracts in a specious manner the whole business of wisdom, and professes a wisdom which it has not studied. To speak briefly, as the beginning of rhetoric is the probable, and an attempted proof the process, and the end persuasion, so the beginning of disputation is what is matter of opinion, and the process a contest, and the end victory. For in the same manner, also, the beginning of sophistry is the apparent, and the process twofold; one of rhetoric, continuous and exhaustive; and the other of logic, and is interrogatory. And its end is admiration. The dialectic in vogue in the schools, on the other hand, is the exercise of a philosopher in matters of opinion, for the sake of the faculty of disputation. But truth is not in these at all. With reason, therefore, the noble apostle, depreciating these superfluous arts occupied about words, says, "If any man do not give heed to wholesome words, but is puffed up by a kind

Clement of Alexandria

of teaching, knowing nothing, but doting (νοσῶν) about questions and strife of words, whereof cometh contention, envy, railings, evil surmising, perverse disputing of men of corrupt minds, destitute of the truth." You see how he is moved against them, calling their art of logic—on which, those to whom this garrulous mischievous art is dear, whether Greeks or barbarians, plume themselves— a disease (νοσος). Very beautifully, therefore, the tragic poet Euripides says in the *Phoenissæ*,—

"But a wrongful speech
Is diseased in itself, and needs skilful medicines."

For the saving Word is called "wholesome," He being the truth; and what is wholesome (healthful) remains ever deathless. But separation from what is healthful and divine is impiety, and a deadly malady. These are rapacious wolves hid in sheep-skins, men-stealers, and glozing soul-seducers, secretly, but proved to be robbers; striving by fraud and force to catch us who are unsophisticated and have less power of speech.

"Often a man, impeded through want of words, carries less weight
In expressing what is right, than the man of eloquence.
But now in fluent mouths the weightiest truths
They disguise, so that they do not seem what they ought to seem,"

says the tragedy. Such are these wranglers, whether they follow the sects, or practice miserable dialectic arts. These are they that "stretch the warp and weave nothing," says the Scripture; prosecuting a bootless task, which the apostle has called "cunning craftiness of men whereby they lie in wait to deceive." "For there are," he says, "many unruly and vain talkers and deceivers." Wherefore it was not said to all, "Ye are the salt of the earth." For there are some even of the hearers of the word who are like the fishes of the sea, which, reared from their birth in brine, yet need salt to dress them for food. Accordingly I wholly approve of the tragedy, when it says:—

"O son, false words can be well spoken,
And truth may be vanquished by beauty of words.
But this is not what is most correct, but nature and what is right;
He who practices eloquence is indeed wise,
But I consider deeds always better than words."

We must not, then, aspire to please the multitude. For we do not practice what will please them, but what we know is remote from their disposition. "Let us not be desirous of vainglory," says the apostle, "provoking one another, envying one another."

Thus the truth-loving Plato says, as if divinely inspired, "Since I am such as to obey nothing but the word, which, after reflection, appears to me the best."

Accordingly he charges those who credit opinions without intelligence and knowledge, with abandoning right and sound reason unwarrantably, and believing him who is a partner in falsehood. For to cheat one's self of the truth is bad; but to speak the truth, and to hold as our opinions positive realities, is good.

Men are deprived of what is good unwillingly. Nevertheless they are deprived either by being deceived or beguiled, or by being compelled and not believing. He who believes not, has already made himself a willing captive; and he who changes his persuasion is cozened, while he forgets that time imperceptibly takes away some things, and reason others. And after an opinion has been entertained, pain and anguish, and on the other hand contentiousness and anger, compel. Above all, men are beguiled who are either bewitched by pleasure or terrified by fear. And all these are voluntary changes, but by none of these will knowledge ever be attained.

CHAPTER IX.—HUMAN KNOWLEDGE NECESSARY FOR THE UNDERSTANDING OF THE SCRIPTURES.

Some, who think themselves naturally gifted, do not wish to touch either philosophy or logic; nay more, they do not wish to learn natural science. They demand bare faith alone, as if they wished, without bestowing any care on the vine, straightway to gather clusters from the first. Now the Lord is figuratively described as the vine, from which, with pains and the art of husbandry, according to the word, the fruit is to be gathered.

We must lop, dig, bind, and perform the other operations. The pruning-knife, I should think, and the pick-axe, and the other agricultural implements, are necessary for the culture of the vine, so that it may produce eatable fruit. And as in husbandry, so also in medicine: he has learned to purpose, who has practiced the various lessons, so as to be able to cultivate and to heal. So also here, I call him truly learned who brings everything to bear on the truth; so that, from geometry, and music, and grammar, and philosophy itself, culling what is useful, he guards the faith against assault. Now, as was said, the athlete is despised who is not furnished for the contest. For instance, too, we praise the experienced helmsman who "has seen the cities of many men," and the physician who has had large experience; thus also some describe the empiric. And he who brings everything to bear on a right life, procuring examples from the Greeks and barbarians, this man is an experienced searcher after truth, and in reality a man of much counsel, like the touch-stone (that is, the Lydian), which is believed to possess the power of distinguishing the spurious from the genuine gold. And our much-knowing gnostic can distinguish sophistry from philosophy, the art of decoration from gymnastics, cookery from physic, and rhetoric from dialectics, and the other sects which are according to the barbarian philosophy, from the truth itself. And how necessary is it for him who desires to be partaker of the power of God, to treat of intellectual subjects by philosophizing! And how serviceable is it to distinguish expressions which are ambiguous, and which in the Testaments are used synonymously! For the Lord, at the time of His temptation, skillfully matched the devil by an ambiguous expression. And I do not yet, in this connection, see how in the world the inventor of philosophy and dialectics, as some suppose, is seduced through being deceived by the form of speech which consists in ambiguity. And if the prophets and apostles knew not the arts by which the exercises of philosophy are exhibited, yet the mind of the prophetic and instructive spirit, uttered secretly, because all have not an intelligent ear, demands skilful modes of teaching in order to clear exposition. For the prophets and disciples of the Spirit knew infallibly their mind. For they knew it by faith, in a way which others could not easily, as the Spirit has said. But it is not possible for those who have not learned to receive it thus. "Write," it is said, "the commandments doubly, in counsel and knowledge, that thou may answer the words of truth to them who send unto thee." What, then, is the knowledge of answering? or what that of asking? It is dialectics. What then? Is not speaking our business, and does not action proceed from the Word? For if we act not for the Word, we shall act against reason. But a rational work is accomplished through God. "And nothing," it is said, "was made without Him"—the Word of God.

And did not the Lord make all things by the Word? Even the beasts work, driven by compelling fear. And do not those who are called orthodox apply themselves to good works, knowing not what they do?

CHAPTER X.—TO ACT WELL OF GREATER CONSEQUENCE THAN TO SPEAK WELL.

Wherefore the Savior, taking the bread, first spoke and blessed. Then breaking the bread, He presented it, that we might eat it, according to reason, and that knowing the Scriptures we might walk obediently. And as those whose speech is evil are no better than those whose practice is evil (for calumny is the servant of the sword, and evil-speaking inflicts pain; and from these proceed disasters in life, such being the effects of evil speech); so also those who are given to good speech are near neighbors to those who accomplish good deeds. Accordingly discourse refreshes the soul and entices it to nobleness; and happy is he who has the use of both his hands. Neither, therefore, is he who can act well to be vilified by him who is able to speak well; nor is he who is able to speak well to be disparaged by him who is capable of acting well. But let each do that for which he is naturally fitted. What the one exhibits as actually done, the other speaks, preparing, as it were, the way for well-doing, and leading the hearers to the practice of good. For there is a saving word, as there is a saving work. Righteousness, accordingly, is not constituted without discourse. And as the receiving of good is abolished if we abolish the doing of good; so obedience and faith are abolished when neither the command, nor one to expound the command, is taken along with us. But now we are benefited mutually and reciprocally by words and deeds; but we must repudiate entirely the art of wrangling and sophistry, since these sentences of the sophists not only bewitch and beguile the many, but sometimes by violence win a Cadmean victory. For true above all is that Psalm, "The just shall live to the end, for he shall not see corruption, when he beholds the wise dying." And whom does he call wise? Hear from the Wisdom of Jesus: "Wisdom is not the knowledge of evil." Such he calls what the arts of speaking and of discussing have invented. "Thou shalt therefore seek wisdom among the wicked, and shalt not find it." And if you inquire again of what sort this is, you are told, "The mouth of the righteous man will distil wisdom." And similarly with truth, the art of sophistry is called wisdom.

But it is my purpose, as I reckon, and not without reason, to live according to the Word, and to understand what is revealed; but never affecting eloquence, to be content merely with indicating my meaning. And by what term that which I wish to present is shown, I care not. For I well know that to be saved, and to aid those who desire to be saved, is the best thing, and not to compose paltry sentences like gewgaws. "And if," says the Pythagorean in the *Politicus* of Plato, "you guard against solicitude about terms, you will be richer in wisdom against old age." And in the *Theoetetus* you will find again, "And carelessness about names, and expressions, and the want of nice scrutiny, is not vulgar and illiberal for the most part, but rather the reverse of this, and is sometimes necessary." This the Scripture has expressed with the greatest possible brevity, when it said, "Be not occupied much about words." For expression is like the dress on the body. The matter is the flesh and sinews. We must not therefore care more for the dress than the safety of the body. For not only a simple mode of life, but also a style of speech devoid of superfluity and nicety, must be cultivated by him who has adopted the true life, if we are to abandon luxury as treacherous and profligate, as the ancient Lacedæmonians adjured ointment and purple, deeming and calling them rightly treacherous garments and treacherous unguents; since neither is that mode of preparing food right where there is more of seasoning than of nutriment; nor is that style of speech elegant which can please rather than benefit the hearers. Pythagoras exhorts us to consider the Muses more pleasant than the Sirens, teaching us to cultivate wisdom apart from pleasure, and exposing the other mode of attracting the soul as deceptive. For sailing past the Sirens one man has sufficient strength, and for answering the Sphinx another one, or, if you please, not even one. We ought never, then, out of desire for vainglory, to make broad the phylacteries. It suffices the Gnostic if only one hearer is found for him. You may hear therefore Pindar the Boeotian, who writes, "Divulge not before all the ancient speech. The way of silence is sometimes the surest. And the mightiest word is a spur to the fight." Accordingly, the blessed apostle very appropriately and urgently exhorts us "not to strive about words to no profit, but to the subverting of the hearers, but to shun profane and vain babblings, for they increase unto more ungodliness, and their word will eat as doth a canker."

CHAPTER XI.—WHAT IS THE PHILOSOPHY WHICH THE APOSTLE BIDS US SHUN?

This, then, "the wisdom of the world is foolishness with God," and of those who are "the wise the Lord knows their thoughts that they are vain." Let no man therefore glory on account of pre-eminence in human thought. For it is written well in Jeremiah, "Let not the wise man glory in his wisdom, and let not the mighty man glory in his might, and let not the rich man glory in his riches: but let him that glories glory in this, that he understand and knows that I am the Lord, that executed mercy and judgment and righteousness upon the earth: for in these things is my delight, says the Lord." "That we should trust not in ourselves, but in God who raises the dead," says the apostle, "who delivered us from so great a death, that our faith should not stand in the wisdom of men, but in the power of God." "For the spiritual man judged all things, but he himself is judged of no man." I hear also those words of his, "And these things I say, lest any man should beguile you with enticing words, or one should enter in to spoil you." And again, "Beware lest any man spoil you through philosophy and vain deceit, after the tradition of men, after the rudiments of the world, and not after Christ;" branding not all philosophy, but the Epicurean, which Paul mentions in the Acts of the Apostles, which abolishes providence and deifies pleasure, and whatever other philosophy honors the elements, but places not over them the efficient cause, nor apprehends the Creator.

The Stoics also, whom he mentions too, say not well that the Deity, being a body, pervades the vilest matter. He calls the jugglery of logic "the tradition of men." Wherefore also he adds, "Avoid juvenile questions. For such contentions are puerile." "But virtue is no lover of boys," says the philosopher Plato. And our struggle, according to Gorgias Leontinus, requires two virtues—boldness and wisdom,—boldness to undergo danger, and wisdom to understand the enigma. For the Word, like the Olympian proclamation, calls him who is willing, and crowns him who is able to continue unmoved as far as the truth is concerned. And, in truth, the Word does not wish him who has believed to be idle. For He says, "Seek, and ye shall find." But seeking ends in finding, driving out the empty trifling, and approving of the contemplation which confirms our faith. "And this I say, lest any man beguile you with enticing words," says the apostle, evidently as having learned to distinguish what was said by him, and as being taught to meet objections. "As ye have therefore received Christ Jesus the Lord, so walk in Him, rooted and built up in Him, and stablished in the faith." Now persuasion is [the means of] being established in the faith. "Beware lest any man spoil you of faith in Christ by philosophy and vain deceit," which does away with providence, "after the tradition of men;" for the philosophy which is in accordance with divine tradition establishes and confirms providence, which, being done away with, the economy of the Savior appears a myth, while we are influenced "after the elements of the world, and not after Christ." For the teaching which is agreeable to Christ deifies the Creator, and traces providence in particular events, and knows the nature of the elements to be capable of change and production, and teaches that we ought to aim at rising up to the power which assimilates to God, and to prefer the dispensation as holding the first rank and superior to all training.

The elements are worshipped,—the air by Diogenes, the water by Thales, the fire by Hippasus; and by those who suppose atoms to be the first principles of things, arrogating the name of philosophers, being wretched creatures devoted to pleasure. "Wherefore I pray," says the apostle, "that your love may abound yet more and more, in knowledge and in all judgment, that ye may approve things that are excellent." "Since, when we were children," says the same apostle, "we were kept in bondage under the rudiments of the world. And the child, though heir, differed nothing from a servant, till the time appointed of the father." Philosophers, then, are children, unless they have been made men by Christ. "For if the son of the bond woman shall not be heir with the son of the free," at least he is the seed of Abraham, though not of promise, receiving what belongs to him by free gift. "But strong meat belongs to those that are of full age, even those who by reason of use have their senses exercised to discern both good and evil." "For every one that uses milk is unskillful in the word of righteousness; for he is a babe," and not yet acquainted with the word, according to which he has believed and works, and not able to give a reason in himself. "Prove all things," the apostle says, "and hold fast that which is good," speaking to spiritual men, who judge what is said according to truth, whether it seems or truly holds by the truth. "He who is not corrected by discipline errs, and stripes and reproofs give the discipline of wisdom," the reproofs manifestly that are with love. "For the right heart seeks knowledge." "For he that seeks the Lord shall find knowledge with righteousness; and they who have sought it rightly have found peace." "And I will know," it is said, "not the speech of those which are puffed up, but the power." In rebuke of those who are wise in appearance, and think themselves wise, but are not in reality wise, he writes: "For the kingdom of God is not in word." It is not in that which is not true, but which is only probable according to opinion; but he said "in power," for the truth alone is powerful. And again: "If any man think that he knows anything, he knows nothing yet as he ought to know." For truth is never mere opinion. But the "supposition of knowledge inflates," and fills with pride; "but charity edifies," which deals not in supposition, but in truth. Whence it is said, "If any man loves, he is known."

CHAPTER XII.—THE MYSTERIES OF THE FAITH NOT TO BE DIVULGED TO ALL.

But since this tradition is not published alone for him who perceives the magnificence of the word; it is requisite, therefore, to hide in a mystery the wisdom spoken, which the Son of God taught. Now, therefore, Isaiah the prophet has his tongue purified by fire, so that he may be able to tell the vision. And we must purify not the tongue alone, but also the ears, if we attempt to be partakers of the truth.

Such were the impediments in the way of my writing. And even now I fear, as it is said, "to cast the pearls before swine, lest they tread them under foot, and turn and rend us." For it is difficult to exhibit the really pure and transparent words respecting the true light, to swinish and untrained hearers. For scarcely could anything which they could hear be more ludicrous than these to the multitude; nor any subjects on the other hand more admirable or more inspiring to those of noble nature. "But the natural man receives not the things of the Spirit of God; for they are foolishness to him." But the wise do not utter with their mouth what they reason in council. "But what ye hear in the ear," says the Lord, "proclaim upon the houses;" bidding them receive the secret traditions of the true knowledge, and expound them aloft and conspicuously; and as we have heard in the ear, so to deliver them to whom it is requisite; but not enjoining us to communicate to all without distinction, what is said to them in parables. But there is only a delineation in the memoranda, which have the truth sowed sparse and broadcast, that it may escape the notice of those who pick up seeds like jackdaws; but when they find a good husbandman, each one of them will germinate and produce corn.

CHAPTER XIII.—ALL SECTS OF PHILOSOPHY CONTAIN A GERM OF TRUTH.

Since, therefore, truth is one (for falsehood has ten thousand by-paths); just as the Bacchantes tore asunder the limbs of Pentheus, so the sects both of barbarian and Hellenic philosophy have done with truth, and each vaunts as the whole truth the portion which has fallen to its lot. But all, in my opinion, are illuminated by the dawn of Light. Let all, therefore, both Greeks and barbarians, who have aspired after the truth,—both those who possess not a little, and those who have any portion,—produce whatever they have of the word of truth.

Eternity, for instance, presents in an instant the future and the present, also the past of time. But truth, much more powerful than limitless duration, can collect its proper germs, though they have fallen on foreign soil. For we shall find that very many of the dogmas that are held by such sects as have not become utterly senseless, and are not cut out from the order of nature (by cutting off Christ, as the women of the fable dismembered the man), though appearing unlike one another, correspond in their origin and with the truth as a whole. For they coincide in one, either as a part, or a species, or a genus. For instance, though the highest note is different from the lowest note, yet both compose one harmony. And in numbers an even number differs from an odd number; but both suit in arithmetic; as also is the case with figure, the circle, and the triangle, and the square, and whatever figures differ from one another. Also, in the whole universe, all the parts, though differing one from another, preserve their relation to the whole. So, then, the barbarian and Hellenic philosophy has torn off a fragment of eternal truth not from the mythology of Dionysus, but from the theology of the ever-living Word. And He who brings again together the separate fragments, and makes them one, will without peril, be assured, contemplate the perfect

Word, the truth. Therefore it is written in Ecclesiastes: "And I added wisdom above all who were before me in Jerusalem; and my heart saw many things; and besides, I knew wisdom and knowledge, parables and understanding. And this also is the choice of the spirit, because in abundance of wisdom is abundance of knowledge." He who is conversant with all kinds of wisdom, will be pre-eminently a gnostic. Now it is written, "Abundance of the knowledge of wisdom will give life to him who is of it." And again, what is said is confirmed more clearly by this saying, "All things are in the sight of those who understand"—all things, both Hellenic and barbarian; but the one or the other is not all. "They are right to those who wish to receive understanding. Choose instruction, and not silver, and knowledge above tested gold," and prefer also sense to pure gold; "for wisdom is better than precious stones, and no precious thing is worth it."

CHAPTER XIV.—SUCCESSION OF PHILOSOPHERS IN GREECE.

The Greeks say, that after Orpheus and Linus, and the most ancient of the poets that appeared among them, the seven, called wise, were the first that were admired for their wisdom. Of whom four were of Asia—Thales of Miletus, and Bias of Priene, Pittacus of Mitylene, and Cleobulus of Lindos; and two of Europe, Solon the Athenian, and Chilon the Lacedæmonian; and the seventh, some say, was Periander of Corinth; others, Anacharsis the Scythian; others, Epimenides the Cretan, whom Paul knew as a Greek prophet, whom he mentions in the Epistle to Titus, where he speaks thus: "One of themselves, a prophet of their own, said, *The Cretans are always liars, evil beasts, slow bellies.* And this witness is true." You see how even to the prophets of the Greeks he attributes something of the truth, and is not ashamed, when discoursing for the edification of some and the shaming of others, to make use of Greek poems. Accordingly to the Corinthians (for this is not the only instance), while discoursing on the resurrection of the dead, he makes use of a tragic Iambic line, when he said,

"What advantaged it me if the dead are not raised? Let us eat and drink, for tomorrow we die. Be not deceived; evil communications corrupt good manners." Others have enumerated Acusilaus the Argive among the seven wise men; and others, Pherecydes of Syros. And Plato substitutes Myso the Chenian for Periander, whom he deemed unworthy of wisdom, on account of his having reigned as a tyrant. That the wise men among the Greeks flourished after the age of Moses, will, a little after, be shown. But the style of philosophy among them, as Hebraic and enigmatical, is now to be considered. They adopted brevity, as suited for exhortation, and most useful. Even Plato says, that of old this mode was purposely in vogue among all the Greeks, especially the Lacedæmonians and Cretans, who enjoyed the best laws.

The expression, "Know thyself," some supposed to be Chilon's. But Chamæleon, in his book *About the Gods*, ascribes it to Thales; Aristotle to the Pythian. It may be an injunction to the pursuit of knowledge. For it is not possible to know the parts without the essence of the whole; and one must study the genesis of the universe, that thereby we may be able to learn the nature of man. Again, to Chilon the Lacedæmonian they attribute, "Let nothing be too much." Strato, in his book *Of Inventions*, ascribes the apophthegm to Stratodemus of Tegea. Didymus assigns it to Solon; as also to Cleobulus the saying, "A middle course is best." And the expression, "Come under a pledge, and mischief is at hand," Cleomenes says, in his book *Concerning Hesiod*, was uttered before by Homer in the lines:—

"Wretched pledges, for the wretched, to be pledged."

The Aristotelians judge it to be Chilon's; but Didymus says the advice was that of Thales. Then, next in order, the saying, "All men are bad," or, "The most of men are bad" (for the same apophthegm is expressed in two ways), Sotades the Byzantian says that it was Bias's. And the aphorism, "Practice conquers everything," they will have it to be Periander's; and likewise the advice, "Know the opportunity," to have been a saying of Pittacus. Solon made laws for the Athenians, Pittacus for the Mitylenians. And at a late date, Pythagoras, the pupil of Pherecydes, first called himself a philosopher. Accordingly, after the aforementioned three men, there were three schools of philosophy, named after the places where they lived: the Italic from Pythagoras, the Ionic from Thales, the Eleatic from Xenophanes. Pythagoras was a Samian, the son of Mnesarchus, as Hippobotus says: according to Aristoxenus, in his life of Pythagoras and Aristarchus and Theopompus, he was a Tuscan; and according to Neanthes, a Syrian or a Tyrian. So that Pythagoras was, according to the most, of barbarian extraction. Thales, too, as Leander and Herodotus relate, was a Phoenician; as some suppose, a Milesian. He alone seems to have met the prophets of the Egyptians. But no one is described as his teacher, nor is any one mentioned as the teacher of Pherecydes of Syros, who had Pythagoras as his pupil. But the Italic philosophy, that of Pythagoras, grew old in Metapontum in Italy. Anaximander of Miletus, the son of Praxiades, succeeded Thales; and was himself succeeded by Anaximenes of Miletus, the son of Eurustratus; after whom came Anaxagoras of Clazomenæ, the son of Hegesibulus. He transferred his school from Ionia to Athens. He was succeeded by Archelaus, whose pupil Socrates was.

> "From these turned aside, the stone-mason;
> Talker about laws; the enchanter of the Greeks,"

says Timon in his *Satirical Poems*, on account of his quitting physics for ethics. Antisthenes, after being a pupil of Socrates, introduced the Cynic philosophy; and Plato withdrew to the Academy. Aristotle, after studying philosophy under Plato, withdrew to the Lyceum, and founded the Peripatetic sect. He was succeeded by Theophrastus, who was succeeded by
Strato, and he by Lycon, then Critolaus, and then Diodorus. Speusippus was the successor of Plato; his successor was

Xenocrates; and the successor of the latter, Polemo. And the disciples of Polemo were Crates and Crantor, in whom the old Academy founded by Plato ceased. Arcesilaus was the associate of Crantor; from whom, down to Hegesilaus, the Middle Academy flourished. Then Carneades succeeded Hegesilaus, and others came in succession. The disciple of Crates was Zeno of Citium, the founder of the Stoic sect. He was succeeded by Cleanthes; and the latter by Chrysippus, and others after him. Xenophanes of Colophon was the founder of the Eleatic school, who, Timæus says, lived in the time of Hiero, lord of Sicily, and Epicharmus the poet; and Apollodorus says that he was born in the fortieth Olympiad, and reached to the times of Darius and Cyrus. Parmenides, accordingly, was the disciple of Xenophanes, and Zeno of him; then came Leucippus, and then Democritus. Disciples of Democritus were Protagoras of Abdera, and Metrodorus of Chios, whose pupil was Diogenes of Smyrna; and his again Anaxarchus, and his Pyrrho, and his Nausiphanes.
Some say that Epicurus was a scholar of his.

Such, in an epitome, is the succession of the philosophers among the Greeks. The periods of the originators of their philosophy are now to be specified successively, in order that, by comparison, we may show that the Hebrew philosophy was older by many generations.

It has been said of Xenophanes that he was the founder of the Eleatic philosophy. And Eudemus, in the *Astrological Histories*, says that Thales foretold the eclipse of the sun, which took place at the time that the Medians and the Lydians fought, in the reign of Cyaxares the father of Astyages over the Medes, and of Alyattus the son of Croesus over the Lydians.
Herodotus in his first book agrees with him. The date is about the fiftieth Olympiad. Pythagoras is ascertained to have lived in the days of Polycrates the tyrant, about the sixty-second Olympiad. Mnesiphilus is described as a follower of Solon, and was a contemporary of Themistocles. Solon therefore flourished about the forty-sixth Olympiad. For Heraclitus, the

son of Bauso, persuaded Melancomas the tyrant to abdicate his sovereignty. He despised the invitation of king Darius to visit the Persians.

CHAPTER XV.—THE GREEK PHILOSOPHY IN GREAT PART DERIVED FROM THE BARBARIANS.

These are the times of the oldest wise men and philosophers among the Greeks. And that the most of them were barbarians by extraction, and were trained among barbarians, what need is there to say? Pythagoras is shown to have been either a Tuscan or a Tyrian. And Antisthenes was a Phrygian. And Orpheus was an Odrysian or a Thracian. The most, too, show Homer to have been an Egyptian. Thales was a Phoenician by birth, and was said to have consorted with the prophets of the Egyptians; as also Pythagoras did with the same persons, by whom he was circumcised, that he might enter the adytum and learn from the Egyptians the mystic philosophy. He held converse with the chief of the Chaldeans and the Magi; and he gave a hint of the church, now so called, in the common hall which he maintained.

And Plato does not deny that he procured all that is most excellent in philosophy from the barbarians; and he admits that he came into Egypt. Whence, writing in the Phoedo that the philosopher can receive aid from all sides, he said: "Great indeed is Greece, O Cebes, in which everywhere there are good men, and many are the races of the barbarians." Thus Plato thinks that some of the barbarians, too, are philosophers. But Epicurus, on the other hand, supposes that only Greeks can philosophize. And in the *Symposium*, Plato, landing the barbarians as practicing philosophy with conspicuous excellence, truly says: "And in many other instances both among Greeks and barbarians, whose temples reared for such sons are already numerous." And it is clear that the barbarians signally honored their lawgivers and teachers, designating them gods. For, according to Plato, "they think that good souls, on quitting the super-celestial region, submit to come to this

Tartarus; and assuming a body, share in all the ills which are involved in birth, from their solicitude for the race of men;" and these make laws and publish philosophy, "than which no greater boon ever came from the gods to the race of men, or will come."

And as appears to me, it was in consequence of perceiving the great benefit which is conferred through wise men, that the men themselves were honored and philosophy cultivated publicly by all the Brahmins, and the Odrysi, and the Getæ. And such were strictly deified by the race of the Egyptians, by the Chaldeans and the Arabians, called the Happy, and those that inhabited Palestine, by not the least portion of the Persian race, and by innumerable other races besides these. And it is well known that Plato is found perpetually celebrating the barbarians, remembering that both himself and Pythagoras learned the most and the noblest of their dogmas among the barbarians. Wherefore he also called the races of the barbarians, "races of barbarian philosophers," recognizing, in the Phoedrus, the Egyptian king, and shows him to us wiser than Theut, whom he knew to be Hermes. But in the Charmides, it is manifest that he knew certain Thracians who were said to make the soul immortal. And Pythagoras is reported to have been a disciple of Sonches the Egyptian arch-prophet; and Plato, of Sechnuphis of Heliopolis; and Eudoxus, of Cnidius of Konuphis, who was also an Egyptian. And in his book, *On the Soul,* Plato again manifestly recognizes prophecy, when he introduces a prophet announcing the word of Lachesis, uttering predictions to the souls whose destiny is becoming fixed. And in the *Timæus* he introduces Solon, the very wise, learning from the barbarian. The substance of the declaration is to the following effect: "O Solon, Solon, you Greeks are always children. And no Greek is an old man. For you have no learning that is hoary with age."

Democritus appropriated the Babylonian ethic discourses, for he is said to have combined with his own compositions a translation of the column of Acicarus. And you may find the distinction notified by him when he writes, "Thus says Democritus." About himself, too, where, pluming himself on his erudition, he says, "I have roamed over the most ground of any man of my time, investigating the most remote parts. I have seen the most skies and lands, and I have heard of learned men in very great numbers. And in composition no one has surpassed me; in demonstration, not even those among the Egyptians who are called Arpenodaptæ, with all of whom I lived in exile up to eighty years." For he went to Babylon, and Persis, and Egypt, to learn from the Magi and the priests.

Zoroaster the Magus, Pythagoras showed to be a Persian. Of the secret books of this man, those who follow the heresy of Prodicus boast to be in possession. Alexander, in his book *On the Pythagorean Symbols*, relates that Pythagoras was a pupil of Nazaratus the Assyrian (some think that he is Ezekiel; but he is not, as will afterwards be shown), and will have it that, in addition to these, Pythagoras was a hearer of the Galatæ and the Brahmins. Clearchus the Peripatetic says that he knew a Jew who associated with Aristotle. Herac-litus says that, not humanly, but rather by God's aid, the Sibyl spoke. They say, accordingly, that at Delphi a stone was shown beside the oracle, on which, it is said, sat the first Sibyl, who came from Helicon, and had been reared by the Muses. But some say that she came from Milea, being the daughter of Lamia of Sidon. And Serapion, in his epic verses, says that the Sibyl, even when dead, ceased not from divination. And he writes that, what proceeded from her into the air after her death, was what gave oracular utterances in voices and omens; and on her body being changed into earth, and the grass as natural growing out of it, whatever beasts happening to be in that place fed on it exhibited to men an accurate knowledge of futurity by their entrails. He thinks also, that the face seen in the moon is her soul. So much for the Sibyl.

Numa the king of the Romans was a Pythagorean, and aided by the precepts of Moses, prohibited from making an image of God in human form, and of the shape of a living creature. Accordingly, during the first hundred and seventy years, though building temples, they made no cast or graven image. For Numa secretly showed them that the Best of Beings could not be apprehended except by the mind alone. Thus philosophy, a thing of the highest utility, flourished in antiquity among the barbarians, shedding its light over the nations.

And afterwards it came to Greece. First in its ranks were the prophets of the Egyptians; and the Chaldeans among the Assyrians; and the Druids among the Gauls; and the Samanæans among the Bactrians; and the philosophers of the Celts; and the Magi of the Persians, who foretold the Savior's birth, and came into the land of Judæa guided by a star. The Indian gymnosophists are also in the number, and the other barbarian philosophers. And of these there are two classes, some of them called Sarmanæ, and others Brahmins. And those of the Sarmanæ who are called Hylobii neither inhabit cities, nor have roofs over them, but are clothed in the bark of trees, feed on nuts, and drink water in their hands. Like those called Encratites in the present day, they know not marriage nor begetting of children.

Some, too, of the Indians obey the precepts of Buddha; whom, on account of his extraordinary sanctity, they have raised to divine honors. Anacharsis was a Scythian, and is recorded to have excelled many philosophers among the Greeks. And the Hyperboreans, Hellanicus relates, dwelt beyond the Riphæan mountains, and inculcated justice, not eating flesh, but using nuts. Those who are sixty years old they take without the gates, and do away with. There are also among the Germans those called sacred women, who, by inspecting the whirlpools of rivers and the eddies, and observing the noises of streams, presage and predict future events. These did not allow the men to fight against Cæsar till the new moon shone.

Of all these, by far the oldest is the Jewish race; and that their philosophy committed to writing has the precedence of philosophy among the Greeks, the Pythagorean Philo shows at large; and, besides him, Aristobulus the Peripatetic, and several others, not to waste time, in going over them by name. Very clearly the author Megasthenes, the contemporary of Seleucus Nicanor, writes as follows in the third of his books, *On Indian Affairs:* "All that was said about nature by the ancients is said also by those who philosophize beyond Greece: some things by the Brahmins among the Indians, and others by those called Jews in Syria." Some more fabulously say that certain of those called the Idæan Dactyli were the first wise men; to whom are attributed the invention of what are called the "Ephesian letters," and of numbers in music. For which reason dactyls in music received their name. And the Idæan Dactyli were Phrygians and barbarians. Herodotus relates that Hercules, having grown a sage and a student of physics, received from the barbarian Atlas, the Phrygian, the columns of the universe; the fable meaning that he received by instruction the knowledge of the heavenly bodies. And Hermippus of Berytus calls Charon the Centaur wise; about whom, he that wrote *The Battle of the Titans* says, "that he first led the race of mortals to righteousness, by teaching them the solemnity of the oath, and propitiatory sacrifices and the figures of Olympus." By him Achilles, who fought at Troy, was taught. And Hippo, the daughter of the Centaur, who dwelt with Æolus, taught him her father's science, the knowledge of physics. Euripides also testifies of Hippo as follows:—

"Who first, by oracles, presaged,
And by the rising stars, events divine."

By this Æolus, Ulysses was received as a guest after the taking of Troy. Mark the epochs by comparison with the age of Moses, and with the high antiquity of the philosophy promulgated by him.

CHAPTER XVI.—THAT THE INVENTORS OF OTHER ARTS WERE MOSTLY BARBARIANS.

And barbarians were inventors not only of philosophy, but almost of every art. The Egyptians were the first to introduce astrology among men. Similarly also the Chaldeans. The Egyptians first showed how to burn lamps, and divided the year into twelve months, prohibited intercourse with women in the temples, and enacted that no one should enter the temples from a woman without bathing. Again, they were the inventors of geometry. There are some who say that the Carians invented prognostication by the stars. The Phrygians were the first who attended to the flight of birds. And the Tuscans, neighbors of Italy, were adepts at the art of the Haruspex. The Isaurians and the Arabians invented augury, as the Telmesians divination by dreams. The Etruscans invented the trumpet, and the Phrygians the flute. For Olympus and Marsyas were Phrygians. And Cadmus, the inventor of letters among the Greeks, as Euphorus says, was a Phoenician; whence also Herodotus writes that they were called Phoenician letters. And they say that the Phoenicians and the Syrians first invented letters; and that Apis, an aboriginal inhabitant of Egypt, invented the healing art before Io came into Egypt. But afterwards they say that Asclepius improved the art. Atlas the Libyan was the first who built a ship and navigated the sea. Kelmis and Damnaneus, Idæan Dactyli, first discovered iron in Cyprus. Another Idæan discovered the tempering of brass; according to Hesiod, a Scythian. The Thracians first invented what is called a scimitar (ἅρπη),—it is a curved sword,—and were the first to use shields on horseback. Similarly also the Illyrians invented the shield (πέλτη). Besides, they say that the Tuscans invented the art of molding clay; and that Itanus (he was a Samnite) first fashioned the oblong shield (θυρέος). Cadmus the Phoenician invented stonecutting, and discovered the gold mines on the Pangæan mountain. Further, another nation, the Cappadocians, first invented the instrument called the nabla, and the Assyrians in the same way the dichord. The Carthaginians were the first that constructed a trireme; and it was built by Bosporus, an aboriginal. Medea, the daughter of Æetas, a Colchian, first invented the dyeing of hair. Besides, the Noropes (they are a Pæonian race, and are now called the Norici) worked copper, and were the first that purified iron. Amycus the king of the Bebryci was the first inventor of boxing-gloves. In music, Olympus the Mysian practiced the Lydian harmony; and the people called Troglodytes invented the sambuca, a musical instrument. It is said that the crooked pipe was invented by Satyrus the Phrygian; likewise also diatonic harmony by Hyagnis, a Phrygian too; and notes by Olympus, a Phrygian; as also the Phrygian harmony, and the half-Phrygian and the half-Lydian, by Marsyas, who belonged to the same region as those mentioned above. And the Doric was invented by Thamyris the Thracian. We have heard that the Persians were the first who fashioned the chariot, and bed, and footstool; and the Sidonians the first to construct a trireme. The Sicilians, close to Italy, were the first inventors of the phorminx, which is not much inferior to the lyre. And they invented castanets. In the time of Semiramis queen of the Assyrians, they relate that linen garments were invented. And Hellanicus says that Atossa queen of the Persians was the first who composed a letter. These things are reported by Scamo of Mitylene, Theophrastus of Ephesus, Cydippus of Mantinea, also Antiphanes, Aristodemus, and Aristotle; and besides these, Philostephanus, and also Strato the Peripatetic, in his books *Concerning Inventions*. I have added a few details from them, in order to confirm the inventive and practically useful genius of the barbarians, by whom the Greeks profited in their studies. And if any one objects to the barbarous language, Anacharsis says, "All the Greeks speak Scythian to me." It was he who was held in admiration by the Greeks, who said, "My covering is a cloak; my supper, milk and cheese." You see that the barbarian philosophy professes deeds, not words. The apostle thus speaks: "So likewise ye, except ye utter by the tongue a word easy to be understood, how shall ye know what is spoken? For ye shall speak into the air. There are, it may be, so many kind of voices in the world, and none of them is without signification. Therefore if I know not the meaning of the voice, I shall be unto him that speaks a barbarian, and he that speaks shall be a barbarian unto me." And, "Let him that speaks in an unknown tongue pray that he may interpret."

Nay more, it was late before the teaching and writing of discourses reached Greece. Alcmæon, the son of Perithus, of Crotona, first composed a treatise on nature. And it is related that Anaxagoras of Clazomenæ, the son of Hegesibulus, first published a book in writing. The first to adapt music to poetical compositions was Terpander of Antissa; and he set the laws of the Lacedæmonians to music. Lasus of Hermione invented the dithyramb; Stesichorus of Himera, the hymn; Alcman the Spartan, the choral song; Anacreon of Teos, love songs; Pindar the Theban, the dance accompanied with song. Timotheus of Miletus was the first to execute those musical compositions called νόμοι on the lyre, with dancing. Moreover, the iambus was invented by Archilochus of Paros, and the choliambus by Hipponax of Ephesus. Tragedy owed its origin to Thespis the Athenian, and comedy to Susarion of Icaria. Their dates are handed down by the grammarians. But it were tedious to specify them accurately: presently, however, Dionysus, on whose account the Dionysian spectacles are celebrated, will be shown to be later than Moses. They say that Antiphon of Rhamnusium, the son of Sophilus, first invented scholastic discourses and rhetorical figures, and was the first who pled causes for a fee, and wrote a forensic speech for delivery, as Diodorus says. And Apollodorus of Cuma first assumed the name of critic, and was called a grammarian. Some say it was Eratosthenes of Cyrene who was first so called, since he published two books which he entitled *Grammatica.* The first who was called a grammarian, as we now use the term, was Praxiphanes, the son of Disnysophenes of Mitylene. Zeleucus the Locrian was reported to have been the first to have framed laws (in writing). Others say that it was Menos the son of Zeus, in the time of Lynceus. He comes after Danaus, in the eleventh generation from Inachus and Moses; as we shall show a little further on. And Lycurgus, who lived many years after the taking of Troy, legislated for the Lacedæmonians a hundred and fifty years before the Olympiads. We have spoken before of the age of Solon. Draco (he was a legislator too) is discovered to have lived about the three hundred and ninth Olympiad. Antilochus, again, who wrote of the learned men from the age of Pythagoras to the death of Epicurus, which took place in the tenth day of the month Gamelion, makes up altogether three hundred and twelve years. Moreover, some say that Phanothea, the wife of Icarius, invented the heroic hexameter; others Themis, one of the Titanides. Didymus, however, in his work *On the Pythagorean Philosophy*, relates that Theano of Crotona was the first woman who cultivated philosophy and composed poems. The Hellenic philosophy then, according to some, apprehended the truth accidentally, dimly, partially; as others will have it, was set a-going by the devil. Several suppose that certain powers, descending from heaven, inspired the whole of philosophy. But if the Hellenic philosophy comprehends not the whole extent of the truth, and besides is destitute of strength to perform the commandments of the Lord, yet it prepares the way for the truly royal teaching; training in some way or other, and molding the character, and fitting him who believes in Providence for the reception of the truth.

CHAPTER XVII.—ON THE SAYING OF THE SAVIOUR, "ALL THAT CAME BEFORE ME WERE THIEVES AND ROBBERS."

But, say they, it is written, "All who were before the Lord's advent are thieves and robbers." All, then, who are in the Word (for it is these that were previous to the incarnation of the Word) are understood generally. But the prophets, being sent and inspired by the Lord, were not thieves, but servants. The Scripture accordingly says, "Wisdom sent her servants, inviting with loud proclamation to a goblet of wine."

But philosophy, it is said, was not sent by the Lord, but came stolen, or given by a thief. It was then some power or angel that had learned something of the truth, but abode not in it, that inspired and taught these things, not without the Lord's knowledge, who knew before the constitution of each essence the issues of futurity, but without His prohibition.

For the theft which reached men then, had some advantage; not that he who perpetrated the theft had utility in his eye, but Providence directed the issue of the audacious deed to utility. I know that many are perpetually assailing us with the allegation, that not to prevent a thing happening, is to be the cause of it happening. For they say, that the man who does not take precaution against a theft, or does not prevent it, is the cause of it: as he is the cause of the conflagration who has not quenched it at the beginning; and the master of the vessel who does not reef the sail, is the cause of the shipwreck. Certainly those who are the causes of such events are punished by the law. For to him who had power to prevent, attaches the blame of what happens. We say to them, that causation is seen in doing, working, acting; but the not preventing is in this respect inoperative. Further, causation attaches to activity; as in the case of the shipbuilder in relation to the origin of the vessel, and the builder in relation to the construction of the house. But that which does not prevent is separated from what takes place. Wherefore the effect will be accomplished; because that which could have prevented neither acts nor prevents. For what activity does that which prevents not exert? Now their assertion is reduced to absurdity, if they shall say that the cause of the wound is not the dart, but the shield, which did not prevent the dart from passing through; and if they blame not the thief, but the man who did not prevent the theft. Let them then say, that it was not Hector that burned the ships of the Greeks, but Achilles; because, having the power to prevent Hector, he did not prevent him; but out of anger (and it depended on himself to be angry or not) did not keep back the fire, and was a concurring cause. Now the devil, being possessed of free-will, was able both to repent and to steal; and it was he who was the author of the theft, not the Lord, who did not prevent him. But neither was the gift hurtful, so as to require that prevention should intervene.

But if strict accuracy must be employed in dealing with them, let them know, that that which does not prevent what we assert to have taken place in the theft, is not a cause at all; but that what prevents is involved in the accusation of being a cause. For he that protects with a shield is the cause of him whom he protects not being wounded; preventing him, as he does, from being wounded. For the demon of Socrates was a cause, not by not preventing, but by exhorting, even if (strictly speaking) he did not exhort. And neither praises nor censures, neither rewards nor punishments, are right, when the soul has not the power of inclination and disinclination, but evil is involuntary. Whence he who prevents is a cause; while he who prevents not judges justly the soul's choice. So in no respect is God the author of evil. But since free choice and inclination originate sins, and a mistaken judgment sometimes prevails, from which, since it is ignorance and stupidity, we do not take pains to recede, punishments are rightly inflicted. For to take fever is involuntary; but when one takes fever through his own fault, from excess, we blame him. Inasmuch, then, as evil is involuntary,—for no one prefers evil as evil; but induced by the pleasure that is in it, and imagining it good, considers it desirable;—such being the case, to free ourselves from ignorance, and from evil and voluptuous choice, and above all, to withhold our assent from those delusive phantasies, depends on ourselves. The devil is called "thief and robber;" having mixed false prophets with the prophets, as tares with the wheat. "All, then, that came before the Lord, were thieves and robbers;" not absolutely all men, but all the false prophets, and all who were not properly sent by Him. For the false prophets possessed the prophetic name dishonestly, being prophets, but prophets of the liar. For the Lord says, "Ye are of your father the devil; and the lusts of your father ye will do. He was a murderer from the beginning, and abode not in the truth, because there is no truth in him. When he speaks a lie, he speaks of his own; for he is a liar, and the father of it." But among the lies, the false prophets also told some true things. And in reality they prophesied "in an ecstasy," as the servants of the apostate. And the Shepherd, the angel of repentance, says to Hermas, of the false prophet: "For he speaks some truths. For the devil fills him with his own spirit, if perchance he may be able to cast down any one from what is right." All things, therefore, are dispensed from heaven for good, "that by the Church may be made known the manifold wisdom of God, according to the eternal foreknowledge, which He purposed in Christ." Nothing withstands God: nothing opposes Him: seeing He is Lord and omnipotent. Further, the counsels and activities of those who have rebelled, being partial, proceed from a bad disposition, as bodily diseases from a bad constitution, but are guided by universal Providence to a salutary issue, even though the cause be productive of disease. It is accordingly the greatest achievement of divine Providence, not to allow the evil, which has sprung from voluntary apostasy, to remain useless, and for no good, and not to become in all respects injurious. For it is the work of the divine wisdom, and excellence, and power, not alone to do good (for this is, so to speak, the nature of God, as it is of fire to warm and of light to illumine), but especially to ensure that what happens through the evils hatched by any, may come to a good and useful issue, and to use to advantage those things which appear to be evils, as also the testimony which accrues from temptation.

    There is then in philosophy, though stolen as the fire by Prometheus, a slender spark, capable of being fanned into flame, a trace of wisdom and an impulse from God. Well, be it so that "the thieves and robbers" are the philosophers among the Greeks, who from the Hebrew prophets before the coming of the Lord received fragments of the truth, not with full knowledge, and claimed these as their own teachings, disguising some points, treating others sophistically by their ingenuity, and discovering other things, for perchance they had "the spirit of perception." Aristotle, too, assented to Scripture, and declared sophistry to have stolen wisdom, as we intimated before. And the apostle says, "Which things we speak, not in the words which man's wisdom teaches, but which the Holy Ghost teaches." For of the prophets it is said, "We have all received of His fullness," that is, of Christ's. So that the prophets are not thieves. "And my doctrine is not Mine," says the Lord, "but the Father's which sent me." And of those who steal He says: "But he that speaks of himself, seeks his own glory." Such are the Greeks, "lovers of their own selves, and boasters." Scripture, when it speaks of these as wise, does not brand those who are really wise, but those who are wise in appearance.

CHAPTER XVIII.—HE ILLUSTRATES THE APOSTLE'S SAYING, "I WILL DESTROY THE WISDOM OF THE WISE."

And of such it is said, "I will destroy the wisdom of the wise: I will bring to nothing the understanding of the prudent." The apostle accordingly adds, "Where is the wise? Where is the scribe? Where is the disputer of this world?" setting in contradistinction to the scribes, the disputers of this world, the philosophers of the Gentiles. "Hath not God made foolish the wisdom of the world?" which is equivalent to, showed it to be foolish, and not true, as they thought. And if you ask the cause of their seeming wisdom, he will say, "because of the blindness of their heart;" since "in the wisdom of God," that is, as proclaimed by the prophets, "the world knew not," in the wisdom "which spoke by the prophets," "Him," that is, God,—"it pleased God by the foolishness of preaching"—what seemed to the Greeks foolishness—"to save them that believe. For the Jews require signs," in order to faith; "and the Greeks seek after wisdom," plainly those reasoning styled "irresistible," and those others, namely, syllogisms. "But we preach Jesus Christ crucified; to the Jews a stumbling-block," because, though knowing prophecy, they did not believe the event: "to the Greeks, foolishness;" for those who in their own estimation are wise, consider it fabulous that the Son of God should speak by man and that God should have a Son, and especially that that Son should have suffered. Whence their preconceived idea inclines them to disbelieve. For the advent of the Savior did not make people foolish, and hard of heart, and unbelieving, but made them understanding, amenable to persuasion, and believing. But those that would not believe, by separating themselves from the voluntary adherence of those who obeyed, were proved to be without understanding, unbelievers and fools. "But to them who are called, both Jews and Greeks, Christ is the power of God, and the wisdom of God." Should we not understand (as is better) the words rendered, "Hath not God made foolish the wisdom of the world?" negatively: "God hath not made foolish the wisdom of the world?"—so that the cause of their hardness of heart may not appear to have proceeded from God, "making foolish the wisdom of the world." For on all accounts, being wise, they incur greater blame in not believing the proclamation. For the preference and choice of truth is voluntary. But that declaration, "I will destroy the wisdom of the wise," declares Him to have sent forth light, by bringing forth in opposition the despised and contemned barbarian philosophy; as the lamp, when shone upon by the sun, is said to be extinguished, on account of its not then exerting the same power. All having been therefore called, those who are willing to obey have been named "called." For there is no unrighteousness with God. Those of either race who have believed, are "a peculiar people." And in the Acts of the Apostles you will find this, word for word, "Those then who received his word were baptized;" but those who would not obey kept themselves aloof. To these prophecy says, "If ye be willing and hear me, ye shall eat the good things of the land;" proving that choice or refusal depends on ourselves. The apostle designates the doctrine which is according to the

Lord, "the wisdom of God," in order to show that the true philosophy has been communicated by the Son. Further, he, who has a show of wisdom, has certain exhortations enjoined on him by the apostle: "That ye put on the new man, which after God is renewed in righteousness and true holiness. Wherefore, putting away lying, speak every man truth. Neither give place to the devil. Let him that stole, steal no more; but rather let him labor, working that which is good" (and to work is to labor in seeking the truth; for it is accompanied with rational well-doing), "that ye may have to give to him that has need," both of worldly wealth and of divine wisdom. For he wishes both that the word be taught, and that the money be put into the bank, accurately tested, to accumulate interest. Whence he adds, "Let no corrupt communication proceed out of your mouth,"—that is "corrupt communication" which proceeds out of conceit,—"but that which is good for the use of edifying, that it may minister grace to the hearers." And the word of the good God must needs be good. And how is it possible that he who saves shall not be good?

CHAPTER XIX.—THAT THE PHILOSOPHERS HAVE ATTAINED TO SOME PORTION OF TRUTH.

Since, then, the Greeks are testified to have laid down some true opinions, we may from this point take a glance at the testimonies. Paul, in the Acts of the Apostles, is recorded to have said to the Areopagites, "I perceive that ye are more than ordinarily religious. For as I passed by, and beheld your devotions, I found an altar with the inscription, To The Unknown God. Whom therefore ye ignorantly worship, Him declare I unto you. God, that made the world and all things therein, seeing that He is Lord of heaven and earth, dwelled not in temples made with hands; neither is worshipped with men's hands, as though He needed anything, seeing He giveth to all life, and breath, and all things; and hath made of one blood all nations of men to dwell on all the face of the earth, and hath determined the times before appointed, and the bounds of their habitation; that they should seek God, if haply they might feel after Him, and find Him; though He be not far from every one of us: for in Him we live, and move, and have our being; as certain also of your own poets have said, For we also are His offspring." Whence it is evident that the apostle, by availing himself of poetical examples from the *Phenomena* of Aratus, approves of what had been well spoken by the Greeks; and intimates that, by the unknown God, God the Creator was in a roundabout way worshipped by the Greeks; but that it was necessary by positive knowledge to apprehend and learn Him by the Son. "Wherefore, then, I send thee to the Gentiles," it is said, "to open their eyes, and to turn them from darkness to light, and from the power of Satan unto God; that they may receive forgiveness of sins, and inheritance among them that are sanctified by faith which is in Me." Such, then, are the eyes of the blind which are opened. The knowledge of the Father by the Son is the comprehension of the "Greek circumlocution;" and to turn from the power of Satan is to change from sin, through which bondage was produced. We do not, indeed, receive absolutely all philosophy, but that of which Socrates speaks in Plato. "For there are (as they say) in the mysteries many bearers of the thyrsus, but few bacchanals;" meaning, "that many are called, but few chosen." He accordingly plainly adds: "These, in my opinion, are none else than those who have philosophized right; to belong to whose number, I myself have left nothing undone in life, as far as I could, but have endeavored in every way. Whether we have endeavored rightly and achieved aught, we shall know when we have gone there, if God will, a little afterwards." Does he not then seem to declare from the Hebrew Scriptures the righteous man's hope, through faith, after death? And in *Demodocus* (if that is really the work of Plato): "And do not imagine that I call it philosophizing to spend life pottering about the arts, or learning many things, but something different; since I, at least, would consider this a disgrace." For he knew, I reckon, "that the knowledge of many things does not educate the mind," according to Heraclitus.

And in the fifth book of the *Republic,* he says, "'Shall we then call all these, and the others which study such things, and those who apply themselves to the meaner arts, philosophers?' 'By no means,' I said, 'but like philosophers.' 'And whom,' said he, 'do you call true?' 'Those,' said I, 'who delight in the contemplation of truth. For philosophy is not in geometry, with its postulates and hypotheses; nor in music, which is conjectural; nor in astronomy, crammed full of physical, fluid, and probable causes. But the knowledge of the good and truth itself
are requisite,—what is good being one thing, and the ways to the good another.'" So that he does not allow that the curriculum of training suffices for the good, but co-operates in rousing and training the soul to intellectual objects. Whether, then, they say that the Greeks gave forth some utterances of the true philosophy by accident, it is the accident of a divine administration (for no one will, for the sake of the present argument with us, deify chance); or by good fortune, good fortune is not unforeseen. Or were one, on the other hand, to say that the Greeks possessed a natural conception of these things, we know the one Creator of nature; just as we also call righteousness natural; or that they had a common intellect, let us reflect who is its father, and what righteousness is in the mental economy. For were one to name "prediction," and assign as its cause "combined utterance," he specifies forms of prophecy. Further, others will have it that some truths were uttered by the philosophers, in appearance.

The divine apostle writes accordingly respecting us: "For now we see as through a glass;" knowing ourselves in it by reflection, and simultaneously contemplating, as we can, the efficient cause, from that, which, in us, is divine. For it is said, "Having seen thy brother, thou hast seen thy God:" methinks that now the Savior God is declared to us. But after the laying aside of the flesh, "face to face,"—then definitely and comprehensively, when the heart becomes pure. And by reflection and direct vision, those among the Greeks who have philosophized accurately, see God. For such, through our weakness, are our true views, as images are seen in the water, and as we see things through pellucid and transparent bodies. Excellently therefore Solomon says: "He who sowed righteousness, worked faith." "And there are those who, sewing their own, make increase." And again: "Take care of the verdure on the plain, and thou shalt cut grass and gather ripe hay, that thou may have sheep for clothing." You see how care must be taken for external clothing and for keeping. "And thou shalt intelligently know the souls of thy flock.""For when the Gentiles, which have not the law, do by nature the things contained in the law, these, having not the law, are a law unto themselves; uncircumcision observing the precepts of the law," according to the apostle, both before the law and before the advent. As if making comparison of those addicted to philosophy with those called heretics, the Word most clearly says: "Better is a friend that is near, than a brother that dwelled afar off." "And he who relies on falsehoods, feeds on the winds, and pursues winged birds." I do not think that philosophy directly declares the Word, although in many instances philosophy attempts and persuasively teaches us probable arguments; but it assails the sects. Accordingly it is added: "For he hath forsaken the ways of his own vineyard, and wandered in the tracks of his own husbandry." Such are the sects which deserted the primitive Church. Now he who has fallen into heresy passes through an arid wilderness, abandoning the only true God, destitute of God, seeking waterless water, reaching an uninhabited and thirsty land, collecting sterility with his hands. And those destitute of prudence, that is, those involved in heresies, "I enjoin," remarks Wisdom, saying, "Touch sweetly stolen bread and the sweet water of theft;" the Scripture manifestly applying the terms bread and water to nothing else but to those heresies, which employ bread and water in the oblation, not according to the canon of the Church. For there are those who celebrate the

Eucharist with mere water. "But begone, stay not in her place:" *place* is the synagogue, not the Church. He calls it by the equivocal name, *place*. Then He subjoins: "For so shalt thou pass through the water of another;" reckoning heretical baptism not proper and true water. "And thou shalt pass over another's river," that rushes along and sweeps down to the sea; into which he is cast who, having diverged from the stability which is according to truth, rushes back into the heathenish and tumultuous waves of life.

CHAPTER XX.—IN WHAT RESPECT PHILOSOPHY CONTRIBUTES TO THE COMPREHENSION OF DIVINE TRUTH.

As many men drawing down the ship, cannot be called many causes, but one cause consisting of many;—for each individual by himself is not the cause of the ship being drawn, but along with the rest;—so also philosophy, being the search for truth, contributes to the comprehension of truth; not as being the cause of comprehension, but a cause along with other things, and co-operator; perhaps also a joint cause. And as the several virtues are causes of the happiness of one individual; and as both the sun, and the fire, and the bath, and clothing are of one getting warm: so while truth is one, many things contribute to its investigation. But its discovery is by the Son. If then we consider, virtue is, in power, one. But it is the case, that when exhibited in some things, it is called prudence, in others temperance, and in others manliness or righteousness. By the same analogy, while truth is one, in geometry there is the truth of geometry; in music, that of music; and in the right philosophy, there will be Hellenic truth. But that is the only authentic truth, unassailable, in which we are instructed by the Son of God. In the same way we say, that the drachma being one and the same, when given to the shipmaster, is called the fare; to the tax-gatherer, tax; to the landlord, rent; to the teacher, fees; to the seller, an earnest. And each, whether it be virtue or truth, called by the same name, is the cause of its own peculiar effect alone; and from the blending of them arises a happy life. For we are not made happy by names alone, when we say that a good life is happiness, and that the man who is adorned in his soul with virtue is happy. But if philosophy contributes remotely to the discovery of truth, by reaching, by diverse essays, after the knowledge which touches close on the truth, the knowledge possessed by us, it aids him who aims at grasping it, in accordance with the Word, to apprehend knowledge. But the Hellenic truth is distinct from that held by us (although it has got the same name), both in respect of extent of knowledge, certainly of demonstration, divine power, and the like. For we are taught of God, being instructed in the truly "sacred letters" by the Son of God. Whence those, to whom we refer, influence souls not in the way we do, but by different teaching. And if, for the sake of those who are fond of fault-finding, we must draw a distinction, by saying that philosophy is a concurrent and cooperating cause of true apprehension, being the search for truth, then we shall avow it to be a preparatory training for the enlightened man (τοῦ γνωστικοῦ); not assigning as the cause that which is but the joint-cause; nor as the upholding cause, what is merely co-operative; nor giving to philosophy the place of a *sine quâ non*. Since almost all of us, without training in arts and sciences, and the Hellenic philosophy, and some even without learning at all, through the influence of a philosophy divine and barbarous, and by power, have through faith received the word concerning God, trained by self-operating wisdom. But that which acts in conjunction with something else, being of itself incapable of operating by itself, we describe as cooperating and concausing, and say that it becomes a cause only in virtue of its being a joint cause, and receives the name of cause only in respect of its concurring with something else, but that it cannot by itself produce the right effect.

Although at one time philosophy justified the Greeks, not conducting them to that entire righteousness to which it is ascertained to cooperate, as the first and second flight of steps help you in your ascent to the upper room, and the grammarian helps the philosopher. Not as if by its abstraction, the perfect Word would be rendered incomplete, or truth perish; since also sight, and hearing, and the voice contribute to truth, but it is the mind which is the appropriate faculty for knowing it. But of those things which co-operate, some contribute a greater amount of power; some, a less. Perspicuity accordingly aids in the communication of truth, and logic in preventing us from falling under the heresies by which we are assailed.

But the teaching, which is according to the Savior, is complete in itself and without defect, being "the power and wisdom of God;" and the Hellenic philosophy does not, by its approach, make the truth more powerful; but rendering powerless the assault of sophistry against it, and frustrating the treacherous plots laid against the truth, is said to be the proper "fence and wall of the vineyard." And the truth which is according to faith is as necessary for life as bread; while the preparatory discipline is like sauce and sweetmeats. "At the end of the dinner, the dessert is pleasant," according to the Theban Pindar. And the Scripture has expressly said, "The innocent will become wiser by understanding, and the wise will receive knowledge." "And he that speaks of himself," says the Lord, "seeks his own glory; but He that seeks His glory that sent Him is true, and there is no unrighteousness in Him." On the other hand, therefore, he who appropriates what belongs to the barbarians, and vaunts it is his own, does wrong, increasing his own glory, and falsifying the truth. It is such a one that is by Scripture called a "thief." It is therefore said, "Son, be not a liar; for falsehood leads to theft." Nevertheless the thief possesses really, what he has possessed himself of dishonestly, whether it be gold, or silver, or speech, or dogma. The ideas, then, which they have stolen, and which are partially true, they know by conjecture and necessary logical deduction: on becoming disciples, therefore, they will know them with intelligent apprehension.

CHAPTER XXI.—THE JEWISH INSTITUTIONS AND LAWS OF FAR HIGHER ANTIQUITY THAN THE PHILOSOPHY OF THE GREEKS.

On the plagiarizing of the dogmas of the philosophers from the Hebrews, we shall treat a little afterwards. But first, as due order demands, we must now speak of the epoch of Moses, by which the philosophy of the Hebrews will be demonstrated beyond all contradiction to be the most ancient of all wisdom. This has been discussed with accuracy by Tatian in his book *To the Greeks*, and by Cassian in the first book of his *Exegetics*. Nevertheless our commentary demands that we too should run over what has been said on the point. Apion, then, the grammarian, surnamed Pleistonices, in the fourth book of *The Egyptian Histories*, although of so hostile a disposition towards the Hebrews, being by race an Egyptian, as to compose a work against the Jews, when referring to Amosis king of the Egyptians, and his exploits, adduces, as a witness, Ptolemy of Mendes. And his remarks are to the following effect: Amosis, who lived in the time of the Argive Inachus, overthrew Athyria, as Ptolemy of Mendes relates in his *Chronology*. Now this Ptolemy was a priest; and setting forth the deeds of the Egyptian kings in three entire books, he says, that the exodus of the Jews from Egypt, under the conduct of Moses, took place while Amosis was king of Egypt. Whence it is seen that Moses flourished in the time of Inachus. And of the Hellenic states, the most ancient is the Argolic, I mean that which took its rise from Inachus, as Dionysius of Halicarnassus teaches in his *Times*. And younger by forty generations than it was Attica, founded by Cecrops, who was an aboriginal of double race, as Tatian expressly says; and Arcadia, founded by Pelasgus, younger too by nine generations; and he, too, is said to have been an aboriginal. And more recent than this last by fifty-two generations, was Pthiotis, founded by Deucalion. And from the time of Inachus to the Trojan war twenty generations or more are reckoned; let us say, four hundred years and more. And if Ctesias says that the Assyrian power is many years older than the Greek, the exodus of Moses from Egypt will appear to have taken place in the forty-second year of the Assyrian empire, in the thirty-second year of the reign of Belochus, in the time of Amosis the Egyptian, and of Inachus the Argive. And in Greece, in the time of Phoroneus, who succeeded Inachus, the flood of Ogyges occurred; and monarchy subsisted in Sicyon first in the person of Ægialeus, then of Europs, then of Telches; in Crete, in the person of Cres. For Acusilaus says that Phoroneus was the first man. Whence, too, the author of *Phoronis* said that he was "the father of mortal men." Thence Plato in the *Timoeus*, following Acusilaus, writes: "And wishing to draw them out into a discussion respecting antiquities, he said that he ventured to speak of the most remote antiquities of this city respecting Phoroneus, called the first man, and Niobe, and what happened after the deluge." And in the time of Phorbus lived Actæus, from whom is derived Actaia, Attica; and in the time of Triopas lived Prometheus, and Atlas, and Epimetheus, and Cecrops of double race, and Ino. And in the time of Crotopus occurred the burning of Phaëthon, and the deluge of Deucalion; and in the time of Sthenelus, the reign of Amphictyon, and the arrival of Danaus in the Peloponnesus; and trader Dardanus happened the building of Dardania, whom, says Homer,

"First cloud-compelling Zeus begat,"—

and the transmigration from Crete into Phoenicia. And in the time of Lynceus took place the abduction of Proserpine, and the dedication of the sacred enclosure in Eleusis, and the husbandry of Triptolemus, and the arrival of Cadmus in Thebes, and the reign of Minos. And in the time of Proetus the war of Eumolpus with the Athenians took place; and in the time of Acrisius, the removal of Pelops from Phrygia, the arrival of Ion at Athens; and the second Cecrops appeared, and the exploits of Perseus and Dionysus took place, and Orpheus and Musæus lived. And in the eighteenth year of the reign of Agamemnon, Troy was taken, in the first year of the reign of

Demophon the son of Theseus at Athens, on the twelfth day of the month Thargelion, as Dionysius the Argive says; but Ægias and Dercylus, in the third book, say that it was on the eighth day of the last division of the month Panemus; Hellanicus says that it was on the twelfth of the month Thargelion; and some of the authors of the *Attica* say that it was on the eighth of the last division of the month in the last year of Menestheus, at full moon.

"It was midnight,"

says the author of the *Little Iliad*,

"And the moon shone clear."

Others say, it took place on the same day of Scirophorion. But Theseus, the rival of Hercules, is older by a generation than the Trojan war. Accordingly Tlepolemus, a son of Hercules, is mentioned by Homer, as having served at Troy.

Moses, then, is shown to have preceded the deification of Dionysus six hundred and four years, if he was deified in the thirty-second year of the reign of Perseus, as Apollodorus says in his *Chronology*. From Bacchus to Hercules and the chiefs that sailed with Jason in the ship Argo, are comprised sixty-three years. Æsculapius and the Dioscuri sailed with them, as Apollonius Rhodius testifies in his *Argonautics*. And from the reign of Hercules, in Argos, to the deification of Hercules and of Æsculapius, are comprised thirty-eight years, according to Apollodorus the chronologist; from this to the deification of Castor and Pollux, fifty-three years. And at this time Troy was taken. And if we may believe the poet Hesiod, let us hear him:—

"Then to Jove, Maia, Atlas' daughter, bore renowned Hermes, Herald of the immortals, having ascended the sacred couch.

And Semele, the daughter of Cadmus, too, bore an illustrious son, Dionysus, the joy-inspiring, when she mingled with him in love."

Cadmus, the father of Semele, came to Thebes in the time of Lynceus, and was the inventor of the Greek letters. Triopas was a contemporary of Isis, in the seventh generation from Inachus. And Isis, who is the same as Io, is so called, it is said, from her going (ἰέναι) roaming over the whole earth. Her, Istrus, in his work on the migration of the Egyptians, calls the daughter of Prometheus. Prometheus lived in the time of Triopas, in the seventh generation after Moses. So that Moses appears to have flourished even before the birth of men, according to the chronology of the Greeks. Leon, who treated of the Egyptian divinities, says that Isis by the Greeks was called Ceres, who lived in the time of Lynceus, in the eleventh generation after Moses. And Apis the king of Argos built Memphis, as Aristippus says in the first book of the *Arcadica*. And Aristeas the Argive says that he was named Serapis, and that it is he that the Egyptians worship. And Nymphodorus of Amphipolis, in the third book of the *Institutions of Asia*, says that the bull Apis, dead and laid in a coffin (σορός), was deposited in the temple of the god (δαίμονος) there worshipped, and thence was called Soroapis, and afterwards Serapis by the custom of the natives. And Apis is third after Inachus. Further, Latona lived in the time of Tityus. "For he dragged Latona, the radiant consort of Zeus." Now Tityus was contemporary with Tantalus. Rightly, therefore, the Boeotian Pindar writes, "And in time was Apollo born;" and no wonder when he is found along with Hercules, serving Admetus "for a long year." Zethus and Amphion, the inventors of music, lived about the age of Cadmus. And should one assert that Phemonoe was the first who sang oracles in verse to Acrisius, let him know that twenty-seven years after Phemonoe, lived Orpheus, and

Musæus, and Linus the teacher of Hercules. And Homer and Hesiod are much more recent than the Trojan war; and after them the legislators among the Greeks are far more recent, Lycurgus and Solon, and the seven wise men, and Pherecydes of Syros, and Pythagoras the great, who lived later, about the Olympiads, as we have shown. We have also demonstrated Moses to be more ancient, not only than those called poets and wise men among the Greeks, but than the most of their deities. Nor he alone, but the Sibyl also is more ancient than Orpheus. For it is said, that respecting her appellation and her oracular utterances there are several accounts; that being a Phrygian, she was called Artemis; and that on her arrival at Delphi, she sang—

> "O Delphians, ministers of far-darting Apollo,
> I come to declare the mind of Ægis-bearing Zeus,
> Enraged as I am at my own brother Apollo."

There is another also, an Erythræan, called Herophile. These are mentioned by Heraclides of Pontus in his work *On Oracles*. I pass over the Egyptian Sibyl, and the Italian, who inhabited the Carmentale in Rome, whose son was Evander, who built the temple of Pan in Rome, called the Lupercal.

It is worth our while, having reached this point, to examine the dates of the other prophets among the Hebrews who succeeded Moses. After the close of Moses's life, Joshua succeeded to the leadership of the people, and he, after warring for sixty-five years, rested in the good land other five-and-twenty. As the book of Joshua relates, the above mentioned man was the successor of Moses twenty-seven years. Then the Hebrews having sinned, were delivered to Chusachar king of Mesopotamia for eight years, as the book of Judges mentions. But having afterwards besought the Lord, they receive for leader Gothoniel, the younger brother of Caleb, of the tribe of Judah, who, having slain the king of Mesopotamia, ruled over the people forty years in succession. And having again sinned, they were delivered into the hands of Æglom king of the Moabites for eighteen years. But on their repentance, Aod, a man who had equal use of both hands, of the tribe of Ephraim, was their leader for eighty years. It was he that dispatched Æglom. On the death of Aod, and on their sinning again, they were delivered into the hand of Jabim king of Canaan twenty years. After him Deborah the wife of Lapidoth, of the tribe of Ephraim, prophesied; and Ozias the son of Rhiesu was high priest. At her instance Barak the son of Bener, of the tribe of Naphtali, commanding the army, having joined battle with Sisera, Jabim's commander-in-chief, conquered him. And after that Deborah ruled, judging the people forty years. On her death, the people having again sinned, were delivered into the hands of the Midianites seven years. After these events, Gideon, of the tribe of Manasseh, the son of Joas, having fought with his three hundred men, and killed a hundred and twenty thousand, ruled forty years; after whom the son of Ahimelech, three years. He was succeeded by Boleas, the son of Bedan, the son of Charran, of the tribe of Ephraim, who ruled twenty-three years. After whom, the people having sinned again, were delivered to the Ammonites eighteen years; and on their repentance were commanded by Jephtha the Gileadite, of the tribe of Manasseh; and he ruled six years. After whom, Abatthan of Bethlehem, of the tribe of Juda, ruled seven years. Then Ebro the Zebulonite, eight years. Then Eglom of Ephraim, eight years. Some add to the seven years of Abatthan the eight of Ebrom. And after him, the people having again transgressed, came under the power of the foreigners, the Philistines, for forty years. But on their returning [to God], they were led by Samson, of the tribe of Dan, who conquered the foreigners in battle. He ruled twenty years. And after him, there being no governor, Eli the priest judged the people for forty years. He was succeeded by Samuel the prophet; contemporaneously with whom Saul reigned, who held sway for twenty-seven years. He anointed David. Samuel died two years before Saul, while Abimelech was high priest. He anointed Saul as king, who was the first that bore regal sway over Israel after the judges; the whole duration of whom, down to Saul, was four hundred and sixty-three years and seven months.

Then in the first book of Kings there are twenty years of Saul, during which he reigned after he was renovated. And after the death of Saul, David the son of Jesse, of the tribe of Judah, reigned next in Hebron, forty years, as is contained in the second book of Kings. And Abiathar the son of Abimelech, of the kindred of Eli, was high priest. In his time Gad and Nathan prophesied. From Joshua the son of Nun, then, till David received the kingdom, there intervene, according to some, four hundred and fifty years. But, as the chronology set forth shows, five hundred and twenty-three years and seven months are comprehended till the death of David.

And after this Solomon the son of David reigned forty years. Under him Nathan continued to prophesy, who also exhorted him respecting the building of the temple. Achias of Shilo also prophesied. And both the kings, David and Solomon, were prophets. And Sadoc the high priest was the first who ministered in the temple which Solomon built, being the eighth from Aaron, the first high priest. From Moses, then, to the age of Solomon, as some say, are five hundred and ninety-five years, and as others, five hundred and seventy-six.

And if you count, along with the four hundred and fifty years from Joshua to David, the forty years of the rule of Moses, and the other eighty years of Moses's life previous to the exodus of the Hebrews from Egypt, you will make up the sum in all of six hundred and ten years. But our chronology will run more correctly, if to the five hundred and twenty-three years and seven months till the death of David, you add the hundred and twenty years of Moses and the forty years of Solomon. For you will make up in all, down to the death of Solomon, six hundred and eighty-three years and seven months.

Hiram gave his daughter to Solomon about the time of the arrival of Menelaus in Phoenicia, after the capture of Troy, as is said by Menander of Pergamus, and Lætus in *The Phoenicia*. And after Solomon, Roboam his son reigned for seventeen years; and Abimelech the son of Sadoc was high priest. In his reign, the kingdom being divided, Jeroboam, of the tribe of Ephraim, the servant of Solomon, reigned in Samaria; and Achias the Shilonite continued to prophesy; also Samæas the son of Amame, and he who came from Judah to Jeroboam, and prophesied against the altar. After him his son Abijam, twenty-three years; and likewise his son Asaman. The last, in his old age, was diseased in his feet; and in his reign prophesied Jehu the son of Ananias.

After him Jehosaphat his son reigned twenty-five years. In his reign prophesied Elias the Thesbite, and Michæas the son of Jebla, and Abdias the son of Ananias. And in the time of Michæas there was also the false prophet Zedekias, the son of Chonaan. These were followed by the reign of Joram the son of Jehosaphat, for eight years; during whose time prophesied Elias; and after Elias, Elisæus the son of Saphat. In his reign the people in Samaria ate doves' dung and their own children. The period of Jehosaphat extends from the close of the third book of Kings to the fourth. And in the reign of Joram, Elias was translated, and Elisæus the son of Saphat commenced prophesying, and prophesied for six years, being forty years old.

Then Ochozias reigned a year. In his time Elisæus continued to prophesy, and along with him Adadonæus. After him the mother of Ozias, Gotholia, reigned eight years, having slain the children of her brother. For she was of the family of Ahab. But the sister of Ozias, Josabæa, stole Joas the son of Ozias, and invested him afterwards with the kingdom. And in the time of this Gotholia, Elisæus was still prophesying. And after her reigned, as I said before, Joash, rescued by Josabæa the wife of Jodæ the high priest, and lived in all forty years.

There are comprised, then, from Solomon to the death of Elisæus the prophet, as some say, one hundred and five years; according to others, one hundred and two; and, as the chronology before us shows, from the reign of Solomon a hundred and eighty-one. Now from the Trojan war to the birth of Homer, according to Philochorus, a hundred and eighty years elapsed; and he was posterior to the Ionic migration. But Aristarchus, in the *Archilochian Memoirs*, says that he lived during the Ionic migration, which took place a hundred and twenty years after the siege of Troy. But Apollodorus alleges it was a hundred and twenty years after the Ionic migration, while Agesilaus son of Doryssæus was king of the Lacedæmonians: so that he brings Lycurgus the legislator, while still a young man, near him. Euthymenes, in the *Chronicles*, says that he flourished contemporaneously with Hesiod, in the time of Acastus, and was born in Chios about the four hundredth year after the capture of Troy. And Archimachus, in the third book of his *Euboean History*, is of this opinion. So that both he and Hesiod were later than Elisæus, the prophet. And if you choose to follow the grammarian Crates, and say that Homer was born about the time of the expedition of the Heraclidæ, eighty years after the taking of Troy, he will be found to be later again than Solomon, in whose days occurred the arrival of Menelaus in Phoenicia, as was said above. Eratosthenes says that Homer's age was two hundred years after the capture of Troy. Further, Theopompus, in the forty-third book of the *Philippics*, relates that Homer was born five hundred years after the war at Troy. And Euphorion, in his book about the *Aleuades*, maintains that he was born in the time of Gyges, who began to reign in the eighteenth Olympiad, who, also he says, was the first that was called tyrant (τύραννος). Sosibius Lacon, again, in his *Record of Dates*, brings Homer down to the eighth year of the reign of Charillus the son of Polydectus. Charillus reigned for sixty-four years, after whom the son of Nicander reigned thirty-nine years. In his thirty-fourth year it is said that the first Olympiad was instituted; so that Homer was ninety years before the introduction of the Olympic games.

After Joas, Amasias his son reigned as his successor thirty-nine years. He in like manner was succeeded by his son Ozias, who reigned for fifty-two years, and died a leper. And in his time prophesied Amos, and Isaiah his son, and Hosea the son of Beeri, and Jonas the son of Amathi, who was of Gethchober, who preached to the Ninevites, and passed through the whale's belly.

Then Jonathan the son of Ozias reigned for sixteen years. In his time Esaias still prophesied, and Hosea, and Michæas the Morasthite, and Joel the son of Bethuel.

Next in succession was his son Ahaz, who reigned for sixteen years. In his time, in the fifteenth year, Israel was carried away to Babylon. And Salmanasar the king of the Assyrians carried away the people of Samaria into the country of the Medes and to Babylon.

Again Ahaz was succeeded by Osee, who reigned for eight years. Then followed Hezekiah, for twenty-nine years. For his sanctity, when he had approached his end, God, by Isaiah, allowed him to live for other fifteen years, giving as a sign the going back of the sun. Up to his times Esaias, Hosea, and Micah continued prophesying.

And these are said to have lived after the age of Lycurgus, the legislator of the Lacedæmonians. For Dieuchidas, in the fourth book of the *Megarics*, places the era of Lycurgus about the two hundred and ninetieth year after the capture of Troy.

After Hezekiah, his son Manasses reigned for fifty-five years. Then his son Amos for two years. After him reigned his son Josias, distinguished for his observance of the law, for thirty-one years. He "laid the carcasses of men upon the carcasses of the idols," as is written in the book of Leviticus. In his reign, in the eighteenth year, the Passover was celebrated, not having been kept from the days of Samuel in the intervening period. Then Chelkias the priest, the father of the prophet Jeremiah, having fallen in with the book of the law, that had been laid up in the temple, read it and died. And in his days Olda prophesied, and Sophonias, and Jeremiah. And in the days of Jeremiah was Ananias the son of Azor, the false prophet. He having disobeyed Jeremiah the prophet, was slain by Pharaoh Necho king of Egypt at the river Euphrates, having encountered the latter, who was marching on the Assyrians.

Josiah was succeeded by Jechoniah, called also Joachas, his son, who reigned three months and ten days. Necho king of Egypt bound him and led him to Egypt, after making his brother Joachim king in his stead, who continued his tributary for eleven years. After him his namesake Joakim reigned for three months. Then Zedekiah reigned for eleven years; and up to his time Jeremiah continued to prophesy. Along with him Ezekiel the son of Buzi, and Urias the son of Samæus, and Ambacum prophesied. Here end the
Hebrew kings.

There are then from the birth of Moses till this captivity nine hundred and seventy-two years; but according to strict chronological accuracy, one thousand and eighty-five, six months, ten days. From the reign of David to the captivity by the Chaldeans, four hundred and fifty-two years and six months; but as the accuracy we have observed in reference to dates makes out, four hundred and eighty-two and six months ten days.

And in the twelfth year of the reign of Zedekiah, forty years before the supremacy of the Persians, Nebuchodonosor made war against the Phoenicians and the Jews, as Berosus asserts in his *Chaldæan Histories*. And Joabas, writing about the Assyrians, acknowledges that he had received the history from Berosus, and testifies to his accuracy. Nebuchodonosor, therefore, having put out the eyes of Zedekiah, took him away to Babylon, and transported the whole people (the captivity lasted seventy years), with the exception of a few who fled to Egypt.

Jeremiah and Ambacum were still prophesying in the time of Zedekiah. In the fifth year of his reign Ezekiel prophesied at Babylon; after him Nahum, then Daniel. After him, again, Haggai and Zechariah prophesied in the time of Darius the First for two years; and then the angel among the twelve. After Haggai and Zechariah, Nehemiah, the chief cup-bearer of Artaxerxes, the son of Acheli the Israelite, built the city of Jerusalem and restored the temple. During the captivity lived Esther and Mordecai, whose book is still extant, as also that of the Maccabees. During this captivity Mishael, Ananias, and Azarias, refusing to worship the image, and being thrown into a furnace of fire, were saved by the appearance of an angel. At that time, on account of the serpent, Daniel was thrown into the den of lions; but being preserved through the providence of God by Ambacub, he is restored on the seventh day. At this period, too, occurred the sign of Jona; and Tobias, through the assistance of the angel Raphael, married Sarah, the demon having killed her seven first suitors; and after the marriage of Tobias, his father Tobit recovered his sight. At that time Zorobabel, having by his wisdom overcome his opponents, and obtained leave from Darius for the rebuilding of Jerusalem, returned with Esdras to his native land; and by him the redemption of the people and the revisal and restoration of the inspired oracles were effected; and the Passover of deliverance celebrated, and marriage with aliens dissolved.

Cyrus had, by proclamation, previously enjoined the restoration of the Hebrews. And his promise being accomplished in the time of Darius, the feast of the dedication was held, as also the feast of tabernacles.

There were in all, taking in the duration of the captivity down to the restoration of the people, from the birth of Moses, one thousand one hundred and fifty-five years, six months, and ten days; and from the reign of David, according to some, four hundred and fifty-two; more correctly, five hundred and seventy-two years, six months, and ten days.

Clement of Alexandria

From the captivity at Babylon, which took place in the time of Jeremiah the prophet, was fulfilled what was spoken by Daniel the prophet as follows: "Seventy weeks are determined upon thy people, and upon thy holy city, to finish the transgression, and to seal sins, and to wipe out and make reconciliation for iniquity, and to bring in everlasting righteousness, and to seal the vision and the prophet, and to anoint the Holy of Holies. Know therefore, and understand, that from the going forth of the word commanding an answer to be given, and Jerusalem to be built, to Christ the Prince, are seven weeks and sixty-two weeks; and the street shall be again built, and the wall; and the times shall be expended. And after the sixty-two weeks the anointing shall be overthrown, and judgment shall not be in him; and he shall destroy the city and the sanctuary along with the coming Prince. And they shall be destroyed in a flood, and to the end of the war shall be cut off by desolations. And he shall confirm the covenant with many for one week; and in the middle of the week the sacrifice and oblation shall be taken away; and in the holy place shall be the abomination of desolations, and until the consummation of time shall the consummation be assigned for desolation.
And in the midst of the week shall he make the incense of sacrifice cease, and of the wing of destruction, even till the consummation, like the destruction of the oblation." That the temple accordingly was built in seven weeks, is evident; for it is written in Esdras. And thus Christ became King of the Jews, reigning in Jerusalem in the fulfilment of the seven weeks. And in the sixty and two weeks the whole of Judæa was quiet, and without wars. And Christ our Lord, "the Holy of Holies," having come and fulfilled the vision and the prophecy, was anointed in His flesh by the Holy Spirit of His Father. In those "sixty and two weeks," as the prophet said, and "in the one week," was He Lord. The half of the week Nero held sway, and in the holy city Jerusalem placed the abomination; and in the half of the week he was taken away, and Otho, and Galba, and Vitellius. And Vespasian rose to the supreme power, and

destroyed Jerusalem, and desolated the holy place. And that such are the facts of the case, is clear to him that is able to understand, as the prophet said.

On the completion, then, of the eleventh year, in the beginning of the following, in the reign of Joachim, occurred the carrying away captive to Babylon by Nabuchodonosor the king, in the seventh year of his reign over the Assyrians, in the second year of the reign of Vaphres over the Egyptians, in the archonship of Philip at Athens, in the first year of the forty-eighth Olympiad. The captivity lasted for seventy years, and ended in the second year of Darius Hystaspes, who had become king of the Persians, Assyrians, and Egyptians; in whose reign, as I said above, Haggai and Zechariah and the angel of the twelve prophesied. And the high priest was Joshua the son of Josedec. And in the second year of the reign of Darius, who, Herodotus says, destroyed the power of the Magi, Zorobabel the son of Salathiel was dispatched to raise and adorn the temple at Jerusalem.

The times of the Persians are accordingly summed up thus: Cyrus reigned thirty years; Cambyses, nineteen; Darius, forty-six; Xerxes, twenty-six; Artaxerxes, forty-one; Darius, eight; Artaxerxes, forty-two; Ochus or Arses, three. The sum total of the years of the Persian monarchy is two hundred and thirty-five years.

Alexander of Macedon, having dispatched this Darius, during this period, began to reign. Similarly, therefore, the times of the Macedonian kings are thus computed: Alexander, eighteen years; Ptolemy the son of Lagus, forty years; Ptolemy Philadelphus, twenty-seven years; then Euergetes, five-and-twenty years; then Philopator, seventeen years; then Epiphanes, four-and-twenty years; he was succeeded by Philometer, who reigned five-and thirty years; after him Physcon, twenty-nine years; then Lathurus, thirty-six years; then he that was surnamed Dionysus, twenty-nine years; and last Cleopatra reigned twenty-two years. And after her was the reign of the Cappadocians for eighteen days.

Accordingly the period embraced by the Macedonian kings is, in all, three hundred and twelve years and eighteen days. Therefore those who prophesied in the time of Darius Hystaspes, about the second year of his reign,—Haggai, and Zechariah, and the angel of the twelve, who prophesied about the first year of the forty-eighth Olympiad,—are demonstrated to be older than Pythagoras, who is said to have lived in the sixty-second Olympiad, and than Thales, the oldest of the wise men of the Greeks, who lived about the fiftieth Olympiad. Those wise men that are classed with Thales were then contemporaneous, as Andron says in the *Tripos*. For Heraclitus being posterior to Pythagoras, mentions him in his book. Whence indisputably the first Olympiad, which was demonstrated to be four hundred and seven years later than the Trojan war, is found to be prior to the age of the above-mentioned prophets, together with those called the seven wise men. Accordingly it is easy to perceive that Solomon, who lived in the time of Menelaus (who was during the Trojan war), was earlier by many years than the wise men among the Greeks. And how many years Moses preceded him we showed, in what we said above. And Alexander, surnamed Polyhistor, in his work on the Jews, has transcribed some letters of Solomon to Vaphres king of Egypt, and to the king of the Phoenicians at Tyre, and theirs to Solomon; in which it is shown that Vaphres sent eighty thousand Egyptian men to him for the building of the temple, and the other as many, along with a Tyrian artificer, the son of a Jewish mother, of the tribe of Dan, as is there written, of the name of Hyperon. Further, Onomacritus the Athenian, who is said to have been the author of the poems ascribed to Orpheus, is ascertained to have lived in the reign of the Pisistratidæ, about the fiftieth Olympiad. And Orpheus, who sailed with Hercules, was the pupil of Musæus. Amphion precedes the Trojan war by two generations. And Demodocus and Phemius were posterior to the capture of Troy; for they were famed for playing on the lyre, the former among the Phæacians, and the latter among the suitors. And the *Oracles* ascribed to Musæus are said to be the production of Onomacritus, and the *Crateres* of Orpheus the production of Zopyrus of Heraclea, and *The Descent to Hades* that of Prodicus of Samos. Ion of Chios relates in the *Triagmi*, that Pythagoras ascribed certain works [of his own] to Orpheus. Epigenes, in his book respecting *The Poetry attributed to Orpheus*, says that *The Descent to Hades* and the *Sacred Discourse* were the production of Cecrops the Pythagorean; and the *Peplus* and the *Physics* of Brontinus. Some also make Terpander out ancient. Hellanicus, accordingly, relates that he lived in the time of Midas: but Phanias, who places Lesches the Lesbian before Terpander, makes Terpander younger than Archilochus, and relates that Lesches contended with Arctinus, and gained the victory. Xanthus the Lydian says that he lived about the eighteenth Olympiad; as also Dionysius says that Thasus was built about the fifteenth Olympiad: so that it is clear that Archilochus was already known after the twentieth Olympiad. He accordingly relates the destruction of Magnetes as having recently taken place. Simonides is assigned to the time of Archilochus. Callinus is not much older; for Archilochus refers to Magnetes as destroyed, while the latter refers to it as flourishing. Eumelus of Corinth being older, is said to have met Archias, who founded Syracuse.

     We were induced to mention these things, because the poets of the epic cycle are placed amongst those of most remote antiquity. Already, too, among the Greeks, many diviners are said to have made their appearance, as the Bacides, one a Boeotian, the other an Arcadian, who uttered many predictions to many. By the counsel of Amphiletus the Athenian, who showed the time for the onset, Pisistratus, too, strengthened his government. For we may pass over in silence Cometes of Crete, Cinyras of Cyprus, Admetus the Thessalian, Aristæas the Cyrenian, Amphiaraus the Athenian, Timoxeus the Corcyræan, Demænetus the Phocian, Epigenes the Thespian, Nicias the Carystian, Aristo the Thessalian,

Clement of Alexandria

Dionysius the Carthaginian, Cleophon the Corinthian, Hippo the daughter of Chiro, and Boeo, and Manto, and the host of Sibyls, the Samian, the Colophonian, the Cumæan, the Erythræan, the Pythian, the Taraxandrian, the Macetian, the Thessalian, and the Thesprotian. And Calchas again, and Mopsus, who lived during the Trojan war. Mopsus, however, was older, having sailed along with the Argonants. And it is said that Battus the Cyrenian composed what is called *the Divination* of Mopsus. Dorotheus in the first *Pandect* relates that Mopsus was the disciple of Alcyon and Corone. And Pythagoras the Great always applied his mind to prognostication, and Abaris the Hyperborean, and Aristæas the Proconnesian, and Epimenides the Cretan, who came to Sparta, and Zoroaster the Mede, and Empedocles of Agrigentum, and Phormion the Lacedæmonian; Polyaratus, too, of Thasus, and Empedotimus of Syracuse; and in addition to these, Socrates the Athenian in particular. "For," he says in the *Theages*, "I am attended by a supernatural intimation, which has been assigned me from a child by divine appointment. This is a voice which, when it comes, prevents what I am about to do, but exhorts never." And Execestus, the tyrant of the Phocians, wore two enchanted rings, and by the sound which they uttered one against the other determined the proper times for actions. But he died, nevertheless, treacherously murdered, although warned beforehand by the sound, as Aristotle says in the *Polity of the Phocians*.

Of those, too, who at one time lived as men among the Egyptians, but were constituted gods by human opinion, were Hermes the Theban, and Asclepius of Memphis; Tireseus and Manto, again, at Thebes, as Euripides says. Helenus, too, and Laocoön, and OEnone, and Crenus in Ilium. For Crenus, one of the Heraclidæ, is said to have been a noted prophet. Another was Jamus in Elis, from whom came the Jamidæ; and Polyidus at Argos and Megara, who is mentioned by the tragedy. Why enumerate Telemus, who, being a prophet of the Cyclops, predicted to Polyphemus the events of Ulysses' wandering; or

Onomacritus at Athens; or Amphiaraus, who campaigned with the seven at Thebes, and is reported to be a generation older than the capture of Troy; or Theoclymenus in Cephalonia, or Telmisus in Caria, or Galeus in Sicily?

There are others, too, besides these: Idmon, who was with the Argonauts, Phemonoe of Delphi, Mopsus the son of Apollo and Manto in Pamphylia, and Amphilochus the son of Amphiaraus in Cilicia, Alcmæon among the Acarnanians, Anias in Delos, Aristander of Telmessus, who was along with Alexander. Philochorus also relates in the first book of the work, *On Divination,* that Orpheus was a seer. And Theopompus, and Ephorus, and Timæus, write of a seer called Orthagoras; as the Samian Pythocles in the fourth book of *The Italics* writes of Caius Julius Nepos.

But some of these "thieves and robbers," as the Scripture says, predicted for the most part from observation and probabilities, as physicians and soothsayers judge from natural signs; and others were excited by demons, or were disturbed by waters, and fumigations, and air of a peculiar kind. But among the Hebrews the prophets were moved by the power and inspiration of God. Before the law, Adam spoke prophetically in respect to the woman, and the naming of the creatures; Noah preached repentance; Abraham, Isaac, and Jacob gave many clear utterances respecting future and present things. Contemporaneous with the law, Moses and Aaron; and after these prophesied Jesus the son of Nave, Samuel, Gad, Nathan, Achias, Samæas, Jehu, Elias, Michæas, Abdiu, Elisæus, Abbadonai, Amos, Esaias, Osee, Jonas, Joel, Jeremias, Sophonias the son of Buzi, Ezekiel, Urias, Ambacum, Naum, Daniel, Misael, who wrote the syllogisms, Aggai, Zacharias, and the angel among the twelve. These are, in all, five-and-thirty prophets. And of women (for these too prophesied), Sara, and Rebecca, and Mariam, and Debbora, and Olda, i.e., Huldah.

Then within the same period John prophesied till the baptism of salvation; and after the birth of Christ, Anna and

Simeon. For Zacaharias, John's father, is said in the Gospels to have prophesied before his son. Let us then draw up the chronology of the Greeks from Moses. From the birth of Moses to the exodus of the Jews from Egypt, eighty years; and the period down to his death, other forty years. The exodus took place in the time of Inachus, before the wandering of Sothis, Moses having gone forth from Egypt three hundred and forty-five years before. From the rule of Moses, and from Inachus to the flood of Deucalion, I mean the second inundation, and to the conflagration of Phaethon, which events happened in the time of Crotopus, forty generations are enumerated (three generations being reckoned for a century). From the flood to the conflagration of Ida, and the discovery of iron, and the Idæan Dactyls, are seventy-three years, according to Thrasyllus; and from the conflagration of Ida to the rape of Ganymede, sixty-five years. From this to the expedition of Perseus, when Glaucus established the Isthmian games in honor of Melicerta, fifteen years; and from the expedition of Perseus to the building of Troy, thirty-four years. From this to the voyage of the Argo, sixty-four years. From this to Theseus and the Minotaur, thirty-two years; then to the seven at Thebes, ten years. And to the Olympic contest, which Hercules instituted in honor of Pelops, three years; and to the expedition of the Amazons against Athens, and the rape of Helen by Theseus, nine years. From this to the deification of Hercules, eleven years; then to the rape of Helen by Alexander, four years. From the taking of Troy to the descent of Æneas and the founding of Lavinium, ten years; and to the government of Ascanius, eight years; and to the descent of the Heraclidæ, sixty-one years; and to the Olympiad of Iphitus, three hundred and thirty-eight years. Eratosthenes thus sets down the dates: "From the capture of Troy to the descent of the Heraclidæ, eighty years. From this to the founding of Ionia, sixty years; and the period following to the protectorate of Lycurgus, a hundred and fifty-nine years; and to the first year of the first Olympiad, a hundred and eight years. From which

Olympiad to the invasion of Xerxes, two hundred and ninety-seven years; from which to the beginning of the Peloponnesian war, forty-eight years; and to its close, and the defeat of the Athenians, twenty-seven years; and to the battle at Leuctra, thirty-four years; after which to the death of Philip, thirty-five years. And after this to the decease of Alexander, twelve years."

Again, from the first Olympiad, some say, to the building of Rome, are comprehended twenty-four years; and after this to the expulsion of the kings, when consuls were created, about two hundred and forty-three years. And from the taking of Babylon to the death of Alexander, a hundred and eighty-six years. From this to the victory of Augustus, when Antony killed himself at Alexandria, two hundred and ninety-four years, when Augustus was made consul for the fourth time. And from this time to the games which Domitian instituted at Rome, are a hundred and fourteen years; and from the first games to the death of Commodus, a hundred and eleven years.

There are some that from Cecrops to Alexander of Macedon reckon a thousand eight hundred and twenty-eight years; and from Demophon, a thousand two hundred and fifty; and from the taking of Troy to the expedition of the Heraclidæ, a hundred and twenty or a hundred and eighty years. From this to the archonship of Evænetus at Athens, in whose time Alexander is said to have marched into Asia, according to Phanias, are seven hundred and fifty years; according to Ephorus, seven hundred and thirty-five; according to Timæus and Clitarchus, eight hundred and twenty; according to Eratosthenes, seven hundred and seventy-four. As also Duris, from the taking of Troy to the march of Alexander into Asia, a thousand years; and from that to the archonship of Hegesias, in whose time Alexander died eleven years. From this date to the reign of Germanicus Claudius Cæsar, three hundred and sixty-five years. From which time the years summed up to the death of Commodus are manifest.

Clement of Alexandria

After the Grecian period, and in accordance with the dates, as computed by the barbarians, very large intervals are to be assigned.

From Adam to the deluge are comprised two thousand one hundred and forty-eight years, four days. From Shem to Abraham, a thousand two hundred and fifty years. From Isaac to the division of the land, six hundred and sixteen years. Then from the judges to Samuel, four hundred and sixty-three years, seven months. And after the judges there were five hundred and seventy-two years, six months, ten days of kings.

After which periods, there were two hundred and thirty-five years of the Persian monarchy. Then of the Macedonian, till the death of Antony, three hundred and twelve years and eighteen days. After which time, the empire of the Romans, till the death of Commodus, lasted for two hundred and twenty-two years.

Then, from the seventy years' captivity, and the restoration of the people into their own land to the captivity in the time of Vespasian, are comprised four hundred and ten years. Finally, from Vespasian to the death of Commodus, there are ascertained to be one hundred and twenty-one years, six months, and twenty-four days.

Demetrius, in his book, *On the Kings in Judæa,* says that the tribes of Juda, Benjamin, and Levi were not taken captive by Sennacherim; but that there were from this captivity to the last, which Nabuchodonosor made out of Jerusalem, a hundred and twenty-eight years and six months; and from the time that the ten tribes were carried captive from Samaria till Ptolemy the Fourth, were five hundred and seventy-three years, nine months; and from the time that the captivity from Jerusalem took place, three hundred and thirty-eight years and three months.

Philo himself set down the kings differently from Demetrius.

Besides, Eupolemus, in a similar work, says that all the years from Adam to the fifth year of Ptolemy Demetrius, who reigned twelve years in Egypt, when added, amount to five thousand a hundred and forty-nine; and from the time that Moses brought out the Jews from Egypt to the above-mentioned date, there are, in all, two thousand five hundred and eighty years. And from this time till the consulship in Rome of Caius Domitian and Casian, a hundred and twenty years are computed.

Euphorus and many other historians say that there are seventy-five nations and tongues, in consequence of hearing the statement made by Moses: "All the souls that sprang from Jacob, which went down into Egypt, were seventy-five." According to the true reckoning, there appear to be seventy-two generic dialects, as our Scriptures hand down. The rest of the vulgar tongues are formed by the blending of two, or three, or more dialects. A dialect is a mode of speech which exhibits a character peculiar to a locality, or a mode of speech which exhibits a character peculiar or common to a race. The Greeks say, that among them are five dialects—the Attic, Ionic, Doric, Æolic, and the fifth the Common; and that the languages of the barbarians, which are innumerable, are not called dialects, but tongues.

Plato attributes a dialect also to the gods, forming this conjecture mainly from dreams and oracles, and especially from demoniacs, who do not speak their own language or dialect, but that of the demons who have taken possession of them. He thinks also that the irrational creatures have dialects, which those that belong to the same genus understand. Accordingly, when an elephant falls into the mud and bellows out any other one that is at hand, on seeing what has happened, shortly turns, and brings with him a herd of elephants, and saves the one that has fallen in. It is said also in Libya, that a scorpion, if it does not succeed in stinging a man, goes away and returns with several more; and that, hanging on one to the other like a chain they make in this way the attempt to succeed in their cunning design.

The irrational creatures do not make use of an obscure intimation, or hint their meaning by assuming a particular attitude, but, as I think, by a dialect of their own. And some others say, that if a fish which has been taken escape by breaking the line, no fish of the same kind will be caught in the same place that day. But the first and generic barbarous dialects have terms by nature, since also men confess that prayers uttered in a barbarian tongue are more powerful. And Plato, in the *Cratylus*, when wishing to interpret πῦρ (*fire*), says that it is a barbaric term. He testifies, accordingly, that the Phrygians use this term with a slight deviation.

And nothing, in my opinion, after these details, need stand in the way of stating the periods of the Roman emperors, in order to the demonstration of the Savior's birth. Augustus, forty-three years; Tiberius, twenty-two years; Caius, four years; Claudius, fourteen years; Nero, fourteen years; Galba, one year; Vespasian, ten years; Titus, three years; Domitian, fifteen years; Nerva, one year; Trajan, nineteen years; Adrian, twenty-one years; Antoninus, twenty-one years; likewise again, Antoninus and Commodus, thirty-two. In all, from Augustus to Commodus, are two hundred and twenty-two years; and from Adam to the death of Commodus, five thousand seven hundred and eighty-four years, two months, twelve days.

Some set down the dates of the Roman emperors thus:—

Caius Julius Cæsar, three years, four months, five days; after him Augustus reigned forty-six years, four months, one day. Then Tiberius, twenty-six years, six months, nineteen days. He was succeeded by Caius Cæsar, who reigned three years, ten months, eight days; and he by Claudius for thirteen years, eight months, twenty-eight days. Nero reigned thirteen years, eight months, twenty-eight days; Galba, seven months and six days; Otho, five months, one day; Vitellius, seven months, one day; Vespasian, eleven years, eleven months, twenty-two days; Titus, two years, two months; Domitian, fifteen years, eight months, five days; Nerva, one year, four months, ten days; Trajan, nineteen years, seven months, ten days; Adrian, twenty years, ten months, twenty-eight days. Antoninus, twenty-two years, three months, and seven days; Marcus Aurelius Antoninus, nineteen years, eleven days; Commodus, twelve years, nine months, fourteen days.

From Julius Cæsar, therefore, to the death of Commodus, are two hundred and thirty-six years, six months. And the whole from Romulus, who founded Rome, till the death of Commodus, amounts to nine hundred and fifty-three years, six months. And our Lord was born in the twenty-eighth year, when first the census was ordered to be taken in the reign of Augustus. And to prove that this is true, it is written in the Gospel by Luke as follows: "And in the fifteenth year, in the reign of Tiberius Cæsar, the word of the Lord came to John, the son of Zacharias." And again in the same book: "And Jesus was coming to His baptism, being about thirty years old," and so on. And that it was necessary for Him to preach only a year, this also is written: "He hath sent Me to proclaim the acceptable year of the Lord." This both the prophet spoke, and the Gospel. Accordingly, in fifteen years of Tiberius and fifteen years of Augustus; so were completed the thirty years till the time He suffered. And from the time that He suffered till the destruction of Jerusalem are forty-two years and three months; and from the destruction of Jerusalem to the death of Commodus, a hundred and twenty-eight years, ten months, and three days. From the birth of Christ, therefore, to the death of Commodus are, in all, a hundred and ninety-four years, one month, thirteen days. And there are those who have determined not only the year of our Lord's birth, but also the day; and they say that it took place in the twenty-eighth year of Augustus, and in the twenty-fifth day of Pachon. And the followers of Basilides hold the day of his baptism as a festival, spending the night before in readings.

And they say that it was the fifteenth year of Tiberius Cæsar, the fifteenth day of the month Tubi; and some that it was the eleventh of the same month. And treating of His passion, with very great accuracy, some say that it took place in the sixteenth year of Tiberius, on the twenty-fifth of Phamenoth; and others the twenty-fifth of Pharmuthi and others say that on the nineteenth of Pharmuthi the Savior suffered. Further, others say that He was born on the twenty-fourth or twenty-fifth of Pharmuthi.

We have still to add to our chronology the following,—I mean the days which Daniel indicates from the desolation of Jerusalem, the seven years and seven months of the reign of Vespasian. For the two years are added to the seventeen months and eighteen days of Otho, and Galba, and Vitellius; and the result is three years and six months, which is "the half of the week," as Daniel the prophet said. For he said that there were two thousand three hundred days from the time that the abomination of Nero stood in the holy city, till its destruction. For thus the declaration, which is subjoined, shows: "How long shall be the vision, the sacrifice taken away, the abomination of desolation, which is given, and the power and the holy place shall be trodden under foot? And he said to him, Till the evening and morning, two thousand three hundred days, and the holy place shall be taken away."

These two thousand three hundred days, then, make six years four months, during the half of which Nero held sway, and it was half a week; and for a half, Vespasian with Otho, Galba, and Vitellius reigned. And on this account Daniel says, "Blessed is he that cometh to the thousand three hundred and thirty-five days." For up to these days was war, and after them it ceased. And this number is demonstrated from a subsequent chapter, which is as follows: "And from the time of the change of continuation, and of the giving of the abomination of desolation, there shall be a thousand two hundred and ninety days. Blessed is he that waited, and cometh to the thousand three hundred and thirty-five days."

Flavius Josephus the Jew, who composed the history of the Jews, computing the periods, says that from Moses to David were five hundred and eighty-five years; from David to the second year of Vespasian, a thousand one hundred and seventy-nine; then from that to the tenth year of Antoninus, seventy-seven. So that from Moses to the tenth year of Antoninus there are, in all, two thousand one hundred and thirty-three years.

Of others, counting from Inachus and Moses to the death of Commodus, some say there were three thousand one hundred and forty-two years; and others, two thousand eight hundred and thirty-one years.

And in the Gospel according to Matthew, the genealogy which begins with Abraham is continued down to Mary the mother of the Lord. "For," it is said, "from Abraham to David are fourteen generations; and from David to the carrying away into Babylon are fourteen generations; and from the carrying away into Babylon till Christ are likewise other fourteen generations,"—three mystic intervals completed in six weeks.

CHAPTER XXII.—ON THE GREEK TRANSLATION OF THE OLD TESTAMENT.

So much for the details respecting dates, as stated variously by many, and as set down by us.

It is said that the Scriptures both of the law and of the prophets were translated from the dialect of the Hebrews into the Greek language in the reign of Ptolemy the son of Lagos, or, according to others, of Ptolemy surnamed Philadelphus; Demetrius Phalereus bringing to this task the greatest earnestness, and employing painstaking accuracy on the materials for the translation. For the Macedonians being still in possession of Asia, and the king being ambitious of adorning the library he had at Alexandria with all writings, desired the people of Jerusalem to translate the prophecies they possessed into the Greek dialect. And they being the subjects of the Macedonians, selected from those of highest character among them seventy elders, versed in the Scriptures, and skilled in the Greek dialect, and sent them to him with the divine books. And each having severally translated each prophetic book, and all the translations being compared together, they agreed both in meaning and expression. For it was the counsel of God carried out for the benefit of Grecian ears. It was not alien to the inspiration of God, who gave the prophecy, also to produce the translation, and make it as it were Greek prophecy. Since the Scriptures having perished in the captivity of Nabuchodonosor, Esdras the Levite, the priest, in the time of Artaxerxes king of the Persians, having become inspired in the exercise of prophecy restored again the whole of the ancient Scriptures. And Aristobulus, in his first book addressed to Philometor, writes in these words: "And Plato followed the laws given to us, and had manifestly studied all that is said in them." And before Demetrius there had been translated by another, previous to the dominion of Alexander and of the Persians, the account of the departure of our countrymen the Hebrews from Egypt, and the fame of all that happened to them, and their taking possession of the land, and the account of the whole code of laws; so that it is perfectly clear that the above-mentioned philosopher derived a great deal from this source, for he was very learned, as also Pythagoras, who transferred many things from our books to his own system of doctrines. And Numenius, the Pythagorean philosopher, expressly writes: "For what is Plato, but Moses speaking in Attic Greek?" This Moses was a theologian and prophet, and as some say, an interpreter of sacred laws. His family, his deeds, and life, are related by the Scriptures themselves, which are worthy of all credit; but have nevertheless to be stated by us also as well as we can.

CHAPTER XXIII.—THE AGE, BIRTH, AND LIFE OF MOSES.

Moses, originally of a Chaldean family, was born in Egypt, his ancestors having migrated from Babylon into Egypt on account of a protracted famine. Born in the seventh generation, and having received a royal education, the following are the circumstances of his history. The Hebrews having increased in Egypt to a great multitude, and the king of the country being afraid of insurrection in consequence of their numbers, he ordered all the female children born to the Hebrews to be reared (woman being unfit for war), but the male to be destroyed, being suspicious of stalwart youth. But the child being goodly, his parents nursed him secretly three months, natural affection being too strong for the monarch's cruelty. But at last, dreading lest they should be destroyed along with the child, they made a basket of the papyrus that grew there, put the child in it, and laid it on the banks of the marshy river. The child's sister stood at a distance, and watched what would happen. In this emergency, the king's daughter, who for a long time had not been pregnant, and who longed for a child, came that day to the river to bathe and wash herself; and hearing the child cry, she ordered it to be brought to her; and touched with pity, sought a nurse. At that moment the child's sister ran up, and said that, if she wished, she could procure for her as nurse one of the Hebrew women who had recently had a child. And on her consenting and desiring her to do so, she brought the child's mother to be nurse for a stipulated fee, as if she had been some other person. Thereupon the queen gave the babe the name of Moses, with etymological propriety, from his being drawn out of "the water,"—for the Egyptians call water "mou,"—in which he had been exposed to die. For they call Moses one who "who breathed [on being taken] from the water." It is clear that previously the parents gave a name to the child on his circumcision; and he was called Joachim. And he had a third name in heaven, after his ascension, as the mystics say—Melchi. Having reached the proper age, he was taught arithmetic, geometry, poetry, harmony, and besides, medicine and music, by those that excelled in these arts among the Egyptians; and besides, the philosophy which is conveyed by symbols, which they point out in the hieroglyphically inscriptions. The rest of the usual course of instruction, Greeks taught him in Egypt as a royal child, as Philo says in his life of Moses. He learned, besides, the literature of the Egyptians, and the knowledge of the heavenly bodies from the Chaldeans and the Egyptians; whence in the Acts he is said "to have been instructed in all the wisdom of the Egyptians." And Eupolemus, in his book *On the Kings in Judea*, says that "Moses was the first wise man, and the first that imparted grammar to the Jews, that the Phoenicians received it from the Jews, and the Greeks from the Phoenicians." And betaking himself to their philosophy, he increased his wisdom, being ardently attached to the training received from his kindred and ancestors, till he struck and slew the Egyptian who wrongfully attacked the Hebrew. And the mystics say that he slew the Egyptian by a word only; as, certainly, Peter in the Acts is related to have slain by speech those who appropriated part of the price of the field, and lied. And so Artapanus, in his work *On the Jews*, relates "that Moses, being shut up in custody by Chenephres, king of the Egyptians, on account of the people demanding to be let go from Egypt, the prison being opened by night, by the interposition of God, went forth, and reaching the palace, stood before the king as he slept, and aroused him; and that the latter, struck with what had taken place, bade Moses tell him the name of the God who had sent him; and that he, bending forward, told him in his ear; and that the king on hearing it fell speechless, but being supported by Moses, revived again." And respecting the education of Moses, we shall find a harmonious account in Ezekiel, the composer of Jewish tragedies in the drama entitled *The Exodus*. He thus writes in the person of Moses:—

> "For, seeing our race abundantly increase,
> His treacherous snares King Pharaoh 'gainst us laid,
> And cruelly in brick-kilns some of us,
> And some, in toilsome works of building, plagued.
> And towns and towers by toil of ill-starred men
> He raised. Then to the Hebrew race proclaimed,
> That each male child should in deep-flowing Nile

> Be drowned. My mother bore and hid me then
> Three months (so afterwards she told). Then took,
> And me adorned with fair array, and placed
> On the deep sedgy marsh by Nilus bank,
> While Miriam, my sister, watched afar.
> Then, with her maids, the daughter of the king,
> To bathe her beauty in the cleansing stream,
> Came near, straight saw, and took and raised me up;
> And knew me for a Hebrew. Miriam
> My sister to the princess ran, and said,
> 'Is it thy pleasure, that I haste and find
> A nurse for thee to rear this child
> Among the Hebrew women?' The princess
> Gave assent. The maiden to her mother sped,
> And told, who quick appeared. My own
> Dear mother took me in her arms. Then said
> The daughter of the king: 'Nurse me this child,
> And I will give thee wages.' And my name
> Moses she called, because she drew and saved
> Me from the waters on the river's bank.
> And when the days of childhood had flown by,
> My mother brought me to the palace where
> The princess dwelt, after disclosing all
> About my ancestry, and God's great gifts.
> In boyhood's years I royal nurture had,
> And in all princely exercise was trained,
> As if the princess's very son. But when
> The circling days had run their course,
> I left the royal palace."

Then, after relating the combat between the Hebrew and the Egyptian, and the burying of the Egyptian in the sand, he says of the other contest:—

> "Why strike one feebler than thyself?
> And he rejoined: Who made thee judge o'er us,

Or ruler? Wilt thou slay me, as thou didst
Him yesterday? And I in terror said,
How is this known?"

Then he fled from Egypt and fed sheep, being thus trained beforehand for pastoral rule. For the shepherd's life is a preparation for sovereignty in the case of him who is destined to rule over the peaceful flock of men, as the chase for those who are by nature warlike. Thence God brought him to lead the Hebrews. Then the Egyptians, oft admonished, continued unwise; and the Hebrews were spectators of the calamities that others suffered, learning in safety the power of God. And when the Egyptians gave no heed to the effects of that power, through their foolish infatuation disbelieving, then, as is said, "the children knew" what was done; and the Hebrews afterwards going forth, departed carrying much spoil from the Egyptians, not for avarice, as the cavilers say, for God did not persuade them to covet what belonged to others. But, in the first place, they took wages for the services they had rendered the Egyptians all the time; and then in a way recompensed the Egyptians, by afflicting them in requital as avaricious, by the abstraction of the booty, as they had done the Hebrews by enslaving them. Whether, then, as may be alleged is done in war, they thought it proper, in the exercise of the rights of conquerors, to take away the property of their enemies, as those who have gained the day do from those who are worsted (and there was just cause of hostilities. The Hebrews came as suppliants to the Egyptians on account of famine; and they, reducing their guests to slavery, compelled them to serve them after the manner of captives, giving them no recompense); or as in peace, took the spoil as wages against the will of those who for a long period had given them no recompense, but rather had robbed them, [it is all one.]

CHAPTER XXIV.—HOW MOSES DISCHARGED THE PART OF A MILITARY LEADER.

Our Moses then is a prophet, a legislator, skilled in military tactics and strategy, a politician, a philosopher. And in what sense he was a prophet, shall be by and by told, when we come to treat of prophecy. Tactics belong to military command, and the ability to command an army is among the attributes of kingly rule. Legislation, again, is also one of the functions of the kingly office, as also judicial authority.

Of the kingly office one kind is divine,—that which is according to God and His holy Son, by whom both the good things which are of the earth, and external and perfect felicity too, are supplied. "For," it is said, "seek what is great, and the little things shall be added." And there is a second kind of royalty, inferior to that administration which is purely rational and divine, which brings to the task of government merely the high mettle of the soul; after which fashion Hercules ruled the Argives, and Alexander the Macedonians. The third kind is what aims after one thing—merely to conquer and overturn; but to turn conquest either to a good or a bad purpose, belongs not to such rule. Such was the aim of the Persians in their campaign against Greece. For, on the one hand, fondness for strife is solely the result of passion, and acquires power solely for the sake of domination; while, on the other, the love of good is characteristic of a soul which uses its high spirit for noble ends. The fourth, the worst of all, is the sovereignty which acts according to the promptings of the passions, as that of Sardanapalus, and those who propose to themselves as their end the gratification of the passions to the utmost. But the instrument of regal sway—the instrument at once of that which overcomes by virtue, and that which does so by force—is the power of managing (or tact). And it varies according to the nature and the material. In the case of arms and of fighting animals the ordering power is the soul and mind, by means animate and inanimate; and in the case of the passions of the soul, which we master by virtue, reason is the ordering power, by affixing the seal of continence and self-restraint, along with holiness, and sound knowledge with truth, making the result of the whole to terminate in piety towards God. For it is wisdom which regulates in the case of those who so practice virtue; and divine things are ordered by wisdom, and human affairs by politics—all things by the kingly faculty. He is a king, then, who governs according to the laws, and possesses the skill to sway willing subjects. Such is the Lord, who receives all who believe on Him and by Him. For the Father has delivered and subjected all to Christ our King, "that at the name of Jesus every knee may bow, of things in heaven, and things in earth, and things under the earth, and every tongue confess that Jesus Christ is Lord, to the glory of God the Father."

Now, generalship involves three ideas: caution, enterprise, and the union of the two. And each of these consists of three things, acting as they do either by word, or by deeds, or by both together. And all this can be accomplished either by persuasion, or by compulsion, or by inflicting harm in the way of taking vengeance on those who ought to be punished; and this either by doing what is right, or by telling what is untrue, or by telling what is true, or by adopting any of these means conjointly at the same time.

Now, the Greeks had the advantage of receiving from Moses all these, and the knowledge of how to make use of each of them. And, for the sake of example, I shall cite one or two instances of leadership. Moses, on leading the people forth, suspecting that the Egyptians would pursue, left the short and direct route, and turned to the desert, and marched mostly by night. For it was another kind of arrangement by which the Hebrews were trained in the great wilderness, and for a protracted time, to belief in the existence of one God alone, being inured by the wise discipline of endurance to which they were subjected. The strategy of Moses, therefore, shows the necessity of discerning what will be of service before the approach of dangers, and so to encounter them. It turned out precisely as he suspected, for the Egyptians pursued with horses and chariots, but were quickly destroyed by the sea breaking on them and overwhelming them with their horses and chariots, so that not a remnant of them was left. Afterwards the pillar of fire, which accompanied them (for it went before them as a guide), conducted the Hebrews by night through an untrodden region, training and bracing them, by toils and hardships, to manliness and endurance, that after their experience of what appeared formidable difficulties, the benefits of the land, to which from the trackless desert he was conducting them, might become apparent. Furthermore, he put to flight and slew the hostile occupants of the land, falling upon them from a desert and rugged line of march (such was the excellence of his generalship). For the taking of the land of those hostile tribes was a work of skill and strategy.

Perceiving this, Miltiades, the Athenian general, who conquered the Persians in battle at Marathon, imitated it in the following fashion. Marching over a trackless desert, he led on the Athenians by night, and eluded the barbarians that were set to watch him. For Hippias, who had deserted from the Athenians, conducted the barbarians into Attica, and seized and held the points of vantage, in consequence of having a knowledge of the ground. The task was then to elude Hippias. Whence rightly Miltiades, traversing the desert and attacking by night the Persians commanded by Dates, led his soldiers to victory.

But further, when Thrasybulus was bringing back the exiles from Phyla, and wished to elude observation, a pillar became his guide as he marched over a trackless region. To Thrasybulus by night, the sky being moonless and stormy, a fire appeared leading the way, which, having conducted them safely, left them near Munychia, where is now the altar of the light-bringer (Phosphorus).

From such an instance, therefore, let our accounts become credible to the Greeks, namely, that it was possible for the omnipotent God to make the pillar of fire, which was their guide on their march, go before the Hebrews by night. It is said also in a certain oracle,—

"A pillar to the Thebans is joy-inspiring Bacchus,"

from the history of the Hebrews. Also Euripides says, in *Antiope*,—

"In the chambers within, the herdsman,
With chaplet of ivy, pillar of the Evoean god."

The pillar indicates that God cannot be portrayed. The pillar of light, too, in addition to its pointing out that God cannot be represented, shows also the stability and the permanent duration of the Deity, and His unchangeable and inexpressible light. Before, then, the invention of the forms of images, the ancients erected pillars, and reverenced them as statues of the Deity. Accordingly, he who composed the *Phoronis* writes,—

"Callithoe, key-bearer of the Olympian queen:
Argive Hera, who first with fillets and with fringes
The queen's tall column all around adorned."

Further, the author of *Europia* relates that the statue of Apollo at Delphi was a pillar in these words:—

"That to the god first-fruits and tithes we may
On sacred pillars and on lofty column hang."

Apollo, interpreted mystically by "privation of many," means the one God. Well, then, that fire like a pillar, and the fire in the desert, is the symbol of the holy light which passed through from earth and returned again to heaven, by the wood [of the cross], by which also the gift of intellectual vision was bestowed on us.

CHAPTER XXV.—PLATO AN IMITATOR OF MOSES IN FRAMING LAWS.

Plato the philosopher, aided in legislation by the books of Moses, censured the polity of Minos, and that of Lycurgus, as having bravery alone as their aim; while he praised as more seemly the polity which expresses some one thing, and directs according to one precept. For he says that it becomes us to philosophize with strength, and dignity, and wisdom,—holding unalterably the same opinions about the same things, with reference to the dignity of heaven. Accordingly, therefore, he interprets what is in the law, enjoining us to look to one God and to do justly. Of politics, he says there are two kinds,—the department of law, and that of politics, strictly so called.

And he refers to the Creator, as the Statesman (ὁ πολιτικός) by way of eminence, in his book of this name (ὁ πολιτικός); and those who lead an active and just life, combined with contemplation, he calls statesmen (πολιτικοί). That department of politics which is called "Law," he divides into administrative magnanimity and private good order, which he calls orderliness; and harmony, and sobriety, which are seen when rulers suit their subjects, and subjects are obedient to their rulers; a result which the system of Moses sedulously aims at effecting. Further, that the department of law is founded on generation, that of politics on friendship and consent, Plato, with the aid he received, affirms; and so, coupled with the laws the philosopher in the *Epinomis*, who knew the course of all generation, which takes place by the instrumentality of the planets; and the other philosopher, *Timæus*, who was an astronomer and student of the motions of the stars, and of their sympathy and association with one another, he consequently joined to the "polity" (or "republic"). Then, in my opinion, the end both of the statesman, and of him who lives according to the law, is contemplation. It is necessary, therefore, that public affairs should be rightly managed. But to philosophize is best. For he who is wise will live concentrating all his energies on knowledge, directing his life by good deeds, despising the opposite, and following the pursuits which contribute to truth. And the law is not what is decided by law (for what is seen is not vision), nor every opinion (not certainly what is evil). But law is the opinion which is good, and what is good is that which is true, and what is true is that which finds "true being," and attains to it. "He who is," says Moses, "sent me." In accordance with which, namely, good opinion, some have called law, right reason, which enjoins what is to be done and forbids what is not to be done.

CHAPTER XXVI.—MOSES RIGHTLY CALLED A DIVINE LEGISLATOR, AND, THOUGH INFERIOR TO CHRIST, FAR SUPERIOR TO THE GREAT LEGISLATORS OF THE GREEKS, MINOS AND LYCURGUS.

Whence the law was rightly said to have been given by Moses, being a rule of right and wrong; and we may call it with accuracy the divine ordinance (θεσμός), inasmuch as it was given by God through Moses. It accordingly conducts to the divine. Paul says: "The law was instituted because of transgressions, till the seed should come, to whom the promise was made." Then, as if in explanation of his meaning, he adds: "But before faith came, we were kept under the law, shut up," manifestly through fear, in consequence of sins, "unto the faith which should afterwards be revealed; so that the law was a schoolmaster to bring us to Christ, that we should be justified by faith." The true legislator is he who assigns to each department of the soul what is suitable to it and to its operations. Now Moses, to speak comprehensively, was a living law, governed by the benign Word. Accordingly, he furnished a good polity, which is the right discipline of men in social life. He also handled the administration of justice, which is that branch of knowledge which deals with the correction of transgressors in the interests of justice. Co-ordinate with it is the faculty of dealing with punishments, which is a knowledge of the due measure to be observed in punishments. And punishment, in virtue of its being so, is the correction of the soul. In a word, the whole system of Moses is suited for the training of such as are capable of becoming good and noble men, and for hunting out men like them; and this is the art of command. And that wisdom, which is capable of treating rightly those who have been caught by the Word, is legislative wisdom. For it is the property of this wisdom, being most kingly, to possess and use.

It is the wise man, therefore, alone whom the philosophers proclaim king, legislator, general, just, holy, God-beloved. And if we discover these qualities in Moses, as shown from the Scriptures themselves, we may, with the most assured persuasion, pronounce Moses to be truly wise. As then we say that it belongs to the shepherd's art to care for the sheep; for so "the good shepherd giveth his life for the sheep;" so also we shall say that legislation, inasmuch as it presides over and cares for the flock of men, establishes the virtue of men, by fanning into flame, as far as it can, what good there is in humanity.

And if the flock figuratively spoken of as belonging to the Lord is nothing but a flock of men, then He Himself is the good Shepherd and Lawgiver of the one flock, "of the sheep who hear Him," the one who cares for them, "seeking," and finding by the law and the word, "that which was lost;" since, in truth, the law is spiritual and leads to felicity. For that which has arisen through the Holy Spirit is spiritual. And he is truly a legislator, who not only announces what is good and noble, but understands it. The law of this man who possesses knowledge is the saving precept; or rather, the law is the precept of knowledge. For the Word is "the power and the wisdom of God." Again, the expounder of the laws is the same one by whom the law was given; the first expounder of the divine commands, who unveiled the bosom of the Father, the only-begotten Son.

Then those who obey the law, since they have some knowledge of Him, cannot disbelieve or be ignorant of the truth. But those who disbelieve, and have shown a repugnance to engage in the works of the law, whoever else may, certainly confess their ignorance of the truth.

What, then, is the unbelief of the Greeks? Is it not their unwillingness to believe the truth which declares that the law was divinely given by Moses, whilst they honor Moses in their own writers? They relate that Minos received the laws from Zeus in nine years, by frequenting the cave of Zeus; and Plato, and Aristotle, and Ephorus write that Lycurgus was trained in legislation by going constantly to Apollo at Delphi. Chamæleo of Heraclea, in his book *On Drunkenness*, and Aristotle in *The Polity of Locrians*, mention that Zaleucus the Locrian received the laws from Athene.

But those who exalt the credit of Greek legislation as far as in them lies, by referring it to a divine source, after the model of Mosaic prophecy, are senseless in not owning the truth, and the archetype of what is related among them.

CHAPTER XXVII.—THE LAW, EVEN IN CORRECTING AND PUNISHING, AIMS AT THE GOOD OF MEN.

Let no, one then, run down law, as if, on account of the penalty, it were not beautiful and good. For shall he who drives away bodily disease appear a benefactor; and shall not he who attempts to deliver the soul from iniquity, as much more appear a friend, as the soul is a more precious thing than the body? Besides, for the sake of bodily health we submit to incisions, and cauterizations, and medicinal draughts; and he who administers them is called savior and healer, even though amputating parts, not from grudge or ill-will towards the patient, but as the principles of the art prescribe, so that the sound parts may not perish along with them, and no one accuses the physician's art of wickedness; and shall we not similarly submit, for the soul's sake, to either banishment, or punishment, or bonds, provided only from unrighteousness we shall attain to righteousness?

For the law, in its solicitude for those who obey, trains up to piety, and prescribes what is to be done, and restrains each one from sins, imposing penalties even on lesser sins.

But when it sees any one in such a condition as to appear incurable, posting to the last stage of wickedness, then in its solicitude for the rest, that they may not be destroyed by it (just as if amputating a part from the whole body), it condemns such a one to death, as the course most conducive to health. "Being judged by the Lord," says the apostle, "we are chastened, that we may not be condemned with the world." For the prophet had said before, "Chastening, the Lord hath chastised me, but hath not given me over unto death." "For in order to teach thee His righteousness," it is said, "He chastised thee and tried thee, and made thee to hunger and thirst in the desert land; that all His statutes and His judgments may be known in thy heart, as I command thee this day; and that thou may know in thine heart, that just as if a man were chastising his son, so the Lord our God shall chastise thee."

And to prove that example corrects, he says directly to the purpose: "A clever man, when he sees the wicked punished, will himself be severely chastised, for the fear of the Lord is the source of wisdom."

But it is the highest and most perfect good, when one is able to lead back any one from the practice of evil to virtue and well-doing, which is the very function of the law. So that, when one fails into any incurable evil,—when taken possession of, for example, by wrong or covetousness,—it will be for his good if he is put to death. For the law is beneficent, being able to make some righteous from unrighteous, if they will only give ear to it, and by releasing others from present evils; for those who have chosen to live temperately and justly, it conducts to immortality. To know the law is characteristic of a good disposition. And again: "Wicked men do not understand the law; but they who seek the Lord shall have understanding in all that is good."

It is essential, certainly, that the providence which manages all, be both supreme and good. For it is the power of both that dispenses salvation—the one correcting by punishment, as supreme, the other showing kindness in the exercise of beneficence, as a benefactor. It is in your power not to be a son of disobedience, but to pass from darkness to life, and lending your ear to wisdom, to be the legal slave of God, in the first instance, and then to become a faithful servant, fearing the Lord God. And if one ascend higher, he is enrolled among the sons.

But when "charity covers the multitude of sins," by the consummation of the blessed hope, then may we welcome him as one who has been enriched in love, and received into the elect adoption, which is called the beloved of God, while he chants the prayer, saying, "Let the Lord be my God."

The beneficent action of the law, the apostle showed in the passage relating to the Jews, writing thus: "Behold, thou art called a Jew and restest in the law, and makes thy boast in God, and knows the will of God, and approves the things that are more excellent, being instructed out of the law, and art confident that thou thyself art a guide of the blind, a light of them who are in darkness, an instructor of the foolish, a teacher of babes, who hast the form of knowledge and of truth in the law." For it is admitted that such is the power of the law, although those whose conduct is not according to the law, make a false pretence, as if they lived in the law. "Blessed is the man that hath found wisdom, and the mortal who has seen understanding; for out of its mouth," manifestly Wisdom's, "proceeds righteousness, and it bears law and mercy on its tongue." For both the law and the Gospel are the energy of one Lord, who is "the power and wisdom of God;" and the terror which the law begets is merciful and in order to salvation. "Let not alms, and faith, and truth fail thee, but hang them around thy neck." In the same way as Paul, prophecy upbraids the people with not understanding the law. "Destruction and misery are in their ways, and the way of peace have they not known." "There is no fear of God before their eyes." "Professing themselves wise, they became fools." "And we know that the law is good, if a man use it lawfully." "Desiring to be teachers of the law, they understand," says the apostle, "neither what they say, nor whereof they affirm." "Now the end of the commandment is charity out of a pure heart, and a good conscience, and faith unfeigned."

CHAPTER XXVIII.—THE FOURFOLD DIVISION OF THE MOSAIC LAW.

The Mosaic philosophy is accordingly divided into four parts,—into the historic, and that which is specially called the legislative, which two properly belong to an ethical treatise; and the third, that which relates to sacrifice, which belongs to physical science; and the fourth, above all, the department of theology, "vision," which Plato predicates of the truly great mysteries. And this species Aristotle calls metaphysics. Dialectics, according to Plato, is, as he says in *The Statesman*, a science devoted to the discovery of the explanation of things. And it is to be acquired by the wise man, not for the sake of saying or doing aught of what we find among men (as the dialecticians, who occupy themselves in sophistry, do), but to be able to say and do, as far as possible, what is pleasing to God. But the true dialectic, being philosophy mixed with truth, by examining things, and testing forces and powers, gradually ascends in relation to the most excellent essence of all, and essays to go beyond to the God of the universe, professing not the knowledge of mortal affairs, but the science of things divine and heavenly; in accordance with which follows a suitable course of practice with respect to words and deeds, even in human affairs. Rightly, therefore, the Scripture, in its desire to make us such dialecticians, exhorts us: "Be ye skilful money-changers" rejecting some things, but retaining what is good. For this true dialectic is the science which analyses the objects of thought, and shows abstractly and by itself the individual substratum of existences, or the power of dividing things into genera, which descends to their most special properties, and presents each individual object to be contemplated simply such as it is.

Wherefore it alone conducts to the true wisdom, which is the divine power which deals with the knowledge of entities as entities, which grasps what is perfect, and is freed from all passion; not without the Savior, who withdraws, by the divine word, the gloom of ignorance arising from evil training, which had overspread the eye of the soul, and bestows the best of gifts,—

"That we might well know or God or man."

It is He who truly shows how we are to know ourselves. It is He who reveals the Father of the universe to whom He wills, and as far as human nature can comprehend. "For no man knows the Son but the Father, nor the Father but the Son, and he to whom the Son shall reveal Him." Rightly, then, the apostle says that it was by revelation that he knew the mystery: "As I wrote afore in few words, according as ye are able to understand my knowledge in the mystery of Christ." "According as ye are able," he said, since he knew that some had received milk only, and had not yet received meat, nor even milk simply. The sense of the law is to be taken in three ways,—either as exhibiting a symbol, or laying down a precept for right conduct, or as uttering a prophecy. But I well know that it belongs to men [of full age] to distinguish and declare these things. For the whole Scripture is not in its meaning a single Myconos, as the proverbial expression has it; but those who hunt after the connection of the divine teaching, must approach it with the utmost perfection of the logical faculty.

CHAPTER XXIX.—THE GREEKS BUT CHILDREN COMPARED WITH THE HEBREWS.

Whence most beautifully the Egyptian priest in Plato said, "O Solon, Solon, you Greeks are always children, not having in your souls a single ancient opinion received through tradition from antiquity. And not one of the Greeks is an old man;" meaning by old, I suppose, those who know what belongs to the more remote antiquity, that is, our literature; and by young, those who treat of what is more recent and made the subject of study by the Greeks,—things of yesterday and of recent date as if they were old and ancient. Wherefore he added, "and no study hoary with time;" for we, in a kind of barbarous way, deal in homely and rugged metaphor. Those, therefore, whose minds are rightly constituted approach the interpretation utterly destitute of artifice. And of the Greeks, he says that their opinions" differ but little from myths." For neither puerile fables nor stories current among children are fit for listening to. And he called the myths themselves "children," as if the progeny of those, wise in their own conceits among the Greeks, who had but little insight; meaning by the "hoary studies" the truth which was possessed by the barbarians, dating from the highest antiquity. To which expression he opposed the phrase "child fable," censuring the mythical character of the attempts of the moderns, as, like children, having nothing of age in them, and affirming both in common—their fables and their speeches—to be puerile.

Divinely, therefore, the power which spoke to Hermas by revelation said, "The visions and revelations are for those who are of double mind, who doubt in their hearts if these things are or are not."

Similarly, also, demonstrations from the resources of erudition, strengthen, confirm, and establish demonstrative reasoning, in so far as men's minds are in a wavering state like young people's. "The good commandment," then, according to the Scripture, "is a lamp, and the law is a light to the path; for instruction corrects the ways of life." "Law is monarch of all, both of mortals and of immortals," says Pindar. I understand, however, by these words, Him who enacted law. And I regard, as spoken of the God of all, the following utterance of Hesiod, though spoken by the poet at random and not with comprehension:—

> "For the Saturnian framed for men this law:
> Fishes, and beasts, and winged birds may eat
> Each other, since no rule of right is theirs;

But Right (by far the best) to men he gave."

Whether, then, it be the law which is connate and natural, or that given afterwards, which is meant, it is certainly of God; and both the law of nature and that of instruction are one. Thus also Plato, in *The Statesman,* says that the lawgiver is one; and in *The Laws,* that he who shall understand music is one; teaching by these words that the Word is one, and God is one. And Moses manifestly calls the Lord a covenant: "Behold I am my Covenant with thee," having previously told him not to seek the covenant in writing. For it is a covenant which God, the Author of all, makes. For God is called Θεός, from θέσις (placing), and order or arrangement. And in the *Preaching* of Peter you will find the Lord called Law and Word. But at this point, let our first Miscellany of gnostic notes, according to the true philosophy, come to a close.

Elucidations.
I.
(Purpose of the *Stromata*)

The Alexandrian Gnostics were the pestilent outgrowth of *pseudo-Platonism;* and nobody could comprehend their root-errors, and their branching thorns and thistles, better than Clement. His superiority in philosophy and classical culture was exhibited, therefore, in his writings, as a necessary preliminary. Like a good nautical combatant, his effort was to "get to windward," and so bear down upon the enemy (to use an anachronism) with heavyshotted broadsides. And we must not blame Clement for his plan of "taking the wind out of their sails," by showing that an eclectic philosophy might be made to harmonize with the Gospel. His plan was that of melting the gold out of divers ores, and throwing the dross away. Pure gold, he argues, is gold wherever it may be found, and even in the purse of "thieves and robbers." So, then, he "takes from them the armor in which they trusted, and divides the spoils." He will not concede to them the name of "Gnostics," but wrests it from them, just as we reclaim the name of "Catholics" from the Tridentine innovators, who have imposed a modern creed (and are constantly adding to it) upon the Latin churches. Here, then, let me quote the *Account* of Bishop Kaye. He says, "The object of Clement, in composing the *Stromata*, was to describe the true 'Gnostic,' or perfect Christian, in order to furnish the believer with a model for his imitation, and to prevent him from being led astray by the representations of the Valentinians and other gnostic sects." ... "Before we proceed to consider his description of the Gnostic, however, it will be necessary briefly to review his opinions respecting the nature and condition of man."

Here follows a luminous analysis (occupying pp. 229–238 of Kaye's work), after which he says,—

"The foregoing brief notice of Clement's opinions respecting man, his soul, and his fallen state, appeared necessary as an introduction to the description of the *true Gnostic*. By γνῶσις, Clement understood the perfect knowledge of all that relates to God, His nature, and dispensations. He speaks of a twofold knowledge,—one, common to all men, and born of sense; the other, the genuine γνῶσις, bred from the intellect, the mind, and its reason.
This latter is not born with men, but must be gained and by practice formed into a habit. *The initiated* find its perfection in a loving mysticism, which this never-failing love makes lasting."

So, further, this learned analyst, not blindly, but always with scientific conscience and judicial impartiality, expounds his author; and, without some such guide, I despair of securing the real interest of the youthful student. Butler's *Analogy* and Aristotle's *Ethics* are always analyzed for learners, by editors of their works; and hence I have ventured to direct attention to this "guide, philosopher, and friend" of my own inquiries.

II.
(Pantænus and His School.)

The catechetical school at Alexandria was already ancient; for Eusebius describes it as ἐξ ἀρχαίου ἔθους and St. Jerome dates its origin from the first planting of Christianity. Many things conspired to make this city the very head of Catholic Christendom, at this time; for the whole East centered here, and the East was Christendom while the West was yet a missionary field almost entirely. Demetrius, then bishop, at the times with which we are now concerned, sent Pantænus to convert the Hindoos, and, whatever his success or failure there, he brought back reports that Christians were there before him, the offspring of St. Bartholomew's preaching; and, in proof thereof, he brought with him a copy of St. Matthew's Gospel in the Hebrew tongue which became one of the treasures of the church on the Nile.

But it deserves note, that, because of the learning concentrated in this place, the bishops of Alexandria were, from the beginning, the great authorities as to the Easter cycle and the annual computation of Easter, which new created the science of astronomy as one result. The Council of Nice, in settling the laws for the observance of the Feast of the Resurrection, extended the function of the Alexandrian See in this respect; for it was charged with the duty of giving notice of the day when Easter should fall every year, to all the churches. And easily might an ambitious primate of Egypt have imagined himself superior to all other bishops at that time; for, as Bingham observes, he was the greatest in the world, "for the absoluteness of his power, and the extent of his jurisdiction." And this greatness of Alexandria was *ancient,* we must remember, at the Nicene epoch; for their celebrated canon (VI.) reads, "*Let ancient customs prevail;* so that in Egypt, Lybia, and Pentapolis, the Bishop of Alexandria shall have power over all these." Similar powers and privileges, over their own regions, were recognized in Rome and Antioch.

The Stromata or Miscellanies

III.
(Tradition.)

The apostles distinguish between vain traditions of the Jews, and their own Christian παραδόσειςthe *tradita apostolica* (2 Tim. i. 13, 14; 2 Tim. ii. 2; 1 Cor. xi. 2; 2 Thess. iii. 6; 1Cor. v. 8; 1 Cor. xvi. 2). Among these were (1) the authentication of their own Scriptures; (2) certain "forms of sound words," afterwards digested into liturgies; (3) the rules for celebrating the Lord's Supper, and of administering baptism; (4) the Christian Passover and the weekly Lord's Day; (5) the Jewish Sabbath and ordinances, how far to be respected while the temple yet stood; (6) the kiss of charity, and other observances of public worship; (7) the *agape*, the rules about widows, etc.

In some degree these were the secret of the Church, with which "strangers intermeddled not" lawfully. The Lord's Supper was celebrated after the catechumens and mere hearers had withdrawn, and nobody was suffered to be present without receiving the sacrament. But, after the conversion of the empire, the canons and constitutions universally dispersed made public all these *tradita;* and the liturgies also were everywhere made known. It is idle, therefore, to shelter under theories of the *Disciplina Arcani*, those Middle-Age inventions, of which antiquity shows no trace but in many ways contradicts emphatically; e.g., the Eucharist, celebrated after the withdrawal of the non-communicants, and received, in both kinds, by all present, cannot be pleaded as the "secret" which justifies a ceremony in an unknown tongue and otherwise utterly different; in which the priest alone partakes, in which the cup is denied to the laity and which is exhibited with great pomp before all comers with no general participation.

IV.
(Esoteric Doctrine)

Early Christians, according to Clement, taught to all alike, (1) all things necessary to salvation, (2) all the whole Scriptures, and (3) all the apostolic traditions. This is evident from passages noted here and hereafter. But, in the presence of the heathen, they remembered our Lord's words, and were careful not "to cast pearls before swine." Like St. Paul before Felix, they "reasoned of righteousness, temperance, and judgment to come," when dealing with men who knew not God, preaching Christ to them in a practical way. In their instructions to the churches, they were able to say with the same apostle, "I am pure from the blood of all men, for I have not shunned to declare unto you *all the counsel of God.*" Yet, even in the Church, they fed babes with milk, and the more intelligent with the meat of God's word. What that meat was, we discover in the *Stromata,* when our author defines the true Gnostic, who follows whithersoever God leads him in *the divinely inspired Scriptures.* He recognizes many who merely taste the Scriptures as *believers;* but the true Gnostic is a *gnomon* of truth, an index to others of the whole knowledge of Christ.

What we teach children in the Sunday school, and what we teach young men in the theological seminary, must illustrate the two ideas; the same truths to babes in element, but to men in all their bearings and relations.

The defenders of the modern creed of Pius the Fourth (a.d. 1564), finding no authority in Holy Scripture for most of its peculiarities, which are all imposed as requisite to salvation as if it were the Apostles' Creed itself, endeavor to support them, by asserting that they belonged to the secret teaching of the early Church, of which they claim Clement as a witness.
But the fallacy is obvious. Either they were thus *secreted,* or they were not. If not, as is most evident (because they contradict what was openly professed), then no ground for the pretence. But suppose they were, what follows? Such secrets

were no part of the faith, and could not become so at a later period. If they were kept secret by the new theologians, and taught to "Gnostics" only, they would still be without primitive example, but might be less objectionable. But, no! they are imposed upon all, as if part of the ancient creeds; imposed, as if articles of the Catholic faith, on the most illiterate peasant, whose mere *doubt* as to any of them excludes him from the Church here, and from salvation hereafter. Such, then, is a fatal departure from Catholic orthodoxy and the traditions of the ancients. The whole system is a novelty, and the product of the most barren and corrupt period of Occidental history.

The Church, as Clement shows, never made any *secret* of any article of the Christian faith; and, as soon as she was free from persecution, the whole testimony of the Ante-Nicene Fathers was summed up in the Nicæno-Constantinopolitan Confession. This only is the Catholic faith, and the council forbade any additions thereto, in the way of a symbol. See Professor Shedd's *Christian Doctrine*, vol. ii. p. 438. Ed. 1864, New York.

V.
(p. 302, note 9, Elucidation III., continued.)

This is a valuable passage for the illustration of our author's views of the nature of tradition, (κατὰ τὸν σεμνὸν τῆς παραδόσεως κανόνα as a canon "from the creation of the world;" a tradition preluding the tradition of true knowledge; a divine mystery preparing for the knowledge of mysteries,— clearing the ground from thorns and weeds, beforehand, so that the seed of the Word may not be choked. Now, in this tradition, he includes a true idea of Gentilism as well as of the Hebrew Church and its covenant relations; in short, whatever a Christian scholar is obliged to learn from "Antiquities" and "Introductions" and "Bible Dictionaries," authenticated by universal and orthodox approbation. These are the
providential provisions of the Divine OEconomy, for the communication of truth. Dr. Watts has a sermon on the *Inward*

Witness to Christianity, which I find quoted by Vicesimus Knox (Works, vol. vii. p. 73, *et seqq.*) in a choice passage that forcibly expands and expounds some of Clement's suggestions, though without referring to our author.

VI.
(Justification, p. 305 note 7.)

Without reference to my own views on this great subject, and desiring merely to illustrate our author, it shall suffice to remark, here, that to suppose that Clement uses the word *technically*, as we now use the language of the schools and of post-Reformation theologians, would hopelessly confuse the argument of our author. It is clear that he has no idea of any justification apart from the merits of Christ: but he uses the term loosely to express his idea, that as the Law led the Hebrews to the great Healer, who rose from the dead for our justification, in that sense, and in no other, *the truth* that was to be found in Greek Philosophy, although a *minimum*, did the same for heathen who loved truth, and followed it so far as they knew. Whether his views even in this were correct, it would not become me, here, to express any opinion. (See below, Elucidation XIV.)

VII.
(Philosophy, p. 305, note 8.)

It is so important to grasp just what our author understands by this "philosophy," that I had designed to introduce, here, a long passage from Bishop Kaye's lucid exposition. Finding, however, that these elucidations are already, perhaps, over multiplied, I content myself with a reference to his *Account*, etc. (pp. 118–121).

VIII.
(Overflow of the Spirit, p. 306, note 1.)

Here, again, I wished to introduce textual citations from several eminent authors: I content myself with a very short one from Kaye, to illustrate the intricacy, not to say the contradictory character, of some of Clement's positions as to the extent of grace bestowed on the heathen. "Clement says that an act, to be right, must be done through the love of God. He says that every action of the heathen is sinful, since it is not sufficient that an action is right: *its object or aim must also be right*" (*Account,* etc., p. 426). For a most interesting, but I venture to think overdrawn, statement of St. Paul's position as to heathen "wisdom," etc., see Farrar's *Life of St. Paul* (p. 20, *et seqq.,* ed. New York). Without relying on this popular author, I cannot but refer the reader to his *Hulsean Lecture* (1870, p. 135, *et seqq.*).

IX.
(Faith without Learning, p. 307, note 5.)

The compassion of Christ for poverty, misery, for childhood, and for ignorance, is everywhere illustrated in Holy Scripture; and *faith,* even "as a grain of mustard seed," is magnified, accordingly, in the infinite love of his teaching. Again I am willing to refer to Farrar (though I read him always with something between the lines, before I can adopt his sweeping generalizations) for a fine passage, I should quote entire, did space permit (*The Witness of History to Christ,* p. 172, ed. London, 1872). See also the noble sermon of Jeremy Taylor on John vii. 17 (*Works,* vol. ii. p. 53, ed. Bohn, 1844).

X.
(The Open Secret, p. 313, note 3.)

The esoteric system of Clement is here expounded in few words: there is nothing in it which may not be proclaimed from the house-tops, for all who have ears to hear. It is the mere swine (with seed-pickers and jack-daws, the σπερμόλογοι of the Athenians) who must be denied the pearls of gnostic truth. And this, on the same merciful principle on which the Master was silent before Pilate, and turned away from cities where they were not prepared to receive his message.

XI.
(Bodily Purity, p. 317, note 1.)

From a familiar quotation, I have often argued that the fine instinct of a woman, even among heathen, enforces a true idea: "If from her husband's bed, as soon as she has bathed: if from adulterous commerce, not at all." This is afterwards noted by our author; but it is extraordinary to find the mind of the great missionary to our Saxon forefathers, troubled about such questions, even in the seventh century. I have less admiration for the elaborate answers of the great Patriarch of Rome (Gregory), to the scrupulous inquiries of Augustine, than for the instinctive and aphoristic wisdom of poor Theano, in all the darkness of her heathenism. (See Ven. Bede, *Eccles. Hist.*, book i. cap. 27, p. 131. Works, ed. London, 1843.)

XII.
(Clement's View of Philosophy, p. 318, note 4.)

I note the concluding words of this chapter (xvi.), as epitomizing the whole of what Clement means to say on this great subject; and, for more, see the Elucidation *infra*, on Justification.

XIII.
(The Ecstacy of Sibyl, etc., p. 319, note 3.)

No need to quote Virgil's description (*Æneid,* vi. 46, with Heyne's references in Excursus V.); but I would compare with his picture of Sibylline inspiration, that of Balaam

(Numbers 24:3, 4, 15, 16), and leave with the student an inquiry, how far we may credit to a divine motion, the oracles of the heathen, i.e., some of them. I wish to refer the student, also, as to a valuable bit of introductory learning, to the essay of Isaac Casaubon (*Exercitationes ad Baronii Prolegom.*, pp. 65–85, ed. Genevæ, 1663).

XIV.
(Justification, p. 323, note 2.)

Casaubon, in the work just quoted above (*Exercitat.*, i.) examines this passage of our author, and others, comparing them with passages from St. Chrysostom and St. Augustine, and with Justin Martyr (see vol. i. p. 178, this series, cap. 46). Bishop Kaye (p. 428) justly remarks: "The apparent incorrectness of Clement's language arises from not making that clear distinction which the controversies at the time of the Reformation introduced." The word "incorrectness," though for myself I do not object to it, might be said "to beg the question;" and hence I should prefer to leave it open to the divers views of readers, by speaking, rather, of his lack of *precision* in the use of a term not then defined with theological delicacy of statement.

XV.
(Chronology, p. 334, note 5.)

Here an invaluable work for comparison and reference must be consulted by the student; viz., the *Chronicon* of Julius Africanus, in Routh's *Reliquiæ* (tom ii. p. 220, *et seqq.*), with learned annotations, in which (e.g., p. 491) Clement's work is cited. Africanus took up chronological science in the imperfect state where it was left by Clement, with whom he was partially contemporary; for he was Bishop of Emmaus in Palestine (called also Nicopolis), and composed his fine books of chronological history, under Marcus Aurelius. On the

Alexandrian era consult a paragraph in *Encyc. Britannica* (vol. v. p. 714). It was adopted for Christian computation, after Africanus. See Eusebius (book vi. cap. 31), and compare (this volume, p. 85) what is said of Theophilus of Antioch, by Abp. Usher.

Book II.

CHAPTER I.—INTRODUCTORY.

As Scripture has called the Greeks pilferers of the Barbarian philosophy, it will next have to be considered how this may be briefly demonstrated. For we shall not only show that they have imitated and copied the marvels recorded in our books; but we shall prove, besides, that they have plagiarized and falsified (our writings being, as we have shown, older) the chief dogmas they hold, both on faith and knowledge and science, and hope and love, and also on repentance and temperance and the fear of God,—a whole swarm, verily, of the virtues of truth.

Whatever the explication necessary on the point in hand shall demand, shall be embraced, and especially what is occult in the barbarian philosophy, the department of symbol and enigma; which those who have subjected the teaching of the ancients to systematic philosophic study have affected, as being in the highest degree serviceable, nay, absolutely necessary to the knowledge of truth. In addition, it will in my opinion form an appropriate sequel to defend those tenets, on account of which the Greeks assail us, making use of a few Scriptures, if perchance the Jew also may listen and be able quietly to turn from what he has believed to Him on whom he has not believed. The ingenuous among the philosophers will then with propriety be taken up in a friendly exposure both of their life and of the discovery of new dogmas, not in the way of our avenging ourselves on our detractors (for that is far from being the case with those who have learned to bless those who curse, even though they needlessly discharge on us words of blasphemy), but with a view to their conversion; if by any means these adepts in wisdom may feel ashamed, being brought to their senses by barbarian demonstration; so as to be able, although late, to see clearly of what sort are the intellectual acquisitions for which they make pilgrimages over the seas. Those they have stolen are to be pointed out, that we may thereby pull down their conceit; and of those on the discovery of which through investigation they plume themselves, the refutation will be furnished. By consequence, also we must treat of what is called the curriculum of study— how far it is serviceable; and of astrology, and mathematics, and magic, and sorcery. For all the Greeks boast of these as the highest sciences. "He who reproves boldly is a peacemaker." We have often said already that we have neither practiced nor do we study the expressing ourselves in pure Greek; for this suits those who seduce the multitude from the truth. But true philosophic demonstration will contribute to the profit not of the listeners' tongues, but of their minds. And, in my opinion, he who is solicitous about truth ought not to frame his language with artfulness and care, but only to try to express his meaning as he best can. For those who are particular about words, and devote their time to them, miss the things. It is a feat fit for the gardener to pluck without injury the rose that is growing among the thorns; and for the craftsman to find out the pearl buried in the oyster's flesh. And they say that fowls have flesh of the most agreeable quality, when, through not being supplied with abundance of food, they pick their sustenance with difficulty, scraping with their feet. If anyone, then, speculating on what is similar, wants to arrive at the truth [that is] in the numerous Greek plausibilities, like the real face beneath masks, he will hunt it out with much pains. For the power that appeared in the vision to Hermas said, "Whatever may be revealed to you, shall be revealed."

CHAPTER II.—THE KNOWLEDGE OF GOD CAN BE ATTAINED ONLY THROUGH FAITH.

"Be not elated on account of thy wisdom," say the Proverbs. "In all thy ways acknowledge her, that she may direct thy ways, and that thy foot may not stumble." By these remarks he means to show that our deeds ought to be conformable to reason, and to manifest further that we ought to select and possess what is useful out of all culture. Now the ways of wisdom are various that lead right to the way of truth. Faith is the way. "Thy foot shall not stumble" is said with reference to some who seem to oppose the one divine administration of Providence. Whence it is added, "Be not wise in thine own eyes," according to the impious ideas which revolt against the administration of God. "But fear God," who alone is powerful. Whence it follows as a consequence that we are not to oppose God. The sequel especially teaches clearly, that "the fear of God is departure from evil;" for it is said, "and depart from all evil." Such is the discipline of wisdom ("for whom the Lord loves He chastens"), causing pain in order to produce understanding, and restoring to peace and immortality. Accordingly, the Barbarian philosophy, which we follow, is in reality perfect and true. And so it is said in the book of Wisdom: "For He hath given me the unerring knowledge of things that exist, to know the constitution of the word," and so forth, down to "and the virtues of roots." Among all these he comprehends natural science, which treats of all the phenomena in the world of sense. And in continuation, he alludes also to intellectual objects in what he subjoins: "And what is hidden or manifest I know; for Wisdom, the artificer of all things, taught me." You have, in brief, the professed aim of our philosophy; and the learning of these branches, when pursued with right course of conduct, leads through Wisdom, the artificer of all things, to the Ruler of all,—a Being difficult to grasp and apprehend, ever receding and withdrawing from him who pursues. But He who is far off has—oh ineffable marvel!—come very near. "I am a God that draws near," says the Lord. He is in essence remote; "for how is it that what is begotten can have approached the Unbegotten?" But He is very near in virtue of that power which holds all things in its embrace. "Shall one do aught in secret, and I see him not?" For the power of God is always present, in contact with us, in the exercise of inspection, of beneficence, of instruction. Whence Moses, persuaded that God is not to be known by human wisdom, said, "Show me Thy glory;" and into the thick darkness where God's voice was, pressed to enter—that is, into the inaccessible and invisible ideas respecting Existence. For God is not in darkness or in place, but above both space and time, and qualities of objects. Wherefore neither is He at any time in a part, either as containing or as contained, either by limitation or by section. "For what house will ye build to Me?" says the Lord. Nay, He has not even built one for Himself, since He cannot be contained. And though heaven be called His throne, not even thus is He contained, but He rests delighted in the creation.

It is clear, then, that the truth has been hidden from us; and if that has been already shown by one example, we shall establish it a little after by several more. How entirely worthy of approbation are they who are both willing to learn, and able, according to Solomon, "to know wisdom and instruction, and to perceive the words of wisdom, to receive knotty words, and to perceive true righteousness," there being another [righteousness as well], not according to the truth, taught by the Greek laws, and by the rest of the philosophers. "And to direct judgments," it is said—not those of the bench, but he means that we must preserve sound and free of error the judicial faculty which is within us—"That I may give subtlety to the simple, to the young man sense and understanding." "For the wise man," who has been persuaded to obey the commandments, "having heard these things, will become wiser" by knowledge; and "the intelligent man will acquire rule, and will understand a parable and a dark word, the sayings and enigmas of the wise." For it is not spurious words which

Clement of Alexandria

those inspired by God and those who are gained over by them adduce, nor is it snares in which the most of the sophists entangle the young, spending their time on naught true. But those who possess the Holy Spirit "search the deep things of God,"—that is, grasp the secret that is in the prophecies. "To impart of holy things to the dogs" is forbidden, so long as they remain beasts. For never ought those who are envious and perturbed, and still infidel in conduct, shameless in barking at investigation, to dip in the divine and clear stream of the living water. "Let not the waters of thy fountain overflow, and let thy waters spread over thine own streets." For it is not many who understand such things as they fall in with; or know them even after learning them, though they think they do, according to the worthy Heraclitus. Does not even he seem to thee to censure those who believe not? "Now my just one shall live by faith," the prophet said. And another prophet also says, "Except ye believe, neither shall ye understand." For how ever could the soul admit the transcendental contemplation of such themes, while unbelief respecting what was to be learned struggled within? But faith, which the Greeks disparage, deeming it futile and barbarous, is a voluntary preconception, the assent of piety—"the subject of things hoped for, the evidence of things not seen," according to the divine apostle. "For hereby," preeminently, "the elders obtained a good report. But without faith it is impossible to please God." Others have defined faith to be a uniting assent to an unseen object, as certainly the proof of an unknown thing is an evident assent. If then it be choice, being desirous of something, the desire is in this instance intellectual. And since choice is the beginning of action, faith is discovered to be the beginning of action, being the foundation of rational choice in the case of any one who exhibits to himself the previous demonstration through faith. Voluntarily to follow what is useful, is the first principle of understanding. Unswerving choice, then, gives considerable momentum in the direction of knowledge. The exercise of faith directly becomes knowledge, reposing on a sure foundation. Knowledge, accordingly, is defined by the sons of the philosophers as a habit, which cannot be overthrown by reason. Is there any other true condition such as this, except piety, of which alone the Word is teacher? I think not. Theophrastus says that sensation is the root of faith. For from it the rudimentary principles extend to the reason that is in us, and the understanding. He who believeth then the divine Scriptures with sure judgment, receives in the voice of God, who bestowed the Scripture, a demonstration that cannot be impugned. Faith, then, is not established by demonstration. "Blessed therefore those who, not having seen, yet have believed." The Siren's songs, exhibiting a power above human, fascinated those that came near, conciliating them, almost against their will, to the reception of what was said.

CHAPTER III.—FAITH NOT A PRODUCT OF NATURE.

Now the followers of Basilides regard faith as natural, as they also refer it to choice, [representing it] as finding ideas by intellectual comprehension without demonstration; while the followers of Valentinus assign faith to us, the simple, but will have it that knowledge springs up in their own selves (who are saved by nature) through the advantage of a germ of superior excellence, saying that it is as far removed from faith as the spiritual is from the animal. Further, the followers of Basilides say that faith as well as choice is proper according to every interval; and that in consequence of the supramundane selection mundane faith accompanies all nature, and that the free gift of faith is conformable to the hope of each. Faith, then, is no longer the direct result of free choice, if it is a natural advantage.

Nor will he who has not believed, not being the author [of his unbelief], meet with a due recompense; and he that has believed is not the cause [of his belief]. And the entire peculiarity and difference of belief and unbelief will not fall under either praise or censure, if we reflect rightly, since there attaches to it the antecedent natural necessity proceeding from the Almighty. And if we are pulled like inanimate things by the puppet-strings of natural powers, willingness and unwillingness, and impulse, which is the antecedent of both, are mere redundancies. And for my part, I am utterly incapable of conceiving such an animal as has its appetencies, which are moved by external causes, under the dominion of necessity. And what place is there any longer for the repentance of him who was once an unbeliever, through which comes forgiveness of sins? So that neither is baptism rational, nor the blessed seal, nor the Son, nor the Father. But God, as I think, turns out to be the distribution to men of natural powers, which has not as the foundation of salvation voluntary faith.

CHAPTER IV.—FAITH THE FOUNDATION OF ALL KNOWLEDGE.

But we, who have heard by the Scriptures that self-determining choice and refusal have been given by the Lord to men, rest in the infallible criterion of faith, manifesting a willing spirit, since we have chosen life and believe God through His voice. And he who has believed the Word knows the matter to be true; for the Word is truth. But he who has disbelieved Him that speaks, has disbelieved God.

"By faith we understand that the worlds were framed by the word of God, so that what is seen was not made of things which appear," says the apostle. "By faith Abel offered to God a fuller sacrifice than Cain, by which he received testimony that he was righteous, God giving testimony to him respecting his gifts; and by it he, being dead, yet speaks," and so forth, down to "than enjoy the pleasures of sin for a season." Faith having, therefore, justified these before the law, made them heirs of the divine promise. Why then should I review and adduce any further testimonies of faith from the history in our hands? "For the time would fail me were I to tell of Gideon, Barak, Samson, Jephtha, David, and Samuel, and the prophets," and what follows. Now, inasmuch as there are four things in which the truth resides—Sensation, Understanding, Knowledge, Opinion,—intellectual apprehension is first in the order of nature; but in our case, and in relation to ourselves, Sensation is first, and of Sensation and Understanding the essence of Knowledge is formed; and evidence is common to Understanding and Sensation. Well, Sensation is the ladder to Knowledge; while Faith, advancing over the pathway of the objects of sense, leaves Opinion behind, and speeds to things free of deception, and reposes in the truth.

Should one say that Knowledge is founded on demonstration by a process of reasoning, let him hear that first principles are incapable of demonstration; for they are known neither by art nor sagacity. For the latter is conversant about objects that are susceptible of change, while the former is practical solely, and not theoretical. Hence it is thought that the first cause of the universe can be apprehended by faith alone. For all knowledge is capable of being taught; and what is capable of being taught is founded on what is known before. But the first cause of the universe was not previously known to the Greeks; neither, accordingly, to Thales, who came to the conclusion that water was the first cause; nor to the other natural philosophers who succeeded him, since it was Anaxagoras who was the first who assigned to Mind the supremacy over material things. But not even he preserved the dignity suited to the efficient cause, describing as he did certain silly vortices, together with the inertia and even foolishness of Mind. Wherefore also the Word says, "Call no man master on earth." For knowledge is a state of mind that results from demonstration; but faith is a grace which from what is indemonstrable conducts to what is universal and simple, what is neither with matter, nor matter, nor under matter. But those who believe not, as to be expected, drag all down from heaven, and the region of the invisible, to earth, "absolutely grasping with their hands rocks and oaks," according to Plato. For, clinging to all such things, they asseverate that that alone exists which can be touched and handled, defining body and essence to be identical: disputing against themselves, they very piously defend the existence of certain intellectual and bodiless forms descending somewhere from above from the invisible world, vehemently maintaining that there is a true essence. "Lo, I make new things," says the Word, "which eye hath not seen, nor ear heard, nor hath it entered into the heart of man." With a new eye, a new ear, a new heart, whatever can be seen and heard is to be apprehended, by the faith and understanding of the disciples of the Lord, who speak, hear, and act spiritually.

For there is genuine coin, and other that is spurious; which no less deceives unprofessionals, that it does not the money-changers; who know through having learned how to separate and distinguish what has a false stamp from what is genuine. So the money-changer only says to the unprofessional man that the coin is counterfeit. But the reason why, only the banker's apprentice, and he that is trained to this department, learns.

Now Aristotle says that the judgment which follows knowledge is in truth faith. Accordingly, faith is something superior to knowledge, and is its criterion. Conjecture, which is only a feeble supposition, counterfeits faith; as the flatterer counterfeits a friend, and the wolf the dog. And as the workman sees that by learning certain things he becomes an artificer, and the helmsman by being instructed in the art will be able to steer; he does not regard the mere wishing to become excellent and good enough, but he must learn it by the exercise of obedience. But to obey the Word, whom we call Instructor, is to believe Him, going against Him in nothing. For how can we take up a position of hostility to God? Knowledge, accordingly, is characterized by faith; and faith, by a kind of divine mutual and reciprocal correspondence, becomes characterized by knowledge.

Epicurus, too, who very greatly preferred pleasure to truth, supposes faith to be a preconception of the mind; and defines preconception to be a grasping at something evident, and at the clear understanding of the thing; and asserts that, without preconception, no one can either inquire, or doubt, or judge, or even argue. How can one, without a preconceived idea of what he is aiming after, learn about that which is the subject of his investigation? He, again, who has learned has already turned his preconception into comprehension. And if he who learns, learns not without a preconceived idea which takes in what is expressed, that man has ears to hear the truth. And happy is the man that speaks to the ears of those who hear; as happy certainly also is he who is a child of obedience. Now to hear is to understand. If, then, faith is nothing else than a preconception of the mind in regard to what is the subject of discourse, and obedience is so called, and understanding and persuasion; no one shall learn aught without faith, since no one [learns aught] without preconception. Consequently there is a more ample demonstration of the complete truth of what was spoken by the prophet, "Unless ye believe, neither will ye understand." Paraphrasing this oracle, Heraclitus of Ephesus says, "If a man hope not, he will not find that which is not hoped for, seeing it is inscrutable and inaccessible." Plato the philosopher, also, in *The Laws*, says, "that he who would be blessed and happy, must be straight from the beginning a partaker of the truth, so as to live true for as long a period as possible; for he is a man of faith. But the unbeliever is one to whom voluntary falsehood is agreeable; and the man to whom involuntary falsehood is agreeable is senseless; neither of which is desirable. For he who is devoid of friendliness, is faithless and ignorant." And does he not enigmatically say in *Euthydemus,* that this is "the regal wisdom"? In *The Statesman* he says expressly, "So that the knowledge of the true king is kingly; and he who possesses it, whether a prince or private person, shall by all means, in consequence of this act, be rightly styled royal." Now those who have believed in Christ both are and are called *Chrestoi* (good), as those who are cared for by the true king are kingly. For as the wise are wise by their wisdom, and those observant of law are so by the law; so also those who belong to Christ the King are kings, and those that are Christ's Christians. Then, in continuation, he adds clearly, "What is right will turn out to be lawful, law being in its nature right reason, and not found in writings or elsewhere." And the stranger of Elea pronounces the kingly and statesmanlike man "*a living law.*" Such is he who fulfils the law, "doing the will of the Father," inscribed on a lofty pillar, and set as an example of divine virtue to all who possess the power of seeing. The Greeks are acquainted with the staves of the Ephori at Lacedæmon, inscribed with the law on wood. But my law, as was said above, is both royal and living; and it is right reason. "Law, which is king of all—of mortals and immortals," as the Boeotian Pindar sings. For Speusippus, in the first book against Cleophon, seems to write like Plato on this wise: "For if royalty be a good thing, and the wise man the only king and ruler, the law, which is right reason, is good;" which is the case. The Stoics teach what is in conformity with this, assigning kinghood, priesthood, prophecy, legislation, riches, true beauty, noble birth, freedom, to the wise man alone. But that he is exceedingly difficult to find, is confessed even by them.

CHAPTER V.—HE PROVES BY SEVERAL EXAMPLES THAT THE GREEKS DREW FROM THE SACRED WRITERS.

Accordingly all those above-mentioned dogmas appear to have been transmitted from Moses the great to the Greeks. That all things belong to the wise man, is taught in these words: "And because God hath showed me mercy, I have all things."And that he is beloved of God, God intimates when He says, "The God of Abraham, the God of Isaac, the God of Jacob." For the first is found to have been expressly called "friend;" and the second is shown to have received a new name, signifying "he that sees God;" while Isaac, God in a figure selected for Himself as a consecrated sacrifice, to be a type to us of the economy of salvation.

Now among the Greeks, Minos the king of nine years' reign, and familiar friend of Zeus, is celebrated in song; they having heard how once God conversed with Moses, "as one speaking with his friend."Moses, then, was a sage, king, legislator. But our Savior surpasses all human nature. He is so lovely, as to be alone loved by us, whose hearts are set on the true beauty, for "He was the true light." He is shown to be a King, as such hailed by unsophisticated children and by the unbelieving and ignorant Jews, and heralded by the prophets. So rich is He, that He despised the whole earth, and the gold above and beneath it, with all glory, when given to Him by the adversary. What need is there to say that He is the only High Priest, who alone possesses the knowledge of the worship of God? He is Melchizedek, "King of peace," the most fit of all to head the race of men. A legislator too, inasmuch as He gave the law by the mouth of the prophets, enjoining and teaching most distinctly what things are to be done, and what not. Who of nobler lineage than He whose only Father is God? Come, then, let us produce Plato assenting to those very dogmas. The wise man he calls rich in the *Phoedrus*, when he says, "O dear Pan, and whatever other gods are here, grant me to become fair within; and whatever external things I have, let them be agreeable to what is within. I would reckon the wise man rich." And the Athenian stranger, finding fault with those who think that those who have many possessions are rich, speaks thus: "For the very rich to be also good is impossible—those, I mean, whom the multitude count rich. Those they call rich, who, among a few men, are owners of the possessions worth most money; which any bad man may possess." "The whole world of wealth belongs to the believer," Solomon says, "but not a penny to the unbeliever." Much more, then, is the Scripture to be believed which says, "It is easier for a camel to go through the eye of a needle, than for a rich man" to lead a philosophic life. But, on the other hand, it blesses "the poor;" as Plato understood when he said, "It is not the diminishing of one's resources, but the augmenting of insatiableness, that is to be considered poverty; for it is not slender means that ever constitutes poverty, but insatiableness, from which the good man being free, will also be rich." And in *Alcibiades* he calls vice a servile thing, and virtue the attribute of freemen. "Take away from you the heavy yoke, and take up the easy one," says the Scripture; as also the poets call [vice] a slavish yoke. And the expression, "Ye have sold yourselves to your sins," agrees with what is said above: "Every one, then, who committed sin is a slave; and the slave abided not in the house for ever. But if the Son shall make you free, then shall ye be free, and the truth shall make you free."

And again, that the wise man is beautiful, the Athenian stranger asserts, in the same way as if one were to affirm that certain persons were just, even should they happen to be ugly in their persons. And in speaking thus with respect to eminent rectitude of character, no one who should assert them to be on this account beautiful would be thought to speak extravagantly. And "His appearance was inferior to all the Sons of men," prophecy predicted.

Plato, moreover, has called the wise man a king, in *The Statesman*. The remark is quoted above.

These points being demonstrated, let us recur again to our discourse on faith. Well, with the fullest demonstration, Plato proves, that there is need of faith everywhere, celebrating peace at the same time: "For no man will ever be trusty and sound in seditions without entire virtue. There are numbers of mercenaries full of fight, and willing to die in war; but, with a very few exceptions, the most of them are desperadoes and villains, insolent and senseless." If these observations are right, "every legislator who is even of slight use, will, in making his laws, have an eye to the greatest virtue. Such is fidelity," which we need at all times, both in peace and in war, and in all the rest of our life, for it appears to embrace the other virtues.

"But the best thing is neither war nor sedition, for the necessity of these is to be deprecated. But peace with one another and kindly feeling are what is best." From these remarks the greatest prayer evidently is to have peace, according to Plato. And faith is the greatest mother of the virtues. Accordingly it is rightly said in Solomon, "Wisdom is in the mouth of the faithful. Since also Xenocrates, in his book on "Intelligence," says "that wisdom is the knowledge of first causes and of intellectual essence." He considers intelligence as twofold, practical and theoretical, which latter is human wisdom. Consequently wisdom is intelligence, but all intelligence is not wisdom. And it has been shown, that the knowledge of the first cause of the universe is of faith, but is not demonstration. For it were strange that the followers of the Samian Pythagoras, rejecting demonstrations of subjects of question, should regard the bare *ipse dixit* as ground of belief; and that this expression alone sufficed for the confirmation of what they heard, while those devoted to the contemplation of the truth, presuming to disbelieve the trustworthy Teacher, God the only Savior, should demand of Him tests of His utterances. But He says, "He that hath ears to hear, let him hear." And who is he? Let Epicharmus say:—

"Mind sees, mind hears; all besides is deaf and blind."

Rating some as unbelievers, Heraclitus says, "Not knowing how to hear or to speak;" aided doubtless by Solomon, who says, "If thou loves to hear, thou shalt comprehend; and if thou incline thine ear, thou shalt be wise."

CHAPTER VI.—THE EXCELLENCE AND UTILITY OF FAITH.

"Lord, who hath believed our report?" Isaiah says. For "faith cometh by hearing, and hearing by the word of God," says the apostle. "How then shall they call on Him in whom they have not believed? And how shall they believe on Him whom they have not heard? And how shall they hear without a preacher? And how shall they preach except they be sent? As it is written, How beautiful are the feet of those that publish glad tidings of good things." You see how he brings faith by hearing, and the preaching of the apostles, up to the word of the Lord, and to the Son of God. We do not yet understand the word of the Lord to be demonstration.

As, then, playing at ball not only depends on one throwing the ball skillfully, but it requires besides one to catch it dexterously, that the game may be gone through according to the rules for ball; so also is it the case that teaching is reliable when faith on the part of those who hear, being, so to speak, a sort of natural art, contributes to the process of learning. So also the earth co-operates, through its productive power, being fit for the sowing of the seed. For there is no good of the very best instruction without the exercise of the receptive faculty on the part of the learner, not even of prophecy, when there is the absence of docility on the part of those who hear. For dry twigs, being ready to receive the power of fire, are kindled with great ease; and the far-famed stone attracts steel through affinity, as the amber tear-drop drags to itself twigs, and the lump sets chaff in motion. And the substances attracted obey them, influenced by a subtle spirit, not as a cause, but as a concurring cause.

There being then a twofold species of vice—that characterized by craft and stealth, and that which leads and drives with violence—the divine Word cries, calling all together; knowing perfectly well those that will not obey; notwithstanding then since to obey or not is in our own power, provided we have not the excuse of ignorance to adduce. He makes a just call, and demands of each according to his strength. For some are able as well as willing, having reached this point through practice and being purified; while others, if they are not yet able, already have the will. Now to will is the act of the soul, but to do is not without the body. Nor are actions estimated by their issue alone; but they are judged also according to the element of free choice in each,—if he chose easily, if he repented of his sins, if he reflected on his failures and repented (μετέγνω), which is (μετὰ ταῦτα ἔγνω) "afterwards knew." For repentance is a tardy knowledge, and primitive innocence is knowledge. Repentance, then, is an effect of faith. For unless a man believe that to which he was addicted to be sin, he will not abandon it; and if he do not believe punishment to be impending over the transgressor, and salvation to be the portion of him who lives according to the commandments, he will not reform.

      Hope, too, is based on faith. Accordingly the followers of Basilides define faith to be, the assent of the soul to any of those things, that do not affect the senses through not being present. And hope is the expectation of the possession of good. Necessarily, then, is expectation founded on faith. Now he is faithful who keeps inviolably what is entrusted to him; and we are entrusted with the utterances respecting God and the divine words, the commands along with the execution of the injunctions. This is the faithful servant, who is praised by the Lord. And when it is said, "God is faithful," it is intimated that He is worthy to be believed when declaring aught. Now His Word declares; and "God" Himself is "faithful." How, then, if to believe is to suppose, do the philosophers think that what proceeds from themselves is sure? For the voluntary assent to a preceding demonstration is not supposition, but it is assent to something sure. Who is more powerful than God? Now unbelief is the feeble negative supposition of one opposed to Him: as incredulity is a condition which admits faith with difficulty. Faith is the voluntary supposition and anticipation of pre-comprehension. Expectation is an opinion about the future, and expectation about other things is opinion about uncertainty. Confidence is a strong judgment about a thing. Wherefore we believe Him in whom we have confidence unto divine glory and salvation. And we confide in Him, who is God alone, whom we know, that those things nobly promised to us, and for this end benevolently created and bestowed by Him on us, will not fail.

      Benevolence is the wishing of good things to another for his sake. For He needs nothing; and the beneficence and benignity which flow from the Lord terminate in us, being divine benevolence, and benevolence resulting in beneficence. And if to Abraham on his believing it was counted for righteousness; and if we are the seed of Abraham, then we must also believe through hearing. For we are Israelites, who are convinced not by signs, but by hearing. Wherefore it is said, "Rejoice, O barren, that barest not; break forth and cry, thou that didst not travail with child: for more are the children of the desolate than of her who hath a husband." "Thou hast lived for the fence of the people, thy children were blessed in the tents of their fathers." And if the same mansions are promised by prophecy to us and to the patriarchs, the God of both the covenants is shown to be one. Accordingly it is added more clearly, "Thou hast inherited the covenant of Israel," speaking to those called from among the nations, that were once barren, being formerly destitute of this husband, who is the Word,—desolate formerly,—of the bridegroom. "Now the just shall live by faith," which is according to the covenant and the commandments; since these, which are two in name and time, given in accordance with the [divine] economy—being in power one—the old and the new, are dispensed through the Son by one God. As the apostle also says in the Epistle to the Romans, "For therein is the righteousness of God revealed from faith to faith," teaching the one salvation which from prophecy to the Gospel is perfected by one and the same Lord. "This charge," he says, "I commit to thee, son Timothy, according to the prophecies which went before on thee, that thou by them might war the good warfare; holding faith, and a good conscience; which some having put away concerning faith have made shipwreck," because they defiled by unbelief the conscience that comes from God. Accordingly, faith may not, any more, with reason, be disparaged in an offhand way, as simple and vulgar, appertaining to anybody. For, if it were a mere human habit, as the Greeks supposed, it would have been extinguished. But if it grow, and there be no place where it is not; then I affirm, that faith, whether founded in love, or in fear, as its disparagers assert, is something divine; which is neither rent asunder by other mundane friendship, nor dissolved by the presence of fear. For love, on account of its friendly alliance with faith, makes men believers; and faith, which is the foundation of love, in its turn introduces the doing of good; since also fear, the pædagogue of the law, is believed to be fear by those, by whom it is believed. For, if its existence is shown in its working, it is yet believed when about to do and threatening, and when not working and present; and being believed to exist, it does not itself generate faith, but is by faith tested and proved trustworthy. Such a change, then, from unbelief to faith—and to trust in hope and fear, is divine. And, in truth, faith is discovered, by us, to be the first movement towards salvation; after which fear, and hope, and repentance, advancing in company with temperance and patience, lead us to love and knowledge. Rightly, therefore, the Apostle Barnabas says, "From the portion I have received I have done my diligence to send by little and little to you; that along with your faith you may also have perfect knowledge. Fear and patience are then helpers of your faith; and our allies are longsuffering and temperance. These, then," he says, "in what respects the Lord, continuing in purity, there rejoice along with them, wisdom, understanding, intelligence, knowledge."

The fore-mentioned virtues being, then, the elements of knowledge; the result is that faith is more elementary, being as necessary to the Gnostic, as respiration to him that lives in this world is to life. And as without the four elements it is not possible to live, so neither can knowledge be attained without faith. It is then the support of truth.

CHAPTER VII.—THE UTILITY OF FEAR. OBJECTIONS ANSWERED

Those, who denounce fear, assail the law; and if the law, plainly also God, who gave the law. For these three elements are of necessity presented in the subject on hand: the ruler, his administration, and the ruled. If, then, according to hypothesis, they abolish the law; then, by necessary consequence, each one who is led by lust, courting pleasure, must neglect what is right and despise the Deity, and fearlessly indulge in impiety and injustice together, having dashed away from the truth.

Yea, say they, fear is an irrational aberration, and perturbation of mind. What says thou? And how can this definition be any longer maintained, seeing the commandment is given me by the Word? But the commandment forbids, hanging fear over the head of those who have incurred admonition for their discipline.

Fear is not then irrational. It is therefore rational. How could it be otherwise, exhorting as it does, *Thou shalt not kill, Thou shalt not commit adultery, Thou shalt not steal, Than shalt not bear false witness?* But if they will quibble about the names, let the philosophers term the fear of the law, cautious fear, (εὐλάβεια) which is a shunning (ἔκκλισις) agreeable to reason. Such Critolaus of Phasela not inaptly called fighters about names (ὀνοματομάκοι). The commandment, then, has already appeared fair and lovely even in the highest degree, when conceived under a change of name. Cautious fear (εὐλάβεια) is therefore shown to be reasonable, being the shunning of what hurts; from which arises repentance for previous sins. "For the fear of the Lord is the beginning of wisdom; good understanding is to all that do it." He calls wisdom a doing, which is the fear of the Lord paving the way for wisdom. But if the law produces fear, the knowledge of the law is the beginning of wisdom; and a man is not wise without law. Therefore those who reject the law are unwise; and in consequence they are reckoned godless (ἄθεοι). Now instruction is the beginning of wisdom. "But the ungodly despise wisdom and instruction," says the Scripture.

Let us see what terrors the law announces. If it is the things which hold an intermediate place between virtue and vice, such as poverty, disease, obscurity, and humble birth, and the like, these things civil laws hold forth, and are praised for so doing. And those of the Peripatetic school, who introduce three kinds of good things, and think that their opposites are evil, this opinion suits. But the law given to us enjoins us to shun what are in reality bad things—adultery, uncleanness, pæderasty, ignorance, wickedness, soul-disease, death (not that which severs the soul from the body, but that which severs the soul from truth). For these are vices in reality, and the workings that proceed from them are dreadful and terrible. "For not unjustly," say the divine oracles, "are the nets spread for birds; for they who are accomplices in blood treasure up evils to themselves." How, then, is the law still said to be not good by certain heresies that clamorously appeal to the apostle, who says, "For by the law is the knowledge of sin?" To whom we say, The law did not cause, but showed sin. For, enjoining what is to be done, it reprehended what ought not to be done. And it is the part of the good to teach what is salutary, and to point out what is deleterious; and to counsel the practice of the one, and to command to shun the other. Now the apostle, whom they do not comprehend, said that by the law the knowledge of sin was manifested, not that from it derived its existence. And how can the law be not good, which trains, which is given as the instructor (παιδαγωγός) to Christ, that being corrected by fear, in the way of discipline, in order to the attainment of the perfection which is by Christ? "I will not," it is said, "the death of the sinner, as his repentance." Now the commandment works repentance; inasmuch as it deters from what ought not to be done, and enjoins good deeds. By ignorance he means, in my opinion, death. "And he that is near the Lord is full of stripes." Plainly, he, that draws near to knowledge, has the benefit of perils, fears, troubles, afflictions, by reason of his desire for the truth. "For the son who is instructed turns out wise, and an intelligent son is saved from burning. And an intelligent son will receive the commandments." And Barnabas the apostle having said, "Woe to those who are wise in their own conceits, clever in their own eyes," added, "Let us become spiritual, a perfect temple to God; let us, as far as in us lies, practice the fear of God, and strive to keep His commands, that we may rejoice in His judgments." Whence "the fear of God" is divinely said to be the beginning of wisdom.

CHAPTER VIII.—THE VAGARIES OF BASILIDES AND VALENTINUS AS TO FEAR BEING THE CAUSE OF THINGS.

Here the followers of Basilides, interpreting this expression, say, "that the Prince, having heard the speech of the Spirit, who was being ministered to, was struck with amazement both with the voice and the vision, having had glad tidings beyond his hopes announced to him; and that his amazement was called fear, which became the origin of wisdom, which distinguishes classes, and discriminates, and perfects, and restores. For not the world alone, but also the election, He that is over all has set apart and sent forth."

And Valentinus appears also in an epistle to have adopted such views. For he writes in these very words: "And as terror fell on the angels at this creature, because he uttered things greater than proceeded from his formation, by reason of the being in him who had invisibly communicated a germ of the supernal essence, and who spoke with free utterance; so also among the tribes of men in the world, the works of men became terrors to those who made them,—as, for example, images and statues. And the hands of all fashion things to bear the name of God: for Adam formed into the name of man inspired the dread attaching to the pre-existent man, as having his being in him; and they were terror-stricken, and speedily marred the work."

But there being but one First Cause, as will be shown afterwards, these men will be shown to be inventors of chattering and chirpings. But since God deemed it advantageous, that from the law and the prophets, men should receive a preparatory discipline by the Lord, the fear of the Lord was called the beginning of wisdom, being given by the Lord, through Moses, to the disobedient and hard of heart. For those whom reason convinces not, fear tames; which also the Instructing Word, foreseeing from the first, and purifying by each of these methods, adapted the instrument suitably for piety. Consternation is, then, fear at a strange apparition, or at an unlooked-for representation—such as, for example, a message; while fear is an excessive wonderment on account of something which arises or is. They do not then perceive that they represent by means of amazement the God who is highest and is extolled by them, as subject to perturbation and antecedent to amazement as having been in ignorance. If indeed ignorance preceded amazement; and if this amazement and fear, which is the beginning of wisdom, is the fear of God, then in all likelihood ignorance as cause preceded both the wisdom of God and all creative work, and not only these, but restoration and even election itself. Whether, then, was it ignorance of what was good or what was evil?

Well, if of good, why does it cease through amazement? And minister and preaching and baptism are [in that case] superfluous to them. And if of evil, how can what is bad be the cause of what is best? For had not ignorance preceded, the minister would not have come down, nor would have amazement seized on "the Prince," as they say; nor would he have attained to a beginning of wisdom from fear, in order to discrimination between the elect and those that are mundane. And if the fear of the pre-existent man made the angels conspire against their own handiwork, under the idea that an invisible germ of the supernal essence was lodged within that creation, or through unfounded suspicion excited envy, which is incredible, the angels became murderers of the creature which had been entrusted to them, as a child might be, they being thus convicted of the grossest ignorance. Or suppose they were influenced by being involved in foreknowledge. But they would not have conspired against what they foreknew in the assault they made; nor would they have been terror-struck at their own work, in consequence of foreknowledge, on their perceiving the supernal germ. Or, finally, suppose, trusting to their knowledge, they dared (but this also were impossible for them), on learning the excellence that is in the Pleroma, to conspire against man. Furthermore also they laid hands on that which was according to the image, in which also is the archetype, and which, along with the knowledge that remains, is indestructible.

To these, then, and certain others, especially the Marcionites, the Scripture cries, though they listen not, "He that hears Me shall rest with confidence in peace, and shall be tranquil, fearless of all evil."

What, then, will they have the law to be? They will not call it evil, but just; distinguishing what is good from what is just. But the Lord, when He enjoins us to dread evil, does not exchange one evil for another, but abolishes what is opposite by its opposite. Now evil is the opposite of good, as what is just is of what is unjust. If, then, that absence of fear, which the fear of the Lord produces, is called the beginning of what is good, fear is a good thing. And the fear which proceeds from the law is not only just, but good, as it takes away evil. But introducing absence of fear by means of fear, it does not produce apathy by means of mental perturbation, but moderation of feeling by discipline. When, then, we hear, "Honor the Lord, and be strong: but fear not another besides Him," we understand it to be meant fearing to sin, and following the commandments given by God, which is the honor that cometh from God. For the fear of God is Δέος [in Greek]. But if fear is perturbation of mind, as some will have it that fear is perturbation of mind, yet all fear is not perturbation. Superstition is indeed perturbation of mind; being the fear of demons, that produce and are subject to the excitement of passion. On the other hand, consequently, the fear of God, who is not subject to perturbation, is free of perturbation. For it is not God, but falling away from God, that the man is terrified for. And he who fears this—that is, falling into evils—fears and dreads those evils. And he who fears a fall, wishes himself to be free of corruption and perturbation. "The wise man, fearing, avoids evil: but the foolish, trusting, mixes himself with it," says the Scripture; and again it says, "In the fear of the Lord is the hope of strength."

The Stromata or Miscellanies

CHAPTER IX.—THE CONNECTION OF THE CHRISTIAN VIRTUES.

Such a fear, accordingly, leads to repentance and hope. Now hope is the expectation of good things, or an expectation sanguine of absent good; and favorable circumstances are assumed in order to good hope, which we have learned leads on to love. Now love turns out to be consent in what pertains to reason, life, and manners, or in brief, fellowship in life, or it is the intensity of friendship and of affection, with right reason, in the enjoyment of associates. And an associate (ἑταῖρος) is another self; just as we call those, brethren, who are regenerated by the same word. And akin to love is hospitality, being a congenial art devoted to the treatment of strangers. And those are strangers, to whom the things of the world are strange. For we regard as worldly those, who hope in the earth and carnal lusts. "Be not conformed," says the apostle, "to this world: but be ye transformed in the renewal of the mind, that ye may prove what is that good, and acceptable, and perfect, will of God."

Hospitality, therefore, is occupied in what is useful for strangers; and guests (ἐπίξενοι) are strangers (ξένοι); and friends are guests; and brethren are friends. "Dear brother," says Homer.

Philanthropy, in order to which also, is natural affection, being a loving treatment of men, and natural affection, which is a congenial habit exercised in the love of friends or domestics, follow in the train of love. And if the real man within us is the spiritual, philanthropy is brotherly love to those who participate, in the same spirit. Natural affection, on the other hand, is the preservation of good-will, or of affection; and affection is its perfect demonstration; and to be beloved is to please in behavior, by drawing and attracting. And persons are brought to sameness by consent, which is the knowledge of the good things that are enjoyed in common. For community of sentiment (ὁμογνωμοσύνη) is harmony of opinions (συμφωνία γνωμῶν). "Let your love be without dissimulation," it is said; "and abhorring what is evil, let us become attached to what is good, to brotherly love," and so on, down to "If it be possible, as much as lie in you, living peaceably with all men." Then "be not overcome of evil," it is said, "but overcome evil with good."And the same apostle owns that he bears witness to the Jews, "that they have a zeal of God, but not according to knowledge. For, being ignorant of God's righteousness, and seeking to establish their own, they have not submitted themselves to the righteousness of God." For they did not know and do the will of the law; but what they supposed, that they thought the law wished. And they did not believe the law as prophesying, but the bare word; and they followed through fear, not through disposition and faith. "For Christ is the end of the law for righteousness," who was prophesied by the law to everyone that believeth. Whence it was said to them by Moses, "I will provoke you to jealousy by them that are not a people; and I will anger you by a foolish nation, that is, by one that has become disposed to obedience."And by Isaiah it is said, "I was found of them that sought Me not; I was made manifest to them that inquired not after Me,"—manifestly previous to the coming of the Lord; after which to Israel, the things prophesied, are now appropriately spoken: "I have stretched out My hands all the day long to a disobedient and gainsaying people." Do you see the cause of the calling from among the nations, clearly declared, by the prophet, to be the disobedience and gainsaying of the people? Then the goodness of God is shown also in their case. For the apostle says, "But through their transgression salvation is come to the Gentiles, to provoke them to jealousy" and to willingness to repent. And the Shepherd, speaking plainly of those who had fallen asleep, recognizes certain righteous among Gentiles and Jews, not only before the appearance of Christ, but before the law, in virtue of acceptance before God,—as Abel, as Noah, as any other righteous man. He says accordingly, "that the apostles and teachers, who had preached the name of the Son of God, and had fallen asleep, in power and by faith, preached to those that had fallen asleep before" Then he subjoins: "And they gave them the seal of preaching. They descended, therefore, with them into the water, and again ascended. But these descended alive, and again ascended alive. But those, who had fallen asleep before, descended dead, but ascended alive. By these, therefore, they were made alive, and knew the name of the Son of God. Wherefore also they ascended with them, and fitted into the structure of the tower, and unhewn were built up together; they fell asleep in righteousness and in great purity, but wanted only this seal." "For when the Gentiles, which have not the law, do by nature the things of the law, these, having not the law, are a law unto themselves," according to the apostle.

As, then, the virtues follow one another, why need I say what has been demonstrated already, that faith hopes through repentance, and fear through faith; and patience and practice in these along with learning terminate in love, which is perfected by knowledge? But that is necessarily to be noticed, that the Divine alone is to be regarded as naturally wise.

Therefore also wisdom, which has taught the truth, is the power of God; and in it the perfection of knowledge is embraced. The philosopher loves and likes the truth, being now considered as a friend, on account of his love, from his being a true servant. The beginning of knowledge is wondering at objects, as Plato says is in his *Theætetus;* and Matthew exhorting in the *Traditions*, says, "Wonder at what is before you;" laying this down first as the foundation of further knowledge. So also in the Gospel to the Hebrews it is written, "He that wonders shall reign, and he that has reigned shall rest. It is impossible, therefore, for an ignorant man, while he remains ignorant, to philosophize, not having apprehended the idea of wisdom; since philosophy is an effort to grasp that which truly is, and the studies that conduce thereto. And it is not the rendering of one accomplished in good habits of conduct, but the knowing how we are to use and act and labor, according as one is assimilated to God. I mean God the Savior, by serving the God of the universe through the High Priest, the Word, by whom what is in truth good and right is beheld. Piety is conduct suitable and corresponding to God.

CHAPTER X.—TO WHAT THE PHILOSOPHER APPLIES HIMSELF.

These three things, therefore, our philosopher attaches himself to: first, speculation; second, the performance of the precepts; third, the forming of good men;—which, concurring, form the Gnostic. Whichever of these is wanting, the elements of knowledge limp. Whence the Scripture divinely says, "And the Lord spoke to Moses, saying, Speak to the children of Israel, and thou shalt say to them, I am the Lord your God. According to the customs of the land of Egypt, in which ye have dwelt, ye shall not do; and according to the customs of Canaan, into which I bring you, ye shall not do; and in their usages ye shall not walk. Ye shall perform My judgments, and keep My precepts, and walk in them: I am the Lord your God. And ye shall keep all My commandments, and do them. He that doeth them shall live in them. I am the Lord your God."Whether, then, Egypt and the land of Canaan be the symbol of the world and of deceit, or of sufferings and afflictions; the oracle shows us what must be abstained from, and what, being divine and not worldly, must be observed. And when it is said, "The man that doeth them shall live in them," it declares both the correction of the Hebrews themselves, and the training and advancement of us who are nigh: it declares at once their life and ours. For "those who were dead in sins are quickened together with Christ," by our covenant. For Scripture, by the frequent reiteration of the expression, "I am the Lord your God," shames in such a way as most powerfully to dissuade, by teaching us to follow God who gave the commandments, and gently admonishes us to seek God and endeavor to know Him as far as possible; which is the highest speculation, that which scans the greatest mysteries, the real knowledge, that which becomes irrefragable by reason. This alone is the knowledge of wisdom, from which rectitude of conduct is never disjoined.

CHAPTER XI.—THE KNOWLEDGE WHICH COMES THROUGH FAITH THE SUREST OF ALL.

But the knowledge of those who think themselves wise, whether the barbarian sects or the philosophers among the Greeks, according to the apostle, "puffed up." But that knowledge, which is the scientific demonstration of what is delivered according to the true philosophy, is founded on faith. Now, we may say that it is that process of reason which, from what is admitted, procures faith in what is disputed. Now, faith being twofold—the faith of knowledge and that of opinion—nothing prevents us from calling demonstration twofold, the one resting on knowledge, the other on opinion; since also knowledge and foreknowledge are designated as twofold, that which is essentially accurate, that which is defective. And is not the demonstration, which we possess, that alone which is true, as being supplied out of the divine Scriptures, the sacred writings, and out of the "God-taught wisdom," according to the apostle? Learning, then, is also obedience to the commandments, which is faith in God. And faith is a power of God, being the strength of the truth. For example, it is said, "If ye have faith as a grain of mustard, ye shall remove the mountain."And again, "According to thy faith let it be to thee."And one is cured, receiving healing by faith; and the dead is raised up in consequence of the power of one believing that he would be raised. The demonstration, however, which rests on opinion is human, and is the result of rhetorical arguments or dialectic syllogisms. For the highest demonstration, to which we have alluded, produces intelligent faith by the adducing and opening up of the Scriptures to the souls of those who desire to learn; the result of which is knowledge (*gnosis*). For if what is adduced in order to prove the point at issue is assumed to be true, as being divine and prophetic, manifestly the conclusion arrived at by inference from it will consequently be inferred truly; and the legitimate result of the demonstration will be knowledge. When, then, the memorial of the celestial and divine food was commanded to be consecrated in the golden

pot, it was said, "The omer was the tenth of the three measures." For in ourselves, by the three measures are indicated three criteria; sensation of objects of sense, speech,— of spoken names and words, and the mind,—of intellectual objects. The Gnostic, therefore, will abstain from errors in speech, and thought, and sensation, and action, having
heard "that he that looks so as to lust hath committed adultery;" and reflecting that "blessed are the pure in heart, for they shall see God;" and knowing this, "that not what enters into the mouth defiles, but that it is what cometh forth by the mouth that defiles the man. For out of the heart proceed thoughts."This, as I think, is the true and just measure according to God, by which things capable of measurement are measured, the decad which is comprehensive of man; which summarily the three above-mentioned measures pointed out. There are body and soul, the five senses, speech, the power of reproduction— the intellectual or the spiritual faculty, or whatever you choose to call it. And we must, in a word, ascending above all the others, stop at the mind; as also certainly in the universe overleaping the nine divisions, the first consisting of the four elements put in one place for equal interchange: and then the seven wandering stars and the one that wanders not, the ninth, to the perfect number, which is above the nine, and the tenth division, we must reach to the knowledge of God, to speak briefly, desiring the Maker after the creation. Wherefore the tithes both of the ephah and of the sacrifices were presented to God; and the paschal feast began with the tenth day, being the transition from all trouble, and from all objects of sense.

The Gnostic is therefore fixed by faith; but the man who thinks himself wise touches not what pertains to the truth, moved as he is by unstable and wavering impulses. It is therefore reasonably written, "Cain went forth from the face of God, and dwelt in the land of Naid, over against Eden." Now Naid is interpreted *commotion*, and Eden *delight;* and Faith, and Knowledge, and Peace are delight, from which he that has disobeyed is cast out. But he that is wise in his own eyes will not so much as listen to the beginning of the divine commandments; but, as if his own teacher, throwing off the reins, plunges voluntarily into a billowy commotion, sinking down to mortal and created things from the uncreated knowledge, holding various opinions at various times. "Those who have no guidance fall like leaves."

Reason, the governing principle, remaining unmoved and guiding the soul, is called its pilot. For access to the Immutable is obtained by a truly immutable means. Thus Abraham was stationed before the Lord, and approaching spoke. And to Moses it is said, "But do thou stand there with Me."And the followers of Simon wish be assimilated in manners to the standing form which they adore. Faith, therefore, and the knowledge of the truth, render the soul, which makes them its choice, always uniform and equable. For congenial to the man of falsehood is shifting, and change, and turning away, as to the Gnostic are calmness, and rest, and peace. As, then, philosophy has been brought into evil repute by pride and self-conceit, so also gnosis by false gnosis called by the same name; of which the apostle writing says, "O Timothy, keep that which is committed to thy trust, avoiding the profane and vain babblings and oppositions of science (gnosis) falsely so called; which some professing, have erred concerning the faith."

Convicted by this utterance, the heretics reject the Epistles to Timothy. Well, then, if the Lord is the truth, and wisdom, and power of God, as in truth He is, it is shown that the real Gnostic is he that knows Him, and His Father by Him. For his sentiments are the same with him who said, "The lips of the righteous know high things."

CHAPTER XII.—TWOFOLD FAITH.

Faith as also Time being double, we shall find virtues in pairs both dwelling together. For memory is related to past time, hope to future. We believe that what is past did, and that what is future will take place. And, on the other hand, we love, persuaded by faith that the past was as it was, and by hope expecting the future. For in everything love attends the Gnostic, who knows one God. "And, behold, all things which He created were very good." He both knows and admires. Godliness adds length of life; and the fear of the Lord adds days. As, then, the days are a portion of life in its progress, so also fear is the beginning of love, becoming by development faith, then love. But it is not as I fear and hate a wild beast (since fear is twofold) that I fear the father, whom I fear and love at once. Again, fearing lest I be punished, I love myself in assuming fear. He who fears to offend his father, loves himself. Blessed then is he who is found possessed of faith, being, as he is, composed of love and fear. And faith is power in order to salvation, and strength to eternal life. Again, prophecy is foreknowledge; and knowledge the understanding of prophecy; being the knowledge of those things known before by the Lord who reveals all things.

The knowledge, then, of those things which have been predicted shows a threefold result— either one that has happened long ago, or exists now, or about to be. Then the extremes either of what is accomplished or of what is hoped for fall under faith; and the present action furnishes persuasive arguments of the confirmation of both the extremes.

For if, prophecy being one, one part is accomplishing and another is fulfilled; hence the truth, both what is hoped for and what is passed is confirmed. For it was first present; then it became past to us; so that the belief of what is past is the apprehension of a past event, and a hope which is future the apprehension of a future event.

And not only the Platonists, but the Stoics, say that assent is in our own power. All opinion then, and judgment, and supposition, and knowledge, by which we live and have perpetual intercourse with the human race, is an assent; which is nothing else than faith. And unbelief being defection from faith, shows both assent and faith to be possessed of power; for non-existence cannot be called privation. And if you consider the truth, you will find man naturally misled so as to give assent to what is false, though possessing the resources necessary for belief in the truth. "The virtue, then, that encloses the Church in its grasp," as the Shepherd says, "is Faith, by which the elect of God are saved; and that which acts the man is Self-restraint. And these are followed by Simplicity, Knowledge, Innocence, Decorum, Love," and all these are the daughters of Faith. And again, "Faith leads the way, fear upbuilds, and love perfects." Accordingly he says, the Lord is to be feared in order to edification, but not the devil to destruction. And again, the works of the Lord—that is, His commandments—are to be loved and done; but the works of the devil are to be dreaded and not done. For the fear of God trains and restores to love; but the fear of the works of the devil has hatred dwelling along with it. The same also says "that repentance is high intelligence. For he that repents of what he did, no longer does or says as he did. But by torturing himself for his sins, he benefits his soul. Forgiveness of sins is therefore different from repentance; but both show what is in our power."

CHAPTER XIII.—ON FIRST AND SECOND REPENTANCE.

He, then, who has received the forgiveness of sins ought to sin no more. For, in addition to the first and only repentance from sins (this is from the previous sins in the first and heathen life—I mean that in ignorance), there is forthwith proposed to those who have been called, the repentance which cleanses the seat of the soul from transgressions, that faith may be established. And the Lord, knowing the heart, and foreknowing the future, foresaw both the fickleness of man and the craft and subtlety of the devil from the first, from the beginning; how that, envying man for the forgiveness of sins, he would present to the servants of God certain causes of sins; skillfully working mischief, that they might fall together with himself. Accordingly, being very merciful, He has vouch-safed, in the case of those who, though in faith, fall into any transgression, a second repentance; so that should anyone be tempted after his calling, overcome by force and fraud, he may receive still a repentance not to be repented of. "For if we sin willfully after that we have received the knowledge of the truth, there remained no more sacrifice for sins, but a certain fearful looking for of judgment and fiery indignation, which shall devour the adversaries." But continual and successive repenting for sins differ nothing from the case of those who have not believed at all, except only in their consciousness that they do sin. And I know not which of the two is worst, whether the case of a man who sins knowingly, or of one who, after having repented of his sins, transgresses again. For in the process of proof sin appears on each side,—the sin which in its commission is condemned by the worker of the iniquity, and that of the man who, foreseeing what is about to be done, yet puts his hand to it as a wickedness. And he who perchance gratifies himself in anger and pleasure, gratifies himself in he knows what; and he who, repenting of that in which he gratified himself, by rushing again into pleasure, is near neighbor to him who has sinned willfully at first. For one, who does again that of which he has repented, and condemning what he does, performs it willingly.

He, then, who from among the Gentiles and from that old life has betaken himself to faith, has obtained forgiveness of sins once. But he who has sinned after this, on his repentance, though he obtain pardon, ought to fear, as one no longer washed to the forgiveness of sins. For not only must the idols which he formerly held as gods, but the works also of his former life, be abandoned by him who has been "born again, not of blood, nor of the will of the flesh," but in the Spirit; which consists in repenting by not giving way to the same fault. For frequent repentance and readiness to change easily from want of training, is the practice of sin again. The frequent asking of forgiveness, then, for those things in which we often transgress, is the semblance of repentance, not repentance itself. "But the righteousness of the blameless cuts straight paths," says the Scripture. And again, "The righteousness of the innocent will make his way right." Nay, "as a father pitied his children, so the Lord pitied them that fear Him." David writes, "They who sow," then, "in tears, shall reap in joy;" those, namely, who confess in penitence. "For blessed are all those that fear the Lord." You see the corresponding blessing in the Gospel. "Fear not," it is said, "when a man is enriched, and when the glory of his house is increased: because when he dies he shall leave all, and his glory shall not descend after him." "But I in Thy I mercy will enter into Thy house. I will worship toward Thy holy temple, in Thy fear: Lord, lead me in Thy righteousness."Appetite is then the movement of the mind to or from something. Passion is an excessive appetite exceeding the measures of reason, or appetite unbridled and disobedient to the word. Passions, then, are a perturbation of the soul contrary to nature, in disobedience to reason. But revolt and distraction and disobedience are in our own power, as obedience is in our power. Wherefore voluntary actions are judged. But should one examine each one of the passions, he will find them irrational impulses.

CHAPTER XIV.—HOW A THING MAY BE INVOLUNTARY.

What is involuntary is not matter for judgment. But this is twofold,—what is done in ignorance, and what is done through necessity. For how will you judge concerning those who are said to sin in involuntary modes? For either one knew not himself, as Cleomenes and Athamas, who were mad; or the thing which he does, as Æschylus, who divulged the mysteries on the stage, who, being tried in the Areopagus, was absolved on his showing that he had not been initiated. Or one knows not what is done, as he who has let off his antagonist, and slain his domestic instead of his enemy; or that by which it is done, as he who, in exercising with spears having buttons on them, has killed someone in consequence of the spear throwing off the button; or knows not the manner how, as he who has killed his antagonist in the stadium, for it was not for his death but for victory that he contended; or knows not the reason why it is done, as the physician gave a salutary antidote and killed, for it was not for this purpose that he gave it, but to save. The law at that time punished him who had killed involuntarily, as e.g., him who was subject involuntarily to gonorrhoea, but not equally with him who did so voluntarily. Although he also shall be punished as for a voluntary action, if one transfer the affection to the truth. For, in reality, he that cannot contain the generative word is to be punished; for this is an irrational passion of the soul approaching garrulity. "The faithful man chooses to conceal things in his spirit." Things, then, that depend on choice are subjects for judgment. "For the Lord searches the hearts and reins.""And he that looked so as to lust" is judged. Wherefore it is said, "Thou shalt not lust."And "this people honored Me with their lips," it is said, "but their heart is far from Me." For God has respect to the very thought, since Lot's wife, who had merely voluntarily turned towards worldly wickedness, He left a senseless mass, rendering her a pillar of salt, and fixed her so that she advanced no further, not as a stupid and useless image, but to season and salt him who has the power of spiritual perception.

CHAPTER XV.—ON THE DIFFERENT KINDS OF VOLUNTARY ACTIONS, AND THE SINS THENCE PROCEEDING.

What is voluntary is either what is by desire, or what is by choice, or what is of intention. Closely allied to each other are these things—sin, mistake, crime. It is sin, for example, to live luxuriously and licentiously; a misfortune, to wound one's friend in ignorance, taking him for an enemy; and crime, to violate graves or commit sacrilege. Sinning arises from being unable to determine what ought to be done, or being unable to do it; as doubtless one falls into a ditch either through not knowing, or through inability to leap across through feebleness of body. But application to the training of ourselves, and subjection to the commandments, is in our own power; with which if we will have nothing to do, by abandoning ourselves wholly to lust, we shall sin, nay rather, wrong our own soul. For the noted Laius says in the tragedy:—

"None of these things of which you admonish me have escaped me; But notwithstanding that I am in my senses, Nature compels me;"

i.e., his abandoning himself to passion. Medea, too, herself cries on the stage:—

> "And I am aware what evils I am to perpetrate,
> But passion is stronger than my resolutions."

Further, not even Ajax is silent; but, when about to kill himself, cries:—

> "No pain gnaws the soul of a free man like dishonor.
> Thus do I suffer; and the deep stain of calamity
> Ever stirs me from the depths, agitated
> By the bitter stings of rage."

Anger made these the subjects of tragedy, and lust made ten thousand others—Phædra, Anthia, Eriphyle,—

> "Who took the precious gold for her dear husband."

For another play represents Thrasonides of the comic drama as saying:—

> "A worthless wench made me her slave."

Mistake is a sin contrary to calculation; and voluntary sin is crime (ἀδικία); and crime is voluntary wickedness. Sin, then, is on my part voluntary. Wherefore says the apostle, "Sin shall not have dominion over you; for ye are not under the law, but under grace." Addressing those who have believed, he says,

"For by His stripes we were healed.""Mistake is the involuntary action of another towards me, while a crime (ἀδικία) alone is voluntary, whether my act or another's. These differences of sins are alluded to by the Psalmist, when he calls those blessed whose iniquities (ἀνομίας) God hath blotted out, and whose sins (ἁμαρτίας) He hath covered. Others He does not impute, and the rest He forgives. For it is written, "Blessed are they whose iniquities are forgiven, whose sins are covered. Blessed is the man to whom the Lord will not impute sin, and in whose mouth there is no fraud." This blessedness came on those who had been chosen by God through Jesus Christ our Lord. For "love hides the multitude of sins." And they are blotted out by Him "who desires the repentance rather than the death of a sinner." And those are not reckoned that are not the effect of choice; "for he who has lusted has already committed adultery," it is said. And the illuminating Word forgives sins: "And in that time, says the Lord, they shall seek for the iniquity of Israel, and it shall not exist; and the sins of Judah, and they shall not be found." "For who is like Me? and who shall stand before My face? You see the one God declared good, rendering according to desert, and forgiving sins. John, too, manifestly teaches the differences of sins, in his larger Epistle, in these words: "If any man see his brother sin a sin that is not unto death, he shall ask, and he shall give him life: for these that sin not unto death," he says. For "there is a sin unto death: I do not say that one is to pray for it. All unrighteousness is sin; and there is a sin not unto death."

David, too, and Moses before David, show the knowledge of the three precepts in the following words: "Blessed is the man who walks not in the counsel of the ungodly;" as the fishes go down to the depths in darkness; for those which have not scales, which Moses prohibits touching, feed at the bottom of the sea. "Nor stands in the way of sinners," as those who, while appearing to fear the Lord, commit sin, like the sow, for when hungry it cries, and when full knows not its owner. "Nor sits in the chair of pestilences," as birds ready for prey. And Moses enjoined not to eat the sow, nor the eagle, nor the hawk, nor the raven, nor any fish without scales. So far Barnabas. And I heard one skilled in such matters say that "the counsel of the ungodly" was the heathen, and "the way of sinners" the Jewish persuasion, and explain "the chair of pestilence" of heresies. And another said, with more propriety, that the first blessing was assigned to those who had not followed wicked sentiments which revolt from God; the second to those who do not remain in the wide and broad road, whether they be those who have been brought up in the law, or Gentiles who have repented. And "the chair of pestilences" will be the theatres and tribunals, or rather the compliance with wicked and deadly powers, and complicity with their deeds. "But his delight is in the law of the Lord." Peter in his *Preaching* called the Lord, Law and Logos. The legislator seems to teach differently the interpretation of the three forms of sin—understanding by the mute fishes sins of word, for there are times in which *silence is better than speech, for silence has a safe recompense;* sins of deed, by the rapacious and carnivorous birds. The sow delights in dirt and dung; and we ought not to have "a conscience" that is "defiled."

Justly, therefore, the prophet says, "The ungodly are not so: but as the chaff which the wind drives away from the face of the earth. Wherefore the ungodly shall not stand in the judgment" (being already condemned, for "he that believeth not is condemned already"), "nor sinners in the counsel of the righteous," inasmuch as they are already condemned, so as not to be united to those that have lived without stumbling. "For the Lord knows the way of the righteous; and the way of the ungodly shall perish."

Again, the Lord clearly shows sins and transgressions to be in our own power, by prescribing modes of cure corresponding to the maladies; showing His wish that we should be corrected by the shepherds, in Ezekiel; blaming, I am of opinion, some of them for not keeping the commandments. "That which was enfeebled ye have not strengthened," and so forth, down to, "and there was none to search out or turn away."

For "great is the joy before the Father when one sinner is saved," says the Lord. So Abraham was much to be praised, because "he walked as the Lord spoke to him." Drawing from this instance, one of the wise men among the Greeks uttered the maxim, "Follow God." "The godly," says Esaias, "framed wise counsels." Now counsel is seeking for the right way of acting in present circumstances, and good counsel is wisdom in our counsels. And what? Does not God, after the pardon bestowed on Cain, suitably not long after introduce Enoch, who had repented? showing that it is the nature of repentance to produce pardon; but pardon does not consist in remission, but in remedy. An instance of the same is the making of the calf by the people before Aaron. Thence one of the wise men among the Greeks uttered the maxim, "Pardon is better than punishment;" as also, "Become surety, and mischief is at hand," is derived from the utterance of Solomon which says, "My son, if thou become surety for thy friend, thou wilt give thine hand to thy enemy; for a man's own lips are a strong snare to him, and he is taken in the words of his own mouth." And the saying, "Know thyself," has been taken rather more mystically from this, "Thou hast seen thy brother, thou hast seen thy God." Thus also, "Thou shalt love the Lord thy God with all thy heart, and thy neighbor as thyself;" for it is said, "On these commandments the law and the prophets hang and are suspended." With these also agree the following: "These things have I spoken to you, that My joy might be fulfilled: and this is My commandment, That ye love one another, as I have loved you." "For the Lord is merciful and pitiful; and gracious is the Lord to all." "Know thyself" is more clearly and often expressed by Moses, when he enjoins, "Take heed to thyself." "By alms then, and acts of faith, sins are purged." "And by the fear of the Lord each one departs from evil." "And the fear of the Lord is instruction and wisdom."

CHAPTER XVI.—HOW WE ARE TO EXPLAIN THE PASSAGES OF SCRIPTURE WHICH ASCRIBE TO GOD HUMAN AFFECTIONS.

Here again arise the cavilers, who say that joy and pain are passions of the soul: for they define joy as a rational elevation and exultation, as rejoicing on account of what is good; and pity as pain for one who suffers undeservedly; and that such affections are moods and passions of the soul. But we, as would appear, do not cease in such matters to understand the Scriptures carnally; and starting from our own affections, interpret the will of the impassible Deity similarly to our perturbations; and as we are capable of hearing; so, supposing the same to be the case with the Omnipotent, err impiously. For the Divine Being cannot be declared as it exists: but as we who are fettered in the flesh were able to listen, so the prophets spoke to us; the Lord savingly accommodating Himself to the weakness of men. Since, then, it is the will of God that he, who is obedient to the commands and repents of his sins should be saved, and we rejoice on account of our salvation, the Lord, speaking by the prophets, appropriated our joy to Himself; as speaking lovingly in the Gospel He says,
"I was hungry, and ye gave Me to eat: I was thirsty, and ye gave Me to drink. For inasmuch as ye did it to one of the least of these, ye did it to Me." As, then, He is nourished, though not personally, by the nourishing of one whom He wishes nourished; so He rejoices, without suffering change, by reason of him who has repented being in joy, as He wished. And since God pities richly, being good, and giving commands by the law and the prophets, and more nearly still by the appearance of his Son, saving and pitying, as was said, those who have found mercy; and properly the greater pities the less; and a man cannot be greater than man, being by nature man; but God in everything is greater than man; if, then, the greater pities the less, it is God alone that will pity us. For a man is made to communicate by righteousness, and bestows what he received from God, in consequence of his natural benevolence and relation, and the commands which he obeys. But God has no natural relation to us, as the authors of the heresies will have it; neither on the supposition of His having made us of nothing,

nor on that of having formed us from matter; since the former did not exist at all, and the latter is totally distinct from God unless we shall dare to say that we are a part of Him, and of the same essence as God. And I know not how one, who knows God, can bear to hear this when he looks to our life, and sees in what evils we are involved. For thus it would turn out, which it were impiety to utter, that God sinned in [certain] portions, if the portions are parts of the whole and complementary of the whole; and if not complementary, neither can they be parts. But God being by nature rich in pity, in consequence of His own goodness, cares for us, though neither portions of Himself, nor by nature His children. And this is the greatest proof of the goodness of God: that such being our relation to Him, and being by nature wholly estranged, He nevertheless cares for us. For the affection in animals to their progeny is natural, and the friendship of kindred minds is the result of intimacy. But the mercy of God is rich toward us, who are in no respect related to Him; I say either in our essence or nature, or in the peculiar energy of our essence, but only in our being the work of His will. And him who willingly, with discipline and teaching, accepts the knowledge of the truth, He calls to adoption, which is the greatest advancement of all. "Transgressions catch a man; and in the cords of his own sins each one is bound."And God is without blame. And in reality, "blessed is the man who fears always through piety."

CHAPTER XVII.—ON THE VARIOUS KINDS OF KNOWLEDGE.

As, then, Knowledge (ἐπιστήμη) is an intellectual state, from which results the act of knowing, and becomes apprehension irrefragable by reason; so also ignorance is a receding impression, which can be dislodged by reason. And that which is overthrown as well as that which is elaborated by reason, is in our power. Akin to Knowledge is *experience*, cognition (εἴδησις), Comprehension (σύνεσις), perception, and Science. Cognition (εἴδησις) is the knowledge of universals by species; and Experience is comprehensive knowledge, which investigates the nature of each thing. Perception (νόησις) is the knowledge of intellectual objects; and Comprehension (σύνεσις) is the knowledge of what is compared, or a comparison that cannot be annulled, or the faculty of comparing the objects with which Judgment and Knowledge are occupied, both of one and each and all that goes to make up one reason. And Science (γνῶσις) is the knowledge of the thing in itself, or the knowledge which harmonizes with what takes place. Truth is the knowledge of the true; and the mental habit of truth is the knowledge of the things which are true. Now knowledge is constituted by the reason, and cannot be overthrown by another reason. What we do not, we do not either from not being able, or not being willing—or both. Accordingly we don't fly, since we neither can nor wish; we do not swim at present, for example, since we can indeed, but do not choose; and we are not as the Lord, since we wish, but cannot be: "for no disciple is above his master, and it is sufficient if we be as the master:" not in essence (for it is impossible for that, which is by adoption, to be equal in substance to that, which is by nature); but [we are as Him] only in our having been made immortal, and our being conversant with the contemplation of realities, and beholding the Father through what belongs to Him.

Therefore volition takes the precedence of all; for the intellectual powers are ministers of the Will. "Will," it is said, "and thou shalt be able."And in the Gnostic, Will, Judgment, and Exertion are identical. For if the determinations are the same, the opinions and judgments will be the same too; so that both his words, and life, and conduct, are conformable to rule. "And a right heart seeks knowledge, and hears it." "God taught me wisdom, and I knew the knowledge of the holy."

CHAPTER XVIII.—THE MOSAIC LAW THE FOUNTAIN OF ALL ETHICS, AND THE SOURCE FROM WHICH THE GREEKS DREW THEIRS.

It is then clear also that all the other virtues, delineated in Moses, supplied the Greeks with the rudiments of the whole department of morals. I mean valor, and temperance, and wisdom, and justice, and endurance, and patience, and decorum, and self-restraint; and in addition to these, piety. But it is clear to everyone that piety, which teaches to worship and honor, is the highest and oldest cause; and the law itself exhibits justice, and teaches wisdom, by abstinence from sensible images, and by inviting to the Maker and Father of the universe. And from this sentiment, as from a fountain, all intelligence increases. "For the sacrifices of the wicked are abomination to the Lord; but the prayers of the upright are acceptable before Him," since "righteousness is more acceptable before God than sacrifice." Such also as the following we find in Isaiah: "To what purpose to me is the multitude of your sacrifices? says the Lord;" and the whole section. "Break every bond of wickedness; for this is the sacrifice that is acceptable to the Lord, a contrite heart that seeks its Maker." "Deceitful balances are abomination before God; but a just balance is acceptable to Him." Thence Pythagoras exhorts "not to step over the balance;" and the profession of heresies is called deceitful righteousness; and "the tongue of the unjust shall be destroyed, but the mouth of the righteous drop wisdom." "For they call the wise and prudent worthless." But it were tedious to adduce testimonies respecting these virtues, since the whole Scripture celebrates them. Since, then, they define manliness to be knowledge of things formidable, and not formidable, and what is intermediate; and temperance to be a state of mind which by choosing and avoiding preserves the judgments of wisdom; and conjoined with manliness is patience, which is called endurance, the knowledge of what is bearable and what is unbearable; and magnanimity is the knowledge which rises superior to circumstances. With temperance also is conjoined caution, which is avoidance in accordance with reason. And observance of the commandments, which is the innoxious keeping of them, is the attainment of a secure life. And there is no endurance without manliness, nor the exercise of self-restraint without temperance. And these virtues follow one another; and with whom are the sequences of the virtues, with him is also salvation, which is the keeping of the state of well-being. Rightly, therefore, in treating of these virtues, we shall inquire into them all; for he that has one virtue gnostically, by reason of their accompanying each other, has them all. Self-restraint is that quality which does not overstep what appears in accordance with right reason. He exercises self-restraint, who curbs the impulses that are contrary to right reason, or curbs himself so as not to indulge in desires contrary to right reason. Temperance, too, is not without manliness; since from the commandments spring both wisdom, which follows God who enjoins, and that which imitates the divine character, namely righteousness; in virtue of which, in the exercise of self-restraint, we address ourselves in purity to piety and the course of conduct thence resulting, in conformity with God; being assimilated to the Lord as far as is possible for us beings mortal in nature. And this is being just and holy with wisdom; for the Divinity needs nothing and suffers nothing; whence it is not, strictly speaking, capable of self-restraint, for it is never subjected to perturbation, over which to exercise control; while our nature, being capable of perturbation, needs self-constraint, by which disciplining itself to the need of little, it endeavors to approximate in character to the divine nature. For the good man, standing as the boundary between an immortal and a mortal nature, has few needs; having wants in consequence of his body, and his birth itself, but taught by rational self-control to want few things.

What reason is there in the law's prohibiting a man from "wearing woman's clothing"? Is it not that it would have us to be manly, and not to be effeminate neither in person and actions, nor in thought and word? For it would have the man, that devotes himself to the truth, to be masculine both in acts of endurance and patience, in life, conduct, word, and discipline by night and by day; even if the necessity were to occur, of witnessing by the shedding of his blood. Again, it is said, "If anyone who has newly built a house, and has not previously inhabited it; or cultivated a newly-planted vine, and not yet partaken of the fruit; or betrothed a virgin, and not yet married her;"—such the humane law orders to be relieved from military service: from military reasons in the first place, lest, bent on their desires, they turn out sluggish in war; for it is those who are untrammeled by passion that boldly encounter perils; and from motives of humanity, since, in view of the uncertainties of war, the law reckoned it not right that one should not enjoy his own labors, and another should without bestowing pains, receive what belonged to those who had labored. The law seems also to point out manliness of soul, by enacting that he who had planted should reap the fruit, and he that built should inhabit, and he that had betrothed should marry: for it is not vain hopes which it provides for those who labor; according to the gnostic word: "For the hope of a good man dead or living does not perish," says Wisdom; "I love them that love me; and they who seek me shall find peace," and so forth. What then? Did not the women of the Midianites, by their beauty, seduce from wisdom into impiety, through licentiousness, the Hebrews when making war against them? For, having seduced them from a grave mode of life, and by their beauty ensnared them in wanton delights, they made them insane upon idol sacrifices and strange women; and overcome by women and by pleasure at once, they revolted from God, and revolted from the law. And the whole people was within a little of falling under the power of the enemy through female stratagem, until, when they were in peril, fear by its admonitions pulled them back. Then the survivors, valiantly undertaking the struggle for piety, got the upper hand of their foes. "The beginning, then, of wisdom is piety, and the knowledge of holy things is understanding; and to know the law is the characteristic of a good understanding." Those, then, who suppose the law to be productive of agitating fear, are neither good at understanding the law, nor have they in reality comprehended it; for "the fear of the Lord causes life, but he who errs shall be afflicted with pangs which knowledge views not." Accordingly, Barnabas says mystically, "May God who rules the universe vouchsafe also to you wisdom, and understanding, and science, and knowledge of His statutes, and patience. Be therefore God-taught, seeking what the Lord seeks from you, that He may find you in the day of judgment lying in wait for these things." "Children of love and peace," he called them gnostically.

Respecting imparting and communicating, though much might be said, let it suffice to remark that the law prohibits a brother from taking usury: designating as a brother not only him who is born of the same parents, but also one of the same race and sentiments, and a participator in the same word; deeming it right not to take usury for money, but with open hands and heart to bestow on those who need. For God, the author and the dispenser of such grace, takes as suitable usury the most precious things to be found among men—mildness, gentleness, magnanimity, reputation, renown. Do you not regard this command as marked by philanthropy? As also the following, "To pay the wages of the poor daily," teaches to discharge without delay the wages due for service; for, as I think, the alacrity of the poor with reference to the future is paralyzed when he has suffered want. Further, it is said, "Let not the creditor enter the debtor's house to take the pledge with violence." But let the former ask it to be brought out, and let not the latter, if he have it, hesitate. And in the harvest the owners are prohibited from appropriating what falls from the handfuls; as also in reaping [the law] enjoins a part to be left unreaped; signally thereby training those who possess to sharing and to large-heartedness, by foregoing of their own to those who are in want, and thus providing means of subsistence for the poor. You see how the law proclaims at once the righteousness and goodness of God, who dispenses food to all ungrudgingly. And in the vintage it prohibited the grape-gatherers from going back again on what had been left, and from gathering the fallen grapes; and the same injunctions are given to the olive-gatherers. Besides, the tithes of the fruits and of the flocks taught both piety towards the Deity, and not covetously to grasp everything, but to communicate gifts of kindness to one's neighbors. For it was from these, I reckon, and from the first-fruits that the priests were maintained. We now therefore understand that we are instructed in piety, and in liberality, and in justice, and in humanity by the law. For does it not command the land to be left fallow in the seventh year, and bids the poor fearlessly use the fruits that grow by divine agency, nature cultivating the ground for behoove of all and sundry? How, then, can it be maintained that the law is not humane, and the teacher of righteousness? Again, in the fiftieth year, it ordered the same things to be performed as in the seventh; besides restoring to each one his own land, if from any circumstance he had parted with it in the meantime; setting bounds to the desires of those who covet possession, by measuring the period of enjoyment, and choosing that those who have paid the penalty of protracted penury should not suffer a life-long punishment. "But alms and acts of faith are royal guards, and blessing is on the head of him who bestows; and he who pities the poor shall be blessed." For he shows love to one like himself, because of his love to the Creator of the human race. The above-mentioned particulars have other explanations more natural, both respecting rest and the recovery of the inheritance; but they are not discussed at present.

Now love is conceived in many ways, in the form of meekness, of mildness, of patience, of liberality, of freedom from envy, of absence of hatred, of forgetfulness of injuries. In all it is incapable of being divided or distinguished: its nature is to communicate. Again, it is said, "If you see the beast of your relatives, or friends, or, in general, of anybody you know, wandering in the wilderness, take it back and restore it; and if the owner be far away, keep it among your own till he return, and restore it." It teaches a natural communication, that what is found is to be regarded as a deposit, and that we are not to bear malice to an enemy. "The command of the Lord being a fountain of life" truly, "causes to turn away from the snare of death." And what? Does it not command us "to love strangers not only as friends and relatives, but as ourselves, both in body and soul?"Nay more, it honored the nations, and bears no grudge against those who have done ill. Accordingly it is expressly said, "Thou shalt not abhor an Egyptian, for thou was a sojourner in Egypt;" designating by the term Egyptian either one of that race, or any one in the world. And enemies, although drawn up before the walls attempting to take the city, are not to be regarded as enemies till they are by the voice of the herald summoned to peace.

Further, it forbids intercourse with a female captive so as to dishonor her. "But allow her," it says, "thirty days to mourn according to her wish, and changing her clothes, associate with her as your lawful wife." For it regards it not right that this should take place either in wantonness or for hire like harlots, but only for the birth of children. Do you see humanity combined with continence? The master who has fallen in love with his captive maid it does not allow to gratify his pleasure, but puts a check on his lust by specifying an interval of time; and further, it cuts off the captive's hair, in order to shame disgraceful love: for if it is reason that induces him to marry, he will cleave to her even after she has become disfigured. Then if one, after his lust, does not care to consort any longer with the captive, it ordains that it shall not be lawful to sell her, or to have her any longer as a servant, but desires her to be freed and released from service, lest on the introduction of another wife she bear any of the intolerable miseries caused through jealousy.

What more? The Lord enjoins to ease and raise up the beasts of enemies when laboring beneath their burdens; remotely teaching us not to indulge in joy at our neighbor's ills, or exult over our enemies; in order to teach those who are trained in these things to pray for their enemies. For He does not allow us either to grieve at our neighbor's good, or to reap joy at our neighbor's ill. And if you find any enemy's beast straying, you are to pass over the incentives of difference, and take it back and restore it. For oblivion of injuries is followed by goodness, and the latter by dissolution of enmity. From this we are fitted for agreement, and this conducts to felicity. And should you suppose one habitually hostile, and discover him to be unreasonably mistaken either through lust or anger, turn him to goodness. Does the law then which conducts to Christ appear humane and mild? And does not the same God, good, while characterized by righteousness from the beginning to the end, employ each kind suitably in order to salvation? "Be merciful," says the Lord, "that you may receive mercy; forgive, that you may be forgiven. As ye do, so shall it be done to you; as ye give, so shall it be given to you; as ye judge, so shall ye be judged; as ye show kindness, so shall kindness be shown to you: with what measure ye mete, it shall be measured to you again." Furthermore, [the law] prohibits those, who are in servitude for their subsistence, to be branded with disgrace; and to those, who have been reduced to slavery through money borrowed, it gives a complete release in the seventh year. Further, it prohibits suppliants from being given up to punishment. True above all, then, is that oracle. "As gold and silver are tried in the furnace, so the Lord chooses men's hearts. The merciful man is long-suffering; and in every one who shows solicitude there is wisdom. For on a wise man solicitude will fall; and exercising thought, he will seek life; and he who seeks God shall find knowledge with righteousness. And they who have sought Him rightly have found peace." And Pythagoras seems to me, to have derived his mildness towards irrational creatures from the law. For instance, he interdicted the immediate use of the young in the flocks of sheep, and goats, and herds of cattle, on the instant of their birth; not even on the pretext of sacrifice allowing it, both on account of the young ones and of the mothers; training man to gentleness by what is beneath him, by means of the irrational creatures. "Resign accordingly," he says, "the young one to its dam for even the first seven days." For if nothing takes place without a cause, and milk comes in a shower to animals in parturition for the sustenance of the progeny, he that tears that, which has been brought forth, away from the supply of the milk, dishonors nature. Let the Greeks, then, feel ashamed, and whoever else inveighs against the law; since it shows mildness in the case of the irrational creatures, while they expose the offspring of men; though long ago and prophetically, the law, in the above-mentioned commandment, threw a check in the way of their cruelty. For if it prohibits the progeny of the irrational creatures to be separated from the dam before sucking, much more in the case of men does it provide beforehand a cure for cruelty and savageness of disposition; so that even if they despise nature, they may not despise teaching. For they are permitted to satiate themselves with kids and lambs, and perhaps there might be some excuse for separating the progeny from its dam. But what cause is there for the exposure of a child? For the man who did not desire to beget children had no right to marry at first; certainly not to have become, through licentious indulgence, the murderer of his children. Again, the humane law forbids slaying the offspring and the dam together on the same day. Thence also the Romans, in the case of a pregnant woman being condemned to death, do not allow her to undergo punishment till she is delivered. The law too, expressly prohibits the slaying of such animals as are pregnant till they have brought forth, remotely restraining the proneness of man to do wrong to man. Thus also it has extended its clemency to the irrational creatures; that from the exercise of humanity in the case of creatures of different species, we might practice among those of the same species a large abundance of it. Those, too, that kick the bellies of certain animals before parturition, in order to feast on flesh mixed with milk, make the womb created for the birth of the *fetus* its grave, though the law expressly commands, "But neither shalt thou seethe a lamb in its mother's milk." For the nourishment of the living animal, it is meant, may not become sauce for that which has been deprived of life; and that, which is the cause of life, may not co-operate in the consumption of the body. And the same law commands "not to muzzle the ox which treaded out the corn: for the laborer must be reckoned worthy of his food."

And it prohibits an ox and ass to be yoked in the plough together; pointing perhaps to the want of agreement in the case of the animals; and at the same time teaching not to wrong any one belonging to another race, and bring him under the yoke, when there is no other cause to allege than difference of race, which is no cause at all, being neither wickedness nor the effect of wickedness. To me the allegory also seems to signify that the husbandry of the Word is not to be assigned equally to the clean and the unclean, the believer and the unbeliever; for the ox is clean, but the ass has been reckoned among the unclean animals. But the benignant Word, abounding in humanity, teaches that neither is it right to cut down cultivated trees, or to cut down the grain before the harvest, for mischiefs sake; nor that cultivated fruit is to be destroyed at all—either the fruit of the soil or that of the soul: for it does not permit the enemy's country to be laid waste.

Further, husbandmen derived advantage from the law in such things. For it orders newly planted trees to be nourished three years in succession, and the superfluous growths to be cut off, to prevent them being loaded and pressed down; and to prevent their strength being exhausted from want, by the nutriment being frittered away, enjoins tilling and digging round them, so that [the tree] may not, by sending out suckers, hinder its growth. And it does not allow imperfect fruit to be plucked from immature trees, but after three years, in the fourth year; dedicating the first-fruits to God after the tree has attained maturity.

This type of husbandry may serve as a mode of instruction, teaching that we must cut the growths of sins, and the useless weeds of the mind that spring up round the vital fruit, till the shoot of faith is perfected and becomes strong. For in the fourth year, since there is need of time to him that is being solidly catechized, the four virtues are consecrated to God, the third alone being already joined to the fourth, the person of the Lord. And a sacrifice of praise is above holocausts: "for He," it is said, "giveth strength to get power." And if your affairs are in the sunshine of prosperity, get and keep strength, and acquire power in knowledge. For by these instances it is shown that both good things and gifts are supplied by God; and that we, becoming ministers of the divine grace, ought to sow the benefits of God, and make those who approach us noble and good; so that, as far as possible, the temperate man may make others continent, he that is manly may make them noble, he that is wise may make them intelligent, and the just may make them just.

CHAPTER XIX.—THE TRUE GNOSTIC IS AN IMITATOR OF GOD, ESPECIALLY IN BENEFICENCE.

He is the Gnostic, who is after the image and likeness of God, who imitates God as far as possible, deficient in none of the things which contribute to the likeness as far as compatible, practicing self-restraint and endurance, living righteously, reigning over the passions, bestowing of what he has as far as possible, and doing good both by word and deed. "He is the greatest," it is said, "in the kingdom who shall do and teach;" imitating God in conferring like benefits. For God's gifts are for the common good. "Whoever shall attempt to do aught with presumption, provokes God," it is said. For haughtiness is a vice of the soul, of which, as of other sins, He commands us to repent; by adjusting our lives from their state of derangement to the change for the better in these three things—mouth, heart, hands. These are signs—the hands of action, the heart of volition, the mouth of speech. Beautifully, therefore, has this oracle been spoken with respect to penitents: "Thou hast chosen God this day to be thy God; and God hath chosen thee this day to be His people." For him who hastes to serve the self-existent One, being a suppliant, God adopts to Himself; and though he be only one in number, he is honored equally with the people. For being a part of the people, he becomes complementary of it, being restored from what he was; and the whole is named from a part.

But nobility is itself exhibited in choosing and practicing what is best. For what benefit to Adam was such a nobility as he had? No mortal was his father; for he himself was father of men that are born. What is base he readily chose, following his wife, and neglected what is true and good; on which account he exchanged his immortal life for a mortal life, but not forever. And Noah, whose origin was not the same as Adam's, was saved by divine care. For he took and consecrated himself to God. And Abraham, who had children by three wives, not for the indulgence of pleasure, but in the hope, as I think, of multiplying the race at the first, was succeeded by one alone, who was heir of his father's blessings, while the rest were separated from the family; and of the twins who sprang from him, the younger having won his father's favor and received his prayers, became heir, and the elder served him. For it is the greatest boon to a bad man not to be master of himself.

And this arrangement was prophetical and typical. And that all things belong to the wise, Scripture clearly indicates when it is said, "Because God hath had mercy on me, I have all things." For it teaches that we are to desire one thing, by which are all things, and what is promised is assigned to the worthy. Accordingly, the good man who has become heir of the kingdom, it registers also as fellow-citizen, through divine wisdom, with the righteous of the olden time, who under the law and before the law lived according to law, whose deeds have become laws to us; and again, teaching that the wise man is king, introduces people of a different race, saying to him, "Thou art a king before God among us;" those who were governed obeying the good man of their own accord, from admiration of his virtue.

Now Plato the philosopher, defining the end of happiness, says that it is likeness to God as far as possible; whether concurring with the precept of the law (for great natures that are free of passions somehow hit the mark respecting the truth, as the Pythagorean Philo says in relating the history of Moses), or whether instructed by certain oracles of the time, thirsting as he always was for instruction. For the law says, "Walk after the Lord your God, and keep my commandments." For the law calls assimilation following; and such a following to the utmost of its power assimilates. "Be," says the Lord, "merciful and pitiful, as your heavenly Father is pitiful." Thence also the Stoics have laid down the doctrine, that living agreeably to nature is the end, fitly altering the name of God into nature; since also nature extends to plants, to seeds, to trees, and to stones. It is therefore plainly said, "Bad men do not understand the law; but they who love the law fortify themselves with a wall." "For the wisdom of the clever knows its ways; but the folly of the foolish is in error." "For on whom will I look, but on him who is mild and gentle, and trembles at my words?" says the prophecy.

We are taught that there are three kinds of friendship: and that of these the first and the best is that which results from virtue, for the love that is founded on reason is firm; that the second and intermediate is by way of recompense, and is social, liberal, and useful for life; for the friendship which is the result of favor is mutual. And the third and last *we* assert to be that which is founded on intimacy; others, again, that it is that variable and changeable form which rests on pleasure. And Hippodamus the Pythagorean seems to me to describe friendships most admirably: "That founded on knowledge of the gods, that founded on the gifts of men, and that on the pleasures of animals." There is the friendship of a philosopher,—that of a man and that of an animal. For the image of God is really the man who does good, in which also he gets good: as the pilot at once saves, and is saved. Wherefore, when one obtains his request, he does not say to the giver, Thou hast given well, but, Thou hast received well. So he receives who gives, and he gives who receives. "But the righteous pity and show mercy." "But the mild shall be inhabitants of the earth, and the innocent shall be left in it. But the transgressors shall be extirpated from it." And Homer seems to me to have said prophetically of the faithful, "Give to thy friend." And an enemy must be aided, that he may not continue an enemy. For by help good feeling is compacted, and enmity dissolved. "But if there be present readiness of mind, according to what a man hath it is acceptable, and not according to what he hath not: for it is not that there be ease to others, but tribulation to you, but of equality at the present time," and so forth. "He hath dispersed, he hath given to the poor; his righteousness endures forever," the Scripture says.

For conformity with the image and likeness is not meant of the body (for it were wrong for what is mortal to be made like what is immortal), but in mind and reason, on which fitly the Lord impresses the seal of likeness, both in respect of doing good and of exercising rule. For governments are directed not by corporeal qualities, but by judgments of the mind. For by the counsels of holy men states are managed well, and the household also.

CHAPTER XX.—THE TRUE GNOSTIC EXERCISES PATIENCE AND SELF-RESTRAINT.

Endurance also itself forces its way to the divine likeness, reaping as its fruit impassibility through patience, if what is related of Ananias be kept in mind; who belonged to a number, of whom Daniel the prophet, filled with divine faith, was one. Daniel dwelt at Babylon, as Lot at Sodom, and Abraham, who a little after became the friend of God, in the land of Chaldea. The king of the Babylonians let Daniel down into a pit full of wild beasts; the King of all, the faithful Lord, took him up unharmed. Such patience will the Gnostic, as a

Gnostic, possess. He will bless when under trial, like the noble Job; like Jonas, when swallowed up by the whale, he will pray, and faith will restore him to prophesy to the Ninevites; and though shut up with lions, he will tame the wild beasts; though cast into the fire, he will be besprinkled with dew, but not consumed. He will give his testimony by night; he will testify by day; by word, by life, by conduct, he will testify. Dwelling with the Lord he will continue his familiar friend, sharing the same hearth according to the Spirit; pure in the flesh, pure in heart, sanctified in word. "The world," it is said, "is crucified to him, and he to the world." He, bearing about the cross of the Savior, will follow the Lord's footsteps, as God, having become holy of holies.

    The divine law, then, while keeping in mind all virtue, trains man especially to self-restraint, laying this as the foundation of the virtues; and disciplines us beforehand to the attainment of self-restraint by forbidding us to partake of such things as are by nature fat, as the breed of swine, which is full-fleshed. For such a use is assigned to epicures. It is accordingly said that one of the philosophers, giving the etymology of ὗς (sow), said that it was θύς, as being fit only for slaughter (θύσιν) and killing; for life was given to this animal for no other purpose than that it might swell in flesh. Similarly, repressing our desires, it forbade partaking of fishes which have neither fins nor scales; for these surpass other fishes in fleshiness and fatness. From this it was, in my opinion, that the mysteries not only prohibited touching certain animals, but also withdrew certain parts of those slain in sacrifice, for reasons which are known to the initiated. If, then, we are to exercise control over the belly, and what is below the belly, it is clear that we have of old heard from the Lord that we are to check lust by the law.

    And this will be completely effected, if we unfeignedly condemn what is the fuel of lust: I mean pleasure. Now they say that the idea of it is a gentle and bland excitement, accompanied with some sensation. Enthralled by this,

Menelaus, they say, after the capture of Troy, having rushed to put Helen to death, as having been the cause of such calamities, was nevertheless not able to effect it, being subdued by her beauty, which made him think of pleasure. Whence the tragedians, jeering, exclaimed insultingly against him:—

> "But thou, when on her breast thou looked, thy sword
> Didst cast away, and with a kiss the traitress,
> Ever-beauteous wretch, thou didst embrace."

And again:—

> "Was the sword then by beauty blunted?"

And I agree with Antisthenes when he says, "Could I catch Aphrodite, I would shoot her; for she has destroyed many of our beautiful and good women." And he says that "Love is a vice of nature, and the wretches who fall under its power call the disease a deity." For in these words it is shown that stupid people are overcome from ignorance of pleasure, to which we ought to give no admittance, even though it be called a god, that is, though it be given by God for the necessity of procreation. And Xenophon, expressly calling pleasure a vice, says: "Wretch, what good dost thou know, or what honorable aim hast thou? Which does not even wait for the appetite for sweet things, eating before being hungry, drinking before being thirsty; and that thou may eat pleasantly, seeking out fine cooks; and that thou may drink pleasantly, procuring costly wines; and in summer runs about seeking snow; and that thou may sleep pleasantly, not only provides soft beds, but also supports to the couches." Whence, as Aristo said, "against the whole tetrachord of pleasure, pain, fear, and lust, there is need of much exercise and struggle."

> "For it is these, it is these that go through our bowels,
> And throw into disorder men's hearts."

"For the minds of those even who are deemed grave, pleasure makes waxen," according to Plato; since "each pleasure and pain nails to the body the soul" of the man, that does not sever and crucify himself from the passions. "He that loses his life," says the Lord, "shall save it;" either giving it up by exposing it to danger for the Lord's sake, as He did for us, or loosing it from fellowship with its habitual life. For if you would loose, and withdraw, and separate (for this is what the cross means) your soul from the delight and pleasure that is in this life, you will possess it, found and resting in the looked-for hope. And this would be the exercise of death, if we would be content with those desires which are measured according to nature alone, which do not pass the limit of those which are in accordance with nature—by going to excess, or going against nature—in which the possibility of sinning arises. "We must therefore put on the panoply of God, that we may be able to stand against the wiles of the devil; since the weapons of our warfare are not carnal, but mighty through God to the pulling down of strongholds, casting down reasoning, and every lofty thing which exalted itself against the knowledge of God, and bringing every thought into captivity unto the obedience of Christ," says the divine apostle. There is need of a man who shall use in a praiseworthy and discriminating manner the things from which passions take their rise, as riches and poverty, honor and dishonor, health and sickness, life and death, toil and pleasure. For, in order that we may treat things, that are different, indifferently, there is need of a great difference in us, as having been previously afflicted with much feebleness, and in the distortion of a bad training and nurture ignorantly indulged ourselves. The simple word, then, of our philosophy declares the passions to be impressions on the soul that is soft and yielding, and, as it were, the signatures of the spiritual powers with whom we have to struggle. For it is the business, in my opinion, of the maleficent powers to endeavor to produce somewhat of their own constitution in everything, so as to overcome and make their own those who have renounced them. And it follows, as might be expected, that some are worsted; but in the case of those who engage in the contest with more athletic energy, the powers mentioned above, after carrying on the conflict in all forms, and advancing even as far as the crown wading in gore, decline the battle, and admire the victors.

For of objects that are moved, some are moved by impulse and appearance, as animals; and some by transposition, as inanimate objects. And of things without life, plants, they say, are moved by transposition in order to growth, if we will concede to them that plants are without life. To stones, then, belongs a permanent state. Plants have a nature; and the irrational animals possess impulse and perception, and likewise the two characteristics already specified. But the reasoning faculty, being peculiar to the human soul, ought not to be impelled similarly with the irrational animals, but ought to discriminate appearances, and not to be carried away by them. The powers, then, of which we have spoken hold out beautiful sights, and honors, and adulteries, and pleasures, and such like alluring phantasies before facile spirits; as those who drive away cattle hold out branches to them. Then, having beguiled those incapable of distinguishing the true from the false pleasure, and the fading and meretricious from the holy beauty, they lead them into slavery. And each deceit, by pressing constantly on the spirit, impresses its image on it; and the soul unwittingly carries about the image of the passion, which takes its rise from the bait and our consent.

The adherents of Basilides are in the habit of calling the passions appendages: saying that these are in essence certain spirits attached to the rational soul, through some original perturbation and confusion; and that, again, other bastard and heterogeneous natures of spirits grow on to them, like that of the wolf, the ape, the lion, the goat, whose properties showing themselves around the soul, they say, assimilate the lusts of the soul to the likeness of the animals. For they imitate the actions of those whose properties they

The Stromata or Miscellanies

bear. And not only are they associated with the impulses and perceptions of the irrational animals, but they affect the motions and the beauties of plants, on account of their bearing also the properties of plants attached to them. They have also the properties of a particular state, as the hardness of steel. But against this dogma we shall argue subsequently, when we treat of the soul. At present this only needs to be pointed out, that man, according to Basilides, preserves the appearance of a wooden horse, according to the poetic myth, embracing as he does in one body a host of such different spirits. Accordingly, Basilides' son himself, Isidorus, in his book, *About the Soul attached to us*, while agreeing in the dogma, as if condemning himself, writes in these words: "For if I persuade any one that the soul is undivided, and that the passions of the wicked are occasioned by the violence of the appendages, the worthless among men will have no slight pretence for saying, 'I was compelled, I was carried away, I did it against my will, I acted unwillingly;' though he himself led the desire of evil things, and did not fight against the assaults of the appendages. But we must, by acquiring superiority in the rational part, show ourselves masters of the inferior creation in us." For he too lays down the hypothesis of two souls in us, like the Pythagoreans, at whom we shall glance afterwards.

Valentinus too, in a letter to certain people, writes in these very words respecting the appendages: "There is one good, by whose presence is the manifestation, which is by the Son, and by Him alone can the heart become pure, by the expulsion of every evil spirit from the heart: for the multitude of spirits dwelling in it do not suffer it to be pure; but each of them performs his own deeds, insulting it oft with unseemly lusts. And the heart seems to be treated somewhat like a caravanserai. For the latter has holes and ruts made in it, and is often filled with dung; men living filthily in it, and taking no care for the place as belonging to others. So fares it with the heart as long as there is no thought taken for it, being unclean, and the abode of many demons. But when the only good Father visits it, it is sanctified, and gleams with light. And he who possesses such a heart is so blessed, that "he shall see God."

What, then, let them tell us, is the cause of such a soul not being cared for from the beginning? Either that it is not worthy (and somehow a care for it comes to it as from repentance), or it is a saved nature, as he would have it; and this, of necessity, from the beginning, being cared for by reason of its affinity, afforded no entrance to the impure spirits, unless by being forced and found feeble. For were he to grant that on repentance it preferred what was better, he will say this unwillingly, being what the truth we hold teaches; namely, that salvation is from a change due to obedience, but not from nature. For as the exhalations which arise from the earth, and from marshes, gather into mists and cloudy masses; so the vapors of fleshly lusts bring on the soul an evil condition, scattering about the idols of pleasure before the soul. Accordingly they spread darkness over the light of intelligence, the spirit attracting the exhalations that arise from lust, and thickening the masses of the passions by persistency in pleasures. Gold is not taken from the earth in the lump, but is purified by smelting; then, when made pure, it is called gold, the earth being purified. For "Ask, and it shall be given you," it is said to those who are able of themselves to choose what is best. And how we say that the powers of the devil, and the unclean spirits, sow into the sinner's soul, requires no more words from me, on adducing as a witness the apostolic Barnabas (and he was one of the seventy, and a fellow-worker of Paul), who speaks in these words: "Before we believed in God, the dwelling-place of our heart was unstable, truly a temple built with hands. For it was full of idolatry, and was a house of demons, through doing what was opposed to God."

He says, then, that sinners exercise activities appropriate to demons; but he does not say that the spirits themselves dwell in the soul of the unbeliever. Wherefore he also adds, "See that the temple of the Lord be gloriously built. Learn, having received remission of sins; and having set our hope on the Name, let us become new, created again from the beginning." For what he says is not that demons are driven out of us, but that the sins which like them we commit before believing are remitted. Rightly thus he puts in opposition what follows: "Wherefore God truly dwells in our home. He dwells in us. How? The word of His faith, the calling of His promise, the wisdom of His statutes, the commandments of His communication, [dwell in us]."

"I know that I have come upon a heresy; and its chief was wont to say that he fought with pleasure by pleasure, this worthy Gnostic advancing on pleasure in feigned combat, for he said he was a Gnostic; since he said it was no great thing for a man that had not tried pleasure to abstain from it, but for one who had mixed in it not to be overcome [was something]; and that therefore by means of it he trained himself in it. The wretched man knew not that he was deceiving himself by the artfulness of voluptuousness. To this opinion, then, manifestly Aristippus the Cyrenian adhered—that of the sophist who boasted of the truth. Accordingly, when reproached for continually cohabiting with the Corinthian courtesan, he said, "I possess Lais, and am not possessed by her."

Such also are those (who say that they follow Nicolaus, quoting an adage of the man, which they pervert, "that the flesh must be abused." But the worthy man showed that it was necessary to check pleasures and lusts, and by such training to waste away the impulses and propensities of the flesh. But they, abandoning themselves to pleasure like goats, as if insulting the body, lead a life of self-indulgence; not knowing that the body is wasted, being by nature subject to dissolution; while their soul is buried in the mire of vice; following as they do the teaching of pleasure itself, not of the apostolic man. For in what do they differ from Sardanapalus, whose life is shown in the epigram:—

"I have what I ate—what I enjoyed wantonly;
And the pleasures I felt in love. But those

Many objects of happiness are left,
For I too am dust, who ruled great Ninus."

For the feeling of pleasure is not at all a necessity, but the accompaniment of certain natural needs—hunger, thirst, cold, marriage. If, then, it were possible to drink without it, or take food, or beget children, no other need of it could be shown. For pleasure is neither a function, nor a state, nor any part of us; but has been introduced into life as an auxiliary, as they say salt was to season food. But when it casts off restraint and rules the house, it generates first concupiscence, which is an irrational propension and impulse towards that which gratifies it; and it induced Epicurus to lay down pleasure as the aim of the philosopher. Accordingly he deifies a sound condition of body, and the certain hope respecting it. For what else is luxury than the voluptuous gluttony and the superfluous abundance of those who are abandoned to self-indulgence? Diogenes writes significantly in a tragedy:—

"Who to the pleasures of effeminate
And filthy luxury attached in heart,
Wish not to undergo the slightest toil."

And what follows, expressed indeed in foul language, but in a manner worthy of the voluptuaries.

Wherefore the divine law appears to me necessarily to menace with fear, that, by caution and attention, the philosopher may acquire and retain absence of anxiety, continuing without fall and without sin in all things. For peace and freedom are not otherwise won, than by ceaseless and unyielding struggles with our lusts. For these stout and Olympic antagonists are keener than wasps, so to speak; and Pleasure especially, not by day only, but by night, is in dreams with witchcraft ensnaringly plotting and biting. How, then, can the Greeks any more be right in running down the law, when they themselves teach that Pleasure is the slave of fear?

Socrates accordingly bids "people guard against enticements to eat when they are not hungry, and to drink when not thirsty, and the glances and kisses of the fair, as fitted to inject a deadlier poison than that of scorpions and spiders." And Antisthenes chose rather "*to be demented than delighted.*" And the Theban Crates says:—

> "Master these, exulting in the disposition of the soul,
> Vanquished neither by gold nor by languishing love,
> Nor are they any longer attendants to the wanton."

And at length infers:—

> "Those, unenslaved and unbended by servile Pleasure,
> Love the immortal kingdom and freedom."

He writes expressly, in other words, "that the stop to the unbridled propensity to amorousness is hunger or a halter."

And the comic poets attest, while they depreciate the teaching of Zeno the Stoic, to be to the following effect:—

> "For he philosophizes a vain philosophy:
> He teaches to want food, and gets pupils
> One loaf, and for seasoning a dry fig, and to drink water."

All these, then, are not ashamed clearly to confess the advantage which accrues from caution. And the wisdom which is true and not contrary to reason, trusting not in mere words and oracular utterances, but in invulnerable armor of defense and energetic mysteries, and devoting itself to divine commands, and exercise, and practice, receives a divine power according to its inspiration from the Word.

Already, then, the ægis of the poetic Jove is described as

"Dreadful, crowned all around by Terror,
And on it Strife and Prowess, and chilling Rout;
On it, too, the Gorgon's head, dread monster,
Terrible, dire, the sign of Ægis-bearing Jove."

But to those, who are able rightly to understand salvation, I know not what will appear dearer than the gravity of the Law, and Reverence, which is its daughter. For when one is said to pitch too high, as also the Lord says, with reference to certain; so that some of those whose desires are towards Him may not sing out of pitch and tune, I do not understand it as pitching too high in reality, but only as spoken with reference to such as will not take up the divine yoke. For to those, who are unstrung and feeble, what is medium seems too high; and to those, who are unrighteous, what befalls them seems severe justice. For those, who, on account of the favor they entertain for sins, are prone to pardon, suppose truth to be harshness, and severity to be savageness, and him who does not sin with them, and is not dragged with them, to be pitiless. Tragedy writes therefore well of Pluto:—

"And to what sort of a deity wilt thou come, dost thou ask,
Who knows neither clemency nor favor,
But loves bare justice alone."

For although you are not yet able to do the things enjoined by the Law, yet, considering that the noblest examples are set before us in it, we are able to nourish and increase the love of liberty; and so we shall profit more eagerly as far as we can, inviting some things, imitating some things, and fearing others. For thus the righteous of the olden time, who lived according to the law, "were not from a storied oak, or from a rock;" because they wish to philosophize truly, took and devoted themselves entirely to God, and were classified under faith. Zeno said well of the Indians, that he would rather have seen one Indian roasted, than have learned the whole of the arguments about bearing pain. But we have exhibited before our eyes every day abundant sources of martyrs that are burnt, impaled, beheaded. All these the fear inspired by the law,— leading as a pædagogue to Christ, trained so as to manifest their piety by their blood. "God stood in the congregation of the gods; He judged in the midst of the gods." Who are they? Those that are superior to Pleasure, who rise above the passions, who know what they do—the Gnostics, who are greater than the world. "I said, Ye are Gods; and all sons of the Highest." To whom speaks the Lord? To those who reject as far as possible all that is of man. And the apostle says, "For ye are not any longer in the flesh, but in the Spirit." And again he says, "Though in the flesh, we do not war after the flesh." "For flesh and blood cannot inherit the kingdom of God, neither doth corruption inherit incorruption." "Lo, ye shall die like men," the Spirit has said, confuting us.

We must then exercise ourselves in taking care about those things which fall under the power of the passions, fleeing like those who are truly philosophers such articles of food as excite lust, and dissolute licentiousness in chambering and luxury; and the sensations that tend to luxury, which are a solid reward to others, must no longer be so to us. For God's greatest gift is self-restraint. For He Himself has said, "I will never leave thee, nor forsake thee," as having judged thee worthy according to the true election. Thus, then, while we attempt piously to advance, we shall have put on us the mild yoke of the Lord from faith to faith, one charioteer driving each of us onward to salvation, that the meet fruit of beatitude may be won. "*Exercise is*" according to Hippocrates of Cos, "*not only the health of the body, but of the soul—fearlessness of labors—a ravenous appetite for food.*"

CHAPTER XXI.—OPINIONS OF VARIOUS PHILOSOPHERS ON THE CHIEF GOOD.

Epicurus, in placing happiness in not being hungry, or thirsty, or cold, uttered that godlike word, saying impiously that he would fight in these points even with Father Jove; teaching, as if it were the case of pigs that live in filth and not that of rational philosophers, that happiness was victory. For of those that are ruled by pleasure are the Cyrenaics and Epicurus; for these expressly said that to live pleasantly was the chief end, and that pleasure was the only perfect good. Epicurus also says that the removal of pain is pleasure; and says that that is to be preferred, which first attracts from itself to itself, being, that is, wholly in motion. Dinomachus and Callipho said that the chief end was for one to do what he could for the attainment and enjoyment of pleasure; and Hieronymus the Peripatetic said the great end was to live unmolested, and that the only final good was happiness; and Diodorus likewise, who belonged to the same sect, pronounces the end to be to live undisturbed and well. Epicurus indeed, and the Cyrenaics, say that pleasure is the first duty; for it is for the sake of pleasure, they say, that virtue was introduced, and produced pleasure. According to the followers of Calliphon, virtue was introduced for the sake of pleasure, but that subsequently, on seeing its own beauty, it made itself equally prized with the first principle, that is, pleasure.

But the Aristotelians lay it down, that to live in accordance with virtue is the end, but that neither happiness nor the end is reached by everyone who has virtue. For the wise man, vexed and involved in involuntary mischances, and wishing gladly on these accounts to flee from life, is neither fortunate nor happy. For virtue needs time; for that is not acquired in one day which exists [only] in the perfect man since, as they say, a child is never happy. But human life is a perfect time, and therefore happiness is completed by the three kinds of good things. Neither, then, the poor, nor the mean nor even the diseased, nor the slave, can be one of them.

Again, on the other hand, Zeno the Stoic thinks the end to be living according to virtue; and, Cleanthes, living agreeably to nature in the right exercise of reason, which he held to consist of the selection of things according to nature. And Antipatrus, his friend, supposes the end to consist in choosing continually and unswervingly the things which are according to nature, and rejecting those contrary to nature. Archedamus, on the other hand, explained the end to be such, that in selecting the greatest and chief things according to nature, it was impossible to overstep it. In addition to these, Panætius pronounced the end to be, to live according to the means given to us by nature. And finally, Posidonius said that it was to live engaged in contemplating the truth and order of the universe, and forming himself as he best can, in nothing influenced by the irrational part of his soul. And some of the later Stoics defined the great end to consist in living agreeably to the constitution of man. Why should I mention Aristo? He said that the end was indifference; but what is indifferent simply abandons the indifferent. Shall I bring forward the opinions of Herillus? Herillus states the end to be to live according to science. For some think that the more recent disciples of the Academy define the end to be, the steady abstraction of the mind to its own impressions.

Further, Lycus the Peripatetic used to say that the final end was the true joy of the soul; as Leucimus, that it was the joy it had in what was good. Critolaus, also a Peripatetic, said that it was the perfection of a life flowing rightly according to nature, referring to the perfection accomplished by the three kinds according to tradition.

We must, however, not rest satisfied with these, but endeavor as we best can to adduce the doctrines laid down on the point by the naturalist; for they say that Anaxagoras of Clazomenæ affirmed contemplation and the freedom flowing from it to be the end of life; Heraclitus the Ephesian, complacency. The Pontic Heraclides relates, that Pythagoras taught that the knowledge of the perfection of the numbers was happiness of the soul. The Abderites also teach the existence of an end. Democritus, in his work *On the Chief End*, said it was cheerfulness, which he also called well-being, and often exclaims, "For delight and its absence are the boundary of those who have reached full age;" Hecatæus, that it was sufficiency to one's self; Apollodotus of Cyzicum, that it was delectation; as Nausiphanes, that it was undauntedness, for he said that it was this that was called by Democritus imperturbability. In addition to these still, Diotimus declared the end to be perfection of what is good, which he said was termed well-being. Again, Antisthenes, that it was humility.

And those called Annicereans, of the Cyrenaic succession, laid down no definite end for the whole of life; but said that to each action belonged, as its proper end, the pleasure accruing from the action. These Cyrenaics reject Epicurus' definition of pleasure, that is the removal of pain, calling that the condition of a dead man; because we rejoice not only on account of pleasures, but companionships and distinctions; while Epicurus thinks that all joy of the soul arises from previous sensations of the flesh. Metrodorus, in his book *On the Source of Happiness in Ourselves being greater than that which arises from Objects*, says: What else is the good of the soul but the sound state of the flesh, and the sure hope of its continuance?

CHAPTER XXII.—PLATO'S OPINION, THAT THE CHIEF GOOD CONSISTS IN ASSIMILATION TO GOD, AND ITS AGREEMENT WITH SCRIPTURE.

Further, Plato the philosopher says that the end is twofold: that which is communicable, and exists first in the ideal forms themselves, which he also calls "the good;" and that which partakes of it, and receives its likeness from it, as is the case in the men who appropriate virtue and true philosophy. Wherefore also Cleanthes, in the second book, *On Pleasure*, says that Socrates everywhere teaches that the just man and the happy are one and the same, and execrated the first man who separated the just from the useful, as having done an impious thing. For those are in truth impious who separate the useful from that which is right according to the law. Plato himself says that happiness (εὐδαιμονία) is to possess rightly the dæmon, and that the ruling faculty of the soul is called the dæmon; and he terms happiness (εὐδαιμονία) the most perfect and complete good. Sometimes he calls it a consistent and harmonious life, sometimes the highest perfection in accordance with virtue; and this he places in the knowledge of the Good, and in likeness to God, demonstrating likeness to be justice and holiness with wisdom. For is it not thus that some of our writers have understood that man straightway on his creation received what is "according to the image," but that what is according "to the likeness" he will receive afterwards on his perfection? Now Plato, teaching that the virtuous man shall have this likeness accompanied with humility, explains the following: "He that humbles himself shall be exalted." He says, accordingly, in *The Laws:* "God indeed, as the ancient saying has it, occupying the beginning, the middle, and the end of all things, goes straight through while He goes round the circumference. And He is always attended by Justice, the avenger of those who revolt from the divine law." You see how he connects fear with the divine law. He adds, therefore: "To which he, who would be happy, cleaving, will follow lowly and beautified." Then, connecting what follows these words, and admonishing by fear, he adds: "What conduct, then, is dear and conformable to God? That which is characterized by one word of old date: *Like will be dear to like*, as to what is in proportion; but things out of proportion are neither dear to one another, nor to those which are in proportion. And that therefore he that would be dear to God, must, to the best of his power, become such as He is. And in virtue of the same reason, our self controlling man is dear to God. But he that has no self-control is unlike and diverse." In saying that it was an ancient dogma, he indicates the teaching which had come to him from the law. And having in the *Theatoetus* admitted that evils make the circuit of mortal nature and of this spot, he adds: "Wherefore we must try to flee hence as soon as possible. For flight is likeness to God as far as possible. And likeness is to become holy and just with wisdom." Speusippus, the nephew of Plato, says that happiness is a perfect state in those who conduct themselves in accordance with nature, or the state of the good: for which condition all men have a desire, but the good only attained to quietude; consequently the virtues are the authors of happiness. And Xenocrates the Chalcedonian defines happiness to be the possession of virtue, strictly so called, and of the power subservient to it. Then he clearly says, that the seat in which it resides is the soul; that by which it is effected, the virtues; and that of these as parts are formed praiseworthy actions, good habits and dispositions, and motions, and relations; and that corporeal and external objects are not without these. For Polemo, the disciple of Xenocrates, seems of the opinion that happiness is sufficiency of all good things, or of the most and greatest. He lays down the doctrine, then, that happiness never exists without virtue; and that virtue, apart from corporeal and external objects, is sufficient for happiness. Let these things be so. The contradictions to the opinions specified shall be adduced in due time. But on us it is incumbent to reach the unaccomplished end, obeying the commands—that is, God—and living according to them, irreproachably and intelligently, through knowledge of the divine will; and assimilation as far as possible in accordance with right reason is the end, and restoration to perfect adoption by the Son, whichever glorifies the Father by the great High Priest who has deigned to call us brethren and fellow-heirs.

And the apostle, succinctly describing the end, writes in the Epistle to the Romans: "But now, being made free from sin, and become servants to God, ye have your fruit unto holiness, and the end everlasting life." And viewing the hope as twofold—that which is expected, and that which has been received—he now teaches the end to be the restitution of the hope. "For patience," he says, "worked experience, and experience hope: and hope makes not ashamed; because the

love of God is shed abroad in our hearts by the Holy Spirit that is given to us." On account of which love and the restoration to hope, he says, in another place, "*which rest* is laid up for us." You will find in Ezekiel the like, as follows: "The soul that sins, it shall die. And the man who shall be righteous, and shall do judgment and justice, who has not eaten on the mountains, nor lifted his eyes to the idols of the house of Israel, and hath not defiled his neighbor's wife, and hath not approached to a woman in the time of her uncleanness (for he does not wish the seed of man to be dishonored), and will not injure a man; will restore the debtor's pledge, and will not take usury; will turn away his hand from wrong; will do true judgment between a man and his neighbor; will walk in my ordinances, and keep my commandments, so as to do the truth; he is righteous, he shall surely live, says Adonai the Lord." Isaiah too, in exhorting him that hath not believed to gravity of life, and the Gnostic to attention, proving that man's virtue and God's are not the same, speaks thus: "Seek the Lord, and on finding Him call on Him. And when He shall draw near to you, let the wicked forsake his ways, and the unrighteous man his ways; and let him return to the Lord, and he shall obtain mercy," down to "and your thoughts from my thoughts." "We," then, according to the noble apostle, "wait for the hope of righteousness by faith. For in Christ neither circumcision availed anything, nor uncircumcision, but faith which worked by love. "And we desire that every one of you show the same diligence to the full assurance of hope," down to "made a high priest forever, after the order of Melchizedek." Similarly with Paul "the All-virtuous Wisdom" says, "H, that hears me shall dwell trusting in hope."For the restoration of hope is called by the same term "hope." To the expression "will dwell" it has most beautifully added "trusting," showing that such a one has obtained rest, having received the hope for which he hoped.
Wherefore also it is added, "and shall be quiet, without fear of any evil." And openly and expressly the apostle, in the first Epistle to the Corinthians says, "Be ye followers of me, as also

I am of Christ," in order that that may take place. If ye are of me, and I am of Christ, then ye are imitators of Christ, and Christ of God. *Assimilation to God, then, so that as far as possible a man becomes righteous and holy with wisdom* he lays down as the aim of faith, and the end to be that restitution of the promise which is effected by faith. From these doctrines gush the fountains, which we specified above, of those who have dogmatized about "the end." But of these enough.

CHAPTER XXIII.—ON MARRIAGE.

Since pleasure and lust seem to fall under marriage, it must also be treated of. Marriage is the first conjunction of man and woman for the procreation of legitimate children. Accordingly Menander the comic poet says:—

"For the begetting of legitimate children,
I give thee my daughter."

We ask if we ought to marry; which is one of the points, which are said to be relative. For some must marry, and a man must be in some condition, and he must marry someone in some condition. For every one is not to marry, nor always. But there is a time in which it is suitable, and a person for whom it is suitable, and an age up to which it is suitable. Neither ought everyone to take a wife, nor is it every woman one is to take, nor always, nor in every way, nor inconsiderately. But only he who is in certain circumstances, and such a one and at such time as is requisite, and for the sake of children, and one who is in every respect similar, and who does not by force or compulsion love the husband who loves her. Hence Abraham, regarding his wife as a sister, says, "She is my sister by my father, but not by my mother; and she became my wife," teaching us that children of the same mothers ought not to enter into matrimony. Let us briefly follow the history. Plato ranks marriage among outward good things, providing for the perpetuity of our race, and handing down as a torch a certain perpetuity to children's children. Democritus repudiates marriage and the procreation of children, on account of the many annoyances thence arising, and abstractions from more necessary things. Epicurus agrees, and those who place good in pleasure, and in the absence of trouble and pain. According to the opinion of the Stoics, marriage and the rearing of children are a thing indifferent; and according to the Peripatetics, a good. In a word, these, following out their dogmas in words, became enslaved to pleasures; some using concubines, some mistresses, and the most youths. And that wise quaternion in the garden with a mistress, honored pleasure by their acts. Those, then, will not escape the curse of yoking an ass with an ox, who, judging certain things not to suit them, command others to do them, or the reverse. This Scripture has briefly showed, when it says, "What thou hates, thou shalt not do to another."

But they who approve of marriage say, Nature has adapted us for marriage, as is evident from the structure of our bodies, which are male and female. And they constantly proclaim that command, "Increase and replenish." And though this is the case, yet it seems to them shameful that man, created by God, should be more licentious than the irrational creatures, which do not mix with many licentiously, but with one of the same species, such as pigeons and ringdoves, and creatures like them. Furthermore, they say, "The childless man fails in the perfection which is according to nature, not having substituted his proper successor in his place. For he is perfect that has produced from himself his like, or rather, when he sees that he has produced the same; that is, when that which is begotten attains to the same nature with him who begat." Therefore we must by all means marry, both for our country's sake, for the succession of children, and as far as we are concerned, the perfection of the world; since the poets also pity a marriage half-perfect and childless, but pronounce the fruitful one happy. But it is the diseases of the body that principally show marriage to be necessary. For a wife's care and the assiduity of her constancy appear to exceed the endurance of all other relations and friends, as much as to excel them in sympathy; and most of all, she takes kindly to patient watching. And in truth, according to Scripture, she is a needful help. The comic poet then, Menander, while running down marriage, and yet alleging on the other side its advantages, replies to one who had said:—

> "I am averse to the thing,
> For you take it awkwardly."

Then he adds:—

> "You see the hardships and the things which annoy you in it.
> But you do not look on the advantages."

And so forth.

Now marriage is a help in the case of those advanced in years, by furnishing a spouse to take care of one, and by rearing children of her to nourish one's old age.

> "For to a man after death his children bring renown,
> Just as corks bear the net,
> Saving the fishing-line from the deep.

according to the tragic poet Sophocles.

Legislators, moreover, do not allow those who are unmarried to discharge the highest magisterial offices. For instance, the legislator of the Spartans imposed a fine not on bachelorhood only, but on monogamy, and late marriage, and single life. And the renowned Plato orders the man who has not married to pay a wife's maintenance into the public treasury, and to give to the magistrates a suitable sum of money as expenses. For if they shall not beget children, not having married, they produce, as far as in them lies, a scarcity of men,

and dissolve states and the world that is composed of them, impiously doing away with divine generation. It is also unmanly and weak to shun living with a wife and children.
For of that of which the loss is an evil, the possession is by all means a good; and this is the case with the rest of things. But the loss of children is, they say, among the chiefest evils: the possession of children is consequently a good thing; and if it be so, so also is marriage. It is said:—

> "Without a father there never could be a child,
> And without a mother conception of a child could not be.
> Marriage makes a father, as a husband a mother."

Accordingly Homer makes a thing to be earnestly prayed for:—

> "A husband and a house;"

yet not simply, but along with good agreement. For the marriage of other people is an agreement for indulgence; but that of philosophers leads to that agreement which is in accordance with reason, bidding wives adorn themselves not in outward appearance, but in character; and enjoining husbands not to treat their wedded wives as mistresses, making corporeal wantonness their aim; but to take advantage of marriage for help in the whole of life, and for the best self-restraint.

Far more excellent, in my opinion, than the seeds of wheat and barley that are sown at appropriate seasons, is man that is sown, for whom all things grow; and those seeds temperate husbandmen ever sow. Every foul and polluting practice must therefore be purged away from marriage; that the intercourse of the irrational animals may not be cast in our teeth, as more accordant with nature than human conjunction in procreation. Some of these, it must be granted, desist at the time in which they are directed, leaving creation to the working of Providence.

By the tragedians, Polyxena, though being murdered, is described nevertheless as having, when dying, taken great care to fall decently,—

"Concealing what ought to be hid from the eyes of men."

Marriage to her was a calamity. To be subjected, then, to the passions, and to yield to them, is the extremest slavery; as to keep them in subjection is the only liberty. The divine Scripture accordingly says, that those who have transgressed the commandments are sold to strangers, that is, to sins alien to nature, till they return and repent. Marriage, then, as a sacred image, must be kept pure from those things which defile it. We are to rise from our slumbers with the Lord, and retire to sleep with thanksgiving and prayer,—

"Both when you sleep, and when the holy light comes,"

confessing the Lord in our whole life; possessing piety in the soul, and extending self-control to the body. For it is pleasing to God to lead decorum from the tongue to our actions. Filthy speech is the way to effrontery; and the end of both is filthy conduct.

Now that the Scripture counsels marriage, and allows no release from the union, is expressly contained in the law, "Thou shalt not put away thy wife, except for the cause of fornication;" and it regards as fornication, the marriage of those separated while the other is alive. Not to deck and adorn herself beyond what is becoming, renders a wife free of calumnious suspicion, while she devotes herself assiduously to prayers and supplications; avoiding frequent departures from the house, and shutting herself up as far as possible from the view of all not related to her, and deeming housekeeping of more consequence than impertinent trifling. "He that taketh a woman that has been put away," it is said, "committed adultery; and if one puts away his wife, he makes her an adulteress," that is, compels her to commit adultery. And not only is he who puts her away guilty of this, but he who takes her, by giving to the woman the opportunity of sinning; for did he not take her, she would return to her husband. What, then, is the law? In order to check the impetuosity of the passions, it commands the adulteress to be put to death, on being convicted of this; and if of priestly family, to be committed to the flames. And the adulterer also is stoned to death, but not in the same place, that not even their death may be in common. And the law is not at variance with the Gospel, but agrees with it. How should it be otherwise, one Lord being the author of both? She who has committed fornication lives in sin, and is dead to the commandments; but she who has repented, being as it were born again by the change in her life, has a regeneration of life; the old harlot being dead, and she who has been regenerated by repentance having come back again to life. The Spirit testifies to what has been said by Ezekiel, declaring, "I desire not the death of the sinner, but that he should turn." Now they are stoned to death; as through hardness of heart dead to the law which they believed not. But in the case of a priestess the punishment is increased, because "to whom much is given, from him shall more be required."

Let us conclude this second book of the *Stromata* at this point, on account of the length and number of the chapters.

Elucidations.

I.
(On the Greeks, cap. i. note 3, p. 347.)

The admirable comments of Stier on the Greeks, who said to Philip, "*We would see Jesus*," seem to me vindicated by the history of the Gospel, and by the part which the Greeks were called to take in its propagation. Clement seems to me the man of Providence, who gives rich significance to "the corn of wheat," and its multiplication in Gentile discipleship. And in this I am a convert to Stier's view, against my preconceptions. That the Greeks who were at Jerusalem at the Passover were other than Hellenistic Jews, or Greek proselytes, always seemed to me improbable; but, more and more, I discover a design in this narrative, which seems to me thoroughly sustained by the history of the Gentile churches, which were Greek everywhere originally, and for the use of which the Septuagint had been prepared in the providence of God. To say nothing of the New-Testament Scriptures, the whole symbolic and liturgical system of the early Christians and all the Catholic councils which were Greek in their topography, language, and legislation, confirm the sublime thought which Stier has elucidated. "The Pharisees said, *The world is gone after him;* and there were certain Greeks," etc. So the story is introduced. Jesus is told of their desire to see him; and he answers, "The hour is come that the Son of man should be glorified;" and he goes on to speak of his death as giving life to the world. I feel grateful to Stier for his bold originality in treating the subject; and I trust others will find that it invests the study of the ante-Nicene Fathers with a fresh interest, and throws back from their writings a peculiar reflex light on the New-Testament Scriptures themselves.

II.
(See p. 352, note 9.)

Μόνος ὁ σοφὸς ἐλεύφερος. Stier, in his comments on St. John (viii. 32–36), may well be compared with this chapter of Clement's. The eighteenth chapter of this book must also be kept in view if we would do full justice to the true position of Clement, who recognizes nothing in heathen philosophy as true wisdom, save as it flows from God, in Moses, and through the Hebrew Church. That Greek philosophy, so viewed, did lead to Christ, and that this great principle is recognized in the apostolic teachings, seems to me indisputable. This illustrates what has been noted above in Elucidation I.

III.
(See p. 359.)

Clement notes that the false Gnostics rejected the Epistles to Timothy, chiefly because of 1 Tim. vi. 20. Beausobre (*Histoire du Manichéisme*, tom. ii. p. v.) doubts as to Basilides, whether he is open to this charge; but Jerome accuses him expressly of rejecting the pastoral epistles, and that to the Hebrews. For this, and Neander's qualifying comment, see Kaye, p. 263. Clement is far from charging Basilides, personally, with an immoral life, or from lending his sanction to impurity; but a study of the Gnostic sects, with whom our Alexandrian doctor was forced to contend, will show that they were introducing, under the pretence of Christianity, such abominations as made their defeat and absolute overthrow a matter of life and death for the Church. To let *such teachers* be confounded with Christians, was to neutralize the very purpose for which the Church existed. Now, it was in the deadly grapple with such loathsome errorists, that the idea of "Catholic orthodoxy" became so precious to the primitive faithful. They were forced to make even the heathen comprehend the existence of that word-wide confederation of churches already explained, and to exhibit their Scriptural creed and purity of discipline, in the strongest contrast with these pestilent "armies of the aliens," who were neither Gnostics nor Christians indeed, much less Catholic or Orthodox teachers and believers.

Now, if in dealing with counterfeits Clement was obliged to meet them on their own grounds, and defeat them on a plan, at once intelligible to the heathen, and enabling all believers to "fight the good fight of faith" successfully, we must concede that he knew better than we can, what was suited to the Alexandrian schools, their intellect, and their false mysticism. His works were a great safeguard to those who came after him; though they led to the false system of exposition by which Origen so greatly impaired his services to the Church, and perhaps to other evils, which, in the issue, shook the great patriarchate of Alexandria to its foundations. It is curious to trace the influence of Clement, through Tertullian and St. Augustine, upon the systems of the schoolmen, and again, through them, on the Teutonic reformers. The mysticism of Fénelon as well, may be traced, more than is generally credited, to the old Alexandrian school, which was itself the product of some of the most subtle elements of our nature, sanctified, but not wholly controlled, by the wisdom that is from above. Compare the interminable controversies of the period, in the writings of Fénelon and Bossuet; and, for a succinct history, see *L'Histoire de l'église de France*, par l'Abbe Guettée, tom. xi. p. 156 *et seqq*.

Book III.

After much consideration, the Editors have deemed it best to give the whole of this book in Latin. [In the former Book, Clement has shown, not without a decided leaning to chaste celibacy, that marriage is a holy estate, and consistent with the perfect man in Christ. He now enters upon the refutation of the false-Gnostics and their licentious tenets. Professing a stricter rule to begin with, and despising the ordinances of the Creator, their result was the grossest immorality in practice. The melancholy consequences of an enforced celibacy are, here, all foreseen and foreshown; and this Book, though necessarily offensive to our Christian tastes, is most useful as a commentary upon the history of monasticism, and the celibacy of priests, in the Western churches. The resolution of the Edinburgh editors to give this Book to scholars *only*, in the Latin, is probably wise. I subjoin a succinct analysis, in the elucidations.]

Since this is a US-English translation only, this version will omit Book III and to Book IV...

Book IV.

CHAPTER I.—ORDER OF CONTENTS.

It will follow, I think, that I should treat of martyrdom, and of who the perfect man is. With these points shall be included what follows in accordance with the demands of the points to be spoken about, and how both bond and free must equally philosophize, whether male or female in sex. And in the sequel, after finishing what is to be said on faith and inquiry, we shall set forth the department of symbols; so that, on cursorily concluding the discourse on ethics, we shall exhibit the advantage which has accrued to the Greeks from the barbarian philosophy. After which sketch, the brief explanation of the Scriptures both against the Greeks and against the Jews will be presented, and whatever points we were unable to embrace in the previous *Miscellanies* (through having respect necessarily to the multitude of matters), in accordance with the commencement of the poem, purposing to finish them in one commentary. In addition to these points, afterwards on completing the sketch, as far as we can in accordance with what we propose, we must give an account of the physical doctrines of the Greeks and of the barbarians, respecting elementary principles, as far as their opinions have reached us, and argue against the principal views excogitated by the philosophers.

It will naturally fall after these, after a cursory view of theology, to discuss the opinions handed down respecting prophecy; so that, having demonstrated that the Scriptures which we believe are valid from their omnipotent authority, we shall be able to go over them consecutively, and to show thence to all the heresies one God and Omnipotent Lord to be truly preached by the law and the prophets, and besides by the blessed Gospel. Many contradictions against the heterodox await us while we attempt, in writing, to do away with the force of the allegations made by them, and to persuade them against their will, proving by the Scriptures themselves.

On completing, then, the whole of what we propose in the commentaries, on which, if the Spirit will, we ministering to the urgent need, (for it is exceedingly necessary, before coming to the truth, to embrace what ought to be said by way of preface), shall address ourselves to the true gnostic science of nature, receiving initiation into the minor mysteries before the greater; so that nothing may be in the way of the truly divine declaration of sacred things, the subjects requiring preliminary detail and statement being cleared away, and sketched beforehand. The science of nature, then, or rather observation, as contained in the gnostic tradition according to the rule of the truth, depends on the discussion concerning cosmogony, ascending thence to the department of theology. Whence, then, we shall begin our account of what is handed down, with the creation as related by the prophets, introducing also the tenets of the heterodox, and endeavoring as far as we can to confute them. But it shall be written if God will, and as He inspires; and now we must proceed to what we proposed, and complete the discourse on ethics.

CHAPTER II.—THE MEANING OF THE NAME STROMATA OR MISCELLANIES.

Let these notes of ours, as we have often said for the sake of those that consult them carelessly and unskillfully, be of varied character—and as the name itself indicates, patched together—passing constantly from one thing to another, and in the series of discussions hinting at one thing and demonstrating another. "For those who seek for gold," says Heraclitus, "dig much earth and find little gold." But those who are of the truly golden race, in mining for what is allied to them, will find the much in little. For the word will find one to understand it. The Miscellanies of notes contribute, then, to the recollection and expression of truth in the case of him who is able to investigate with reason. And you must prosecute, in addition to these, other labors and researches; since, in the case of people who are setting out on a road with which they are unacquainted, it is sufficient merely to point out the direction. After this they must walk and find out the rest for themselves. As, they say, when a certain slave once asked at the oracle what he should do to please his master, the Pythian priestess replied, "You will find if you seek." It is truly a difficult matter, then, as turns out, to find out latent good; since

> "Before virtue is placed exertion,
> And long and steep is the way to it,
> And rough at first; but when the summit is reached,
> Then is it easy, though difficult [before]."

"For narrow," in truth, "and strait is the way" of the Lord. And it is to the "violent that the kingdom of God belongs."

Whence, "Seek, and ye shall find," holding on by the truly royal road, and not deviating. As we might expect, then, the generative power of the seeds of the doctrines comprehended in this treatise is great in small space, as the "universal herbage of the field," as Scripture says. Thus the Miscellanies of notes have their proper title, wonderfully like that ancient oblation culled from all sorts of things of which Sophocles writes:—

> "For there was a sheep's fleece, and there was a vine,
> And a libation, and grapes well stored;
> And there was mixed with it fruit of all kinds,
> And the fat of the olive, and the most curious
> Wax-formed work of the yellow bee."

Just so our *Stromata*, according to the husbandman of the comic poet Timocles, produce "figs, olives, dried figs, honey, as from an all-fruitful field;" on account of which exuberance he adds:—

> "Thou speaks of a harvest-wreath not of husbandry."

For the Athenians were wont to cry:—

> "The harvest-wreath bears figs and fat loaves,
> And honey in a cup, and olive oil to anoint you."

We must then often, as in winnowing sieves, shake and toss up this the great mixture of seeds, in order to separate the wheat.

CHAPTER III.—THE TRUE EXCELLENCE OF MAN.

The most of men have a disposition unstable and heedless, like the nature of storms. "Want of faith has done many good things, and faith evil things." And Epicharmus says, "Don't forget to exercise incredulity; for it is the sinews of the soul." Now, to disbelieve truth brings death, as to believe, life; and again, to believe the lie and to disbelieve the truth hurries to destruction. The same is the case with self-restraint and licentiousness. To restrain one's self from doing good is the work of vice; but to keep from wrong is the beginning of salvation. So the Sabbath, by abstinence from evils, seems to indicate self-restraint. And what, I ask, is it in which man differs from beasts, and the angels of God, on the other hand, are wiser than he? "Thou made him a little lower than the angels." For some do not interpret this Scripture of the Lord, although He also bore flesh, but of the perfect man and the gnostic, inferior in comparison with the angels in time, and by reason of the vesture [of the body]. I call then wisdom nothing but science, since life differs not from life. For to live is common to the mortal nature, that is to man, with that to which has been vouchsafed immortality; as also the faculty of contemplation and of self-restraint, one of the two being more excellent. On this ground Pythagoras seems to me to have said that God alone is wise, since also the apostle writes in the Epistle to the Romans, "For the obedience of the faith among all nations, being made known to the only wise God through Jesus Christ;" and that he himself was a philosopher, on account of his friendship with God. Accordingly it is said, "God talked with Moses as a friend with a friend." That, then, which is true being clear to God, forthwith generates truth. And the gnostic loves the truth. "Go," it is said, "to the ant, thou sluggard, and be the disciple of the bee;" thus speaks Solomon. For if there is one function belonging to the peculiar nature of each creature, alike of the ox, and horse, and dog, what shall we say is the peculiar function of man? He is like, it appears to me, the Centaur, a Thessalian figment, compounded of a rational and irrational part, of soul and body. Well, the body tills the ground, and hastes to it; but the soul is raised to God: trained in the true philosophy, it speeds to its kindred above, turning away from the lusts of the body, and besides these, from toil and fear, although we have shown that patience and fear belong to the good man. For if "by the law is the knowledge of sin," as those allege who disparage the law, and "till the law sin was in the world;" yet "without the law sin was dead," we oppose them. For when you take away the cause of fear, sin, you have taken away fear; and much more, punishment, when you have taken away that which gives rise to lust. "For the law is not made for the just man," says the Scripture. Well, then, says Heraclitus, "They would not have known the name of Justice if these things had not been." And Socrates says, "that the law was not made for the sake of the good." But the cavilers did not know even this, as the apostle says, "that he who loves his brother worked not evil;" for this, "Thou shalt not kill, thou shalt not commit adultery, thou shalt not steal; and if there be any other commandment, it is comprehended in the word, Thou shall love thy neighbor as thyself." So also is it said, "Thou shall love the Lord thy God with all thy heart, and thou shalt love thy neighbor as thyself."And "if he that loves his neighbor worked no evil," and if "every commandment is comprehended in this, the loving our neighbor," the commandments, by menacing with fear, work love, not hatred. Wherefore the law is productive of the emotion of fear. "So that the law is holy," and in truth "spiritual," according to the apostle. We must, then, as is fit, in investigating the nature of the body and the essence of the soul, apprehend the end of each, and not regard death as an evil. "For when ye were the servants of sin," says the apostle, "ye were free from righteousness. What fruit had ye then in those things in which ye are now ashamed? For the end of those things is death. But now, being made free from sin, and become servants to God, ye have your fruit unto holiness, and the end everlasting life. For the wages of sin is death: but the gift of God is eternal life, through Jesus Christ our Lord." The assertion, then, may be hazarded, that it has been shown that death is the fellowship of the soul in a state of sin with the body; and life the separation from sin. And many are the stakes and ditches of lust which impede us, and the pits of wrath and anger which must be overleaped, and all the machinations we must avoid of those who plot against us,—who would no longer see the knowledge of God "through a glass."

> "The half of virtue the far-seeing Zeus takes
> From man, when he reduces him to a state of slavery."

As slaves the Scripture views those "under sin" and "sold to sin," the lovers of pleasure and of the body; and beasts rather than men, "those who have become like to cattle, horses, neighing after their neighbors' wives." The licentious is "the lustful ass," the covetous is the "savage wolf," and the deceiver is "a serpent." The severance, therefore, of the soul from the body, made a life-long study, produces in the philosopher gnostic alacrity, so that he is easily able to bear natural death, which is the dissolution of the chains which bind the soul to the body. "For the world is crucified to me, and I to the world," the [apostle] says; "and now I live, though in the flesh, as having my conversation in heaven."

CHAPTER IV.—THE PRAISES OF MARTYRDOM.

Whence, as is reasonable, the gnostic, when Galled, obeys easily, and gives up his body to him who asks; and, previously divesting himself of the affections of this carcass, not insulting the tempter, but rather, in my opinion, training him and convincing him,—

"From what honor and what extent of wealth fallen,"

as says Empedocles, here for the future he walks with mortals. He, in truth, bears witness to himself that he is faithful and loyal towards God; and to the tempter, that he in vain envied him who is faithful through love; and to the Lord, of the inspired persuasion in reference to His doctrine, from which he will not depart through fear of death; further, he confirms also the truth of preaching by his deed, showing that God to whom he hastes is powerful. You will wonder at his love, which he conspicuously shows with thankfulness, in being united to what is allied to him, and besides by his precious blood, shaming the unbelievers. He then avoids denying Christ through fear by reason of the command; nor does he sell his faith in the hope of the gifts prepared, but in love to the Lord he will most gladly depart from this life; perhaps giving thanks both to him who afforded the cause of his departure hence, and to him who laid the plot against him, for receiving an honorable reason which he himself furnished not, for showing what he is, to him by his patience, and to the Lord in love, by which even before his birth he was manifested to the Lord, who knew the martyr's choice. With good courage, then, he goes to the Lord, his friend, for whom he voluntarily gave his body, and, as his judges hoped, his soul, hearing from our Savior the words of poetry, "Dear brother," by reason of the similarity of his life. We call martyrdom perfection, not because the man comes to the end of his life as others, but because he has exhibited the perfect work of love. And the ancients laud the death of those among the Greeks who died in war, not that they advised people to die a violent death, but because he who ends his life in war is released without the dread of dying, severed from the body without experiencing previous suffering or being enfeebled in his soul, as the people that suffer in diseases. For they depart in a state of effeminacy and desiring to live; and therefore they do not yield up the soul pure, but bearing with it their lusts like weights of lead; all but those who have been conspicuous in virtue. Some die in battle with their lusts, these being in no respect different from what they would have been if they had wasted away by disease.

If the confession to God is martyrdom, each soul which has lived purely in the knowledge of God, which has obeyed the commandments, is a witness both by life and word, in whatever way it may be released from the body,—shedding faith as blood along its whole life till its departure. For instance, the Lord says in the Gospel, "Whosoever shall leave father, or mother, or brethren," and so forth, "for the sake of the Gospel and my name," he is blessed; not indicating simple martyrdom, but the gnostic martyrdom, as of the man who has conducted himself according to the rule of the Gospel, in love to the Lord (for the knowledge of the Name and the understanding of the Gospel point out the gnosis, but not the bare appellation), so as to leave his worldly kindred, and wealth, and every possession, in order to lead a life free from passion. "Mother" figuratively means country and sustenance; "fathers" are the laws of civil polity: which must be contemned thankfully by the high-souled just man; for the sake of being the friend of God, and of obtaining the right hand in the holy place, as the Apostles have done.

Then Heraclitus says, "Gods and men honor those slain in battle;" and Plato in the fifth book of the *Republic* writes, "Of those who die in military service, whoever dies after winning renown, shall we not say that he is chief of the golden race? Most assuredly." But the golden race is with the gods, who are in heaven, in the fixed sphere, who chiefly hold command in the providence exercised towards men. Now some of the heretics who have misunderstood the Lord, have at once an impious and cowardly love of life; saying that the true martyrdom is the knowledge of the only true God (which we also admit), and that the man is a self-murderer and a suicide who makes confession by death; and adducing other similar sophisms of cowardice. To these we shall reply at the proper time; for they differ with us in regard to first principles. Now we, too, say that those who have rushed on death (for there are some, not belonging to us, but sharing the name merely, who are in haste to give themselves up, the poor wretches dying through hatred to the Creator)—these, we say, banish themselves without being martyrs, even though they are punished publicly. For they do not preserve the characteristic mark of believing martyrdom, inasmuch as they have not known the only true God, but give themselves up to a vain death, as the Gymnosophists of the Indians to useless fire.

But since these falsely named calumniate the body, let them learn that the harmonious mechanism of the body contributes to the understanding which leads to goodness of nature. Wherefore in the third book of the *Republic,* Plato, whom they appeal to loudly as an authority that disparages generation, says, "that for the sake of harmony of soul, care must be taken for the body," by which, he who announces the proclamation of the truth, finds it possible to live, and to live well. For it is by the path of life and health that we learn gnosis. But is he who cannot advance to the height without being occupied with necessary things, and through them doing what tends to knowledge, not to choose to live well? In living, then, living well is secured. And he who in the body has devoted himself to a good life, is being sent on to the state of immortality.

CHAPTER V.—ON CONTEMPT FOR PAIN, POVERTY, AND OTHER EXTERNAL THINGS.

Fit objects for admiration are the Stoics, who say that the soul is not affected by the body, either to vice by disease, or to virtue by health; but both these things, they say, are indifferent. And indeed Job, through exceeding continence, and excellence of faith, when from rich he became poor, from being held in honor dishonored, from being comely unsightly, and sick from being healthy, is depicted as a good example, putting the Tempter to shame, blessing his Creator; bearing what came second, as the first, and most clearly teaching that it is possible for the gnostic to make an excellent use of all circumstances. And that ancient achievements are proposed as images for our correction, the apostle shows, when he says, "So that my bonds in Christ are become manifest in all the palace, and to all the rest; and several of the brethren in the Lord, waxing confident by my bonds, are much more bold to speak the word of God without fear,"—since martyrs' testimonies are examples of conversion gloriously sanctified. "For what things the Scripture speaks were written for our instruction, that we, through patience and the consolation of the Scriptures, might have the hope of consolation." When pain is present, the soul appears to decline from it, and to deem release from present pain a precious thing. At that moment it slackens from studies, when the other virtues also are neglected. And yet we do not say that it is virtue itself which suffers, for virtue is not affected by disease. But he who is partaker of both, of virtue and the disease, is afflicted by the pressure of the latter; and if he who has not yet attained the habit of self-command be not a high-souled man, he is distraught; and the inability to endure it is found equivalent to fleeing from it.

The same holds good also in the case of poverty. For it compels the soul to desist from necessary things, I mean contemplation and from pure sinlessness, forcing him, who has not wholly dedicated himself to God in love, to occupy himself about provisions; as, again, health and abundance of necessaries keep the soul free and unimpeded, and capable of making a good use of what is at hand. "For," says the apostle, "such shall have trouble in the flesh. But I spare you. For I would have you without anxiety, in order to decorum and assiduity for the Lord, without distraction."

These things, then, are to be abstained from, not for their own sakes, but for the sake of the body; and care for the body is exercised for the sake of the soul, to which it has reference. For on this account it is necessary for the man who lives as a gnostic to know what is suitable. Since the fact that pleasure is not a good thing is admitted from the fact that certain pleasures are evil, by this reason good appears evil, and evil good. And then, if we choose some pleasures and shun others, it is not every pleasure that is a good thing.

Similarly, also, the same rule holds with pains, some of which we endure, and others we shun. But choice and avoidance are exercised according to knowledge; so that it is not pleasure that is the good thing, but knowledge by which we shall choose a pleasure at a certain time, and of a certain kind. Now the martyr chooses the pleasure that exists in prospect through the present pain. If pain is conceived as existing in thirst, and pleasure in drinking, the pain that has preceded becomes the efficient cause of pleasure. But evil cannot be the efficient cause of good. Neither, then, is the one thing nor the other evil. Simonides accordingly (as also Aristotle) writes, "that to be in good health is the best thing, and the second best thing is to be handsome, and the third best thing is to be rich without cheating."

And Theognis of Megara says:—

"You must, to escape poverty, throw
Yourself, O Cyrnus down from
The steep rocks into the deep sea."

On the other hand, Antiphanes, the comic poet, says, "Plutus (Wealth), when it has taken hold of those who see better than others, makes them blind." Now by the poets he is proclaimed as blind from his birth:—

"And brought him forth blind who saw not the sun."

Says the Chalcidian Euphorion:—

"Riches, then, and extravagant luxuries,
Were for men the worst training for manliness."

Wrote Euripides in *Alexander:*—

"And it is said,
Penury has attained wisdom through misfortune;

> But much wealth will capture not
> Sparta alone, but every city."

"It is not then the only coin that mortals have, that which is white silver or golden, but virtue too," as Sophocles says.

CHAPTER VI.—SOME POINTS IN THE BEATITUDES.

Our holy Savior applied poverty and riches, and the like, both to spiritual things and objects of sense. For when He said, "Blessed are they that are persecuted for righteousness' sake," He clearly taught us in every circumstance to seek for the martyr who, if poor for righteousness' sake, witnesses that the righteousness which he loves is a good thing; and if he "hunger and thirst for righteousness' sake," testifies that righteousness is the best thing. Likewise he, that weeps and mourns for righteousness' sake, testifies to the best law that it is beautiful. As, then, "those that are persecuted," so also "those that hunger and thirst" for righteousness' sake, are called "blessed" by Him who approves of the true desire, which not even famine can put a stop to. And if "they hunger after righteousness itself," they are blessed. "And blessed are the poor," whether "in spirit" or in circumstance"—that is, if for righteousness' sake. It is not the poor simply, but those that have wished to become poor for righteousness' sake, that He pronounces blessed—those who have despised the honors of this world in order to attain "the good;" likewise also those who, through chastity, have become comely in person and character, and those who are of noble birth, and honorable, having through righteousness attained to adoption, and therefore "have received power to become the sons of God," and "to tread on serpents and scorpions," and to rule over demons and "the host of the adversary." And, in fine, the Lord's discipline draws the soul away gladly from the body, even if it wrench itself away in its removal. "For he that loves his life shall lose it, and he that loses his life shall find it," if we only join that which is mortal of us with the immortality of

God. It is the will of God [that we should attain] the knowledge of God, which is the communication of immortality. He therefore, who, in accordance with the word of repentance, knows his life to be sinful will lose it—losing it from sin, from which it is wrenched; but losing it, will find it, according to the obedience which lives again to faith, but dies to sin. This, then, is what it is "to find one's life," "to know one's self."

The conversion, however, which leads to divine things, the Stoics say, is affected by a change, the soul being changed to wisdom. And Plato: "On the soul taking a turn to what is better, and a change from a kind of nocturnal day." Now the philosophers also allow the good man an exit from life in accordance with reason, in the case of one depriving him of active exertion, so that the hope of action is no longer left him. And the judge who compels us to deny Him whom we love, I regard as showing who is and who is not the friend of God.

In that case there is not left ground for even examining what one prefers—the menaces of man or the love of God. And abstinence from vicious acts is found, somehow, [to result in] the diminution and extinction of vicious propensities, their energy being destroyed by inaction. And this is the import of "Sell what thou hast, and give to the poor, and come, follow Me"—that is, follow what is said by the Lord. Some say that by what "thou hast" He designated the things in the soul, of a nature not akin to it, though how these are bestowed on the poor they are not able to say. For God dispenses to all according to desert, His distribution being righteous. Despising, therefore, the possessions which God apportions to thee in thy magnificence, comply with what is spoken by me; haste to the ascent of the Spirit, being not only justified by abstinence from what is evil, but in addition also perfected, by Christ like beneficence. In this instance He convicted the man, who boasted that he had fulfilled the injunctions of the law, of not loving his neighbor; and it is by beneficence that the love which, according to the gnostic ascending scale, is Lord of the Sabbath, proclaims itself. We must then, according to my view, have recourse to the word of salvation neither from fear of punishment nor promise of a gift, but on account of the good itself. Such, as do so, stand on the right hand of the sanctuary; but those who think that by the gift of what is perishable they shall receive in exchange what belongs to immortality are in the parable of the two brothers called "hirelings." And is there not some light thrown here on the expression "in the likeness and image," in the fact that some live according to the likeness of Christ, while those who stand on the left hand live according to their image? There are then two things proceeding from the truth, one root lying beneath both,—the choice being, however, not equal, or rather the difference that is in the choice not being equal. To choose by way of imitation differs, as appears to me, from the choice of him who chooses according to knowledge, as that which is set on fire differs from that which is illuminated. Israel, then, is the light of the likeness which is according to the Scripture. But the image is another thing.

What means the parable of Lazarus, by showing the image of the rich and poor? And what the saying, "No man can serve two masters, God and Mammon?"—the Lord so terming the love of money. For instance, the covetous, who were invited, responded not to the invitation to the supper, not because of their possessing property, but of their inordinate affection to what they possessed. "The foxes," then, have holes. He called those evil and earthly men who are occupied about the wealth which is mined and dug from the ground, foxes. Thus also, in reference to Herod: "Go, tell that fox, Behold, I cast out devils, and perform cures today and tomorrow, and the third day I shall be perfected." For He applied the name "fowls of the air" to those who were distinct from the other birds—those really pure, those that have the power of flying to the knowledge of the heavenly Word. For not riches only, but also honor, and marriage, and poverty, have ten thousand cares for him who is unfit for them. And those cares He indicated in the parable of the fourfold seed, when He said that "the seed of the word which fell unto the thorns" and hedges was choked by them, and could not bring forth fruit. It is therefore necessary to learn how to make use of every occurrence, so as by a good life, according to knowledge, to be trained for the state of eternal life. For it said, "I saw the wicked exalted and towering as the cedars of Lebanon; and I passed," says the Scripture, "and, lo, he was not; and I sought him, and his place was not found. Keep innocence, and look on uprightness: for there is a remnant to the man of peace." Such will he be who believes unfeignedly with his whole heart, and is tranquil in his whole soul. "For the different people honor me with their lips, but their heart is far from the Lord." "They bless with their mouth, but they curse in their heart." "They loved Him with their mouth, and lied to Him with their tongue; but their heart was not right with Him, and they were not faithful to His covenant." Wherefore "let the false lips become speechless, and let the Lord destroy the boastful tongue: those who say, We shall magnify our tongue, and our lips are our own; who is Lord over us? For the affliction of the poor and the groaning of the needy now will I arise, says the Lord; I will set him in safety; I will speak out in his case." For it is to the humble that Christ belongs, who do not exalt themselves against His flock. "Lay not up for yourselves, therefore, treasures on the earth, where moth and rust destroy, and thieves break through and steal," says the Lord, in reproach perchance of the covetous, and perchance also of those who are simply anxious and full of cares, and those too who indulge their bodies. For amours, and diseases, and evil thoughts "breakthrough" the mind and the whole man. But our true "treasure" is where what is allied to our mind is, since it bestows the communicative power of righteousness, showing that we must assign to the habit of our old conversation what we have acquired by it, and have recourse to God, beseeching mercy. He is, in truth, "the bag that waxed not old," the provisions of eternal life, "the treasure that fails not in heaven." "For I will have mercy on whom I will have mercy," says the Lord. And they say those things to those who wish to be poor for righteousness' sake. For they have heard in the commandment that "the broad and wide way leads to destruction, and many there are who go in by it." It is not of anything else that the assertion is made, but of profligacy, and love of women, and love of glory, and ambition, and similar passions. For so He says, "Fool, this night shall thy soul be required of thee; and whose shall those things be which thou hast prepared?" And the commandment is expressed in these very words, "Take heed, therefore, of covetousness. For a man's life does not consist in the abundance of those things which he possesses. For what shall it profit a man, if he shall gain the whole world, and lose his own soul? Or what shall a man give in exchange for his soul?" "Wherefore I say, Take no thought for your life, what ye shall eat; neither for your body, what ye shall put on. For your life is more than meat, and your body than raiment."And again, "For your Father knows that ye have need of all these things." "But seek first the kingdom of heaven, and its righteousness," for these are the great things, and the things which are small and appertain to this life "shall be added to you." Does He not plainly then exhort us to follow the gnostic life, and enjoin us to seek the truth in word and deed? Therefore Christ, who trains the soul, reckons one rich, not by his gifts, but by his choice. It is said, therefore, that Zaccheus, or, according to some, Matthew, the chief of the publicans, on hearing that the Lord had deigned to come to him, said, "Lord, and if I have taken anything by false accusation, I restore him fourfold;" on which the Savior said, "The Son of man, on coming to-day, has found that which was lost."Again, on seeing the rich cast into the treasury according to their wealth, and the widow two mites, He said "that the widow had cast in more than they all," for "they had contributed of their abundance, but she of her destitution." And because He brought all things to bear on the discipline of the soul, He said, "Blessed are the meek: for they shall inherit the earth."And the meek are those who have quelled the battle of unbelief in the soul, the battle of wrath, and lust, and the other forms that are subject to them. And He praises those meek by choice, not by necessity. For there are with the Lord both rewards and "many mansions," corresponding to men's lives. "Whosoever shall receive," says He, "a prophet in the name of a prophet, shall receive a prophet's reward; and whosoever shall receive a righteous man in the name of a righteous man, shall receive a righteous man's reward; and whoso shall receive one of the least of these my disciples, shall not lose his reward." And again, the differences of virtue according to merit, and the noble rewards, He indicated by the hours unequal in number; and in addition, by the equal reward given to each of the laborers—that is, salvation, which is meant by the penny—He indicated the equality of justice; and the difference of those called He intimated, by those who worked for unequal portions of time. They shall work, therefore, in accordance with the appropriate mansions of which they have been deemed worthy as rewards, being fellow-workers in the ineffable administration and service."Those, then," says Plato, "who seem called to a holy life, are those who, freed and released from those earthly localities as from prisons, have reached the pure dwelling-place on high." In clearer terms again he expresses the same thing: "Those who by philosophy have been sufficiently purged from those things, live without bodies entirely for all time. Although they are enveloped in certain shapes; in the case of some, of air, and others, of fire." He adds further: "And they reach abodes fairer than those, which it is not easy, nor is there sufficient time now to describe." Whence with reason, "blessed are they that mourn: for they shall be comforted;"for they who have repented of their former evil life shall attain to "the calling" (κλῆσιν), for this is the meaning of being comforted (παρακληθῆναι). And there are two styles of penitents. That which is more common is fear on account of what is done; but the other which is more special, the shame which the spirit feels in itself arising from conscience. Whether then, here or elsewhere (for no place is devoid of the beneficence of God), He again says, "Blessed are the merciful: for they shall obtain mercy." And mercy is not, as

some of the philosophers have imagined, pain on account of others' calamities, but rather something good, as the prophets say. For it is said, "I will have mercy, and not sacrifice." And He means by the merciful, not only those who do acts of mercy, but those who wish to do them, though they be not able; who do as far as purpose is concerned. For sometimes we wish by the gift of money or by
personal effort to do mercy, as to assist one in want, or help one who is sick, or stand by one who is in any emergency; and are not able either from poverty, or disease, or old age (for this also is natural disease), to carry out our purpose, in reference to the things to which we are impelled, being unable to conduct them to the end we wished. Those, who have entertained the wish whose purpose is equal, share in the same honor with those who have the ability, although others have the advantage in point of resources. And since there are two paths of reaching the perfection of salvation, works and knowledge, He called the "pure in heart blessed, for they shall see God." And if we really look to the truth of the matter, knowledge is the purification of the leading faculty of the soul, and is a good activity. Some things accordingly are good in themselves, and others by participation in what is good, as we say good actions are good. But without things intermediate which hold the place of material, neither good nor bad actions are constituted, such I mean as life, and health, and other necessary things or circumstantials. Pure then as respects corporeal lusts, and pure in respect of holy thoughts, he means those are, who attain to the knowledge of God, when the chief faculty of the soul has nothing spurious to stand in the way of its power. When, therefore, he who partakes gnostically of this holy quality devotes himself to contemplation, communing in purity with the divine, he enters more nearly into the state of impassible identity, so as no longer to have science and possess knowledge, but to be science and knowledge.

"Blessed, then, are the peacemakers," who have subdued and tamed the law which wars against the disposition of the mind, the menaces of anger, and the baits of lust, and the other passions which war against the reason; who, having lived in the knowledge both of good works and true reason, shall be reinstated in adoption, which is dearer. It follows that the perfect peacemaking is that which keeps unchanged in all circumstances what is peaceful; calls Providence holy and good; and has its being in the knowledge of divine and human affairs, by which it deems the opposites that are in the world to be the fairest harmony of creation. They also are peacemakers, who teach those who war against the stratagems of sin to have recourse to faith and peace. And it is the sum of all virtue, in my opinion, when the Lord teaches us that for love to God we must gnostically despise death. "Blessed are they," says He, "who are persecuted for righteousness' sake, for they shall be called the sons of God;"or, as some of those who transpose the Gospels say, "Blessed are they who are persecuted by righteousness, for they shall be perfect." And, "Blessed are they who are persecuted for my sake; for they shall have a place where they shall not be persecuted." And, "Blessed are ye when men shall hate you, when they shall separate you, when they shall cast out your name as evil, for the Son of man's sake;" if we do not detest our persecutors, and undergo punishments at their hands, not hating them under the idea that we have been put to trial more tardily than we looked for; but knowing this also, that every instance of trial is an occasion for testifying.

CHAPTER VII.—THE BLESSEDNESS OF THE MARTYR.

Then he who has lied and shown himself unfaithful, and revolted to the devil's army, in what evil do we think him to be? He belies, therefore, the Lord, or rather he is cheated of his own hope who believes not God; and he believes not who does not what He has commanded.

And what? Does not he, who denies the Lord, deny himself? For does he not rob his Master of His authority, who deprives himself of his relation to Him? He, then, who denies the Savior, denies life; for "the light was life." He does not term those men of little faith, but faithless and hypocrites, who have the name inscribed on them, but deny that they are really believers. But the faithful is called both servant and friend. So that if one loves himself, he loves the Lord, and confesses to salvation that he may save his soul. Though you die for your neighbor out of love, and regard the Savior as our neighbor (for God who saves is said to be nigh in respect to what is saved); you do so, choosing death on account of life, and suffering for your own sake rather than his. And is it not for this that he is called brother? he who, suffering out of love to God, suffered for his own salvation; while he, on the other hand, who dies for his own salvation, endures for love to the Lord. For he being life, in what he suffered wished to suffer that we might live by his suffering.

"Why call ye me Lord, Lord," He says, "and do not the things which I say?" For "the people that loves with their lips, but have their heart far away from the Lord," is another people, and trust in another, and have willingly sold themselves to another; but those who perform the commandments of the Lord, in every action "testify," by doing what He wishes, and consistently naming the Lord's name; and "testifying" by deed to Him in whom they trust, that they are those "who have crucified the flesh, with the affections and lusts." "If we live in the Spirit, let us also walk in the Spirit." "He that sowed to his flesh, shall of the flesh reap corruption; but he that sowed to the Spirit, shall of the Spirit reap life everlasting."

But to those miserable men, witness to the Lord by blood seems a most violent death, not knowing that such a gate of death is the beginning of the true life; and they will understand neither the honors after death, which belong to those who have lived holily, nor the punishments of those who have lived unrighteously and impurely. I do not say only from our Scriptures (for almost all the commandments indicate them); but they will not even hear their own discourses. For the Pythagorean Theano writes, "Life were indeed a feast to the wicked, who, having done evil, then die; were not the soul immortal, death would be a godsend." And Plato in the *Phædo,* "For if death were release from everything," and so forth. We are not then to think according to the *Telephus* of Æschylus, "that a single path leads to Hades." The ways are many, and the sins that lead thither. Such deeply erring ones as the unfaithful are, Aristophanes properly makes the subjects of comedy. "Come," he says, "ye men of obscure life, ye that are like the race of leaves, feeble, wax figures, shadowy tribes, evanescent, fleeting, ephemeral." And Epicharmus, "This nature of men is inflated skins." And the Savior has said to us, "The spirit is willing, but the flesh is weak." "Because the carnal mind is enmity against God," explains the apostle: "for it is not subject to the law of God, neither indeed, can be. And they that are in the flesh cannot please God." And in further explanation continues, that no one may, like Marcion regard the creature as evil. "But if Christ be in you, the body is dead because of sin; but the Spirit is life because of righteousness." And again: "For if ye live after the flesh, ye shall die. For I reckon that the sufferings of this present time are not worthy to be compared to the glory which shall be revealed in us. If we suffer with Him, that we also may be glorified together as joint-heirs of Christ. And we know that all things work together for good to them that love God, to them that are called according to the purpose. For whom He did foreknow, He also did predestinate to be conformed to the image of His Son, that He might be the first-born among many brethren. And whom He did predestinate, them He also called; and whom He called, them He also justified; and whom He justified, them He also glorified."

You see that martyrdom for love's sake is taught. And should you wish to be a martyr for the recompense of advantages, you shall hear again. "For we are saved by hope: but hope that is seen is not hope: for what a man sees, why doth he yet hope for? But if we hope for that we see not, then do we with patience wait for it." "But if we also suffer for righteousness' sake," says Peter, "blessed are we. Be not afraid of their fear, neither be troubled. But sanctify the Lord God in your hearts: and be ready always to give an answer to him that asks a reason of the hope that is in you, but with meekness and fear, having a good conscience; so that in reference to that for which you are spoken against, they may be ashamed who calumniate your good conversation in Christ. For it is better to suffer for well-doing, if the will of God, than for evil-doing." But if one should captiously say, And how is it possible for feeble flesh to resist the energies and spirits of the Powers? well, let him know this, that, confiding in the Almighty and the Lord, we war against the principalities of darkness, and against death. "Whilst thou art yet speaking," He says, "Lo, here am I." See the invincible Helper who shields us. "Think it not strange, therefore, concerning the burning sent for your trial, as though some strange thing happened to you; But, as you are partaken in the sufferings of Christ, rejoice; that at the revelation of His glory ye may rejoice exultant. If ye be reproached in the name of Christ, happy are ye; for the Spirit of glory and of God rested on you." As it is written, "Because for Thy sake we are killed all the day long; we are accounted as sheep for the slaughter. Nay, in all these things we are more than conquerors, through Him that loved us."

> "What you wish to ascertain from my mind,
> You shall not ascertain, not were you to apply
> Horrid saws from the crown of my head to the soles of my feet,
> Not were you to load me with chains,"

says a woman acting manfully in the tragedy. And Antigone, contemning the proclamation of Creon, says boldly:—

> "It was not Zeus who uttered this proclamation."

But it is God that makes proclamation to us, and He must be believed. "For with the heart man believeth unto righteousness; and with the mouth confession is made unto salvation.

Wherefore the Scripture says, "Whosoever believeth on Him shall not be put to shame." Accordingly Simonides justly writes, "It is said that virtue dwells among all but inaccessible rocks, but that she speedily traverses a pure place. Nor is she visible to the eyes of all mortals. He who is not penetrated by heart-vexing sweat will not scale the summit of manliness." And Pindar says:—

"But the anxious thoughts of youths, revolving with toils,
Will find glory: and in time their deeds
Will in resplendent ether splendid shine."

Æschylus, too, having grasped this thought, says:—

> "To him who toils is due,
> As product of his toil, glory from the gods."

"For great Fates attain great destinies," according to Heraclitus:—

> "And what slave is there, who is careless of death?"

"For God hath not given us the spirit of bondage again to fear; but of power, and love, and of a sound mind. Be not therefore ashamed of the testimony of our Lord, or of me his prisoner," he writes to Timothy. Such shall he be "who cleaves to that which is good," according to the apostle, "who hates evil, having love unfeigned; for he that loves another fulfills the law." If, then, this God, to whom we bear witness, be as He is, the God of hope, we acknowledge our hope, speeding on to hope, "saturated with goodness, filled with all knowledge."

The Indian sages say to Alexander of Macedon: "You transport men's bodies from place to place. But you shall not force our souls to do what we do not wish. Fire is to men the greatest torture, this we despise." Hence Heraclitus preferred one thing, glory, to all else; and professes "that he allows the crowd to stuff themselves to satiety like cattle."

"For on account of the body are many toils,
For it we have invented a roofed house,
And discovered how to dig up silver, and sow the land,
And all the rest which we know by names."

To the multitude, then, this vain labor is desirable. But to us the apostle says, "Now we know this, that our old man is crucified with Him, that the body of sin might be destroyed, that henceforth we should not serve sin."Does not the apostle then plainly add the following, to show the contempt for faith in the case of the multitude? "For I think that God hath set forth us the apostles last, as appointed to death: we are made a spectacle to the world, and to angels, and to men. Up to this present hour we both hunger, and thirst, and are naked, and are beaten, and are feeble, and labor, working with our hands. Being reviled, we bless; being persecuted, we endure; being defamed, we entreat; we are become as it were the offscourings of the world." Such also are the words of Plato in the *Republic:* "The just man, though stretched on the rack, though his eyes are dug out, will be happy." The Gnostic will never then have the chief end placed in life, but in being always happy and blessed, and a kingly friend of God. Although visited with ignominy and exile, and confiscation, and above all, death, he will never be wrenched from his freedom, and signal love to God. "The charity which bears all things, endures all things," is assured that Divine Providence orders all things well. "I exhort you," therefore it is said, "Be followers of me." The first step to salvation is the instruction accompanied with fear, in consequence of which we abstain from what is wrong; and the second is hope, by reason of which we desire the best things; but love, as is fitting, perfects, by training now according to knowledge. For the Greeks, I know not how, attributing events to unreasoning necessity, own that they yield to them unwillingly. Accordingly Euripides says:—

> "What I declare, receive from me, madam:
> No mortal exists who has not toil;
> He buries children, and begets others,
> And he himself dies. And thus mortals are afflicted."

Then he adds:—

> "We must bear those things which are inevitable according to nature, and go through them:
> Not one of the things which are necessary is formidable for mortals."

And for those who are aiming at perfection there is proposed the rational gnosis, the foundation of which is "the sacred Triad." "Faith, hope, love; but the greatest of these is love." Truly, "all things are lawful, but all things are not expedient," says the apostle: "all things are lawful for me, but all things edify not."And, "Let no one seek his own advantage, but also that of his neighbor," so as to be able at once to do and to teach, building and building up. For that "the earth is the Lord's, and the fullness thereof," is admitted; but the conscience of the weak is supported. "Conscience, I say, not his own, but that of the other; for why is my liberty judged of by another conscience? For if I by grace am partaker, why am I evil spoken of for that for which I give thanks? Whether therefore ye eat, or drink, or whatsoever ye do, do all to the glory of God." "For though we walk in the flesh, we do not war after the flesh; for the weapons of our warfare are not carnal, but mighty through God to the demolition of fortifications, demolishing thoughts, and every high thing which exalted itself against the knowledge of Christ." Equipped with these weapons, the Gnostic says: O Lord, give opportunity, and receive demonstration; let this dread event pass; I contemn dangers for the love I bear to Thee.

> "Because alone of human things
> Virtue receives not a recompense from without,
> But has itself as the reward of its toils."

"Put on therefore, as the elect of God, holy and beloved, bowels of mercies, kindness, humbleness, meekness, long-suffering. And above all these, love, which is the bond of perfection. And let the peace of God reign in your hearts, to which also ye are called in one body; and be thankful," ye who, while still in the body, like the just men of old, enjoy impassibility and tranquility of soul.

CHAPTER VIII.—WOMEN AS WELL AS MEN, SLAVES AS WELL AS FREEMEN, CANDIDATES FOR THE MARTYR'S CROWN.

Since, then, not only the Æsopians, and Macedonians, and the Lacedæmonians endured when subjected to torture, as Eratosthenes says in his work, *On Things Good and Evil;* but also Zeno of Elea, when subjected to compulsion to divulge a secret, held out against the tortures, and confessed nothing; who, when expiring, bit out his tongue and spat it at the tyrant, whom some term Nearchus, and some Demulus. Theodotus the Pythagorean acted also similarly, and Paulus the friend of Lacydes, as Timotheus of Pergamus says in his work on *The Fortitude of Philosophers*, and Achaicus in *The Ethics*. Posthumus also, the Roman, when captured by Peucetion, did not divulge a single secret; but putting his hand on the fire, held it to it as if to a piece of brass, without moving a muscle of his face. I omit the case of Anaxarchus, who exclaimed, "Pound away at the sack which holds Anaxarchus, for it is not Anaxarchus you are pounding," when by the tyrant's orders he was being pounded with iron pestles. Neither, then, the hope of happiness nor the love of God takes what befalls ill, but remains free, although thrown among the wildest beasts or into the all-devouring fire; though racked with a tyrant's tortures. Depending as it does on the divine favor, it ascends aloft unenslaved, surrendering the body to those who can touch it alone. A barbarous nation, not cumbered with philosophy, select, it is said, annually an ambassador to the hero Zamolxis. Zamolxis was one of the disciples of Pythagoras. The one, then, who is judged of the most sterling worth is put to death, to the distress of those who have practiced philosophy, but have not been selected, at being reckoned unworthy of a happy service.

So the Church is full of those, as well chaste women as men, who all their life have contemplated the death which rouses up to Christ. For the individual whose life is framed as ours is, may philosophize without Learning, whether barbarian, whether Greek, whether slave—whether an old man, or a boy, or a woman. For self-control is common to all human beings who have made choice of it. And we admit that the same nature exists in every race, and the same virtue. As far as respects human nature, the woman does not possess one nature, and the man exhibit another, but the same: so also with virtue. If, consequently, a self-restraint and righteousness, and whatever qualities are regarded as following them, is the virtue of the male, it belongs to the male alone to be virtuous, and to the woman to be licentious and unjust. But it is offensive even to say this. Accordingly woman is to practice self-restraint and righteousness, and every other virtue, as well as man, both bond and free; since it is a fit consequence that the same nature possesses one and the same virtue. We do not say that woman's nature is the same as man's, as she is woman. For undoubtedly it stands to reason that some difference should exist between each of them, in virtue of which one is male and the other female. Pregnancy and parturition, accordingly, we say belong to woman, as she is woman, and not as she is a human being. But if there were no difference between man and woman, both would do and suffer the same things. As then there is sameness, as far as respects the soul, she will attain to the same virtue; but as there is difference as respects the peculiar construction of the body, she is destined for child-bearing and housekeeping. "For I would have you know," says the apostle, "that the head of every man is Christ; and the head of the woman is the man: for the man is not of the woman, but the woman of the man. For neither is the woman without the man, nor the man without the woman, in the Lord." For as we say that the man ought to be continent, and superior to pleasures; so also we reckon that the woman should be continent and practiced in fighting against pleasures. "But I say, Walk in the Spirit, and ye shall not fulfil the lusts of the flesh," counsels the apostolic command; "for the flesh lusted against the spirit, and the spirit against the flesh. These, then, are contrary" (not as good to evil, but as fighting advantageously), he adds therefore, so that ye cannot do the things that ye would. Now the works of the flesh are manifest, which are, fornication uncleanness, profligacy, idolatry, witchcrafts, enmities, strife, jealousies, wrath, contentions, dissensions, heresies, envying, drunkenness, reveling, and such like; of which I tell you before, as I have also said before, that they which do such things shall not inherit the kingdom of God. But the fruit of the Spirit is love, joy, peace, long-suffering, gentleness, temperance, goodness, faith, meekness." He calls sinners, as I think, "flesh," and the righteous "spirit." Further, manliness is to be assumed in order to produce confidence and forbearance, so as "to him that strikes on the one cheek, to give to him the other; and to him that takes away the cloak, to yield to him the coat also," strongly, restraining anger. For we do not train our women like Amazons to manliness in war; since we wish the men even to be peaceable. I hear that the Sarmatian women practice war no less than the men; and the women of the Sacæ besides, who shoot backwards, feigning flight as well as the men. I am aware, too, that the women near Iberia practice manly work and toil, not refraining from their tasks even though near their delivery; but even in the very struggle of her pains, the woman, on being delivered, taking up the infant, carries it home. Further, the females no less than the males manage the house, and hunt, and keep the flocks:—

> "Cressa the hound ran keenly in the stag's track."

Women are therefore to philosophize equally with men, though the males are preferable at everything, unless they have become effeminate. To the whole human race, then, discipline and virtue are a necessity, if they would pursue after happiness. And how recklessly Euripides writes sometimes this and sometimes that! On one occasion, "For every wife is inferior to her husband, though the most excellent one marry her that is of fair fame." And on another:—

> "For the chaste is her husband's slave,
> While she that is unchaste in her folly despises her consort.
> .... For nothing is better and more excellent,
> Than when as husband and wife ye keep house,
> Harmonious in your sentiments."

The ruling power is therefore the head. And if "the Lord is head of the man, and the man is head of the woman," the man, "being the image and glory of God, is lord of the woman." Wherefore also in the Epistle to the Ephesians it is written, "Subjecting yourselves one to another in the fear of God. Wives, submit yourselves to your own husbands, as to the Lord. For the husband is head of the wife, as also Christ is the head of the Church; and He is the Savior of the body. Husbands, love your wives, as also Christ loved the Church.
So also ought men to love their wives as their own bodies: he that loves his wife loves himself. For no man ever yet hated his own flesh."And in that to the Colossians it is said, "Wives, submit yourselves to your own husbands, as is fit in the Lord. Husbands, love your wives, and be not bitter against them. Children, obey your parents in all things; for this is well

pleasing to the Lord. Fathers, provoke not your children to anger, lest they be discouraged. Servants, be obedient in all things to those who are your masters according to the flesh; not with eye-service, as men-pleasers; but with singleness of heart, fearing the Lord. And whatsoever ye do, do it heartily, as serving the Lord and not men; knowing that of the Lord ye shall receive the reward of the inheritance: for ye serve the Lord Christ. For the wrongdoer shall receive the wrong, which he hath done; and there is no respect of persons. Masters, render to your servants justice and equity; knowing that ye also have a Master in heaven, where there is neither Greek nor Jew, circumcision and uncircumcision, barbarian, Scythian, bond, free: but Christ is all, and in all."And the earthly Church is the image of the heavenly, as we pray also "that the will of God may be done upon the earth as in heaven." "Putting on, therefore, bowels of mercy, gentleness, humbleness, meekness, long-suffering; forbearing one another, and forgiving one another, if one have a quarrel against any man; as also Christ hath forgiven us, so also let us. And above all these things put on charity, which is the bond of perfectness. And let the peace of God rule in your hearts, to which ye are called in one body; and be thankful." For there is no obstacle to adducing frequently the same Scripture in order to put Marcion to the blush, if perchance he be persuaded and converted; by learning that the faithful ought to be grateful to God the Creator, who hath called us, and who preached the Gospel in the body. From these considerations the unity of the faith is clear, and it is shown who is the perfect man; so that though some are reluctant, and offer as much resistance as they can, though menaced with punishments at the hand of husband or master, both the domestic and the wife will philosophize. Moreover, the free, though threatened with death at a tyrant's hands, and brought before the tribunals, and all his substances imperiled, will by no means abandon piety; nor will the wife who dwells with a wicked husband, or the son if he has a bad father, or the domestic if he has a bad master, ever fail in holding nobly to virtue. But as it is noble for a man to die for virtue, and for liberty, and for himself, so also is it for a woman. For this is not peculiar to the nature of males, but to the nature of the good. Accordingly, both the old man, the young, and the servant will live faithfully, and if need be die; which will be to be made alive by death. So we know that both children, and women, and servants have often, against their fathers', and masters', and husbands' will, reached the highest degree of excellence. Wherefore those who are determined to live piously ought none the less to exhibit alacrity, when some seem to exercise compulsion on them; but much more, I think, does it become them to show eagerness, and to strive with uncommon vigor, lest, being overcome, they abandon the best and most indispensable counsels. For it does not, I think, admit of comparison, whether it be better to be a follower of the Almighty than to choose the darkness of demons. For the things which are done by us on account of others we are to do always, endeavoring to have respect to those for whose sake it is proper that they be done, regarding the gratification rendered in their case, as what is to be our rule; but the things which are done for our own sake rather than that of others, are to be done with equal earnestness, whether they are like to please certain people or not. If some indifferent things have obtained such honor as to appear worthy of adoption, though against the will of some; much more is virtue to be regarded by us as worth contending for, looking the while to nothing but what can be rightly done, whether it seem good to others or not. Well then, Epicurus, writing to Menoeceus, says, "Let not him who is young delay philosophizing, and let not the old man grow weary of philosophizing; for no one is either not of age or past age for attending to the health of his soul. And he who says that the time for philosophizing is not come or is past, is like the man who says that the time for happiness is not come or has gone. So that young as well as old ought to philosophize: the one, in order that, while growing old, he may grow young in good things out of favor accruing from what is past; and the other, that he may be at once young and old, from want of fear for the future."

CHAPTER IX.—CHRIST'S SAYINGS RESPECTING MARTYRDOM.

On martyrdom the Lord hath spoken explicitly, and what is written in different places we bring together. "But I say unto you, Whosoever shall confess in Me before men, the Son of man also shall confess before the angels of God; but whosoever shall deny Me before men, him will I deny before the angels." "Whosoever shall be ashamed of Me or of My words in this adulterous and sinful generation, of him shall the Son of man also be ashamed when He cometh in the glory of His Father with His angels. Whosoever therefore shall confess in Me before men, him will I also confess before my Father in heaven. "And when they bring you before synagogues, and rulers, and powers, think not beforehand how ye shall make your defense, or what ye shall say. For the Holy Spirit shall teach you in the same hour what ye must say." In explanation of this passage, Heracleon, the most distinguished of the school of Valentinians, says expressly, "that there is a confession by faith and conduct, and one with the voice. The confession that is made with the voice, and before the authorities, is what the most reckon the only confession. Not soundly: and hypocrites also can confess with this confession. But neither will this utterance be found to be spoken universally; for all the saved have confessed with the confession made by the voice, and departed. Of whom are Matthew, Philip, Thomas, Levi, and many others. And confession by the lip is not universal, but partial. But that which He specifies now is universal, that which is by deeds and actions corresponding to faith in Him. This confession is followed by that which is partial, that before the authorities, if necessary, and reason dictate. For he will confess rightly with his voice who has first confessed by his disposition. And he has well used, with regard to those who confess, the expression 'in Me,' and applied to those who deny the expression 'Me.' For those, though they confess Him with the voice, yet deny Him, not confessing Him in their conduct. But those alone confess 'in Him,' who live in the confession and conduct according to Him, in which He also confesses, who is contained in them and held by them. Wherefore 'He never can deny Himself.' And those deny Him who are not in Him. For He said not, 'Whosoever shall deny' in Me, but 'Me.' For no one who is in Him will ever deny Him. And the expression 'before men' applies both to the saved and the heathen similarly by conduct before the one, and by voice before the other. Wherefore they never can deny Him. But those deny Him who are not in Him." So far Heracleon. And in other things he seems to be of the same sentiments with us in this section; but he has not adverted to this, that if some have not by conduct and in their life "confessed Christ before men," they are manifested to have believed with the heart; by confessing Him with the mouth at the tribunals, and not denying Him when tortured to the death. And the disposition being confessed, and especially not being changed by death at any time, cuts away all passions which were engendered by corporeal desire. For there is, so to speak, at the close of life a sudden repentance in action, and a true confession toward Christ, in the testimony of the voice. But if the Spirit of the Father testifies in us, how can we be any more hypocrites, who are said to bear testimony with the voice alone? But it will be given to some, if expedient, to make a defense, that by their witness and confession all may be benefited—those in the Church being confirmed, and those of the heathen who have devoted themselves to the search after salvation wondering and being led to the faith; and the rest seized with amazement. So that confession is by all means necessary. For it is in our power. But to make a defense for our faith is not universally necessary. For that does not depend on us. "But he that endures to the end shall be saved." For who of those who are wise would not choose to reign in God, and even to serve? So some "confess that they know God," according to the apostle; "but in works they deny Him, being abominable and disobedient, and to every good work reprobate." And these, though they confess nothing but this, will have done at the end one good work. Their witness, then, appears to be the cleansing away of sins with glory. For instance, the Shepherd says: "You will escape the energy of the wild beast, if your heart become pure and blameless." Also the Lord Himself says: "Satan hath desired to sift you; but I have prayed."Alone, therefore, the Lord, for the purification of the men who plotted against Him and disbelieved Him, "drank the cup;" in imitation of whom the apostles, that they might be in reality Gnostics, and perfect, suffered for the Churches which they founded. So, then, also the Gnostics who tread in the footsteps of the apostles ought to be sinless, and, out of love to the Lord, to love also their brother; so that, if occasion call, enduring without stumbling, afflictions for the Church, "they may drink the cup." Those who witness in their life by deed, and at the tribunal by word, whether entertaining hope or surmising fear, are better than those who confess salvation by their mouth alone. But if one ascend also to love, he is a really blessed and true martyr, having confessed perfectly both to the commandments and to God, by the Lord; whom having loved, he acknowledged a brother, giving himself up wholly for God, resigning pleasantly and lovingly the man when asked, like a deposit.

CHAPTER X.—THOSE WHO OFFERED THEMSELVES FOR MARTYRDOM REPROVED.

When, again, He says, "When they persecute you in this city, flee ye to the other," He does not advise flight, as if persecution were an evil thing; nor does He enjoin them by flight to avoid death, as if in dread of it, but wishes us neither to be the authors nor abettors of any evil to any one, either to ourselves or the persecutor and murderer. For He, in a way, bids us take care of ourselves. But he who disobeys is rash and foolhardy. If he who kills a man of God sins against God, he also who presents himself before the judgment-seat becomes guilty of his death. And such is also the case with him who does not avoid persecution, but out of daring presents himself for capture. Such a one, as far as in him lies, becomes an accomplice in the crime of the persecutor. And if he also uses provocation, he is wholly guilty, challenging the wild beast. And similarly, if he afford any cause for conflict or punishment, or retribution or enmity, he gives occasion for persecution. Wherefore, then, we are enjoined not to cling to anything that belongs to this life; but "to him that takes our cloak to give our coat," not only that we may continue destitute of inordinate affection, but that we may not by retaliating make our persecutors savage against ourselves, and stir them up to blaspheme the name.

CHAPTER XI.—THE OBJECTION, WHY DO YOU SUFFER IF GOD CARES FOR YOU, ANSWERED.

But, say they, if God cares for you, why are you persecuted and put to death? Has He delivered you to this? No, we do not suppose that the Lord wishes us to be involved in calamities, but that He foretold prophetically what would happen—that we should be persecuted for His name's sake, slaughtered, and impaled. So that it was not that He wished us to be persecuted, but He intimated beforehand what we shall suffer by the prediction of what would take place, training us to endurance, to which He promised the inheritance, although we are punished not alone, but along with many. But those, it is said, being malefactors, are righteously punished. Accordingly, they unwillingly bear testimony to our righteousness, we being unjustly punished for righteousness' sake. But the injustice of the judge does not affect the providence of God. For the judge must be master of his own opinion—not pulled by strings, like inanimate machines, set in motion only by external causes. Accordingly he is judged in respect to his judgment, as we also, in accordance with our choice of things desirable, and our endurance. Although we do not wrong, yet the judge looks on us as doing wrong, for he neither knows nor wishes to know about us, but is influenced by unwarranted prejudice;

wherefore also he is judged. Accordingly they persecute us, not from the supposition that we are wrong-doers, but imagining that by the very fact of our being Christians we sin against life in so conducting ourselves, and exhorting others to adopt the like life.

But why are you not helped when persecuted? say they. What wrong is done us, as far as we are concerned, in being released by death to go to the Lord, and so undergoing a change of life, as if a change from one time of life to another? Did we think rightly, we should feel obliged to those who have afforded the means for speedy departure, if it is for love that we bear witness; and if not, we should appear to the multitude to be base men. Had they also known the truth, all would have bounded on to the way, and there would have been no choice. But our faith, being the light of the world, reproves unbelief. "Should Anytus and Melitus kill me, they will not hurt me in the least; for I do not think it right for the better to be hurt by the worse," [says Socrates]. So that each one of us may with confidence say, "The Lord is my helper; I will not fear: what shall man do to me?" "For the souls of the righteous are in the hand of the Lord, and no plague shall touch them."

CHAPTER XII.—BASILIDES' IDEA OF MARTYRDOM REFUTED.

Basilides, in the twenty-third book of the *Exegetics*, respecting those that are punished by martyrdom, expresses himself in the following language: "For I say this, Whosoever fall under the afflictions mentioned, in consequence of unconsciously transgressing in other matters, are brought to this good end by the kindness of Him who brings them, but accused on other grounds; so that they may not suffer as condemned for what are owned to be iniquities, nor reproached as the adulterer or the murderer, but because they are Christians; which will console them, so that they do not appear to suffer. And if one who has not sinned at all incur suffering— a rare case—yet even he will not suffer aught through the machinations of power, but will suffer as the child which seems not to have sinned would suffer." Then further on he adds: "As, then, the child which has not sinned before, or committed actual sin in itself, but has that which committed sin, when subjected to suffering, gets good, reaping the advantage of many difficulties; so also, although a perfect man may not have sinned in act, while he endures afflictions, he suffers similarly with the child. Having within him the sinful principle, but not embracing the opportunity of committing sin, he does not sin; so that he is not to be reckoned as not having sinned. For as he who wishes to commit adultery is an adulterer, although he does not succeed in committing adultery; and he that wishes to commit murder is a murderer, although he is unable to kill; so also, if I see the man without sin, whom I specify, suffering, though he have done nothing bad, I should call him bad, on account of his wishing to sin. For I will affirm anything rather than call Providence evil." Then, in continuation, he says expressly concerning the Lord, as concerning man: "If then, passing from all these observations, you were to proceed to put me to shame by saying, perchance impersonating certain parties, This man has then sinned; for this man has suffered;—if you permit, I will say, He has not sinned; but was like a child suffering. If you were to insist more urgently, I would say, That the man you name is man, but that God is righteous: "For no one is pure," as one said, 'from pollution.'" But the hypothesis of Basilides says that the soul, having sinned before in another life, endures punishment in this—the elect soul with honor by martyrdom, the other purged by appropriate punishment.

How can this be true, when the confessing and suffering punishment or not depends on ourselves? For in the case of the man who shall deny, Providence, as held by Basilides, is done away with. I will ask him, then, in the case of a confessor who has been arrested, whether he will confess and be punished in virtue of Providence or not? For in the case of denying he will not be punished. But if, for the sake of escaping and evading the necessity of punishing such a one, he shall say that the destruction of those who shall deny is of Providence, he will be a martyr against his will. And how any more is it the case, that there is laid up in heaven the very glorious recompense to him who has witnessed, for his witnessing? If Providence did not permit the sinner to get the length of sinning, it is unjust in both cases; both in not rescuing the man who is dragged to punishment for righteousness' sake, and in having rescued him who wished to do wrong, he having done it as far as volition was concerned, but [Providence] having prevented the deed, and unjustly favored the sinner. And how impious, in deifying the devil, and in daring to call the Lord a sinful man! For the devil tempting us, knowing what we are, but not knowing if we will hold out, but wishing to dislodge us from the faith, attempts also to bring us into subjection to himself. Which is all that is allowed to him, partly from the necessity of saving us, who have taken occasion from the commandment, from ourselves; partly for the confusion of him who has tempted and failed; for the confirmation of the members of the Church, and the conscience of those who admire the constancy [displayed]. But if martyrdom be retribution by way of punishment, then also faith and doctrine, on account of which martyrdom comes, are co-operators in punishment—than which, what other absurdity could be greater? But with reference to these dogmas, whether the soul is changed to another body, also of the devil, at the proper time mention will be made. But at present, to what has been already said, let us add the following: Where any more is faith in the retribution of sins committed before martyrdom takes place? And where is love to God, which is persecuted and endures for the truth? And where is the praise of him who has confessed, or the censure of him who has denied? And for what use is right conduct, the mortification of the lusts, and the hating of no creature? But if, as Basilides himself says, we suppose one part of the declared will of God to be the loving of all things because all things bear a relation to the whole, and another "not to lust after anything," and a third "not to hate anything," by the will of God these also will be punishments, which it were impious to think. For neither did the Lord suffer by the will of the Father, nor are those who are persecuted persecuted by the will of God; since either of two things is the case: either persecution in consequence of the will of God is a good thing, or those who decree and afflict are guiltless. But nothing is without the will of the Lord of the universe. It remains to say that such things happen without the prevention of God; for this alone saves both the providence and the goodness of God. We must not therefore think that He actively produces afflictions (far be it that we should think this!); but we must be persuaded that He does not prevent those that cause them, but overrules for good the crimes of His enemies: "I will therefore," He says, "destroy the wall, and it shall be for treading under foot." Providence being a disciplinary art; in the case of others for each individual's sins, and in the case of the Lord and His apostles for ours. To this point says the divine apostle: "For this is the will of God, even your sanctification, that ye abstain from fornication: that each one of you should know how to possess his vessel in sanctification and honor; not in the lust of concupiscence, as the Gentiles who know not the Lord: that none of you should overreach or take advantage of his brother in any matter; because the Lord is the avenger in respect of all such, as we also told you before, and testified. For God hath not called us unto uncleanness, but to holiness. Wherefore he that despises, despises not man, but God, who hath also given His Holy Spirit to you." Wherefore the Lord was not prohibited from this sanctification of ours. If, then, one of them were to say, in reply, that the martyr is punished for sins committed before this embodying, and that he will again reap the fruit of his conduct in this life, for that such are the arrangements of the [divine administration], we shall ask him if the retribution takes place by Providence. For if it be not of the divine administration, the economy of expiations is gone, and their hypothesis falls to the ground; but if expiations are by Providence, punishments are by Providence too. But Providence, although it begins, so to speak, to move with the Ruler, yet is implanted in substances along with their origin by the God of the universe. Such being the case, they must confess either that punishment is not just, and those who condemn and persecute the martyrs do right, or that persecutions even are wrought by the will of God. Labor and fear are not, then, as they say, incident to affairs as rust to iron, but come upon the soul through its own will. And on these points there is much to say, which will be reserved for future consideration, taking them up in due course.

CHAPTER XIII.—VALENTINIAN'S VAGARIES ABOUT THE ABOLITION OF DEATH REFUTED.

Valentinian, in a homily, writes in these words: "Ye are originally immortal, and children of eternal life, and ye would have death distributed to you, that ye may spend and lavish it, and that death may die in you and by you; for when we dissolve the world, and are not yourselves dissolved, ye have dominion over creation and all corruption." For he also, similarly with Basilides, supposes a class saved by nature, and that this different race has come hither to us from above for the abolition of death, and that the origin of death is the work of the Creator of the world. Wherefore also he so expounds that Scripture, "No man shall see the face of God, and live," as if He were the cause of death. Respecting this God, he makes those allusions when writing in these expressions: "As much as the image is inferior to the living face, so much is the world inferior to the living Æon. What is, then, the cause of the image? The majesty of the face, which exhibits the figure to the painter, to be honored by his name; for the form is not found exactly to the life, but the name supplies what is wanting in the effigy. The invisibility of God co-operates also in order to the faith of that which has been fashioned." For the Creator, called God and Father, he designated as "Painter," and "Wisdom," whose image that which is formed is, to the glory of the invisible One; since the things which proceed from a pair are complements, and those which proceed from one are images. But since what is seen is no part of Him, the soul comes from what is intermediate, which is different; and this is the inspiration of the different spirit, and generally what is breathed into the soul, which is the image of the spirit. And in general, what is said of the Creator, who was made according to the image, they say was foretold by a sensible image in the book of Genesis respecting the origin of man; and the likeness they transfer to themselves, teaching that the addition of the different spirit was made; unknown to the Creator. When, then, we treat of the unity of the God who is proclaimed in the law, the prophets, and the Gospel, we shall also discuss this; for the topic is supreme. But we must advance to that which is urgent. If for the purpose of doing away with death the peculiar race has come, it is not Christ who has abolished death, unless He also is said to be of the same essence with them. And if He abolished it to this end, that it might not touch the peculiar race, it is not these, the rivals of the Creator, who breathe into the image of their intermediate spirit the life from above—in accordance with the principle of their dogma—that abolish death. But should they say that this takes place by His mother, or should they say that they, along with Christ, war against death, let them own their secret dogma that they have the hardihood to assail the divine power of the Creator, by setting to rights His creation, as if they were superior, endeavoring to save the vital image which He was not able to rescue from corruption. Then the Lord would be superior to God the Creator; for the son would never contend with the father, especially among the gods. But the point that the Creator of all things, the omnipotent Lord, is the Father of the Son, we have deferred till the discussion of these points, in which we have undertaken to dispute against the heresies, showing that He alone is the God proclaimed by Him.

But the apostle, writing to us with reference to the endurance of afflictions, says, "And this is of God, that it is given to you on behalf of Christ, not only to believe on Him, but also to suffer for His sake; having the same conflict which ye saw in me, and now hear to be in me. If there is therefore any consolation in Christ, if any comfort of love, if any communion of spirit, if any bowels and mercies, fulfil ye my joy, that ye may be of the same mind, having the same love, unanimous, thinking one thing. And if he is offered on the sacrifice and service of faith, joying and rejoicing" with the Philippians, to whom the apostle speaks, calling them "fellow-partakers of joy," how does he say that they are of one soul, and having a soul? Likewise, also, writing respecting Timothy and himself, he says, "For I have no one like-souled, who will nobly care for your state. For all seek their own, not the things which are Jesus Christ's."

Let not the above-mentioned people, then, call us, by way of reproach, "natural men" (ψυκικοί), nor the Phrygians either; for these now call those who do not apply themselves to the new prophecy "natural men" (ψυκικοί), with whom we shall discuss in our remarks on "Prophecy." The perfect man ought therefore to practice love, and thence to haste to the divine friendship, fulfilling the commandments from love. And loving one's enemies does not mean loving wickedness, or impiety, or adultery, or theft; but the thief, the impious, the adulterer, not as far as he sins, and in respect of the actions by which he stains the name of man, but as he is a man, and the work of God. Assuredly sin is an activity, not an existence: and therefore it is not a work of God. Now sinners are called enemies of God—enemies, that is, of the commands which they do not obey, as those who obey become friends, the one named so from their fellowship, the others from their estrangement, which is the result of free choice; for there is neither enmity nor sin without the enemy and the sinner. And the command "to covet nothing," not as if the things to be desired did not belong to us, does not teach us not to entertain desire, as those suppose who teach that the Creator is different from the first God, not as if creation was loathsome and bad (for such opinions are impious). But we say that the things of the world are *not our own*, not as if they were monstrous, not as if they did not belong to God, the Lord of the universe, but because we do not continue among them forever; being, in respect of possession, not ours, and passing from one to another in succession; but belonging to us, for whom they were made in respect of use, so long as it is necessary to continue with them. In accordance, therefore, with natural appetite, things disallowed are to be used rightly, avoiding all excess and inordinate affection.

CHAPTER XIV.—THE LOVE OF ALL, EVEN OF OUR ENEMIES.

How great also is benignity! "Love your enemies," it is said, "bless them who curse you, and pray for them who despitefully use you," and the like; to which it is added, "that ye may be the children of your Father who is in heaven," in allusion to resemblance to God. Again, it is said, "Agree with thine adversary quickly, whilst thou art in the way with him." The adversary is not the body, as some would have it, but the devil, and those assimilated to him, who walks along with us in the person of men, who emulate his deeds in this earthly life. It is inevitable, then, that those who confess themselves to belong to Christ, but find themselves in the midst of the devil's works, suffer the most hostile treatment. For it is written, "Lest he deliver thee to the judge, and the judge deliver thee to the officers of Satan's kingdom." "For I am persuaded that neither death," through the assault of persecutors, "nor life" in this world, "nor angels," the apostate ones, "nor powers" (and Satan's power is the life which he chose, for such are the powers and principalities of darkness belonging to him), "nor things present," amid which we exist during the time of life, as the hope entertained by the soldier, and the merchant's gain, "nor height, nor depth, nor any other creature," in consequence of the energy proper to a man,—opposes the faith of him who acts according to free choice. "Creature" is synonymous with activity, being our work, and such activity "shall not be able to separate us from the love of God, which is in Christ Jesus our Lord." You have got a compendious account of the gnostic martyr.

CHAPTER XV.—ON AVOIDING OFFENCE.

"We know that we all have knowledge"—common knowledge in common things, and the knowledge that there is one God. For he was writing to believers; whence he adds, "But knowledge (*gnosis*) is not in all," being communicated to few. And there are those who say that the knowledge about things sacrificed to idols is not promulgated among all, "lest our liberty prove a stumbling-block to the weak. For by thy knowledge he that is weak is destroyed." Should they say, "Whatsoever is sold in the shambles, ought that to be bought?" adding, by way of interrogation, "asking no questions," as if equivalent to "asking questions," they give a ridiculous interpretation. For the apostle says, "All other things buy out of the shambles, asking no questions," with the exception of the things mentioned in the Catholic epistle of all the apostles, "with the consent of the Holy Ghost," which is written in the Acts of the Apostles, and conveyed to the faithful by the hands of Paul himself. For they intimated "that they must of necessity abstain from things offered to idols, and from blood, and from things strangled, and from fornication, from which keeping themselves, they should do well." It is a different matter, then, which is expressed by the apostle: "Have we not power to eat and to drink? Have we not power to lead about a sister, a wife, as the rest of the apostles, as the brethren of the Lord and Cephas? But we have not used this power," he says, "but bear all things, lest we should occasion hindrance to the Gospel of Christ;" namely, by bearing about burdens, when it was necessary to be untrammeled for all things; or to become an example to those who wish to exercise temperance, not encouraging each other to eat greedily of what is set before us, and not to consort inconsiderately with woman. And especially is it incumbent on those entrusted with such a dispensation to exhibit to disciples a pure example. "For though I be free from all men, I have made myself servant to all," it is said, "that I might gain all. And every one that strives for mastery is temperate in all things." "But the earth is the Lord's, and the fullness thereof." For conscience' sake, then, we are to abstain from what we ought to abstain. "Conscience, I say, not his own," for it is endued with knowledge, "but that of the other," lest he be trained badly, and by imitating in ignorance what he knows not, he become a despiser instead of a strong-minded man. "For why is my liberty judged of by another conscience? For if I by grace am a partaker, why am I evil spoken of for that for which I give thanks? Whatever ye do, do all to the glory of God"—what you are commanded to do by the rule of faith.

CHAPTER XVI.—PASSAGES OF SCRIPTURE RESPECTING THE CONSTANCY, PATIENCE, AND LOVE OF THE MARTYRS.

"With the heart man believeth unto righteousness, and with the mouth confession is made unto salvation. Wherefore the Scripture says, Whosoever believeth on Him shall not be ashamed; that is, the word of faith which we preach: for if thou confess the word with thy mouth that Jesus is Lord, and believe in thy heart that God hath raised Him from the dead, thou shalt be saved." There is clearly described the perfect righteousness, fulfilled both in practice and contemplation. Wherefore we are "to bless those who persecute us. Bless, and curse not." "For our rejoicing is this, the testimony of a good conscience, that in holiness and sincerity we know God" by this inconsiderable instance exhibiting the work of love, that "not in fleshly wisdom, but by the grace of God, we have had our conversation in the world." So far the apostle respecting knowledge; and in the second Epistle to the Corinthians he calls the common "teaching of faith" the savor of knowledge. "For unto this day the same veil remains on many in the reading of the Old Testament," not being uncovered by turning to the Lord. Wherefore also to those capable of perceiving he showed resurrection, that of the life still in the flesh, creeping on its belly. Whence also he applied the name "brood of vipers" to the voluptuous, who serve the belly and the pudenda, and cut off one another's heads for the sake of worldly pleasures. "Little children, let us not love in word, or in tongue," says John, teaching them to be perfect, "but in deed and in truth; hereby shall we know that we are of the truth." And if "God be love," piety also is love: "there is no fear in love; but perfect love casted out fear." "This is the love of God, that we keep His commandments." And again, to him who desires to become a Gnostic, it is written, "But be thou an example of the believers, in word, in conversation, in love, in faith, in purity." For perfection in faith differs, I think, from ordinary faith. And the divine apostle furnishes the rule for the Gnostic in these words, writing as follows: "For I have learned, in whatsoever state I am, to be content. I know both how to be abased, and I know how to abound. Everywhere and in all things I am instructed both to be full and to be hungry, both to abound and to lack. I can do all things through Him who strengthened me." And also when discussing with others in order to put them, to shame, he does not shrink from saying, "But call to mind the former days, in which, after ye were illuminated, ye endured a great fight of afflictions; partly, whilst ye were made a gazing-stock, both by reproaches and afflictions; and partly, whilst ye became companions of them that were so used. For ye had compassion of me in my bonds, and took with joy the spoiling of your goods, knowing that you have a better and enduring substance. Cast not away therefore your confidence, which hath great recompense of reward. For ye have need of patience, that, after doing the will of God, ye may obtain the promise. For yet a little while, and He that cometh will come, and will not tarry. Now the just shall live by faith: and if any man draw back, my soul shall have no pleasure in him. But we are not of them that draw back unto perdition, but of them that believe to the saving of the soul." He then brings forward a swarm of divine examples. For was it not "by faith," he says, this endurance, that they acted nobly who "had trial of mockeries and scourgings, and, moreover, of bonds and imprisonments? They were stoned, they were tempted, were slain with the sword. They wandered about in sheep-skins and goat-skins, being destitute, afflicted, tormented, of whom the world was not worthy. They wandered in deserts, in mountains, in dens, and caves of the earth. And all having received a good report, through faith, received not the promise of God" (what is expressed by a parasiopesis is left to be understood, viz., "alone"). He adds accordingly, "God having provided some better thing for us (for He was good), that they should not without us be made perfect. Wherefore also, having encompassing us such a cloud," holy and transparent, "of witnesses, laying aside every weight, and the sin which doth so easily beset us, let us run with patience the race set before us, looking unto Jesus, the author and finisher of our faith." Since, then, he specifies one salvation in Christ of the righteous, and of us he has expressed the former unambiguously, and saying nothing less respecting Moses, adds, "Esteeming the reproach of Christ greater riches than the treasures of Egypt: for he had respect to the recompense of the reward. By faith he forsook Egypt, not fearing the wrath of the king: for he endured as seeing Him who is invisible." The divine Wisdom says of the martyrs, "They seemed in the eyes of the foolish to die, and their departure was reckoned a calamity, and their migration from us an affliction. But they are in peace. For though in the sight of men they were punished, their hope was full of immortality." He then adds, teaching martyrdom to be a glorious purification, "And being chastened a little, they shall be benefited much; because God proved them," that is, suffered them to be tried, to put them to the proof, and to put to shame the author of their trial, "and found them worthy of Himself," plainly to be called sons. "As gold in the furnace He proved them, and as a whole burned-offering of sacrifice He accepted them. And in the time of their visitation they will shine forth, even as sparks run along the stubble. They shall judge the nations, and rule over the peoples, and the Lord shall reign over them forever."

CHAPTER XVII.—PASSAGES FROM CLEMENT'S EPISTLE TO THE CORINTHIANS ON MARTYRDOM.

Moreover, in the Epistle to the Corinthians, the Apostle Clement also, drawing a picture of the Gnostic, says: "For who that has sojourned among you has not proved your perfect and firm faith? and has not admired your sound and gentle piety? and has not celebrated the munificent style of your hospitality? and has not felicitated your complete and sure knowledge? For ye did all things impartially, and walked in the ordinances of God;" and so forth.

Then more clearly: "Let us fix our eyes on those who have yielded perfect service to His magnificent glory. Let us take Enoch, who, being by his obedience found righteous, was translated; and Noah, who, having believed, was saved; and Abraham, who for his faith and hospitality was called the friend of God, and was the father of Isaac." "For hospitality and piety, Lot was saved from Sodom." "For faith and hospitality, Rahab the harlot was saved." "From patience and faith they walked about in goat-skins, and sheep-skins, and folds of camels' hair, proclaiming the kingdom of Christ. We name His prophets Elias, and Eliseus, and Ezekiel, and John."

"For Abraham, who for his free faith was called 'the friend of God,' was not elated by glory, but modestly said, 'I am dust and ashes.' And of Job it is thus written: 'Job was just and blameless, true and pious, abstaining from all evil.'"He it was who overcame the tempter by patience, and at once testified and was testified to by God; who keeps hold of humility, and says, "No one is pure from defilement, not even if his life were but for one day." "Moses, 'the servant who was faithful in all his house,' said to Him who uttered the oracles from the bush, 'Who am I, that Thou sends me? I am slow of speech, and of a stammering tongue,' to minister the voice of God in human speech. And again: 'I am smoke from a pot.'" "For God resisted the proud, but giveth grace to the humble."

"David too, of whom the Lord, testifying, says, 'I found a man after my own heart, David the son of Jesse. With my holy oil I anointed him.' But he also says to God, 'Pity me, O God, according to Thy mercy; and according to the multitude of Thy tender mercies, blot out my transgression. Wash me thoroughly from mine iniquity, and cleanse me from my sin. For I know my transgression, and my sin is ever before me.'" Then, alluding to sin which is not subject to the law, in the exercise of the moderation of true knowledge, he adds, "Against Thee only have I sinned, and done evil in Thy sight." For the Scripture somewhere says, "The Spirit of the Lord is a lamp, searching the recesses of the belly." And the more of a Gnostic a man becomes by doing right, the nearer is the illuminating Spirit to him. "Thus the Lord draws near to the righteous, and none of the thoughts and reasoning of which we are the authors escape Him—I mean the Lord Jesus," the scrutinizer by His omnipotent will of our heart, "whose blood was consecrated for us. Let us therefore respect those who are over us, and reverence the elders; let us honor the young, and let us teach the discipline of God." For blessed is he who shall do and teach the Lord's commands worthily; and he is of a magnanimous mind, and of a mind contemplative of truth. "Let us direct our wives to what is good; let them exhibit," says he, "the lovable disposition of chastity; let them show the guileless will of their meekness; let them manifest the gentleness of their tongue by silence; let them give their love not according to their inclinations, but equal love in sanctity to all that fear God. Let our children share in the discipline that is in Christ; let them learn what humility avails before God; what is the power of holy love before God, how lovely and great is the fear of the Lord, saving all that walk in it holily; with a pure heart: for He is the Searcher of the thoughts and sentiments, whose breath is in us, and when He wills He will take it away."

"Now all those things are confirmed by the faith that is in Christ. 'Come, ye children,' says the Lord, 'hearken to me, and I will teach you the fear of the Lord. Who is the man that desires life, that loves to see good days? ' Then He subjoins the gnostic mystery of the numbers seven and eight.'Stop thy tongue from evil, and thy lips from speaking guile. Depart from evil, and do good. Seek peace, and pursue it.' For in these words He alludes to knowledge (*gnosis*), with abstinence from evil and the doing of what is good, teaching that it is to be perfected by word and deed. 'The eyes of the Lord are on the righteous, and His ears are to their prayer. But the face of God is against those that do evil, to root out their memory from the earth. The righteous cried, and the Lord heard, and delivered him out of all his distresses.' 'Many are the stripes of sinners; but those who hope in the Lord, mercy shall compass about.'" "A multitude of mercy," he nobly says, "surrounds him that trusts in the Lord."

For it is written in the Epistle to the Corinthians, "Through Jesus Christ our foolish and darkened mind springs up to the light. By Him the Sovereign Lord wished us to taste the knowledge that is immortal." And, showing more expressly the peculiar nature of knowledge, he added: "These things, then, being clear to us, looking into the depths of divine knowledge, we ought to do all things in order which the Sovereign Lord commanded us to perform at the appointed seasons. Let the wise man, then, show his wisdom not in words only, but in good deeds. Let the humble not testify to himself, but allow testimony to be borne to him by another. Let not him who is pure in the flesh boast, knowing that it is another who furnishes him with continence. Ye see, brethren, that the more we are subjected to peril, the more knowledge are we counted worthy of."

CHAPTER XVIII.—ON LOVE, AND THE REPRESSING OF OUR DESIRES.

"The decorous tendency of our philanthropy, therefore," according to Clement, "seeks the common good;" whether by suffering martyrdom, or by teaching by deed and word,—the latter being twofold, unwritten and written. This is love, to love God and our neighbor. "This conducts to the height which is unutterable. 'Love covers a multitude of sins. Love bears all things, suffers all things.' Love joins us to God, does all things in concord. In love, all the chosen of God were perfected. Apart from love, nothing is well pleasing to God." "Of its perfection there is no unfolding," it is said. "Who is fit to be found in it, except those whom God counts worthy?" To the point the Apostle Paul speaks, "If I give my body, and have not love, I am sounding brass, and a tinkling cymbal." If it is not from a disposition determined by gnostic love that I shall testify, he means; but if through fear and expected reward, moving my lips in order to testify to the Lord that I shall confess the Lord, I am a common man, sounding the Lord's name, not knowing Him. "For there is the people that loves with the lips; and there is another which gives the body to be burned." "And if I give all my goods in alms," he says, not according to the principle of loving communication, but on account of recompense, either from him who has received the benefit, or the Lord who has promised; "and if I have all faith so as to remove mountains," and cast away obscuring passions, and be not faithful to the Lord from love, "I am nothing," as in comparison of him who testifies as a Gnostic, and the crowd, and being reckoned nothing better.

"Now all the generations from Adam to this day are gone. But they who have been perfected in love, through the grace of God, hold the place of the godly, who shall be manifested at the visitation of the kingdom of Christ." Love permits not to sin; but if it fall into any such case, by reason of the interference of the adversary, in imitation of David, it will sing: "I will confess unto the Lord, and it will please Him above a young bullock that has horns and hoofs. Let the poor see it, and be glad." For he says, "Sacrifice to God a sacrifice of praise, and pay to the Lord thy vows; and call upon me in the day of trouble, and I will deliver thee, and thou shalt glorify me.""For the sacrifice of God is a broken spirit."

"God," then, being good, "is love," it is said. Whose "love worked no ill to his neighbor," neither injuring nor revenging ever, but, in a word, doing good to all according to the image of God. "Love is," then, "the fulfilling of the law;"

like as Christ, that is the presence of the Lord who loves us; and our loving teaching of, and discipline according to Christ. By love, then, the commands not to commit adultery, and not to covet one's neighbor's wife, are fulfilled, [these sins being] formerly prohibited by fear.

The same work, then, presents a difference, according as it is done by fear, or accomplished by love, and is wrought by faith or by knowledge. Rightly, therefore, their rewards are different. To the Gnostic "are prepared what eye hath not seen, nor ear heard, nor hath entered into the heart of man;" but to him who has exercised simple faith He testifies a hundredfold in return for what he has left,—a promise which has turned out to fall within human comprehension.

Come to this point, I recollect one who called himself a Gnostic. For, expounding the words, "But I say unto you, he that looked on a woman to lust after, hath committed adultery," he thought that it was not bare desire that was condemned; but if through the desire the act that results from it proceeding beyond the desire is accomplished in it. For dream employs phantasy and the body. Accordingly, the historians relate the following decision of Bocchoris the just. A youth, falling in love with a courtesan, persuades the girl, for a stipulated reward, to come to him next day. But his desire being unexpectedly satiated, by laying hold of the girl in a dream, by anticipation, when the object of his love came according to stipulation, he prohibited her from coming in. But she, on learning what had taken place, demanded the reward, saying that in this way she had sated the lover's desire. They came accordingly to the judge. He, ordering the youth to hold out the purse containing the reward in the sun, bade the courtesan take hold of the shadow; facetiously bidding him pay the image of a reward for the image of an embrace.

Accordingly one dreams, the soul assenting to the vision. But he dreams waking, who looks so as to lust; not only, as that Gnostic said, if along with the sight of the woman he imagine in his mind intercourse, for this is already the act of lust, as lust; but if one looks on beauty of person (the Word says), and the flesh seem to him in the way of lust to be fair, looking on carnally and sinfully, he is judged because he admired. For, on the other hand, he who in chaste love looks on beauty, thinks not that the flesh is beautiful, but the spirit, admiring, as I judge, the body as an image, by whose beauty he transports himself to the Artist, and to the true beauty; exhibiting the sacred symbol, the bright impress of righteousness to the angels that wait on the ascension; I mean the unction of acceptance, the quality of disposition which resides in the soul that is gladdened by the communication of the Holy Spirit. This glory, which shone forth on the face of Moses, the people could not look on. Wherefore he took a veil for the glory, to those who looked carnally. For those, who demand toll, detain those who bring in any worldly things, who are burdened with their own passions. But him that is free of all things which are subject to duty, and is full of knowledge, and of the righteousness of works, they pass on with their good wishes, blessing the man with his work. "And his life shall not fall away"—the leaf of the living tree that is nourished "by the water-courses." Now the righteous is likened to fruit-bearing trees, and not only to such as are of the nature of tall-growing ones. And in the sacrificial oblations, according to the law, there were those who looked for blemishes in the sacrifices.

They who are skilled in such matters distinguish propension (ὄρεξις) from lust (ἐπιθυμία); and assign the latter, as being irrational, to pleasures and licentiousness; and propension, as being a rational movement, they assign to the necessities of nature.

CHAP. XIX.—WOMEN AS WELL AS MEN CAPABLE OF PERFECTION.

In this perfection it is possible for man and woman equally to share. It is not only Moses, then, that heard from God, "I have spoken to thee once, and twice, saying, I have seen this people, and lo, it is stiff-necked. Suffer me to exterminate them, and blot out their name from under heaven;

and I will make thee into a great and wonderful nation much greater than this;" who answers not regarding himself, but the common salvation: "By no means, O Lord; forgive this people their sin, or blot me out of the book of the living." How great was his perfection, in wishing to die together with the people, rather than be saved alone!

But Judith too, who became perfect among women, in the siege of the city, at the entreaty of the elders went forth into the strangers' camp, despising all danger for her country's sake, giving herself into the enemy's hand in faith in God; and straightway she obtained the reward of her faith,—though a woman, prevailing over the enemy of her faith, and gaining possession of the head of Holofernes. And again, Esther perfect by faith, who rescued Israel from the power of the king and the satrap's cruelty: a woman alone, afflicted with fasting, held back ten thousand armed hands, annulling by her faith the tyrant's decree; him indeed she appeased, Haman she restrained, and Israel she preserved scathless by her perfect prayer to God. I pass over in silence Susanna and the sister of Moses, since the latter was the prophet's associate in commanding the host, being superior to all the women among the Hebrews who were in repute for their wisdom; and the former in her surpassing modesty, going even to death condemned by licentious admirers, remained the unwavering martyr of chastity.

Dion, too, the philosopher, tells that a certain woman Lysidica, through excess of modesty, bathed in her clothes; and that Philotera, when she was to enter the bath, gradually drew back her tunic as the water covered the naked parts; and then rising by degrees, put it on. And did not Leæna of Attica manfully bear the torture? She being privy to the conspiracy of Harmodius and Aristogeiton against Hipparchus, uttered not a word, though severely tortured. And they say that the Argolic women, under the guidance of Telesilla the poetess, turned to flight the doughty Spartans by merely showing themselves; and that she produced in them fearlessness of death. Similarly speaks he who composed the Danais respecting the daughters of Danaus:—

"And then the daughters of Danaus swiftly armed themselves, Before the fair-flowing river, majestic Nile,"

and so forth.
    And the rest of the poets sing of Atalanta's swiftness in the chase, of Anticlea's love for children, of Alcestis's love for her husband, of the courage of Makæria and of the Hyacinthides. What shall I say? Did not Theano the Pythagorean make such progress in philosophy, that to him who looked intently at her, and said, "Your arm is beautiful," she answered "Yes, but it is not public." Characterized by the same propriety, there is also reported the following reply. When asked when a woman after being with her husband attends the Thesmophoria, said, "From her own husband at once, from a stranger never." Themisto too, of Lampsacus, the daughter of Zoilus, the wife of Leontes of Lampsacus, studied the Epicurean philosophy, as Myia the daughter of Theano the Pythagorean, and Arignote, who wrote the history of Dionysius.
    And the daughters of Diodorus, who was called Kronus, all became dialecticians, as Philo the dialectician says in the *Menexenus*, whose names are mentioned as follows— Menexene, Argia, Theognis, Artemesia, Pantaclea. I also recollect a female Cynic,—she was called Hipparchia, a Maronite, the wife of Crates,—in whose case the so-called dog-wedding was celebrated in the Poecile. Arete of Cyrene, too, the daughter of Aristippus, educated her son Aristippus, who was surnamed Mother-taught. Lastheneia of Arcis, and Axiothea of Phlius, studied philosophy with Plato. Besides, Aspasia of Miletus, of whom the writers of comedy write much, was trained by Socrates in philosophy, by Pericles in rhetoric. I omit, on account of the length of the discourse, the rest; enumerating neither the poetesses Corinna, Telesilla,

Myia, and Sappho; nor the painters, as Irene the daughter of Cratinus, and Anaxandra the daughter of Nealces, according to the account of Didymus in the Symposiaci. The daughter of Cleobulus, the sage and monarch of the Lindii, was not ashamed to wash the feet of her father's guests. Also the wife of Abraham, the blessed Sarah, in her own person prepared the cakes baked in the ashes for the angels; and princely maidens among the Hebrews fed sheep. Whence also the Nausicaä of Homer went to the washing-tubs.

The wise woman, then, will first choose to persuade her husband to be her associate in what is conducive to happiness. And should that be found impracticable, let her by herself earnestly aim at virtue, gaining her husband's consent in everything, so as never to do anything against his will, with exception of what is reckoned as contributing to virtue and salvation. But if one keeps from such a mode of life either wife or maid-servant, whose heart is set on it; what such a person in that case plainly does is nothing else than determine to drive her away from righteousness and sobriety, and to choose to make his own house wicked and licentious.

It is not then possible that man or woman can be conversant with anything whatever, without the advantage of education, and application, and training; and virtue, we have said, depends not on others, but on ourselves above all. Other things one can repress, by waging war against them; but with what depends on one's self, this is entirely out of the question, even with the most strenuous persistence. For the gift is one conferred by God, and not in the power of any other. Whence licentiousness should be regarded as the evil of no other one than of him who is guilty of licentiousness; and temperance, on the other hand, as the good of him who is able to practice it.

CHAPTER XX.—A GOOD WIFE.

The woman who, with propriety, loves her husband, Euripides describes, while admonishing,—

"That when her husband says aught,
She ought to regard him as speaking well if she say nothing;
And if she will say anything, to do her endeavor to gratify her husband."

And again he subjoins the like:—

"And that the wife should sweetly look sad with her husband,
Should aught evil befall him,
And have in common a share of sorrow and joy."

Then, describing her as gentle and kind even in misfortunes, he adds:—

"And I, when you are ill, will, sharing your sickness bear it;
And I will bear my share in your misfortunes."

And:—

> "Nothing is bitter to me,
> For with friends one ought to be happy,
> For what else is friendship but this?"

The marriage, then, that is consummated according to the word, is sanctified, if the union be under subjection to God, and be conducted "with a true heart, in full assurance of faith, having hearts sprinkled from an evil conscience, and the body washed with pure water, and holding the confession of hope; for He is faithful that promised." And the happiness of marriage ought never to be estimated either by wealth or beauty, but by virtue.

"Beauty," says the tragedy,—

> "Helps no wife with her husband;
> But virtue has helped many; for every good wife

Who is attached to her husband knows how to practice sobriety."

Then, as giving admonitions, he says:—

"First, then, this is incumbent on her who is endowed with mind,
That even if her husband be ugly, he must appear good-looking;
For it is for the mind, not the eye, to judge."

And so forth.

For with perfect propriety Scripture has said that woman is given by God as "a help" to man. It is evident, then, in my opinion, that she will charge herself with remedying, by good sense and persuasion, each of the annoyances that originate with her husband in domestic economy. And if he do not yield, then she will endeavor, as far as possible for human nature, to lead a sinless life; whether it be necessary to die, in accordance with reason, or to live; considering that God is her helper and associate in such a course of conduct, her true defender and Savior both for the present and for the future; making Him the leader and guide of all her actions, reckoning sobriety and righteousness her work, and making the favor of God her end. Gracefully, therefore, the apostle says in the Epistle to Titus, "that the elder women should be of godly behavior, should not be slanderers, not enslaved to much wine; that they should counsel the young women to be lovers of their husbands, lovers of their children, discreet, chaste, housekeepers, good, subject to their own husbands; that the word of God be not blasphemed." But rather, he says, "Follow peace with all men, and holiness, without which no man shall see the Lord: looking diligently, lest there be any fornicator or profane person, as Esau, who for one morsel surrendered his birth-right; and lest any root of bitterness springing up trouble you, and thereby many be defiled." And then, as putting the finishing stroke to the question about marriage, he adds: "Marriage is honorable in all, and the bed undefiled: but whoremongers and adulterers God will judge." And one aim and one end, as far as regards perfection, being demonstrated to belong to the man and the woman, Peter in his Epistle says, "Though now for a season, if need be, ye are in heaviness through manifold temptations; that the trial of your faith, being much more precious than that of gold which perishes, though it be tried with fire, might be found unto praise, and honor, and glory at the revelation of Jesus Christ; whom, having not seen, ye love; in whom, though now ye see Him not, yet believing, ye rejoice with joy unspeakable, and full of glory, receiving the end of your faith, the salvation of your souls." Wherefore also Paul rejoices for Christ's sake that he was "in labors, more abundantly, in stripes above measure, in deaths oft."

CHAPTER XXI.—DESCRIPTION OF THE PERFECT MAN, OR GNOSTIC.

Here I find perfection apprehended variously in relation to Him who excels in every virtue. Accordingly one is perfected as pious, and as patient, and as continent, and as a worker, and as a martyr, and as a Gnostic. But I know no one of men perfect in all things at once, while still human, though according to the mere letter of the law, except Him alone who for us clothed Himself with humanity. Who then is perfect? He who professes abstinence from what is bad. Well, this is the way to the Gospel and to well-doing. But gnostic perfection in the case of the legal man is the acceptance of the Gospel, that he that is after the law may be perfect. For so he, who was after the law, Moses, foretold that it was necessary to hear in order that we might, according to the apostle, receive Christ, the fullness of the law. But now in the Gospel the Gnostic attains proficiency not only by making use of the law as a step, but by understanding and comprehending it, as the Lord who gave the Covenants delivered it to the apostles. And if he conduct himself rightly (as assuredly it is impossible to attain knowledge (*gnosis*) by bad conduct); and if, further, having made an eminently right confession, he become a martyr out of love, obtaining considerable renown as among men; not even thus will he be called perfect in the flesh beforehand; since it is the close of life which claims this appellation, when the gnostic martyr has first shown the perfect work, and rightly exhibited it, and having thankfully shed his blood, has yielded up the ghost: blessed then will he be, and truly proclaimed perfect, "that the excellency of the power may be of God, and not of us," as the apostle says. Only let us preserve free-will and love: "troubled on every side, yet not distressed; perplexed, but not in despair; persecuted, but not forsaken; cast down, but not destroyed." For those who strive after perfection, according to the same apostle, must "give no offence in anything, but in everything approve themselves not to men, but to God." And, as a consequence, also they ought to yield to men; for it is reasonable, on account of abusive calumnies. Here is the specification: "in much patience, in afflictions, in necessities, in distresses, in stripes, in imprisonments, in tumults, in labors, in watching, in fasting, in pureness, in knowledge, in long-suffering, in kindness, in the Holy Ghost, in love unfeigned, in the word of truth, in the power of God," that we may be the temples of God, purified "from all filthiness of the flesh and of the spirit." "And I," He says, "will receive you; and I will be to you for a Father, and ye shall be to Me for sons and daughters, says the Lord Almighty." "Let us then," he says, "perfect holiness in the fear of God." For though fear beget pain, "I rejoice," he says, "not that ye were made sorry, but that ye showed susceptibility to repentance. For ye sorrowed after a godly sort, that ye might receive damage by us in nothing. For godly sorrow worked repentance unto salvation not to be regretted; but the sorrow of the world worked death. For this same thing that ye sorrowed after a godly sort, what earnestness it wrought in you; yea, what clearing of yourselves; yea, what compunction; yea, what fear; yea, what desire; yea, what zeal; yea, revenge!

In all things ye have showed yourselves clear in the matter." Such are the preparatory exercises of gnostic discipline. And since the omnipotent God Himself "gave some apostles, and some prophets, and some evangelists, and some pastors and teachers, for the perfecting of the saints, for the work of the ministry, for the edifying of the body of Christ, till we all attain to the unity of the faith, and of the knowledge of the Son of God, to a perfect man, to the measure of the stature of the fullness of Christ;" we are then to strive to reach manhood as befits the Gnostic, and to be as perfect as we can while still abiding in the flesh, making it our study with perfect concord here to concur with the will of God, to the restoration of what is the truly perfect nobleness and relationship, to the fullness of Christ, that which perfectly depends on our perfection.

And now we perceive where, and how, and when the divine apostle mentions the perfect man, and how he shows the differences of the perfect. And again, on the other hand: "The manifestation of the Spirit is given for our profit. For to one is given the word of wisdom by the Spirit; to another the word of knowledge according to the same Spirit; to another faith through the same Spirit; to another the gifts of healing through the same Spirit; to another the working of miracles; to another prophecy; to another discernment of spirits; to another diversities of tongues; to another the interpretation of tongues: and all these worked the one and the same Spirit, distributing to each one according as He wills." Such being the case, the prophets are perfect in prophecy, the righteous in righteousness, and the martyrs in confession, and others in preaching, not that they are not sharers in the common virtues, but are proficient in those to which they are appointed. For what man in his senses would say that a prophet was not righteous? For what? did not righteous men like Abraham prophesy?

"For to one God has given warlike deeds,
To another the accomplishment of the dance,

To another the lyre and song," says Homer. "But each has his own proper gift of God"—one in one way, another in another. But the apostles were perfected in all. You will find, then, if you choose, in their acts and writings, knowledge, life, preaching, righteousness, purity, prophecy. We must know, then, that if Paul is young in respect to time—having flourished immediately after the Lord's ascension—yet his writings depend on the Old Testament, breathing and speaking of them. For faith in Christ and the knowledge of the Gospel are the explanation and fulfilment of the law; and therefore it was said to the Hebrews, "If ye believe not, neither shall you understand;" that is, unless you believe what is prophesied in the law, and oracularly delivered by the law, you will not understand the Old Testament, which He by His coming expounded.

CHAPTER XXII.—THE TRUE GNOSTIC DOES GOOD, NOT FROM FEAR OF PUNISHMENT OR HOPE OF REWARD, BUT ONLY FOR THE SAKE OF GOOD ITSELF.

The man of understanding and perspicacity is, then, a Gnostic. And his business is not abstinence from what is evil (for this is a step to the highest perfection), or the doing of good out of fear. For it is written, "Whither shall I flee, and where shall I hide myself from Thy presence? If I ascend into heaven, Thou art there; if I go away to the uttermost parts of the sea, there is Thy right hand; if I go down into the depths, there is Thy Spirit." Nor any more is he to do so from hope of promised recompense. For it is said, "Behold the Lord, and His reward is before His face, to give to everyone according to his works; what eye hath not seen, and ear hath not heard, and hath not entered into the heart of man what God hath prepared for them that love Him." But only the doing of good out of love, and for the sake of its own excellence, is to be the Gnostic's choice. Now, in the person of God it is said to the Lord, "Ask of Me, and I will give the heathen for Thine inheritance;"teaching Him to ask a truly regal request—that is, the salvation of men without price, that we may inherit and possess the Lord. For, on the contrary, to desire knowledge about God for any practical purpose, that this may be done, or that may not be done, is not proper to the Gnostic; but the knowledge itself suffices as the reason for contemplation. For I will dare aver that it is not because he wishes to be saved that he, who devotes himself to knowledge for the sake of the divine science itself, chooses knowledge. For the exertion of the intellect by exercise is prolonged to a perpetual exertion. And the perpetual exertion of the intellect is the essence of an intelligent being, which results from an uninterrupted process of admixture, and remains eternal contemplation, a living substance. Could we, then, suppose anyone proposing to the Gnostic whether he would choose the knowledge of God or everlasting salvation; and if these, which are entirely identical, were separable, he would without the least hesitation choose the knowledge of God, deeming that property of faith, which from love ascends to knowledge, desirable, for its own sake. This, then, is the perfect man's first form of doing good, when it is done not for any advantage in what pertains to him, but because he judges it right to do good; and the energy being vigorously exerted in all things, in the very act becomes good; not, good in some things, and not good in others; but consisting in the habit of doing good, neither for glory, nor, as the philosophers say, for reputation, nor from reward either from men or God; but so as to pass life after the image and likeness of the Lord.

And if, in doing good, he be met with anything adverse, he will let the recompense pass without resentment as if it were good, he being just and good "to the just and the unjust." To such the Lord says, "Be ye, as your Father is perfect."

To him the flesh is dead; but he himself lives alone, having consecrated the sepulcher into a holy temple to the Lord, having turned towards God the old sinful soul.

Such a one is no longer continent, but has reached a state of passionlessness, waiting to put on the divine image. "If thou doest alms," it is said, "let no one know it; and if thou fastest, anoint thyself, that God alone may know," and not a single human being. Not even he himself who shows mercy ought to know that he does show mercy; for in this way he will be sometimes merciful, sometimes not. And when he shall do good by habit, he will imitate the nature of good, and his disposition will be his nature and his practice. There is no necessity for removing those who are raised on high, but there is necessity for those who are walking to reach the requisite goal, by passing over the whole of the narrow way. For this is to be drawn by the Father, to become worthy to receive the power of grace from God, so as to run without hindrance. And if some hate the elect, such a one knows their ignorance, and pities their minds for its folly.

As is right, then, knowledge itself loves and teaches the ignorant, and instructs the whole creation to honor God Almighty. And if such a one teaches to love God, he will not hold virtue as a thing to be lost in any case, either awake or in a dream, or in any vision; since the habit never goes out of itself by falling from being a habit. Whether, then, knowledge be said to be habit or disposition; on account of diverse sentiments never obtaining access, the guiding faculty, remaining unaltered, admits no alteration of appearances by framing in dreams visionary conceptions out of its movements by day. Wherefore also the Lord enjoins "to watch," so that our soul may never be perturbed with passion, even in dreams; but also to keep the life of the night pure and stainless, as if spent in the day. For assimilation to God, as far as we can, is preserving the mind in its relation to the same things. And this is the relation of mind as mind.

But the variety of disposition arises from inordinate affection to material things. And for this reason, as they appear to me, to have called night Euphrone; since then the soul, released from the perceptions of sense, turns in on itself, and

has a truer hold of intelligence (φρόνησις). Wherefore the mysteries are for the most part celebrated by night, indicating the withdrawal of the soul from the body, which takes place by night. "Let us not then sleep, as do others; but let us watch and be sober. For they that sleep, sleep in the night; and they that are drunken, are drunken in the night. But let us who are of the day be sober, putting on the breastplate of faith and love, and as a helmet the hope of salvation." And as to what, again, they say of sleep, the very same things are to be understood of death. For each exhibits the departure of the soul, the one more, the other less; as we may also get this in Heraclitus: "Man touches night in himself, when dead and his light quenched; and alive, when he sleeps he touches the dead; and awake, when he shuts his eyes, he touches the sleeper." "For blessed are those that have seen the Lord," according to the apostle;
"for it is high time to awake out of sleep. For now is our salvation nearer than when we believed. The night is far spent, the day is at hand. Let us therefore cast off the works of darkness, and put on the armor of light."By day and light he designates figuratively the Son, and by the armor of light metaphorically the promises.

So it is said that we ought to go washed to sacrifices and prayers, clean and bright; and that this external adornment and purification are practiced for a sign. Now purity is to think holy thoughts. Further, there is the image of baptism, which also was handed down to the poets from Moses as follows:—

"And she having drawn water, and wearing on her body clean clothes."

It is Penelope that is going to prayer:—

"And Telemachus,
Having washed his hands in the hoary sea, prayed to Athene."

It was a custom of the Jews to wash frequently after being in bed. It was then well said,—

"Be pure, not by washing of water, but in the mind."

For sanctity, as I conceive it, is perfect pureness of mind, and deeds, and thoughts, and words too, and in its last degree sinlessness in dreams.

And sufficient purification to a man, I reckon, is thorough and sure repentance. If, condemning ourselves for our former actions, we go forward, after these things taking thought, and divesting our mind both of the things which please us through the senses, and of our former transgressions.

If, then, we are to give the etymology of ἐπιστήμη, knowledge, its signification is to be derived from στάσις, placing; for our soul, which was formerly borne, now in one way, now in another, it settles in objects. Similarly faith is to be explained etymologically, as the settling (στάσις) of our soul respecting that which is.

But we desire to learn about the man who is always and in all things righteous; who, neither dreading the penalty proceeding from the law, nor fearing to entertain hatred of evil in the case of those who live with him and who prosecute the injured, nor dreading danger at the hands of those who do wrong, remains righteous. For he who, on account of these considerations, abstains from anything wrong, is not voluntarily kind, but is good from fear. Even Epicurus says, that the man who in his estimation was wise, "would not do wrong to anyone for the sake of gain; for he could not persuade himself that he would escape detection." So that, if he knew he would not be detected, he would, according to him, do evil.
And such are the doctrines of darkness. If, too, one shall abstain from doing wrong from hope of the recompense given by God on account of righteous deeds, he is not on this supposition spontaneously good. For as fear makes that man just, so reward makes this one; or rather, makes him appear to

be just. But with the hope after death—a good hope to the good, to the bad the reverse—not only they who follow after Barbarian wisdom, but also the Pythagoreans, are acquainted. For the latter also proposed hope as an end to those who philosophize. Whereas Socrates also, in the *Phædo*, says "that good souls depart hence with a good hope;" and again, denouncing the wicked, he sets against this the assertion,
"For they live with an evil hope." With him Heraclitus manifestly agrees in his dissertations concerning men: "There awaits man after death what they neither hope nor think." Divinely, therefore, Paul writes expressly, "Tribulation worked, patience, and patience experience, and experience hope; and hope makes not ashamed." For the patience is on account of the hope in the future. Now hope is synonymous with the recompense and restitution of hope; which makes not ashamed, not being any more vilified.

But he who obeys the mere call, as he is called, neither for fear, nor for enjoyments, is on his way to knowledge (γνῶσις). For he does not consider whether any extrinsic lucrative gain or enjoyment follows to him; but drawn by the love of Him who is the true object of love, and led to what is requisite, practices piety. So that not even were we to suppose him to receive from God leave to do things forbidden with impunity; not even if he were to get the promise that he would receive as a reward the good things of the blessed; but besides, not even if he could persuade himself that God would be hoodwinked with reference to what he does (which is impossible), would he ever wish to do aught contrary to right reason, having once made choice of what is truly good and worthy of choice on its own account, and therefore to be loved. For it is not in the food of the belly, that we have heard good to be situated. But he has heard that "meat will not commend us," nor marriage, nor abstinence from marriage in ignorance; but virtuous gnostic conduct. For the dog, which is an irrational animal, may be said to be continent, dreading as it does the uplifted stick, and therefore keeping away from the meat. But let the predicted promise be taken away, and the threatened dread cancelled, and the impending danger removed, and the disposition of such people will be revealed.

CHAPTER XXIII.—THE SAME SUBJECT CONTINUED.

For it is not suitable to the nature of the thing itself, that they should apprehend in the truly gnostic manner the truth, that all things which were created for our use are good; as, for example, marriage and procreation, when used in moderation; and that it is better than good to become free of passion, and virtuous by assimilation to the divine. But in the case of external things, agreeable or disagreeable, from some they abstain, from others not. But in those things from which they abstain from disgust, they plainly find fault with the creature and the Creator; and though in appearance they walk faithfully, the opinion they maintain is impious. That command, "Thou shall not lust," needs neither the necessity arising from fear, which compels to keep from things that are pleasant; nor the reward, which by promise persuades to restrain the impulses of passion.

And those who obey God through the promise, caught by the bait of pleasure, choose obedience not for the sake of the commandment, but for the sake of the promise. Nor will turning away from objects of sense, as a matter of necessary consequence, produce attachment to intellectual objects. On the contrary, the attachment to intellectual objects naturally becomes to the Gnostic an influence which draws away from the objects of sense; inasmuch as he, in virtue of the selection of what is good, has chosen what is good according to knowledge (γνωστικῶς), admiring generation, and by sanctifying the Creator sanctifying assimilation to the divine. But I shall free myself from lust, let him say, O Lord, for the sake of alliance with Thee. For the economy of creation is good, and all things are well administered: nothing happens without a cause. I must be in what is Thine, O Omnipotent One. And if I am there, I am near Thee. And I would be free of fear that I may be able to draw near to Thee, and to be satisfied with little, practicing Thy just choice between things good and things like.

Right mystically and sacredly the apostle, teaching us the choice which is truly gracious, not in the way of rejection of other things as bad, but so as to do things better than what is good, has spoken, saying, "So he that giveth his virgin in marriage doeth well; and he that giveth her not doeth better; as far as respects seemliness and undistracted attendance on the Lord."

Now we know that things which are difficult are not essential; but that things which are essential have been graciously made easy of attainment by God. Wherefore Democritus well says, that "nature and instruction" are like each other. And we have briefly assigned the cause. For instruction harmonizes man, and by harmonizing makes him natural; and it is no matter whether one was made such as he is by nature, or transformed by time and education. The Lord has furnished both; that which is by creation, and that which is by creating again and renewal through the covenant. And that is preferable which is advantageous to what is superior; but what is superior to everything is mind. So, then, what is really good is seen to be most pleasant, and of itself produces the fruit which is desired—tranquility of soul. "And he who hears Me," it is said, "shall rest in peace, confident, and shall be calm without fear of any evil." "Rely with all thy heart and thy mind on God."

On this wise it is possible for the Gnostic already to have become God. "I said, Ye are gods, and sons of the highest." And Empedocles says that the souls of the wise become gods, writing as follows:—

"At last prophets, minstrels, and physicians,
And the foremost among mortal men, approach;
Whence spring gods supreme in honors."

Man, then, genetically considered, is formed in accordance with the idea of the connate spirit. For he is not created formless and shapeless in the workshop of nature, where mystically the production of man is accomplished, both art and essence being common. But the individual man is stamped according to the impression produced in the soul by the objects of his choice. Thus we say that Adam was perfect, as far as respects his formation; for none of the distinctive characteristics of the idea and form of man were wanting to him; but in the act of coming into being he received perfection. And he was justified by obedience; this was reaching manhood, as far as depended on him. And the cause lay in his choosing, and especially in his choosing what was forbidden. God was not the cause.

For production is twofold—of things procreated, and of things that grow. And manliness in man, who is subject to perturbation, as they say, makes him who partakes of it essentially fearless and invincible; and anger is the mind's satellite in patience, and endurance, and the like; and self-constraint and salutary sense are set over desire. But God is impassible, free of anger, destitute of desire. And He is not free of fear, in the sense of avoiding what is terrible; or temperate, in the sense of having command of desires. For neither can the nature of God fall in with anything terrible, nor does God flee fear; just as He will not feel desire, so as to rule over desires. Accordingly that Pythagorean saying was mystically uttered respecting us, "that man ought to become one;" for the high priest himself is one, God being one in the immutable state of the perpetual flow of good things. Now the Savior has taken away wrath in and with lust, wrath being lust of vengeance. For universally liability to feeling belongs to every kind of desire; and man, when deified purely into a passionless state, becomes a unit. As, then, those, who at sea are held by an anchor, pull at the anchor, but do not drag it to them, but drag themselves to the anchor; so those who, according to the gnostic life, draw God towards them, imperceptibly bring themselves to God: for he who reverences God, reverences himself. In the contemplative life, then, one in worshipping God attends to himself, and through his own spotless purification beholds the holy God holily; for self-control, being present, surveying and contemplating itself uninterruptedly, is as far as possible assimilated to God.

CHAPTER XXIV.—THE REASON AND END OF DIVINE PUNISHMENTS.

Now that is in our power, of which equally with its opposite we are masters,—as, say to philosophize or not, to believe or disbelieve. In consequence, then, of our being equally masters of each of the opposites, what depends on us is found possible. Now the commandments may be done or not done by us, who, as is reasonable, are liable to praise and blame. And those, again, who are punished on account of sins committed by them, are punished for them alone; for what is done is past, and what is done can never be undone. The sins committed before faith are accordingly forgiven by the Lord, not that they may be undone, but as if they had not been done. "But not all," says Basilides, "but only sins involuntary and in ignorance, are forgiven;" as would be the case were it a man, and not God, that conferred such a boon. To such a one Scripture says, "Thou thought that I would be like thee." But if we are punished for voluntary sins, we are punished not that the sins which are done may be undone, but because they were done. But punishment does not avail to him who has sinned, to undo his sin, but that he may sin no more, and that no one else fall into the like. Therefore the good God corrects for these three causes: First, that he who is corrected may become better than his former self; then that those who are capable of being saved by examples may be driven back, being admonished; and thirdly, that he who is injured may not be readily despised, and be apt to receive injury. And there are two methods of correction—the instructive and the punitive, which we have called the disciplinary. It ought to be known, then, that those who fall into sin after baptism are those who are subjected to discipline; for the deeds done before are remitted, and those done after are purged. It is in reference to the unbelieving that it is said, "that they are reckoned as the chaff which the wind drives from the face of the earth, and the drop which falls from a vessel."

CHAPTER XXV.—TRUE PERFECTION CONSISTS IN THE KNOWLEDGE AND LOVE OF GOD.

"Happy he who possesses the culture of knowledge, and is not moved to the injury of the citizens or to wrong actions, but contemplates the undecaying order of immortal nature, how and in what way and manner it subsists. To such the practice of base deeds attaches not," Rightly, then, Plato says, "that the man who devotes himself to the contemplation of ideas will live as a god among men; now the mind is the place of ideas, and God is mind." He says that he who contemplates the unseen God lives as a god among men. And in the *Sophist*, Socrates calls the stranger of Elea, who was a dialectician, "god:" "Such are the gods who, like stranger guests, frequent cities. For when the soul, rising above the sphere of generation, is by itself apart, and dwells amidst ideas," like the Coryphæus in Theætetus, now become as an angel, it will be with Christ, being rapt in contemplation, ever keeping in view the will of God; in reality

"Alone wise, while these flit like shadows."

"For the dead bury their dead." Whence Jeremiah says: "I will fill it with the earth-born dead whom mine anger has smitten."

God, then, being not a subject for demonstration, cannot be the object of science. But the Son is wisdom, and knowledge, and truth, and all else that has affinity thereto. He is also susceptible of demonstration and of description. And all the powers of the Spirit, becoming collectively one thing, terminate in the same point—that is, in the Son. But He is incapable of being declared, in respect of the idea of each one of His powers. And the Son is neither simply one thing as one thing, nor many things as parts, but one thing as all things; whence also He is all things. For He is the circle of all powers rolled and united into one unity. Wherefore the Word is called the Alpha and the Omega, of whom alone the end becomes beginning, and ends again at the original beginning without any break. Wherefore also to believe in Him, and by Him, is to become a unit, being indissolubly united in Him; and to disbelieve is to be separated, disjoined, divided.

"Wherefore thus says the Lord, Every alien son is uncircumcised in heart, and uncircumcised in flesh" (that is, unclean in body and soul): "there shall not enter one of the strangers into the midst of the house of Israel, but the Levites." He calls those that would not believe, but would disbelieve, strangers. Only those who live purely being true priests of God. Wherefore, of all the circumcised tribes, those anointed to be high priests, and kings, and prophets, were reckoned more holy. Whence He commands them not to touch dead bodies, or approach the dead; not that the body was polluted, but that sin and disobedience were incarnate, and embodied, and dead, and therefore abominable. It was only, then, when a father and mother, a son and daughter died, that the priest was allowed to enter, because these were related only by flesh and seed, to whom the priest was indebted for the immediate cause of his entrance into life. And they purify themselves seven days, the period in which Creation was consummated. For on the seventh day the rest is celebrated; and on the eighth he brings a propitiation, as is written in Ezekiel, according to which propitiation the promise is to be received. And the perfect propitiation, I take it, is that propitious faith in the Gospel which is by the law and the prophets, and the purity which shows itself in universal obedience, with the abandonment of the things of the world; in order to that grateful surrender of the tabernacle, which results from the enjoyment of the soul. Whether, then, the time be that which through the seven periods enumerated returns to the chiefest rest, or the seven

Clement of Alexandria

heavens, which some reckon one above the other; or whether also the fixed sphere which borders on the intellectual world be called the eighth, the expression denotes that the Gnostic ought to rise out of the sphere of creation and of sin. After these seven days, sacrifices are offered for sins. For there is still fear of change, and it touches the seventh circle. The righteous Job says: "Naked came I out of my mother's womb, and naked shall I return there;" not naked of possessions, for that were a trivial and common thing; but, as a just man, he departs naked of evil and sin, and of the unsightly shape which follows those who have led bad lives. For this was what was said, "Unless ye be converted, and become as children," pure in flesh, holy in soul by abstinence from evil deeds; showing that He would have us to be such as also He generated us from our mother—the water. For the intent of one generation succeeding another is to immortalize by progress. "But the lamp of the wicked shall be put out." That purity in body and soul which the Gnostic partakes of, the all-wise Moses indicated, by employing repetition in describing the incorruptibility of body and of soul in the person of Rebecca, thus: "Now the virgin was fair, and man had not known her." And Rebecca, interpreted, means "glory of God;" and the glory of God is immortality. This is in reality righteousness, not to desire other things, but to be entirely the consecrated temple of the Lord. Righteousness is peace of life and a well-conditioned state, to which the Lord dismissed her when He said, "Depart into peace." For Salem is, by interpretation, peace; of which our Savior is enrolled King, as Moses says, Melchizedek king of Salem, priest of the most high God, who gave bread and wine, furnishing consecrated food for a type of the Eucharist. And Melchizedek is interpreted "righteous king;" and the name is a synonym for righteousness and peace. Basilides, however, supposes that Righteousness and her daughter Peace dwell stationed in the eighth sphere.

But we must pass from physics to ethics, which are clearer; for the discourse concerning these will follow after the treatise in hand. The Savior Himself, then, plainly initiates us into the mysteries, according to the words of the tragedy:—

"Seeing those who see, he also gives the orgies."

And if you ask,

"These orgies, what is their nature?"

You will hear again:—

"It is forbidden to mortals uninitiated in the Bacchic rites to know."

And if anyone will inquire curiously what they are, let him hear:—

"It is not lawful for thee to hear, but they are worth knowing; The rites of the God detest him who practices impiety."

Now God, who is without beginning, is the perfect beginning of the universe, and the producer of the beginning. As, then, He is being, He is the first principle of the department of action, as He is good, of morals; as He is mind, on the other hand, He is the first principle of reasoning and of judgment. Whence also He alone is Teacher, who is the only Son of the Most High Father, the Instructor of men.

CHAPTER XXVI.—HOW THE PERFECT MAN TREATS THE BODY AND THE THINGS OF THE WORLD.

Those, then, who run down created existence and vilify the body are wrong; not considering that the frame of man was formed erect for the contemplation of heaven, and that the organization of the senses tends to knowledge; and that the members and parts are arranged for good, not for pleasure. Whence this abode becomes receptive of the soul which is most precious to God; and is dignified with the Holy Spirit through the sanctification of soul and body, perfected with the perfection of the Savior. And the succession of the three virtues is found in the Gnostic, who morally, physically, and logically occupies himself with God. For wisdom is the knowledge of things divine and human; and righteousness is the concord of the parts of the soul; and holiness is the service of God. But if one were to say that he disparaged the flesh, and generation on account of it, by quoting Isaiah, who says, "All flesh is grass, and all the glory of man as the flower of grass: the grass is withered, and the flower has fallen; but the word of the Lord endures forever;" let him hear the Spirit interpreting the matter in question by Jeremiah, "And I scattered them like dry sticks, that are made to fly by the wind into the desert. This is the lot and portion of your disobedience, says the Lord. As thou hast forgotten Me, and hast trusted in lies, so will I discover thy hinder parts to thy face; and thy disgrace shall be seen, thy adultery, and thy neighing," and so on. For "the flower of grass," and "walking after the flesh," and "being carnal," according to the apostle, are those who are in their sins. The soul of man is confessedly the better part of man, and the body the inferior. But neither is the soul good by nature, nor, on the other hand, is the body bad by nature. Nor is that which is not good straightway bad. For there are things which occupy a middle place, and among them are things to be preferred, and things to be rejected. The constitution of man, then, which has its place among things of sense, was necessarily composed of things diverse, but not opposite—body and soul.

Always therefore the good actions, as better, attach to the better and ruling spirit; and voluptuous and sinful actions are attributed to the worse, the sinful one.

Now the soul of the wise man and Gnostic, as sojourning in the body, conducts itself towards it gravely and respectfully, not with inordinate affections, as about to leave the tabernacle if the time of departure summon. "I am a stranger in the earth, and a sojourner with you," it is said. And hence Basilides says, that he apprehends that the election are strangers to the world, being supramundane by nature. But this is not the case. For all things are of one God. And no one is a stranger to the world by nature, their essence being one, and God one. But the elect man dwells as a sojourner, knowing all things to be possessed and disposed of; and he makes use of the things which the Pythagoreans make out to be the threefold good things. The body, too, as one sent on a distant pilgrimage, uses inns and dwellings by the way, having care of the things of the world, of the places where he halts; but leaving his dwelling-place and property without excessive emotion; readily following him that leads him away from life; by no means and on no occasion turning back; giving thanks for his sojourn, and blessing [God] for his departure, embracing the mansion that is in heaven. "For we know, that, if the earthly house of our tabernacle be dissolved, we have a building of God, a house not made with hands, eternal in the heavens. For we that are in this tabernacle do groan, desiring to be clothed upon with our house which is from heaven: if so be that being clothed we shall not be found naked. For we walk by faith, not by sight," as the apostle says; "and we are willing rather to be absent from the body, and present with God." The rather is in comparison. And comparison obtains in the case of things that fall under resemblance; as the more valiant man is more valiant among the valiant, and most valiant among cowards. Whence he adds, "Wherefore we strive, whether present or absent, to be accepted with Him," that is, God, whose work and creation are all things, both the world and things supramundane. I admire Epicharmus, who clearly says:—

> "Endowed with pious mind, you will not, in dying,
> Suffer aught evil. The spirit will dwell in heaven above;"

and the minstrel who sings:—
"The souls of the wicked flit about below the skies on earth,

In murderous pains beneath inevitable yokes of evils;
But those of the pious dwell in the heavens,
Hymning in songs the Great, the Blessed One."

The soul is not then sent down from heaven to what is worse. For God works all things up to what is better. But the soul which has chosen the best life—the life that is from God and righteousness—exchanges earth for heaven. With reason therefore, Job, who had attained to knowledge, said, "Now I know that thou canst do all things; and nothing is impossible to Thee. For who tells me of what I know not, great and wonderful things with which I was unacquainted? And I felt myself vile, considering myself to be earth and ashes." For he who, being in a state of ignorance, is sinful, "is earth and ashes;" while he who is in a state of knowledge, being assimilated as far as possible to God, is already spiritual, and so elect. And that Scripture calls the senseless and disobedient "earth," will be made clear by Jeremiah the prophet, saying, in reference to Joachim and his brethren "Earth, earth, hear the word of the Lord; Write this man, as man excommunicated." And another prophet says again, "Hear, O heaven; and give ear, O earth," calling understanding "ear," and the soul of the Gnostic, that of the man who has applied himself to the contemplation of heaven and divine things, and in this way has become an Israelite, "heaven." For again he calls him who has made ignorance and hardness of heart his choice, "earth." And the expression "give ear" he derives from the "organs of hearing," "the ears," attributing carnal things to those who cleave to the things of sense. Such are they of whom Micah the prophet says, "Hear the word of the Lord, ye peoples who dwell with pangs." And Abraham said, "By no means. The Lord is He who judged the earth;" "since he that believeth not, is," according to the utterance of the Savior, "condemned already." And there is written in the Kings the judgment and sentence of the Lord, which stands thus: "The Lord hears the righteous, but the wicked He saved not, because they do not desire to know God." For the Almighty will not accomplish what is absurd. What do the heresies say to this utterance, seeing Scripture proclaims the Almighty God to be good, and not the author of evil and wrong, if indeed ignorance arises from one not knowing? But God does nothing absurd. "For this God," it is said, "is our God, and there is none to save besides Him." "For there is no unrighteousness with God," according to the apostle. And clearly yet the prophet teaches the will of God, and the gnostic proficiency, in these words: "And now, Israel, what doth the Lord God require of thee, but to fear the Lord thy God, and walk in all His ways, and love Him, and serve Him alone?" He asks of thee, who hast the power of choosing salvation. What is it, then, that the Pythagoreans mean when they bid us "pray with the voice"? As seems to me, not that they thought the Divinity could not hear those who speak silently, but because they wished prayers to be right, which no one would be ashamed to make in the knowledge of many. We shall, however, treat of prayer in due course by and by. But we ought to have works that cry aloud, as becoming "those who walk in the day." "Let thy works shine," and behold a man and his works before his face. "For behold God and His works." For the gnostic must, as far as is possible, imitate God. And the poets call the elect in their pages godlike and gods, and equal to the gods, and equal in sagacity to Zeus, and having counsels like the gods, and resembling the gods,—nibbling, as seems to me, at the expression, "in the image and likeness."

Euripides accordingly says, "Golden wings are round my back, and I am shod with the winged sandals of the Sirens; and I shall go aloft into the wide ether, to hold convene with Zeus."

But I shall pray the Spirit of Christ to wing me to my Jerusalem. For the Stoics say that heaven is properly a city, but places here on earth are not cities; for they are called so, but are not. For a city is an important thing, and the people a decorous body, and a multitude of men regulated by law as the church by the word—a city on earth impregnable—free from tyranny; a product of the divine will on earth as in heaven. Images of this city the poets create with their pen. For the Hyperboreans, and the Arimaspian cities, and the Elysian plains, are commonwealths of just men. And we know Plato's city placed as a pattern in heaven.

Elucidations.

I.
(The Lord's Discipline, book iv. cap. vi. p. 413.)

ἡ κυριακὴ ἄσκησις. Casaubon explains this as *Dominica exercitatio* (the *religion* which the Lord taught), and quotes the apostolic canons (li. and lii.), which, using this word (ἄσκησις), ordain certain fasts *on account of pious exercise.* Baronius, *more suo,* grasps at this word ἄσκησις, as a peg to hang the system of monkery upon. Casaubon answers: "If so, then all the early Christians were monks and nuns; as this word is always used by the Fathers for the Christian discipline, or Christianity itself." Such are the original *ascetics,* nothing more. The Christian Fathers transferred the word from heathen use to that of the Church, to signify the training to which *all the faithful* should subject themselves, in obedience to St. Paul (1 Cor. ix. 24–27). See Isaaci Casauboni, *De Annalibus Baronianis Exercitationes,* p. 171.

II.
(Theano, cap. xix. p. 431.)

The translator has not been happy in this rendering, but I retain it as in the Edinburgh Edition, which leaves one in doubt whether this second saying was Theano's; for, possibly, the translator meant to leave it so. But the Migne note is very good: "Jamblichus mentions two Theanos, one the wife of Brontinus, or Brotinus, and the other of Pythagoras. Both alike were devoted to the Pythagorean philosophy; and it is not certain, therefore, to which of them these *dicta* belong." Theodoret quotes both, but decides not this doubt. Hoffman says, "There were many of the name;" and he mentions five different ones. Suidas makes mention of Theano of Crotona as the wife of Pythagoras, "the first woman who philosophized and wrote poetry;" and Hoffman doubts not this lady is the one quoted by Clement. She seems to have presided over the school of her husband after his death. Of the beauty and morality of the second *dictum*, I have spoken already (p. 348, Elucidation XI.); and I think it worth whole volumes of casuistry on a subject which (naturâ duce, sub lege Logi) the Gospel modestly leaves to natural decency and enlightened conscience. (See Clement's fine remarks, on p. 435.

III.
(St. Paul, note 4, p. 434.)

Better rendered, "Paul is more recent (or later) in respect of time." This seems a strangely apologetic way to speak of this glorious apostle; though the reference may be to his own words (1 Cor. xv. 8), "as of one born out of due time." And it suggests to me, that, among the Alexandrian Christians, there were many Jewish converts who said, "I am of Apollos," and with whom the name of the great apostle of the Gentiles was still unsavory. This goes to confirm the Pauline origin of the Epistle to the Hebrews, so far as it accounts for (what is testified by Eusebius, vi. 14) his omission of his own name from his treatise, lest it should prejudice his argument with his Hebrew kinsmen. Apollos may have sent it to Alexandria.

IV.
(Socrates, cap. xxii. p. 436.)

Who can read the *Phædo*, and think of Plato and Socrates, without hope that the mystery of redemption applies to them in some effectual way, under St. Paul's maxims (Rom. ii. 26)? It would torture me in reading such sayings as are quoted here, were I not able reverently to indulge such hope, and then *to desist from speculation*. Cannot we be silent where

Scripture is silent, and leave all to Him who loved the Gentiles, and died for them on the cross? I suspect the itch of our times, on this and like subjects, to be presumption (2 Cor. x. 5) "against the obedience of Christ." As if our own concern for the heathen were greater than His who died for the unjust, praying for His murderers! Why not leave the ransomed world to the world's Redeemer? The cross bore the inscription in Greek, and Latin also; for the Jews scorned it in Hebrew: and who can doubt that those outstretched arms embraced all mankind?

V.
(Basilides answered, cap. xxiv. p. 437.)

Note the pith and point of this chapter, and the beauty of Clement's *dictum*, "So it would be, were it a man and not God that justifies! As it is written, Thou thought that I was altogether such a one as thyself." (Compare Matt. xx. 14.) But let us not overlook his exposition of the ends and purposes of chastisement. The great principle which he lays down destroys the whole Trent theology about penance, and annihilates the logical base of its figment about "Purgatory." "Punishment does not avail to him who has sinned, to undo his sin." The precious blood of Christ "speaks better things."

VI.
(Sin after Baptism, cap. xxiv. p. 438.)

Not to broach any opinion of my own, it is enough to remark, that this reference to primitive discipline shows that a defined penitential system in the early Church was aimed at by the Montanists, and inspired their deadly animosity, not merely as a theory, but as a system. Although differing on many points with Dr. Bunsen (he is both Baron and Doctor, and I give him the more honorable title of the two), I feel it due to my contract with the reader of this series to refer him to what he says of the baptismal vow, etc. (*Hippol.*, iii. p. 187), as furnishing a valuable commentary on the text, and on the whole plan of Alexandrian teaching and discipline.

VII.
(Jubilee, cap. xxv. p. 438.)

Here the reader may feel that an Elucidation is requisite to any intelligent idea of what Clement means to say. "We wish he would explain his explanation" of Ezekiel. Let me give a brief rendering of the annotations in Migne, as all that can here be furnished. (1) The *tabernacle* is the body, as St. Paul uses the word (2 Cor. v. 1–4), and St. Peter (2 Ep. i. 13, 14). (2) The *seven periods* are the Sabbatical weeks of years leading up to the year of Jubilee. (3) The ἀπλανὴς χώρα refers to the old system of astronomy, and its division of the heavens into an octave of *spheres,* of which the seven inner spheres are those of the seven planets; the fixt stars being in the eighth, which "borders on the intellectual world,"—the abode of spirits, according to Clement.

The Miltonic student will recall the perplexity with which, perhaps, in early years, he first read:—

"They pass the planets seven, and pass the fixt,
And that crystalline sphere whose balance weighs
The trepidation talked, and that first moved.

Paradise Lost, book iii. 481.

The Copernican system was, even in Milton's time, not generally accepted; but, for one who had personally conversed with Galileo, this seems incorrigibly bad. The true system would have given greater dignity, and in fact a better topography, to his great poem.

VIII.

(Rebecca, p. 439.)

Le Nourry, as well as Barbeyrac (see Kaye, pp. 109 and 473), regards Clement as ignorant of the Hebrew language. Kaye, though he shows that some of the attempts to demonstrate this are fanciful, inclines to the same opinion; remarking that he borrows his interpretations from Philo. On the passage here under consideration, he observes, that, "having said repeatedly that Rebekah in Hebrew is equivalent to ὑπομονὴ in Greek, he now makes it equivalent to Θεοῦ δόξα. He elsewhere refers our Savior's exclamation, Eli, Eli, etc., to the Greek word ἥλιος, and the name Jesus to ἰᾶσθαι."

IX.
(Plato's City, cap. xxvi. p. 441.)

This is worth quoting from the *Republic* (book ix. p. 423, Jowett): "In heaven there is laid up a pattern of such a city; and he who desires may behold this, and, beholding, govern himself accordingly; He will act according to the laws of that city, and of no other." Sublime old Gentile! Did not the apostle of the Gentiles think of Socrates, when he wrote Heb. xii. 28, and xiii. 14? On this noble passage, of which Clement has evidently thought very seriously, Schleiermacher's remarks seem to me cold and unsatisfactory. (See his *Introductions*, translated by Dobson; ed. Cambridge, 1836.)

Book V.

CHAP. I.—ON FAITH.

Of the Gnostic so much has been cursorily, as it were, written. We proceed now to the sequel, and must again contemplate faith; for there are some that draw the distinction, that faith has reference to the Son, and knowledge to the Spirit. But it has escaped their notice that, in order to believe truly in the Son, we must believe that He is the Son, and that He came, and how, and for what, and respecting His passion; and we must know who is the Son of God. Now neither is knowledge without faith, nor faith without knowledge. Nor is the Father without the Son; for the Son is with the Father. And the Son is the true teacher respecting the Father; and that we may believe in the Son, we must know the Father, with whom also is the Son. Again, in order that we may know the Father, we must believe in the Son, that it is the Son of God who teaches; for from faith to knowledge by the Son is the Father. And the knowledge of the Son and Father, which is according to the gnostic rule—that which in reality is gnostic—is the attainment and comprehension of the truth by the truth.

We, then, are those who are believers in what is not believed, and who are Gnostics as to what is unknown; that is, Gnostics as to what is unknown and disbelieved by all, but believed and known by a few; and Gnostics, not describing actions by speech, but Gnostics in the exercise of contemplation. Happy is he who speaks in the ears of the hearing. Now faith is the ear of the soul. And such the Lord intimates faith to be, when He says, "He that hath ears to hear, let him hear;" so that by believing he may comprehend what He says, as He says it. Homer, too, the oldest of the poets, using the word "hear" instead of "perceive"— the specific for the generic term—writes:—

"Him most they heard."

For, in fine, the agreement and harmony of the faith of both contribute to one end—salvation. We have in the apostle an unerring witness: "For I desire to see you, that I may impart unto you some spiritual gift, in order that ye may be strengthened; that is, that I may be comforted in you, by the mutual faith of you and me." And further on again he adds, "The righteousness of God is revealed from faith to faith." The apostle, then, manifestly announces a twofold faith, or rather one which admits of growth and perfection; for the common faith lies beneath as a foundation. To those, therefore, who desire to be healed, and are moved by faith, He added, "Thy faith hath saved thee." But that which is excellently built upon is consummated in the believer, and is again perfected by the faith which results from instruction and the word, in order to the performance of the commandments. Such were the apostles, in whose case it is said that "faith removed mountains and transplanted trees." Whence, perceiving the greatness of its power, they asked "that faith might be added to them;" a faith which salutarily bites the soil "like a grain of mustard," and grows magnificently in it, to such a degree that the reasons of things sublime rest on it. For if one by nature knows God, as Basilides thinks, who calls intelligence of a superior order at once faith and kingship, and a creation worthy of the essence of the Creator; and explains that near Him exists not power, but essence and nature and substance; and says that faith is not the rational assent of the soul exercising free-will, but an undefined beauty, belonging immediately to the creature;—the precepts both of the Old and of the New Testament are, then, superfluous, if one is saved by nature, as Valentinus would have it, and is a believer and an elect man by nature, as Basilides thinks; and nature would have been able, one time or other, to have shone forth, apart from the Savior's appearance. But were they to say that the visit of the Savior was necessary, then the properties of nature are gone from them, the elect being saved by instruction, and purification, and the doing of good works. Abraham, accordingly, who through hearing believed the voice, which promised under the oak in Mamre, "I will give this land to thee, and to thy seed," was either elect or not. But if he was not, how did he straightway believe, as it were naturally? And if he was elect, their hypothesis is done away with, inasmuch as even previous to the coming of the Lord an election was found, and that saved: "For it was reckoned to him for righteousness." For if any one, following Marcion, should dare to say that the Creator (Δημιουργόν) saved the man that believed on him, even before the advent of the Lord, (the election being saved with their own proper salvation); the power of the good Being will be eclipsed; inasmuch as late only, and subsequent to the Creator spoken of by them in words of good omen, it made the attempt to save, and by instruction, and in imitation of him. But if, being such, the good Being save, according to them; neither is it his own that he saves, nor is it with the consent of him who formed the creation that he essays salvation, but by force or fraud. And how can he any more be good, acting thus, and being posterior? But if the locality is different, and the dwelling-place of the Omnipotent is remote from the dwelling-place of the good God; yet the will of him who saves, having been the first to begin, is not inferior to that of the good God. From what has been previously proved, those who believe not are proved senseless:

"For their paths are perverted, and they know not peace," says the prophet. "But foolish and unlearned questions" the divine Paul exhorted to "avoid, because they gender strife." And Æschylus exclaims:—

"In what profits not, labor not in vain."

For that investigation, which accords with faith, which builds, on the foundation of faith, the august knowledge of the truth, we know to be the best. Now we know that neither things which are clear are made subjects of investigation, such as if it is day, while it is day; nor things unknown, and never destined to become clear, as whether the stars are even or odd in number; nor things convertible; and those are so which can be said equally by those who take the opposite side, as if what is in the womb is a living creature or not. A fourth mode is, when, from either side of those, there is advanced an unanswerable and irrefragable argument. If, then, the ground of inquiry, according to all of these modes, is removed, faith is established. For we advance to them the unanswerable consideration, that it is God who speaks and comes to our help in writing, respecting each one of the points regarding which I investigate. Who, then, is so impious as to disbelieve God, and to demand proofs from God as from men? Again, some questions demand the evidence of the senses, as if one were to ask whether the fire be warm, or the snow white; and some admonition and rebuke, as the question if you ought to honor your parents. And there are those that deserve punishment, as to ask proofs of the existence of Providence. There being then a Providence, it were impious to think that the whole of prophecy and the economy in reference to a Savior did not take place in accordance with Providence. And perchance one should not even attempt to demonstrate such points, the divine Providence being evident from the sight of all its skilful and wise works which are seen, some of which take place in order, and some appear in order. And He who communicated to us being and life, has communicated to us also reason, wishing us to live rationally and rightly. For the Word of the Father of the universe is not the uttered word (λόγος προφορικός), but the wisdom and most manifest kindness of God, and His power too, which is almighty and truly divine, and not incapable of being conceived by those who do not confess—the all-potent will. But since some are unbelieving, and some are disputatious, all do not attain to the perfection of the good. For neither is it possible to attain it without the exercise of free choice; nor does the whole depend on our own purpose; as, for example, what is defined to happen. "For by grace we are saved:" not, indeed, without good works; but we must, by being formed for what is good, acquire an inclination for it. And we must possess the healthy mind which is fixed on the pursuit of the good; in order to which we have the greatest need of divine grace, and of right teaching, and of holy susceptibility, and of the drawing of the Father to Him. For, bound in this earthly body, we apprehend the objects of sense by means of the body; but we grasp intellectual objects by means of the logical faculty itself. But if one expect to apprehend all things by the senses, he has fallen far from the truth. Spiritually, therefore, the apostle writes respecting the knowledge of God, "For now we see as through a glass, but then face to face." For the vision of the truth is given but to few. Accordingly, Plato says in the *Epinomis*, "I do not say that it is possible for all to be blessed and happy; only a few. Whilst we live, I pronounce this to be the case. But there is a good hope that after death I shall attain all." To the same effect is what we find in Moses: "No man shall see My face, and live." For it is evident that no one during the period of life has been able to apprehend God clearly. But "the pure in heart shall see God," when they arrive at the final perfection. For since the soul became too enfeebled for the apprehension of realities, we needed a divine teacher. The Savior is sent down—a teacher and leader in the acquisition of the good—the secret and sacred token of the great Providence. "Where, then, is the scribe? where is the searcher of this world? Hath not God made foolish the wisdom of this world?" it is said. And again, "I will destroy the wisdom of the wise, and bring to nothing the understanding of the prudent," plainly of those wise in their own eyes, and disputatious. Excellently therefore Jeremiah says, "Thus says the Lord, Stand in the ways, and ask for the eternal paths, what is the good way, and walk in it, and ye shall find expiation for your souls."Ask, he says, and inquire of those who know, without contention and dispute. And on learning the way of truth, let us walk on the right way, without turning till we attain to what we desire. It was therefore with reason that the king of the Romans (his name was Numa), being a Pythagorean, first of all men, erected a temple to Faith and Peace. "And to Abraham, on believing, righteousness was reckoned." He, prosecuting the lofty philosophy of aerial phenomena, and the sublime philosophy of the movements in the heavens, was called Abram, which is interpreted "sublime father." But afterwards, on looking up to heaven, whether it was that he saw the Son in the spirit, as some explain, or a glorious angel, or in any other way recognized God to be superior to the creation, and all the order in it, he receives in addition the Alpha, the knowledge of the one and only God, and is called Abraam, having, instead of a natural philosopher, become wise, and a lover of God. For it is interpreted, "elect father of sound." For by sound is the uttered word: the mind is its father; and the mind of the good man is elect. I cannot forbear praising exceedingly the poet of Agrigentum, who celebrates faith as follows:—

> "Friends, I know, then, that there is truth in the myths
> Which I will relate. But very difficult to men,
> And irksome to the mind, is the attempt of faith."

Wherefore also the apostle exhorts, "that your faith should not be in the wisdom of men," who profess to persuade, "but in the power of God," which alone without proofs, by mere faith, is able to save. "For the most approved of those that are reputable knows how to keep watch. And justice will apprehend the forgers and witnesses of lies," says the Ephesian. For he, having derived his knowledge from the barbarian philosophy, is acquainted with the purification by fire of those who have led bad lives, which the Stoics afterwards called the Conflagration (ἐκπύρωσις), in which also they teach that each will arise exactly as he was, so treating of the resurrection; while Plato says as follows, that the earth at certain periods is purified by fire and water: "There have been many destructions of men in many ways; and there shall be very great ones by fire and water; and others briefer by innumerable causes." And after a little he adds: "And, in truth, there is a change of the objects which revolve about earth and heaven; and in the course of long periods there is the destruction of the objects on earth by a great conflagration." Then he subjoins respecting the deluge: "But when, again, the gods deluge the earth to purify it with water, those on the mountains, herdsmen and shepherds, are saved; those in your cities are carried down by the rivers into the sea." And we showed in the first Miscellany that the philosophers of the Greeks are called thieves, inasmuch as they have taken without acknowledgment their principal dogmas from Moses and the prophets. To which also we shall add, that the angels who had obtained the superior rank, having sunk into pleasures, told to the women the secrets which had come to their knowledge; while the rest of the angels concealed them, or rather, kept them against the coming of the Lord. Thence emanated the doctrine of providence, and the revelation of high things; and prophecy having already been imparted to the philosophers of the Greeks, the treatment of dogma arose among the philosophers, sometimes true when they hit the mark, and sometimes erroneous, when they comprehended not the secret of the prophetic allegory. And this it is proposed briefly to indicate in running over the points requiring mention. Faith, then, we say, we are to show must not be inert and alone, but accompanied with investigation. For I do not say that we are not to inquire at all. For "Search, and thou shalt find," it is said.

> "What is sought may be captured,
> But what is neglected escapes,"

according to Sophocles.
The like also says Menander the comic poet:—

> "All things sought,
> The wisest say, need anxious thought.

But we ought to direct the visual faculty of the soul a right to discovery, and to clear away obstacles; and to cast clean away contention, and envy, and strife, destined to perish miserably from among men.
For very beautifully does Timon of Phlius write:—

> "And Strife, the Plague of Mortals, stalks vainly shrieking,
> The sister of Murderous Quarrel and Discord,

Which rolls blindly over all things. But then
It sets its head towards men, and casts them on hope."

Then a little below he adds:—

"For who hath set these to fight in deadly strife?
A rabble keeping pace with Echo; for, enraged at those silent,
It raised an evil disease against men, and many perished;"

of the speech which denies what is false, and of the dilemma, of that which is concealed, of the Sorites, and of the Crocodilean, of that which is open, and of ambiguities and sophisms. To inquire, then, respecting God, if it tend not to strife, but to discovery, is salutary. For it is written in David, "The poor eat, and shall be filled; and they shall praise the Lord that seek Him. Your heart shall live forever." For they who seek Him after the true search, praising the Lord, shall be filled with the gift that comes from God, that is, knowledge. And their soul shall live; for the soul is figuratively termed the heart, which ministers life: for by the Son is the Father known.

We ought not to surrender our ears to all who speak and write rashly. For cups also, which are taken hold of by many by the ears, are dirtied, and lose the ears; and besides, when they fall they are broken. In the same way also, those, who have polluted the pure hearing of faith by many trifles, at last becoming deaf to the truth, become useless and fall to the earth. It is not, then, without reason that we commanded boys to kiss their relations, holding them by the ears; indicating this, that the feeling of love is engendered by hearing. And
"God," who is known to those who love, "is love," as "God," who by instruction is communicated to the faithful, "is faithful;" and we must be allied to Him by divine love: so that by like we may see like, hearing the word of truth guilelessly and purely, as children who obey us. And this was what he,

whoever he was, indicated who wrote on the entrance to the temple at Epidaurus the inscription:—

"Pure he must be who goes within
The incense-perfumed fane."

And purity is "to think holy thoughts." "Except ye become as these little children, ye shall not enter," it is said, "into the kingdom of heaven." For there the temple of God is seen established on three foundations—faith, hope, and love.

CHAP. II.—ON HOPE.

Respecting faith we have adduced sufficient testimonies of writings among the Greeks. But in order not to exceed bounds, through eagerness to collect a very great many also respecting hope and love, suffice it merely to say that in the *Crito* Socrates, who prefers a good life and death to life itself, thinks that we have hope of another life after death.

Also in the *Phoedrus* he says, "That only when in a separate state can the soul become partaker of the wisdom which is true, and surpasses human power; and when, having reached the end of hope by philosophic love, desire shall waft it to heaven, then," says he, "does it receive the commencement of another, an immortal life." And in the *Symposium* he says, "That there is instilled into all the natural love of generating what is like, and in men of generating men alone, and in the good man of the generation of the counterpart of himself.
But it is impossible for the good man to do this without possessing the perfect virtues, in which he will train the youth who have recourse to him." And as he says in the *Theoetetus,* "He will beget and finish men. For some procreate by the body, others by the soul;" since also with the barbarian philosophers to teach and enlighten is called to regenerate; and "I have begotten you in Jesus Christ," says the good apostle somewhere.

Empedocles, too, enumerates friendship among the elements, conceiving it as a combining love:—

"Which do you look at with your mind; and don't sit gaping with your eyes."

Parmenides, too, in his poem, alluding to hope, speaks thus:—

> "Yet look with the mind certainly on what is absent as present,
> For it will not sever that which is from the grasp it has of that which is
> Not, even if scattered in every direction over the world or combined."

CHAPTER III.—THE OBJECTS OF FAITH AND HOPE PERCEIVED BY THE MIND ALONE.

For he who hopes, as he who believes, sees intellectual objects and future things with the mind. If, then, we affirm that aught is just, and affirm it to be good, and we also say that truth is something, yet we have never seen any of such objects with our eyes, but with our mind alone. Now the Word of God says, "I am the truth." The Word is then to be contemplated by the mind. "Do you aver," it was said, "that there are any true philosophers?" "Yes," said I, "those who love to contemplate the truth." In the *Phoedrus* also, Plato, speaking of the truth, shows it as an idea. Now an idea is a conception of God; and this the barbarians have termed the Word of God. The words are as follow: "For one must then dare to speak the truth, especially in speaking of the truth. For the essence of the soul, being colorless, formless, and intangible, is visible only to God, its guide." Now the Word issuing forth was the cause of creation; then also he generated himself, "when the Word had become flesh," that He might be seen. The righteous man will seek the discovery that flows from love, to which if he hastes he prospers. For it is said, "To him that knocked, it shall be opened: ask, and it shall be given to you." "For the violent that storm the kingdom" are not so in disputatious speeches; but by continuance in a right life and unceasing prayers, are said "to take it by force," wiping away the blots left by their previous sins.

> "You may obtain wickedness, even in great abundance.
> And him who toils God helps;
> For the gifts of the Muses, hard to win,
> Lie not before you, for anyone to bear away."

The knowledge of ignorance is, then, the first lesson in walking according to the Word. An ignorant man has sought, and having sought, he finds the teacher; and finding has believed, and believing has hoped; and henceforward having loved, is assimilated to what was loved—endeavoring to be what he first loved. Such is the method Socrates shows Alcibiades, who thus questions: "Do you not think that I shall know about what is right otherwise?" "Yes, if you have found out." "But you don't think I have found out?" "Certainly, if you have sought."

"Then you don't think that I have sought?" "Yes, if you think you do not know." So with the lamps of the wise virgins, lighted at night in the great darkness of ignorance, which the Scripture signified by "night." Wise souls, pure as virgins, understanding themselves to be situated amidst the ignorance of the world, kindle the light, and rouse the mind, and illumine the darkness, and dispel ignorance, and seek truth, and await the appearance of the Teacher.

"The mob, then," said I, "cannot become philosopher."

"Many rod-bearers there are, but few Bacchi," according to Plato. "For many are called, but few chosen." "Knowledge is not in all," says the apostle. "And pray that we may be delivered from unreasonable and wicked men: for all men have not faith."And the *Poetics* of Cleanthes, the Stoic, writes to the following effect:—

> "Look not to glory, wishing to be suddenly wise,
> And fear not the undiscerning and rash opinion of the many;
> For the multitude has not an intelligent, or wise, or right judgment,
> And it is in few men that you will find this."

And more sententiously the comic poet briefly says:—

> "It is a shame to judge of what is right by much noise."

For they heard, I think, that excellent wisdom, which says to us, "Watch your opportunity in the midst of the foolish, and in the midst of the intelligent continue."And again, "The wise will conceal sense." For the many demand demonstration as a pledge of truth, not satisfied with the bare salvation by faith.

> "But it is strongly incumbent to disbelieve the dominant wicked,
> And as is enjoined by the assurance of our muse,
> Know by dissecting the utterance within your breast."

"For this is habitual to the wicked," says Empedocles, "to wish to overbear what is true by disbelieving it." And that our tenets are probable and worthy of belief, the Greeks shall know, the point being more thoroughly investigated in what follows. For we are taught what is like by what is like. For says Solomon, "Answer a fool according to his folly." Wherefore also, to those that ask the wisdom that is with us, we are to hold out things suitable, that with the greatest possible ease they may, through their own ideas, be likely to arrive at faith in the truth. For "I became all things to all men, that I might gain all men." Since also "the rain" of the divine grace is sent down "on the just and the unjust." "Is He the God of the Jews only, and not also of the Gentiles? Yes, also of the Gentiles: if indeed He is one God," exclaims the noble apostle.

CHAPTER IV.—DIVINE THINGS WRAPPED UP IN FIGURES BOTH IN THE SACRED AND IN HEATHEN WRITERS.

But since they will believe neither in what is good justly nor in knowledge unto salvation, we ourselves reckoning what they claim as belonging to us, because all things are God's; and especially since what is good proceeded from us to the Greeks, let us handle those things as they are capable of hearing. For intelligence or rectitude this great crowd estimates not by truth, but by what they are delighted with. And they will be pleased not more with other things than with what is like themselves. For he who is still blind and dumb, not having understanding, or the undazzled and keen vision of the contemplative soul, which the Savior confers, like the uninitiated at the mysteries, or the unmusical at dances, not being yet pure and worthy of the pure truth, but still discordant and disordered and material, must stand outside of the divine choir. "For we compare spiritual things with spiritual." Wherefore, in accordance with the method of concealment, the truly sacred Word, truly divine and most necessary for us, deposited in the shrine of truth, was by the Egyptians indicated by what were called among them *adyta,* and by the Hebrews by the veil. Only the consecrated—that is, those devoted to God, circumcised in the desire of the passions for the sake of love to that which is alone divine—were allowed access to them. For Plato also thought it not lawful for "the impure to touch the pure."

Thence the prophecies and oracles are spoken in enigmas, and the mysteries are not exhibited incontinently to all and sundry, but only after certain purifications and previous instructions.

"For the Muse was not then
Greedy of gain or mercenary;

> Nor were Terpsichore's sweet,
> Honey-toned, silvery soft-voiced
> Strains made merchandise of."

Now those instructed among the Egyptians learned first of all that style of the Egyptian letters which is called Epistolographic; and second, the Hieratic, which the sacred scribes practice; and finally, and last of all, the Hieroglyphic, of which one kind which is by the first elements is literal (Kyriologic), and the other Symbolic. Of the Symbolic, one kind speaks literally by imitation, and another writes as it were figuratively; and another is quite allegorical, using certain enigmas.

Wishing to express Sun in writing, they make a circle; and Moon, a figure like the Moon, like its proper shape. But in using the figurative style, by transposing and transferring, by changing and by transforming in many ways as suits them, they draw characters. In relating the praises of the kings in theological myths, they write in anaglyphs. Let the following stand as a specimen of the third species—the Enigmatic. For the rest of the stars, on account of their oblique course, they have figured like the bodies of serpents; but the sun, like that of a beetle, because it makes a round figure of ox-dung, and rolls it before its face. And they say that this creature lives six months under ground, and the other division of the year above ground, and emits its seed into the ball, and brings forth; and that there is not a female beetle. All then, in a word, who have spoken of divine things, both Barbarians and Greeks, have veiled the first principles of things, and delivered the truth in enigmas, and symbols, and allegories, and metaphors, and such like tropes. Such also are the oracles among the Greeks. And the Pythian Apollo is called Loxias. Also the maxims of those among the Greeks called wise men, in a few sayings indicate the unfolding of matter of considerable importance. Such certainly is that maxim, "Spare Time:" either because life is short, and we ought not to expend this time in vain; or, on the other hand, it bids you spare your personal expenses; so that, though you live many years, necessaries may not fail you. Similarly also the maxim "*Know thyself*" shows many things; both that thou art mortal, and that thou was born a human being; and also that, in comparison with the other excellences of life, thou art of no account, because thou says that thou art rich or renowned; or, on the other hand, that, being rich or renowned, you are not honored on account of your advantages alone. And it says, Know for what thou wert born, and whose image thou art; and what is thy essence, and what thy creation, and what thy relation to God, and the like. And the Spirit says by Isaiah the prophet, "I will give thee treasures, hidden, dark." Now wisdom, hard to hunt, is the treasures of God and unfailing riches. But those, taught in theology by those prophets, the poets, philosophize much by way of a hidden sense. I mean Orpheus, Linus, Musæus, Homer, and Hesiod, and those in this fashion wise. The persuasive style of poetry is for them a veil for the many. Dreams and signs are all more or less obscure to men, not from jealousy (for it were wrong to conceive of God as subject to passions), but in order that research, introducing to the understanding of enigmas, may haste to the discovery of truth. Thus Sophocles the tragic poet somewhere says:—

> "And God I know to be such a one,
> Ever the revealer of enigmas to the wise,
> But to the perverse bad, although a teacher in few words,"—

putting bad instead of simple. Expressly then respecting all our Scripture, as if spoken in a parable, it is written in the Psalms, "Hear, O My people, My law: incline your ear to the words of My mouth. I will open My mouth in parables, I will utter My problems from the beginning." Similarly speaks the noble apostle to the following effect: "Howbeit we speak wisdom among those that are perfect; yet not the wisdom of this world, nor of the princes of this world, that come to naught. But we speak the wisdom of God hidden in a mystery; which none of the princes of this world knew. For had they known it, they would not have crucified the Lord of glory."

The philosophers did not exert themselves in contemning the appearance of the Lord. It therefore follows that it is the opinion of the wise among the Jews which the apostle inveighs against. Wherefore he adds, "But we preach, as it is written, what eye hath not seen, and ear hath not heard, and hath not entered into the heart of man, what God hath prepared for them that love Him. For God hath revealed it to us by the Spirit. For the Spirit searches all things, even the deep things of God." For he recognizes the spiritual man and the Gnostic as the disciple of the Holy Spirit dispensed by God, which is the mind of Christ. "But the natural man receives not the things of the Spirit, for they are foolishness to him." Now the apostle, in contradistinction to gnostic perfection, calls the common faith *the foundation,* and sometimes *milk,* writing on this wise: "Brethren, I could not speak to you as to spiritual, but as to carnal, to babes in Christ. I have fed you with milk, not with meat: for ye were not able. Neither yet are ye now able. For ye are yet carnal: for whereas there is among you envy and strife, are ye not carnal, and walk as men?" Which things are the choice of those men who are sinners. But those who abstain from these things give their thoughts to divine things, and partake of gnostic food. "According to the grace," it is said, "given to me as a wise master builder, I have laid the foundation. And another built on it gold and silver, precious stones."Such is the gnostic superstructure on the foundation of faith in Christ Jesus. But "the stubble, and the wood, and the hay," are the additions of heresies. "But the fire shall try every man's work, of what sort it is." In allusion to the gnostic edifice also in the Epistle to the Romans, he says, "For I desire to see you, that I may impart unto you a spiritual gift, that ye may be established." It was impossible that gifts of this sort could be written without disguise.

CHAPTER V.—ON THE SYMBOLS OF PYTHAGORAS.

Now the Pythagorean symbols were connected with the Barbarian philosophy in the most recondite way. For instance, the Samian counsels "not to have a swallow in the house;" that is, not to receive a loquacious, whispering, garrulous man, who cannot contain what has been communicated to him. "For the swallow, and the turtle, and the sparrows of the field, know the times of their entrance," says the Scripture; and one ought never to dwell with trifles. And the turtle-dove murmuring shows the thankless slander of fault-finding, and is rightly expelled the house.

"Don't mutter against me, sitting by one in one place, another in another."

The swallow too, which suggests the fable of Pandion, seeing it is right to detest the incidents reported of it, some of which we hear Tereus suffered, and some of which he inflicted. It pursues also the musical grasshoppers, whence he who is a persecutor of the word ought to be driven away.

"By scepter-bearing Here, whose eye surveys Olympus,
I have a rusty closet for tongues,"

says Poetry. Æschylus also says:—

"But, I, too, have a key as a guard on my tongue."

Again Pythagoras commanded, "When the pot is lifted off the fire, not to leave its mark in the ashes, but to scatter them;" and "people on getting up from bed, to shake the bed-clothes." For he intimated that it was necessary not only to efface the mark, but not to leave even a trace of anger; and that on its ceasing to boil, it was to be composed, and all memory of injury to be wiped out. "And let not the sun," says the Scripture, "go down upon your wrath." And he that said, "Thou shall not desire," took away all memory of wrong; for wrath is found to be the impulse of concupiscence in a mild soul, especially seeking irrational revenge. In the same way "the bed is ordered to be shaken up," so that there may be no recollection of effusion in sleep, or sleep in the day-time; nor, besides, of pleasure during the night. And he intimated that the vision of the dark ought to be dissipated speedily by the light of truth. "Be angry, and sin not," says David, teaching us that we ought not to assent to the impression, and not to follow it up by action, and so confirm wrath.

Again, "Don't sail on land" is a Pythagorean saw, and shows that taxes and similar contracts, being troublesome and fluctuating, ought to be declined. Wherefore also the Word says that the tax-gatherers shall be saved with difficulty.

And again, "Don't wear a ring, nor engrave on it the images of the gods," enjoins Pythagoras; as Moses ages before enacted expressly, that neither a graven, nor molten, nor molded, nor painted likeness should be made; so that we may not cleave to things of sense, but pass to intellectual objects: for familiarity with the sight disparages the reverence of what is divine; and to worship that which is immaterial by matter, is to dishonor it by sense. Wherefore the wisest of the Egyptian priests decided that the temple of Athene should be hypæthral, just as the Hebrews constructed the temple without an image. And some, in worshipping God, make a representation of heaven containing the stars; and so worship, although Scripture says, "Let Us make man in Our image and likeness." I think it worthwhile also to adduce the utterance of Eurysus the Pythagorean, which is as follows, who in his book *On Fortune*, having said that the "Creator, on making man, took Himself as an exemplar," added, "And the body is like the other things, as being made of the same material, and fashioned by the best workman, who wrought it, taking Himself as the archetype."

And, in fine, Pythagoras and his followers, with Plato also, and most of the other philosophers, were best acquainted with the

Lawgiver, as may be concluded from their doctrine. And by a happy utterance of divination, not without divine help, concurring in certain prophetic declarations, and, seizing the truth in portions and aspects, in terms not obscure, and not going beyond the explanation of the things, they honored it on as certaining the appearance of relation with the truth. Whence the Hellenic philosophy is like the torch of wick which men kindle, artificially stealing the light from the sun. But on the proclamation of the Word all that holy light shone forth. Then in houses by night the stolen light is useful; but by day the fire blazes, and all the night is illuminated by such a sun of intellectual light.

Now Pythagoras made an epitome of the statements on righteousness in Moses, when he said, "Do not step over the balance;" that is, do not transgress equality in distribution, honoring justice so.

> "Which friends to friends forever, binds,
> To cities, cities—to allies, allies,
> For equality is what is right for men;
> But less to greater ever hostile grows,
> And days of hate begin,"

as is said with poetic grace.

Wherefore the Lord says, "Take My yoke, for it is gentle and light." And on the disciples, striving for the pre-eminence, He enjoins equality with simplicity, saying "that they must become as little children." Likewise also the apostle writes, that "no one in Christ is bond or free, or Greek or Jew. For the creation in Christ Jesus is new, is equality, free of strife—not grasping—just." For envy, and jealousy, and bitterness, stand without the divine choir.

Thus also those skilled in the mysteries forbid "to eat the heart;" teaching that we ought not to gnaw and consume the soul by idleness and by vexation, on account of things which happen against one's wishes. Wretched, accordingly, was the man whom Homer also says, wandering alone, "ate his own heart." But again, seeing the Gospel supposes two ways—the apostles, too, similarly with all the prophets—and seeing they call that one "narrow and confined" which is circumscribed according to the commandments and prohibitions, and the opposite one, which leads to perdition, "broad and roomy," open to pleasures and wrath, and say, "Blessed is the man who walks not in the counsel of the ungodly, and stands not in the way of sinners." Hence also comes the fable of Prodicus of Ceus about Virtue and Vice. And Pythagoras shrinks not from prohibiting to walk on the public thoroughfares, enjoining the necessity of not following the sentiments of the many, which are crude and inconsistent. And Aristocritus, in the first book of his *Positions against Heracliodorus*, mentions a letter to this effect: "Atoeeas king of the Scythians to the people of Byzantium: Do not impair my revenues in case my mares drink your water;" for the Barbarian indicated symbolically that he would make war on them. Likewise also the poet Euphorion introduces Nestor saying,—

"We have not yet wet the Achæan steeds in Simois."

Therefore also the Egyptians place Sphinxes before their temples, to signify that the doctrine respecting God is enigmatical and obscure; perhaps also that we ought both to love and fear the Divine Being: to love Him as gentle and benign to the pious; to fear Him as inexorably just to the impious; for the sphinx shows the image of a wild beast and of a man together.

CHAPTER VI.—THE MYSTIC MEANING OF THE TABERNACLE AND ITS FURNITURE.

It were tedious to go over all the Prophets and the Law, specifying what is spoken in enigmas; for almost the whole Scripture gives its utterances in this way. It may suffice, I think, for any one possessed of intelligence, for the proof of the point in hand, to select a few examples.

Now concealment is evinced in the reference of the seven circuits around the temple, which are made mention of among the Hebrews; and the equipment on the robe, indicating by the various symbols, which had reference to visible objects, the agreement which from heaven reaches down to earth. And the covering and the veil were variegated with blue, and purple, and scarlet, and linen. And so it was suggested that the nature of the elements contained the revelation of God. For purple is from water, linen from the earth; blue, being dark, is like the air, as scarlet is like fire.

In the midst of the covering and veil, where the priests were allowed to enter, was situated the altar of incense, the symbol of the earth placed in the middle of this universe; and from it came the fumes of incense. And that place intermediate between the inner veil, where the high priest alone, on prescribed days, was permitted to enter, and the external court which surrounded it—free to all the Hebrews—was, they say, the middlemost point of heaven and earth. But others say it was the symbol of the intellectual world, and that of sense. The covering, then, the barrier of popular unbelief, was stretched in front of the five pillars, keeping back those in the surrounding space.

So very mystically the five loaves are broken by the Savior, and fill the crowd of the listeners. For great is the crowd that keep to the things of sense, as if they were the only things in existence. "Cast your eyes round, and see," says Plato, "that none of the uninitiated listen." Such are they who think that nothing else exists, but what they can hold tight with their hands; but do not admit as in the department of existence, actions and processes of generation, and the whole of the unseen. For such are those who keep by the five senses.
But the knowledge of God is a thing inaccessible to the ears and like organs of this kind of people. Hence the Son is said to be the Father's face, being the revealer of the Father's character

to the five senses by clothing Himself with flesh. "But if we live in the Spirit, let us also walk in the Spirit." "For we walk by faith, not by sight," the noble apostle says. Within the veil, then, is concealed the sacerdotal service; and it keeps those engaged in it far from those without.

Again, there is the veil of the entrance into the holy of holies. Four pillars there are, the sign of the sacred tetrad of the ancient covenants. Further, the mystic name of four letters which was affixed to those alone to whom the adytum was accessible, is called Jave, which is interpreted, "Who is and shall be." The name of God, too, among the Greeks contains four letters.

Now the Lord, having come alone into the intellectual world, enters by His sufferings, introduced into the knowledge of the Ineffable, ascending above every name which is known by sound. The lamp, too, was placed to the south of the altar of incense; and by it were shown the motions of the seven planets, that perform their revolutions towards the south. For three branches rose on either side of the lamp, and lights on them; since also the sun, like the lamp, set in the midst of all the planets, dispenses with a kind of divine music the light to those above and to those below.

The golden lamp conveys another enigma as a symbol of Christ, not in respect of form alone, but in his casting light, "at sundry times and divers manners," on those who believe on Him and hope, and who see by means of the ministry of the First-born. And they say that the seven eyes of the Lord "are the seven spirits resting on the rod that springs from the root of Jesse."

North of the altar of incense was placed a table, on which there was "the exhibition of the loaves;" for the most nourishing of the winds are those of the north. And thus are signified certain seats of churches conspiring so as to form one body and one assemblage.

And the things recorded of the sacred ark signify the properties of the world of thought, which is hidden and closed to the many.

And those golden figures, each of them with six wings, signify either the two bears, as some will have it, or rather the two hemispheres. And the name cherubim meant "much knowledge." But both together have twelve wings, and by the zodiac and time, which moves on it, point out the world of sense. It is of them, I think, that Tragedy, discoursing of Nature, says:—

> "Unwearied Time circles full in perennial flow,
> Producing itself. And the twin-bears
> On the swift wandering motions of their wings,
> Keep the Atlantean pole."

And Atlas, the unsuffering pole, may mean the fixed sphere, or better perhaps, motionless eternity. But I think it better to regard the ark, so called from the Hebrew word *Thebotha*, as signifying something else. It is interpreted, *one instead of one in all places*. Whether, then, it is the eighth region and the world of thought, or God, all-embracing, and without shape, and invisible, that is indicated, we may for the present defer saying. But it signifies the repose which dwells with the adoring spirits, which are meant by the cherubim.

For He who prohibited the making of a graven image, would never Himself have made an image in the likeness of holy things. Nor is there at all any composite thing, and creature endowed with sensation, of the sort in heaven. But the face is a symbol of the rational soul, and the wings are the lofty ministers and energies of powers right and left; and the voice is delightsome glory in ceaseless contemplation. Let it suffice that the mystic interpretation has advanced so far.

Now the high priest's robe is the symbol of the world of sense. The seven planets are represented by the five stones and the two carbuncles, for Saturn and the Moon. The former is southern, and moist, and earthy, and heavy; the latter aerial, whence she is called by some Artemis, as if Ærotomos (cutting the air); and the air is cloudy. And cooperating as they did in the production of things here below, those that by Divine Providence are set over the planets are rightly represented as placed on the breast and shoulders; and by them was the work of creation, the first week. And the breast is the seat of the heart and soul.

Differently, the stones might be the various phases of salvation; some occupying the upper, some the lower parts of the entire body saved. The three hundred and sixty bells, suspended from the robe, is the space of a year, "the acceptable year of the Lord," proclaiming and resounding the stupendous manifestation of the Savior. Further, the broad gold mitre indicates the regal power of the Lord, "since the Head of the Church" is the Savor. The mitre that is on it [i.e., the head] is, then, a sign of most princely rule; and otherwise we have heard it said, "The Head of Christ is the God and Father of our Lord Jesus Christ." Moreover, there was the breastplate, comprising the ephod, which is the symbol of work, and the oracle (λογίον); and this indicated the Word (λόγος) by which it was framed, and is the symbol of heaven, made by the Word, and subjected to Christ, the Head of all things, inasmuch as it moves in the same way, and in a like manner. The luminous emerald stones, therefore, in the ephod, signify the sun and moon, the helpers of nature. The shoulder, I take it, is the commencement of the hand.

The twelve stones, set in four rows on the breast, describe for us the circle of the zodiac, in the four changes of the year. It was otherwise requisite that the law and the prophets should be placed beneath the Lord's head, because in both Testaments mention is made of the righteous. For were we to say that the apostles were at once prophets and righteous, we should say well, "since one and the self-same Holy Spirit works in all." And as the Lord is above the whole world, yea, above the world of thought, so the name engraven on the plate has been regarded to signify, above all rule and authority; and it was inscribed with reference both to the written commandments and the manifestation to sense. And it is the name of God that is expressed; since, as the Son sees the goodness of the Father, God the Savior works, being called the first principle of all things, which was imaged forth from the invisible God first, and before the ages, and which fashioned all things which came into being after itself. Nay more, the oracle exhibits the prophecy which by the Word cries and preaches, and the judgment that is to come; since it is the same Word which prophesies, and judges, and discriminates all things.

And they say that the robe prophesied the ministry in the flesh, by which He was seen in closer relation to the world. So the high priest, putting off his consecrated robe (the universe, and the creation in the universe, were consecrated by Him assenting that, what was made, was good), washes himself, and puts on the other tunic—a holy-of-holies one, so to speak—which is to accompany him into the adytum; exhibiting, as seems to me, the Levite and Gnostic, as the chief of other priests (those bathed in water, and clothed in faith alone, and expecting their own individual abode), himself distinguishing the objects of the intellect from the things of sense, rising above other priests, hasting to the entrance to the world of ideas, to wash himself from the things here below, not in water, as formerly one was cleansed on being enrolled in the tribe of Levi. But purified already by the gnostic Word in his whole heart, and thoroughly regulated, and having improved that mode of life received from the priest to the highest pitch, being quite sanctified both in word and life, and having put on the bright array of glory, and received the ineffable inheritance of that spiritual and perfect man, "which eye hath not seen and ear hath not heard, and it hath not entered into the heart of man;" and having become son and friend, he is now replenished with insatiable contemplation face to face. For there is nothing like hearing the Word Himself, who by means of the Scripture inspires fuller intelligence. For so it is said, "And he shall put off the linen robe, which he had put on when he entered into the holy place; and shall lay it aside there, and wash his body in water in the holy place, and put on his robe." But in one way, as I think, the Lord puts off and puts on by descending into the region of sense; and in another, he who through Him has believed puts off and puts on, as the apostle intimated, the consecrated stole. Thence, after the image of the Lord the worthiest were chosen from the sacred tribes to be high priests, and those elected to the kingly office and to prophecy were anointed.

CHAPTER VII.—THE EGYPTIAN SYMBOLS AND ENIGMAS OF SACRED THINGS.

Whence also the Egyptians did not entrust the mysteries they possessed to all and sundry, and did not divulge the knowledge of divine things to the profane; but only to those destined to ascend the throne, and those of the priests that were judged the worthiest, from their nurture, culture, and birth. Similar, then, to the Hebrew enigmas in respect to concealment, are those of the Egyptians also. Of the Egyptians, some show the sun on a ship, others on a crocodile. And they signify hereby, that the sun, making a passage through the delicious and moist air, generates time; which is symbolized by the crocodile in some other sacerdotal account. Further, at Diospolis in Egypt, on the temple called Pylon, there was figured a boy as the symbol of production, and an old man as that of decay. A hawk, on the other hand, was the symbol of God, as a fish of hate; and, according to a different symbolism, the crocodile of impudence. The whole symbol, then, when put together, appears to teach this: "Oh ye who are born and die, God hates impudence."

And there are those who fashion ears and eyes of costly material, and consecrate them, dedicating them in the temples to the gods—by this plainly indicating that God sees and hears all things. Besides, the lion is with them the symbol of strength and prowess, as the ox clearly is of the earth itself, and husbandry and food, and the horse of fortitude and confidence; while, on the other hand, the sphinx, of strength combined with intelligence—as it had a body entirely that of a lion, and the face of a man. Similarly to these, to indicate intelligence, and memory, and power, and art, a man is sculptured in the temples. And in what is called among them the Komasiæ of the gods, they carry about golden images—two dogs, one hawk, and one ibis; and the four figures of the images they call four letters. For the dogs are symbols of the two hemispheres, which, as it were, go round and keep watch; the hawk, of the sun, for it is fiery and destructive (so they attribute pestilential diseases to the sun); the ibis, of the moon, likening the shady parts to that which is dark in plumage, and the luminous to the light. And some will have it that by the dogs are meant the tropics, which guard and watch the sun's passage to the south and north. The hawk signifies the equinoctial line, which is high and parched with heat, as the ibis the ecliptic. For the ibis seems, above other animals, to have furnished to the Egyptians the first rudiments of the invention of number and measure, as the oblique line did of circles.

CHAPTER VIII.—THE USE OF THE SYMBOLIC STYLE BY POETS AND PHILOSOPHERS.

But it was not only the most highly intellectual of the Egyptians, but also such of other barbarians as prosecuted philosophy, that affected the symbolical style. They say, then, that Idanthuris king of the Scythians, as Pherecydes of Syros relates, sent to Darius, on his passing the Ister in threat of war, a symbol, instead of a letter, consisting of a mouse, a frog, a bird, a javelin, a plough. And there being a doubt in reference to them, as was to be expected, Orontopagas the Chiliarch said that they were to resign the kingdom; taking dwellings to be meant by the mouse, waters by the frog, air by the bird, land by the plough, arms by the javelin. But Xiphodres interpreted the contrary; for he said, "If we do not take our flight like birds, or like mice get below the earth, or like frogs beneath the water, we shall not escape their arrows; for we are not lords of the territory."

It is said that Anacharsis the Scythian, while asleep, covered the pudenda with his left hand, and his mouth with his right, to intimate that both ought to be mastered, but that it was a greater thing to master the tongue than voluptuousness.

And why should I linger over the barbarians, when I can adduce the Greeks as exceedingly addicted to the use of the method of concealment? Androcydes the Pythagorean says the far-famed so-called Ephesian letters were of the class of symbols. For he said that ἄσκιον (shadowless) meant darkness, for it has no shadow; and κατάσκιον (shadowy) light, since it casts with its rays the shadow; and λίξ if is the earth, according to an ancient' appellation; and τετράς is the year, in reference to the seasons; and δαμναμενεύς is the sun, which overpowers (δαμάζων); and τὰ αἴσια is the true voice. And then the symbol intimates that divine things have been arranged in harmonious order—darkness to light, the sun to the year, and the earth to nature's processes of production of every sort. Also Dionysius Thrax, the grammarian, in his book, *Respecting the Exposition of the Symbolical Signification in Circles,* says expressly, "Some signified actions not by words only, but also by symbols: by words, as is the case of what are called the Delphic maxims, 'Nothing in excess,' 'Know thyself,' and the like; and by symbols, as the wheel that is turned in the temples of the gods, derived from the Egyptians, and the branches that are given to the worshippers. For the Thracian Orpheus says:—

> "Whatever works of branches are a care to men on earth,
> Not one has one fate in the mind, but all things
> Revolve around; and it is not lawful to stand at one point,
> But each one keeps an equal part of the race as they began."

The branches either stand as the symbol of the first food, or they are that the multitude may know that fruits spring and grow universally, remaining a very long time; but that the duration of life allotted to themselves is brief. And it is on this account that they will have it that the branches are given; and perhaps also that they may know, that as these, on the other hand, are burned, so also they themselves speedily leave this life, and will become fuel for fire.

Very useful, then, is the mode of symbolic interpretation for many purposes; and it is helpful to the right theology, and to piety, and to the display of intelligence, and the practice of brevity, and the exhibition of wisdom. "For the use of symbolical speech is characteristic of the wise man," appositely remarks the grammarian Didymus, "and the explanation of what is signified by it." And indeed the most elementary instruction of children embraces the interpretation of the four elements; for it is said that the Phrygians call water Bedu, as also Orpheus says:—

> "And bright water is poured down, the Bedu of the nymphs."

Dion Thytes also seems to write similarly:—

> And taking Bedu, pour it on your hands, and turn to divination."

On the other hand, the comic poet, Philydeus, understands by Bedu the air, as being (Biodoros) life-giver, in the following lines:—

> "I pray that I may inhale the salutary Bedu,
> Which is the most essential part of health;
> Inhale the pure, the unsullied air."

In the same opinion also concurs Neanthes of Cyzicum, who writes that the Macedonian priests invoke Bedu, which they interpret to mean *the air,* to be propitious to them and to their children. And Zaps some have ignorantly taken for fire (from ζέσιν, *boiling*); for so the sea is called, as Euphorion, in his reply to Theoridas:—

"And Zaps, destroyer of ships, wrecked it on the rocks."

And Dionysius Iambus similarly:—

"Briny Zaps moans about the maddened deep."

Similarly Cratinus the younger, the comic poet:—

"Zaps casts forth shrimps and little fishes."

And Simmias of Rhodes:—

"Parent of the Ignetes and the Telchines briny Zaps was born."

And χθών is the carth (κεχυμένη) spread forth to bigness. And Plectron, according to some, is the sky (πόλος), according to others, it is the air, which strikes (πλήσσοντα) and moves to nature and increase, and which fills all things. But these have not read Cleanthes the philosopher, who expressly calls Plectron the sun; for darting his beams in the east, as if striking the world, he leads the light to its harmonious course. And from the sun it signifies also the rest of the stars.

And the Sphinx is not the comprehension of the universe, and the revolution of the world, according to the poet Aratus; but perhaps it is the spiritual tone which pervades and holds together the universe. But it is better to regard it as the ether, which holds together and presses all things; as also Empedocles says:—

"But come now, first will I speak of the Sun, the first principle of all things,
From which all, that we look upon, has sprung,
Both earth, and billowy deep, and humid air;
Titan and Ether too, which binds all things around."

And Apollodorus of Corcyra says that these lines were recited by Branchus the seer, when purifying the Milesians from plague; for he, sprinkling the multitude with branches of laurel, led off the hymn somehow as follows:—

"Sing Boys Hecaergus and Hecaerga."

And the people accompanied him, saying, "Bedu, Zaps, Chthon, Plectron, Sphinx, Cnaxzbi, Chthyptes, Phlegmos, Drops." Callimachus relates the story in iambics. Cnaxzbi is, by derivation, the plague, from its gnawing (κναίειν) and destroying (διαφθείρειν), and θῦψαι is to consume with a thunderbolt. Thespis the tragic poet says that something else was signified by these, writing thus: "Lo, I offer to thee a libation of white Cnaxzbi, having pressed it from the yellow nurses. Lo, to thee, O two-horned Pan, mixing Chthyptes cheese with red honey, I place it on thy sacred altars. Lo, to thee I pour as a libation the sparkling gleam of Bromius." He signifies, as I think, the soul's first milk-like nutriment of the four and- twenty elements, after which solidified milk comes as food. And last, he teaches of the blood of the vine of the Word, the sparkling wine, the perfecting gladness of instruction.
And Drops is the operating Word, which, beginning with elementary training, and advancing to the growth of the man, inflames and illumines man up to the measure of maturity.

The third is said to be a writing copy for children—μάρπτες, σφίγξ, κλώψ, ζυγχθηδόν. And it signifies, in my opinion, that by the arrangement of the elements and of the world, we must advance to the knowledge of what is more perfect, since eternal salvation is attained by force and toil; for μάρψαι is to grasp. And the harmony of the world is meant by the Sphinx; and ζυνχθηδόν means difficulty; and κλώψ means at once the secret knowledge of the Lord and day. Well! does not Epigenes, in his book on the *Poetry of Orpheus*, in exhibiting the peculiarities found in Orpheus, say that by "the curved rods" (κεραίσι) is meant "ploughs;" and by the warp (στήμοσι), the furrows; and the woof (μίτος) is a figurative expression for the seed; and that the tears of Zeus signify a shower; and that the "parts" (μοῖραι) are, again, the phases of the moon, the thirtieth day, and the fifteenth, and the new moon, and that Orpheus accordingly calls them "white-robed," as being parts of the light? Again, that the Spring is called "flowery," from its nature; and Night "still," on account of rest; and the Moon "Gorgonian," on account of the face in it; and that the time in which it is necessary to sow is called Aphrodite by the "Theologian." In the same way, too, the Pythagoreans figuratively called the planets the "dogs of Persephone;" and to the sea they applied the metaphorical appellation of "the tears of Kronus." Myriads on myriads of enigmatical utterances by both poets and philosophers are to be found; and there are also whole books which present the mind of the writer veiled, as that of Heraclitus *On Nature*, who on this very account is called "Obscure." Similar to this book is the *Theology* of Pherecydes of Syrus; for Euphorion the poet, and the *Causes* of Callimachus, and the *Alexandra* of Lycophron, and the like, are proposed as an exercise in exposition to all the grammarians.

It is, then, proper that the Barbarian philosophy, on which it is our business to speak, should prophecy also obscurely and by symbols, as was evinced. Such are the injunctions of Moses: "These common things, the sow, the hawk, the eagle, and the raven, are not to be eaten." For the sow is the emblem of voluptuous and unclean lust of food, and lecherous and filthy licentiousness in venery, always prurient, and material, and lying in the mire, and fattening for slaughter and destruction.

Again, he commands to eat that which parts the hoof and ruminates; "intimating," says Barnabas, "that we ought to cleave to those who fear the Lord, and meditate in their heart on that portion of the word which they have received, to those who speak and keep the Lord's statutes, to those to whom meditation is a work of gladness, and who ruminate on the word of the Lord. And what is the parted hoof? That the righteous walks in this world, and expects the holy eternity to come." Then he adds, "See how well Moses enacted. But whence could they understand or comprehend these things? We who have rightly understood speak the commandments as the Lord wished; wherefore He circumcised our ears and hearts, that we may comprehend these things. And when he says, 'Thou shalt not eat the eagle, the hawk, the kite, and the crow;' he says, 'Thou shalt not adhere to or become like those men who know not how to procure for themselves subsistence by toil and sweat, but live by plunder, and lawlessly.' For the eagle indicates robbery, the hawk injustice, and the raven greed. It is also written, 'With the innocent man thou wilt be innocent, and with the chosen choice, and with the perverse thou shall pervert.' It is incumbent on us to cleave to the saints, because they that cleave to them shall be sanctified." Thence Theognis writes:—

> "For from the good you will learn good things;
> But if you mix with the bad, you will destroy any mind you may have."

And when, again, it is said in the ode, "For He hath triumphed gloriously: the horse and his rider hath He cast into the sea;" the many-limbed and brutal affection, lust, with the rider mounted, who gives the reins to pleasures, "He has cast into the sea," throwing them away into the disorders of the world. Thus also Plato, in his book *On the Soul*, says that the charioteer and the horse that ran off—the irrational part, which is divided in two, into anger and concupiscence—fall down; and so the myth intimates that it was through the licentiousness of the steeds that Phaëthon was thrown out. Also in the case of Joseph: the brothers having envied this young man, who by his knowledge was possessed of uncommon foresight, stripped off the coat of many colors, and took and threw him into a pit (the pit was empty, it had no water), rejecting the good man's varied knowledge, springing from his love of instruction; or, in the exercise of the bare faith, which is according to the law, they threw him into the pit empty of water, selling him into Egypt, which was destitute of the divine word. And the pit was destitute of knowledge; into which being thrown and stripped of his knowledge, he that had become unconsciously wise, stripped of knowledge, seemed like his brethren. Otherwise interpreted, the coat of many colors is lust, which takes its way into a yawning pit. "And if one open up or hew out a pit," it is said, "and do not cover it, and there fall in there a calf or ass, the owner of the pit shall pay the price in money, and give it to his neighbor; and the dead body shall be his. Here add that prophecy: "The ox knows his owner, and the ass his master's crib: but Israel hath not understood Me." In order, then, that none of those, who have fallen in with the knowledge taught by thee, may become incapable of holding the truth, and disobey and fall away, it is said, Be thou sure in the treatment of the word, and shut up the living spring in the depth from those who approach irrationally, but reach drink to those that thirst for truth. Conceal it, then, from those who are unfit to receive the depth of knowledge, and so cover the pit. The owner of the pit, then, the Gnostic, shall himself be punished, incurring the blame of the others stumbling, and of being overwhelmed by the greatness of the word, he himself being of small capacity; or transferring the worker into the region of speculation, and on that account dislodging him from off-hand faith. "And will pay money," rendering a reckoning, and submitting his accounts to the "omnipotent Will."

This, then, is the type of "the law and the prophets which were until John;" while he, though speaking more perspicuously as no longer prophesying, but pointing out as now present, Him, who was proclaimed symbolically from the beginning, nevertheless said, "I am not worthy to loose the latchet of the Lord's shoe." For he confesses that he is not worthy to baptize so great a Power; for it behooves those, who purify others, to free the soul from the body and its sins, as the foot from the thong. Perhaps also this signified the final exertion of the Savior's power toward us—the immediate, I mean—that by His presence, concealed in the enigma of prophecy, inasmuch as he, by pointing out to sight Him that had been prophesied of, and indicating the Presence which had come, walking forth into the light, loosed the latchet of the oracles of the [old] economy, by unveiling the meaning of the symbols.

And the observances practiced by the Romans in the case of wills have a place here; those balances and small coins to denote justice, and freeing of slaves, and rubbing of the ears. For these observances are, that things may be transacted with justice; and those for the dispensing of honor; and the last, that he who happens to be near, as if a burden were imposed on him, should stand and hear and take the post of mediator.

CHAPTER IX.—REASONS FOR VEILING THE TRUTH IN SYMBOLS.

But, as appears, I have, in my eagerness to establish my point, insensibly gone beyond what is requisite. For life would fail me to adduce the multitude of those who philosophize in a symbolical manner. For the sake, then, of memory and brevity, and of attracting to the truth, such are the Scriptures of the Barbarian philosophy.

For only to those who often approach them, and have given them a trial by faith and in their whole life, will they supply the real philosophy and the true theology. They also wish us to require an interpreter and guide. For so they considered, that, receiving truth at the hands of those who knew it well, we would be more earnest and less liable to deception, and those worthy of them would profit. Besides, all things that shine through a veil show the truth grander and more imposing; as fruits shining through water, and figures through veils, which give added reflections to them. For, in addition to the fact that things unconcealed are perceived in one way, the rays of light shining round reveal defects. Since, then, we may draw several meanings, as we do from what is expressed in veiled form, such being the case, the ignorant and unlearned man fails. But the Gnostior apprehends. Now, then, it is not wished that all things should be exposed indiscriminately to all and sundry, or the benefits of wisdom communicated to those who have not even in a dream been purified in soul, (for it is not allowed to hand to every chance comer what has been procured with such laborious efforts); nor are the mysteries of the word to be expounded to the profane.

They say, then, that Hipparchus the Pythagorean, being guilty of writing the tenets of Pythagoras in plain language, was expelled from the school, and a pillar raised for him as if he had been dead. Wherefore also in the Barbarian philosophy they call those dead who have fallen away from the dogmas, and have placed the mind in subjection to carnal passions.
"For what fellowship hath righteousness and iniquity?" according to the divine apostle. "Or what communion hath light with darkness? or what concord hath Christ with Belial? Or what portion hath the believer with the unbeliever?" For the honors of the Olympians and of mortals lie apart. "Wherefore also go forth from the midst of them, and be separated, says the Lord, and touch not the unclean thing; and I will receive you, and will be to you for a Father, and ye shall be my sons and daughters."

It was not only the Pythagoreans and Plato then, that concealed many things; but the Epicureans too say that they have things that may not be uttered, and do not allow all to peruse those writings. The Stoics also say that by the first Zeno things were written which they do not readily allow disciples to read, without their first giving proof whether or not they are genuine philosophers. And the disciples of Aristotle say that some of their treatises are esoteric, and others common and exoteric. Further, those who instituted the mysteries, being philosophers, buried their doctrines in myths, so as not to be obvious to all. Did they then, by veiling human opinions, prevent the ignorant from handling them; and was it not more beneficial for the holy and blessed contemplation of realities to be concealed? But it was not only the tenets of the Barbarian philosophy, or the Pythagorean myths. But even those myths in Plato (in the *Republic*, that of Hero the Armenian; and in the *Gorgias*, that of Æacus and Rhadamanthus; and in the *Phædo*, that of Tartarus; and in the *Protagoras*, that of Prometheus and Epimetheus; and besides these, that of the war between the Atlantini and the Athenians in the Atlanticum) are to be expounded allegorically, not absolutely in all their expressions, but in those which express the general sense. And these we shall find indicated by symbols under the veil of allegory. Also the association of Pythagoras, and the twofold intercourse with the associates which designates the majority, hearers (ἀκουσματικοί), and the others that have a genuine attachment to philosophy, disciples (μαθηματικοί), yet signified that something was spoken to the multitude, and something concealed from them. Perchance, too, the twofold species of the Peripatetic teaching—that called probable, and that called knowable—came very near the distinction between opinion on the one hand, and glory and truth on the other.

> "To win the flowers of fair renown from men,
> Be not induced to speak aught more than right."

The Ionic muses accordingly expressly say, "That the majority of people, wise in their own estimation, follow minstrels and make use of laws, knowing that many are bad, few good; but that the best pursue glory: for the best make choice of the everlasting glory of men above all. But the multitude cram themselves like brutes, measuring happiness by the belly and the pudenda, and the basest things in us." And the great Parmenides of Elea is introduced describing thus the teaching of the two ways:—

> "The one is the dauntless heart of convincing truth;
> The other is in the opinions of men, in whom is no true faith."

CHAPTER X.—THE OPINION OF THE APOSTLES ON VEILING THE MYSTERIES OF THE FAITH.

Rightly, therefore, the divine apostle says, "By revelation the mystery was made known to me (as I wrote before in brief, in accordance with which, when ye read, ye may understand my knowledge in the mystery of Christ), which in other ages was not made known to the sons of men, as it is now revealed to His holy apostles and prophets." For there is an instruction of the perfect, of which, writing to the Colossians, he says, "We cease not to pray for you, and beseech that ye may be filled with the knowledge of His will in all wisdom and spiritual understanding; that ye may walk worthy of the Lord to all pleasing; being fruitful in every good work, and increasing in the knowledge of God; strengthened with all might according to the glory of His power." And again he says, "According to the disposition of the grace of God which is given me, that ye may fulfil the word of God; the mystery which has been hid from ages and generations, which now is manifested to His saints: to whom God wished to make known what is the riches of the glory of this mystery among the nations." So that, on the one hand, then, are the mysteries which were hid till the time of the apostles, and were delivered by them as they received from the Lord, and, concealed in the Old Testament, were manifested to the saints. And, on the other hand, there is "the riches of the glory of the mystery in the Gentiles," which is faith and hope in Christ; which in another place he has called the "foundation." And again, as if in eagerness to divulge this knowledge, he thus writes: "Warning every man in all wisdom, that we may present every man (the whole man) perfect in Christ;" not every man simply, since no one would be unbelieving. Nor does he call every man who believes in Christ perfect; but he says all the man, as if he said the whole man, as if purified in body and soul. For that the knowledge does not appertain to all, he expressly adds: "Being knit together in love, and unto all the riches of the full assurance of knowledge, to the acknowledgment of the mystery of God in Christ, in whom are hid all the treasures of wisdom and of knowledge." "Continue in prayer, watching therein with thanksgiving." And thanksgiving has place not for the soul and spiritual blessings alone, but also for the body, and for the good things of the body. And he still more clearly reveals that knowledge belongs not to all, by adding: "Praying at the same time for you, that God would open to us a door to speak the mystery of Christ, for which I am bound; that I may make it known as I ought to speak." For there were certainly, among the Hebrews, some things delivered unwritten. "For when ye ought to be teachers for the time," it is said, as if they had grown old in the Old Testament, "ye have again need that one teach you which be the first principles of the oracles of God; and are become such as have need of milk, and not of solid food. For every one that partakes of milk is unskillful in the word of righteousness; for he is a babe, being instructed with the first lessons. But solid food belongs to those who are of full age, who by reason of use have their senses exercised so as to distinguish between good and evil. Wherefore, leaving the first principles of the doctrine of Christ, let us go on to perfection."

Barnabas, too, who in person preached the word along with the apostle in the ministry of the Gentiles, says, "I write to you most simply, that ye may understand." Then below, exhibiting already a clearer trace of gnostic tradition, he says, "What says the other prophet Moses to them? Lo, thus says the Lord God, Enter ye into the good land which the Lord God swore, the God of Abraham, and Isaac, and Jacob; and ye received for an inheritance that land, flowing with milk and honey." What says knowledge? Learn, hope, it says, in Jesus, who is to be manifested to you in the flesh. For man is the suffering land; for from the face of the ground was the formation of Adam. What, then, does it say in reference to the good land, flowing with milk and honey? Blessed be our Lord, brethren, who has put into our hearts wisdom, and the understanding of His secrets. For the prophet says, "Who shall understand the Lord's parable but the wise and understanding, and he that loves his Lord?" It is but for few to comprehend these things. For it is not in the way of envy that the Lord announced in a Gospel, "My mystery is to me, and to the sons of my house;" placing the election in safety, and beyond anxiety; so that the things pertaining to what it has chosen and taken may be above the reach of envy. For he who has not the knowledge of good is wicked: for there is one good, the Father; and to be ignorant of the Father is death, as to know Him is eternal life, through participation in the power of the incorrupt One. And to be incorruptible is to participate in divinity; but revolt from the knowledge of God brings corruption. Again the prophet says: "And I will give thee treasures, concealed, dark, unseen; that they may know that I am the Lord." Similarly David sings: "For, lo, Thou hast loved truth; the obscure and hidden things of wisdom hast Thou showed me." "Day utters speech to day" (what is clearly written), "and night to night proclaims knowledge" (which is hidden in a mystic veil); "and there are no words or utterances whose voices shall not be heard" by God, who said, "Shall one do what is secret, and I shall not see him?"

Wherefore instruction, which reveals hidden things, is called illumination, as it is the teacher only who uncovers the lid of the ark, contrary to what the poets say, that "Zeus stops up the jar of good things, but opens that of evil." "For I know," says the apostle, "that when I come to you, I shall come in the fullness of the blessing of Christ;"designating the spiritual gift, and the gnostic communication, which being present he desires to impart to them present as "the fullness of Christ, according to the revelation of the mystery sealed in the ages of eternity, but now manifested by the prophetic Scriptures, according to the command of the eternal God, made known to all the nations, in order to the obedience of faith," that is, those of the nations who believe that it is. But only to a few of them is shown what those things are which are contained in the mystery.

Rightly then, Plato, in the Epistles, treating of God, says: "We must speak in enigmas; that should the tablet come by any mischance on its leaves either by sea or land, he who reads may remain ignorant." For the God of the universe, who is above all speech, all conception, all thought, can never be committed to writing, being inexpressible even by His own power. And this too Plato showed, by saying: "Considering, then, these things, take care lest some time or other you repent on account of the present things, departing in a manner unworthy. The greatest safeguard is not to write, but learn; for it is utterly impossible that what is written will not vanish."

Akin to this is what the holy Apostle Paul says, preserving the prophetic and truly ancient secret from which the teachings that were good were derived by the Greeks: "Howbeit we speak wisdom among them who are perfect; but not the wisdom of this world, or of the princes of this world, that come to naught; but we speak the wisdom of God hidden in a mystery." Then proceeding, he thus inculcates the caution against the divulging of his words to the multitude in the following terms: "And I, brethren, could not speak to you as to spiritual, but as to carnal, even to babes in Christ. I have fed you with milk, not with meat: for ye were not yet able; neither are ye now able. For ye are yet carnal."

If, then, "the milk" is said by the apostle to belong to the babes, and "meat" to be the food of the full-grown, milk will be understood to be catechetical instruction—the first food, as it were, of the soul. And meat is the mystic contemplation; for this is the flesh and the blood of the Word, that is, the comprehension of the divine power and essence. "Taste and see that the Lord is Christ," it is said. For so He imparts of Himself to those who partake of such food in a more spiritual manner; when now the soul nourishes itself, according to the truth-loving Plato. For the knowledge of the divine essence is the meat and drink of the divine Word. Wherefore also Plato says, in the second book of the *Republic*, "It is those that sacrifice not a sow, but some great and difficult sacrifice," who ought to inquire respecting God. And the apostle writes, "Christ our Passover was sacrificed for us;"—a sacrifice hard to procure, in truth, the Son of God consecrated for us.

CHAPTER XI.—ABSTRACTION FROM MATERIAL THINGS NECESSARY IN ORDER TO ATTAIN TO THE TRUE KNOWLEDGE OF GOD.

Now the sacrifice which is acceptable to God is unswerving abstraction from the body and its passions. This is the really true piety. And is not, on this account, philosophy rightly called by Socrates the practice of Death? For he who neither employs his eyes in the exercise of thought, nor draws aught from his other senses, but with pure mind itself applies to objects, practices the true philosophy. This is, then, the import of the silence of five years prescribed by Pythagoras, which he enjoined on his disciples; that, abstracting themselves from the objects of sense, they might with the mind alone contemplate the Deity. It was from Moses that the chief of the Greeks drew these philosophical tenets. For he commands holocausts to be skinned and divided into parts. For the gnostic soul must be consecrated to the light, stripped of the integuments of matter, devoid of the frivolousness of the body and of all the passions, which are acquired through vain and lying opinions, and divested of the lusts of the flesh. But the most of men, clothed with what is perishable, like cockles, and rolled all round in a ball in their excesses, like hedgehogs, entertain the same ideas of the blessed and incorruptible God as of themselves. But it has escaped their notice, though they be near us, that God has bestowed on us ten thousand things in which He does not share: birth, being Himself unborn; food, He wanting nothing; and growth, He being always equal; and long life and immortality, He being immortal and incapable of growing old. Wherefore let no one imagine that hands, and feet, and mouth, and eyes, and going in and coming out, and resentments and threats, are said by the Hebrews to be attributes of God. By no means; but that certain of these appellations are used more sacredly in an allegorical sense, which, as the discourse proceeds, we shall explain at the proper time.

"Wisdom of all medicines is the Panacea," writes Callimachus in the *Epigrams*. "And one becomes wise from another, both in past times and at present," says Bacchylides in the *Poeans;* "for it is not very easy to find the portals of unutterable words." Beautifully, therefore, Isocrates writes in the *Panathenaic*, having put the question, "Who, then, are well trained?" adds, "First, those who manage well the things which occur each day, whose opinion jumps with opportunity, and is able for the most part to hit on what is beneficial; then those who behave becomingly and rightly to those who approach them, who take lightly and easily annoyances and molestations offered by others, but conduct themselves as far as possible, to those with whom they have intercourse, with consummate care and moderation; further, those who have the command of their pleasures, and are not too much overcome by misfortunes, but conduct themselves in the midst of them with manliness, and in a way worthy of the nature which we share; fourth—and this is the greatest—those who are not corrupted by prosperity, and are not put beside themselves, or made haughty, but continue in the class of sensible people." Then he puts on the top-stone of the discourse: "Those who have the disposition of their soul well suited not to one only of these things, but to them all—those I assert to be wise and perfect men, and to possess all the virtues."

Do you see how the Greeks deify the gnostic life (though not knowing how to become acquainted with it)? And what knowledge it is, they know not even in a dream. If, then, it is agreed among us that knowledge is the food of reason, "blessed truly are they," according to the Scripture, "who hunger and thirst after truth: for they shall be filled" with everlasting food. In the most wonderful harmony with these words, Euripides, the philosopher of the drama, is found in the following words,—making allusion, I know not how, at once to the Father and the Son:—

> "To thee, the Lord of all, I bring
> Cakes and libations too, O Zeus,
> Or Hades wouldn't thou choose be called;
> Do thou accept my offering of all fruits,
> Rare, full, poured forth."

For a whole burnt-offering and rare sacrifice for us is Christ. And that unwittingly he mentions the Savior, he will make plain, as he adds:—

> "For thou who, 'midst the heavenly gods,
> Jove's scepter sway's, dost also share
> The rule of those on earth."

Then he says expressly:—

> "Send light to human souls that fain would know
> Whence conflicts spring, and what the root of ills,
> And of the blessed gods to whom due rites
> Of sacrifice we needs must pay, that so
> We may from troubles find repose."

It is not then without reason that in the mysteries that obtain among the Greeks, lustrations hold the first place; as also the laver among the Barbarians. After these are the minor mysteries, which have some foundation of instruction and of preliminary preparation for what is to come after; and the great mysteries, in which nothing remains to be learned of the universe, but only to contemplate and comprehend nature and things.

We shall understand the mode of purification by confession, and that of contemplation by analysis, advancing by analysis to the first notion, beginning with the properties underlying it; abstracting from the body its physical properties, taking away the dimension of depth, then that of breadth, and then that of length. For the point which remains is a unit, so to speak, having position; from which if we abstract position, there is the conception of unity.

If, then, abstracting all that belongs to bodies and things called incorporeal, we cast ourselves into the greatness of Christ, and thence advance into immensity by holiness, we may reach somehow to the conception of the Almighty, knowing not what He is, but what He is not. And form and motion, or standing, or a throne, or place, or right hand or left, are not at all to be conceived as belonging to the Father of the universe, although it is so written. But what each of these means will be shown in its proper place. The First Cause is not then in space, but above both space, and time, and name, and conception.

Wherefore also Moses says, "Show Thyself to me,"—intimating most clearly that God is not capable of being taught by man, or expressed in speech, but to be known only by His own power. For inquiry was obscure and dim; but the grace of knowledge is from Him by the Son. Most clearly Solomon shall testify to us, speaking thus: "The prudence of man is not in me: but God giveth me wisdom, and I know holy things." Now Moses, describing allegorically the divine prudence, called it the tree of life planted in Paradise; which Paradise may be the world in which all things proceeding from creation grow. In it also the Word blossomed and bore fruit, being "made flesh," and gave life to those "who had tasted of His graciousness;" since it was not without the wood of the tree that He came to our knowledge. For our life was hung on it, in order that we might believe. And Solomon again says: "She is a tree of immortality to those who take hold of her." "Behold, I set before thy face life and death, to love the Lord thy God, and to walk in His ways, and hear His voice, and trust in life. But if ye transgress the statutes and the judgments which I have given you, ye shall be destroyed with destruction. For this is life, and the length of thy days, to love the Lord thy God."

Again: "Abraham, when he came to the place which God told him of on the third day, looking up, saw the place afar off." For the first day is that which is constituted by the sight of good things; and the second is the soul's best desire; on the third, the mind perceives spiritual things, the eyes of the understanding being opened by the Teacher who rose on the third day. The three days may be the mystery of the seal, in which God is really believed. It is consequently afar off that he sees the place. For the region of God is hard to attain; which Plato called the region of ideas, having learned from Moses that it was a place which contained all things universally. But it is seen by Abraham afar off, rightly, because of his being in the realms of generation, and he is forthwith initiated by the angel. Thence says the apostle: "Now we see as through a glass, but then face to face," by those sole pure and incorporeal applications of the intellect. In reasoning, it is possible to divine respecting God, if one attempt without any of the senses, by reason, to reach what is individual; and do not quit the sphere of existences, till, rising up to the things which transcend it, he apprehends by the intellect itself that which is good, moving in the very confines of the world of thought, according to Plato.

Again, Moses, not allowing altars and temples to be constructed in many places, but raising one temple of God, announced that the world was only-begotten, as Basilides says, and that God is one, as does not as yet appear to Basilides. And since the gnostic Moses does not circumscribe within space Him that cannot be circumscribed, he set up no image in the temple to be worshipped; showing that God was invisible, and incapable of being circumscribed; and somehow leading the Hebrews to the conception of God by the honor for His name in the temple. Further, the Word, prohibiting the constructing of temples and all sacrifices, intimates that the Almighty is not contained in anything, by what He says: "What house will ye build to Me? says the Lord. Heaven is my throne," and so on. Similarly respecting sacrifices: "I do not desire the blood of bulls and the fat of lambs," and what the Holy Spirit by the prophet in the sequel forbids.

Most excellently, therefore, Euripides accords with these, when he writes:—

> "What house constructed by the workmen's hands,
> With folds of walls, can clothe the shape divine?"

And of sacrifices he thus speaks:—

> "For God needs naught, if He is truly God.
> These of the minstrels are the wretched myths."

"For it was not from need that God made the world; that He might reap honors from men and the other gods and demons, winning a kind of revenue from creation, and from us, fumes, and from the gods and demons, their proper ministries," says Plato. Most instructively, therefore, says Paul in the Acts of the Apostles: "The God that made the world, and all things in it, being the Lord of heaven and earth, dwelled not in temples made with hands; neither is worshipped by men's hands, as if He needed anything; seeing that it is He Himself that giveth to all breath, and life, and all things." And Zeno, the founder of the Stoic sect, says in this book of the *Republic*, "that we ought to make neither temples nor images; for that no work is worthy of the gods." And he was not afraid to write in these very words: "There will be no need to build temples. For a temple is not worth much, and ought not to be regarded as holy. For nothing is worth much, and holy, which is the work of builders and mechanics." Rightly, therefore, Plato too, recognizing the world as God's temple, pointed out to the citizens a spot in the city where their idols were to be laid up.

"Let not, then, any one again," he says, "consecrate temples to the gods. For gold and silver in other states, in the case of private individuals and in the temples, is an invidious possession; and ivory, a body which has abandoned the life, is not a sacred votive offering; and steel and brass are the instruments of wars; but whatever one wishes to dedicate, let it be wood of one tree, as also stone for common temples." Rightly, then, in the great Epistle he says: "For it is not capable of expression, like other branches of study. But as the result of great intimacy with this subject, and living with it, a sudden light, like that kindled by a coruscating fire, arising in the soul, feeds itself." Are not these statements like those of Zephaniah the prophet? "And the Spirit of the Lord took me, and brought me up to the fifth heaven, and I beheld angels called Lords; and their diadem was set on in the Holy Spirit; and each of them had a throne sevenfold brighter than the light of the rising sun; and they dwelt in temples of salvation, and hymned the ineffable, Most High God."

CHAPTER XII.—GOD CANNOT BE EMBRACED IN WORDS OR BY THE MIND.

"For both is it a difficult task to discover the Father and Maker of this universe; and having found Him, it is impossible to declare Him to all. For this is by no means capable of expression, like the other subjects of instruction," says the truth-loving Plato. For he that had heard right well that the all-wise Moses, ascending the mount for holy contemplation, to the summit of intellectual objects, necessarily commands that the whole people do not accompany him. And when the Scripture says, "Moses entered into the thick darkness where God was," this shows to those capable of understanding, that God is invisible and beyond expression by words. And "the darkness"—which is, in truth, the unbelief and ignorance of the multitude—obstructs the gleam of truth. And again Orpheus, the theologian, aided from this quarter, says:—

"One is perfect in himself, and all things are made the progeny of one,"

or, "are born;" for so also is it written. He adds:—

> "Him
> No one of mortals has seen, but He sees all."

And he adds more clearly:—

> "Him see I not, for round about, a cloud
> Has settled; for in mortal eyes are small,
> And mortal pupils—only flesh and bones grow there."

To these statements the apostle will testify: "I know a man in Christ, caught up into the third heaven, and thence into Paradise, who heard unutterable words which it is not lawful for a man to speak,"—intimating thus the impossibility of expressing God, and indicating that what is divine is unutterable by human power; if, indeed, he begins to speak above the third heaven, as it is lawful to initiate the elect souls in the mysteries there. For I know what is in Plato (for the examples from the barbarian philosophy, which are many, are suggested now by the composition which, in accordance with promises previously given, waits the suitable time). For doubting, in *Timæus*, whether we ought to regard several worlds as to be understood by many heavens, or this one, he makes no distinction in the names, calling the world and heaven by the same name. But the words of the statement are as follows: "Whether, then, have we rightly spoken of one heaven, or of many and infinite? It were more correct to say one, if indeed it was created according to the model." Further, in the Epistle of the Romans to the Corinthians it is written, "An ocean illimitable by men and the worlds after it." Consequently, therefore, the noble apostle exclaims, "Oh the depth of the riches both of the wisdom and the knowledge of God!"

And was it not this which the prophet meant, when he ordered unleavened cakes to be made, intimating that the truly sacred mystic word, respecting the unbegotten and His powers, ought to be concealed? In confirmation of these things, in the Epistle to the Corinthians the apostle plainly says: "Howbeit we speak wisdom among those who are perfect, but not the wisdom of this world, or of the princes of this world, that come to naught. But we speak the wisdom of God hidden in a mystery." And again in another place he says: "To the acknowledgment of the mystery of God in Christ, in whom are hid all the treasures of wisdom and knowledge." These things the Savior Himself seals when He says: "To you it is given to know the mysteries of the kingdom of heaven." And again the Gospel says that the Savior spoke to the apostles the word in a mystery. For prophecy says of Him: "He will open His mouth in parables, and will utter things kept secret from the foundation of the world." And now, by the parable of the leaven, the Lord shows concealment; for He says, "The kingdom of heaven is like leaven, which a woman took and hid in three measures of meal, till the whole was leavened." For the tripartite soul is saved by obedience, through the spiritual power hidden in it by faith; or because the power of the word which is given to us, being strong and powerful, draws to itself secretly and invisibly everyone who receives it, and keeps it within himself, and brings his whole system into unity.

Accordingly Solon has written most wisely respecting God thus:—

"It is most difficult to apprehend the mind's invisible measure
Which alone holds the boundaries of all things."

For "the divine," says the poet of Agrigentum,—

"Is not capable of being approached with our eyes,

> Or grasped with our hands; but the highway
> Of persuasion, highest of all, leads to men's minds."

And John the apostle says: "No man hath seen God at any time. The only-begotten God, who is in the bosom of the Father, He hath declared Him,"—calling invisibility and ineffableness the bosom of God. Hence some have called it the Depth, as containing and embosoming all things, inaccessible and boundless.

This discourse respecting God is most difficult to handle. For since the first principle of everything is difficult to find out, the absolutely first and oldest principle, which is the cause of all other things being and having been, is difficult to exhibit. For how can that be expressed which is neither genus, nor difference, nor species, nor individual, nor number; nay more, is neither an event, nor that to which an event happens? No one can rightly express Him wholly. For on account of His greatness He is ranked as the All, and is the Father of the universe. Nor are any parts to be predicated of Him. For the One is indivisible; wherefore also it is infinite, not considered with reference to inscrutability, but with reference to its being without dimensions, and not having a limit. And therefore it is without form and name. And if we name it, we do not do so properly, terming it either the One, or the Good, or Mind, or Absolute Being, or Father, or God, or Creator, or Lord. We speak not as supplying His name; but for want, we use good names, in order that the mind may have these as points of support, so as not to err in other respects. For each one by itself does not express God; but all together are indicative of the power of the Omnipotent. For predicates are expressed either from what belongs to things themselves, or from their mutual relation. But none of these are admissible in reference to God. Nor any more is He apprehended by the science of demonstration. For it depends on primary and better known principles. But there is nothing antecedent to the Unbegotten.

It remains that we understand, then, the Unknown, by divine grace, and by the word alone that proceeds from Him; as Luke in the Acts of the Apostles relates that Paul said, "Men of Athens, I perceive that in all things ye are too superstitious. For in walking about, and beholding the objects of your worship, I found an altar on which was inscribed, To the Unknown God. Whom therefore ye ignorantly worship, Him declare I unto you."

CHAPTER XIII.—THE KNOWLEDGE OF GOD A DIVINE GIFT, ACCORDING TO THE PHILOSOPHERS.

Everything, then, which falls under a name, is originated, whether they will or not. Whether, then, the Father Himself draws to Himself everyone who has led a pure life, and has reached the conception of the blessed and incorruptible nature; or whether the free-will which is in us, by reaching the knowledge of the good, leaps and bounds over the barriers, as the gymnasts say; yet it is not without eminent grace that the soul is winged, and soars, and is raised above the higher spheres, laying aside all that is heavy, and surrendering itself to its kindred element.

Plato, too, in *Meno*, says that virtue is God-given, as the following expressions show: "From this argument then, O Meno, virtue is shown to come to those, in whom it is found, by divine providence." Does it not then appear that "the gnostic disposition" which has come to all is enigmatically called "divine providence?" And he adds more explicitly: "If, then, in this whole treatise we have investigated well, it results that virtue is neither by nature, nor is it taught, but is produced by divine providence, not without intelligence, in those in whom it is found." Wisdom which is God-given, as being the power of the Father, rouses indeed our free-will, and admits faith, and repays the application of the elect with its crowning fellowship.

And now I will adduce Plato himself, who clearly deems it fit to believe the children of God. For, discoursing on gods that are visible and born, in *Timæus*, he says: "But to speak of the other demons, and to know their birth, is too much for us. But we must credit those who have formerly spoken, they being the offspring of the gods, as they said, and knowing well their progenitors, although they speak without probable and necessary proofs." I do not think it possible that clearer testimony could be borne by the Greeks, that our Savior, and those anointed to prophesy (the latter being called the sons of God, and the Lord being His own Son), are the true witnesses respecting divine things. Wherefore also they ought to be believed, being inspired, he added. And were one to say in a more tragic vein, that we ought not to believe,

"For it was not Zeus that told me these things,"

yet let him know that it was God Himself that promulgated the Scriptures by His Son. And he, who announces what is his own, is to be believed. "No one," says the Lord, "hath known the Father but the Son, and he to whom the Son shall reveal Him." This, then, is to be believed, according to Plato, though it is announced and spoken "without probable and necessary proofs," but in the Old and New Testament. "For except ye believe," says the Lord, "ye shall die in your sins." And again: "He that believeth hath everlasting life." "Blessed are all they that put their trust in Him." For trusting is more than faith. For when one has believed that the Son of God is our teacher, he trusts that his teaching is true. And as "instruction," according to Empedocles, "makes the mind grow," so trust in the Lord makes faith grow.

    We say, then, that it is characteristic of the same persons to vilify philosophy, and run down faith, and to praise iniquity and felicitate a libidinous life. But now faith, if it is the voluntary assent of the soul, is still the doer of good things, the foundation of right conduct; and if Aristotle defines strictly when he teaches that ποιεῖν is applied to the irrational creatures and to inanimate things, while πράττειν is applicable to men only, let him correct those who say that God is the maker (ποιητής) of the universe. And what is done (πρακτόν), he says, is as good or as necessary. To do wrong, then, is not good, for no one does wrong except for some other thing; and nothing that is necessary is voluntary. To do wrong, then, is voluntary, so that it is not necessary. But the good differ especially from the bad in inclinations and good desires. For all depravity of soul is accompanied with want of restraint; and he who acts from passion, acts from want of restraint and from depravity.

I cannot help admiring in every particular that divine utterance: "Verily, verily, I say unto you, He that entered not in by the door into the sheepfold, but climbed up some other way, the same is a thief and a robber. But he that entered in by the door is the shepherd of the sheep. To him the porter opened." Then the Lord says in explanation, "I am the door of the sheep." Men must then be saved by learning the truth through Christ, even if they attain philosophy. For now that is clearly shown "which was not made known to other ages, which is now revealed to the sons of men." For there was always a natural manifestation of the one Almighty God, among all right-thinking men; and the most, who had not quite divested themselves of shame with respect to the truth, apprehended the eternal beneficence in divine providence. In fine, then, Xenocrates the Chalcedonian was not quite without hope that the notion of the Divinity existed even in the irrational creatures. And Democritus, though against his will, will make this avowal by the consequences of his dogmas; for he represents the same images as issuing, from the divine essence, on men and on the irrational animals. Far from destitute of a divine idea is man, who, it is written in Genesis, partook of inspiration, being endowed with a purer essence than the other animate creatures. Hence the Pythagoreans say that mind comes to man by divine providence, as Plato and Aristotle avow; but we assert that the Holy Spirit inspires him who has believed. The Platonists hold that mind is an effluence of divine dispensation in the soul, and they place the soul in the body. For it is expressly said by Joel, one of the twelve prophets, "And it shall come to pass after these things, I will pour out of My Spirit on all flesh, and your sons and your daughters shall prophesy." But it is not as a portion of God that the Spirit is in each of us. But how this dispensation takes place, and what the Holy Spirit is, shall be shown by us in the books on prophecy, and in those on the soul. But "incredulity is good at concealing the depths of knowledge," according to Heraclitus; "for incredulity escapes from ignorance."

CHAPTER XIV.—GREEK PLAGIARISM FROM THE HEBREWS.

Let us add in completion what follows, and exhibit now with greater clearness the plagiarism of the Greeks from the Barbarian philosophy.

Now the Stoics say that God, like the soul, is essentially body and spirit. You will find all this explicitly in their writings. Do not consider at present their allegories as the Gnostic truth presents them; whether they show one thing and mean another, like the dexterous athletes. Well, they say that God pervades all being; while we call Him solely Maker, and Maker by the Word. They were misled by what is said in the book of Wisdom: "He pervades and passes through all by reason of His purity;" since they did not understand that this was said of Wisdom, which was the first of the creation of God.

So be it, they say. But the philosophers, the Stoics, and Plato, and Pythagoras, nay more, Aristotle the Peripatetic, suppose the existence of matter among the first principles; and not one first principle. Let them then know that what is called matter by them, is said by them to be without quality, and without form, and more daringly said by Plato to be non-existence. And does he not say very mystically, knowing that the true and real first cause is one, in these very words: "Now, then, let our opinion be so. As to the first principle or principles of the universe, or what opinion we ought to entertain about all these points, we are not now to speak, for no other cause than on account of its being difficult to explain our sentiments in accordance with the present form of discourse." But undoubtedly that prophetic expression, "Now the earth was invisible and formless," supplied them with the ground of material essence.

And the introduction of "chance" was hence suggested to Epicurus, who misapprehended the statement, "Vanity of vanities, and all is vanity." And it occurred to Aristotle to extend Providence as far as the moon from this psalm: "Lord, Thy mercy is in the heavens; and Thy truth reaches to the clouds." For the explanation of the prophetic mysteries had not yet been revealed previous to the advent of the Lord.

Punishments after death, on the other hand, and penal retribution by fire, were pilfered from the Barbarian philosophy both by all the poetic Muses and by the Hellenic philosophy. Plato, accordingly, in the last book of the *Republic,* says in these express terms: "Then these men fierce and fiery to look on, standing by, and hearing the sound, seized and took some aside; and binding Aridæus and the rest hand, foot, and head, and throwing them down, and flaying them, dragged them along the way, tearing their flesh with thorns." For the fiery men are meant to signify the angels, who seize and punish the wicked. "Who makes," it is said, "His angels spirits; His ministers flaming fire." It follows from this that the soul is immortal. For what is tortured or corrected being in a state of sensation lives, though said to suffer. Well! Did not Plato know of the rivers of fire and the depth of the earth, and Tartarus, called by the Barbarians Gehenna, naming, as he does prophetically, Cocytus, and Acheron, and Pyriphlegethon, and introducing such corrective tortures for discipline?

But indicating "the angels" as the Scripture says, "of the little ones, and of the least, which see God," and also the oversight reaching to us exercised by the tutelary angels, he shrinks not from writing, "That when all the souls have selected their several lives, according as it has fallen to their lot, they advance in order to Lachesis; and she sends along with each one, as his guide in life, and the joint accomplisher of his purposes, the demon which he has chosen." Perhaps also the demon of Socrates suggested to him something similar.

Nay, the philosophers. having so heard from Moses, taught that the world was created. And so Plato expressly said, "Whether was it that the world had no beginning of its existence, or derived its beginning from some beginning? For being visible, it is tangible; and being tangible, it has a body." Again, when he says, "It is a difficult task to find the
Maker and Father of this universe," he not only showed that the universe was created, but points out that it was generated by him as a son, and that he is called its father, as deriving its being from him alone, and springing from non-existence. The Stoics, too, hold the tenet that the world was created.

And that the devil so spoken of by the Barbarian philosophy, the prince of the demons, is a wicked spirit, Plato asserts in the tenth book of the *Laws,* in these words: "Must we not say that spirit which pervades the things that are moved on all sides, pervades also heaven? Well, what? One or more? Several, say I, in reply for you. Let us not suppose fewer than two—that which is beneficent, and that which is able to accomplish the opposite." Similarly in the *Phoedrus* he writes as follows: "Now there are other evils. But some demon has mingled pleasure with the most things at present." Further, in the tenth book of the *Laws,* he expressly emits that apostolic sentiment, "Our contest is not with flesh and blood, but principalities, with powers, with the spiritual things of those which are in heaven;" writing thus: "For since we are agreed that heaven is full of many good beings; but it is also full of the opposite of these, and more of these; and as we assert such a contest is deathless, and requiring marvelous watchfulness."

Again the Barbarian philosophy knows the world of thought and the world of sense—the former archetypal, and the latter the image of that which is called the model; and assigns the former to the Monad, as being perceived by the mind, and the world of sense to the number six. For six is called by the Pythagoreans marriage, as being the genital number; and he places in the Monad the invisible heaven and the holy earth, and intellectual light. For "in the beginning," it is said, "God made the heaven and the earth; and the earth was invisible." And it is added, "And God said, Let there be light; and there was light." And in the material cosmogony He creates a solid heaven (and what is solid is capable of being perceived by sense), and a visible earth, and a light that is seen. Does not Plato hence appear to have left the ideas of living creatures in the intellectual world, and to make intellectual objects into sensible species according to their genera? Rightly then Moses says, that the body which Plato calls "the earthly tabernacle" was formed of the ground, but that the rational soul was breathed by God into man's face. For there, they say, the ruling faculty is situated; interpreting the access by the senses into the first man as the addition of the soul.

    Wherefore also man is said "to have been made in [God's] image and likeness." For the image of God is the divine and royal Word, the impassible man; and the image of the image is the human mind. And if you wish to apprehend the likeness by another name, you will find it named in Moses, a divine correspondence. For he says, "Walk after the Lord your God, and keep His commandments." And I reckon all the virtuous, servants and followers of God. Hence the Stoics say that the end of philosophy is to live agreeable to nature; and Plato, likeness to God, as we have shown in the second Miscellany. And Zeno the Stoic, borrowing from Plato, and he from the Barbarian philosophy, says that all the good are friends of one another. For Socrates says in the *Phoedrus*, "that it has not been ordained that the bad should be a friend to the bad, nor the good be not a friend to the good;" as also he showed sufficiently in the *Lysis*, that friendship is never preserved in wickedness and vice. And the Athenian stranger similarly says, "that there is conduct pleasing and conformable to God, based on one ancient ground-principle, That like loves like, provided it be within measure. But things beyond measure are congenial neither to what is within nor what is beyond measure. Now it is the case that God is the measure to us of all things." Then proceeding, Plato adds: "For every good man is like every other good man; and so being like to God, he is liked by every good man and by God." At this point I have just recollected the following. In the end of the *Timæus* he says: "You must necessarily assimilate that which perceives to that which is perceived, according to its original nature; and it is by so assimilating it that you attain to the end of the highest life proposed by the gods to men, for the present or the future time." For those have equal power with these. He, who seeks, will not stop till he find; and having found, he will wonder; and wondering, he will reign; and reigning, he will rest. And what? Were not also those expressions of Thales derived from these? The fact that God is glorified forever, and that He is expressly called by us the Searcher of hearts, he interprets. For Thales being asked, What is the divinity? said, What has neither beginning nor end. And on another asking, "If a man could elude the knowledge of the Divine Being while doing aught?" said, "How could he who cannot do so while thinking?"

Further, the Barbarian philosophy recognizes good as alone excellent, and virtue as sufficient for happiness, when it says, "Behold, I have set before your eyes good and evil, life and death, that ye may choose life." For it calls good, "life," and the choice of it excellent, and the choice of the opposite "evil." And the end of good and of life is to become a lover of God: "For this is thy life and length of days," to love that which tends to the truth. And these points are yet clearer. For the Savior, in enjoining to love God and our neighbor, says, "that on these two commandments hang the whole law and the prophets." Such are the tenets promulgated by the Stoics; and before these, by Socrates, in the *Phoedrus*, who prays, "O Pan, and ye other gods, give me to be beautiful within." And in the *Theoetetus* he says expressly, "For he that speaks well (καλῶς) is both beautiful and good." And in the *Protagoras* he avers to the companions of Protagoras that he has met with one more beautiful than Alcibiades, if indeed that which is wisest is most beautiful. For he said that virtue was the soul's beauty, and, on the contrary, that vice was the soul's deformity. Accordingly, Antipatrus the Stoic, who composed three books on the point, "That, according to Plato, only the beautiful is good," shows that, according to him, virtue is sufficient for happiness; and adduces several other dogmas agreeing with the Stoics. And by Aristobulus, who lived in the time of Ptolemy Philadelphus, who is mentioned by the composer of the epitome of the books of the Maccabees, there were abundant books to show that the Peripatetic philosophy was derived from the law of Moses and from the other prophets. Let such be the case.

Plato plainly calls us brethren, as being of one God and one teacher, in the following words: "For ye who are in the state are entirely brethren (as we shall say to them, continuing our story). But the God who formed you, mixed gold in the composition of those of you who are fit to rule, at your birth, wherefore you are most highly honored; and silver in the case of those who are helpers; and steel and brass in the case of farmers and other workers." Whence, of necessity, some embrace and love those things to which knowledge pertains; and others matters of opinion. Perchance he prophesies of that elect nature which is bent on knowledge; if by the supposition he makes of three natures he does not describe three politics, as some supposed: that of the Jews, the silver; that of the Greeks, the third; and that of the Christians, with whom has been mingled the regal gold, the Holy Spirit, the golden.

And exhibiting the Christian life, he writes in the *Theætetus* in these words: "Let us now speak of the highest principles. For why should we speak of those who make an abuse of philosophy? These know neither the way to the forum, nor know they the court or the senate house, or any other public assembly of the state. As for laws and decrees spoken or written, they neither see nor hear them. But party feelings of political associations and public meetings, and revels with musicians [occupy them]; but they never even dream of taking part in affairs. Has anyone conducted himself either well or ill in the state, or has aught evil descended to a man from his forefathers?—it escapes their attention as much as do the sands of the sea. And the man does not even know that he does not know all these things; but in reality his body alone is situated and dwells in the state, while the man himself flies, according to Pindar, beneath the earth and above the sky, astronomizing, and exploring all nature on all sides.

Again, with the Lord's saying, "Let your yea be yea, and your nay be nay," may be compared the following: "But to admit a falsehood, and destroy a truth, is in nowise lawful." With the prohibition, also, against swearing agrees the saying in the tenth book of the *Laws:* "Let praise and an oath in everything be absent."

And in general, Pythagoras, and Socrates, and Plato say that they hear God's voice while closely contemplating the fabric of the universe, made and preserved unceasingly by God. For they heard Moses say, "He said, and it was done," describing the word of God as an act.

And founding on the formation of man from the dust, the philosophers constantly term the body earthy. Homer, too, does not hesitate to put the following as an imprecation:—

"But may you all become earth and water."

As Esaias says, "And trample them down as clay." And Callimachus clearly writes:—

"That was the year in which
Birds, fishes, quadrupeds,
Spoke like Prometheus' clay."

And the same again:—

"If thee Prometheus formed,
And thou art not of other clay."

Hesiod says of Pandora:—

> "And bade Hephæstus, famed, with all his speed,
> Knead earth with water, and man's voice and mind
> Infuse."

The Stoics, accordingly, define nature to be artificial fire, advancing systematically to generation. And God and His Word are by Scripture figuratively termed fire and light. But how? Does not Homer himself, is not Homer himself, paraphrasing the retreat of the water from the land, and the clear uncovering of the dry land, when he says of Tethys and Oceanus:—

> "For now for a long time they abstain from
> Each other's bed and love?"

Again, power in all things is by the most intellectual among the Greeks ascribed to God; Epicharmus—he was a Pythagorean—saying:—

> "Nothing escapes the divine. This it behooves thee to know.
> He is our observer. To God naught is impossible."

And the lyric poet:—

> "And God from gloomy night
> Can raise unstained light,
> And can in darksome gloom obscure
> The day's refulgence pure."

He alone who is able to make night during the period of day is God.

In the *Phoenomena* Aratus writes thus:—

> "With Zeus let us begin; whom let us ne'er,

> Being men, leave unexpressed. All full of Zeus,
> The streets, and throngs of men, and full the sea,
> And shores, and everywhere we Zeus enjoy."

He adds:—

> "For we also are
> His offspring; . ."
> that is, by creation.

> "Who, bland to men,
> Propitious signs displays, and to their tasks
> Arouses. For these signs in heaven He fixed,
> The constellations spread, and crowned the year
> With stars; to show to men the seasons' tasks,
> That all things may proceed in order sure.
> Him ever first, Him last too, they adore:
> Hail Father, marvel great—great boon to men."

And before him, Homer, framing the world in accordance with Moses on the Vulcan wrought shield, says:—

> "On it he fashioned earth, and sky, and sea,
> And all the signs with which the heaven is crowned."

For the Zeus celebrated in poems and prose compositions leads the mind up to God. And already, so to speak, Democritus writes, "that a few men are in the light, who stretch out their hands to that place which we Greeks now call the air. Zeus speaks all, and he hears all, and distributes and takes away, and he is king of all." And more mystically the Boeotian Pindar, being a Pythagorean, says:—

> "One is the race of gods and men,
> And of one mother both have breath;"

that is, of matter: and names the one creator of these things, whom he calls Father, chief artificer, who furnishes the means of advancement on to divinity, according to merit.

For I pass over Plato; he plainly, in the Epistle to Erastus and Coriscus, is seen to exhibit the Father and Son somehow or other from the Hebrew Scriptures, exhorting in these words: "In invoking by oath, with not illiterate gravity, and with culture, the sister of gravity, God the author of all, and invoking Him by oath as the Lord, the Father of the Leader, and author; whom if ye study with a truly philosophical spirit, ye shall know." And the address in the *Timoeus* calls the creator, Father, speaking thus: "Ye gods of gods, of whom I am Father; and the Creator of your works." So that when he says, "Around the king of all, all things are, and because of Him are all things; and he [or that] is the cause of all good things; and around the second are the things second in order; and around the third, the third," I understand nothing else than the Holy Trinity to be meant; for the third is the Holy Spirit, and the Son is the second, by whom all things were made according to the will of the Father.

And the same, in the tenth book of the *Republic,* mentions Eros the son of Armenius, who is Zoroaster. Zoroaster, then, writes: "These were composed by Zoroaster, the son of Armenius, a Pamphylian by birth: having died in battle, and been in Hades, I learned them of the gods." This Zoroaster, Plato says, having been placed on the funeral pyre, rose again to life in twelve days. He alludes perchance to the resurrection, or perchance to the fact that the path for souls to ascension lies through the twelve signs of the zodiac; and he himself says, that the descending pathway to birth is the same. In the same way we are to understand the twelve labors of Hercules, after which the soul obtains release from this entire world.

I do not pass over Empedocles, who speaks thus physically of the renewal of all things, as consisting in a transmutation into the essence of fire, which is to take place.

And most plainly of the same opinion is Heraclitus of Ephesus, who considered that there was a world everlasting, and recognized one perishable—that is, in its arrangement, not being different from the former, viewed in a certain aspect. But that he knew the imperishable world which consists of the universal essence to be everlastingly of a certain nature, he makes clear by speaking thus: "The same world of all things, neither any of the gods, nor any one of men, made. But there was, and is, and will be ever-living fire, kindled according to measure, and quenched according to measure." And that he taught it to be generated and perishable, is shown by what follows: "There are transmutations of fire,—first, the sea; and of the sea the half is land, the half fiery vapor." For he says that these are the effects of power. For fire is by the Word of God, which governs all things, changed by the air into moisture, which is, as it were, the germ of cosmical change; and this he calls sea. And out of it again is produced earth, and sky, and all that they contain. How, again, they are restored and ignited, he shows clearly in these words: "The sea is diffused and measured according to the same rule which subsisted before it became earth." Similarly also respecting the other elements, the same is to be understood. The most renowned of the Stoics teach similar doctrines with him, in treating of the conflagration and the government of the world, and both the world and man properly so called, and of the continuance of our souls.

Plato, again, in the seventh book of the *Republic,* has called "the day here nocturnal," as I suppose, on account of "the world-rulers of this darkness;" and the descent of the soul into the body, sleep and death, similarly with Heraclitus. And was not this announced, oracularly, of the Savior, by the Spirit, saying by David, "I slept, and slumbered; I awoke: for the Lord will sustain me; "For He not only figuratively calls the resurrection of Christ rising from sleep; but to the descent of the Lord into the flesh he also applies the figurative term sleep. The Savior Himself enjoins, "Watch;" as much as to say,

"Study how to live, and endeavor to separate the soul from the body."

And the Lord's day Plato prophetically speaks of in the tenth book of the *Republic,* in these words: "And when seven days have passed to each of them in the meadow, on the eighth they are to set out and arrive in four days." By the meadow is to be understood the fixed sphere, as being a mild and genial spot, and the locality of the pious; and by the seven days each motion of the seven planets, and the whole practical art which speeds to the end of rest. But after the wandering orbs the journey leads to heaven, that is, to the eighth motion and day. And he says that souls are gone on the fourth day, pointing out the passage through the four elements. But the seventh day is recognized as sacred, not by the Hebrews only, but also by the Greeks; according to which the whole world of all animals and plants revolve. Hesiod says of it:—

"The first, and fourth, and seventh day were held sacred."

And again:—

"And on the seventh the sun's resplendent orb."

And Homer:—

"And on the seventh then came the sacred day."

And:—

"The seventh was sacred."

And again:—

"It was the seventh day, and all things were accomplished."

And again:—

"And on the seventh morn we leave the stream of Acheron."

Callimachus the poet also writes:—

"It was the seventh morn, and they had all things done."

And again:—

"Among good days is the seventh day, and the seventh race."

And:—

"The seventh is among the prime, and the seventh is perfect."

And:—

"Now all the seven were made in starry heaven,
In circles shining as the years appear."

The Elegies of Solon, too, intensely deify the seventh day.
    And how? Is it not similar to Scripture when it says, "Let us remove the righteous man from us, because he is troublesome to us?" when Plato, all but predicting the economy of salvation, says in the second book of the *Republic* as follows: "Thus he who is constituted just shall be scourged, shall be stretched on the rack, shall be bound, have his eyes put out; and at last, having suffered all evils, shall be crucified."
    And the Socratic Antisthenes, paraphrasing that prophetic utterance, "To whom have ye likened me? says the Lord," says that "God is like no one; wherefore no one can come to the knowledge of Him from an image."

Xenophon too, the Athenian, utters these similar sentiments in the following words: "He who shakes all things, and is Himself immoveable, is manifestly one great and powerful. But what He is in form, appears not. No more does the sun, who wishes to shine in all directions, deem it right to permit any one to look on himself. But if one gaze on him audaciously, he loses his eyesight."

> "What flesh can see with eyes the Heavenly, True,
> Immortal God, whose dwelling is the poles?
> Not even before the bright beams of the sun
> Are men, as being mortal, fit to stand,"—

the Sibyl had said before. Rightly, then, Xenophanes of Colophon, teaching that God is one and incorporeal, adds:—

> "One God there is 'midst gods and men supreme;
> In form, in mind, unlike to mortal men."

And again:—

> "But men have the idea that gods are born,
> And wear their clothes, and have both voice and shape."

And again:—

> "But had the oxen or the lions hands,
> Or could with hands depict a work like men,
> Were beasts to draw the semblance of the gods,
> The horses would them like to horses sketch,
> To oxen, oxen, and their bodies make
> Of such a shape as to themselves belongs."

Let us hear, then, the lyric poet Bacchylides speaking of the divine:—

> "Who to diseases dire never succumb,
> And blameless are; in naught resembling men."

And also Cleanthes, the Stoic, who writes thus in a poem on the Deity:—

> "If you ask what is the nature of the good, listen—
> That which is regular, just, holy, pious,
> Self-governing, useful, fair, fitting,
> Grave, independent, always beneficial,
> That feels no fear or grief, profitable, painless,
> Helpful, pleasant, safe, friendly,
> Held in esteem, agreeing with itself: honorable,
> Humble, careful, meek, zealous,
> Perennial, blameless, ever-during."

And the same, tacitly vilifying the idolatry of the multitude, adds:—

> "Base is everyone who looks to opinion,
> With the view of deriving any good from it."

We are not, then, to think of God according to the opinion of the multitude.

> "For I do not think that secretly,
> Imitating the guise of a scoundrel,
> He would go to thy bed as a man,"

says Amphion to Antiope. And Sophocles plainly writes:—

> "His mother Zeus espoused,
> Not in the likeness of gold, nor covered
> With swan's plumage, as the Pleuronian girl
> He impregnated; but an out and out man."

He further proceeds, and adds:—

> "And quick the adulterer stood on the bridal steps."

Then he details still more plainly the licentiousness of the fabled Zeus:—

> "But he nor food nor cleansing water touched,
> But heart-stung went to bed, and that whole night
> Wantoned."

But let these be resigned to the follies of the theatre.

Heraclius plainly says: "But of the word which is eternal men are not able to understand, both before they have heard it, and on first hearing it." And the lyrist Melanippides says in song:—

> "Hear me, O Father, Wonder of men,
> Ruler of the ever-living soul."

And Parmenides the great, as Plato says in the *Sophist*, writes of God thus:—

"Very much, since unborn and indestructible He is,
Whole, only-begotten, and immoveable, and unoriginated."

Hesiod also says:—

> "For He of the immortals all is King and Lord.
> With God none else in might may strive."

Nay more, Tragedy, drawing away from idols, teaches to look up to heaven. Sophocles, as Hecatæus, who composed the histories in the work about Abraham and the Egyptians, says, exclaims plainly on the stage:—

> "One in very truth, God is One,
> Who made the heaven and the far-stretching earth,
> The Deep's blue billow, and the might of winds.
> But of us mortals, many erring far
> In heart, as solace for our woes, have raised
> Images of gods—of stone, or else of brass,
> Or figures wrought of gold or ivory;
> And sacrifices and vain festivals
> To these appointing, deem ourselves devout."

And Euripides on the stage, in tragedy, says:—

> "Does thou this lofty, boundless Ether see,
> Which holds the earth around in the embrace
> Of humid arms? This reckon Zeus,
> And this regard as God."

And in the drama of Pirithous, the same writes those lines in tragic vein:—

> "Thee, self-sprung, who on Ether's wheel
> Hast universal nature spun,
> Around whom Light and dusky spangled Night,
> The countless host of stars, too, ceaseless dance."

For there he says that the creative mind is self-sprung. What follows applies to the universe, in which are the opposites of light and darkness.

Æschylus also, the son of Euphorion, says with very great solemnity of God:—

> "Ether is Zeus, Zeus earth, and Zeus the heaven;
> The universe is Zeus, and all above."

I am aware that Plato assents to Heraclitus, who writes: "The one thing that is wise alone will not be expressed, and means the name of Zeus." And again, "Law is to obey the will of one." And if you wish to adduce that saying, "He that hath ears to hear, let him hear," you will find it expressed by the Ephesian to the following effect: "Those that hear without understanding are like the deaf. The proverb witnesses against them, that when present they are absent."

But do you want to hear from the Greeks expressly of one first principle? Timæus the Locrian, in the work on Nature, shall testify in the following words: "There is one first principle of all things unoriginated. For were it originated, it would be no longer the first principle; but the first principle would be that from which it originated." For this true opinion was derived from what follows: "Hear," it is said, "O Israel; the Lord thy God is one, and Him only shalt thou serve."

"Lo He all sure and all unerring is,"

says the Sibyl.

Homer also manifestly mentions the Father and the Son by a happy hit of divination in the following words:—

"If Outis, alone as thou art, offers thee violence,
And there is no escaping disease sent by Zeus,—
For the Cyclopes heed not Ægis-bearing Zeus."

And before him Orpheus said, speaking of the point in hand:—

"Son of great Zeus, Father of Ægis-bearing Zeus."

And Xenocrates the Chalcedonian, who mentions the supreme Zeus and the inferior Zeus, leaves an indication of the Father and the Son. Homer, while representing the gods as subject to human passions, appears to know the Divine Being, whom Epicurus does not so revere.
He says accordingly:—

"Why, son of Peleus, mortal as thou art,

> With swift feet me pursues, a god
> Immortal? Hast thou not yet known
> That I am a god?"

For he shows that the Divinity cannot be captured by a mortal, or apprehended either with feet, or hands, or eyes, or by the body at all. "To whom have ye likened the Lord? or to what likeness have ye likened Him?" says the Scripture. Has not the artificer made the image? or the goldsmith, melting the gold, has gilded it, and what follows.

The comic poet Epicharmus speaks in the *Republic* clearly of the Word in the following terms:—

> "The life of men needs calculation and number alone,
> And we live by number and calculation, for these save mortals."

He then adds expressly:—

> "Reason governs mortals, and alone preserves manners."

Then:—

> "There is in man reasoning; and there is a divine Reason.
> Reason is implanted in man to provide for life and sustenance,
> But divine Reason attends the arts in the case of all,
> Teaching them always what it is advantageous to do.
> For it was not man that discovered art, but God brought it;
> And the Reason of man derives its origin from the divine Reason."

The Spirit also cries by Isaiah: "Wherefore the multitude of sacrifices? says the Lord. I am full of holocausts of rams, and the fat of lambs and the blood of bulls I wish not;" and a little after adds: "Wash you, and be clean. Put away wickedness from your souls," and so forth.

Menander, the comic poet, writes in these very words:—

> "If one by offering sacrifice, a crowd
> Of bulls or kids, O Pamphilus, by Zeus.
> Or such like things; by making works of art,
> Garments of gold or purple, images
> Of ivory or emerald, deems by these
> God can be made propitious, he does err,
> And has an empty mind. For the man must prove
> A man of worth, who neither maids deflowers,
> Nor an adulterer is, nor steals, nor kills
> For love of worldly wealth, O Pamphilus.
> Nay, covet not a needle's thread. For God
> Thee sees, being near beside thee." . . .

"I am a God at hand," it is said by Jeremiah, "and not a God afar off. Shall a man do aught in secret places, and I shall not see him?"

And again Menander, paraphrasing that Scripture, "Sacrifice a sacrifice of righteousness, and trust in the Lord," thus writes:—

> "And not a needle even that is
> Another's ever covet, dearest friend;
> For God in righteous works delights, and so
> Permits him to increase his worldly wealth,
> Who toils, and ploughs the land both night and day.
> But sacrifice to God, and righteous be,
> Shining not in bright robes, but in thy heart;
> And when thou hears the thunder, do not flee,
> Being conscious to thyself of naught amiss,
> Good sir, for thee God ever present sees."

"Whilst thou art yet speaking," says the Scripture, "I will say, Lo, here I am."

Again Diphilus, the comic poet, discourses as, follows on the judgment:—

> "Think's thou, O Niceratus, that the dead,
> Who in all kinds of luxury in life have shared,
> Escape the Deity, as if forgot?
> There is an eye of justice, which sees all.
> For two ways, as we deem, to Hades lead—
> One for the good, the other for the bad.
> But if the earth hides both forever, then
> Go plunder, steal, rob, and be turbulent.
> But err not. For in Hades judgment is,
> Which God the Lord of all will execute,
> Whose name too dreadful is for me to name,
> Who gives to sinners length of earthly life.
> If any mortal thinks, that day by day,
> While doing ill, he eludes the gods' keen sight,
> His thoughts are evil; and when justice has
> The leisure, he shall then detected be
> So thinking. Look, whoe'er you be that say
> That there is not a God. There is, there is.
> If one, by nature evil, evil does,
> Let him redeem the time; for such as he
> Shall by and by due punishment receive."

And with this agrees the tragedy in the following lines:—

> "For there shall come, shall come that point of time,
> When Ether, golden-eyed, shall ope its store
> Of treasured fire; and the devouring flame,
> Raging, shall burn all things on earth below,
> And all above." ...

And after a little he adds:—

> "And when the whole world fades,

> And vanished all the abyss of ocean's waves,
> And earth of trees is bare; and wrapt in flames,
> The air no more begets the winged tribes;
> Then He who all destroyed, shall all restore."

We shall find expressions similar to these also in the Orphic hymns, written as follows:—

> "For having hidden all, brought them again
> To gladsome light, forth from his sacred heart,
> Solicitous."

And if we live throughout holily and righteously, we are happy here, and shall be happier after our departure hence; not possessing happiness for a time, but enabled to rest in eternity.

> "At the same hearth and table as the rest
> Of the immortal gods, we sit all free
> Of human ills, unharmed,"

says the philosophic poetry of Empedocles. And so, according to the Greeks, none is so great as to be above judgment, none so insignificant as to escape its notice.

And the same Orpheus speaks thus:—

> "But to the word divine, looking, attend,
> Keeping aright the heart's receptacle
> Of intellect, and tread the straight path well,
> And only to the world's immortal King
> Direct thy gaze."

And again, respecting God, saying that He was invisible, and that He was known to but one, a Chaldean by race—meaning either by this Abraham or his son—he speaks as follows:—

> "But one a scion of Chaldean race;
> For he the sun's path knew right well,

> And how the motion of the sphere about
> The earth proceeds, in circle moving
> Equally around its axis, how the winds
> Their chariot guide o'er air and sea."

Then, as if paraphrasing the expression, "Heaven is my throne, and earth is my footstool," he adds:—

> "But in great heaven, He is seated firm
> Upon a throne of gold, and 'neath His feet
> The earth. His right hand round the ocean's bound
> He stretches; and the hills' foundations shake
> To the center at His wrath, nor can endure
> His mighty strength. He all celestial is,
> And all things finishes upon the earth.
> He the Beginning, Middle is, and End.
> But Thee I dare not speak. In limbs
> And mind I tremble. He rules from on high."

And so forth. For in these he indicates these prophetic utterances: "If Thou opens the heaven, trembling shall seize the mountains from Thy presence; and they shall melt, as wax melted before the fire;" and in Isaiah, "Who hath measured the heaven with a span, and the whole earth with His fist? Again, when it is said:—

> "Ruler of Ether, Hades, Sea, and Land,
> Who with Thy bolts Olympus' strong-built home
> Does shake. Whom demons dread, and whom the throng
> Of gods do fear. Whom, too, the Fates obey,
> Relentless though they be. O deathless One,
> Our mother's Sire! whose wrath makes all things reel;
> Who mov'st the winds, and shroud'st in clouds the world,
> Broad Ether cleaving with Thy lightning gleams,—
> Thine is the order 'mongst the stars, which run

> As Thine unchangeable behests direct.
> Before Thy burning throne the angels wait,
> Much-working, charged to do all things, for men.
> Thy young Spring shines, all prank'd with purple flowers;
> Thy Winter with its chilling clouds assails;
> Thine Autumn noisy Bacchus distributes."

Then he adds, naming expressly the Almighty God:—

> "Deathless Immortal, capable of being
> To the immortals only uttered! Come,
> Greatest of gods, with strong Necessity.
> Dread, invincible, great, deathless One,
> Whom Ether crowns." ...

By the expression "Sire of our Mother" (μητροπάτωρ) he not only intimates creation out of nothing, but gives occasion to those who introduce emissions of imagining a consort of the Deity. And he paraphrases those prophetic Scripture—that in Isaiah, "I am He that fixes the thunder, and creates the wind; whose hands have founded the host of heaven;" and that in Moses, "Behold, behold that I am He, and there is no god beside me: I will kill, and I will make to live; I will smite, and I will heal: and there is none that shall deliver out of my hands."

> "And He, from good, to mortals planted ill,
> And cruel war, and tearful woes,"

according to Orpheus.

Such also are the words of the Parian Archilochus.

> "O Zeus, thine is the power of heaven, and thou
> Inflict'st on men things violent and wrong."

Again let the Thracian Orpheus sing to us:—

> "His right hand all around to ocean's bound
> He stretches; and beneath His feet is earth."

These are plainly derived from the following: "The Lord will save the inhabited cities, and grasp the whole land in His hand like a nest;" "It is the Lord that made the earth by His power," as says Jeremiah, "and set up the earth by His wisdom." Further, in addition to these, Phocylides, who calls the angels demons, explains in the following words that some of them are good, and others bad (for we also have learned that some are apostate):—

> "Demons there are—some here, some there—set over men;
> Some, on man's entrance [into life], to ward off ill."

Rightly, then, also Philemon, the comic poet demolishes idolatry in these words:—

> "Fortune is no divinity to us:
> There's no such god. But what befalls by chance
> And of itself to each, is Fortune called."

And Sophocles the tragedian says:—

> "Not even the gods have all things as they choose,
> Excepting Zeus; for he beginning is and end."

And Orpheus:—

> "One Might, the great, the flaming heaven, was
> One Deity. All things one Being were; in whom
> All these revolve fire, water, and the earth."

And so forth.

Pindar, the lyric poet, as if in Bacchic frenzy, plainly says:—

"What is God? The All."

And again:—

"God, who makes all mortals."

And when he says,—

"How little, being a man, dost thou expect
Wisdom for man? 'Tis hard for mortal mind
The counsels of the gods to scan; and thou
Wast of a mortal mother born,"

he drew the thought from the following: "Who hath known the mind of the Lord, or who was His counsellor?" Hesiod, too, agrees with what is said above, in what he writes:—

"No prophet, sprung of men that dwell on earth,
Can know the mind of Ægis-bearing Zeus."

Similarly, then, Solon the Athenian, in the *Elegies*, following Hesiod, writes:—

"The immortal's mind to men is quite unknown."

Again Moses, having prophesied that the woman would bring forth in trouble and pain, on account of transgression, a poet not undistinguished writes:—

"Never by day
From toil and woe shall they have rest, nor yet
By night from groans. Sad cares the gods to men
Shall give."

Further, when Homer says,—

> "The Sire himself the golden balance held,"

he intimates that God is just.

And Menander, the comic poet, in exhibiting God, says:—

> "To each man, on his birth, there is assigned
> A tutelary Demon, as his life's good guide.
> For that the Demon evil is, and harms
> A good life, is not to be thought."

Then he adds:—

"Ἅπαντα δ' ἀγαθὸν εἶναι τὸν Θεόν,"

meaning either "that every one good is God," or, what is preferable, "that God in all things is good."

Again, Æschylus the tragedian, setting forth the power of God, does not shrink from calling Him the Highest, in these words:—

> "Place God apart from mortals; and think not
> That He is, like thyself, corporeal.
> Thou know'st Him not. Now He appears as fire,
> Dread force; as water now; and now as gloom;
> And in the beasts is dimly shadowed forth,
> In wind, and cloud, in lightning, thunder, rain;
> And minister to Him the seas and rocks,
> Each fountain and the water's floods and streams.
> The mountains tremble, and the earth, the vast
> Abyss of sea, and towering height of hills,
> When on them looks the Sovereign's awful eye:
> Almighty is the glory of the Most High God."

Does he not seem to you to paraphrase that text, "At the presence of the Lord the earth trembles?" In addition to these, the most prophetic Apollo is compelled—thus testifying to the glory of God—to say of Athene, when the Medes made war against Greece, that she besought and supplicated Zeus for Attica. The oracle is as follows:—

> "Pallas cannot Olympian Zeus propitiate,
> Although with many words and sage advice she prays;
> But he will give to the devouring fire many temples of the immortals,
> Who now stand shaking with terror, and bathed in sweat;"

and so forth.

Thearidas, in his book *On Nature*, writes: "There was then one really true beginning [first principle] of all that exist"—one. For that Being in the beginning is one and alone." "Nor is there any other except the Great King," says Orpheus. In accordance with whom, the comic poet Diphilus says very sententiously, the

> "Father of all,
> To Him alone incessant reverence pay,
> The inventor and the author of such blessings."

Rightly therefore Plato "accustoms the best natures to attain to that study which formerly we said was the highest, both to see the good and to accomplish that ascent. And this, as appears, is not the throwing of the potsherds; but the turning round of the soul from a nocturnal day to that which is a true return to that which really is, which we shall assert to be the true philosophy." Such as are partakers of this he judges to belong to the golden race, when he says: "Ye are all brethren; and those who are of the golden race are most capable of judging most accurately in every respect."

The Father, then, and Maker of all things is apprehended by all things, agreeably to all, by innate power and without teaching,—things inanimate, sympathizing with the animate creation; and of living beings some are already immoral, working in the light of day. But of those that are still mortal, some are in fear, and carried still in their mother's womb; and others regulate themselves by their own independent reason. And of men all are Greeks and Barbarians. But no race anywhere of tillers of the soil, or nomads, and not even of dwellers in cities, can live, without being imbued with the faith of a superior being. Wherefore every eastern nation, and every nation touching the western shore; or the north, and each one towards the south,—all have one and the same preconception respecting Him who hath appointed government; since the most universal of His operations equally pervade all.

Much more did the philosophers among the Greeks, devoted to investigation, starting from the Barbarian philosophy, attribute providence to the "Invisible, and sole, and most powerful, and most skillful and supreme cause of all things most beautiful;"—not knowing the inferences from these truths, unless instructed by us, and not even how God is to be known naturally; but only, as we have already often said, by a true periphrasis. Rightly therefore the apostle says, "Is He the God of the Jews only, and not also of the Greeks?"—not only saying prophetically that of the Greeks believing Greeks would know God; but also intimating that in power the Lord is the God of all, and truly Universal King. For they know neither what He is, nor how He is Lord, and Father, and Maker, nor the rest of the system of the truth, without being taught by it. Thus also the prophetic utterances have the same force as the apostolic word. For Isaiah says, "If ye say, We trust in the Lord our God: now make an alliance with my Lord the king of the Assyrians." And he adds: "And now, was it without the Lord that we came up to this land to make war against it?" And Jonah, himself a prophet, intimates the same thing in what he says: "And the shipmaster came to him, and said to him, Why dost thou snore? Rise, call on thy God, that He may save us, and that we may not perish." For the expression "thy God" he makes as if to one who knew Him by way of knowledge; and the expression, "that God may save us," revealed the consciousness in the minds of heathens who had applied their mind to the Ruler of all, but had not yet believed. And again the same: "And he said to them, I am the servant of the Lord; and I fear the Lord, the God of heaven." And again the same: "And he said, Let us by no means perish for the life of this man." And Malachi the prophet plainly exhibits God saying, "I will not accept sacrifice at your hands. For from the rising of the sun to its going down, My name is glorified among the Gentiles; and in every place sacrifice is offered to Me." And again: "Because I am a great King, says the Lord omnipotent; and My name is manifest among the nations." What name? The Son declaring the Father among the Greeks who have believed.

Plato in what follows gives an exhibition of free-will: "Virtue owns not a master; and in proportion as each one honors or dishonors it, in that proportion he will be a partaker of it. The blame lies in the exercise of free choice." But God is blameless. For He is never the author of evil.

"O warlike Trojans," says the lyric poet,—

> "High ruling Zeus, who beholds all things,
> Is not the cause of great woes to mortals;
> But it is in the power of all men to find
> Justice, holy, pure,
> Companion of order,
> And of wise Themis
> The sons of the blessed are ye
> In finding her as your associate."

And Pindar expressly introduces also Zeus Soter, the consort of Themis, proclaiming him King, Savior, Just, in the following lines:—

> "First, prudent Themis, of celestial birth,
> On golden steeds, by Ocean's rock,
> The Fates brought to the stair sublime,
> The shining entrance of Olympus,
> Of Savior Zeus for aye to be the spouse,
> And she, the Hours, gold-diademed, fair-fruited, good, brought forth."

He, then, who is not obedient to the truth, and is puffed up with human teaching, is wretched and miserable, according to Euripides:—

> "Who these things seeing, yet apprehends not God,
> But mouthing lofty themes, casts far
> Perverse deceits; stubborn in which, the tongue
> Its shafts discharges, about things unseen,
> Devoid of sense."

Let him who wishes, then, approaching to the true instruction, learn from Parmenides the Eleatic, who promises:—

> "Ethereal nature, then, and all the signs
> In Ether thou shall know, and the effects,
> All viewless, of the sacred Sun's clear torch
> And whence produced. The round-eyed Moon's
> Revolving influences and nature thou
> Shall learn; and the ensphering heaven shall know;
> Whence sprung; and how Necessity took it
> And chained so as to keep the starry bounds."

And Metrodorus, though an Epicurean, spoke thus, divinely inspired: "Remember, O Menestratus, that, being a mortal endowed with a circumscribed life, thou hast in thy soul ascended, till thou hast seen endless time, and the infinity of things; and what is to be, and what has been;" when with the blessed choir, according to Plato, we shall gaze on the blessed sight and vision; we following with Zeus, and others with other deities, if we may be permitted so to say, to receive initiation into the most blessed mystery: which we shall celebrate, ourselves being perfect and untroubled by the ills which awaited us at the end of our time; and introduced to the knowledge of perfect and tranquil visions, and contemplating them in pure sunlight; we ourselves pure, and now no longer distinguished by that, which, when carrying it about, we call the body, being bound to it like an oyster to its shell.

The Pythagoreans call heaven the Antichthon [the opposite Earth]. And in this land, it is said by Jeremiah, "I will place thee among the children, and give thee the chosen land as inheritance of God Omnipotent;" and they who inherit it shall reign over the earth. Myriads on myriads of examples rush on my mind which might adduce. But for the sake of symmetry the discourse must now stop, in order that we may not exemplify the saying of Agatho the tragedian:—

"Treating our by-work as work,
And doing our work as by-work."

It having been, then, as I think, clearly shown in what way it is to be understood that the Greeks were called thieves by the Lord, I willingly leave the dogmas of the philosophers. For were we to go over their sayings, we should gather together directly such a quantity of notes, in showing that the whole of the Hellenic wisdom was derived from the Barbarian philosophy. But this speculation, we shall, nevertheless, again touch on, as necessity requires, when we collect the opinions current among the Greeks respecting first principles.

But from what has been said, it tacitly devolves on us to consider in what way the Hellenic books are to be perused by the man who is able to pass through the billows in them. Therefore

"Happy is he who possesses the wealth of the divine mind,"

as appears according to Empedocles,

> "But wretched he, who cares for dark opinion about the Gods."

He divinely showed knowledge and ignorance to be the boundaries of happiness and misery. "For it behooves philosophers to be acquainted with very many things," according to Heraclitus; and truly must

> "He, who seeks to be good, err in many things."

It is then now clear to us, from what has been said, that the beneficence of God is eternal, and that, from an unbeginning principle, equal natural righteousness reached all, according to the worth of each several race,—never having had a beginning. For God did not make a beginning of being Lord and Good, being always what He is. Nor will He ever cease to do good, although He bring all things to an end. And each one of us is a partaker of His beneficence, as far as He wills. For the difference of the elect is made by the intervention of a choice worthy of the soul, and by exercise.

Thus, then, let our fifth Miscellany of gnostic notes in accordance with the true philosophy be brought to a close.

Elucidations.
I.
(Clement's Hebrew, p. 446, note 8.)

On this matter having spoken in a former Elucidation (see Elucidation VIII. p. 443), I must here translate a few words from Philo Judæus. He says, "Before Abram was called, such was his name; but afterward he was named *Abraam*, by the simple duplication of one letter, which nevertheless enfolds a great significance. For Abram is expounded to mean *sublime father*, but *Abraam* means *elect father of sound*." Philo goes on to give his personal fancies in explication of this whim. But, with Clement, Philo was an *expert*, to whom all knowledge was to be credited in his specialty. This passage, however, confirms the opinion of those who pronounce Clement destitute of Hebrew, even in its elements. No need to say that *Abram* means something like what Philo gives us, but *Abraham* is expounded in the Bible itself (Genesis 17:3). The text of the LXX, seems to have been dubious to our author's mind, and hence he fails back on Philo. But this of itself appears decisive as to Clement's Hebrew scholarship.

II.
(The Beetle, cap. iv. p. 449, note 6.)

Cicero notes the *scarabæus* on the tongue, as identifying Apis, the calf-god of the Egyptians. Now, this passage of our author seems to me to clear up the Scriptural word *gillulim* in Deut. xxix. 17, where the English margin reads, literally enough, *dungy-gods*. The word means, *things rolled about* (Lev. xxvi. 30; Hab. ii. 18, 19; 1 Kings xv. 12); on which compare Leighton (*St. Peter*, pp. 239, 746, and note). Scripture seems to prove that this story of Clement's about the beetle of the Egyptians, was known to the ancient Hebrews, and was the point in their references to the *gillulim* (see *Herod.*, book iii. cap. 28., or Rawlinson's *Trans.*, vol. ii. 353). The note in Migne *ad loc.* is also well-worthy to be consulted.

III.
(The Tetrad, cap. vi. p. 452, note 4.)

It is important to observe that "the patriarchal dispensation," as we too carelessly speak, is pluralized by Clement. He clearly distinguishes the *three* patriarchal dispensations, as given in Adam, Noah, and Abraham; and then comes the Mosaic. The editor begs to be pardoned for referring to his venerated and gifted father's division (sustained by Clement's authority), which he used to insist should be further enlarged so as to subdivide the first and the last, making *seven* complete, and thus honoring the system of sevens which runs through all Scripture. Thus *Adam* embraces *Paradise*, and the *first covenant* after the fall; and the *Christian covenant* embraces a *millennial period*. So that we have (1) *Paradise*, (2) Adam, (3) Noah (4) Abraham, (5) Moses, (6) Christ (7) *a millennial period*, preluding the Judgment and the Everlasting Kingdom. My venerated and most erudite instructor in theology, the late Dr. Jarvis, in his *Church of the Redeemed*, expounds a dispensation as identified by (1) a covenant, original or renewed, (2) a sign or sacrament, and (3) a closing judgment. (See pp. 4, 5, and elsewhere in the great work I have named.) Thus (1) the Tree of Life, (2) the institution of sacrifice, (3) the rainbow, (4) circumcision, (5) the ark, (6) the baptismal and Eucharistic sacraments, and (7) the same renewed and glorified by the conversion of nations are the symbols. The covenants and the judgments are easily identified, ending with the universal Judgment. Dr. Jarvis died, leaving his work unfinished; but the *Church of the Redeemed* is a book complete in itself, embodying the results of a vast erudition, and of a devout familiarity with Scripture. It begins with Adam, and ends with the downfall of Jerusalem (the typical judgment), which closed the Mosaic dispensation. It is written in a pellucid style, and with a fastidious use of the English language; and it is the noblest introduction to the understanding of the New Testament, with which I am acquainted. That such a work should be almost unknown in American literature, of which it should be a conspicuous ornament, is a sad commentary upon the taste of the period when it was given to the public.

IV.
(The Golden Candlestick, cap. vi. p. 452, note 6.)

The seven gifts of the Spirit seem to be prefigured in this symbol, corresponding to the seven (spirits) lamps before the throne in the vision of St. John (see Rev. i. 4, iii. 1, iv. 5, and v. 6; also Isa. xi. 1, 2, and Zech. iii. 9, and iv. 10). The prediction of Isaiah intimates the anointing of Jesus at his baptism, and the outpouring of these gifts upon the Christian Church.

V.
(Symbols, cap. vi. p. 453, note 3.)

Clement regards the symbols of the divine law as *symbols* merely, and not *images* in the sense of the Decalogue. Whatever we may think of this distinction, his argument destroys the fallacy of the *Trent Catechism*, which pleads the Levitical symbols in favor of *images* in "the likeness of holy things," and which virtually abrogates the second commandment. Images of God the Father (crowned with the Papal tiara) are everywhere to be seen in the Latin churches, and countless images of all heavenly things are everywhere *worshipped* under the fallacy which Clement rejects. Pascal exposes the distinctions without a difference, by which God's laws are evacuated of all force in Jesuit theology; but the hairsplitting distinctions, about "bowing down to images and *worshipping* them," which infect the Trent theology, are equal to the worst of Pascal's instances. It is with profound regret that I insert this testimony; but it seems necessary, because garbling of patristic authorities, which begin to appear in America, make an accurate and intelligent study of the *Ante-Nicene Fathers* a necessity for the American theologian.

VI.
(Perfection, cap. x. p. 459, note 2.)

The τέλειοι of the ancient canons were rather the *complete* than the *perfect,* as understood by the ancients. Clement's *Gnostic* is "complete," and goes on to moral perfection. Now, does not St. Paul make a similar distinction between babes in Christ, and those "*complete* in Him?"(Col. ii. 10.) The πεπληρωμένοι of this passage, referring to the "thoroughly furnished" Christian (fully equipped for his work

The Stromata or Miscellanies

and warfare), has thrown light on many passages of the fathers and of the old canons, in my experience; and I merely make the suggestion for what it may be worth. See Bunsen's *Church and Home Book* (*Hippol.*, iii. 82, 83, *et seqq.*) for the rules (1) governing all Christians, and (2) those called "the faithful," by way of eminence. So, in our days, not all *believers* are *communicants*.

VII.
(The Unknown God, cap. xii. p. 464, note 1.)

Must we retain "too superstitious," even in the Revised Version? (Which see *ad loc.*) Bunsen's rendering of δεισιδαιμονία, by *demon-fear*, is not English; but it suggests the common view of scholars, upon the passage, and leads me to suppose that the learned and venerable company of revisers could not agree on any English that would answer. That St.
Paul paid the Athenians a compliment, as *devout in their way*, i.e., God fearing towards their divinities, will not be denied. Clement seems to have so understood it, and hence his constant effort to show that we must recognize, in dealing with Gentiles, whatever of elementary good God has permitted to exist among them. May we not admit this principle, at least so far as to believe that Divine Providence led the Athenians to set up the very inscription which was to prompt Christ's apostle to an ingenious interpretation, and to an equally ingenious use of it, so avoiding a direct conflict with their laws? This they had charged on him (Acts xvii. 18), as before on Socrates.

VIII.
(Xenocrates and Democritus, cap. xiii. p. 465, note 3.)

My grave and studious reader will forgive me, here, for a reference to *Stromata* of a widely different sort. *Dulce est desipere*, etc. One sometimes finds instruction and relief amid the intense nonsense of "agnostic" and other "philosophies" of our days, in turning to a healthful intellect which "answers fools according to their folly." I confess myself an occasional reader of the vastly entertaining and suggestive *Noctes* of Christopher North, which may be excused by the famous example of a Father of the Church, who delighted in Aristophanes. To illustrate this passage of Clement, then, let me refer to Professor Wilson's intense sympathy with animals. See the real eloquence of his reference to the dogs of Homer and of Sir Walter Scott. "The Ettrick Shepherd" somewhere wondered, whether some dogs are not gifted with souls; and, in the passage referred to, it is asked, whether the dog of Ulysses could have been destitute of an immortal spirit. On another occasion, Christopher breaks out with something like this: "Let me prefer the man who thinks so, to the miserable atheist whose creed is dust." He looks upon his dog "Fro," and continues (while the noble animal seems listening), "Yes, better a thousand times, O Fro, to believe that 'my faithful dog shall bear me company,' than that the soul of a Newton perishes at death," etc. How often have I regaled myself with the wholesome tonic of such dog loving sport, after turning with disgust from some God hating and man destroying argument of "modern science," falsely so called.

IX.
(Plato's Prophecy, cap. xiv. p. 470, note 2.)

My references at this point are worthy of being enlarged upon. I subjoin the following as additional. On this sublime passage, Jones of Nayland remarks, "The greatest moral philosopher of the Greeks declared, with a kind of prescience, that, if a man *perfectly just* were to come upon earth, he would be impoverished and scourged, and bound as a criminal; and, when he had suffered all manner of indignities, would be put to the shameful death of (suspension or) crucifixion." "Several of the Fathers," he adds, "have taken notice of this extraordinary passage in Plato, looking upon it as a prediction of the sufferings of the Just One, Jesus Christ." He refers us to Grotius (*De Veritate*, iv. sec. 12) and to Meric

Casaubon (*On Credulity*, p. 135). The passage from Plato (*Rep.*, ii. 5) impressed the mind of Cicero. (See his *Rep.*, iii. 17.)

Book VI.

CHAPTER I.—PLAN.

The sixth and also the seventh Miscellany of gnostic notes, in accordance with the true philosophy, having delineated as well as possible the ethical argument conveyed in them, and having exhibited what the Gnostic is in his life, proceed to show the philosophers that he is by no means impious, as they suppose, but that he alone is truly pious, by a compendious exhibition of the Gnostic's form of religion, as far as it is possible, without danger, to commit it to writing in a book of reference. For the Lord enjoined "to labor for the meat which endures to eternity." And the prophet says, "Blessed is he that sowed into all waters, whose ox and ass tread," [that is,] the people, from the Law and from the Gentiles, gathered into one faith.

"Now the weak eats herbs," according to the noble apostle. *The Instructor*, divided by us into three books, has already exhibited the training and nurture up from the state of childhood, that is, the course of life which from elementary instruction grows by faith; and in the case of those enrolled in the number of men, prepares beforehand the soul, endued with virtue, for the reception of gnostic knowledge. The Greeks, then, clearly learning, from what shall be said by us in these pages, that in profanely persecuting the God-loving man, they themselves act impiously; then, as the notes advance, in accordance with the style of the *Miscellanies*, we must solve the difficulties raised both by Greeks and Barbarians with respect to the coming of the Lord.

In a meadow the flowers blooming variously, and in a park the plantations of fruit trees, are not separated according to their species from those of other kinds. If some, culling varieties, have composed learned collections, Meadows, and Helicons, and Honeycombs, and Robes; then, with the things which come to recollection by haphazard, and are expurgated neither in order nor expression, but purposely scattered, the form of the *Miscellanies* is promiscuously variegated like a meadow. And such being the case, my notes shall serve as kindling sparks; and in the case of him, who is fit for knowledge, if he chance to fall in with them, research made with exertion will turn out to his benefit and advantage. For it is right that labor should precede not only food but also, much more knowledge, in the case of those that are advancing to the eternal and blessed salvation by the "straight and narrow way," which is truly the Lord's.

Our knowledge, and our spiritual garden, is the Savior Himself; into whom we are planted, being transferred and transplanted, from our old life, into the good land. And transplanting contributes to fruitfulness. The Lord, then, into whom we have been transplanted, is the Light and the true Knowledge.

Now knowledge is otherwise spoken of in a twofold sense: that, commonly so called, which appears in all men (similarly also comprehension and apprehension), universally, in the knowledge of individual objects; in which not only the rational powers, but equally the irrational, share, which I would never term knowledge, inasmuch as the apprehension of
things through the senses comes naturally. But that which *par excellence* is termed knowledge, bears the impress of judgment and reason, in the exercise of which there will be rational
cognitions alone, applying purely to objects of thought, and resulting from the bare energy of the soul. "He is a good man," says David, "who pities" (those ruined through error), "and lends" (from the communication of the word of truth) not at haphazard, for "he will dispense his words in judgment:" with profound calculation, "he hath dispersed, he hath given to the poor."

CHAPTER II.—THE SUBJECT OF PLAGIARISMS RESUMED. THE GREEKS PLAGIARIZED FROM ONE ANOTHER.

Before handling the point proposed, we must, by way of preface, add to the close of the fifth book what is wanting. For since we have shown that the symbolical style was ancient, and was employed not only by our prophets, but also by the majority of the ancient Greeks, and by not a few of the rest of the Gentile Barbarians, it was requisite to proceed to the mysteries of the initiated. I postpone the elucidation of these till we advance to the confutation of what is said by the Greeks on first principles; for we shall show that the mysteries belong to the same branch of speculation. And having proved that the declaration of Hellenic thought is illuminated all round by the truth, bestowed on us in the Scriptures, taking it according to the sense, we have proved, not to say what is invidious, that the theft of the truth passed to them.

Come, and let us adduce the Greeks as witnesses against themselves to the theft. For, inasmuch as they pilfer from one another, they establish the fact that they are thieves; and although against their will, they are detected, clandestinely appropriating to those of their own race the truth which belongs to us. For if they do not keep their hands from each other, they will hardly do it from our authors. I shall say nothing of philosophic dogmas, since the very persons who are the authors of the divisions into sects, confess in writing, so as not to be convicted of ingratitude, that they have received from Socrates the most important of their dogmas. But after availing myself of a few testimonies of men most talked of, and of repute among the Greeks, and exposing their plagiarizing style, and selecting them from various periods, I shall turn to what follows.

Orpheus, then, having composed the line:—

"Since nothing else is more shameless and wretched than woman,"

Homer plainly says:—

> "Since nothing else is more dreadful and shameless than a woman."

And Musæus having written:—

> "Since art is greatly superior to strength,"—

Homer says:—

> "By art rather than strength is the woodcutter greatly superior."

Again, Musæus having composed the lines:—

> "And as the fruitful field produces leaves,
> And on the ash trees some fade, others grow,
> So whirls the race of man its leaf,"—

Homer transcribes:—

> "Some of the leaves the wind strews on the ground.
> The budding wood bears some; in time of spring,
> They come. So springs one race of men, and one departs."

Again, Homer having said:—

> "It is unholy to exult over dead men,"

Archilochus and Cratinus write, the former:—

> "It is not noble at dead men to sneer;"

and Cratinus in the *Lacones:*—

> "For men 'tis dreadful to exult
> Much o'er the stalwart dead."

Again, Archilochus, transferring that Homeric line:—

> "I erred, nor say I nay: instead of many"—

writes thus:—

> "I erred, and this mischief hath somehow seized another."

As certainly also that line:—

> "Even-handed war the slayer slays."

He also, altering, has given forth thus:—

> "I will do it.
> For Mars to men in truth is evenhanded."

Also, translating the following:—

> "The issues of victory among men depend on the gods,"

he openly encourages youth, in the following iambic:—

> "Victory's issues on the gods depend."

Again, Homer having said:—

> "With feet unwashed sleeping on the ground,"

Euripides writes in *Erechtheus*:—

> "Upon the plain spread with no couch they sleep,

Nor in the streams of water lave their feet."

Archilochus having likewise said:—

> "But one with this and one with that
> His heart delights,"—

in correspondence with the Homeric line:—

> "For one in these deeds, one in those delights,"—

Euripides says in *OEneus:*—

> "But one in these ways, one in those, has more delight."

And I have heard Æschylus saying:—

> "He who is happy ought to stay at home;
> There should he also stay, who speeds not well."

And Euripides, too, shouting the like on the stage:—

> "Happy the man who, prosperous, stays at home."

Menander, too, on comedy, saying:—

> "He ought at home to stay, and free remain,
> Or be no longer rightly happy."

Again, Theognis having said:—

> "The exile has no comrade dear and true,"—

Euripides has written:—

"Far from the poor flies every friend."

And Epicharmus, saying:—

"Daughter, woe worth the day!
Thee who art old I marry to a youth;" and adding:—

"For the young husband takes some other girl,
And for another husband longs the wife,"—

Euripides writes:—

"'Tis bad to yoke an old wife to a youth;
For he desires to share another's bed,
And she, by him deserted, mischief plots."

Euripides having, besides, said in the *Medea:*—

"For no good do a bad man's gifts,"—

Sophocles in *Ajax Flagellifer* utters this iambic:—

"For foes' gifts are no gifts, nor any boon."

Solon having written:—

"For surfeit insolence begets,
When store of wealth attends."

Theognis writes in the same way:—

"For surfeit insolence begets,
When store of wealth attends the bad."

Whence also Thucydides, in the *Histories*, says: "Many men, to whom in a great degree, and in a short time, unlooked-for prosperity comes, are wont to turn to insolence." And Philistus likewise imitates the same sentiment, expressing himself thus: "And the many things which turn out prosperously to men, in accordance with reason, have an incredibly dangerous tendency to misfortune. For those who meet with unlooked success beyond their expectations, are for the most part wont to turn to insolence." Again, Euripides having written:—

> "For children sprung of parents who have led
> A hard and toilsome life, superior are;"

Critias writes: "For I begin with a man's origin: how far the best and strongest in body will he be, if his father exercises himself, and eats in a hardy way, and subjects his body to toilsome labor; and if the mother of the future child be strong in body, and give herself exercise."

Again, Homer having said of the Hephæstus-made shield:—

> "Upon it earth and heaven and sea he made,
> And Ocean's rivers' mighty strength portrayed,"

Pherecydes of Syros says:—"Zas makes a cloak large and beautiful, and works on it earth and Ogenus, and the palace of Ogenus."

And Homer having said:—

> "Shame, which greatly hurts a man or helps,"—

Euripides writes in *Erechtheus:*—

> "Of shame I find it hard to judge;
> 'Tis needed. 'Tis at times a great mischief."

Take, by way of parallel, such plagiarisms as the following, from those who flourished together, and were rivals of each other. From the *Orestes* of Euripides:—

> "Dear charm of sleep, aid in disease."

From the *Eriphyle* of Sophocles:—

> "Hie thee to sleep, healer of that disease."

And from the *Antigone* of Sophocles:—

> "Bastardy is opprobrious in name; but the nature is equal;"

And from the *Aleuades* of Sophocles:—

> "Each good thing has its nature equal."

Again, in the *Ctimenus* of Euripides:—

> "For him who toils, God helps;"

And in the *Minos* of Sophocles;

> "To those who act not, fortune is no ally;"

And from the *Alexander* of Euripides:—

> "But time will show; and learning, by that test, I shall know whether thou art good or bad;"

And from the *Hipponos* of Sophocles:—

> "Besides, conceal thou naught; since Time,
> That sees all, hears all, all things will unfold."

But let us similarly run over the following; for Eumelus having composed the line,

> "Of Memory and Olympian Zeus the daughters nine,"

Solon thus begins the elegy:—

> "Of Memory and Olympian Zeus the children bright."

Again, Euripides, paraphrasing the Homeric line:—

"What, whence art thou? Thy city and thy parents, where?"

employs the following iambics in *Ægeus:*—

> "What country shall we say that thou hast left
> To roam in exile, what thy land—the bound
> Of thine own native soil? Who thee begat?
> And of what father dost thou call thyself the son?"

And what? Theognis having said:—

> "Wine largely drunk is bad; but if one use
> It with discretion, 'tis not bad, but good,"

does not Panyasis write?

> "Above the gods' best gift to men ranks wine,
> In measure drunk; but in excess the worst."

Hesiod, too, saying:—

> "But for the fire to thee I'll give a plague,
> For all men to delight themselves withal,"—

Euripides writes:—

> "And for the fire
> Another fire greater and unconquerable,
> Sprung up in the shape of women"

And in addition, Homer, saying:—

> "There is no satiating the greedy paunch,
> Baneful, which many plagues has caused to men."

Euripides says:—

> "Dire need and baneful paunch me overcome;
> From which all evils come."

Besides, Callias the comic poet having written:—

> "With madmen, all men must be mad, they say,"—

Menander, in the *Poloumenoi*, expresses himself similarly, saying:—

> "The presence of wisdom is not always suitable:
> One sometimes must with others play the fool."

And Antimachus of Teos having said:—

> "From gifts, to mortals many ills arise,"—

Augias composed the line:—

> "For gifts men's mind and acts deceive."

And Hesiod having said:—

> "Than a good wife, no man a better thing
> Ere gained; than a bad wife, a worse,"—

Simonides said:—

> "A better prize than a good wife no man
> Ere gained, than a bad one naught worse."

Again, Epicharmas having said:—

> "As destined long to live, and yet not long,
> Think of thyself."—

Euripides writes:—

> "Why? seeing the wealth we have uncertain is,
> Why don't we live as free from care, as pleasant As we may?"

Similarly also, the comic poet Diphilus having said:—

> "The life of men is prone to change,"—

Posidippus says:—

> "No man of mortal mold his life has passed
> From suffering free. Nor to the end again
> Has continued prosperous."

Similarly speaks to thee Plato, writing of man as a creature subject to change. Again, Euripides having said:—

> "Oh life to mortal men of trouble full,
> How slippery in everything art thou!
> Now grow'st thou, and thou now decay'st away.
> And there is set no limit, no, not one,
> For mortals of their course to make an end,
> Except when Death's remorseless final end
> Comes, sent from Zeus,"—

Diphilus writes:—

> "There is no life which has not its own ills,
> Pains, cares, thefts, and anxieties, disease;
> And Death, as a physician, coming, gives
> Rest to their victims in his quiet sleep."

Furthermore, Euripides having said:—

> "Many are fortune's shapes,
> And many things contrary to expectation the gods perform,"—

The tragic poet Theodectes similarly writes:—

> "The instability of mortals' fates."

And Bacchylides having said:—

> "To few alone of mortals is it given
> To reach hoary age, being prosperous all the while,
> And not meet with calamities,"—

Moschion, the comic poet, writes:—

> "But he of all men is most blest,
> Who leads throughout an equal life."

And you will find that, Theognis having said:—

> "For no advantage to a man grown old
> A young wife is, who will not, as a ship
> The helm, obey,"—

Aristophanes, the comic poet, writes:—

> "An old man to a young wife suits but ill."

Clement of Alexandria

For Anacreon, having written:—

> "Luxurious love I sing,
> With flowery garlands graced,
> He is of gods the king,
> He mortal men subdues,—

Euripides writes:—

> "For love not only men attacks,
> And women; but disturbs
> The souls of gods above, and to the sea
> Descends."

But not to protract the discourse further, in our anxiety to show the propensity of the Greeks to plagiarism in expressions and dogmas, allow us to adduce the express testimony of Hippias, the sophist of Elea, who discourses on the point in hand, and speaks thus: "Of these things some perchance are said by Orpheus, some briefly by Musæus; some in one place, others in other places; some by Hesiod, some by Homer, some by the rest of the poets; and some in prose compositions, some by Greeks, some by Barbarians. And I from all these, placing together the things of most importance and of kindred character, will make the present discourse new and varied."

And in order that we may see that philosophy and history, and even rhetoric, are not free of a like reproach, it is right to adduce a few instances from them. For Alcmæon of Crotona having said, "It is easier to guard against a man who is an enemy than a friend," Sophocles wrote in the *Antigone:*—

"For what sore more grievous than a bad friend?"

And Xenophon said: "No man can injure enemies in any way other than by appearing to be a friend."

And Euripides having said in *Telephus:*—

"Shall we Greeks be slaves to Barbarians?"—

Thrasymachus, in the oration for the Larissæans, says: "Shall we be slaves to Archelaus—Greeks to a Barbarian?"
And Orpheus having said:—

> "Water is the change for soul, and death for water;
> From water is earth, and what comes from earth is again water,
> And from that, soul, which changes the whole ether;"

and Heraclitus, putting together the expressions from these lines, writes thus:—

> "It is death for souls to become water, and death for water to become earth; and from earth comes water, and from water soul."

And Athamas the Pythagorean having said, "Thus was produced the beginning of the universe; and there are four roots—fire, water, air, earth: for from these is the origination of what is produced,"—Empedocles of Agrigentum wrote:—

> "The four roots of all things first do thou hear—
> Fire, water, earth, and ether's boundless height:
> For of these all that was, is, shall be, comes."

And Plato having said, "Wherefore also the gods, knowing men, release sooner from life those they value most," Menander wrote:—

> "Whom the gods love, dies young."

And Euripides having written in the *OEnomaus:*—

"We judge of things obscure from what we see;"

and in the *Phoenix:*—

"By signs the obscure is fairly grasped,"—

Hyperides says, "But we must investigate things unseen by learning from signs and probabilities." And Isocrates having said, "We must conjecture the future by the past," Andocides does not shrink from saying, "For we must make use of what has happened previously as signs in reference to what is to be." Besides, Theognis having said:—

> "The evil of counterfeit silver and gold is not intolerable,
> O Cyrnus, and to a wise man is not difficult of detection;
> But if the mind of a friend is hidden in his breast,
> If he is false, and has a treacherous heart within,
> This is the basest thing for mortals, caused by God,
> And of all things the hardest to detect,"—

Euripides writes:—

> "Oh Zeus, why hast thou given to men clear tests
> Of spurious gold, while on the body grows
> No mark sufficing to discover clear
> The wicked man?"

Hyperides himself also says, "There is no feature of the mind impressed on the countenance of men."
Again, Stasinus having composed the line:—

> "Fool, who, having slain the father, leaves the children,"—

Xenophon says, "For I seem to myself to have acted in like manner, as if one who killed the father should spare his children." And Sophocles having written in the *Antigone:*—

> "Mother and father being in Hades now,
> No brother ever can to me spring forth,"—

Herodotus says, "Mother and father being no more, I shall not have another brother." In addition to these, Theopompus having written:—

> "Twice children are old men in very truth;"

And before him Sophocles in *Peleus:*—

> "Peleus, the son of Æacus, I, sole housekeeper,
> Guide, old as he is now, and train again,
> For the aged man is once again a child,"—

Antipho the orator says, "For the nursing of the old is like the nursing of children." Also the philosopher Plato says, "The old man then, as seems, will be twice a child." Further, Thucydides having said, "We alone bore the brunt at Marathon,"—Demosthenes said, "By those who bore the brunt at Marathon." Nor will I omit the following. Cratinus having said in the *Pytine:*—

> "The preparation perchance you know,"

Andocides the orator says, "The preparation, gentlemen of the jury, and the eagerness of our enemies, almost all of you know." Similarly also Nicias, in the speech on the deposit, against Lysias, says, "The preparation and the eagerness of the adversaries, ye see, O gentlemen of the jury." After him Æschines says, "You see the preparation, O men of Athens, and the line of battle." Again, Demosthenes having said, "What zeal and what canvassing, O men of Athens, have been employed in this contest, I think almost all of you are aware;" and Philinus similarly, "What zeal, what forming of the line of battle, gentlemen of the jury, have taken place in this contest, I think not one of you is ignorant." Isocrates, again, having said, "As if she were related to his wealth, not him," Lysias says in the *Orphics*, "And he was plainly related not to the persons, but to the money." Since Homer also having written:—

> "O friend, if in this war, by taking flight,
> We should from age and death exemption win,
> I would not fight among the first myself,
> Nor would I send thee to the glorious fray;
> But now—for myriad fates of death attend
> In any case, which man may not escape
> Or shun—come on. To some one we shall bring
> Renown, or someone shall to us,"—

Theopompus writes, "For if, by avoiding the present danger, we were to pass the rest of our time in security, to show love of life would not be wonderful. But now, so many fatalities are incident to life, that death in battle seems preferable." And what? Child the sophist having uttered the apophthegm, "Become surety, and mischief is at hand," did not Epicharmus utter the same sentiment in other terms, when he said, "Suretyship is the daughter of mischief, and loss that of suretyship?" Further, Hippocrates the physician having written, "You must look to time, and locality, and age, and disease," Euripides says in *Hexameters:*—

> "Those who the healing art would practice well,
> Must study people's modes of life, and note
> The soil, and the diseases so consider."

Homer again, having written:—

"I say no mortal man can doom escape,"—

Archinus says, "All men are bound to die either sooner or later;" and Demosthenes, "To all men death is the end of life, though one should keep himself shut up in a coop."
And Herodotus, again, having said, in his discourse about Glaucus the Spartan, that the Pythian said, "In the case of the Deity, to say and to do are equivalent," Aristophanes said:—

"For to think and to do are equivalent."

And before him, Parmenides of Elea said:—

"For thinking and being are the same."

And Plato having said, "And we shall show, not absurdly perhaps, that the beginning of love is sight; and hope diminishes the passion, memory nourishes it, and intercourse preserves it;" does not Philemon the comic poet write:—

"First all see, then admire;
Then gaze, then come to hope;
And thus arises love?"

Further, Demosthenes having said, "For to all of us death is a debt," and so forth, Phanocles writes in *Loves*, or *The Beautiful*:—

"But from the Fates' unbroken thread escape
Is none for those that feed on earth."

You will also find that Plato having said, "For the first sprout of each plant, having got a fair start, according to the virtue of its own nature, is most powerful in inducing the appropriate end;" the historian writes, "Further, it is not natural for one of the wild plants to become cultivated, after they have passed the earlier period of growth;" and the following of Empedocles:—

> "For I already have been boy and girl,
> And bush, and bird, and mute fish in the sea,"—

Euripides transcribes in *Chrysippus:*—

> "But nothing dies
> Of things that are; but being dissolved,
> One from the other,
> Shows another form."

And Plato having said, in the *Republic*, that women were common, Euripides writes in the *Protesilaus:*—

> "For common, then, is woman's bed."

Further, Euripides having written:—

> "For to the temperate enough sufficient is"—

Epicurus expressly says, "Sufficiency is the greatest riches of all."

Again, Aristophanes having written:—

> "Life thou securely shalt enjoy, being just
> And free from turmoil, and from fear live well,"—

Epicurus says, "The greatest fruit of righteousness is tranquility."

Let these species, then, of Greek plagiarism of sentiments, being such, stand as sufficient for a clear specimen to him who is capable of perceiving.

And not only have they been detected pirating and paraphrasing thoughts and expressions, as will be shown; but

they will also be convicted of the possession of what is entirely stolen. For stealing entirely what is the production of others, they have published it as their own; as Eugamon of Cyrene did the entire book on the Thesprotians from Musæus, and
Pisander of Camirus the Heraclea of Pisinus of Lindus, and Panyasis of Halicarnassus, the capture of OEchalia from Cleophilus of Samos.

You will also find that Homer, the great poet, took from Orpheus, from the *Disappearance* of Dionysus, those words and what follows verbatim:—

"As a man trains a luxuriant shoot of olive."

And in the *Theogony*, it is said by Orpheus of Kronos:—

"He lay, his thick neck bent aside; and him
All-conquering Sleep had seized."

These Homer transferred to the Cyclops. And Hesiod writes of Melampous:—

"Gladly to hear, what the immortals have assigned
To men, the brave from cowards clearly marks;"

and so forth, taking it word for word from the poet Musæus.

And Aristophanes the comic poet has, in the first of the *Thesmophoriazusæ*, transferred the words from the *Empiprameni* of Cratinus. And Plato the comic poet, and Aristophanes in *Dædalus*, steal from one another. *Cocalus*, composed by Araros, the son of Aristophanes, was by the comic poet Philemon altered, and made into the comedy called *Hypobolimoens*.

Eumelus and Acusilaus the historiographers changed the contents of Hesiod into prose, and published them as their own. Gorgias of Leontium and Eudemus of Naxus, the historians, stole from Melesagoras. And, besides, there is Bion of Proconnesus, who epitomized and transcribed the writings of the ancient Cadmus, and Archilochus, and Aristotle, and Leandrus, and Hellanicus, and Hecatæus, and Androtion, and Philochorus. Dieuchidas of Megara transferred the beginning of his treatise from the *Deucalion* of Hellanicus. I pass over in silence Heraclitus of Ephesus, who took a very great deal from Orpheus.

From Pythagoras Plato derived the immortality of the soul; and he from the Egyptians. And many of the Platonists composed books, in which they show that the Stoics, as we said in the beginning, and Aristotle, took the most and principal of their dogmas from Plato. Epicurus also pilfered his leading dogmas from Democritus. Let these things then be so. For life would fail me, were I to undertake to go over the subject in detail, to expose the selfish plagiarism of the Greeks, and how they claim the discovery of the best of their doctrines, which they have received from us.

CHAPTER III.—PLAGIARISM BY THE GREEKS OF THE MIRACLES RELATED IN THE SACRED BOOKS OF THE HEBREWS.

And now they are convicted not only of borrowing doctrines from the Barbarians, but also of relating as prodigies of Hellenic mythology the marvels found in our records, wrought through divine power from above, by those who led holy lives, while devoting attention to us. And we shall ask at them whether those things which they relate are true or false. But they will not say that they are false; for they will not with their will condemn themselves of the very great silliness of composing falsehoods, but of necessity admit them to be true. And how will the prodigies enacted by Moses and the other prophets any longer appear to them incredible? For the Almighty God, in His care for all men, turns some to salvation by commands, some by threats, some by miraculous signs, some by gentle promises.

Well, the Greeks, when once a drought had wasted Greece for a protracted period, and a dearth of the fruits of the earth ensued, it is said, those that survived of them, having,

because of the famine, come as suppliants to Delphi, asked the Pythian priestess how they should be released from the calamity. She announced that the only help in their distress was, that they should avail themselves of the prayers of Æacus. Prevailed on by them, Æacus, ascending the Hellenic hill, and stretching out pure hands to heaven, and invoking the
Common God, besought him to pity wasted Greece. And as he prayed, thunder sounded, out of the usual course of things, and the whole surrounding atmosphere was covered with clouds. And impetuous and continued rains, bursting down, filled the whole region. The result was a copious and rich fertility wrought by the husbandry of the prayers of Æacus.

"And Samuel called on the Lord," it is said, "and the Lord gave forth His voice, and rain in the day of harvest." Do you see that "He who sendeth His rain on the just and on the unjust" by the subject powers is the one God? And the whole of our Scripture is full of instances of God, in reference to the prayers of the just, hearing and performing each one of their petitions.

Again, the Greeks relate, that in the case of a failure once of the Etesian winds, Aristæus once sacrificed in Ceus to Isthmian Zeus. For there was great devastation, everything being burnt up with the heat in consequence of the winds which had been wont to refresh the productions of the earth, not blowing, and he easily called them back.

And at Delphi, on the expedition of Xerxes against Greece, the Pythian priestess having made answer:—

"O Delphians, pray the winds, and it will be better,"—

they having erected an altar and performed sacrifice to the winds, had them as their helpers. For, blowing violently around Cape Sepias, they shivered the whole preparations of the
Persian expedition. Empedocles of Agrigentum was called "Checker of Winds." Accordingly it is said, that when, on a time, a wind blew from the mountain of Agrigentum, heavy

and pestiferous for the inhabitants, and the cause also of barrenness to their wives, he made the wind to cease. Wherefore he himself writes in the lines:—

> "Thou shalt the might of the unwearied winds make still,
> Which rushing to the earth spoil mortals' crops,
> And at thy will bring back the avenging blasts."

And they say that he was followed by some that used divinations, and some that had been long vexed by sore diseases. They plainly, then, believed in the performance of cures, and signs and wonders, from our Scriptures. For if certain powers move the winds and dispense showers, let them hear the psalmist: "How amiable are thy tabernacles, O Lord of hosts!" This is the Lord of powers, and principalities, and authorities, of whom Moses speaks; so that we may be with Him. "And ye shall circumcise your hard heart, and shall not harden your neck any more. For He is Lord of lords and God of gods, the great God and strong," unit so forth. And Isaiah says, "Lift your eyes to the height, and see who hath produced all these things."

And some say that plagues, and hail-storms, and tempests, and the like, are wont to take place, not alone in consequence of material disturbance, but also through anger of demons and bad angels. For instance, they say that the Magi at Cleone, watching the phenomena of the skies, when the clouds are about to discharge hail, avert the threatening of wrath by incantations and sacrifices. And if at any time there is the want of an animal, they are satisfied with bleeding their own finger for a sacrifice. The prophetess Diotima, by the Athenians offering sacrifice previous to the pestilence, effected a delay of the plague for ten years. The sacrifices, too, of Epimenides of Crete, put off the Persian war for an equal period. And it is considered to be all the same whether we call these spirits gods or angels. And those skilled in the matter of consecrating statues, in many of the temples have erected tombs of the dead, calling the souls of these Dæmons, and teaching them to be worshipped by men; as having, in consequence of the purity of their life, by the divine foreknowledge, received the power of wandering about the space around the earth in order to minister to men. For they knew that some souls were by nature kept in the body. But of these, as the work proceeds, in the treatise on the angels, we shall discourse.

Democritus, who predicted many things from observation of celestial phenomena, was called "Wisdom" (Σοφία). On his meeting a cordial reception from his brother Damasus, he predicted that there would be much rain, judging from certain stars. Some, accordingly, convinced by him, gathered their crops; for being in summer-time, they were still on the threshing-floor. But others lost all, unexpected and heavy showers having burst down.

How then shall the Greeks any longer disbelieve the divine appearance on Mount Sinai, when the fire burned, consuming none of the things that grew on the mount; and the sound of trumpets issued forth, breathed without instruments? For that which is called the descent on the mount of God is the advent of divine power, pervading the whole world, and proclaiming "the light that is inaccessible."

For such is the allegory, according to the Scripture. But the fire was seen, as Aristobulus says, while the whole multitude, amounting to not less than a million, besides those under age, were congregated around the mountain, the circuit of the mount not being less than five days' journey. Over the whole place of the vision the burning fire was seen by them all encamped as it were around; so that the descent was not local. For God is everywhere.

Now the compilers of narratives say that in the island of Britain there is a cave situated under a mountain, and a chasm on its summit; and that, accordingly, when the wind falls into the cave, and rushes into the bosom of the cleft, a sound is heard like cymbals clashing musically. And often in the woods, when the leaves are moved by a sudden gust of wind, a sound is emitted like the song of birds.

Those also who composed the *Persics* relate that in the uplands, in the country of the Magi, three mountains are situated on an extended plain, and that those who travel through the locality, on coming to the first mountain, hear a confused sound as of several myriads shouting, as if in battle array; and on reaching the middle one, they hear a clamor louder and more distinct; and at the end hear people singing a pæan, as if victorious. And the cause, in my opinion, of the whole sound, is the smoothness and cavernous character of the localities; and the air, entering in, being sent back and going to the same point, sounds with considerable force. Let these things be so. But it is possible for God Almighty, even without a medium, to produce a voice and vision through the ear, showing that His greatness has a natural order beyond what is customary, in order to the conversion of the hitherto unbelieving soul, and the reception of the commandment given. But there being a cloud and a lofty mountain, how is it not possible to hear a different sound, the wind moving by the active cause? Wherefore also the prophet says, "Ye heard the voice of words, and saw no similitude." You see how the Lord's voice, the Word, without shape, the power of the Word, the luminous word of the Lord, the truth from heaven, from above, coming to the assembly of the Church, wrought by the luminous immediate ministry.

CHAPTER IV.—THE GREEKS DREW MANY OF THEIR PHILOSOPHICAL TENETS FROM THE EGYPTIAN AND INDIAN GYMNOSOPHISTS.

We shall find another testimony in confirmation, in the fact that the best of the philosophers, having appropriated their most excellent dogmas from us, boast, as it were, of certain of the tenets which pertain to each sect being culled from other Barbarians, chiefly from the Egyptians—both other tenets, and that especially of the transmigration of the soul. For the Egyptians pursue a philosophy of their own. This is principally shown by their sacred ceremonial. For first advances the Singer, bearing some one of the symbols of music. For they say that he must learn two of the books of Hermes, the one of which contains the hymns of the gods, the second the regulations for the king's life. And after the Singer advances the Astrologer, with a horologe in his hand, and a palm, the symbols of astrology. He must have the astrological books of Hermes, which are four in number, always in his mouth. Of these, one is about the order of the fixed stars that are visible, and another about the conjunctions and luminous appearances of the sun and moon; and the rest respecting their risings. Next in order advances the sacred Scribe, with wings on his head, and in his hand a book and rule, in which were writing ink and the reed, with which they write. And he must be acquainted with what are called hieroglyphics, and know about cosmography and geography, the position of the sun and moon, and about the five planets; also the description of Egypt, and the chart of the Nile; and the description of the equipment of the priests and of the places consecrated to them, and about the measures and the things in use in the sacred rites. Then the Stole-keeper follows those previously mentioned, with the cubit of justice and the cup for libations. He is acquainted with all points called Pædeutic (relating to training) and Moschophatic (sacrificial). There are also ten books which relate to the honor paid by them to their gods, and containing the Egyptian worship; as that relating to sacrifices, first-fruits, hymns, prayers, processions, festivals, and the like. And behind all walks the Prophet, with the water-vase carried openly in his arms; who is followed by those who carry the issue of loaves. He, as being the governor of the temple, learns the ten books called "Hieratic;" and they contain all about the laws, and the gods, and the whole of the training of the priests. For the Prophet is, among the Egyptians, also over the distribution of the revenues. There are then forty-two books of Hermes indispensably necessary; of which the six-and-thirty containing the whole philosophy of the Egyptians are learned by the aforementioned personages; and the other six, which are medical, by the Pastophoroi (image-bearers),— treating of the structure of the body, and of diseases, and instruments, and medicines, and about the eyes, and the last about women. Such are the customs of the Egyptians, to speak briefly.

The philosophy of the Indians, too, has been celebrated. Alexander of Macedon, having taken ten of the Indian Gymnosophists, that seemed the best and most sententious, proposed to them problems, threatening to put to death him that did not answer to the purpose; ordering one, who was the eldest of them, to decide.

The first, then, being asked whether he thought that the living were more in number than the dead, said, The living; for that the dead were not. The second, on being asked whether the sea or the land maintained larger beasts, said, The land; for the sea was part of it. And the third being asked which was the most cunning of animals? The one, which has not hitherto been known, man. And the fourth being interrogated, For what reason they had made Sabba, who was their prince, revolt, answered, Because they wished him to live well rather than die ill. And the fifth being asked, Whether he thought that day or night was first, said, One day. For puzzling questions must have puzzling answers. And the sixth being posed with the query, How shall one be loved most? By being most powerful; in order that he may not be timid. And the seventh being asked, How any one of men could become God? said, If he do what it is impossible for man to do. And the eighth being asked, Which is the stronger, life or death? said, Life, which bears such ills. And the ninth being interrogated, Up to what point it is good for a man to live? said, Till he does not think that to die is better than to live. And on Alexander ordering the tenth to say something, for he was judge, he said, "One spoke worse than another." And on Alexander saying, Shall you not, then, die first, having given such a judgment? he said, And how, O king, wilt thou prove true, after saying that thou would kill first the first man that answered very badly?

And that the Greeks are called pilferers of all manner of writing, is, as I think, sufficiently demonstrated by abundant proofs.

CHAPTER V.—THE GREEKS HAD SOME KNOWLEDGE OF THE TRUE GOD.

And that the men of highest repute among the Greeks knew God, not by positive knowledge, but by indirect expression, Peter says in the *Preaching:* "Know then that there is one God, who made the beginning of all things, and holds the power of the end; and is the Invisible, who sees all things; incapable of being contained, who contains all things; needing nothing, whom all things need, and by whom they are; incomprehensible, everlasting, unmade, who made all things by the 'Word of His power,' that is, according to the Gnostic scripture, His Son."

Then he adds: "Worship this God not as the Greeks,"—signifying plainly, that the excellent among the Greeks worshipped the same God as we, but that they had not learned by perfect knowledge that which was delivered by the Son. "Do not then worship," he did not say, the God whom the Greeks worship, but "as the Greeks,"—changing the manner of the worship of God, not announcing another God. What, then, the expression "not as the Greeks" means, Peter himself shall explain, as he adds: "Since they are carried away by ignorance, and know not God" (as we do, according to the perfect knowledge); "but giving shape to the things of which He gave them the power for use—stocks and stones, brass and iron, gold and silver—matter;—and setting up the things which are slaves for use and possession, worship them. And what God hath given to them for food—the fowls of the air, and the fish of the sea, and the creeping things of the earth, and the wild beasts with the four-footed cattle of the field, weasels and mice, cats and dogs and apes, and their own proper food—they sacrifice as sacrifices to mortals; and offering dead things to the dead, as to gods, are unthankful to God, denying His existence by these things." And that it is said, that we and the Greeks know the same God, though not in the same way, he will infer thus: "Neither worship as the Jews; for they, thinking that they only know God, do not know Him, adoring as they do angels and archangels, the month and the moon. And if the moon be not visible, they do not hold the Sabbath, which is called the first; nor do they hold the new moon, nor the feast of unleavened bread, nor the feast, nor the great day." Then he gives the finishing stroke to the question: "So that do ye also, learning holily and righteously what we deliver to you; keep them, worshipping God in a new way, by Christ." For we find in the Scriptures, as the Lord says: "Behold, I make with you a new covenant, not as I made with your fathers in Mount Horeb." He made a new covenant with us; for what belonged to the Greeks and Jews is old. But we, who worship Him in a new way, in the third form, are Christians. For clearly, as I think, he showed that the one and only God was known by the Greeks in a Gentile way, by the Jews Judaically, and in a new and spiritual way by us.

And further, that the same God that furnished both the Covenants was the giver of Greek philosophy to the Greeks, by which the Almighty is glorified among the Greeks, he shows. And it is clear from this. Accordingly, then, from the Hellenic training, and also from that of the law are gathered into the one race of the saved people those who accept faith: not that the three peoples are separated by time, so that one might suppose three natures, but trained in different Covenants of the one Lord, by the word of the one Lord. For that, as God wished to save the Jews by giving to them prophets, so also by raising up prophets of their own in their own tongue, as they were able to receive God's beneficence, He distinguished the most excellent of the Greeks from the common herd, in addition to *"Peter's Preaching,"* the Apostle Paul will show, saying: "Take also the Hellenic books, read the Sibyl, how it is shown that God is one, and how the future is indicated. And taking Hystaspes, read, and you will find much more luminously and distinctly the Son of God described, and how many kings shall draw up their forces against Christ, hating Him and those that bear His name, and His faithful ones, and His patience, and His coming." Then in one word he asks us, "Whose is the world, and all that is in the world? Are they not God's?" Wherefore Peter says, that the Lord said to the apostles: "If any one of Israel then, wishes to repent, and by my name to believe in God, his sins shall be forgiven him, after twelve years. Go forth into the world, that no one may say, We have not heard."

CHAPTER VI.—THE GOSPEL WAS PREACHED TO JEWS AND GENTILES IN HADES.

But as the proclamation [of the Gospel] has come now at the fit time, so also at the fit time were the Law and the Prophets given to the Barbarians, and Philosophy to the Greeks, to fit their ears for the Gospel. "Therefore," says the Lord who delivered Israel, "in an acceptable time have I heard thee, and in a day of salvation have I helped thee. And I have given thee for a Covenant to the nations; that thou mightest inhabit the earth, and receive the inheritance of the wilderness; saying to those that are in bonds, Come forth; and to those that are in darkness, Show yourselves." For if the "prisoners" are the Jews, of whom the Lord said, "Come forth, ye that will, from your bonds,"—meaning the voluntary bound, and who have taken on them "*the burdens grievous to be borne*" by human injunction—it is plain that "those in darkness" are they who have the ruling faculty of the soul buried in idolatry.

For to those who were righteous according to the law, faith was wanting. Wherefore also the Lord, in healing them, said, "Thy faith hath saved thee." But to those that were righteous according to philosophy, not only faith in the Lord, but also the abandonment of idolatry, were necessary. Straightway, on the revelation of the truth, they also repented of their previous conduct.

Wherefore the Lord preached the Gospel to those in Hades. Accordingly the Scripture says, "Hades says to

Destruction, We have not seen His form, but we have heard His voice." It is not plainly the place, which, the words above say, heard the voice, but those who have been put in Hades, and have abandoned themselves to destruction, as persons who have thrown themselves voluntarily from a ship into the sea. They, then, are those that hear the divine power and voice. For who in his senses can suppose the souls of the righteous and those of sinners in the same condemnation, charging Providence with injustice?

But how? Do not [the Scriptures] show that the Lord preached the Gospel to those that perished in the flood, or rather had been chained, and to those kept "in ward and guard"? And it has been shown also, in the second book of the *Stromata*, that the apostles, following the Lord, preached the Gospel to those in Hades. For it was requisite, in my opinion, that as here, so also there, the best of the disciples should be imitators of the Master; so that He should bring to repentance those belonging to the Hebrews, and they the Gentiles; that is, those who had lived in righteousness according to the Law and Philosophy, who had ended life not perfectly, but sinfully. For it was suitable to the divine administration, that those possessed of greater worth in righteousness, and whose life had been pre-eminent, on repenting of their transgressions, though found in another place, yet being confessedly of the number of the people of God Almighty, should be saved, each one according to his individual knowledge.

And, as I think, the Savior also exerts His might because it is His work to save; which accordingly He also did by drawing to salvation those who became willing, by the preaching [of the Gospel], to believe on Him, wherever they were. If, then, the Lord descended to Hades for no other end but to preach the Gospel, as He did descend; it was either to preach the Gospel to all or to the Hebrews only. If, accordingly, to all, then all who believe shall be saved, although they may be of the Gentiles, on making their profession there; since God's punishments are saving and disciplinary, leading to conversion, and choosing rather the repentance them the death of a sinner; and especially since souls, although darkened by passions, when released from their bodies, are able to perceive more clearly, because of their being no longer obstructed by the paltry flesh.

If, then, He preached only to the Jews, who wanted the knowledge and faith of the Savior, it is plain that, since God is no respecter of persons, the apostles also, as here, so there preached the Gospel to those of the heathen who were ready for conversion. And it is well said by the Shepherd, "They went down with them therefore into the water, and again ascended. But these descended alive, and again ascended alive. But those who had fallen asleep, descended dead, but ascended alive." Further the Gospel says, "that many bodies of those that slept arose,"—plainly as having been translated to a better state. There took place, then, a universal movement and translation through the economy of the Savior.

One righteous man, then, differs not, as righteous, from another righteous man, whether he be of the Law or a Greek. For God is not only Lord of the Jews, but of all men, and more nearly the Father of those who know Him. For if to live well and according to the law is to live, also to live rationally according to the law is to live; and those who lived rightly before the Law were classed under faith, and judged to be righteous,—it is evident that those, too, who were outside of the Law, having lived rightly, in consequence of the peculiar nature of the voice, though they are in Hades and in ward, on hearing the voice of the Lord, whether that of His own person or that acting through His apostles, with all speed turned and believed. For we remember that the Lord is "the power of God," and power can never be weak.

So I think it is demonstrated that the God being good, and the Lord powerful, they save with a righteousness and equality which extend to all that turn to Him, whether here or elsewhere. For it is not here alone that the active power of God is beforehand, but it is everywhere and is always at work.

Accordingly, in the *Preaching of Peter*, the Lord says to the disciples after the resurrection, "I have chosen you twelve disciples, judging you worthy of me," whom the Lord wished to be apostles, having judged them faithful, sending them into the world to the men on the earth, that they may know that there is one God, showing clearly what would take place by the faith of Christ; that they who heard and believed should be saved; and that those who believed not, after having heard, should bear witness, not having the excuse to allege, We have not heard.

What then? Did not the same dispensation obtain in Hades, so that even there, all the souls, on hearing the proclamation, might either exhibit repentance, or confess that their punishment was just, because they believed not? And it were the exercise of no ordinary arbitrariness, for those who had departed before the advent of the Lord (not having the Gospel preached to them, and having afforded no ground from themselves, in consequence of believing or not) to obtain either salvation or punishment. For it is not right that these should be condemned without trial, and that those alone who lived after the advent should have the advantage of the divine righteousness. But to all rational souls it was said from above, "Whatever one of you has done in ignorance, without clearly knowing God, if, on becoming conscious, he repent, all his sins will be forgiven him." "For, behold," it is said, "I have set before your face death and life, that ye may choose life." God says that He set, not that He made both, in order to the comparison of choice. And in another Scripture He says, "If ye hear Me, and be willing, ye shall eat the good of the land. But if ye hear Me not, and are not willing, the sword shall devour you: for the mouth of the Lord hath spoken these things."

Again, David expressly (or rather the Lord in the person of the saint, and the same from the foundation of the world is each one who at different periods is saved, and shall be saved by faith) says, "My heart was glad, and my tongue rejoiced, and my flesh shall still rest in hope. For Thou shalt not leave my soul in hell, nor wilt Thou give Thine holy one to see corruption. Thou hast made known to me the paths of life, Thou wilt make me full of joy in Thy presence."As, then, the people was precious to the Lord, so also is the entire holy people; he also who is converted from the Gentiles, who was prophesied under the name of proselyte, along with the Jew. For rightly the Scripture says, that "the ox and the bear shall come together." For the Jew is designated by the ox, from the animal under the yoke being reckoned clean, according to the law; for the ox both parts the hoof and chews the cud. And the Gentile is designated by the bear, which is an unclean and wild beast. And this animal brings forth a shapeless lump of flesh, which it shapes into the likeness of a beast solely by its tongue. For he who is convened from among the Gentiles is formed from a beastlike life to gentleness by the word; and, when once tamed, is made clean, just as the ox. For example, the prophet says, "The sirens, and the daughters of the sparrows, and all the beasts of the field, shall bless me." Of the number of unclean animals, the wild beasts of the field are known to be, that is, of the world; since those who are wild in respect of faith, and polluted in life, and not purified by the righteousness which is according to the law, are called wild beasts. But changed from wild beasts by the faith of the Lord, they become men of God, advancing from the wish to change to the fact. For some the Lord exhorts, and to those who have already made the attempt he stretches forth His hand, and draws them up. "For the Lord dreads not the face of any one, nor will He regard greatness; for He hath made small and great, and cares alike for all." And David says, "For the heathen are fixed in the destruction they have caused; their foot is taken in the snare which they hid.""But the Lord was a refuge to the poor, a help in season also in affliction." Those, then, that were in affliction had the Gospel seasonably proclaimed. And therefore it said, "Declare among the heathen his pursuits," that they may not be judged unjustly.

If, then, He preached the Gospel to those in the flesh that they might not be condemned unjustly, how is it conceivable that He did not for the same cause preach the Gospel to those who had departed this life before His advent? "For the righteous Lord loves righteousness: His countenance beholds uprightness."'"But he that loves wickedness hated his own soul."

If, then, in the deluge all sinful flesh perished, punishment having been inflicted on them for correction, we must first believe that the will of God, which is disciplinary and beneficent, saves those who turn to Him. Then, too, the more subtle substance, the soul, could never receive any injury from the grosser element of water, its subtle and simple nature rendering it impalpable, called as it is incorporeal. But whatever is gross, made so in consequence of sin, this is cast away along with the carnal spirit which lusts against the soul.

Now also Valentinus, the Coryphæus of those who herald community, in his book on *The Intercourse of Friends*, writes in these words: "Many of the things that are written, though in common books, are found written in the church of God. For those sayings which proceed from the heart are vain. For the law written in the heart is the People of the Beloved—loved and loving Him." For whether it be the Jewish writings or those of the philosophers that he calls "the Common Books," he makes the truth common. And Isidore, at once son and disciple to Basilides, in the first book of the *Expositions of the Prophet Parchor*, writes also in these words: "The Attics say that certain things were intimated to Socrates, in consequence of a dæmon attending on him. And Aristotle says that all men are provided with dæmons, that attend on them during the time they are in the body,—having taken this piece of prophetic instruction and transferred it to his own books, without acknowledging whence he had abstracted this statement." And again, in the second book of his work, he thus writes: "And let no one think that what we say is peculiar to the elect, was said before by any philosophers. For it is not a discovery of theirs.

For having appropriated it from our prophets, they attributed it to him who is wise according to them." Again, in the same: "For to me it appears that those who profess to philosophize, do so that they may learn what is the winged oak, and the variegated robe on it, all of which Pherecydes has employed as theological allegories, having taken them from the prophecy of Cham."

CHAPTER VII.—WHAT TRUE PHILOSOPHY IS, AND WHENCE SO CALLED.

As we have long ago pointed out, what we propose as our subject is not the discipline which obtains in each sect, but that which is really philosophy, strictly systematic Wisdom, which furnishes acquaintance with the things which pertain to life. And we define Wisdom to be certain knowledge, being a sure and irrefragable apprehension of things divine and human, comprehending the present, past, and future, which the Lord hath taught us, both by His advent and by the prophets. And it is irrefragable by reason, inasmuch as it has been communicated. And so it is wholly true according to [God's] intention, as being known through means of the Son. And in one aspect it is eternal, and in another it becomes useful in time. Partly it is one and the same, partly many and indifferent—partly without any movement of passion, partly with passionate desire—partly perfect, partly incomplete.

This wisdom, then—rectitude of soul and of reason, and purity of life—is the object of the desire of philosophy, which is kindly and lovingly disposed towards wisdom, and does everything to attain it.

Now those are called philosophers, among us, who love Wisdom, the Creator and Teacher of all things, that is, the knowledge of the Son of God; and among the Greeks, those who undertake arguments on virtue. Philosophy, then, consists of such dogmas found in each sect (I mean those of philosophy) as cannot be impugned, with a corresponding life, collected into one selection; and these, stolen from the

Barbarian God-given grace, have been adorned by Greek speech. For some they have borrowed, and others they have misunderstood. And in the case of others, what they have spoken, in consequence of being moved, they have not yet perfectly worked out; and others by human conjecture and reasoning, in which also they stumble. And they think that they have hit the truth perfectly; but as we understand them, only partially. They know, then, nothing more than this world. And it is just like geometry, which treats of measures and magnitudes and forms, by delineation on plane-surfaces; and just as painting appears to take in the whole field of view in the scenes represented. But it gives a false description of the view, according to the rules of the art, employing the signs that result from the incidents of the lines of vision. By this means, the higher and lower points in the view, and those between, are preserved; and some objects seem to appear in the foreground, and others in the background, and others to appear in some other way, on the smooth and level surface. So also the philosophers copy the truth, after the manner of painting. And always in the case of each one of them, their self-love is the cause of all their mistakes. Wherefore one ought not, in the desire for the glory that terminates in men, to be animated by self-love; but loving God, to become really holy with wisdom. If, then, one treats what is particular as universal, and regards that, which serves, as the Lord, he misses the truth, not understanding what was spoken by David by way of confession: "I have eaten earth [ashes] like bread." Now, self-love and self-conceit are, in his view, earth and error. But if so, science and knowledge are derived from instruction.

And if there is instruction, you must seek for the master. Cleanthes claims Zeno, and Metrodorus Epicurus, and Theophrastus Aristotle, and Plato Socrates. But if I come to Pythagoras, and Pherecydes, and Thales, and the first wise men, I come to a stand in my search for their teacher. Should you say the Egyptians, the Indians, the Babylonians, and the Magi themselves, I will not stop from asking their teacher. And

I lead you up to the first generation of men; and from that point I begin to investigate Who is their teacher. No one of men; for they had not yet learned. Nor yet any of the angels: for in the way that angels, in virtue of being angels, speak, men do not hear; nor, as we have ears, have they a tongue to correspond; nor would any one attribute to the angels organs of speech, lips I mean, and the parts contiguous, throat, and windpipe, and chest, breath and air to vibrate. And God is far from calling aloud in the unapproachable sanctity, separated as He is from even the archangels.

And we also have already heard that angels learned the truth, and their rulers over them; for they had a beginning. It remains, then, for us, ascending to seek their teacher. And since the unoriginated Being is one, the Omnipotent God; one, too, is the First-begotten, "by whom all things were made, and without whom not one thing ever was made." "For one, in truth, is God, who formed the beginning of all things;" pointing out "the first-begotten Son," Peter writes, accurately comprehending the statement, "In the beginning God made the heaven and the earth." And He is called Wisdom by all the prophets. This is He who is the Teacher of all created beings, the Fellow-counsellor of God, who foreknew all things; and He from above, from the first foundation of the world, "in many ways and many times," trains and perfects; whence it is rightly said, "Call no man your teacher on earth."

You see whence the true philosophy has its handles; though the Law be the image and shadow of the truth: for the Law is the shadow of the truth. But the self-love of the Greeks proclaims certain men as their teachers. As, then, the whole family runs back to God the Creator; so also all the teaching of good things, which justifies, does to the Lord, and leads and contributes to this.

But if from any creature they received in any way whatever the seeds of the Truth, they did not nourish them; but committing them to a barren and rainless soil, they choked them with weeds, as the Pharisees revolted from the Law, by introducing human teachings,—the cause of these being not the Teacher, but those who choose to disobey. But those of them who believed the Lord's advent and the plain teaching of the Scriptures, attain to the knowledge of the law; as also those addicted to philosophy, by the teaching of the Lord, are introduced into the knowledge of the true philosophy: "For the oracles of the Lord are pure oracles, melted in the fire, tried in the earth, purified seven times." Just as silver often purified, so is the just man brought to the test, becoming the Lord's coin and receiving the royal image. Or, since Solomon also calls the "tongue of the righteous man gold that has been subjected to fire," intimating that the doctrine which has been proved, and is wise, is to be praised and received, whenever it is amply tried by the earth: that is, when the Gnostic soul is in manifold ways sanctified, through withdrawal from earthy fires. And the body in which it dwells is purified, being appropriated to the pureness of a holy temple. But the first purification which takes place in the body, the soul being first, is abstinence from evil things, which some consider perfection, and is, in truth, the perfection of the common believer—Jew and Greek. But in the case of the Gnostic, after that which is reckoned perfection in others, his righteousness advances to activity in well-doing. And in whomsoever the increased force of righteousness advances to the doing of good, in his case perfection abides in the fixed habit of well-doing after the likeness of God. For those who are the seed of Abraham, and besides servants of God, are "the called;" and the sons of Jacob are the elect—they who have tripped up the energy of wickedness.

If, then, we assert that Christ Himself is Wisdom, and that it was His working which showed itself in the prophets, by which the gnostic tradition may be learned, as He Himself taught the apostles during His presence; then it follows that the *gnosis,* which is the knowledge and apprehension of things present, future, and past, which is sure and reliable, as being imparted and revealed by the Son of God, is wisdom.

And if, too, the end of the wise man is contemplation, that of those who are still philosophers aims at it, but never attains it, unless by the process of learning it receives the prophetic utterance which has been made known, by which it future, and the past—how they are, were, and shall be.

And the *gnosis* itself is that which has descended by transmission to a few, having been imparted unwritten by the apostles. Hence, then, knowledge or wisdom ought to be exercised up to the eternal and unchangeable habit of contemplation.

CHAPTER VIII.—PHILOSOPHY IS KNOWLEDGE GIVEN BY GOD.

For Paul too, in the Epistles, plainly does not disparage philosophy; but deems it unworthy of the man who has attained to the elevation of the Gnostic, any more to go back to the Hellenic "philosophy," figuratively calling it "the rudiments of this world," as being most rudimentary, and a preparatory training for the truth. Wherefore also, writing to the Hebrews, who were declining again from faith to the law, he says, "Have ye not need again of one to teach you which are the first principles of the oracles of God, and are become such as have need of milk, and not of strong meat?" So also to the Colossians, who were Greek converts, "Beware lest any man spoil you by philosophy and vain deceit, after the tradition of men, after the rudiments of this world, and not after Christ,"—enticing them again to return to philosophy, the elementary doctrine.

And should one say that it was through human understanding that philosophy was discovered by the Greeks, still I find the Scriptures saying that understanding is sent by God. The psalmist, accordingly, considers understanding as the greatest free gift, and beseeches, saying, "I am Thy servant; give me understanding." And does not David, while asking the abundant experience of knowledge, write, "Teach me gentleness, and discipline, and knowledge: for I have believed in Thy commandments?" He confessed the covenants to be of the highest authority, and that they were given to the more excellent. Accordingly the psalm again says of God, "He hath not done thus to any nation; and He hath not shown His judgments to them." The expression "He hath not done so" shows that *He hath done*, but not "thus." The "thus," then, is put comparatively, with reference to pre-eminence, which obtains in our case. The prophet might have said simply, "He hath not done," without the "thus."

Further, Peter in the Acts says, "Of a truth, I perceive that God is no respecter of persons; but in every nation he that fears Him, and worked righteousness, is accepted by Him."

The absence of respect of persons in God is not then in time, but from eternity. Nor had His beneficence a beginning; nor any more is it limited to places or persons. For His beneficence is not confined to parts. "Open ye the gates of righteousness," it is said; "entering into them, I will confess to the Lord. This is the gate of the Lord. The righteous shall enter by it." Explaining the prophet's saying, Barnabas adds, "There being many gates open, that which is in righteousness is the gate which is in Christ, by which all who enter are blessed." Bordering on the same meaning is also the following prophetic utterance: "The Lord is on many waters;" not the different covenants alone, but the modes of teaching, those among the Greek and those among the Barbarians, conducing to righteousness. And already clearly David, bearing testimony to the truth, sings, "Let sinners be turned into Hades, and all the nations that forget God." They forget, plainly, Him whom they formerly remembered, and dismiss Him whom they knew previous to forgetting Him. There was then a dim knowledge of God also among the nations. So much for those points.

Now the Gnostic must be erudite. And since the Greeks say that Protagoras having led the way, the opposing of one argument by another was invented, it is fitting that something be said with reference to arguments of this sort. For Scripture says, "He that says much, shall also hear in his turn." And who shall understand a parable of the Lord, but the wise, the intelligent, and he that loves his Lord? Let such a man be faithful; let him be capable of uttering his knowledge; let him be wise in the discrimination of words; let him be dexterous in action; let him be pure. "The greater he seems to be, the more humble should he be," says Clement in the Epistle to the Corinthians,—"such a one as is capable of complying with the precept, 'And some pluck from the fire, and on others have compassion, making a difference,'"

The pruning-hook is made, certainly, principally for pruning; but with it we separate twigs that have got intertwined, cut the thorns which grow along with the vines, which it is not very easy to reach. And all these things have a reference to pruning. Again, man is made principally for the knowledge of God; but he also measures land, practices agriculture, and philosophizes; of which pursuits, one conduces to life, another to living well, a third to the study of the things which are capable of demonstration. Further, let those who say that philosophy took its rise from the devil know this, that the Scripture says that "the devil is transformed into an angel of light." When about to do what? Plainly, when about to prophesy. But if he prophesies as an angel of light, he will speak what is true. And if he prophesies what is angelical, and of the light, then he prophesies what is beneficial when he is transformed according to the likeness of the operation, though he be different with respect to the matter of apostasy. For how could he deceive any one, without drawing the lover of knowledge into fellowship, and so drawing him afterwards into falsehood? Especially he will be found to know the truth, if not so as to comprehend it, yet so as not to be unacquainted with it.

Philosophy is not then false, though the thief and the liar speak truth, through a transformation of operation. Nor is sentence of condemnation to be pronounced ignorantly against what is said, on account of him who says it (which also is to be kept in view, in the case of those who are now alleged to prophesy); but what is said must be looked at, to see if it keep by the truth.

And in general terms, we shall not err in alleging that all things necessary and profitable for life came to us from God, and that philosophy more especially was given to the Greeks, as a covenant peculiar to them—being, as it is, a stepping-stone to the philosophy which is according to Christ—although those who applied themselves to the philosophy of the Greeks shut their ears voluntarily to the truth, despising the voice of Barbarians, or also dreading the danger suspended over the believer, by the laws of the state.

And as in the Barbarian philosophy, so also in the Hellenic, "tares were sown" by the proper husbandman of the tares; whence also heresies grew up among us along with the productive wheat; and those who in the Hellenic philosophy preach the impiety and voluptuousness of Epicurus, and whatever other tenets are disseminated contrary to right reason, exist among the Greeks as spurious fruits of the divinely bestowed husbandry. This voluptuous and selfish philosophy the apostle calls "the wisdom of this world;" in consequence of its teaching the things of this world and about it alone, and its consequent subjection, as far as respects ascendancy, to those who rule here. Wherefore also this fragmentary philosophy is very elementary, while truly perfect science deals with intellectual objects, which are beyond the sphere of the world, and with the objects still more spiritual than those which "eye saw not, and ear heard not, nor did it enter into the heart of men," till the Teacher told the account of them to us; unveiling the holy of holies; and in ascending order, things still holier than these, to those who are truly and not spuriously heirs of the Lord's adoption. For we now dare aver (for here is the faith that is characterized by knowledge) that such a one knows all things, and comprehends all things in the exercise of sure apprehension, respecting matters difficult for us, and really pertaining to the true gnosis such as were James, Peter, John, Paul, and the rest of the apostles. For prophecy is full of knowledge (*gnosis*), inasmuch as it was given by the Lord, and again explained by the Lord to the apostles. And is not knowledge (*gnosis*) an attribute of the rational soul, which trains itself for this, that by knowledge it may become entitled to immortality? For both are powers of the soul, both knowledge and impulse. And impulse is found to be a movement after an assent. For he who has an impulse towards an action, first receives the knowledge of the action, and secondly the impulse. Let us further devote our attention to this. For since learning is older than action; (for naturally, he who does what he wishes to do learns it first; and knowledge comes from learning, and impulse follows knowledge; after which comes action;) knowledge turns out the beginning and author of all rational action. So that rightly the peculiar nature of the rational soul is characterized by this alone; for in reality impulse, like knowledge, is excited by existing objects. And knowledge (*gnosis*) is essentially a contemplation of existences on the part of the soul, either of a certain thing or of certain things, and when perfected, of all together. Although some say that the wise man is persuaded that there are some things incomprehensible, in such wise as to have respecting them a kind of comprehension, inasmuch as he comprehends that things incomprehensible are incomprehensible; which is common, and pertains to those who are capable of perceiving little. For such a man affirms that there are some things incomprehensible.

But that Gnostic of whom I speak, himself comprehends what seems to be incomprehensible to others; believing that nothing is incomprehensible to the Son of God, whence nothing incapable of being taught. For He who suffered out of His love for us, would have suppressed no element of knowledge requisite for our instruction. Accordingly this faith becomes sure demonstration; since truth follows what has been delivered by God. But if one desires extensive knowledge, "he knows things ancient, and conjectures things future; he understands knotty sayings, and the solutions of enigmas. The disciple of wisdom foreknows signs and omens, and the issues of seasons and of times."

CHAPTER IX.—THE GNOSTIC FREE OF ALL PERTURBATIONS OF THE SOUL.

The Gnostic is such, that he is subject only to the affections that exist for the maintenance of the body, such as hunger, thirst, and the like. But in the case of the Savior, it were ludicrous [to suppose] that the body, as a body, demanded the necessary aids in order to its duration. For He ate, not for the sake of the body, which was kept together by a holy energy, but in order that it might not enter into the minds of those who were with Him to entertain a different opinion of Him; in like manner as certainly some afterwards supposed that He appeared in a phantasmal shape (δοκήσει). But He was entirely impassible (ἀπαθής); inaccessible to any movement of feeling—either pleasure or pain. While the apostles, having most gnostically mastered, through the Lord's teaching, anger and fear, and lust, were not liable even to such of the movements of feeling, as seem good, courage, zeal, joy, desire, through a steady condition of mind, not changing a whit; but ever continuing unvarying in a state of training after the resurrection of the Lord.

And should it be granted that the affections specified above, when produced rationally, are good, yet they are nevertheless inadmissible in the case of the perfect man, who is incapable of exercising courage: for neither does he meet what inspires fear, as he regards none of the things that occur in life as to be dreaded; nor can aught dislodge him from this—the love he has towards God. Nor does he need cheerfulness of mind; for he does not fall into pain, being persuaded that all things happen well. Nor is he angry; for there is nothing to move him to anger, seeing he ever loves God, and is entirely turned towards Him alone, and therefore hates none of God's creatures. No more does he envy; for nothing is wanting to him, that is requisite to assimilation, in order that he may be excellent and good. Nor does he consequently love any one with this common affection, but loves the Creator in the creatures. Nor, consequently, does he fall into any desire and eagerness; nor does he want, as far as respects his soul, aught appertaining to others, now that he associates through love with the Beloved One, to whom he is allied by free choice, and by the habit which results from training, approaches closer to Him, and is blessed through the abundance of good things.

So that on these accounts he is compelled to become like his Teacher in impassibility. For the Word of God is intellectual, according as the image of mind is seen in man alone. Thus also the good man is godlike in form and semblance as respects his soul. And, on the other hand, God is like man. For the distinctive form of each one is the mind by which we are characterized. Consequently, also, those who sin against man are unholy and impious. For it were ridiculous to say that the gnostic and perfect man must not eradicate anger and courage, inasmuch as without these he will not struggle against circumstances, or abide what is terrible. But if we take from him desire, he will be quite overwhelmed by troubles, and therefore depart from this life very basely. Unless possessed of it, as some suppose, he will not conceive a desire for what is like the excellent and the good. If, then, all alliance with what is good is accompanied with desire, how, it is said, does he remain impassible who desires what is excellent?

But these people know not, as appears, the divinity of love. For love is not desire on the part of him who loves; but is a relation of affection, restoring the Gnostic to the unity of the faith,—independent of time and place. But he who by love is already in the midst of that in which he is destined to be, and has anticipated hope by knowledge, does not desire anything, having, as far as possible, the very thing desired. Accordingly, as to be expected, he continues in the exercise of gnostic love, in the one unvarying state.

Nor will he, therefore, eagerly desire to be assimilated to what is beautiful, possessing, as he does, beauty by love. What more need of courage and of desire to him, who has obtained the affinity to the impassible God which arises from love, and by love has enrolled himself among the friends of God?

We must therefore rescue the gnostic and perfect man from all passion of the soul. For knowledge (*gnosis*) produces practice, and practice habit or disposition; and such a state as this produces impassibility, not moderation of passion. And the complete eradication of desire reaps as its fruit impassibility. But the Gnostic does not share either in those affections that are commonly celebrated as good, that is, the good things of the affections which are allied to the passions: such, I mean, as gladness, which is allied to pleasure; and dejection, for this is conjoined with pain; and caution, for it is subject to fear. Nor yet does he share in high spirit, for it takes its place alongside of wrath; although some say that these are no longer evil, but already good. For it is impossible that he who has been once made perfect by love, and feasts eternally and insatiably on the boundless joy of contemplation, should delight in small and groveling things. For what rational cause remains any more to the man who has gained "the light inaccessible," for revering to the good things of the world? Although not yet true as to time and place, yet by that gnostic love through which the inheritance and perfect restitution follow, the giver of the reward makes good by deeds what the Gnostic, by gnostic choice, had grasped by anticipation through love.

For by going away to the Lord, for the love he bears Him, though his tabernacle be visible on earth, he does not withdraw himself from life. For that is not permitted to him. But he has withdrawn his soul from the passions. For that is granted to him. And on the other hand he lives, having put to death his lusts, and no longer makes use of the body, but allows it the use of necessaries, that he may not give cause for dissolution.

How, then, has he any more need of fortitude, who is not in the midst of dangers, being not present, but already wholly with the object of love? And what necessity for self-restraint to him who has not need of it? For to have such desires, as require self-restraint in order to their control, is characteristic of one who is not yet pure, but subject to passion. Now, fortitude is assumed by reason of fear and cowardice. For it were no longer seemly that the friend of God, whom "God hath fore-ordained before the foundation of the world" to be enrolled in the highest "adoption," should fall into pleasures or fears, and be occupied in the repression of the passions. For I venture to assert, that as he is predestinated through what he shall do, and what he shall obtain, so also has he predestinated himself by reason of what he knew and whom he loved; not having the future indistinct, as the multitude live, conjecturing it, but having grasped by gnostic faith what is hidden from others. And through love, the future is for him already present. For he has believed, through prophecy and the advent, on God who lies not. And what he believes he possesses, and keeps hold of the promise. And He who hath promised is truth. And through the trustworthiness of Him who has promised, he has firmly laid hold of the end of the promise by knowledge. And he, who knows the sure comprehension of the future which there is in the circumstances, in which he is placed, by love goes to meet the future. So he, that is persuaded that he will obtain the things that are really good, will not pray to obtain what is here, but that he may always cling to the faith which hits the mark and succeeds. And besides, he will pray that as many as possible may become like him, to the glory of God, which is perfected through knowledge. For he who is made like the Savior is also devoted to saving; performing unerringly the commandments as far as the human nature may admit of the image. And this is to worship God by deeds and knowledge of the true righteousness. The Lord will not wait for the voice of this man in prayer. "Ask," He says, "and I will do it; think, and I will give."

For, in fine, it is impossible that the immutable should assume firmness and consistency in the mutable. But the ruling faculty being in perpetual change, and therefore unstable, the force of habit is not maintained. For how can he who is perpetually changed by external occurrences and accidents, ever possess habit and disposition, and in a word, grasp of scientific knowledge (ἐπιστήμη)? Further, also, the philosophers regard the virtues as habits, dispositions, and sciences. And as knowledge (*gnosis*) is not born with men, but is acquired, and the acquiring of it in its elements demands application, and training, and progress; and then from incessant practice it passes into a habit; so, when perfected in the mystic habit, it abides, being infallible through love. For not only has he apprehended the first Cause, and the Cause produced by it, and is sure about them, possessing firmly firm and irrefragable and immoveable reasons; but also respecting what is good and what is evil, and respecting all production, and to speak comprehensively, respecting all about which the Lord has spoken, he has learned, from the truth itself, the most exact truth from the foundation of the world to the end. Not preferring to the truth itself what appears plausible, or, according to Hellenic reasoning, necessary; but what has been spoken by the Lord he accepts as clear and evident, though concealed from others; and he has already received the knowledge of all things. And the oracles we possess give their utterances respecting what exists, as it is; and respecting what is future, as it shall be; and respecting what is past, as it was.

In scientific matters, as being alone possessed of scientific knowledge, he will hold the preeminence, and will discourse on the discussion respecting the good, ever intent on intellectual objects, tracing out his procedure in human affairs from the archetypes above; as navigators direct the ship according to the star; prepared to hold himself in readiness for every suitable action; accustomed to despise all difficulties and dangers when it is necessary to undergo them; never doing anything precipitate or incongruous either to himself or the common weal; foreseeing; and inflexible by pleasures both of waking hours and of dreams. For, accustomed to spare living and frugality, he is moderate, active, and grave; requiring few necessaries for life; occupying himself with nothing superfluous. But desiring not even these things as chief, but by reason of fellowship in life, as necessary for his sojourn in life, as far as necessary.

CHAPTER X.—THE GNOSTIC AVAILS HIMSELF OF THE HELP OF ALL HUMAN KNOWLEDGE.

For to him knowledge (*gnosis*) is the principal thing. Consequently, therefore, he applies to the subjects that are a training for knowledge, taking from each branch of study its contribution to the truth. Prosecuting, then, the proportion of harmonies in music; and in arithmetic noting the increasing and decreasing of numbers, and their relations to one another, and how the most of things fall under some proportion of numbers; studying geometry, which is abstract essence, he perceives a continuous distance, and an immutable essence which is different from these bodies. And by astronomy, again, raised from the earth in his mind, he is elevated along with heaven, and will revolve with its revolution; studying ever divine things, and their harmony with each other; from which Abraham starting, ascended to the knowledge of Him who created them. Further, the Gnostic will avail himself of dialectics, fixing on the distinction of genera into species, and will master the distinction of existences, till he come to what are primary and simple.

But the multitude are frightened at the Hellenic philosophy, as children are at masks, being afraid lest it lead them astray. But if the faith (for I cannot call it knowledge) which they possess be such as to be dissolved by plausible speech, let it be by all means dissolved, and let them confess that they will not retain the truth. For truth is immoveable; but false opinion dissolves. We choose, for instance, one purple by comparison with another purple. So that, if one confesses that he has not a heart that has been made right, he has not the table of the money-changers or the test of words. And how can he be any longer a moneychanger, who is not able to prove and distinguish spurious coin, even offhand?

Now David cried, "The righteous shall not be shaken forever;" neither, consequently, by deceptive speech nor by erring pleasure. Whence he shall never be shaken from his own heritage. "He shall not be afraid of evil tidings;" consequently neither of unfounded calumny, nor of the false opinion around him. No more will he dread cunning words, who is capable of distinguishing them, or of answering rightly to questions asked. Such a bulwark are dialectics, that truth cannot be trampled underfoot by the Sophists. "For it behooves those who praise in the holy name of the Lord," according to the prophet, "to rejoice in heart, seeking the Lord. Seek then Him, and be strong. Seek His face continually in every way." "For, having spoken at sundry times and in divers manners," it is not in one way only that He is known.

It is, then, not by availing himself of these as virtues that our Gnostic will be deeply learned. But by using them as helps in distinguishing what is common and what is peculiar, he will admit the truth. For the cause of all error and false opinion, is inability to distinguish in what respect things are common, and in what respects they differ. For unless, in things that are distinct, one closely watch speech, he will inadvertently confound what is common and what is peculiar. And where this takes place, he must of necessity fall into pathless tracts and error.

The distinction of names and things also in the Scriptures themselves produces great light in men's souls. For it is necessary to understand expressions which signify several things, and several expressions when they signify one thing. The result of which is accurate answering. But it is necessary to avoid the great futility which occupies itself in irrelevant matters; since the Gnostic avails himself of branches of learning as auxiliary preparatory exercises, in order to the accurate communication of the truth, as far as attainable and with as little distraction as possible, and for defense against reasoning that plot for the extinction of the truth. He will not then be deficient in what contributes to proficiency in the curriculum of studies and the Hellenic philosophy; but not principally, but necessarily, secondarily, and on account of circumstances. For what those laboring in heresies use wickedly, the Gnostic will use rightly.

Therefore the truth that appears in the Hellenic philosophy, being partial, the real truth, like the sun glancing on the colors both white and black, shows what like each of them is. So also it exposes all sophistical plausibility. Rightly, then, was it proclaimed also by the Greeks:—"Truth the queen is the beginning of great virtue."

CHAPTER XI.—THE MYSTICAL MEANINGS IN THE PROPORTIONS OF NUMBERS, GEOMETRICAL RATIOS, AND MUSIC.

As then in astronomy we have Abraham as an instance, so also in arithmetic we have the same Abraham. "For, hearing that Lot was taken captive, and having numbered his own servants, born in his house, 318 (τιή)," he defeats a very great number of the enemy.

They say, then, that the character representing 300 is, as to shape, the type of the Lord's sign, and that the *Iota* and the *Eta* indicate the Savior's name; that it was indicated, accordingly, that Abraham's domestics were in salvation, who having fled to the Sign and the Name became lords of the captives, and of the very many unbelieving nations that followed them.

Now the number 300 is, 3 by 100. Ten is allowed to be the perfect number. And 8 is the first cube, which is equality in all the dimensions—length, breadth, depth. "The days of men shall be," it is said, "120 (ρκ′) years." And the sum is made up of the numbers from 1 to 15 added together. And the moon at 15 days is full.

On another principle, 120 is a triangular number, and consists of the equality of the number 64, [which consists of eight of the odd numbers beginning with unity], the addition of which (1, 3, 5, 7, 9, 11, 13, 15) in succession generate squares; and of the inequality of the number 56, consisting of seven of the even numbers beginning with 2 (2, 4, 6, 8, 10, 12, 14), which produce the numbers that are not squares.

Again, according to another way of indicating, the number 120 consists of four numbers—of one triangle, 15; of another, a square, 25; of a third, a pentagon, 35; and of a fourth, a hexagon, 45. The 5 is taken according to the same ratio in each mode. For in triangular numbers, from the unity 5 comes 15; and in squares, 25; and of those in succession, proportionally. Now 25, which is the number 5 from unity, is said to be the symbol of the Levitical tribe. And the number 35 depends also on the arithmetic, geometric, and harmonic scale of doubles—6, 8, 9, 12; the addition of which makes 35. In these days, the Jews say that seven months' children are formed. And the number 45 depends on the scale of triples—6, 9, 12, 18—the addition of which makes 45; and similarly, in these days they say that nine months' children are formed.

Such, then, is the style of the example in arithmetic. And let the testimony of geometry be the tabernacle that was constructed, and the ark that was fashioned,—constructed in most regular proportions, and through divine ideas, by the gift of understanding, which leads us from things of sense to intellectual objects, or rather from these to holy things, and to the holy of holies. For the squares of wood indicate that the square form, producing right angles, pervades all, and points out security. And the length of the structure was three hundred cubits, and the breadth fifty, and the height thirty; and above, the ark ends in a cubit, narrowing to a cubit from the broad base like a pyramid, the symbol of those who are purified and tested by fire. And this geometrical proportion has a place, for the transport of those holy abodes, whose differences are indicated by the differences of the numbers set down below.

And the numbers introduced are six-fold, as three hundred is six times fifty; and tenfold, as three hundred is ten times thirty; and containing one and two-thirds (επιδίμοιροι), for fifty is one and two-thirds of thirty.

Now there are some who say that three hundred cubits are the symbol of the Lord's sign; and fifty, of hope and of the remission given at Pentecost; and thirty, or as in some, twelve, they say points out the preaching [of the Gospel]; because the Lord preached in His thirtieth year; and the apostles were twelve. And the structure's terminating in a cubit is the symbol of the advancement of the righteous to oneness and to "the unity of the faith."

And the table which was in the temple was six cubits; and its four feet were about a cubit and a half.

They add, then, the twelve cubits, agreeably to the revolution of the twelve months, in the annual circle, during which the earth produces and matures all things; adapting itself to the four seasons. And the table, in my opinion, exhibits the image of the earth, supported as it is on four feet, summer, autumn, spring, winter, by which the year travels. Wherefore also it is said that the table has "wavy chains;" either because the universe revolves in the circuits of the times, or perhaps it indicated the earth surrounded with ocean's tide.

Further, as an example of music, let us adduce David, playing at once and prophesying, melodiously praising God. Now the Enarmonic suits best the Dorian harmony, and the Diatonic the Phrygian, as Aristoxenus says. The harmony, therefore, of the Barbarian psaltery, which exhibited gravity of strain, being the most ancient, most certainly became a model for Terpander, for the Dorian harmony, who sings the praise of Zeus thus:—

"O Zeus, of all things the Beginning, Ruler of all;
O Zeus, I send thee this beginning of hymns."

The lyre, according to its primary signification, may by the psalmist be used figuratively for the Lord; according to its secondary, for those who continually strike the chords of their souls under the direction of the Choir-master, the Lord. And if the people saved be called the lyre, it will be understood to be in consequence of their giving glory musically, through the inspiration of the Word and the knowledge of God, being struck by the Word so as to produce faith. You may take music in another way, as the ecclesiastical symphony at once of the law and the prophets, and the apostles along with the Gospel, and the harmony which obtained in each prophet, in the transitions of the persons.

But, as seems, the most of those who are inscribed with the Name, like the companions of Ulysses, handle the word unskillfully, passing by not the Sirens, but the rhythm and the melody, stopping their ears with ignorance; since they know that, after lending their ears to Hellenic studies, they will never subsequently be able to retrace their steps.

But he who culls what is useful for the advantage of the catechumens, and especially when they are Greeks (and the earth is the Lord's, and the fullness thereof), must not abstain from erudition, like irrational animals; but he must collect as many aids as possible for his hearers. But he must by no means linger over these studies, except solely for the advantage accruing from them; so that, on grasping and obtaining this, he may be able to take his departure home to the true philosophy, which is a strong cable for the soul, providing security from everything.

Music is then to be handled for the sake of the embellishment and composure of manners. For instance, at a banquet we pledge each other while the music is playing; soothing by song the eagerness of our desires, and glorifying God for the copious gift of human enjoyments, for His perpetual supply of the food necessary for the growth of the body and of the soul. But we must reject superfluous music, which enervates men's souls, and leads to variety,— now mournful, and then licentious and voluptuous, and then frenzied and frantic.

The same holds also of astronomy. For treating of the description of the celestial objects, about the form of the universe, and the revolution of the heavens, and the motion of the stars, leading the soul nearer to the creative power, it teaches to quickness in perceiving the seasons of the year, the changes of the air, and the appearance of the stars; since also navigation and husbandry derive from this much benefit, as architecture and building from geometry. This branch of learning, too, makes the soul in the highest degree observant, capable of perceiving the true and detecting the false, of discovering correspondences and proportions, so as to hunt out for similarity in things dissimilar; and conducts us to the discovery of length without breadth, and superficial extent without thickness, and an indivisible point, and transports to intellectual objects from those of sense.

The studies of philosophy, therefore, and philosophy itself, are aids in treating of the truth. For instance, the cloak was once a fleece; then it was shorn, and became warp and woof; and then it was woven. Accordingly the soul must be prepared and variously exercised, if it would become in the highest degree good. For there is the scientific and the practical element in truth; and the latter flows from the speculative; and there is need of great practice, and exercise, and experience.

But in speculation, one element relates to one's neighbors and another to one's self. Wherefore also training ought to be so molded as to be adapted to both. He, then, who has acquired a competent acquaintance with the subjects which embrace the principles which conduce to scientific knowledge (*gnosis*), may stop and remain for the future in quiet, directing his actions in l conformity with his theory.

But for the benefit of one's neighbors, in the case of those who have proclivities for writing, and those who set themselves to deliver the word, both is other culture beneficial, and the reading of the Scriptures of the Lord is necessary, in order to the demonstration of what is said, and especially if those who hear are accessions from Hellenic culture.

Such David describes the Church: "The queen stood on thy right hand, enveloped in a golden robe, variegated;" and with Hellenic and superabundant accomplishments, "clothed variegated with gold-fringed garments." And the Truth says by the Lord, "For who had known Thy counsel, had Thou not given wisdom, and sent Thy Holy Spirit from the Highest; and so the ways of those on earth were corrected, and men learned Thy decrees, and were saved by wisdom?" For the Gnostic knows things ancient by the Scripture, and conjectures things future: he understands the involutions of words and the solutions of enigmas. He knows beforehand signs and wonders, and the issues of seasons and periods, as we have said already. See thou the fountain of instructions that takes its rise from wisdom? But to those who object, What use is there in knowing the causes of the manner of the sun's motion, for example, and the rest of the heavenly bodies, or in having studied the theorems of geometry or logic, and each of the other branches of study?—for these are of no service in the discharge of duties, and the Hellenic philosophy is human wisdom, for it is incapable of teaching the truth—the following remarks are to be made. First, that they stumble in reference to the highest of things—namely, the mind's free choice. "For they," it is said, "who keep holy holy things, shall be made holy; and those who have been taught will find an answer." For the Gnostic alone will do holily, in accordance with reason all that has to be done, as he hath learned through the Lord's teaching, received through men.

Again, on the other hand, we may hear: "For in His hand, that is, in His power and wisdom, are both we and our words, and all wisdom and skill in works; for God loves nothing but the man that dwells with wisdom." And again, they have not read what is said by Solomon; for, treating of the construction of the temple, he says expressly, "And it was Wisdom as artificer that framed it; and Thy providence, O Father, governs throughout." And how irrational, to regard philosophy as inferior to architecture and shipbuilding!
And the Lord fed the multitude of those that reclined on the grass opposite to Tiberias with the two fishes and the five barley loaves, indicating the preparatory training of the Greeks

and Jews previous to the divine grain, which is the food cultivated by the law. For barley is sooner ripe for the harvest than wheat; and the fishes signified the Hellenic philosophy that was produced and moved in the midst of the Gentile billow, given, as they were, for copious food to those lying on the ground, increasing no more, like the fragments of the loaves, but having partaken of the Lord's blessing, and breathed into them the resurrection of Godhead through the power of the Word. But if you are curious, understand one of the fishes to mean the curriculum of study, and the other the philosophy which supervenes. The gatherings point out the word of the Lord. says the Tragic Muse somewhere.

"I must decrease," said the prophet John, and the Word of the Lord alone, in which the law terminates, "increase." Understand now for me the mystery of the truth, granting pardon if I shrink from advancing further in the treatment of it, by announcing this alone: "All things were made by Him, and without Him was not even one thing." Certainly He is called "the chief corner stone; in whom the whole building, fitly joined together, grows into a holy temple of God," according to the divine apostle.

I pass over in silence at present the parable which says in the Gospel: "The kingdom of heaven is like a man who cast a net into the sea and out of the multitude of the fishes caught, makes a selection of the better ones."

And now the wisdom which we possess announces the four virtues in such a way as to show that the sources of them were communicated by the Hebrews to the Greeks. This may be learned from the following: "And if one loves justice, its toils are virtues. For temperance and prudence teach justice and fortitude; and than these there is nothing more useful in life to men."

Above all, this ought to be known, that by nature we are adapted for virtue; not so as to be possessed of it from our birth, but so as to be adapted for acquiring it.

CHAPTER XII.—HUMAN NATURE POSSESSES AN ADAPTATION FOR PERFECTION; THE GNOSTIC ALONE ATTAINS IT.

By which consideration is solved the question propounded to us by the heretics. Whether Adam was created perfect or imperfect? Well, if imperfect, how could the work of a perfect God—above all, that work being man—be imperfect? And if perfect, how did he transgress the commandments? For they shall hear from us that he was not perfect in his creation, but adapted to the reception of virtue. For it is of great importance in regard to virtue to be made fit for its attainment. And it is intended that we should be saved by ourselves. This, then, is the nature of the soul, to move of itself. Then, as we are rational, and philosophy being rational, we have some affinity with it. Now an aptitude is a movement towards virtue, not virtue itself. All, then, as I said, are naturally constituted for the acquisition of virtue.

But one man applies less, one more, to learning and training. Wherefore also some have been competent to attain to perfect virtue, and others have attained to a kind of it. And some, on the other hand, through negligence, although in other respects of good dispositions, have turned to the opposite. Now much more is that knowledge which excels all branches of culture in greatness and in truth, most difficult to acquire, and is attained with much toil. "But, as seems, they know not the mysteries of God. For God created man for immortality, and made him an image of His own nature;" according to which nature of Him who knows all, he who is a Gnostic, and righteous, and holy with prudence, hastes to reach the measure of perfect manhood. For not only are actions and thoughts, but words also, pure in the case of the Gnostic: "Thou hast proved mine heart; Thou hast visited me by night," it is said; "Thou hast subjected me to the fire, and unrighteousness was not found in me: so that my mouth shall not speak the works of men."

And why do I say the works of men? He recognizes sin itself, which is not brought forward in order to repentance (for this is common to all believers); but what sin is. Nor does he condemn this or that sin, but simply all sin; nor is it what one has done ill that he brings up, but what ought not to be done. Whence also repentance is twofold: that which is common, on account of having transgressed; and that which, from learning the nature of sin, persuades, in the first instance, to keep from sinning, the result of which is not sinning.

Let them not then say, that he who does wrong and sins transgresses through the agency of demons; for then he would be guiltless. But by choosing the same things as demons, by sinning; being unstable, and light, and fickle in his desires, like a demon, he becomes a demoniac man. Now he who is bad, having become, through evil, sinful by nature, becomes depraved, having what he has chosen; and being sinful, sins also in his actions. And again, the good man does right. Wherefore we call not only the virtues, but also right actions, good. And of things that are good we know that some are desirable for themselves, as knowledge; for we hunt for nothing from it when we have it, but only [seek] that it be with us, and that we be in uninterrupted contemplation, and strive to reach it for its own sake. But other things are desirable for other considerations, such as faith, for escape from punishment, and the advantage arising from reward, which accrue from it. For, in the case of many, fear is the cause of their not sinning; and the promise is the means of pursuing obedience, by which comes salvation. Knowledge, then, desirable as it is for its own sake, is the most perfect good; and consequently the things which follow by means of it are good. And punishment is the cause of correction to him who is punished; and to those who are able to see before them he becomes an example, to prevent them falling into the like.

Let us then receive knowledge, not desiring its results, but embracing itself for the sake of knowing. For the first advantage is the habit of knowledge (γνωστική), which furnishes harmless pleasures and exultation both for the present and the future. And exultation is said to be gladness, being a reflection of the virtue which is according to truth, through a kind of exhilaration and relaxation of soul. And the acts which partake of knowledge are good and fair actions. For abundance in the actions that are according to virtue, is the true riches, and destitution in decorous desires is poverty. For the use and enjoyment of necessaries are not injurious in quality, but in quantity, when in excess. Wherefore the Gnostic circumscribes his desires in reference both to possession and to enjoyment, not exceeding the limit of necessity. Therefore, regarding life in this world as necessary for the increase of science (ἐπιστήμη) and the acquisition of knowledge (γνῶσις), he will value highest, not living, but living well. He will therefore prefer neither children, nor marriage, nor parents, to love for God, and righteousness in life. To such a one, his wife, after conception, is as a sister, and is judged as if of the same father; then only recollecting her husband, when she looks on the children; as being destined to become a sister in reality after putting off the flesh, which separates and limits the knowledge of those who are spiritual by the peculiar characteristics of the sexes. For souls, themselves by themselves, are equal. Souls are neither male nor female, when they no longer marry nor are given in marriage. And is not woman translated into man, when she is become equally unfeminine, and manly, and perfect? Such, then, was the laughter of Sarah when she received the good news of the birth of a son; not, in my opinion, that she disbelieved the angel, but that she felt ashamed of the intercourse by means of which she was destined to become the mother of a son.

And did not Abraham, when he was in danger on account of Sarah's beauty, with the king of Egypt, properly call her sister, being of the same father, but not of the same mother?

To those, then, who have repented and not firmly believed, God grants their requests through their supplications. But to those who live sinlessly and gnostically, He gives, when they have but merely entertained the thought. For example, to Anna, on her merely conceiving the thought, conception was vouchsafed of the child Samuel. "Ask," says the Scripture, "and I will do. Think, and I will give." For we have heard that God knows the heart, not judging the soul from [external] movement, as we men; nor yet from the event. For it is ridiculous to think so. Nor was it as the architect praises the work when accomplished that God, on making the light and then seeing it, called it good. But He, knowing before He made it what it would be, praised that which was made, He having potentially made good, from the first by His purpose that had no beginning, what was destined to be good actually. Now that which has future He already said beforehand was good, the phrase concealing the truth by hyperbaton. Therefore the Gnostic prays in thought during every hour, being by love allied to God. And first he will ask forgiveness of sins; and after, that he may sin no more; and further, the power of well-doing and of comprehending the whole creation and administration by the Lord, that, becoming pure in heart through the knowledge, which is by the Son of God, he may be initiated into the beatific vision face to face, having heard the Scripture which says, "Fasting with prayer is a good thing."

Now fasting signify abstinence from all evils whatsoever, both in action and in word, and in thought itself. As appears, then, righteousness is quadrangular; on all sides equal and like in word, in deed, in abstinence from evils, in beneficence, in gnostic perfection; nowhere, and in no respect halting, so that he does not appear unjust and unequal. As one, then, is righteous, so certainly is he a believer. But as he is a believer, he is not yet also righteous—I mean according to the righteousness of progress and perfection, according to which the Gnostic is called righteous.

For instance, on Abraham becoming a believer, it was reckoned to him for righteousness, he having advanced to the greater and more perfect degree of faith. For he who merely abstains from evil conduct is not just, unless he also attain besides beneficence and knowledge; and for this reason some things are to be abstained from, others are to be done. "By the armor of righteousness on the right hand and on the left," the apostle says, the righteous man is sent on to the inheritance above,—by some [arms] defended, by others putting forth his might. For the defense of his panoply alone, and abstinence from sins, are not sufficient for perfection, unless he assume in addition the work of righteousness—activity in doing good.

Then our dexterous man and Gnostic is revealed in righteousness already even here, as Moses, glorified in the face of the soul, as we have formerly said, the body bears the stamp of the righteous soul. For as the mordant of the dyeing process, remaining in the wool, produces in it a certain quality and diversity from other wool; so also in the soul the pain is gone, but the good remains; and the sweet is left, but the base is wiped away. For these are two qualities characteristic of each soul, by which is known that which is glorified, and that which is condemned.

And as in the case of Moses, from his righteous conduct, and from his uninterrupted intercourse with God, who spoke to him, a kind of glorified hue settled on his face; so also a divine power of goodness clinging to the righteous soul in contemplation and in prophecy, and in the exercise of the function of governing, impresses on it something, as it were, of intellectual radiance, like the solar ray, as a visible sign of righteousness, uniting the soul with light, through unbroken love, which is God-bearing and God-borne. Thence assimilation to God the Savior arises to the Gnostic, as far as permitted to human nature, he being made perfect "as the Father who is in heaven."

It is He Himself who says, "Little children, a little while I am still with you." Since also God Himself remains blessed and immortal, neither molested nor molesting another; not in consequence of being by nature good, but in consequence of doing good in a manner peculiar to Himself. God being essentially, and proving Himself actually, both

Father and good, continues immutably in the self-same goodness. For what is the use of good that does not act and do good?

CHAPTER XIII.—DEGREES OF GLORY IN HEAVEN CORRESPONDING WITH THE DIGNITIES OF THE CHURCH BELOW.

He, then, who has first moderated his passions and trained himself for impassibility, and developed to the beneficence of gnostic perfection, is here equal to the angels. Luminous already, and like the sun shining in the exercise of beneficence, he speeds by righteous knowledge through the love of God to the sacred abode, like as the apostles. Not that they became apostles through being chosen for some distinguished peculiarity of nature, since also Judas was chosen along with them. But they were capable of becoming apostles on being chosen by Him who foresees even ultimate issues. Matthias, accordingly, who was not chosen along with them, on showing himself worthy of becoming an apostle, is substituted for Judas.

Those, then, also now, who have exercised themselves in the Lord's commandments, and lived perfectly and gnostically according to the Gospel, may be enrolled in the chosen body of the apostles. Such a one is in reality a presbyter of the Church, and a true minister (deacon) of the will of God, if he do and teach what is the Lord's; not as being ordained by men, nor regarded righteous because a presbyter, but enrolled in the presbyterate because righteous. And although here upon earth he be not honored with the chief seat, he will sit down on the four-and-twenty thrones, judging the people, as John says in the Apocalypse.

For, in truth, the covenant of salvation, reaching down to us from the foundation of the world, through different generations and times, is one, though conceived as different in respect of gift. For it follows that there is one unchangeable gift of salvation given by one God, through one Lord, benefiting in many ways. For which cause the middle wall which separated the Greek from the Jew is taken away, in order that there might be a peculiar people. And so both meet in the one unity of faith; and the selection out of both is one. And the chosen of the chosen are those who by reason of perfect knowledge are called [as the best] from the Church itself, and honored with the most august glory—the judges and rulers—four-and-twenty (the grace being doubled) equally from Jews and Greeks. Since, according to my opinion, the grades here in the Church, of bishops, presbyters, deacons, are imitations of the angelic glory, and of that economy which, the Scriptures say, awaits those who, following the footsteps of the apostles, have lived in perfection of righteousness according to the Gospel. For these taken up in the clouds, the apostle writes, will first minister [as deacons], then be classed in the presbyterate, by promotion in glory (for glory differs from glory) till they grow into "a perfect man."

CHAPTER XIV.—DEGREES OF GLORY IN HEAVEN.

Such, according to David, "rest in the holy hill of God," in the Church far on high, in which are gathered the philosophers of God, "who are Israelites indeed, who are pure in heart, in whom there is no guile;" who do not remain in the seventh seat, the place of rest, but are promoted, through the active beneficence of the divine likeness, to the heritage of beneficence which is the eighth grade; devoting themselves to the pure vision of insatiable contemplation.

"And other sheep there are also," says the Lord, "which are not of this fold"—deemed worthy of another fold and mansion, in proportion to their faith. "But My sheep hear My voice," understanding gnostically the commandments. And this is to be taken in a magnanimous and worthy acceptation, along with also the recompense and accompaniment of works. So that when we hear, "Thy faith hath saved thee," we do not understand Him to say absolutely that those who have believed in any way whatever shall be saved, unless also works follow. But it was to the Jews alone that He spoke this utterance, who kept the law and lived blamelessly, who wanted only faith in the Lord. No one, then, can be a believer and at the same time be licentious; but though he quit the flesh, he must put off the passions, so as to be capable of reaching his own mansion.

Now to know is more than to believe, as to be dignified with the highest honor after being saved is a greater thing than being saved. Accordingly the believer, through great discipline, divesting himself of the passions, passes to the mansion which is better than the former one, viz., to the greatest torment, taking with him the characteristic of repentance from the sins he has committed after baptism. He is tortured then still more—not yet or not quite attaining what he sees others to have acquired. Besides, he is also ashamed of his transgressions. The greatest torments, indeed, are assigned to the believer. For God's righteousness is good, and His goodness is righteous. And though the punishments cease in the course of the completion of the expiation and purification of each one, yet those have very great and permanent grief who are found worthy of the other fold, on account of not being along with those that have been glorified through righteousness.

For instance, Solomon, calling the Gnostic, wise, speaks thus of those who admire the dignity of his mansion: "For they shall see the end of the wise, and to what a degree the Lord has established him." And of his glory they will say, "This was he whom we once held up to derision, and made a byword of reproach; fools that we were! We thought his life madness, and his end dishonorable. How is he reckoned among the sons of God, and his inheritance among the saints?"

Not only then the believer, but even the heathen, is judged most righteously. For since God knew in virtue of His prescience that he would not believe, He nevertheless, in order that he might receive his own perfection gave him philosophy, but gave it him previous to faith. And He gave the sun, and the moon, and the stars to be worshipped; "which God," the Law says, made for the nations, that they might not become altogether atheistical, and so utterly perish. But they, also in the instance of this commandment, having become devoid of sense, and addicting themselves to graven images, are judged unless they repent; some of them because, though able, they would not believe God; and others because, though willing, they did not take the necessary pains to become believers. There were also, however, those who, from the worship of the heavenly bodies, did not return to the Maker of them.

For this was the sway given to the nations to rise up to God, by means of the worship of the heavenly bodies. But those who would not abide by those heavenly bodies assigned to them, but fell away from them to stocks and stones, "were counted," it is said, "as chaff-dust and as a drop from a jar," beyond salvation, cast away from the body.

As, then, to be simply saved is the result of medium actions, but to be saved rightly and becoming is right action, so also all action of the Gnostic may be called right action; that of the simple believer, intermediate action, not yet perfected according to reason, not yet made right according to knowledge; but that of every heathen again is sinful. For it is not simply doing well, but doing actions with a certain aim, and acting according to reason, that the Scriptures exhibit as requisite.

As, then, lyres ought not to be touched by those who are destitute of skill in playing the lyre, nor flutes by those who are unskilled in flute-playing, neither are those to put their hand to affairs who have not knowledge, and know not how to use them in the whole of life.

The struggle for freedom, then, is waged not alone by the athletes of battles in wars, but also in banquets, and in bed, and in the tribunals, by those who are anointed by the word, who are ashamed to become the captives of pleasures.

"I would never part with virtue for unrighteous gain." But plainly, unrighteous gain is pleasure and pain, toil and fear; and, to speak comprehensively, the passions of the soul, the present of which is delightful, the future vexatious. "For what is the profit," it is said, "if you gain the world and lose the soul?" It is clear, then, that those who do not perform good actions, do not know what is for their own advantage. And if so, neither are they capable of praying aright, so as to receive from God good things; nor, should they receive them, will they be sensible of the boon; nor, should they enjoy them, will they enjoy worthily what they know not; both from their want of knowledge how to use the good things given them, and from their excessive stupidity, being ignorant of the way to avail themselves of the divine gifts.

Now stupidity is the cause of ignorance. And it appears to me that it is the vaunt of a boastful soul, though of one with a good conscience, to exclaim against what happens through circumstances:—

"Therefore let them do what they may;
For it shall be well with me; and Right
Shall be my ally, and I shall not be caught doing evil."

But such a good conscience preserves sanctity towards God and justice towards men; keeping the soul pure with grave thoughts, and pure words, and just deeds. By thus receiving the Lord's power, the soul studies to be God; regarding nothing bad but ignorance, and action contrary to right reason. And giving thanks always for all things to God, by righteous hearing and divine reading, by true investigation, by holy oblation, by blessed prayer; lauding, hymning, blessing, praising, such a soul is never at any time separated from God. Rightly then is it said, "And they who trust in Him shall understand the truth, and those faithful in love shall abide by Him." You see what statements Wisdom makes about the Gnostics.

Conformably, therefore, there are various abodes, according to the worth of those who have believed. To the point Solomon says, "For there shall be given to him the choice grace of faith, and a more pleasant lot in the temple of the

Lord." For the comparative shows that there are lower parts in the temple of God, which is the whole Church. And the superlative remains to be conceived, where the Lord is. These chosen abodes, which are three, are indicated by the numbers in the Gospel—the thirty, the sixty, the hundred. And the perfect inheritance belongs to those who attain to "a perfect man," according to the image of the Lord. And the likeness is not, as some imagine, that of the human form; for this consideration is impious. Nor is the likeness to the first cause that which consists in virtue. For this utterance is also impious, being that of those who have imagined that virtue in man and in the sovereign God is the same. "Thou hast supposed iniquity," He says, "[in imagining] that I will be like to thee."But "it is enough for the disciple to become as the Master," says the Master. To the likeness of God, then, he that is introduced into adoption and the friendship of God, to the just inheritance of the lords and gods is brought; if he be perfected, according to the Gospel, as the Lord Himself taught.

CHAPTER XV.—DIFFERENT DEGREES OF KNOWLEDGE.

The Gnostic, then, is impressed with the closest likeness, that is, with the mind of the Master; which He being possessed of, commanded and recommended to His disciples and to the prudent. Comprehending this, as He who taught wished, and receiving it in its grand sense, he teaches worthily "on the housetops" those capable of being built to a lofty height; and begins the doing of what is spoken, in accordance with the example of life. For He enjoined what is possible. And, in truth, the kingly man and Christian ought to be ruler and leader. For we are commanded to be lords over not only the wild beasts without us, but also over the wild passions within ourselves.

Through the knowledge, then, as appears, of a bad and good life is the Gnostic saved, understanding and executing "more than the scribes and Pharisees." "Exert thyself, and prosper, and reign" writes David, "because of truth, and meekness, and righteousness; and thy right hand shall guide thee marvelously,"that is, the Lord. "Who then is the wise? and he shall understand these things. Prudent? and he shall know them. For the ways of the Lord are right," says the prophet, showing that the Gnostic alone is able to understand and explain the things spoken by the Spirit obscurely. "And he who understands in that time shall hold his peace," says the Scripture, plainly in the way of declaring them to the unworthy. For the Lord says, "He that hath ears to hear, let him hear," declaring that hearing and understanding belong not to all. To the point David writes: "Dark water is in the clouds of the skies. At the gleam before Him the clouds passed, hail and coals of fire;"showing that the holy words are hidden. He intimates that transparent and resplendent to the Gnostics, like the innocuous hail, they are sent down from God; but that they are dark to the multitude, like extinguished coals out of the fire, which, unless kindled and set on fire, will not give forth fire or light. "The Lord, therefore," it is said, "gives me the tongue of instruction, so as to know in season when it is requisite to speak a word;" not in the way of testimony alone, but also in the way of question and answer. "And the instruction of the Lord opens my mouth." It is the prerogative of the Gnostic, then, to know how to make use of speech, and when, and how, and to whom. And already the apostle, by saying, "After the rudiments of the world, and not after Christ," makes the asseveration that the Hellenic teaching is elementary, and that of Christ perfect, as we have already intimated before.

"Now the wild olive is inserted into the fatness of the olive," and is indeed of the same species as the cultivated olives. For the graft uses as soil the tree in which it is engrafted. Now all the plants sprouted forth simultaneously in consequence of the divine order. Wherefore also, though the wild olive be wild, it crowns the Olympic victors. And the elm teaches the vine to be fruitful, by leading it up to a height. Now we see that wild trees attract more nutriment, because they cannot ripen. The wild trees, therefore, have less power of secretion than those that are cultivated. And the cause of their wildness is the want of the power of secretion. The engrafted olive accordingly receives more nutriment from its growing in the wild one; and it gets accustomed, as it were, to secrete the nutriment, becoming thus assimilated to the fatness of the cultivated tree.

So also the philosopher, resembling the wild olive, in having much that is undigested, on account of his devotion to the search, his propensity to follow, and his eagerness to seize the fatness of the truth; if he get besides the divine power, through faith, by being transplanted into the good and mild knowledge, like the wild olive, engrafted in the truly fair and merciful Word, he both assimilates the nutriment that is supplied, and becomes a fair and good olive tree. For engrafting makes worthless shoots noble, and compels the barren to be fruitful by the art of culture and by gnostic skill.

Different modes of engrafting illustrative of different kinds of conversion.

They say that engrafting is effected in four modes: one, that in which the graft must be fitted in between the wood and the bark; resembling the way in which we instruct plain people belonging to the Gentiles, who receive the word superficially. Another is, when the wood is cleft, and there is inserted in it the cultivated branch. And this applies to the case of those who have studied philosophy; for on cutting through their dogmas, the acknowledgment of the truth is produced in them. So also in the case of the Jews, by opening up the Old Testament, the new and noble plant of the olive is inserted. The third mode of engrafting applies to rustics and heretics, who are brought by force to the truth. For after smoothing off both suckers with a sharp pruning-hook, till the pith is laid bare, but not wounded, they are bound together. And the fourth is that form of engrafting called budding. For a bud (eye) is cut out of a trunk of a good sort, a circle being drawn round in the bark along with it, of the size of the palm. Then the trunk is stripped, to suit the eye, over an equal circumference. And so the graft is inserted, tied round, and daubed with clay, the bud being kept uninjured and unstained. This is the style of gnostic teaching, which is capable of looking into things themselves. This mode is, in truth, of most service in the case of cultivated trees.

And "the engrafting into the good olive" mentioned by the apostle, may be [engrafting into] Christ Himself; the uncultivated and unbelieving nature being transplanted into Christ—that is, in the case of those who believe in Christ. But it is better [to understand it] of the engrafting of each one's faith in the soul itself. For also the Holy Spirit is thus somehow transplanted by distribution, according to the circumscribed capacity of each one, but without being circumscribed.

Knowledge and love.

Now, discoursing on knowledge, Solomon speaks thus: "For wisdom is resplendent and fadeless, and is easily beheld by those who love her. She is beforehand in making herself known to those who desire her. He that rises early for her shall not toil wearily. For to think about her is the perfection of good sense. And he that keeps vigils for her shall quickly be relieved of anxiety. For she goes about, herself seeking those worthy of her (for knowledge belongs not to all); and in all ways she benignly shows herself to them."Now the paths are the conduct of life, and the variety that exists in the covenants. Presently he adds: "And in every thought she meets them,"being variously contemplated, that is, by all discipline. Then he subjoins, adducing love, which perfects by syllogistic reasoning and true propositions, drawing thus a most convincing and true inference, "For the beginning of her is the truest desire of instruction," that is, of knowledge; "prudence is the love of instruction, and love is the keeping of its laws; and attention to its laws is the confirmation of immortality; and immortality causes nearness to God. The desire of wisdom leads, then, to the kingdom."

For he teaches, as I think, that true instruction is desire for knowledge; and the practical exercise of instruction produces love of knowledge. And love is the keeping of the commandments which lead to knowledge. And the keeping of them is the establishment of the commandments, from which immortality results. "And immortality brings us near to God."

True knowledge found in the teaching of Christ alone.

If, then, the love of knowledge produces immortality, and leads the kingly man near to God the King, knowledge ought to be sought till it is found. Now seeking is an effort at grasping, and finds the subject by means of certain signs. And discovery is the end and cessation of inquiry, which has now its object in its gasp. And this is knowledge. And this discovery, properly so called, is knowledge, which is the apprehension of the object of search. And they say that a proof is either the antecedent, or the coincident, or the consequent. The discovery, then, of what is sought respecting God, is the teaching through the Son; and the proof of our Savior being the very Son of God is the prophecies which preceded His coming, announcing Him; and the testimonies regarding Him which attended His birth in the world; in addition, His powers proclaimed and openly shown after His ascension.

The proof of the truth being with us, is the fact of the Son of God Himself having taught us. For if in every inquiry these universals are found, a person and a subject, that which is truly the truth is shown to be in our hands alone. For the Son of God is the person of the truth which is exhibited; and the subject is the power of faith, which prevails over the opposition of every one whatever, and the assault of the whole world.

But since this is confessedly established by eternal facts and reasons, and each one who thinks that there is no Providence has already been seen to deserve punishment and not contradiction, and is truly an atheist, it is our aim to discover what doing, and in what manner living, we shall reach the knowledge of the sovereign God, and how, honoring the

Divinity, we may become authors of our own salvation. Knowing and learning, not from the Sophists, but from God Himself, what is well-pleasing to Him, we endeavor to do what is just and holy. Now it is well-pleasing to Him that we should be saved; and salvation is effected through both well-doing and knowledge, of both of which the Lord is the teacher.

If, then, according to Plato, it is only possible to learn the truth either from God or from the progeny of God, with reason we, selecting testimonies from the divine oracles, boast of learning the truth by the Son of God, prophesied at first, and then explained.

Philosophy and heresies, aids in discovering the truth.

But the things which co-operate in the discovery of truth are not to be rejected. Philosophy, accordingly, which proclaims a Providence, and the recompense of a life of felicity, and the punishment, on the other hand, of a life of misery, teaches theology comprehensively; but it does not preserve accuracy and particular points; for neither respecting the Son of God, nor respecting the economy of Providence, does it treat similarly with us; for it did not know the worship of God.

Wherefore also the heresies of the Barbarian philosophy, although they speak of one God, though they sing the praises of Christ, speak without accuracy, not in accordance with truth; for they discover another God, and receive Christ not as the prophecies deliver. But their false dogmas, while they oppose the conduct that is according to the truth, are against us. For instance, Paul circumcised Timothy because of the Jews who believed, in order that those who had received their training from the law might not revolt from the faith through his breaking such points of the law as were understood more carnally, knowing right well that circumcision does not justify; for he professed that "all things were for all" by conformity, preserving those of the dogmas that were essential, "that he might gain all." And Daniel, under the king of the

Persians, wore "the chain," though he despised not the afflictions of the people.

The liars, then, in reality are not those who for the sake of the scheme of salvation conform, nor those who err in minute points, but those who are wrong in essentials, and reject the Lord, and as far as in them lies deprive the Lord of the true teaching; who do not quote or deliver the Scriptures in a manner worthy of God and of the Lord; for the deposit rendered to God, according to the teaching of the Lord by His apostles, is the understanding and the practice of the godly tradition. "And what ye hear in the ear"—that is, in a hidden manner, and in a mystery (for such things are figuratively said to be spoken in the ear)—"proclaim," He says, "on the housetops," understanding them sublimely, and delivering them in a lofty strain, and according to the canon of the truth explaining the Scriptures; for neither prophecy nor the Savior Himself announced the divine mysteries simply so as to be easily apprehended by all and sundry, but express them in parables. The apostles accordingly say of the Lord, that "He spoke all things in parables, and without a parable spoke He nothing unto them;" and if "all things were made by Him, and without Him was not anything made that was made," consequently also prophecy and the law were by Him, and were spoken by Him in parables. "But all things are right," says the Scripture, "before those who understand," that is, those who receive and observe, according to the ecclesiastical rule, the exposition of the Scriptures explained by Him; and the ecclesiastical rule is the concord and harmony of the law and the prophets in the covenant delivered at the coming of the Lord. Knowledge is then followed by practical wisdom, and practical wisdom by self-control: for it may be said that practical wisdom is divine knowledge, and exists in those who are deified; but that self-control is mortal, and subsists in those who philosophize, and are not yet wise. But if virtue is divine, so is also the knowledge of it; while self-control is a sort of imperfect wisdom which aspires after wisdom, and exerts itself laboriously, and is not contemplative. As certainly righteousness, being human, is, as being a common thing, subordinate to holiness, which subsists through the divine righteousness; for the righteousness of the perfect man does not rest on civil contracts, or on the prohibition of law, but flows from his own spontaneous action and his love to God.

Reasons for the meaning of Scripture being veiled.

For many reasons, then, the Scriptures hide the sense. First, that we may become inquisitive, and be ever on the watch for the discovery of the words of salvation. Then it was not suitable for all to understand, so that they might not receive harm in consequence of taking in another sense the things declared for salvation by the Holy Spirit. Wherefore the holy mysteries of the prophecies are veiled in the parables— preserved for chosen men, selected to knowledge in consequence of their faith; for the style of the Scriptures is parabolic.

Wherefore also the Lord, who was not of the world, came as one who was of the world to men. For He was clothed with all virtue; and it was His aim to lead man, the foster-child of the world, up to the objects of intellect, and to the most essential truths by knowledge, from one world to another.

Wherefore also He employed metaphorical description; for such is the parable,—a narration based on some subject which is not the principal subject, but similar to the principal subject, and leading him who understands to what is the true and principal thing; or, as some say, a mode of speech presenting with vigor, by means of other circumstances, what is the principal subject.

And now also the whole economy which prophesied of the Lord appears indeed a parable to those who know not the truth, when one speaks and the rest hear that the Son of God— of Him who made the universe—assumed flesh, and was conceived in the virgin's womb (as His material body was produced), and subsequently, as was the case, suffered and rose again, being "to the Jews a stumbling-block, and to the Greeks foolishness," as the apostle says.

But on the Scriptures being opened up, and declaring the truth to those who have ears, they proclaim the very suffering endured by the flesh, which the Lord assumed, to be "the power and wisdom of God." And finally, the parabolic style of Scripture being of the greatest antiquity, as we have shown, abounded most, as was to be expected, in the prophets, in order that the Holy Spirit might show that the philosophers among the Greeks, and the wise men among the Barbarians besides, were ignorant of the future coming of the Lord, and of the mystic teaching that was to be delivered by Him. Rightly then, prophecy, in proclaiming the Lord, in order not to seem to some to blaspheme while speaking what was beyond the ideas of the multitude, embodied its declarations in expressions capable of leading to other conceptions. Now all the prophets who foretold the Lord's coming, and the holy mysteries accompanying it, were persecuted and killed. As also the Lord Himself, in explaining the Scriptures to them, and His disciples who preached the word like Him, and subsequently to His life, used parables. Whence also Peter, in his Preaching, speaking of the apostles, says: "But we, unrolling the books of the prophets which we possess, who name Jesus Christ, partly in parables, partly in enigmas, partly expressly and in so many words, find His coming and death, and cross, and all the rest of the tortures which the Jews inflicted on Him, and His resurrection and assumption to heaven previous to the capture of Jerusalem. As it is written, *These things are all that He behooves to suffer, and what should be after Him.* Recognizing them, therefore, we have believed in God in consequence of what is written respecting Him."

And after a little again he draws the inference that the Scriptures owed their origin to the divine providence, asserting as follows: "For we know that God enjoined these things, and we say nothing apart from the Scriptures."

Now the Hebrew dialect, like all the rest, has certain properties, consisting in a mode of speech which exhibits the national character. Dialect is accordingly defined as a style of speech produced by the national character. But prophecy is not marked by those dialects. For in the Hellenic writings, what are called changes of figures purposely produce onscurations, deduced after the style of our prophecies. But this is effected through the voluntary departure from direct speech which takes place in metrical or offhand diction. A figure, then, is a form of speech transferred from what is literal to what is not literal, for the sake of the composition, and on account of a diction useful in speech.

But prophecy does not employ figurative forms in the expressions for the sake of beauty of diction. But from the fact that truth appertains not to all, it is veiled in manifold ways, causing the light to arise only on those who are initiated into knowledge, who seek the truth through love. The proverb, according to the Barbarian philosophy, is called a mode of prophecy, and the parable is so called, and the enigma in addition. Further also, they are called "wisdom;" and again, as something different from it, "instruction and words of prudence," and "turnings of words," and "true righteousness;" and again, "teaching to direct judgment," and "subtlety to the simple," which is the result of training, "and perception and thought," with which the young catechumen is imbued. "He who hears these prophets, being wise, will be wiser. And the intelligent man will acquire rule, and will understand a parable and a dark saying, the words and enigmas of the wise."

And if it was the case that the Hellenic dialects received their appellation from Hellen, the son of Zeus, surnamed Deucalion, from the chronology which we have already exhibited, it is comparatively easy to perceive by how many generations the dialects that obtained among the Greeks are posterior to the language of the Hebrews.

But as the work advances, we shall in each section, noting the figures of speech mentioned above by the prophet, exhibit the gnostic mode of life, showing it systematically according to the rule of the truth.

Did not the Power also, that appeared to Hermas in the Vision, in the form of the Church, give for transcription the book which she wished to be made known to the elect? And this, he says, he transcribed to the letter, without finding how to complete the syllables. And this signified that the Scripture is clear to all, when taken according to the bare reading; and that this is the faith which occupies the place of the rudiments. Wherefore also the figurative expression is employed, "reading according to the letter;" while we understand that the gnostic unfolding of the Scriptures, when faith has already reached an advanced state, is likened to reading according to the syllables.

Further, Esaias the prophet is ordered to take "a new book, and write in it" certain things: the Spirit prophesying that through the exposition of the Scriptures there would come afterwards the sacred knowledge, which at that period was still unwritten, because not yet known. For it was spoken from the beginning to those only who understand. Now that the Savior has taught the apostles, the unwritten rendering of the written [Scripture] has been handed down also to us, inscribed by the power of God on hearts new, according to the renovation of the book. Thus those of highest repute among the Greeks, dedicate the fruit of the pomegranate to Hermes, who they say is speech, on account of its interpretation. For speech conceals much. Rightly, therefore, Jesus the son of Nave saw Moses, when taken up [to heaven], double,—one Moses with the angels, and one on the mountains, honored with burial in their ravines. And Jesus saw this spectacle below, being elevated by the Spirit, along also with Caleb. But both do not see similarly. But the one descended with greater speed, as if the weight he carried was great; while the other, on descending after him, subsequently related the glory which he beheld, being able to perceive more than the other as having grown purer; the narrative, in my opinion, showing that knowledge is not the privilege of all. Since some look at the body of the Scriptures, the expressions and the names as to the body of Moses; while others see through to the thoughts and what it is signified by the names, seeking the Moses that is with the angels.

Many also of those who called to the Lord said, "Son of David, have mercy on me." A few, too, knew Him as the Son of God; as Peter, whom also He pronounced blessed, "for flesh and blood revealed not the truth to him, but His Father in heaven,"—showing that the Gnostic recognizes the Son of the Omnipotent, not by His flesh conceived in the womb, but by the Father's own power. That it is therefore not only to those who read simply that the acquisition of the truth is so difficult, but that not even to those whose prerogative the knowledge of the truth is, is the contemplation of it vouch-safed all at once, the history of Moses teaches, until, accustomed to gaze, at the Hebrews on the glory of Moses, and the prophets of Israel on the visions of angels, so we also become able to look the splendors of truth in the face.

CHAPTER XVI.—GNOSTIC EXPOSITION OF THE DECALOGUE.

Let the Decalogue be set forth cursorily by us as a specimen for gnostic exposition.

The number "Ten."

That ten is a sacred number, it is superfluous to say now. And if the tables that were written were the work of God, they will be found to exhibit physical creation. For by the "finger of God" is understood the power of God, by which the creation of heaven and earth is accomplished; of both of which the tables will be understood to be symbols. For the writing and handiwork of God put on the table is the creation of the world.

And the Decalogue, viewed as an image of heaven, embraces sun and moon, stars, clouds, light, wind, water, air, darkness, fire. This is the physical Decalogue of the heaven.

And the representation of the earth contains men, cattle, reptiles, wild beasts; and of the inhabitants of the water, fishes and whales; and again, of the winged tribes, those that are carnivorous, and those that use mild food; and of plants likewise, both fruit-bearing and barren. This is the physical Decalogue of the earth.

And the ark which held them will then be the knowledge of divine and human things and wisdom.

And perhaps the two tables themselves may be the prophecy of the two covenants. They were accordingly mystically renewed, as ignorance along with sin abounded. The commandments are written, then, doubly, as appears, for twofold spirits, the ruling and the subject.
"For the flesh lusted against the Spirit, and the Spirit against the flesh."

And there is a ten in man himself: the five senses, and the power of speech, and that of reproduction; and the eighth is the spiritual principle communicated at his creation; and the ninth the ruling faculty of the soul; and tenth, there is the distinctive characteristic of the Holy Spirit, which comes to him through faith.

Besides, in addition to these ten human parts, the law appear to give its injunctions to sight, and hearing, and smell, and touch, and taste, and to the organs subservient to these, which are double—the hands and the feet. For such is the formation of man. And the soul is introduced, and previous to it the ruling faculty, by which we reason, not produced in procreation; so that without it there is made up the number ten, of the faculties by which all the activity of man is carried out. For in order, straightway on man's entering existence, his life begins with sensations. We accordingly assert that rational and ruling power is the cause of the constitution of the living creature; also that this, the irrational part, is animated, and is a part of it. Now the vital force, in which is comprehended the power of nutrition and growth, and generally of motion, is assigned to the carnal spirit, which has great susceptibility
of motion, and passes in all directions through the senses and the rest of the body, and through the body is the primary

subject of sensations. But the power of choice, in which investigation, and study, and knowledge, reside, belongs to the ruling faculty. But all the faculties are placed in relation to one—the ruling faculty: it is through that man lives, and lives in a certain way.

Through the corporeal spirit, then, man perceives, desires, rejoices, is angry, is nourished, grows. It is by it, too, that thoughts and conceptions advance to actions. And when it masters the desires, the ruling faculty reigns.

The commandment, then, "Thou shalt not lust," says, thou shalt not serve the carnal spirit, but shall rule over it; "For the flesh lusted against the Spirit," and excites to disorderly conduct against nature; "and the Spirit against the flesh" exercises sway, in order that the conduct of the man may be according to nature.

Is not man, then, rightly said "to have been made in the image of God?"—not in the form of his [corporeal] structure; but inasmuch as God creates all things by the Word (λόγῳ), and the man who has become a Gnostic performs good actions by the faculty of reason (τῷ λογικῷ), properly therefore the two tables are also said to mean the commandments that were given to the twofold spirits,—those communicated before the law to that which was created, and to the ruling faculty; and the movements of the senses are both copied in the mind, and manifested in the activity which proceeds from the body. For apprehension results from both combined. Again, as sensation is related to the world of sense, so is thought to that of intellect. And actions are twofold—those of thought, those of act.

The First Commandment.

The first commandment of the Decalogue shows that there is one only Sovereign God; who led the people from the land of Egypt through the desert to their fatherland; that they might apprehend His power, as they were able, by means of the divine works, and withdraw from the idolatry of created things, putting all their hope in the true God.

The Second Commandment.

The second word intimated that men ought not to take and confer the august power of God (which is the name, for this alone were many even yet capable of learning), and transfer His title to things created and vain, which human artificers have made, among which "He that is" is not ranked. For in His uncreated identity, "He that is" is absolutely alone.

The Fourth Commandment.

And the fourth word is that which intimates that the world was created by God, and that He gave us the seventh day as a rest, on account of the trouble that there is in life.
For God is incapable of weariness, and suffering, and want. But we who bear flesh need rest. The seventh day, therefore, is proclaimed a rest—abstraction from ills—preparing for the
Primal Day, our true rest; which, in truth, is the first creation of light, in which all things are viewed and possessed. From this day the first wisdom and knowledge illuminate us. For the light of truth—a light true, casting no shadow, is the Spirit of God indivisibly divided to all, who are sanctified by faith, holding the place of a luminary, in order to the knowledge of real existences. By following Him, therefore, through our whole life, we become impassible; and this is to rest.

Wherefore Solomon also says, that before heaven, and earth, and all existences, Wisdom had arisen in the Almighty; the participation of which—that which is by power, I mean, not that by essence—teaches a man to know by apprehension things divine and human. Having reached this point, we must mention these things by the way; since the discourse has turned on the seventh and the eighth. For the eighth may possibly turn out to be properly the seventh, and the seventh manifestly the sixth, and the latter properly the Sabbath, and the seventh a day of work. For the creation of the world was concluded in six days. For the motion of the sun from solstice to solstice is completed in six months—in the course of which, at one time the leaves fall, and at another plants bud and seeds come to maturity. And they say that the embryo is perfected exactly in the sixth month, that is, in one hundred and eighty days in addition to the two and a half, as Polybus the physician relates in his book *On the Eighth Month*, and Aristotle the philosopher in his book *On Nature*. Hence the Pythagoreans, as I think, reckon six the perfect number, from the creation of the world, according to the prophet, and call it Meseuthys and Marriage, from its being the middle of the even numbers, that is, of ten and two. For it is manifestly at an equal distance from both.

And as marriage generates from male and female, so six is generated from the odd number three, which is called the masculine number, and the even number two, which is considered the feminine. For twice three are six.

Such, again, is the number of the most general motions, according to which all origination takes place—up, down, to the right, to the left, forward, backward. Rightly, then, they reckon the number seven motherless and childless, interpreting the Sabbath, and figuratively expressing the nature of the rest, in which "they neither marry nor are given in marriage anymore." For neither by taking from one number and adding to another of those within ten is seven produced; nor when added to any number within the ten does it make up any of them.

And they called eight a cube, counting the fixed sphere along with the seven revolving ones, by which is produced "the great year," as a kind of period of recompense of what has been promised.

Thus the Lord, who ascended the mountain, the fourth, becomes the sixth, and is illuminated all round with spiritual light, by laying bare the power proceeding from Him, as far as those selected to see were able to behold it, by the Seventh, the Voice, proclaimed to be the Son of God; in order that they, persuaded respecting Him, might have rest; while He by His birth, which was indicated by the sixth conspicuously marked, becoming the eighth, might appear to be God in a body of flesh, by displaying His power, being numbered indeed as a man, but being concealed as to who He was. For six is reckoned in the order of numbers, but the succession of the letters acknowledges the character which is not written. In this case, in the numbers themselves, each unit is preserved in its order up to seven and eight. But in the number of the characters, *Zeta* becomes six and *Eta* seven.

And the character having somehow slipped into writing, should we follow it out thus, the seven became six, and the eight seven.

Wherefore also man is said to have been made on the sixth day, who became faithful to Him who is the sign (τῷ ἐπισήμῳ), so as straightway to receive the rest of the Lord's inheritance. Some such thing also is indicated by the sixth hour in the scheme of salvation, in which man was perfected. Further, of the eight, the intermediates are seven; and of the seven, the intervals are shown to be six. For that is another ground, in which seven glorifies eight, and "the heavens declare to the heavens the glory of God."

The sensible types of these, then, are the sounds we pronounce. Thus the Lord Himself is called "Alpha and Omega, the beginning and the end," "by whom all things were made, and without whom not even one thing was made."God's resting is not, then, as some conceive, that God ceased from doing. For, being good, if He should ever cease from doing good, then would He cease from being God, which it is sacrilege even to say. The resting is, therefore, the ordering that the order of created things should be preserved inviolate, and that each of the creatures should cease from the ancient disorder. For the creations on the different days followed in a most important succession; so that all things brought into existence might have honor from priority, created together in thought, but not being of equal worth. Nor was the creation of each signified by the voice, inasmuch as the creative work is said to have made them at once. For something must needs have been named first.

Wherefore those things were announced first, from which came those that were second, all things being originated together from one essence by one power. For the will of God was one, in one identity. And how could creation take place in time, seeing time was born along with things which exist.

And now the whole world of creatures born alive, and things that grow, revolves in sevens. The first-born princes of the angels, who have the greatest power, are seven. The mathematicians also say that the planets, which perform their course around the earth, are seven; by which the Chaldeans think that all which concerns mortal life is effected through sympathy, in consequence of which they also undertake to tell things respecting the future.

And of the fixed stars, the Pleiades are seven. And the Bears, by the help of which agriculture and navigation are carried through, consist of seven stars. And in periods of seven days the moon undergoes its changes. In the first week she becomes half-moon; in the second, full moon; and in the third, in her wane, again half-moon; and in the fourth she disappears. Further, as Seleucus the mathematician lays down, she has seven phases. First, from being invisible she becomes crescent-shaped, then half-moon, then gibbous and full; and in her wane again gibbous, and in like manner half-moon and crescent-shaped.

"On a seven-stringed lyre we shall sing new hymns,"

writes a poet of note, teaching us that the ancient lyre was seven-toned. The organs of the senses situated on our face are also seven—two eyes, two passages of hearing, two nostrils, and the seventh the mouth.

And that the changes in the periods of life take place by sevens, the *Elegies of Solon* teach thus:—

"The child, while still an infant, in seven years,
Produces and puts forth its fence of teeth;

> And when God seven years more completes,
> He shows of puberty's approach the signs;
> And in the third, the beard on growing cheek
> With down o'erspreads the bloom of changing skin;
> And in the fourth septenniad, at his best
> In strength, of manliness he shows the signs;
> And in the fifth, of marriage, now mature,
> And of posterity, the man bethinks;
> Nor does he yet desire vain works to see.
> The seventh and eighth septenniads see him now
> In mind and speech mature, till fifty years;
> And in the ninth he still has vigor left,
> But strength and body are for virtue great
> Less than of yore; when, seven years more, God brings
> To end, then not too soon may he submit to die."

Again, in diseases the seventh day is that of the crisis; and the fourteenth, in which nature struggles against the causes of the diseases. And a myriad such instances are adduced by
Hermippus of Berytus, in his book *On the Number Seven*, regarding it as holy. And the blessed David delivers clearly to those who know the mystic account of seven and eight, praising thus: "Our years were exercised like a spider. The days of our years in them are seventy years; but if in strength, eighty years. And that will be to reign." That, then, we may be taught that the world was originated, and not suppose that God made it in time, prophecy adds: "This is the book of the generation: also of the things in them, when they were created in the day that God made heaven and earth." For the expression "when they were created" intimates an indefinite and dateless production. But the expression "in the day that God made," that is, in and by which God made "all things," and "without which not even one thing was made," points out the activity exerted by the Son. As David says, "This is the day which the Lord hath made; let us be glad and rejoice in it;" that is, in consequence of the knowledge imparted by Him, let us

celebrate the divine festival; for the Word that throws light on things hidden, and by whom each created thing came into life and being, is called day.

And, in fine, the Decalogue, by the letter *Iota,* signifies the blessed name, presenting Jesus, who is the Word.

The Fifth Commandment.

Now the fifth in order is the command on the honor of father and mother. And it clearly announces God as Father and Lord. Wherefore also it calls those who know Him sons and gods. The Creator of the universe is their Lord and Father; and the mother is not, as some say, the essence from which we sprang, nor, as others teach, the Church, but the divine knowledge and wisdom, as Solomon says, when he terms wisdom "the mother of the just," and says that it is desirable for its own sake. And the knowledge of all, again, that is lovely and venerable, proceeds from God through the Son.

The Sixth Commandment.

Then follows the command about murder. Now murder is a sure destruction. He, then, that wishes to extirpate the true doctrine of God and of immortality, in order to introduce falsehood, alleging either that the universe is not under Providence, or that the world is uncreated, or affirming anything against true doctrine, is most pernicious.

The Seventh Commandment.

This is followed by the command respecting adultery. Now it is adultery, if one, abandoning the ecclesiastical and true knowledge, and the persuasion respecting God, accedes to false and incongruous opinion, either by deifying any created object, or by making an idol of anything that exists not, so as to overstep, or rather step from, knowledge. And to the Gnostic false opinion is foreign, as the true belongs to him, and is allied with him. Wherefore the noble apostle calls one of the kinds of fornication, idolatry, in following the prophet, who says: "[My people] hath committed fornication with stock and stone. They have said to the stock, Thou art my father; and to the stone, Thou hast begotten me."

The Eighth Commandment.

And after this is the command respecting theft. As, then, he that steals what is another's, doing great wrong, rightly incurs ills suitable to his deserts; so also does he, who arrogates to himself divine works by the art of the statuary or the painter, and pronounces himself to be the maker of animals and plants. Likewise those, too, who mimic the true philosophy are thieves. Whether one be a husbandman or the father of a child, he is an agent in depositing seeds. But it is God who, ministering the growth and perfection of all things, brings the things produced to what is in accordance with their nature. But the most, in common also with the philosophers, attribute growth and changes to the stars as the primary cause, robbing the Father of the universe, as far as in them lies, of His tireless might.

The elements, however, and the stars—that is, the administrative powers— are ordained for the accomplishment of what is essential to the administration, and are influenced and moved by what is commanded to them, in the way in which the Word of the Lord leads, since it is the nature of the divine power to work all things secretly. He, accordingly, who alleges that he has conceived or made anything which pertains to creation, will suffer the punishment of his impious audacity.

The Tenth Commandment.

And the tenth is the command respecting all lusts. As, then, he who entertains unbecoming desires is called to account; in the same way he is not allowed to desire things false, or to suppose that, of created objects, those that are animate have power of themselves, and that inanimate things can at all save or hurt. And should one say that an antidote cannot heal or hemlock kill, he is unwittingly deceived. For none of these operates except one makes use of the plant and the drug; just as the axe does not without one to cut with it, or a saw without one sawing with it. And as they do not work by themselves, but have certain physical qualities which accomplish their proper work by the exertion of the artisan; so also, by the universal providence of God, through the medium of secondary causes, the operative power is propagated in succession to individual objects.

CHAPTER XVII.—PHILOSOPHY CONVEYS ONLY AN IMPERFECT KNOWLEDGE OF GOD.

But, as appears, the philosophers of the Greeks, while naming God, do not know Him. But their philosophical speculations, according to Empedocles, "as passing over the tongue of the multitude, are poured out of mouths that know little of the whole." For as art changes the light of the sun into fire by passing it through a glass vessel full of water, so also philosophy, catching a spark from the divine Scripture, is visible in a few. Also, as all animals breathe the same air, some in one way, others in another, and to a different purpose; so also a considerable number of people occupy themselves with the truth, or rather with discourse concerning the truth. For they do not say aught respecting God, but expound Him by attributing their own affections to God. For they spend life in seeking the probable, not the true. But truth is not taught by imitation, but by instruction. For it is not that we may seem good that we believe in Christ, as it is not alone for the purpose of being seen, while in the sun, that we pass into the sun. But in the one case for the purpose of being warmed; and in the other, we are compelled to be Christians in order to be excellent and good. For the kingdom belongs pre-eminently to the violent, who, from investigation, and study, and discipline, reap this fruit, that they become kings.

He, then, who imitates opinion shows also preconception. When then one, having got an inkling of the subject, kindles it within in his soul by desire and study, he sets everything in motion afterwards in order to know it. For that which one does not apprehend, neither does he desire it, nor does he embrace the advantage flowing from it. Subsequently, therefore, the Gnostic at last imitates the Lord, as far as allowed to men, having received a sort of quality akin to the Lord Himself, in order to assimilation to God. But those who are not proficient in knowledge cannot judge the truth by rule. It is not therefore possible to share in the gnostic contemplations, unless we empty ourselves of our previous notions. For the truth in regard to every object of intellect and of sense is thus simply universally declared. For instance, we may distinguish the truth of painting from that which is vulgar, and decorous music from licentious. There is, then, also a truth of philosophy as distinct from the other philosophies, and a true beauty as distinct from the spurious. It is not then the partial truths, of which truth is predicated, but the truth itself, that we are to investigate, not seeking to learn names. For what is to be investigated respecting God is not one thing, but ten thousand.

There is a difference between declaring God, and declaring things about God. And to speak generally, in everything the accidents are to be distinguished from the essence.

Suffice it for me to say, that the Lord of all is God; and I say the Lord of all absolutely, nothing being left by way of exception.

Since, then, the forms of truth are two—the names and the things—some discourse of names, occupying themselves with the beauties of words: such are the philosophers among the Greeks. But we who are Barbarians have the things. Now it was not in vain that the Lord chose to make use of a mean form of body; so that no one praising the grace and admiring the beauty might turn his back on what was said, and attending to what ought to be abandoned, might be cut off from what is intellectual. We must therefore occupy ourselves not with the expression, but the meaning.

To those, then, who are not gifted with the power of apprehension, and are not inclined to knowledge, the word is not entrusted; since also the ravens imitate human voices, having no understanding of the thing which they say. And intellectual apprehension depends on faith. Thus also Homer said:—

"Father of men and gods,"—

knowing not who the Father is, or how He is Father.

And as to him who has hands it is natural to grasp, and to him who has sound eyes to see the light; so it is the natural prerogative of him who has received faith to apprehend knowledge, if he desires, on "the foundation" laid, to work, and build up "gold, silver, precious stones."

Accordingly he does not profess to wish to participate, but begins to do so. Nor does it belong to him to *intend*, but to *be* regal, and illuminated, and gnostic. Nor does it appertain to him to wish to grasp things in name, but in fact.

For God, being good, on account of the principal part of the whole creation, seeing He wishes to save it, was induced to make the rest also; conferring on them at the beginning this first boon, that of existence. For that to be is far better than not to be, will be admitted by everyone. Then, according to the capabilities of their nature, each one was and is made, advancing to that which is better.

So there is no absurdity in philosophy having been given by Divine Providence as a preparatory discipline for the perfection which is by Christ; unless philosophy is ashamed at learning from Barbarian knowledge how to advance to truth. But if "the very hairs are numbered, and the most insignificant motions," how shall not philosophy be taken into account? For to Samson power was given in his hair, in order that he might perceive that the worthless arts that refer to the things in this life, which lie and remain on the ground after the departure of the soul, were not given without divine power.

But it is said Providence, from above, from what is of prime importance, as from the head, reaches to all, "as the ointment," it is said, "which descends to Aaron's beard, and to the skirt of his garment" (that is, of the great High Priest, "by whom all things were made, and without whom not even one thing was made"); not to the ornament of the body; for Philosophy is outside of the People, like raiment. The philosophers, therefore, who, trained to their own peculiar power of perception by the spirit of perception, when they investigate, not a part of philosophy, but philosophy absolutely, testify to the truth in a truth-loving and humble spirit; if in the case of good things said by those even who are of different sentiments they advance to understanding, through the divine administration, and the ineffable Goodness, which always, as far as possible, leads the nature of existences to that which is better. Then, by cultivating the acquaintance not of Greeks alone, but also of Barbarians, from the exercise common to their proper intelligence, they are conducted to Faith. And when they have embraced the foundation of truth, they receive in addition the power of advancing further to investigation. And thence they love to be learners, and aspiring after knowledge, haste to salvation.

Thus Scripture says, that "the spirit of perception" was given to the artificers from God. And this is nothing else than Understanding, a faculty of the soul, capable of studying existences,—of distinguishing and comparing what succeeds as like and unlike,—of enjoining and forbidding, and of conjecturing the future. And it extends not to the arts alone, but even to philosophy itself.

Why, then, is the serpent called wise? Because even in its wiles there may be found a connection, and distinction, and combination, and conjecturing of the future. And so very many crimes are concealed; because the wicked arrange for themselves so as by all means to escape punishment.

And Wisdom being manifold, pervading the whole world, and all human affairs, varies its appellation in each case. When it applies itself to first causes, it is called Understanding (νόησις). When, however, it confirms this by demonstrative reasoning, it is termed Knowledge, and Wisdom, and Science. When it is occupied in what pertains to piety, and receives without speculation the primal Word in consequence of the maintenance of the operation in it, it is called Faith. In the sphere of things of sense, establishing that which appears as being truest, it is Right Opinion. In operations, again, performed by skill of hand, it is Art. But when, on the other hand, without the study of primary causes, by the observation of similarities, and by transposition, it makes any attempt or combination, it is called Experiment. But belonging to it, and supreme and essential, is the Holy Spirit, which above all he who, in consequence of [divine] guidance, has believed, receives after strong faith. Philosophy, then, partaking of a more exquisite perception, as has been shown from the above statements, participates in Wisdom.

Logical discussion, then, of intellectual subjects, with selection and assent, is called Dialectics; which establishes, by demonstration, allegations respecting truth, and demolishes the doubts brought forward.

Those, then, who assert that philosophy did not come hither from God, all but say that God does not know each particular thing, and that He is not the cause of all good things; if, indeed, each of these belongs to the class of individual things. But nothing that exists could have subsisted at all, had God not willed. And if He willed, then philosophy is from God, He having willed it to be such as it is, for the sake of those who not otherwise than by its means would abstain from what is evil. For God knows all things—not those only which exist, but those also which shall be—and how each thing shall be. And foreseeing the particular movements, "He surveys all things, and hears all things," seeing the soul naked within; and possesses from eternity the idea of each thing individually. And what applies to theatres, and to the parts of each object, in looking at, looking round, and taking in the whole in one view, applies also to God. For in one glance He views all things together, and each thing by itself; but not all things, by way of primary intent.

Now, then, many things in life take their rise in some exercise of human reason, having received the kindling spark from God. For instance, health by medicine, and soundness of body through gymnastics, and wealth by trade, have their origin and existence in consequence of Divine Providence indeed, but in consequence, too, of human co-operation. Understanding also is from God.

But God's will is especially obeyed by the free-will of good men. Since many advantages are common to good and bad men: yet they are nevertheless advantageous only to men of goodness and probity, for whose sake God created them. For it was for the use of good men that the influence which is in God's gifts was originated. Besides, the thoughts of virtuous men are produced through the inspiration of God; the soul being disposed in the way it is, and the divine will being conveyed to human souls, particular divine ministers contributing to such services. For regiments of angels are distributed over the nations and cities. And, perchance, some are assigned to individuals.

The Shepherd, then, cares for each of his sheep; and his closest inspection is given to those who are excellent in their natures, and are capable of being most useful. Such are those fit to lead and teach, in whom the action of Providence is conspicuously seen; whenever either by instruction, or government, or administration, God wishes to benefit. But He wishes at all times. Wherefore He moves those who are adapted to useful exertion in the things which pertain to virtue, and peace, and beneficence. But all that is characterized by virtue proceeds from virtue, and leads back to virtue. And it is given either in order that men may become good, or that those who are so may make use of their natural advantages. For it co-operates both in what is general and what is particular. How absurd, then, is it, to those who attribute disorder and wickedness to the devil, to make him the bestower of philosophy, a virtuous thing! For he is thus all but made more benignant to the Greeks, in respect of making men good, than the divine providence and mind.

Again, I reckon it is the part of law and of right reason to assign to each one what is appropriate to him, and belongs to him, and falls to him. For as the lyre is only for the harper, and the flute for the flute-player; so good things are the possessions of good men. As the nature of the beneficent is to do good, as it is of the fire to warm, and the light to give light, and a good man will not do evil, or light produce darkness, or fire cold; so, again, vice cannot do aught virtuous. For its activity is to do evil, as that of darkness to dim the eyes.

Philosophy is not, then, the product of vice, since it makes men virtuous; it follows, then, that it is the work of God, whose work it is solely to do good. And all things given by God are given and received well.

Further, if the practice of philosophy does not belong to the wicked, but was accorded to the best of the Greeks, it is clear also from what source it was bestowed—manifestly from Providence, which assigns to each what is befitting in accordance with his deserts."

Rightly, then, to the Jews belonged the Law, and to the Greeks Philosophy, until the Advent; and after that came the universal calling to be a peculiar people of righteousness, through the teaching which flows from faith, brought together by one Lord, the only God of both Greeks and Barbarians, or rather of the whole race of men. We have often called by the name philosophy that portion of truth attained through philosophy, although but partial.

Now, too what is good in the arts as arts, have their beginning from God. For as the doing of anything artistically is embraced in the rules of art, so also acting sagaciously is classed under the head of sagacity (φρόνησις). Now sagacity is virtue, and it is its function to know other things, but much more especially what belongs to itself. And Wisdom (Σοφία) being power, is nothing but the knowledge of good things, divine and human.

But "the earth is God's, and the fullness thereof," says the Scripture, teaching that good things come from God to men; it being through divine power and might that the distribution of them comes to the help of man.

Now the modes of all help and communication from one to another are three. One is, by attending to another, as the master of gymnastics, in training the boy. The second is, by assimilation, as in the case of one who exhorts another to benevolence by practicing it before. The one co-operates with the learner, and the other benefits him who receives. The third mode is that by command, when the gymnastic master, no longer training the learner, nor showing in his own person the exercise for the boy to imitate, prescribes the exercise by name to him, as already proficient in it.

The Gnostic, accordingly, having received from God the power to be of service, benefits some by disciplining them, by bestowing attention on them; others, by exhorting them, by assimilation; and others, by training and teaching them, by command. And certainly he himself is equally benefited by the Lord. Thus, then, the benefit that comes from God to men becomes known—angels at the same time lending encouragement. For by angels, whether seen or not, the divine power bestows good things. Such was the mode adopted in the advent of the Lord. And sometimes also the power "breathes" in men's thoughts and reasoning, and "puts in" their hearts "strength" and a keener perception, and furnishes "prowess" and "boldness of alacrity" both for researches and deeds.

But exposed for imitation and assimilation are truly admirable and holy examples of virtue in the actions put on record. Further, the department of action is most conspicuous both in the testaments of the Lord, and in the laws in force among the Greeks, and also in the precepts of philosophy.

And to speak comprehensively, all benefit appertaining to life, in its highest reason, proceeding from the Sovereign God, the Father who is over all, is consummated by the Son, who also on this account "is the Savior of all men," says the apostle, "but especially of those who believe." But in respect of its immediate reason, it is from those next to each, in accordance with the command and injunction of Him who is nearest the First Cause, that is, the Lord.

CHAPTER XVIII.—THE USE OF PHILOSOPHY TO THE GNOSTIC.

Greek philosophy the recreation of the Gnostic.

Now our Gnostic always occupies himself with the things of highest importance. But if at any time he has leisure and time for relaxation from what is of prime consequence, he applies himself to Hellenic philosophy in preference to other recreation, feasting on it as a kind of dessert at supper. Not that he neglects what is superior; but that he takes this in addition, as long as proper, for the reasons I mentioned above. But those who give their mind to the unnecessary and superfluous points of philosophy, and addict themselves to wrangling sophisms alone, abandon what is necessary and most essential, pursuing plainly the shadows of words.

It is well indeed to know all. But the man whose soul is destitute of the ability to reach to acquaintance with many subjects of study, will select the principal and better subjects alone. For real science (ἐπιστήμη, which we affirm the Gnostic alone possesses) is a sure comprehension (κατάληψις), leading up through true and sure reasons to the knowledge (γνῶσις) of the cause. And he, who is acquainted with what is true respecting any one subject, becomes of course acquainted with what is false respecting it.

Philosophy necessary.

For truly it appears to me to be a proper point for discussion. Whether we ought to philosophize: for its terms are consistent. But if we are not to philosophize, what then? (For no one can condemn a thing without first knowing it): the consequence, even in that case, is that we must philosophize.

First of all, idols are to be rejected.

Such, then, being the case, the Greeks ought by the Law and the Prophets to learn to worship one God only, the only Sovereign; then to be taught by the apostle, "but to us an idol is nothing in the world," since nothing among created things can be a likeness of God; and further, to be taught that none of those images which they worship can be similitudes: for the race of souls is not in form such as the Greeks fashion their idols. For souls are invisible; not only those that are rational, but those also of the other animals. And their bodies never become parts of the souls themselves, but organs—partly as seats, partly as vehicles—and in other cases possessions in various ways. But it is not possible to copy accurately even the likenesses of the organs; since, were it so, one might model the sun, as it is seen, and take the likeness of the rainbow in colors.

After abandoning idols, then, they will hear the Scripture, "Unless your righteousness exceed the righteousness of the scribes and Pharisees" (who justified themselves in the way of abstinence from what was evil),—so as, along with such perfection as they evinced, and "the loving of your neighbor," to be able also to do good, you shall not "be kingly."

For intensification of the righteousness which is according to the law shows the Gnostic. So one who is placed in the head, which is that which rules its own body—and who advances to the summit of faith, which is the knowledge (*gnosis*) itself, for which all the organs of perception exist— will likewise obtain the highest inheritance.

The primacy of knowledge the apostle shows to those capable of reflection, in writing to those Greeks of Corinth, in the following terms: "But having hope, when your faith is increased, that we shall be magnified in you according to our rule abundantly, to preach the Gospel beyond you." He does not mean the extension of his preaching locally: for he says also that in Achaia faith abounded; and it is related also in the Acts of the Apostles that he preached the word in Athens. But he teaches that knowledge (*gnosis*), which is the perfection of faith, goes beyond catechetical instruction, in accordance with the magnitude of the Lord's teaching and the rule of the Church. Wherefore also he proceeds to add, "And if I am rude in speech, yet I am not in knowledge."

Whence is the knowledge of truth?

But let those who vaunt on account of having apprehended the truth tell us from whom they boast of having heard it. They will not say from God, but will admit that it was from men. And if so, it is either from themselves that they have learned it lately, as some of them arrogantly boast, or from others like them. But human teachers, speaking of God, are not reliable, as men. For he that is man cannot speak worthily the truth concerning God: the feeble and mortal [cannot speak worthily] of the Unoriginated and Incorruptible—the work, of the Workman. Then he who is incapable of speaking what is true respecting himself, is he not much less reliable in what concerns God? For just as far as man is inferior to God in power, so much feebler is man's speech than Him; although he do not declare God, but only speak about God and the divine word. For human speech is by nature feeble, and incapable of uttering God. I do not say His name. For to name it is common, not to philosophers only, but also to poets. Nor [do I say] His essence; for this is impossible, but the power and the works of God.

Those even who claim God as their teacher, with difficulty attain to a conception of God, grace aiding them to the attainment of their modicum of knowledge; accustomed as they are to contemplate the will [of God] by the will, and the Holy Spirit by the Holy Spirit. "For the Spirit searches the deep things of God. But the natural man receives not the things of the Spirit."

The only wisdom, therefore, is the God-taught wisdom we possess; on which depend all the sources of wisdom, which make conjectures at the truth.

Intimations of the Teacher's advent

Assuredly of the coming of the Lord, who has taught us, to men, there were a myriad indicators, heralds, preparers, precursors, from the beginning, from the foundation of the world, intimating beforehand by deeds and words, prophesying that He would come, and where, and how, what should be the signs. From afar certainly Law and Prophecy kept Him in view beforehand. And then the precursor pointed Him out as present. After whom the heralds point out by their teaching the virtue of His manifestation.

Universal diffusion of the Gospel a contrast to philosophy.

The philosophers, however, chose to [teach philosophy] to the Greeks alone, and not even to all of them; but Socrates to Plato, and Plato to Xenocrates, Aristotle to Theophrastus, and Zeno to Cleanthes, who persuaded their own followers alone.

But the word of our Teacher remained not in Judea alone, as philosophy did in Greece; but was diffused over the whole world, over every nation, and village, and town, bringing already over to the truth whole houses, and each individual of those who heard it by him himself, and not a few of the philosophers themselves.

And if any one ruler whatever prohibit the Greek philosophy, it vanishes forthwith. But our doctrine on its very first proclamation was prohibited by kings and tyrants together, as well as particular rulers and governors, with all their mercenaries, and in addition by innumerable men, warring against us, and endeavoring as far as they could to exterminate it. But it flourishes the more. For it dies not, as human doctrine dies, nor fades as a fragile gift. For no gift of God is fragile. But it remains unchecked, though prophesied as destined to be persecuted to the end. Thus Plato writes of poetry: "A poet is a light and a sacred thing, and cannot write poetry till he be inspired and lose his senses." And Democritus similarly: "Whatever things a poet writes with divine afflatus, and with a sacred spirit, are very beautiful." And we know what sort of things poets say. And shall no one be amazed at the prophets of God Almighty becoming the organs of the divine voice?

Having then molded, as it were, a statue of the Gnostic, we have now shown who he is; indicating in outline, as it were, both the greatness and beauty of his character. What he is as to the study of physical phenomena shall be shown afterwards, when we begin to treat of the creation of the world.

Elucidations.

I.
(Gentlemen of the Jury, cap. ii. p. 485.)

This strange rendering of ὦ ἄνδρες δικασταὶ (which we were taught to translate *O judices*, in our school-days) occurs three times on this page, and I felt bound to retain it. But why import such an anachronism into the author's work, and the forensic eloquence of the Athenians? Better do violence to idiom, like our English Bible ("men and brethren"), and say, *O men and judges*. Why not *judges*? See Sharon Turner (*Anglo-Saxons,* i. p. 476) and Freeman (*Norman Conquest,* v. p. 451).

II.
(Aristobulus, cap. iii. p. 487, note 7.)

In addition to the note *in loc.*, it may be well to mention the *Stromata* (book i. cap. xv. p. 316), as another place where this name occurs. The learned Calmet (Works, tom. ix. p. 121), in his *Dict. Critic.*, has a valuable statement as to the difficulties connected with this name and the probability that there were two so called, who have been confused in the citations and references of authors.

III.
(Egyptians, cap. iv. p. 488.)

The paradoxical genius of Warburton ought not to dissuade us from enjoying the amusement and instruction to be found in his *Divine Legation*. In many respects he reminds me of this great Alexandrian Father, and they are worthy of being studied together. Let me instance, in connection with this subject, the second book, e. g. p. 151, on *Metempsychosis* (Hurd's Edition, vol. ii. 1811).

IV.
(Egyptian Women, book vi. cap. iv. p. 488.)

"*Last*, about women," says our author; and one would infer *least*. But Rawlinson (*Herod.*, vol. ii. p. 47, ed. New York) has a long and learned note on this subject. "Queens made offerings with the kings, and the monuments show that an order of women were employed in the service of the gods." ... Then he says, "A sort of monastic institution seems to have originated in Egypt at an early time, and to have been imitated afterwards, when *the real conventual system* was set on foot by the Christians, in the same country." This may be worthy of being borne in mind, when we come to the coenobitic life of the Thebaid, which lies, indeed, beyond the limits of our ante-Nicene researches. But persecution had already driven Christians to the desert; and the ascetic type of piety, with which the age and its necessities imprinted the souls of many devout women, may have led them at a very early period to the "imitation" of which Rawlinson speaks. The "widows" recognized by the ante-Nicene canons, would naturally become the founders of "widows' houses," such as are to be seen among the pious Moravians in our times. (See Bunsen, *Hippol.*, iii. p. 81.)

V.
(Philosophy, cap. vii. p. 493.)

In justice to Clement's eulogies of philosophy, we must constantly bear in mind his reiterated definitions. We have here a very important outline of his *Christian Eclecticism*, which, so far from clashing with St. Paul's scornful references to Gentile wisdom, seems to me in absolute correspondence with his reference to "science *falsely so called*" (1 Tim. vi. 20). So, when the apostle identifies philosophy with "the rudiments of the world," he adds, "and not after Christ." Now, Clement's eclectic system yokes all true philosophy to the chariot-wheels of the Messiah, as in this instance; making all true science hinge upon "the knowledge of the Son of God." How these chapters shine in contrast even with Plato.

VI.
(Numbers, cap. xi. p. 499.)

The marvelous system of numbers which runs through all revelation, and which gives us the name *Palmoni* (English margin) in a remarkable passage of Dan. viii. 13, has lately excited fresh interest among the learned in England and America. Doubtless the language of St. John (Rev. xiii. 18), "Here is wisdom," etc., influenced the early Church in what seems to us purely fanciful conjectures and combinations like these. Two unpretending little books have lately struck me as quite in the spirit of the Ante-Nicene Fathers: *The Number Counted*, and the *Name Counted*, by J. A. Upjohn (Appleton, Wis., 1883).

VII.
(The Gnostic, cap. xi. p. 501.)

The Gnostic "conjectures things future," i.e., by the Scriptures. "He shall show you things to come," said the Divine Master, speaking of the Blessed Comforter. To what extent did these ancients, in their esoteric conjectures, anticipate the conversion of the empire, and the evils that were to follow? This they could not publish; but the inquiry deserves thought, and there are dues for inquirers.

VIII.
(Ultimate Issues, cap. xiii. p. 504.)

With reference to the choice of Judas to be an apostle, and like mysteries, this seems to me a bit of calm philosophy, worthy of the childlike faith of the early Christians. I confess great obligations to a neglected American author, with reference to such discussions (see Bledsoe, *Theodicy*, New York, 1854).

IX.
(Enigmas, cap. xv. p. 510.)

We are often troubled by this Oriental tendency to teach by myth and mysteries; but the text here quoted from the Proverbs, goes far to show that it is rooted in human nature, and that God himself has condescended to adopt it. Like every gift of God, it is subject to almost inevitable corruption and abuse.

X.
(Omissions, cap. xvi. p. 515.)

The omissions in Clement's Decalogue are worthy of remark, and I can only account for them by supposing a defective text. Kaye might have said more on the subject; but he suggests this as the solution of the difficulty, when he says (p. 201), "*As the text now stands*, Clement interprets only eight out of the ten." P.S.—I have foreborne to say anything on "the descent into hell," in my annotations (on cap. vi.), for obvious reasons of propriety; but, for an entire system of references to the whole subject, I name Ezra Abbot's *Catalogue*, appended to Alger's *History*, etc. (Philadelphia, 1864.)

BOOK VII.

CHAPTER I.—THE GNOSTIC A TRUE WORSHIPPER OF GOD, AND UNJUSTLY CALUMNIATED BY UNBELIEVERS AS AN ATHEIST.

It is now time to show the Greeks that the Gnostic alone is truly pious; so that the philosophers, learning of what description the true Christian is, may condemn their own stupidity in rashly and inconsiderately persecuting the [Christian] name, and without reason calling those impious who know the true God. And clearer arguments must be employed, I reckon, with the philosophers, so that they may be able, from the exercise they have already had through their own training, to understand, although they have not yet shown themselves worthy to partake of the power of believing.

The prophetic sayings we shall not at present advert to, as we are to avail ourselves of the Scriptures subsequently at the proper places. But we shall point out summarily the points indicated by them, in our delineation of Christianity, so that by taking the Scriptures at once (especially as they do not yet comprehend their utterances), we may not interrupt the continuity of the discourse. But after pointing out the things indicated, proofs shall be shown in abundance to those who have believed.

But if the assertions made by us appear to certain of the multitude to be different from the Scriptures of the Lord, let it be known that it is from that source that they have breath and life; and taking their rise from them, they profess to adduce the sense only, not the words. For further treatment, not being seasonable, will rightly appear superfluous. Thus, not to look at what is urgent would be excessively indolent and defective;

and "blessed, in truth, are they who, investigating the testimonies of the Lord, shall seek Him with their whole heart." And the law and the prophets witness of the Lord.

It is, then, our purpose to prove that the Gnostic alone is holy and pious, and worships the true God in a manner worthy of Him; and that worship meet for God is followed by loving and being loved by God. He accordingly judges all excellence to be honorable according to its worth; and judges that among the objects perceived by our senses, we are to esteem rulers, and parents, and every one advanced in years; and among subjects of instruction, the most ancient philosophy and primeval prophecy; and among intellectual ideas, what is oldest in origin, the timeless and unoriginated First Principle, and Beginning of existences—the Son—from whom we are to learn the remoter Cause, the Father, of the universe, the most ancient and the most beneficent of all; not capable of expression by the voice, but to be reverenced with reverence, and silence, and holy wonder, and supremely venerated; declared by the Lord, as far as those who learned were capable of comprehending, and understood by those chosen by the Lord to acknowledge; "whose senses," says the apostle, "were exercised."

The service of God, then, in the case of the Gnostic, is his soul's continual study and occupation, bestowed on the Deity in ceaseless love. For of the service bestowed on men, one kind is that whose aim is improvement, the other ministerial. The improvement of the body is the object of the medical art, of the soul of philosophy. Ministerial service is rendered to parents by children, to rulers by subjects.

Similarly, also, in the Church, the elders attend to the department which has improvement for its object; and the deacons to the ministerial. In both these ministries the angels serve God, in the management of earthly affairs; and the Gnostic himself ministers to God, and exhibits to men the scheme of improvement, in the way in which he has been appointed to discipline men for their amendment. For he is alone pious that serves God rightly and unblameably in human affairs. For as that treatment of plants is best through which their fruits are produced and gathered in, through knowledge and skill in husbandry, affording men the benefit accruing from them; so the piety of the Gnostic, taking to itself the fruits of the men who by his means have believed, when not a few attain to knowledge and are saved by it, achieves by his skill the best harvest. And as Godliness (θεοπρέπεια) is the habit which preserves what is becoming to God, the godly man is the only lover of God, and such will he be who knows what is becoming, both in respect of knowledge and of the life which must be lived by him, who is destined to be divine (θεῷ), and is already being assimilated to God. So then he is in the first place a lover of God. For as he who honors his father is a lover of his father, so he who honors God is a lover of God.

Thus also it appears to me that there are three effects of gnostic power: the knowledge of things; second, the performance of whatever the Word suggests; and the third, the capability of delivering, in a way suitable to God, the secrets veiled in the truth.

He, then, who is persuaded that God is omnipotent, and has learned the divine mysteries from His only-begotten Son, how can he be an atheist (ἄθπεος)? Foa he is an atheist who thinks that God does not exist. And he is superstitious who dreads the demons; who deifies all things, both wood and stone; and reduces to bondage spirit, and man who possesses the life of reason.

CHAPTER II.—THE SON THE RULER AND SAVIOUR OF ALL.

To know God is, then, the first step of faith; then, through confidence in the teaching of the Savior, to consider the doing of wrong in any way as not suitable to the knowledge of God.

So the best thing on earth is the most pious man; and the best thing in heaven, the nearer in place and purer, is an angel, the partaker of the eternal and blessed life. But the nature of the Son, which is nearest to Him who is alone the Almighty One, is the most perfect, and most holy, and most potent, and most princely, and most kingly, and most beneficent. This is the highest excellence, which orders all things in accordance with the Father's will, and holds the helm of the universe in the best way, with unwearied and tireless power, working all things in which it operates, keeping in view its hidden designs. For from His own point of view the Son of God is never displaced; not being divided, not severed, not passing from place to place; being always everywhere, and being contained nowhere; complete mind, the complete paternal light; all eyes, seeing all things, hearing all things, knowing all things, by His power scrutinizing the powers. To Him is placed in subjection all the host of angels and gods; He, the paternal Word, exhibiting a holy administration for Him who put [all] in subjection to Him.

Wherefore also all men are His; some through knowledge, and others not yet so; and some as friends, some as faithful servants, some as servants merely. This is the Teacher, who trains the Gnostic by mysteries, and the believer by good hopes, and the hard of heart by corrective discipline through sensible operation. Thence His providence is in private, in public, and everywhere.

And that He whom we call Savior and Lord is the Son of God, the prophetic Scriptures explicitly prove. So the Lord of all, of Greeks and of Barbarians, persuades those who are willing. For He does not compel him who (through choosing and fulfilling, from Him, what pertains to laying hold of it the hope) is able to receive salvation from Him.

It is He who also gave philosophy to the Greeks by means of the inferior angels. For by an ancient and divine order the angels are distributed among the nations. But the glory of those who believe is "the Lord's portion." For either the Lord does not care for all men; and this is the case either because He is unable (which is not to be thought, for it would be a proof of weakness), or because He is unwilling, which is not the attribute of a good being. And He who for our sakes assumed flesh capable of suffering, is far from being luxuriously indolent. Or He does care for all, which is befitting for Him who has become Lord of all. For He is Savior; not [the Savior] of some, and of others not. But in proportion to the adaptation possessed by each, He has dispensed His beneficence both to Greeks and Barbarians, even to those of them that were predestinated, and in due time called, the faithful and elect. Nor can He who called all equally, and assigned special honors to those who have believed in a specially excellent way, ever envy any. Nor can He who is the Lord of all, and serves above all the will of the good and almighty Father, ever be hindered by another. But neither does envy touch the Lord, who without beginning was impassible; nor are the things of men such as to be envied by the Lord. But it is another, he whom passion hath touched, who envies. And it cannot be said that it is from ignorance that the Lord is not willing to save humanity, because He knows not how each one is to be cared for. For ignorance applies not to the God who, before the foundation of the world, was the counsellor of the Father. For He was the Wisdom "in which" the Sovereign God "delighted." For the Son is the power of God, as being the Father's most ancient Word before the production of all things, and His Wisdom. He is then properly called the Teacher of the beings formed by Him. Nor does He ever abandon care for men, by being drawn aside from pleasure, who, having assumed flesh, which by nature is susceptible of suffering, trained it to the condition of impassibility.

And how is He Savior and Lord, if not the Savior and Lord of all? But He is the Savior of those who have believed, because of their wishing to know; and the Lord of those who have not believed, till, being enabled to confess him, they obtain the peculiar and appropriate boon which comes by Him.

Now the energy of the Lord has a reference to the Almighty; and the Son is, so to speak, an energy of the Father. Therefore, a hater of man, the Savior can never be; who, for

His exceeding love to human flesh, despising not its susceptibility to suffering, but investing Himself with it, came for the common salvation of men; for the faith of those who have chosen it, is common. Nay more, He will never neglect His own work, because man alone of all the other living creatures was in his creation endowed with a conception of God. Nor can there be any other better and more suitable government for men than that which is appointed by God.

It is then always proper for the one who is superior by nature to be over the inferior, and for him who is capable of managing aught well to have the management of it assigned to him. Now that which truly rules and presides is the Divine Word and His providence, which inspects all things, and despises the care of nothing belonging to it.

Those, then, who choose to belong to Him, are those who are perfected through faith. He, the Son, is, by the will of the Almighty Father, the cause of all good things, being the first efficient cause of motion—a power incapable of being apprehended by sensation. For what He was, was not seen by those who, through the weakness of the flesh, were incapable of taking in [the reality]. But, having assumed sensitive flesh, He came to show man what was possible through obedience to the commandments. Being, then, the Father's power, He easily prevails in what He wishes, leaving not even the minutest point of His administration unattended to. For otherwise the whole would not have been well executed by Him.

But, as I think, characteristic of the highest power is the accurate scrutiny of all the parts, reaching even to the minutest, terminating in the first Administrator of the universe, who by the will of the Father directs the salvation of all; some overlooking, who are set under others, who are set over them, till you come to the great High Priest. For on one original first Principle, which acts according to the [Father's] will, the first and the second and the third depend. Then at the highest extremity of the visible world is the blessed band of angels;

and down to ourselves there are ranged, some under others, those who, from One and by One, both are saved and save.

As, then, the minutest particle of steel is moved by the spirit of the Heraclean stone, when diffused over many steel rings; so also, attracted by the Holy Spirit, the virtuous are added by affinity to the first abode, and the others in succession down to the last. But those who are bad from infirmity, having fallen from vicious insatiableness into a depraved state, neither controlling nor controlled, rush round and round, whirled about by the passions, and fall down to the ground.

For this was the law from the first, that virtue should be the object of voluntary choice. Wherefore also the commandments, according to the Law, and before the Law, not given to the upright (for the law is not appointed for a righteous man), ordained that he should receive eternal life and the blessed prize, who chose them.

But, on the other hand, they allowed him who had been delighted with vice to consort with the objects of his choice; and, on the other hand, that the soul, which is ever improving in the acquisition of virtue and the increase of righteousness, should obtain a better place in the universe, as tending in each step of advancement towards the habit of impassibility, till "it come to a perfect man," to the excellence at once of knowledge and of inheritance.

These salutary revolutions, in accordance with the order of change, are distinguished both by times, and places, and honors, and cognitions, and heritages, and ministries, according to the particular order of each change, up to the transcendent and continual contemplation of the Lord in eternity.

Now that which is lovable leads, to the contemplation of itself, each one who, from love of knowledge, applies himself entirely to contemplation. Wherefore also the Lord, drawing the commandments, both the first which He gave, and the second, from one fountain, neither allowed those who were before the law to be without law, nor permitted those who were unacquainted with the principles of the Barbarian philosophy to be without restraint. For, having furnished the one with the commandments, and the other with philosophy, He shut up unbelief to the Advent. Whence everyone who believes not is without excuse. For by a different process of advancement, both Greek and Barbarian, He leads to the perfection which is by faith.

And if any one of the Greeks, passing over the preliminary training of the Hellenic philosophy, proceeds directly to the true teaching, he distances others, though an unlettered man, by choosing the compendious process of salvation by faith to perfection.

Everything, then, which did not hinder a man's choice from being free, He made and rendered auxiliary to virtue, in order that there might be revealed somehow or other, even to those capable of seeing but dimly, the one only almighty, good God—from eternity to eternity saving by His Son.

And, on the other hand, He is in no respect whatever the cause of evil. For all things are arranged with a view to the salvation of the universe by the Lord of the universe, both generally and particularly. It is then the function of the righteousness of salvation to improve everything as far as practicable. For even minor matters are arranged with a view to the salvation of that which is better, and for an abode suitable for people's character. Now everything that is virtuous changes for the better; having as the proper cause of change the free choice of knowledge, which the soul has in its own power. But necessary corrections, through the goodness of the great overseeing Judge, both by the attendant angels, and by various acts of anticipative judgment, and by the perfect judgment, compel egregious sinners to repent.

CHAPTER III.—THE GNOSTIC AIMS AT THE NEAREST LIKENESS POSSIBLE TO GOD AND HIS SON.

Now I pass over other things in silence, glorifying the Lord. But I affirm that Gnostic souls, that surpass in the grandeur of contemplation the mode of life of each of the holy ranks, among whom the blessed abodes of the gods are allotted by distribution, reckoned holy among the holy, transferred entire from among the entire, reaching places better than the better places, embracing the divine vision not in mirrors or by means of mirrors, but in the transcendently clear and absolutely pure insatiable vision which is the privilege of intensely loving souls, holding festival through endless ages, remain honored with the indentity of all excellence. Such is the vision attainable by "the pure in heart." This is the function of the Gnostic, who has been perfected, to have converse with God through the great High Priest, being made like the Lord, up to the measure of his capacity, in the whole service of God, which tends to the salvation of men, through care of the beneficence which has us for its object; and on the other side through worship, through teaching and through beneficence in deeds. The Gnostic even forms and creates himself; and besides also, he, like to God, adorns those who hear him; assimilating as far as possible the moderation which, arising from practice, tends to impassibility, to Him who by nature possesses impassibility; and especially having uninterrupted converse and fellowship with the Lord. Mildness, I think, and philanthropy, and eminent piety, are the rules of gnostic assimilation. I affirm that these virtues "are a sacrifice acceptable in the sight of God;" Scripture alleging that "the humble heart with right knowledge is the holocaust of God;" each man who is admitted to holiness being illuminated in order to indissoluble union.

For "to bring themselves into captivity," and to slay themselves, putting to death "the old man, who is through lusts corrupt," and raising the new man from death, "from the old conversation," by abandoning the passions, and becoming free of sin, both the Gospel and the apostle enjoin.

It was this, consequently, which the Law intimated, by ordering the sinner to be cut off, and translated from death to life, to the impassibility that is the result of faith; which the teachers of the Law, not comprehending, inasmuch as they regarded the law as contentious, they have given a handle to those who attempt idly to calumniate the Law. And for this reason we rightly do not sacrifice to God, who, needing nothing, supplies all men with all things; but we glorify Him who gave Himself in sacrifice for us, we also sacrificing ourselves; from that which needs nothing to that which needs nothing, and to that which is impassible from that which is impassible. For in our salvation alone God delights. We do not therefore, and with reason too, offer sacrifice to Him who is not overcome by pleasures, inasmuch as the fumes of the smoke stop far beneath, and do not even reach the thickest clouds; but those they reach are far from them. The Deity neither is, then, in want of aught, nor loves pleasure, or gain, or money, being full, and supplying all things to everything that has received being and has wants. And neither by sacrifices nor offerings, nor on the other hand by glory and honor, is the Deity won over; nor is He influenced by any such things; but He appears only to excellent and good men, who will never betray justice for threatened fear, nor by the promise of considerable gifts.

But those who have not seen the self-determination of the human soul, and its incapability of being treated as a slave in what respects the choice of life, being disgusted at what is done through rude injustice, do not think that there is a God. On a par with these in opinion, are they who, falling into licentiousness in pleasures, and grievous pains, and unlooked-for accidents, and bidding defiance to events, say that there is no God, or that, though existing, He does not oversee all things. And others there are, who are persuaded that those they reckon gods are capable of being prevailed upon by sacrifices and gifts, favoring, so to speak, their profligacies; and will not believe that He is the only true God, who exists in the invariableness of righteous goodness.

The Gnostic, then, is pious, who cares first for himself, then for his neighbors, that they may become very good. For the son gratifies a good father, by showing himself good and like his father; and in like manner the subject, the governor. For believing and obeying are in our own power.

But should any one suppose the cause of evils to be the weakness of matter, and the involuntary impulses of ignorance, and (in his stupidity) irrational necessities; he who has become a Gnostic has through instruction superiority over these, as if they were wild beasts; and in imitation of the divine plan, he does good to such as are willing, as far as he can. And if ever placed in authority, like Moses, he will rule for the salvation of the governed; and will tame wildness and faithlessness, by recording honor for the most excellent, and punishment for the wicked, in accordance with reason for the sake of discipline.

For pre-eminently a divine image, resembling God, is the soul of a righteous man; in which, through obedience to the commands, as in a consecrated spot, is enclosed and enshrined the Leader of mortals and of immortals, King and Parent of what is good, who is truly law, and right, and eternal Word, being the one Savior individually to each, and in common to all.

He is the true Only-begotten, the express image of the glory of the universal King and Almighty Father, who impresses on the Gnostic the seal of the perfect contemplation, according to His own image; so that there is now a third divine image, made as far as possible like the Second Cause, the Essential Life, through which we live the true life; the Gnostic, as we regard him, being described as moving amid things sure and wholly immutable.

Ruling, then, over himself and what belongs to him, and possessing a sure grasp, of divine science, he makes a genuine approach to the truth. For the knowledge and apprehension of intellectual objects must necessarily be called certain scientific knowledge, whose function in reference to divine things is to consider what is the First Cause, and what that "by whom all things were made, and without whom nothing was made;" and what things, on the other hand, are as pervasive, and what is comprehensive; what conjoined, what disjoined; and what is the position which each one of them holds, and what power and what service each contributes. And again, among human things, what man himself is, and what he has naturally or preternaturally; and how, again, it becomes him to do or to suffer; and what are his virtues and what his vices; and about things good, bad, and indifferent; also about fortitude, and prudence, and self-restraint, and the virtue which is in all respects complete, namely, righteousness.

Further, he employs prudence and righteousness in the acquisition of wisdom, and fortitude, not only in the endurance of circumstances, but also in restraining pleasure and desire, grief and anger; and, in general, to withstand everything which either by any force or fraud entices us. For it is not necessary to endure vices and virtues, but it is to be persuaded to bear things that inspire fear.

Accordingly, pain is found beneficial in the healing art, and in discipline, and in punishment; and by it men's manners are corrected to their advantage. Forms of fortitude are endurance, magnanimity, high spirit, liberality, and grandeur. And for this reason he neither meets with the blame or the bad opinion of the multitude; nor is he subjected to opinions or flatteries. But in the endurance of toils and at the same time in the discharge of any duty, and in his manly superiority to all circumstances, he appears truly a man (ἀνήρ) among the rest of human beings. And, on the other hand, maintaining prudence, he exercises moderation in the calmness of his soul; receptive of what is commanded, as of what belongs to him, entertaining aversion to what is base, as alien to him; become decorous and supramundane, he does everything with decorum and in order, and transgresses in no respect, and in nothing. Rich he is in the highest degree in desiring nothing, as having few wants; and being in the midst of abundance of all good through the knowledge of the good. For it is the first effect of his righteousness, to love to spend his time and associate with those of his own race both in earth and heaven. So also he is liberal of what he possesses. And being a lover of men, he is a hater of the wicked, entertaining a perfect aversion to all villainy. He must consequently learn to be faithful both to himself and his neighbors, and obedient to the commandments. For he is the true servant of God who spontaneously subjects himself to His commands. And he who already, not through the commandments, but through knowledge itself, is pure in heart, is the friend of God. For neither are we born by nature possessing virtue, nor after we are born does it grow naturally, as certain parts of the body; since then it would neither be voluntary nor praiseworthy. Nor is virtue, like speech, perfected by the practice that results from everyday occurrences (for this is very much the way in which vice originates). For it is not by any art, either those of acquisition, or those which relate to the care of the body, that knowledge is attained. No more is it from the curriculum of instruction. For that is satisfied if it can only prepare and sharpen the soul. For the laws of the state are perchance able to restrain bad actions; but persuasive words, which but touch the surface, cannot produce a scientific permanence of the truth.

Now the Greek philosophy, as it were, purges the soul, and prepares it beforehand for the reception of faith, on which the Truth builds up the edifice of knowledge.

This is the true athlete—he who in the great stadium, the fair world, is crowned for the true victory over all the passions. For He who prescribes the contest is the Almighty God, and He who awards the prize is the only-begotten Son of God. Angels and gods are spectators; and the contest, embracing all the varied exercises, is "not against flesh and blood," but against the spiritual powers of inordinate passions that work through the flesh. He who obtains the mastery in these struggles, and overthrows the tempter, menacing, as it were, with certain contests, wins immortality. For the sentence of God in most righteous judgment is infallible. The spectators are summoned to the contest, and the athletes contend in the stadium; the one, who has obeyed the directions of the trainer, wins the day. For to all, all rewards proposed by God are equal; and He Himself is unimpeachable. And he who has power receives mercy, and he that has exercised will is mighty.

So also we have received mind, that we may know what we do. And the maxim "Know thyself" means here to know for what we are born. And we are born to obey the commandments, if we choose to be willing to be saved. Such is the Nemesis, through which there is no escaping from God. Man's duty, then, is obedience to God, who has proclaimed salvation manifold by the commandments. And confession is thanksgiving. For the beneficent first begins to do good. And he who on fitting considerations readily receives and keeps the commandments, is faithful (πιστός); and he who by love requites benefits as far as he is able, is already a friend. One recompense on the part of men is of paramount importance— the doing of what is pleasing to God. As being His own production, and a result akin to Himself, the Teacher and Savior receives acts of assistance and of improvement on the part of men as a personal favor and honor; as also He regards the injuries inflicted on those who believe on Him as ingratitude and dishonor to Himself. For what other dishonor can touch God? Wherefore it is impossible to render a recompense at all equivalent to the boon received from the Lord.

And as those who maltreat property insult the owners, and those who maltreat soldiers insult the commander, so also the ill-usage of His consecrated ones is contempt for the Lord.

For, just as the sun not only illumines heaven and the whole world, shining over land and sea, but also through windows and small chinks sends his beams into the innermost recesses of houses, so the Word diffused everywhere casts His eye-glance on the minutest circumstances of the actions of life.

CHAPTER IV.—THE HEATHENS MADE GODS LIKE THEMSELVES, WHENCE SPRINGS ALL SUPERSTITION.

Now, as the Greeks represent the gods as possessing human forms, so also do they as possessing human passions. And as each of them depict their forms similar to themselves, as Xenophanes says, "Ethiopians as black and apes, the Thracians ruddy and tawny;" so also they assimilate their souls to those who form them: the Barbarians, for instance, who make them savage and wild; and the Greeks, who make them more civilized, yet subject to passion.

Wherefore it stands to reason, that the ideas entertained of God by wicked men must be bad, and those by good men most excellent. And therefore he who is in soul truly kingly and gnostic, being likewise pious and free from superstition, is persuaded that He who alone is God is honorable, venerable, august, beneficent, the doer of good, the author of all good things, but not the cause of evil. And respecting the Hellenic superstition we have, as I think, shown enough in the book entitled by us *The Exhortation,* availing ourselves abundantly of the history bearing on the point. There is no need, then, again to make a long story of what has already been clearly stated. But in as far as necessity requires to be pointed out on coming to the topic, suffice it to adduce a few out of many considerations in proof of the impiety of those who make the Divinity resemble the worst men. For either those Gods of theirs are injured by men, and are shown to be inferior to men on being injured by us; or, if not so, how is it that they are incensed at those by whom they are not injured, like a testy old wife roused to wrath?

As they say that Artemis was enraged at the Ætolians on account of OEneus. For how, being a goddess, did she not consider that he had neglected to sacrifice, not through contempt, but out of inadvertence, or under the idea that he had sacrificed?

And Latona, arguing her case with Athene, on account of the latter being incensed at her for having brought forth in the temple, says:—

> "Man-slaying spoils
> Torn from the dead you love to see. And these
> To you are not unclean. But you regard
> My parturition here a horrid thing,
> Though other creatures in the temple do
> No harm by bringing forth their young."

It is natural, then, that having a superstitious dread of those irascible [gods], they imagine that all events are signs and causes of evils. If a mouse bore through an altar built of clay, and for want of something else gnaw through an oil flask; if a cock that is being fattened crow in the evening, they determine this to be a sign of something.

Of such a one Menander gives a comic description in *The Superstitious Man:*—

> "*A.* Good luck be mine, ye honored gods!
> Tying my, right shoe's string,
> I broke it."
> "*B.* Most likely, silly fool,
> For it was rotten, and you, niggard, you
> Would not buy new ones."

It was a clever remark of Antiphon, who (when one regarded it as an ill omen that the sow had eaten her pigs), on seeing her emaciated through the niggardliness of the person that kept her, said, Congratulate yourself on the omen that, being so hungry, she did not eat your own children.

"And what wonder is it," says Bion, "if the mouse, finding nothing to eat, gnaws the bag?" For it were wonderful if (as Arcesilaus argued in fun) "the bag had eaten the mouse."

Diogenes accordingly remarked well to one who wondered at finding a serpent coiled round a pestle: "Don't wonder; for it would have been more surprising if you had seen the pestle coiled round the serpent, and the serpent straight."

For the irrational creatures must run, and scamper, and fight, and breed, and die; and these things being natural to them, can never be unnatural to us.

"And many birds beneath the sunbeams walk."

And the comic poet Philemon treats such points in comedy:—

"When I see one who watches who has sneezed,
Or who has spoken; or looking, who goes on,
I straightway in the market sell him off.
Each one of us walks, talks, and sneezes too,
For his own self, not for the citizens:
According to their nature things turn out."

Then by the practice of temperance men seek health: and by cramming themselves, and wallowing in potations at feasts, they attract diseases.

There are many, too, that dread inscriptions set up. Very cleverly Diogenes, on finding in the house of a bad man the inscription, "Hercules, for victory famed, dwells here; let nothing bad enter," remarked, "And how shall the master of the house go in?"

The same people, who worship every stick and greasy stone, as the saying is, dreads tufts of tawny wool, and lumps of salt, and torches, and squills, and sulphur, bewitched by sorcerers, in certain impure rites of expiation. But God, the true God, recognizes as holy only the character of the righteous man,—as unholy, wrong and wickedness.

You may see the eggs, taken from those who have been purified, hatched if subjected to the necessary warmth. But this could not take place if they had had transferred to them the sins of the man that had undergone purification. Accordingly the comic poet Diphilus facetiously writes, in comedy, of sorcerers, in the following words:—

"Purifying Proetus' daughters, and their father
Proetus Abantades, and fifth, an old wife to boot,
So many people's persons with one torch, one squill,

> With sulphur and asphalt of the loud-sounding sea,
> From the placid-flowing, deep-flowing ocean.
> But blest air through the clouds send Anticyra
> That I may make this bug into a drone."

For well Menander remarks:—

> "Had you, O Phidias, any real ill,
> You needs must seek for it a real cure;
> Now 'tis not so. And for the unreal ill
> I've found an unreal cure. Believe that it
> Will do thee good. Let women in a ring
> Wipe thee, and from three fountains water bring.
> Add salt and lentils; sprinkle then thyself.
> Each one is pure, who's conscious of no sin."

For instance, the tragedy says:—

> *Menelaus.* "What disease, Orestes, is destroying thee?"
> *Orestes.* "Conscience. For horrid deeds I know I've done."

For in reality there is no other purity but abstinence from sins. Excellently then Epicharmus says:—

> "If a pure mind thou hast,
> In thy whole body thou art pure."

Now also we say that it is requisite to purify the soul from corrupt and bad doctrines by right reason; and so thereafter to the recollection of the principal heads of doctrine. Since also before the communication of the mysteries they think it right to apply certain purifications to those who are to be initiated; so it is requisite for men to abandon impious opinion, and thus turn to the true tradition.

CHAPTER V.—THE HOLY SOUL A MORE EXCELLENT TEMPLE THAN ANY EDIFICE BUILT BY MAN.

For is it not the case that rightly and truly we do not circumscribe in any place that which cannot be circumscribed; nor do we shut up in temples made with hands that which contains all things? What work of builders, and stonecutters, and mechanical art can be holy? Superior to these are not they who think that the air, and the enclosing space, or rather the whole world and the universe, are meet for the excellency of God?

It were indeed ridiculous, as the philosophers themselves say, for man, the plaything of God, to make God, and for God to be the plaything of art; since what is made is similar and the same to that of which it is made, as that which is made of ivory is ivory, and that which is made of gold golden. Now the images and temples constructed by mechanics are made of inert matter; so that they too are inert, and material, and profane; and if you perfect the art, they partake of mechanical coarseness. Works of art cannot then be sacred and divine.

And what can be localized, there being nothing that is not localized? Since all things are in a place. And that which is localized having been formerly not localized, is localized by something. If, then, God is localized by men, He was once not localized, and did not exist at all. For the non-existent is what is not localized; since whatever does not exist is not localized.

And what exists cannot be localized by what does not exist; nor by another entity. For it is also an entity. It follows that it must be by itself. And how shall anything generate itself? Or how shall that which exists place itself as to being? Whether, being formerly not localized, has it localized itself? But it was not in existence; since what exists not is not localized. And its localization being supposed, how can it afterwards make itself what it previously was?

But how can He, to whom the things that are belong, need anything? But were God possessed of a human form, He would need, equally with man, food, and shelter, and house, and the attendant incidents. Those who are like in form and affections will require similar sustenance. And if sacred (τo ἱερόν) has a twofold application, designating both God Himself and the structure raised to His honor, how shall we not with propriety call the Church holy, through knowledge, made for the honor of God, sacred (ἱερόν) to God, of great value, and not constructed by mechanical art, nor embellished by the hand of an impostor, but by the will of God fashioned into a temple? For it is not now the place, but the assemblage of the elect, that I call the Church. This temple is better for the reception of the greatness of the dignity of God. For the living creature which is of high value, is made sacred by that which is worth all, or rather which has no equivalent, in virtue of the exceeding sanctity of the latter. Now this is the Gnostic, who is of great value, who is honored by God, in whom God is enshrined, that is, the knowledge respecting God is consecrated. Here, too, we shall find the divine likeness and the holy image in the righteous soul, when it is blessed in being purified and performing blessed deeds. Here also we shall find that which is localized, and that which is being localized,—the former in the case of those who are already Gnostics, and the latter in the case of those capable of becoming so, although not yet worthy of receiving the knowledge of God. For every being destined to believe is already faithful in the sight of God, and set up for His honor, an image, endowed with virtue, dedicated to God.

CHAPTER VI.—PRAYERS AND PRAISE FROM A PURE MIND, CEASELESSLY OFFERED, FAR BETTER THAN SACRIFICES.

As, then, God is not circumscribed by place, neither is ever represented by the form of a living creature; so neither has He similar passions, nor has He wants like the creatures, so as to desire sacrifice, from hunger, by way of food. Those creatures which are affected by passion are all mortal. And it is useless to bring food to one who is not nourished.

And that comic poet Pherecrates, in *The Fugitives*, facetiously represents the gods themselves as finding fault with men on the score of their sacred rites:—

> "When to the gods you sacrifice,
> Selecting what our portion is,
> 'Tis shame to tell, do ye not take,
> And both the thighs, clean to the groins,
> The loins quite bare, the backbone, too,
> Clean scrape as with a file,
> Them swallow, and the remnant give
> To us as if to dogs? And then,
> As if of one another 'shamed,
> With heaps of salted barley hide."

And Eubulus, also a comic poet, thus writes respecting sacrifices:—

> "But to the gods the tail alone
> And thigh, as if to pæderasts you sacrifice."

And introducing Dionysus in Semele, he represents him disputing:—

> "First if they offer ought to me, there are
> Who offer blood, the bladder, not the heart
> Or call. For I no flesh do ever eat
> That's sweeter than the thigh."

And Menander writes:—

> "The end of the loin,
> The bile, the bones uneatable, they set
> Before the gods; the rest themselves consume."

Clement of Alexandria

For is not the savor of the holocausts avoided by the beasts? And if in reality the savor is the guerdon of the gods of the Greeks, should they not first deify the cooks, who are dignified with equal happiness, and worship the chimney itself, which is closer still to the much-prized savor?

And Hesiod says that Zeus, cheated in a division of flesh by Prometheus, received the white bones of an ox, concealed with cunning art, in shining fat:—

> "Whence to the immortal gods the tribes of men
> The victim's white bones on the altars burn."

But they will by no means say that the Deity, enfeebled through the desire that springs from want, is nourished. Accordingly, they will represent Him as nourished without desire like a plant, and like beasts that burrow. They say that these grow innoxiously, nourished either by the density in the air, or from the exhalations proceeding from their own body.
Though if the Deity, though needing nothing, is according to them nourished, what necessity has He for food, wanting nothing? But if, by nature needing nothing, He delights to be honored, it is not without reason that we honor God in prayer; and thus the best and holiest sacrifice with righteousness we bring, presenting it as an offering to the most righteous Word, by whom we receive knowledge, giving glory by Him for what we have learned.

The altar, then, that is with us here, the terrestrial one, is the congregation of those who devote themselves to prayers, having as it were one common voice and one mind.

Now, if nourishing substances taken in by the nostrils are diviner than those taken in by the mouth, yet they infer respiration. What, then, do they say of God? Whether does He exhale like the tribe of oaks? Or does He only inhale, like the aquatic animals, by the dilatation of their gills? Or does He breathe all round, like the insects, by the compression of the section by means of their wings? But no one, if he is in his senses, will liken God to any of these.

And the creatures that breathe by the expansion of the lung towards the thorax draw in the air. Then if they assign to God viscera, and arteries, and veins, and nerves, and parts, they will make Him in nothing different from man.

Now breathing together (σύμπνοια) is properly said of the Church. For the sacrifice of the Church is the word breathing as incense from holy souls, the sacrifice and the whole mind being at the same time unveiled to God. Now the very ancient altar in Delos they celebrated as holy; which alone, being undefiled by slaughter and death, they say Pythagoras approached. And will they not believe us when we say that the righteous soul is the truly sacred altar, and that incense arising from it is holy prayer? But I believe sacrifices were invented by men to be a pretext for eating flesh. But without such idolatry he who wished might have partaken of flesh.

For the sacrifices of the Law express figuratively the piety which we practice, as the turtle-dove and the pigeon offered for sins point out that the cleansing of the irrational part of the soul is acceptable to God. But if any one of the righteous does not burden his soul by the eating of flesh, he has the advantage of a rational reason, not as Pythagoras and his followers dream of the transmigration of the soul.

Now Xenocrates, treating by himself of "the food derived from animals," and Polemon in his work *On Life according to Nature*, seem clearly to say that animal food is unwholesome, inasmuch as it has already been elaborated and assimilated to the souls of the irrational creatures.

So also, in particular, the Jews abstain from swine's flesh on the ground of this animal being unclean; since more than the other animals it roots up, and destroys the productions of the ground. But if they say that the animals were assigned to men—and we agree with them—yet it was not entirely for food. Nor was it all animals, but such as do not work.

Wherefore the comic poet Plato says not badly in the drama of *The Feasts:* —

> "For of the quadrupeds we should not slay
> In future aught but swine. For these have flesh
> Most toothsome; and about the pig is naught
> For us, excepting bristles, mud, and noise."

Whence Æsop said not badly, that "swine squeaked out very loudly, because, when they were dragged, they knew that they were good for nothing but for sacrifice."

Wherefore also Cleanthes says, "that they have soul instead of salt," that their flesh may not putrefy. Some, then, eat them as useless, others as destructive of fruits. And others do not eat them, because the animal has a strong sensual propensity.

So, then, the law sacrifices not the goat, except in the sole case of the banishment of sins; since pleasure is the metropolis of vice. It is to the point also that it is said that the eating of goat's flesh contributes to epilepsy. And they say that the greatest increase is produced by swine's flesh. Wherefore it is beneficial to those who exercise the body; but to those who devote themselves to the development of the soul it is not so, on account of the hebetude that results from the eating of flesh. Perchance also some Gnostic will abstain from the eating of flesh for the sake of training, and in order that the flesh may not grow wanton in amorousness. "For wine," says Androcydes, "and gluttonous feeds of flesh make the body strong, but the soul more sluggish." Accordingly such food, in order to clear understanding, is to be rejected.

Wherefore also the Egyptians, in the purifications practiced among them, do not allow the priests to feed on flesh; but they use chickens, as lightest; and they do not touch fish, on account of certain fables, but especially on account of such food making the flesh flabby. But now terrestrial animals and birds breathe the same air as our vital spirits, being possessed of a vital principle cognate with the air. But it is said that fishes do not breathe this air, but that which was mixed with the water at the instant of its first creation, as well as with the rest of the elements, which is also a sign of the permanence of matter.

Wherefore we ought to offer to God sacrifices not costly, but such as He loves. And that compounded incense which is mentioned in the Law, is that which consists of many tongues and voices in prayer, or rather of different nations and natures, prepared by the gift vouchsafed in the dispensation for "the unity of the faith," and brought together in praises, with a pure mind, and just and right conduct, from holy works and righteous prayer. For in the elegant language of poetry,—

> "Who is so great a fool, and among men
> So very easy of belief, as thinks
> The gods, with fraud of fleshless bones and bile
> All burnt, not fit for hungry dogs to eat,
> Delighted are, and take this as their prize,
> And favor show to those who treat them thus,"

though they happen to be tyrants and robbers?

But we say that the fire sanctifies not flesh, but sinful souls; meaning not the all devouring vulgar fire but that of wisdom, which pervades the soul passing through the fire.

CHAPTER VII.—WHAT SORT OF PRAYER THE GNOSTIC EMPLOYS, AND HOW IT IS HEARD BY GOD.

Now we are commanded to reverence and to honor the same one, being persuaded that He is Word, Savior, and Leader, and by Him, the Father, not on special days, as some others, but doing this continually in our whole life, and in every way. Certainly the elect race justified by the precept says, "Seven times a day have I praised Thee." Whence not in a specified place, or selected temple, or at certain festivals and on appointed days, but during his whole life, the Gnostic in every place, even if he be alone by himself, and wherever he has any of those who have exercised the like faith, honors God, that is, acknowledges his gratitude for the knowledge of the way to live.

And if the presence of a good man, through the respect and reverence which he inspires, always improves him with whom he associates, with much more reason does not he who always holds uninterrupted converse with God by knowledge, life, and thanksgiving, grow at every step superior to himself in all respects—in conduct, in words, in disposition? Such a one is persuaded that God is ever beside him, and does not suppose that He is confined in certain limited places; so that under the idea that at times he is without Him, he may indulge in excesses night and day.

Holding festival, then, in our whole life, persuaded that God is altogether on every side present, we cultivate our fields, praising; we sail the sea, hymning; in all the rest of our conversation we conduct ourselves according to rule. The Gnostic, then, is very closely allied to God, being at once grave and cheerful in all things,—grave on account of the bent of his soul towards the Divinity, and cheerful on account of his consideration of the blessings of humanity which God hath given us.

Now the excellence of knowledge is evidently presented by the prophet when he says, "Benignity, and instruction, and knowledge teach me," magnifying the supremacy of perfection by a climax.

He is, then, the truly kingly man; he is the sacred high priest of God. And this is even now observed among the most sagacious of the Barbarians, in advancing the sacerdotal caste to the royal power. He, therefore, never surrenders himself to the rabble that rules supreme over the theatres, and gives no admittance even in a dream to the things which are spoken, done, and seen for the sake of alluring pleasures; neither, therefore, to the pleasures of sight, nor the various pleasures which are found in other enjoyments, as costly incense and odors, which bewitch the nostrils, or preparations of meats, and indulgences in different wines, which ensnare the palate, or fragrant bouquets of many flowers, which through the senses effeminate the soul. But always tracing up to God the grave enjoyment of all things, he offers the first-fruits of food, and drink, and unguents to the Giver of all, acknowledging his thanks in the gift and in the use of them by the Word given to him. He rarely goes to convivial banquets of all and sundry, unless the announcement to him of the friendly and harmonious character of the entertainment induce him to go. For he is convinced that God knows and perceives all things—not the words only, but also the thought; since even our sense of hearing, which acts through the passages of the body, has the apprehension [belonging to it] not through corporeal power, but through a psychical perception, and the intelligence which distinguishes significant sounds. God is not, then, possessed of human form, so as to hear; nor needs He senses, as the Stoics have decided, "especially hearing and sight; for He could never otherwise apprehend." But the susceptibility of the air, and the intensely keen perception of the angels, and the power which reaches the soul's consciousness, by ineffable power and without sensible hearing, know all things at the moment of thought. And should anyone say that the voice does not reach God, but is rolled downwards in the air, yet the thoughts of the saints cleave not the air only, but the whole world. And the divine power, with the speed of light, sees through the whole soul. Well! Do not also volitions speak to God, uttering their voice? And are they not conveyed by conscience? And what voice shall He wait for, who, according to His purpose, knows the elect already, even before his birth, knows what is to be as already existent? Does not the light of power shine down to the very bottom of the whole soul; "the lamp of knowledge," as the Scripture says, searching "the recesses"? God is all ear and all eye, if we may be permitted to use these expressions.

In general, then, an unworthy opinion of God preserves no piety, either in hymns, or discourses, or writings, or dogmas, but diverts to groveling and unseemly ideas and notions.

Whence the commendation of the multitude differs nothing from censure, in consequence of their ignorance of the truth. The objects, then, of desires and aspirations, and, in a word, of the mind's impulses, are the subjects of prayers. Wherefore, no man desires a draught, but to drink what is drinkable; and no man desires an inheritance, but to inherit. And in like manner no man desires knowledge, but to know; or a right government, but to take part in the government. The subjects of our prayers, then, are the subjects of our requests, and the subjects of requests are the objects of desires. Prayer, then, and desire, follow in order, with the view of possessing the blessings and advantages offered.

The Gnostic, then, who is such by possession, makes his prayer and request for the truly good things which appertain to the soul, and prays, he himself also contributing his efforts to attain to the habit of goodness, so as no longer to have the things that are good as certain lessons belonging to him, but to be good.

Wherefore also it is most incumbent on such to pray, knowing as they do the Divinity rightly, and having the moral excellence suitable to him; who know what things are really good, and what are to be asked, and when and how in each individual case. It is the extremest stupidity to ask of them who are no gods, as if they were gods; or to ask those things which are not beneficial, begging evils for themselves under the appearance of good things.

Whence, as is right, there being only one good God, that some good things be given from Him alone, and that some remain, we and the angels pray. But not similarly. For it is not the same thing to pray that the gift remain, and to endeavor to obtain it for the first time.

The averting of evils is a species of prayer; but such prayer is never to be used for the injury of men, except that the Gnostic, in devoting attention to righteousness, may make use of this petition in the case of those who are past feeling.

Prayer is, then, to speak more boldly, converse with God. Though whispering, consequently, and not opening the lips, we speak in silence, yet we cry inwardly. For God hears continually all the inward converse. So also we raise the head and lift the hands to heaven, and set the feet in motion at the closing utterance of the prayer, following the eagerness of the spirit directed towards the intellectual essence; and endeavoring to abstract the body from the earth, along with the discourse, raising the soul aloft, winged with longing for better things, we compel it to advance to the region of holiness, magnanimously despising the chain of the flesh. For we know right well, that the Gnostic willingly passes over the whole world, as the Jews certainly did over Egypt, showing clearly, above all, that he will be as near as possible to God.

Now, if some assign definite hours for prayer—as, for example, the third, and sixth, and ninth—yet the Gnostic prays throughout his whole life, endeavoring by prayer to have fellowship with God. And, briefly, having reached to this, he leaves behind him all that is of no service, as having now received the perfection of the man that acts by love. But the distribution of the hours into a threefold division, honored with as many prayers, those are acquainted with, who know the blessed triad of the holy abodes.

Having got to this point, I recollect the doctrines about there being no necessity to pray, introduced by certain of the heterodox, that is, the followers of the heresy of Prodicus. That they may not then be inflated with conceit about this godless wisdom of theirs, as if it were strange, let them learn that it was embraced before by the philosophers called Cyrenaics. Nevertheless, the unholy knowledge (*gnosis*) of those falsely called [Gnostics] shall meet with confutation at a fitting time; so that the assault on them, by no means brief, may not, by being introduced into the commentary, break the discourse in hand, in which we are showing that the only really holy and pious man is he who is truly a Gnostic according to the rule of the Church, to whom alone the petition made in accordance with the will of God is granted, on asking and on thinking. For as God can do all that He wishes, so the Gnostic receives all that he asks. For, universally, God knows those who are and those who are not worthy of good things; whence He gives to each what is suitable. Wherefore to those that are unworthy, though they ask often, He will not give; but He will give to those who are worthy.

Nor is petition superfluous, though good things are given without claim.

Now thanksgiving and request for the conversion of our neighbors is the function of the Gnostic; as also the Lord prayed, giving thanks for the accomplishment of His ministry, praying that as many as possible might attain to knowledge; that in the saved, by salvation, through knowledge, God might be glorified, and He who is alone good and alone Savior might be acknowledged through the Son from age to age. But also faith, that one will receive, is a species of prayer gnostically laid up in store.

But if any occasion of converse with God becomes prayer, no opportunity of access to God ought to be omitted. Without doubt, the holiness of the Gnostic, in union with [God's] blessed Providence, exhibits in voluntary confession the perfect beneficence of God. For the holiness of the Gnostic, and the reciprocal benevolence of the friend of God, are a kind of corresponding movement of providence. For neither is God involuntarily good, as the fire is warming; but in Him the imparting of good things is voluntary, even if He receive the request previously. Nor shall he who is saved be saved against his will, for he is not inanimate; but he will above all voluntarily and of free choice speed to salvation. Wherefore also man received the commandments in order that he might be self-impelled, to whatever he wished of things to be chosen and to be avoided. Wherefore God does not do good by necessity, but from His free choice benefits those who spontaneously turn. For the Providence which extends to us from God is not ministerial, as that service which proceeds from inferiors to superiors. But in pity for our weakness, the continual dispensations of Providence work, as the care of shepherds towards the sheep, and of a king towards his subjects; we ourselves also conducting ourselves obediently towards our superiors, who take the management of us, as appointed, in accordance with the commission from God with which they are invested.

Consequently those who render the most free and kingly service, which is the result of a pious mind and of knowledge, are servants and attendants of the Divinity. Each place, then, and time, in which we entertain the idea of God, is in reality sacred.

When, then, the man who chooses what is right, and is at the same time of thankful heart, makes his request in prayer, he contributes to the obtaining of it, gladly taking hold in prayer of the thing desired. For when the Giver of good things perceives the susceptibility on our part, all good things follow at once the conception of them. Certainly in prayer the character is sifted, how it stands with respect to duty.

But if voice and expression are given us, for the sake of understanding, how can God not hear the soul itself, and the mind, since assuredly soul hears soul, and mind, mind?
Whence God does not wait for loquacious tongues, as interpreters among men, but knows absolutely the thoughts of all; and what the voice intimates to us, that our thought, which even before the creation He knew would come into our mind, speaks to God. Prayer, then, may be uttered without the voice, by concentrating the whole spiritual nature within on expression by the mind, in un-distracted turning towards God.

And since the dawn is an image of the day of birth, and from that point the light which has shone forth at first from the darkness increases, there has also dawned on those involved in darkness a day of the knowledge of truth. In correspondence with the manner of the sun's rising, prayers are made looking towards the sunrise in the east. Whence also the most ancient temples looked towards the west, that people might be taught to turn to the east when facing the images. "Let my prayer be directed before Thee as incense, the uplifting of my hands as the evening sacrifice," say the Psalms.

In the case of wicked men, therefore, prayer is most injurious, not to others alone, but to themselves also. If, then, they should ask and receive what they call pieces of good fortune, these injure them after they receive them, being ignorant how to use them. For they pray to possess what they have not, and they ask things which seem, but are not, good things. But the Gnostic will ask the permanence of the things he possesses, adaptation for what is to take place, and the eternity of those things which he shall receive. And the things which are really good, the things which concern the soul, he prays that they may belong to him, and remain with him. And so he desires not anything that is absent, being content with what is present. For he is not deficient in the good things which are proper to him; being already sufficient for himself, through divine grace and knowledge. But having become sufficient in himself, he stands in no want of other things. But knowing the sovereign will, and possessing as soon as he prays, being brought into close contact with the almighty power, and earnestly desiring to be spiritual, through boundless love, he is united to the Spirit.

Thus he, being magnanimous, possessing, through knowledge, what is the most precious of all, the best of all, being quick in applying himself to contemplation, retains in his soul the permanent energy of the objects of his contemplation, that is the perspicacious keenness of knowledge. And this power he strives to his utmost to acquire, by obtaining command of all the influences which war against the mind; and by applying himself without intermission to speculation, by exercising himself in the training of abstinence from pleasures, and of right conduct in what he does; and besides, furnished with great experience both in study and in life, he has freedom of speech, not the power of a babbling tongue, but a power which employs plain language, and which neither for favor nor fear conceals aught of the things which may be worthily said at the fitting time, in which it is highly necessary to say them. He, then, having received the things respecting God from the mystic choir of the truth itself, employs language which urges the magnitude of virtue in accordance with its worth; and shows its results with an inspired elevation of prayer, being associated gnostically, as far as possible, with intellectual and spiritual objects.

Whence he is always mild and meek, accessible, affable, long-suffering, grateful, endued with a good conscience. Such a man is rigid, not alone so as not to be corrupted, but so as not to be tempted. For he never exposes his soul to submission, or capture at the hands of Pleasure and Pain. If the Word, who is Judge, call; he, having grown inflexible, and not indulging a whit the passions, walks unswervingly where justice advises him to go; being very well persuaded that all things are managed consummately well, and that progress to what is better goes on in the case of souls that have chosen virtue, till they come to the Good itself, to the Father's vestibule, so to speak, close to the great High Priest. Such is our Gnostic, faithful, persuaded that the affairs of the universe are managed in the best way. Particularly, he is well pleased with all that happens. In accordance with reason, then, he asks for none of those things in life required for necessary use; being persuaded that God, who knows all things, supplies the good with whatever is for their benefit, even though they do not ask.

For my view is, that as all things are supplied to the man of art according to the rules of art, and to the Gentile in a Gentile way, so also to the Gnostic all things are supplied gnostically. And the man who turns from among the Gentiles will ask for faith, while he that ascends to knowledge will ask for the perfection of love. And the Gnostic, who has reached the summit, will pray that contemplation may grow and abide, as the common man will for continual good health.

Nay, he will pray that he may never fall from virtue; giving his most strenuous co-operation in order that he may become infallible. For he knows that some of the angels, through carelessness, were hurled to the earth, not having yet quite reached that state of oneness, by extricating themselves from the propensity to that of duality.

But him, who from this has trained himself to the summit of knowledge and the elevated height of the perfect man, all things relating to time and place help on, now that he has made it his choice to live infallibly, and subjects himself to training in order to the attainment of the stability of knowledge on each side. But in the case of those in whom there is still a heavy corner, leaning downwards, even that part which has been elevated by faith is dragged down. In him, then, who by gnostic training has acquired virtue which cannot be lost, habit becomes nature. And just as weight in a stone, so the knowledge of such a one is incapable of being lost. Not without, but through the exercise of will, and by the force of reason, and knowledge, and Providence, is it brought to become incapable of being lost. Through care it becomes incapable of being lost. He will employ caution so as to avoid sinning, and consideration to prevent the loss of virtue.

Now knowledge appears to produce consideration, by teaching to perceive the things that are capable of contributing to the permanence of virtue. The highest thing is, then, the knowledge of God; wherefore also by it virtue is so preserved as to be incapable of being lost. And he who knows God is holy and pious. The Gnostic has consequently been demonstrated by us to be the only pious man.

He rejoices in good things present, and is glad on account of those promised, as if they were already present. For they do not elude his notice, as if they were still absent, because he knows by anticipation what sort they are. Being then persuaded by knowledge how each future thing shall be, he possesses it. For want and defect are measured with reference to what appertains to one. If, then, he possesses wisdom, and wisdom is a divine thing, he who partakes of what has no want will himself have no want. For the imparting of wisdom does not take place by activity and receptivity moving and stopping each other, or by aught being abstracted or becoming defective. Activity is therefore shown to be undiminished in the act of communication. So, then, our Gnostic possesses all good things, as far as possible; but not likewise in number; since otherwise he would be incapable of changing his place through the due inspired stages of advancement and acts of administration.

Him God helps, by honoring him with closer oversight. For were not all things made for the sake of good men, for their possession and advantage, or rather salvation? He will not then deprive, of the things which exist for the sake of virtue, those for whose sake they were created. For, evidently in honor of their excellent nature and their holy choice, he inspires those who have made choice of a good life with strength for the rest of their salvation; exhorting some, and helping others, who of themselves have become worthy. For all good is capable of being produced in the Gnostic; if indeed it is his aim to know and do everything intelligently. And as the physician ministers health to those who co-operate with him in order to health, so also God ministers eternal salvation to those who co-operate for the attainment of knowledge and good conduct; and since what the commandments enjoin are in our own power, along with the performance of them, the promise is accomplished.

And what follows seems to me to be excellently said by the Greeks. An athlete of no mean reputation among those of old, having for a long time subjected his body to thorough training in order to the attainment of manly strength, ongoing up to the Olympic games, cast his eye on the statue of the Pisæan Zeus, and said: "O Zeus, if all the requisite preparations for the contest have been made by me, come, give me the victory, as is right." For so, in the case of the Gnostic, who has unblameably and with a good conscience fulfilled all that depends on him, in the direction of learning, and training, and well-doing, and pleasing God, the whole contributes to carry salvation on to perfection. From us, then, are demanded the things which are in our own power, and of the things which pertain to us, both present and absent, the choice, and desire, and possession, and use, and permanence.

Wherefore also he who holds converse with God must have his soul immaculate and stainlessly pure, it being essential to have made himself perfectly good.

But also it becomes him to make all his prayers gently with the good. For it is a dangerous thing to take part in others' sins. Accordingly the Gnostic will pray along with those who have more recently believed, for those things in respect of which it is their duty to act together. And his whole life is a holy festival. His sacrifices are prayers, and praises, and readings in the Scriptures before meals, and psalms and hymns during meals and before bed, and prayers also again during night. By these he unites himself to the divine choir, from continual recollection, engaged in contemplation which has everlasting remembrance.

And what? Does he not also know the other kind of sacrifice, which consists in the giving both of doctrines and of money to those who need? Assuredly. But he does not use wordy prayer by his mouth; having learned to ask of the Lord what is requisite. In every place, therefore, but not ostensibly and visibly to the multitude, he will pray. But while engaged in walking, in conversation, while in silence, while engaged in reading and in works according to reason, he in every mood prays. If he but form the thought in the secret chamber of his soul, and call on the Father "with unspoken groaning," He is near, and is at his side, while yet speaking. Inasmuch as there are but three ends of all action, he does everything for its excellence and utility; but doing aught for the sake of pleasure, he leaves to those who pursue the common life.

CHAPTER VIII.—THE GNOSTIC SO ADDICTED TO TRUTH AS NOT TO NEED TO USE AN OATH.

The man of proved character in such piety is far from being apt to lie and to swear. For an oath is a decisive affirmation, with the taking of the divine name. For how can he, that is once faithful, show himself unfaithful, so as to require an oath; and so that his life may not be a sure and decisive oath? He lives, and walks, and shows the trustworthiness of his affirmation in an unwavering and sure life and speech. And if the wrong lies in the judgment of one who does and says [something], and not in the suffering of one who has been wronged, he will neither lie nor commit perjury so as to wrong the Deity, knowing that it by nature is incapable of being harmed. Nor yet will he lie or commit any transgression, for the sake of the neighbor whom he has learned to love, though he be not on terms of intimacy. Much more, consequently, will he not lie or perjure himself on his own account, since he never with his will can be found doing wrong to himself.

But he does not even swear, preferring to make averment, in affirmation by "yea," and in denial by "nay." For it is an oath to swear, or to produce anything from the mind in the way of confirmation in the shape of an oath. It suffices, then, with him, to add to an affirmation or denial the expression "I say truly," for confirmation to those who do not perceive the certainty of his answer. For he ought, I think, to maintain a life calculated to inspire confidence towards those without, so that an oath may not even be asked; and towards himself and those with whom he associates good feeling, which is voluntary righteousness.

The Gnostic swears truly, but is not apt to swear, having rarely recourse to an oath, just as we have said. And his speaking truth on oath arises from his accord with the truth. This speaking truth on oath, then, is found to be the result of correctness in duties. Where, then, is the necessity for an oath to him who lives in accordance with the extreme of truth? He, then, that does not even swear will be far from perjuring himself. And he who does not transgress in what is ratified by compacts, will never swear; since the ratification of the violation and of the fulfilment is by actions; as certainly lying and perjury in affirming and swearing are contrary to duty. But he who lives justly, transgressing in none of his duties, when the judgment of truth is scrutinized, swears truth by his acts. Accordingly, testimony by the tongue is in his case superfluous.

Therefore, persuaded always that God is everywhere, and fearing not to speak the truth, and knowing that it is unworthy of him to lie, he is satisfied with the divine consciousness and his own alone. And so he lies not, nor does aught contrary to his compacts. And so he swears not even when asked for his oath; nor does he ever deny, so as to speak falsehood, though he should die by tortures.

CHAPTER IX.—THOSE WHO TEACH OTHERS, OUGHT TO EXCEL IN VIRTUES.

The gnostic dignity is augmented and increased by him who has undertaken the first place in the teaching of others, and received the dispensation by word and deed of the greatest good on earth, by which he mediates contact and fellowship with the Divinity. And as those who worship terrestrial things pray to them as if they heard, confirming compacts before them; so, in men who are living images, the true majesty of the Word is received by the trustworthy teacher; and the beneficence exerted towards them is carried up to the Lord, after whose image he who is a true man by instruction creates and harmonizes, renewing to salvation the man who receives instruction. For as the Greeks called steel *Ares,* and wine *Dionysus,* on account of a certain relation; so the Gnostic considering the benefit of his neighbors as his own salvation, may be called a living image of the Lord, not as respects the peculiarity of form, but the symbol of power and similarity of preaching.

Whatever, therefore, he has in his mind, he bears on his tongue, to those who are worthy to hear, speaking as well as living from assent and inclination. For he both thinks and speaks the truth; unless at any time, medicinally, as a physician for the safety of the sick, he may deceive or tell an untruth, according to the Sophists.

To illustrate: the noble apostle circumcised Timothy, though loudly declaring and writing that circumcision made with hands profits nothing. But that he might not, by dragging all at once away from the law to the circumcision of the heart through faith those of the Hebrews who were reluctant listeners, compel them to break away from the synagogue, he, "accommodating himself to the Jews, became a Jew that he might gain all." He, then, who submits to accommodate himself merely for the benefit of his neighbors, for the salvation of those for whose sake he accommodates himself, not partaking in any dissimulation through the peril impending over the just from those who envy them, such a one by no means acts with compulsion. But for the benefit of his neighbors alone, he will do things which would not have been done by him primarily, if he did not do them on their account. Such a one gives himself for the Church, for the disciples whom he has begotten in faith; for an example to those who are capable of receiving the supreme economy of the philanthropic and God-loving Instructor, for confirmation of the truth of his words, for the exercise of love to the Lord. Such a one is unenslaved by fear, true in word, enduring in labor, never willing to lie by uttered word, and in it always securing sinlessness; since falsehood, being spoken with a certain deceit, is not an inert word, but operates to mischief.

On every hand, then, the Gnostic alone testifies to the truth in deed and word. For he always does rightly in all things, both in word and action, and in thought itself.

Such, then, to speak cursorily, is the piety of the Christian. If, then, he does these things according to duty and right reason, he does them piously and justly. And if such be the case, the Gnostic alone is really both pious, and just, and God-fearing.

The Christian is not impious. For this was the point incumbent on us to demonstrate to the philosophers; so that he will never in any way do aught bad or base (which is unjust). Consequently, therefore, he is not impious; but he alone fears God, holily and dutifully worshipping the true God, the universal Ruler, and King, and Sovereign, with the true piety.

CHAPTER X.—STEPS TO PERFECTION.

For knowledge (*gnosis*), to speak generally, a perfecting of man as man, is consummated by acquaintance with divine things, in character, life, and word, accordant and conformable to itself and to the divine Word. For by it faith is perfected, inasmuch as it is solely by it that the believer becomes perfect. Faith is an internal good, and without searching for God, confesses His existence, and glorifies Him as existent. Whence by starting from this faith, and being developed by it, through the grace of God, the knowledge respecting Him is to be acquired as far as possible.

Now we assert that knowledge (*gnosis*) differs from the wisdom (σοφία), which is the result of teaching. For as far as anything is knowledge, so far is it certainly wisdom; but in as far as aught is wisdom, it is not certainly knowledge. For the term wisdom appears only in the knowledge of the uttered word.

But it is not doubting in reference to God, but believing, that is the foundation of knowledge. But Christ is both the foundation and the superstructure, by whom are both the beginning and the ends. And the extreme points, the beginning and the end—I mean faith and love—are not taught. But knowledge, conveyed from communication through the grace of God as a deposit, is entrusted to those who show themselves worthy of it; and from it the worth of love beams forth from light to light. For it is said, "To him that hath shall be given:" to faith, knowledge; and to knowledge, love; and to love, the inheritance.

And this takes place, whenever one hangs on the Lord by faith, by knowledge, by love, and ascends along with Him to where the God and guard of our faith and love is. Whence at last (on account of the necessity for very great preparation and previous training in order both to hear what is said, and for the composure of life, and for advancing intelligently to a point beyond the righteousness of the law) it is that knowledge is committed to those fit and selected for it. It leads us to the endless and perfect end, teaching us beforehand the future life that we shall lead, according to God, and with gods; after we are freed from all punishment and penalty which we undergo, in consequence of our sins, for salutary discipline. After which redemption the reward and the honors are assigned to those who have become perfect; when they have got done with purification, and ceased from all service, though it be holy service, and among saints. Then become pure in heart, and near to the Lord, there awaits them restoration to everlasting contemplation; and they are called by the appellation of gods, being destined to sit on thrones with the other gods that have been first put in their places by the Savior.

Knowledge is therefore quick in purifying, and fit for that acceptable transformation to the better. Whence also with ease it removes [the soul] to what is akin to the soul, divine and holy, and by its own light conveys man through the mystic stages of advancement; till it restores the pure in heart to the crowning place of rest; teaching to gaze on God, face to face, with knowledge and comprehension. For in this consists the perfection of the Gnostic soul, in its being with the Lord, where it is in immediate subjection to Him, after rising above all purification and service.

Faith is then, so to speak, a comprehensive knowledge of the essentials; and knowledge is the strong and sure demonstration of what is received by faith, built upon faith by the Lord's teaching, conveying [the soul] on to infallibility, science, and comprehension. And, in my view, the first saving change is that from heathenism to faith, as I said before; and the second, that from faith to knowledge. And the latter terminating in love, thereafter gives the loving to the loved, that which knows to that which is known. And, perchance, such an one has already attained the condition of "being equal to the angels." Accordingly, after the highest excellence in the flesh, changing always duly to the better, he urges his flight to the ancestral hall, through the holy septenniad [of heavenly abodes] to the Lord's own mansion; to be a light, steady, and continuing eternally, entirely and in every part immutable.

The first mode of the Lord's operation mentioned by us is an exhibition of the recompense resulting from piety. Of the very great number of testimonies that there are, I shall adduce one, thus summarily expressed by the prophet David: "Who shall ascend to the hill of the Lord, or who shall stand in His holy place? He who is guiltless in his hands, and pure in his heart; who hath not lifted up his soul to vanity, or sworn deceitfully to his neighbor. He shall receive blessing from the Lord, and mercy from God his Savior. This is the generation of them that seek the Lord, that seek the face of the God of Jacob." The prophet has, in my opinion, concisely indicated the Gnostic. David, as appears, has cursorily demonstrated the Savior to be God, by calling Him "the face of the God of Jacob," who preached and taught concerning the Spirit. Wherefore also the apostle designates as "the express image (χαρακτῆρα) of the glory of the Father" the Son, who taught the truth respecting God, and expressed the fact that the Almighty is the one and only God and Father, "whom no man knows but the Son, and he to whom the Son shall reveal Him." That God is one is intimated by those "who seek the face of the God of Jacob;" whom being the only God, our Savior and God characterizes as the Good Father. And "the generation of those that seek Him" is the elect race, devoted to inquiry after knowledge. Wherefore also the apostle says, "I shall profit you nothing, unless I speak to you, either by revelation, or by knowledge, or by prophecy, or by doctrine."

Although even by those who are not Gnostics some things are done rightly, yet not according to reason; as in the case of fortitude. For some who are naturally high-spirited, and have afterwards without reason fostered this disposition, rush to many things, and act like brave men, so as sometimes to succeed in achieving the same things; just as endurance is easy for mechanics. But it is not from the same cause, or with the same object; not were they to give their whole body. "For they have not love," according to the apostle.

All the action, then, of a man possessed of knowledge is right action; and that done by a man not possessed of knowledge is wrong action, though he observe a plan; since it is not from reflection that he acts bravely, nor does he direct his action in those things which proceed from virtue to virtue, to any useful purpose.

The same holds also with the other virtues. So too the analogy is preserved in religion. Our Gnostic, then, not only is such in reference to holiness; but corresponding to the piety of knowledge are the commands respecting the rest of the conduct of life. For it is our purpose at present to describe the life of the Gnostic, not to present the system of dogmas, which we shall afterwards explain at the fitting time, preserving the order of topics.

CHAPTER XI.—DESCRIPTION OF THE GNOSTIC'S LIFE.

Respecting the universe, he conceives truly and grandly in virtue of his reception of divine teaching. Beginning, then, with admiration of the Creation, and affording of himself a proof of his capability for receiving knowledge, he becomes a ready pupil of the Lord. Directly on hearing of God and Providence, he believed in consequence of the admiration he entertained. Through the power of impulse thence derived he devotes his energies in every way to learning, doing all those things by means of which he shall be able to acquire the knowledge of what he desires. And desire blended with inquiry arises as faith advances. And this is to become worthy of speculation, of such a character, and such importance. So shall the Gnostic taste of the will of God. For it is not his ears, but his soul, that he yields up to the things signified by what is spoken. Accordingly, apprehending essences and things through the words, he brings his soul, as is fit, to what is essential; apprehending (e.g.) in the peculiar way in which they are spoken to the Gnostic, the commands, "Do not commit adultery," "Do not kill;" and not as they are understood by other people. Training himself, then, in scientific speculation, he proceeds to exercise himself in larger generalizations and grander propositions; knowing right well that "He that teaches man knowledge," according to the prophet, is the Lord, the Lord acting by man's mouth. So also He assumed flesh.

As is right, then, he never prefers the pleasant to the useful; not even if a beautiful woman were to entice him, when overtaken by circumstances, by wantonly urging him: since Joseph's master's wife was not able to seduce him from his steadfastness; but as she violently held his coat, divested himself of it,—becoming bare of sin, but clothed with seemliness of character. For if the eyes of the master—the Egyptian, I mean—saw not Joseph, yet those of the Almighty looked on. For we hear the voice, and see the bodily forms; but God scrutinizes the thing itself, from which the speaking and the looking proceed.

Consequently, therefore, though disease, and accident, and what is most terrible of all, death, come upon the Gnostic, he remains inflexible in soul,—knowing that all such things are a necessity of creation, and that, also by the power of God, they become the medicine of salvation, benefiting by discipline those who are difficult to reform; allotted according to desert, by Providence, which is truly good.

Using the creatures, then, when the Word prescribes, and to the extent it prescribes, in the exercise of thankfulness to the Creator, he becomes master of the enjoyment of them.

He never cherishes resentment or harbors a grudge against any one, though deserving of hatred for his conduct.

For he worships the Maker, and loves him, who shares life, pitying and praying for him on account of his ignorance. He indeed partakes of the affections of the body, to which, susceptible as it is of suffering by nature, he is bound. But in sensation he is not the primary subject of it.

Accordingly, then, in involuntary circumstances, by withdrawing himself from troubles to the things which really belong to him, he is not carried away with what is foreign to him. And it is only to things that are necessary for him that he accommodates himself, in so far as the soul is preserved unharmed. For it is not in supposition or seeming that he wishes to be faithful; but in knowledge and truth, that is, in sure deed and effectual word. Wherefore he not only praises what is noble, but endeavors himself to be noble; changing by love from a good and faithful servant into a friend, through the perfection of habit, which he has acquired in purity from true instruction and great discipline.

Striving, then, to attain to the summit of knowledge (*gnosis*); decorous in character; composed in mien; possessing all those advantages which belong to the true Gnostic; fixing his eye on fair models, on the many patriarchs who have lived rightly, and on very many prophets and angels reckoned without number, and above all, on the Lord, who taught and showed it to be possible for him to attain that highest life of all,—he therefore loves not all the good things of the world, which are within his grasp, that he may not remain on the ground, but the things hoped for, or rather already known, being hoped for so as to be apprehended.

So then he undergoes toils, and trials, and afflictions, not as those among the philosophers who are endowed with manliness, in the hope of present troubles ceasing, and of sharing again in what is pleasant; but knowledge has inspired him with the firmest persuasion of receiving the hopes of the future. Wherefore he contemns not alone the pains of this world, but all its pleasures.

They say, accordingly, that the blessed Peter, on seeing his wife led to death, rejoiced on account of her call and conveyance home, and called very encouragingly and comfortingly, addressing her by name, "Remember thou the Lord." Such was the marriage of the blessed and their perfect disposition towards those dearest to them.

Thus also the apostle says, "that he who marries should be as though he married not," and deem his marriage free of inordinate affection, and inseparable from love to the Lord; to which the true husband exhorted his wife to cling on her departure out of this life to the Lord.

Was not then faith in the hope after death conspicuous in the case of those who gave thanks to God even in the very extremities of their punishments? For firm, in my opinion, was the faith they possessed, which was followed by works of faith.

In all circumstances, then, is the soul of the Gnostic strong, in a condition of extreme health and strength, like the body of an athlete.

For he is prudent in human affairs, in judging what ought to be done by the just man; having obtained the principles from God from above, and having acquired, in order to the divine resemblance, moderation in bodily pains and pleasures. And he struggles against fears boldly, trusting in God. Certainly, then, the gnostic soul, adorned with perfect virtue, is the earthly image of the divine power; its development being the joint result of nature, of training, of reason, all together. This beauty of the soul becomes a temple of the Holy Spirit, when it acquires a disposition in the whole of life corresponding to the Gospel. Such an one consequently withstands all fear of everything terrible, not only of death, but also poverty and disease, and ignominy, and things akin to these; being unconquered by pleasure, and lord over irrational desires. For he well knows what is and what is not to be done; being perfectly aware what things are really to be dreaded, and what not. Whence he bears intelligently what the Word intimates to him to be requisite and necessary; intelligently discriminating what is really safe (that is, good), from what appears so; and things to be dreaded from what seems so, such as death, disease, and poverty; which are rather so in opinion than in truth.

This is the really good man, who is without passions; having, through the habit or disposition of the soul endued with virtue, transcended the whole life of passion. He has everything dependent on himself for the attainment of the end. For those accidents which are called terrible are not formidable to the good man, because they are not evil. And those which are really to be dreaded are foreign to the gnostic Christian, being diametrically opposed to what is good, because evil; and it is impossible for contraries to meet in the same person at the same time. He, then, who faultlessly acts the drama of life which God has given him to play, knows both what is to be done and what is to be endured.

Is it not then from ignorance of what is and what is not to be dreaded that cowardice arises? Consequently the only man of courage is the Gnostic, who knows both present and future good things; along with these, knowing, as I have said, also the things which are in reality not to be dreaded. Because, knowing vice alone to be hateful, and destructive of what contributes to knowledge, protected by the armor of the Lord, he makes war against it.

For if anything is caused through folly, and the operation or rather co-operation of the devil, this thing is not straightway the devil or folly. For no action is wisdom. For wisdom is a habit. And no action is a habit. The action, then, that arises from ignorance, is not already ignorance, but an evil through ignorance, but not ignorance. For neither perturbations of mind nor sins are vices, though proceeding from vice.

No one, then, who is irrationally brave is a Gnostic; since one might call children brave, who, through ignorance of what is to be dreaded, undergo things that are frightful.
So they touch fire even. And the wild beasts that rush close on the points of spears, having a brute courage, might be called

valiant. And such people might perhaps call jugglers valiant, who tumble on swords with a certain dexterity, practicing a mischievous art for sorry gain. But he who is truly brave, with the peril arising from the bad feeling of the multitude before his eyes, courageously awaits whatever comes. In this way he is distinguished from others that are called martyrs, inasmuch as some furnish occasions for themselves, and rush into the heart of dangers, I know not how (for it is right to use mild language); while they, in accordance with right reason, protect themselves; then, on God really calling them, promptly surrender themselves, and confirm the call, from being conscious of no precipitancy, and present the man to be proved in the exercise of true rational fortitude. Neither, then, enduring lesser dangers from fear of greater, like other people, nor dreading censure at the hands of their equals, and those of like sentiments, do they continue in the confession of their calling; but from love to God they willingly obey the call, with no other aim in view than pleasing God, and not for the sake of the reward of their toils.

For some suffer from love of glory, and others from fear of some other sharper punishment, and others for the sake of pleasures and delights after death, being children in faith; blessed indeed, but not yet become men in love to God, as the Gnostic is. For there are, as in the gymnastic contests, so also in the Church, crowns for men and for children. But love is to be chosen for itself, and for nothing else. Therefore in the Gnostic, along with knowledge, the perfection of fortitude is developed from the discipline of life, he having always studied to acquire mastery over the passions.

Accordingly, love makes its own athlete fearless and dauntless, and confident in the Lord, anointing and training him; as righteousness secures for him truthfulness in his whole life. For it was a compendium of righteousness to say, "Let your yea be yea; and your nay, nay."

And the same holds with self-control. For it is neither for love of honor, as the athletes for the sake of crowns and fame; nor on the other hand, for love of money, as some pretend to exercise self-control, pursuing what is good with terrible suffering. Nor is it from love of the body for the sake of health. Nor any more is any man who is temperate from rusticity, who has not tasted pleasures, truly a man of self-control. Certainly those who have led a laborious life, on tasting pleasures, forthwith break down the inflexibility of temperance into pleasures. Such are they who are restrained by law and fear. For on finding a favorable opportunity they defraud the law, by giving what is good the slip. But self-control, desirable for its own sake, perfected through knowledge, abiding ever, makes the man lord and master of himself; so that the Gnostic is temperate and passionless, incapable of being dissolved by pleasures and pains, as they say adamant is by fire.

The cause of these, then, is love, of all science the most sacred and most sovereign.

For by the service of what is best and most exalted, which is characterized by unity, it renders the Gnostic at once friend and son, having in truth grown "a perfect man, up to the measure of full stature."

Further, agreement in the same thing is consent. But what is the same is one. And friendship is consummated in likeness; the community lying in oneness. The Gnostic, consequently, in virtue of being a lover of the one true God, is the really perfect man and friend of God, and is placed in the rank of son. For these are names of nobility and knowledge, and perfection in the contemplation of God; which crowning step of advancement the gnostic soul receives, when it has become quite pure, reckoned worthy to behold everlastingly God Almighty, "face," it is said, "to face." For having become wholly spiritual, and having in the spiritual Church gone to what is of kindred nature, it abides in the rest of God.

CHAPTER XII.—THE TRUE GNOSTIC IS BENEFICENT, CONTINENT, AND DESPISES WORLDLY THINGS.

Let these things, then, be so. And such being the attitude of the Gnostic towards the body and the soul—towards his neighbors, whether it be a domestic, or a lawful enemy, or whosoever—he is found equal and like. For he does not "despise his brother," who, according to the divine law, is of the same father and mother. Certainly he relieves the afflicted, helping him with consolations, encouragements, and the necessaries of life; giving to all that need, though not similarly, but justly, according to desert; furthermore, to him who persecutes and hates, even if he need it; caring little for those who say to him that he has given out of fear, if it is not out of fear that he does so, but to give help. For how much more are those, who towards their enemies are devoid of love of money, and are haters of evil, animated with love to those who belong to them?

Such a one from this proceeds to the accurate knowledge of whom he ought chiefly to give to, and how much, and when, and how.

And who could with any reason become the enemy of a man who gives no cause for enmity in any way? And is it not just as in the case of God? We say that God is the adversary of no one, and the enemy of no one (for He is the Creator of all, and nothing that exists is what He wills it not to be; but we assert that the disobedient, and those who walk not according to His commandments, are enemies to Him, as being those who are hostile to His covenant). We shall find the very same to be the case with the Gnostic, for he can never in anyway become an enemy to any one; but those may be regarded enemies to him who turn to the contrary path.

In particular, the habit of liberality which prevails among us is called "righteousness;" but the power of discriminating according to desert, as to greater and less, with reference to those who am proper subjects of it, is a form of the very highest righteousness.

There are things practiced in a vulgar style by some people, such as control over pleasures. For as, among the heathen, there are those who, from the impossibility of obtaining what one sees, and from fear of men, and also for the sake of greater pleasures, abstain from the delights that are before them; so also, in the case of faith, some practice self-restraint, either out of regard to the promise or from fear of God. Well, such self-restraint is the basis of knowledge, and an approach to something better, and an effort after perfection. For "the fear of the Lord," it is said, "is the beginning of wisdom." But the perfect man, out of love, "bears all things, endures all things," "as not pleasing man, but God." Although praise follows him as a consequence, it is not for his own advantage, but for the imitation and benefit of those who praise him.

According to another view, it is not he who merely controls his passions that is called a continent man, but he who has also achieved the mastery over good things, and has acquired surely the great accomplishments of science, from which he produces as fruits the activities of virtue. Thus the Gnostic is never, on the occurrence of an emergency, dislodged from the habit peculiar to him. For the scientific possession of what is good is firm and unchangeable, being the knowledge of things divine and human. Knowledge, then, never becomes ignorance nor does good change into evil. Wherefore also he eats, and drinks, and marries, not as principal ends of existence, but as necessary. I name marriage even, if the Word prescribe, and as is suitable. For having become perfect, he has the apostles for examples; and one is not really shown to be a man in the choice of single life; but he surpasses men, who, disciplined by marriage, procreation of children, and care for the house, without pleasure or pain, in his solicitude for the house has been inseparable from God's love, and withstood all temptation arising through children, and wife, and domestics, and possessions. But he that has no family is in a great degree free of temptation. Caring, then, for himself alone, he is surpassed by him who is inferior, as far as his own personal salvation is concerned, but who is superior in the conduct of life, preserving certainly, in his care for the truth, a minute image.

But we must as much as possible subject the soul to varied preparatory exercise, that it may become susceptible to the reception of knowledge. Do you not see how wax is softened and copper purified, in order to receive the stamp applied to it? Just as death is the separation of the soul from the body, so is knowledge as it were the rational death urging the spirit away, and separating it from the passions, and leading it on to the life of well-doing, that it may then say with confidence to God, "I live as Thou wishes." For he who makes it his purpose to please men cannot please God, since the multitude choose not what is profitable, but what is pleasant. But in pleasing God, one as a consequence gets the favor of the good among men. How, then, can what relates to meat, and drink, and amorous pleasure, be agreeable to such an one? since he views with suspicion even a word that produces pleasure, and a pleasant movement and act of the mind. "For no one can serve two masters, God and Mammon," it is said; meaning not simply money, but the resources arising from money bestowed on various pleasures. In reality, it is not possible for him who magnanimously and truly knows God, to serve antagonistic pleasures.

There is one alone, then, who from the beginning was free of concupiscence—the philanthropic Lord, who for us became man. And whosoever endeavor to be assimilated to the impress given by Him, strive, from exercise, to become free of concupiscence. For he who has exercised concupiscence and then restrained himself, is like a widow who becomes again a virgin by continence. Such is the reward of knowledge, rendered to the Savior and Teacher, which He Himself asked for,—abstinence from what is evil, activity in doing good, by which salvation is acquired.

As, then, those who have learned the arts procure their living by what they have been taught, so also is the Gnostic saved, procuring life by what he knows. For he who has not formed the wish to extirpate the passion of the soul, kills himself. But, as seems, ignorance is the starvation of the soul, and knowledge its sustenance.

Such are the gnostic souls, which the Gospel likened to the consecrated virgins who wait for the Lord. For they are virgins, in respect of their abstaining from what is evil. And in respect of their waiting out of love for the Lord and kindling their light for the contemplation of things, they are wise souls, saying, "Lord, for long we have desired to receive Thee; we have lived according to what Thou hast enjoined, transgressing none of Thy commandments. Wherefore also we claim the promises. And we pray for what is beneficial, since it is not requisite to ask of Thee what is most excellent. And we shall take everything for good; even though the exercises that meet us, which Thine arrangement brings to us for the discipline of our steadfastness, appear to be evil."

The Gnostic, then, from his exceeding holiness, is better prepared to fail when he asks, than to get when he does not ask.

His whole life is prayer and converse with God. And if he be pure from sins, he will by all means obtain what he wishes. For God says to the righteous man, "Ask, and I will give thee; think, and I will do." If beneficial, he will receive it at once; and if injurious, he will never ask it, and therefore he will not receive it. So it shall be as he wishes.

But if one say to us, that some sinners even obtain according to their requests, [we should say] that this rarely takes place, by reason of the righteous goodness of God. And it is granted to those who are capable of doing others good. Whence the gift is not made for the sake of him that asked it; but the divine dispensation, foreseeing that one would be saved by his means, renders the boon again righteous. And to those who are worthy, things which are really good are given, even without their asking.

Whenever, then, one is righteous, not from necessity or out of fear or hope, but from free choice, this is called the royal road, which the royal race travel. But the byways are slippery and precipitous. If, then, one take away fear and honor, I do not know if the illustrious among the philosophers, who use such freedom of speech, will any longer endure afflictions.

Now lusts and other sins are called "briars and thorns." Accordingly the Gnostic labors in the Lord's vineyard, planting, pruning, watering; being the divine husbandman of what is planted in faith. Those, then, who have not done evil, think it right to receive the wages of ease. But he who has done good out of free choice, demands the recompense as a good workman. He certainly shall receive double wages—both for what he has not done, and for what good he has done.

Such a Gnostic is tempted by no one except with God's permission, and that for the benefit of those who are with him; and he strengthens them for faith, encouraging them by manly endurance. And assuredly it was for this end, for the establishment and confirmation of the Churches, that the blessed apostles were brought into trial and to martyrdom.

The Gnostic, then, hearing a voice ringing in his ear, which says, "Whom I shall strike, do thou pity," beseeches that those who hate him may repent. For the punishment of malefactors, to be consummated in the highways, is for children to behold; for there is no possibility of the Gnostic, who has from choice trained himself to be excellent and good, ever being instructed or delighted with such spectacles. And so, having become incapable of being softened by pleasures, and never falling into sins, he is not corrected by the examples of other men's sufferings. And far from being pleased with earthly pleasures and spectacles is he who has shown a noble contempt for the prospects held out in this world, although they are divine.

"Not everyone," therefore, "that says Lord, Lord, shall enter into the kingdom of God; but he that doeth the will of God." Such is the gnostic laborer, who has the mastery of worldly desires even while still in the flesh; and who, in regard to things future and still invisible, which he knows, has a sure persuasion, so that he regards them as more present than the things within reach. This able workman rejoices in what he knows, but is cramped on account of his being involved in the necessities of life; not yet deemed worthy of the active participation in what he knows. So he uses this life as if it belonged to another,—so far, that is, as is necessary.

He knows also the enigmas of the fasting of those days—I mean the Fourth and the Preparation. For the one has its name from Hermes, and the other from Aphrodite. He fasts in his life, in respect of covetousness and voluptuousness, from which all the vices grow. For we have already often above shown the three varieties of fornication, according to the apostle—love of pleasure, love of money, idolatry. He fasts, then, according to the Law, abstaining from bad deeds, and, according to the perfection of the Gospel, from evil thoughts.
Temptations are applied to him, not for his purification, but, as we have said, for the good of his neighbors, if, making trial of toils and pains, he has despised and passed them by.

The same holds of pleasure. For it is the highest achievement for one who has had trial of it, afterwards to abstain. For what great thing is it, if a man restrains himself in what he knows not? He, in fulfilment of the precept, according to the Gospel, keeps the Lord's day, when he abandons an evil disposition, and assumes that of the Gnostic, glorifying the Lord's resurrection in himself. Further, also, when he has received the comprehension of scientific speculation, he deems that he sees the Lord, directing his eyes towards things invisible, although he seems to look on what he does not wish to look on; chastising the faculty of vision, when he perceives himself pleasurably affected by the application of his eyes; since he wishes to see and hear that alone which concerns him.

In the act of contemplating the souls of the brethren, he beholds the beauty of the flesh also, with the soul itself, which has become habituated to look solely upon that which is good, without carnal pleasure. And they are really brethren; inasmuch as, by reason of their elect creation, and their oneness of character, and the nature of their deeds, they do, and think, and speak the same holy and good works, in accordance with the sentiments with which the Lord wished them as elect to be inspired.

For faith shows itself in their making choice of the same things; and knowledge, in learning and thinking the same things; and hope, in desiring the same things.

And if, through the necessity of life, he spend a small portion of time about his sustenance, he thinks himself defrauded, being diverted by business. Thus not even in dreams does he look on aught that is unsuitable to an elect man. For thoroughly a stranger and sojourner in the whole of life is every such one, who, inhabiting the city, despises the things in the city which are admired by others, and lives in the city as in a desert, so that the place may not compel him, but his mode of life show him to be just.

This Gnostic, to speak compendiously, makes up for the absence of the apostles, by the rectitude of his life, the accuracy of his knowledge, by benefiting his relations, by "removing the mountains" of his neighbors, and putting away the irregularities of their soul. Although each of us is his own vineyard and laborer.

He, too, while doing the most excellent things, wishes to elude the notice of men, persuading the Lord along with himself that he is living in accordance with the commandments, preferring these things from believing them to exist. "For where any one's mind is, there also is his treasure."

He impoverishes himself, in order that he may never overlook a brother who has been brought into affliction, through the perfection that is in love, especially if he know that he will bear want himself easier than his brother. He considers, accordingly, the other's pain his own grief; and if, by contributing from his own indigence in order to do good, he suffer any hardship, he does not fret at this, but augments his beneficence still more. For he possesses in its sincerity the faith which is exercised in reference to the affairs of life, and praises the Gospel in practice and contemplation. And, in truth, he wins his praise "not from men, but from God," by the performance of what the Lord has taught.

He, attracted by his own hope, tastes not the good things that are in the world, entertaining a noble contempt for all things here; pitying those that are chastised after death, who through punishment unwillingly make confession; having a clear conscience with reference to his departure, and being always ready, as "a stranger and pilgrim," with regard to the inheritances here; mindful only of those that are his own, and regarding all things here as not his own; not only admiring the Lord's commandments, but, so to speak, being by knowledge itself partaker of the divine will; a truly chosen intimate of the Lord and His commands in virtue of being righteous; and princely and kingly as being a Gnostic; despising all the gold on earth and under the earth, and dominion from shore to shore of ocean, so that he may cling to the sole service of the Lord. Wherefore also, in eating, and drinking, and marrying (if the Word enjoin), and even in seeing dreams, he does and thinks what is holy.

So is he always pure for prayer. He also prays in the society of angels, as being already of angelic rank, and he is never out of their holy keeping; and though he pray alone, he has the choir of the saints standing with him.

He recognizes a twofold [element in faith], both the activity of him who believes, and the excellence of that which is believed according to its worth; since also righteousness is twofold, that which is out of love, and that from fear. Accordingly it is said, "The fear of the Lord is pure, remaining for ever and ever." For those that from fear turn to faith and righteousness, remain forever. Now fear works abstinence from what is evil; but love exhorts to the doing of good, by building up to the point of spontaneousness; that one may hear from the Lord, "I call you no longer servants, but friends," and may now with confidence apply himself to prayer.

And the form of his prayer is thanksgiving for the past, for the present, and for the future as already through faith present. This is preceded by the reception of knowledge. And he asks to live the allotted life in the flesh as a Gnostic, as free from the flesh, and to attain to the best things, and flee from the worse. He asks, too, relief in those things in which we have sinned, and conversion to the acknowledgment of them.

He follows, on his departure, Him who calls, as quickly, so to speak, as He who goes before calls, hasting by reason of a good conscience to give thanks; and having got there with Christ shows himself worthy, through his purity, to possess, by a process of blending, the power of God communicated by Christ. For he does not wish to be warm by participation in heat, or luminous by participation in flame, but to be wholly light.

He knows accurately the declaration, "Unless ye hate father and mother, and besides your own life, and unless ye bear the sign [of the cross]." For he hates the inordinate affections of the flesh, which possess the powerful spell of pleasure; and entertains a noble contempt for all that belongs to the creation and nutriment of the flesh. He also withstands the corporeal soul, putting a bridle-bit on the restive irrational spirit: "For the flesh lusted against the Spirit." And "to bear the sign of [the cross]" is to bear about death, by taking farewell of all things while still alive; since there is not equal love in "having sown the flesh," and in having formed the soul for knowledge.

He having acquired the habit of doing good, exercises beneficence well, quicker than speaking; praying that he may get a share in the sins of his brethren, in order to confession and conversion on the part of his kindred; and eager to give a share to those dearest to him of his own good things. And so these are to him, friends. Promoting, then, the growth of the seeds deposited in him, according to the husbandry enjoined by the Lord, he continues free of sin, and becomes continent, and lives in spirit with those who are like him, among the choirs of the saints, though still detained on earth.

He, all day and night, speaking and doing the Lord's commands, rejoices exceedingly, not only on rising in the morning and at noon, but also when walking about, when asleep, when dressing and undressing; and he teaches his son, if he has a son. He is inseparable from the commandment and from hope, and is ever giving thanks to God, like the living creatures figuratively spoken of by Esaias, and submissive in every trial, he says, "The Lord gave, and the Lord hath taken away." For such also was Job; who after the spoiling of his effects, along with the health of his body, resigned all through love to the Lord. For "he was," it is said, "just, holy, and kept apart from all wickedness." Now the word "holy" points out all duties toward God, and the entire course of life. Knowing which, he was a Gnostic. For we must neither cling too much to such things, even if they are good, seeing they are human, nor on the other hand detest them, if they are bad; but we must be above both [good and bad], trampling the latter under foot, and passing on the former to those who need them. But the Gnostic is cautious in accommodation, lest he be not perceived, or lest the accommodation become disposition.

CHAPTER XIII.—DESCRIPTION OF THE GNOSTIC CONTINUED.

He never remembers those who have sinned against him, but forgives them. Wherefore also he righteously prays, saying, "Forgive us; for we also forgive." For this also is one of the things which God wishes, to covet nothing, to hate no one. For all men are the work of one will. And is it not the Savior, who wishes the Gnostic to be perfect as "the heavenly
Father," that is, Himself, who says, "Come, ye children, hear from me the fear of the Lord?" He wishes him no longer to stand in need of help by angels, but to receive it from Himself, having become worthy, and to have protection from Himself by obedience.

Such a one demands from the Lord, and does not merely ask. And in the case of his brethren in want, the Gnostic will not ask himself for abundance of wealth to bestow, but will pray that the supply of what they need may be furnished to them. For so the Gnostic gives his prayer to those who are in need, and by his prayer they are supplied, without his knowledge, and without vanity.

Penury and disease, and such trials, are often sent for admonition, for the correction of the past, and for care for the future. Such a one prays for relief from them, in virtue of possessing the prerogative of knowledge, not out of vainglory; but from the very fact of his being a Gnostic, he works beneficence, having become the instrument of the goodness of God.

They say in the traditions that Matthew the apostle constantly said, that "if the neighbor of an elect man sin, the elect man has sinned. For had he conducted himself as the Word prescribes, his neighbor also would have been filled with such reverence for the life he led as not to sin."

What, then, shall we say of the Gnostic himself? "Know ye not," says the apostle, "that ye are the temple of God?" The Gnostic is consequently divine, and already holy, God bearing, and God-borne. Now the Scripture, showing that sinning is foreign to him, sells those who have fallen away to strangers, saying, "Look not on a strange woman, to lust," plainly pronounces sin foreign and contrary to the nature of the temple of God. Now the temple is great, as the Church, and it is small, as the man who preserves the seed of Abraham. He, therefore, who has God resting in him will not desire aught else. At once leaving all hindrances, and despising all matter which distracts him, he cleaves the heaven by knowledge. And passing through the spiritual Essences, and all rule and authority, he touches the highest thrones, hasting to that alone for the sake of which alone he knew.

Mixing, then, "the serpent with the dove," he lives at once perfectly and with a good conscience, mingling faith with hope, in order to the expectation of the future. For he is conscious of the boon he has received, having become worthy of obtaining it; and is translated from slavery to adoption, as the consequence of knowledge; knowing God, or rather known of Him, for the end, he puts forth energies corresponding to the worth of grace. For works follow knowledge, as the shadow the body.

Rightly, then, he is not disturbed by anything which happens; nor does he suspect those things, which, through divine arrangement, take place for good. Nor is he ashamed to die, having a good conscience, and being fit to be seen by the Powers. Cleansed, so to speak, from all the stains of the soul, he knows right well that it will be better with him after his departure.

Whence he never prefers pleasure and profit to the divine arrangement, since he trains himself by the commands, that in all things he may be well pleasing to the Lord, and praiseworthy in the sight of the world, since all things depend on the one Sovereign God. The Son of God, it is said, came to His own, and His own received Him not. Wherefore also in the use of the things of the world he not only gives thanks and praises the creation, but also, while using them as is right, is praised; since the end he has in view terminates in contemplation by gnostic activity in accordance with the commandments.

Thence now, by knowledge collecting materials to be the food of contemplation, having embraced nobly the magnitude of knowledge, he advances to the holy recompense of translation hence. For he has heard the Psalm which says: "Encircle Zion, and encompass it, tell upon its towers." For it intimates, I think, those who have sublimely embraced the Word, so as to become lofty towers, and to stand firmly in faith and knowledge.

Let these statements concerning the Gnostic, containing the germs of the matter in as brief terms as possible, be made to the Greeks. But let it be known that if the [mere] believer do rightly one or a second of these things, yet he will not do so in all nor with the highest knowledge, like the Gnostic.

CHAPTER XIV.—DESCRIPTION OF THE GNOSTIC FURNISHED BY AN EXPOSITION OF 1 COR. VI. 1, ETC.

Now, of what I may call the passionlessness which we attribute to the Gnostic (in which the perfection of the believer, "advancing by love, comes to a perfect man, to the measure of full stature," by being assimilated to God, and by becoming truly angelic), many other testimonies from the Scripture, occur to me to adduce. But I think it better, on account of the length of the discourse, that such an honor should be devolved on those who wish to take pains, and leave it to them to elaborate the dogmas by the selection of Scriptures.

One passage, accordingly, I shall in the briefest terms advert to, so as not to leave the topic unexplained.

For in the first Epistle to the Corinthians the divine apostle says: "Dare any of you, having a matter against the other, go to law before the unrighteous, and not before the saints? Know ye not that the saints shall judge the world?" and so on.

The section being very long, we shall exhibit the meaning of the apostle's utterance by employing such of the apostolic expressions as are most pertinent, and in the briefest language, and in a sort of cursory way, interpreting the discourse in which he describes the perfection of the Gnostic. For he does not merely instance the Gnostic as characterized by suffering wrong rather than do wrong; but he teaches that he is not mindful of injuries, and does not allow him even to pray against the man who has done him wrong. For he knows that the Lord expressly enjoined "to pray for enemies."

To say, then, that the man who has been injured goes to law before the unrighteous, is nothing else than to say that he shows a wish to retaliate, and a desire to injure the second in return, which is also to do wrong likewise himself.

And his saying, that he wishes "some to go to law before the saints," points out those who ask by prayer that those who have done wrong should suffer retaliation for their injustice, and intimates that the second are better than the former; but they are not yet obedient, if they do not, having become entirely free of resentment, pray even for their enemies.

It is well, then, for them to receive right dispositions from repentance, which results in faith. For if the truth seems to get enemies who entertain bad feeling, yet it is not hostile to anyone. "For God makes His sun to shine on the just and on the unjust," and sent the Lord Himself to the just and the unjust. And he that earnestly strives to be assimilated to God, in the exercise of great absence of resentment, forgives seventy times seven times, as it were all his life through, and in all his course in this world (that being indicated by the enumeration of sevens) shows clemency to each and any one; if any during the whole time of his life in the flesh do the Gnostic wrong. For he not only deems it right that the good man should resign his property alone to others, being of the number of those who have done him wrong; but also wishes that the righteous man should ask of those judges forgiveness for the offences of those who have done him wrong. And with reason, if indeed it is only in that which is external and concerns the body, though it go to the extent of death even, that those who attempt to wrong him take advantage of him; none of which truly belong to the Gnostic.

And how shall one "judge" the apostate "angels," who has become himself an apostate from that forgetfulness of injuries, which is according to the Gospel? "Why do ye not rather suffer wrong?" he says; "why are ye not rather defrauded? Yea, ye do wrong and defraud," manifestly by praying against those who transgress in ignorance, and deprive of the philanthropy and goodness of God, as far as in you lies, those against whom you pray, "and these your brethren,"—not meaning those in the faith only, but also the proselytes. For whether he who now is hostile shall afterwards believe, we know not as yet. From which the conclusion follows clearly, if all are not yet brethren to us, they ought to be regarded in that light. And now it is only the man of knowledge who recognizes all men to be the work of one God, and invested with one image in one nature, although some may be more turbid than others; and in the creatures he recognizes the operation, by which again he adores the will of God.

"Know ye not that the unrighteous shall not inherit the kingdom of God?" He acts unrighteously who retaliates, whether by deed or word, or by the conception of a wish, which, after the training of the Law, the Gospel rejects.

"And such were some of you"—such manifestly as those still are whom you do not forgive; "but ye are washed," not simply as the rest, but with knowledge; ye have cast off the passions of the soul, in order to become assimilated, as far as possible, to the goodness of God's providence by long-suffering, and by forgiveness "towards the just and the unjust," casting on them the gleam of benignity in word and deeds, as the sun.

The Gnostic will achieve this either by greatness of mind, or by imitation of what is better. And that is a third cause. "Forgive, and it shall be forgiven you;" the commandment, as it were, compelling to salvation through superabundance of goodness.

"But ye are sanctified." For he who has come to this state is in a condition to be holy, falling into none of the passions in any way, but as it were already disembodied and already grown holy without this earth.

"Wherefore," he says, "ye are justified in the name of the Lord." Ye are made, so to speak, by Him to be righteous as He is, and are blended as far as possible with the Holy Spirit. For "are not all things lawful to me? yet I will not be brought under the power of any," so as to do, or think, or speak aught contrary to the Gospel. "Meats for the belly, and the belly for meats, which God shall destroy,"—that is, such as think and live as if they were made for eating, and do not eat that they may live as a consequence, and apply to knowledge as the primary end. And does he not say that these are, as it were, the fleshy parts of the holy body? As a body, the Church of the Lord, the spiritual and holy choir, is symbolized. Whence those, who are merely called, but do not live in accordance with the word, are the fleshy parts. "Now" this spiritual "body," the holy Church, "is not for fornication." Nor are those things which belong to heathen life to be adopted by apostasy from the Gospel. For he who conducts himself heathenishly in the Church, whether in deed, or word, or even in thought, commits fornication with reference to the Church and his own body. He who in this way "is joined to the harlot," that is, to conduct contrary to the Covenant becomes another "body," not holy, "and one flesh," and has a heathenish life and another hope. "But he that is joined to the Lord in spirit" becomes a spiritual body by a different kind of conjunction.

Such a one is wholly a son, an holy man, passionless, gnostic, perfect, formed by the teaching of the Lord; in order that in deed, in word, and in spirit itself, being brought close to the Lord, he may receive the mansion that is due to him who has reached manhood thus.

Let the specimen suffice to those who have ears. For it is not required to unfold the mystery, but only to indicate what is sufficient for those who are partakers in knowledge to bring it to mind; who also will comprehend how it was said by the Lord, "Be ye perfect as your father, perfectly," by forgiving sins, and forgetting injuries, and living in the habit of passionlessness. For as we call a physician perfect, and a philosopher perfect, so also, in my view, do we call a Gnostic perfect. But not one of those points, although of the greatest importance, is assumed in order to the likeness of God. For we do not say, as the Stoics do most impiously, that virtue in man and God is the same. Ought we not then to be perfect, as the Father wills? For it is utterly impossible for anyone to become perfect as God is. Now the Father wishes us to be perfect by living blamelessly, according to the obedience of the Gospel.

If, then, the statement being elliptical, we understand what is wanting, in order to complete the section for those who are incapable of understanding what is left out, we shall both know the will of God, and shall walk at once piously and magnanimously, as befits the dignity of the commandment.

CHAPTER XV.—THE OBJECTION TO JOIN THE CHURCH ON ACCOUNT OF THE DIVERSITY OF HERESIES ANSWERED.

Since it comes next to reply to the objections alleged against us by Greeks and Jews; and since, in some of the questions previously discussed, the sects also who adhere to other teaching give, their help, it will be well first to clear away the obstacles before us, and then, prepared thus for the solution of the difficulties, to advance to the succeeding Miscellany.

First, then, they make this objection to us, saying, that they ought not to believe on account of the discord of the sects. For the truth is warped when some teach one set of dogmas, others another.

To whom we say, that among you who are Jews, and among the most famous of the philosophers among the Greeks, very many sects have sprung up. And yet you do not say that one ought to hesitate to philosophize or Judaize, because of the want of agreement of the sects among you between themselves. And then, that heresies should be sown among the truth, as "tares among the wheat," was foretold by the Lord; and what was predicted to take place could not but happen. And the cause of this is, that everything that is fair is followed by a foul blot. If one, then, violate his engagements, and go aside from the confession which he makes before us, are we not to stick to the truth because he has belied his profession? But as the good man must not prove false or fail to ratify what he has promised, although others violate their engagements; so also are we bound in no way to transgress the canon of the Church. And especially do we keep our profession in the most important points, while they traverse it.

Those, then, are to be believed, who hold firmly to the truth. And we may broadly make use of this reply, and say to them, that physicians holding opposite opinions according to their own schools, yet equally in point of fact treat patients. Does one, then, who is ill in body and needing treatment, not have recourse to a physician, on account of the different schools in medicine? No more, then, may he who in soul is sick and full of idols, make a pretext of the heresies, in reference to the recovery of health and conversion to God.

Further, it is said that it is on account of "those that are approved that heresies exist." [The apostle] calls "approved," either those who in reaching faith apply to the teaching of the Lord with some discrimination (as those are called skillful money-changers, who distinguish the spurious coin from the genuine by the false stamp), or those who have already become approved both in life and knowledge.

For this reason, then, we require greater attention and consideration in order to investigate how precisely we ought to live, and what is the true piety. For it is plain that, from the very reason that truth is difficult and arduous of attainment, questions arise from which spring the heresies, savoring of self-love and vanity, of those who have not learned or apprehended truly, but only caught up a mere conceit of knowledge. With the greater care, therefore, are we to examine the real truth, which alone has for its object the true God. And the toil is followed by sweet discovery and reminiscence.

On account of the heresies, therefore, the toil of discovery must be undertaken; but we must not at all abandon [the truth]. For, on fruit being set before us, some real and ripe, and some made of wax, as like the real as possible, we are not to abstain from both on account of the resemblance. But by the exercise of the apprehension of contemplation, and by reasoning of the most decisive character, we must distinguish the true from the seeming.

And as, while there is one royal highway, there are many others, some leading to a precipice, some to a rushing river or to a deep sea, no one will shrink from travelling by reason of the diversity, but will make use of the safe, and royal, and frequented way; so, though some say this, some that, concerning the truth, we must not abandon it; but must seek out the most accurate knowledge respecting it. Since also among garden-grown vegetables weeds also spring up, are the husbandmen, then, to desist from gardening?

Having then from nature abundant means for examining the statements made, we ought to discover the sequence of the truth. Wherefore also we are rightly condemned, if we do not assent to what we ought to obey, and do not distinguish what is hostile, and unseemly, and unnatural, and false, from what is true, consistent, and seemly, and according to nature. And these means must be employed in order to attain to the knowledge of the real truth.

This pretext is then, in the case of the Greeks, futile; for those who are willing may find the truth. But in the case of those who adduce unreasonable excuses, their condemnation is unanswerable. For whether do they deny or admit that there is such a thing as demonstration? I am of opinion that all will make the admission, except those who take away the senses.

There being demonstration, then, it is necessary to condescend to questions, and to ascertain by way of demonstration by the Scriptures themselves how the heresies failed, and how in the truth alone and in the ancient Church is both the exactest knowledge, and the truly best set of principles (αἵρεσις).

Now, of those who diverge from the truth, some attempt to deceive themselves alone, and some also their neighbors. Those, then, who are called (δοξόσοφοι) wise in their own opinions, who think that they have found the truth, but have no true demonstration, deceive themselves in thinking that they have reached a resting place. And of whom there is no inconsiderable multitude, who avoid investigations for fear of refutations, and shun instructions for fear of condemnation. But those who deceive those who seek access to them are very astute; who, aware that they know nothing, yet darken the truth with plausible arguments.

But, in my opinion, the nature of plausible arguments is of one character, and that of true arguments of another. And we know that it is necessary that the appellation of the heresies should be expressed in contradistinction to the truth; from which the Sophists, drawing certain things for the destruction of men, and burying them in human arts invented by themselves, glory rather in being at the head of a School than presiding over the Church.

CHAPTER XVI.—SCRIPTURE THE CRITERION BY WHICH TRUTH AND HERESY ARE DISTINGUISHED.

But those who are ready to toil in the most excellent pursuits, will not desist from the search after truth, till they get the demonstration from the Scriptures themselves.

There are certain criteria common to men, as the senses; and others that belong to those who have employed their wills and energies in what is true,—the methods which are pursued by the mind and reason, to distinguish between true and false propositions.

Now, it is a very great thing to abandon opinion, by taking one's stand between accurate knowledge and the rash wisdom of opinion, and to know that he who hopes for everlasting rest knows also that the entrance to it is toilsome "and straight." And let him who has once received the Gospel, even in the very hour in which he has come to the knowledge of salvation, "not turn back, like Lot's wife," as is said; and let him not go back either to his former life, which adheres to the things of sense, or to heresies. For they form the character, not knowing the true God. "For he that loves father or mother more than Me," the Father and Teacher of the truth, who regenerates and creates anew, and nourishes the elect soul, "is not worthy of Me"—He means, to be a son of God and a disciple of God, and at the same time also to be a friend, and of kindred nature.

"For no man who looks back, and puts his hand to the plough, is fit for the kingdom of God."

But, as appears, many even down to our own time regard Mary, on account of the birth of her child, as having been in the puerperal state, although she was not. For some say that, after she brought forth, she was found, when examined, to be a virgin.

Now such to us are the Scriptures of the Lord, which gave birth to the truth and continue virgin, in the concealment of the mysteries of the truth. "And she brought forth, and yet brought not forth," says the Scripture; as having conceived of herself, and not from conjunction. Wherefore the Scriptures have conceived to Gnostics; but the heresies, not having learned them, dismissed them as not having conceived.

Now all men, having the same judgment, some, following the Word speaking, frame for themselves proofs; while others, giving themselves up to pleasures, wrest Scripture, in accordance with their lusts. And the lover of truth, as I think, needs force of soul. For those who make the greatest attempts must fail in things of the highest importance; unless, receiving from the truth itself the rule of the truth, they cleave to the truth. But such people, in consequence of falling away from the right path, err in most individual points; as you might expect from not having the faculty for judging of what is true and false, strictly trained to select what is essential. For if they had, they would have obeyed the Scriptures.

As, then, if a man should, similarly to those drugged by Circe, become a beast; so he, who has spurned the ecclesiastical tradition, and darted off to the opinions of heretical men, has ceased to be a man of God and to remain faithful to the Lord. But he who has returned from this deception, on hearing the Scriptures, and turned his life to the truth, is, as it were, from being a man made a god.

For we have, as the source of teaching, the Lord, both by the prophets, the Gospel, and the blessed apostles, "in divers manners and at sundry times," leading from the beginning of knowledge to the end. But if one should suppose that another origin was required, then no longer truly could an origin be preserved.

He, then, who of himself believes the Scripture and voice of the Lord, which by the Lord acts to the benefiting of men, is rightly [regarded] faithful. Certainly we use it as a criterion in the discovery of things. What is subjected to criticism is not believed till it is so subjected; so that what needs criticism cannot be a first principle. Therefore, as is reasonable, grasping by faith the indemonstrable first principle, and receiving in abundance, from the first principle itself, demonstrations in reference to the first principle, we are by the voice of the Lord trained up to the knowledge of the truth.

For we may not give our adhesion to men on a bare statement by them, who might equally state the opposite. But if it is not enough merely to state the opinion, but if what is stated must be confirmed, we do not wait for the testimony of men, but we establish the matter that is in question by the voice of the Lord, which is the surest of all demonstrations, or rather is the only demonstration; in which knowledge those who have merely tasted the Scriptures are believers; while those who, having advanced further, and become correct expounders of the truth, are Gnostics. Since also, in what pertains to life, craftsmen are superior to ordinary people, and model what is beyond common notions; so, consequently, we also, giving a complete exhibition of the Scriptures from the Scriptures themselves, from faith persuade by demonstration.

And if those also who follow heresies venture to avail themselves of the prophetic Scriptures; in the first place they will not make use of all the Scriptures, and then they will not quote them entire, nor as the body and texture of prophecy prescribe. But, selecting ambiguous expressions, they wrest them to their own opinions, gathering a few expressions here and there; not looking to the sense, but making use of the mere words. For in almost all the quotations they make, you will find that they attend to the names alone, while they alter the meanings; neither knowing, as they affirm, nor using the quotations they adduce, according to their true nature.

But the truth is not found by changing the meanings (for so people subvert all true teaching), but in the consideration of what perfectly belongs to and becomes the Sovereign God, and in establishing each one of the points demonstrated in the Scriptures again from similar Scriptures. Neither, then, do they want to turn to the truth, being ashamed to abandon the claims of self-love; nor are they able to manage their opinions, by doing violence to the Scriptures. But having first promulgated false dogmas to men; plainly fighting against almost the whole Scriptures, and constantly confuted by us who contradict them; for the rest, even now partly they hold out against admitting the prophetic Scriptures, and partly disparage us as of a different nature, and incapable of understanding what is peculiar to them. And sometimes even they deny their own dogmas, when these are confuted, being ashamed openly to own what in private they glory in teaching. For this may be seen in all the heresies, when you examine the iniquities of their dogmas. For when they are overturned by our clearly showing that they are opposed to the Scriptures, one of two things may be seen to have been done by those who defend the dogma. For they either despise the consistency of their own dogmas, or despise the prophecy itself, or rather their own hope. And they invariably prefer what seems to them to be more evident to what has been spoken by the Lord through the prophets and by the Gospel, and, besides, attested and confirmed by the apostles.

Seeing, therefore, the danger that they are in (not in respect of one dogma, but in reference to the maintenance of the heresies) of not discovering the truth; for while reading the books we have ready at hand, they despise them as useless, but in their eagerness to surpass common faith, they have diverged from the truth. For, in consequence of not learning the mysteries of ecclesiastical knowledge, and not having capacity for the grandeur of the truth, too indolent to descend to the bottom of things, reading superficially, they have dismissed the Scriptures. Elated, then, by vain opinion, they are incessantly wrangling, and plainly care more to *seem* than to *be* philosophers. Not laying as foundations the necessary first principles of things; and influenced by human opinions, then making the end to suit them, by compulsion; on account of being confuted, they spar with those who are engaged in the prosecution of the true philosophy, and undergo everything, and, as they say, ply every oar, even going the length of impiety, by disbelieving the Scriptures, rather than be removed from the honors of the heresy and the boasted first seat in their churches; on account of which also they eagerly embrace that convivial couch of honor in the Agape, falsely so called.

The knowledge of the truth among us from what is already believed, produces faith in what is not yet believed; which [faith] is, so to speak, the essence of demonstration. But, as appears, no heresy has at all ears to hear what is useful, but opened only to what leads to pleasure. Since also, if one of them would only obey the truth, he would be healed.

Now the cure of self-conceit (as of every ailment) is threefold: the ascertaining of the cause, and the mode of its removal; and thirdly, the training of the soul, and the accustoming it to assume a right attitude to the judgments come to. For, just like a disordered eye, so also the soul that has been darkened by unnatural dogmas cannot perceive distinctly the light of truth, but even overlooks what is before it.

They say, then, that in muddy water eels are caught by being blinded. And just as knavish boys bar out the teacher, so do these shut out the prophecies from their Church, regarding them with suspicion by reason of rebuke and admonition. In fact, they stitch together a multitude of lies and figments, that they may appear acting in accordance with reason in not admitting the Scriptures. So, then, they are not pious, inasmuch as they are not pleased with the divine commands, that is, with the Holy Spirit. And as those almonds are called empty in which the contents are worthless, not those in which there is nothing; so also we call those heretics empty, who are destitute of the counsels of God and the traditions of Christ; bitter, in truth, like the wild almond, their dogmas originating with themselves, with the exception of such truths as they could not, by reason of their evidence, discard and conceal.

As, then, in war the soldier must not leave the post which the commander has assigned him, so neither must we desert the post assigned by the Word, whom we have received as the guide of knowledge and of life. But the most have not even inquired, if there is one that we ought to follow, and who this is, and how he is to be followed. For as is the Word, such also must the believer's life be, so as to be able to follow God, who brings all things to end from the beginning by the right course.

But when one has transgressed against the Word, and thereby against God; if it is through becoming powerless in consequence of some impression being suddenly made, he ought to see to have the impressions of reasons at hand. And if it is that he has become "common," as the Scripture says, in consequence of being overcome the habits which formerly had sway by over him, the habits must be entirely put a stop to, and the soul trained to oppose them. And if it appears that conflicting dogmas draw some away, these must be taken out of the way, and recourse is to be had to those who reconcile dogmas, and subdue by the charm of the Scriptures such of the untutored as are timid, by explaining the truth by the connection of the Testaments.

But, as appears, we incline to ideas founded on opinion, though they be contrary, rather than to the truth. For it is austere and grave. Now, since there are three states of the soul—ignorance, opinion, knowledge—those who are in ignorance are the Gentiles, those in knowledge, the true Church, and those in opinion, the Heretics. Nothing, then, can be more clearly seen than those, who know, making affirmations about what they know, and the others respecting what they hold on the strength of opinion, as far as respects affirmation without proof.

They accordingly despise and laugh at one another. And it happens that the same thought is held in the highest estimation by some, and by others condemned for insanity. And, indeed, we have learned that voluptuousness, which is to be attributed to the Gentiles, is one thing; and wrangling, which is preferred among the heretical sects, is another; and joy, which is to be appropriated to the Church, another; and delight, which is to be assigned to the true Gnostic, another. And as, if one devote himself to Ischomachus, he will make him a farmer; and to Lampis, a mariner; and to Charidemus, a military commander; and to Simon, an equestrian; and to Perdices, a trader; and to Crobylus, a cook; and to Archelaus, a dancer; and to Homer, a poet; and to Pyrrho, a wrangler; and to Demosthenes, an orator; and to Chrysippus, a dialectician; and to Aristotle, a naturalist; and to Plato, a philosopher: so he who listens to the Lord, and follows the prophecy given by Him, will be formed perfectly in the likeness of the teacher—made a god going about in flesh.

Accordingly, those fall from this eminence who follow not God whither He leads. And He leads us in the inspired Scriptures.

Though men's actions are ten thousand in number, the sources of all sin are but two, ignorance and inability. And both depend on ourselves; inasmuch as we will not learn, nor, on the other hand, restrain lust. And of these, the one is that, in consequence of which people do not judge well, and the other that, in consequence of which they cannot comply with right judgments. For neither will one who is deluded in his mind be able to act rightly, though perfectly able to do what he knows; nor, though capable of judging what is requisite, will he keep himself free of blame, if destitute of power in action. Consequently, then, there are assigned two kinds of correction applicable to both kinds of sin: for the one, knowledge and clear demonstration from the testimony of the Scriptures; and for the other, the training according to the Word, which is regulated by the discipline of faith and fear. And both develop into perfect love. For the end of the Gnostic here is, in my judgment, twofold,—partly scientific contemplation, partly action.

Would, then, that these heretics would learn and be set right by these notes, and turn to the sovereign God! But if, like the deaf serpents, they listen not to the song called new, though very old, may they be chastised by God, and undergo paternal admonitions previous to the Judgment, till they become ashamed and repent, but not rush through headlong unbelief, and precipitate themselves into judgment.

For there are partial corrections, which are called chastisements, which many of us who have been in transgression incur, by falling away from the Lord's people. But as children are chastised by their teacher, or their father, so are we by Providence. But God does not punish, for punishment is retaliation for evil. He chastises, however, for good to those who are chastised, collectively and individually.

I have adduced these things from a wish to avert those, who are eager to learn, from the liability to fall into heresies, and out of a desire to stop them from superficial ignorance, or stupidity, or bad disposition, or whatever it should be called. And in the attempt to persuade and lead to the truth those who are not entirely incurable, I have made use of these words.
For there are some who cannot bear at all to listen to those who exhort them to turn to the truth; and they attempt to trifle, pouring out blasphemies against the truth, claiming for themselves the knowledge of the greatest things in the universe, without having learned, or inquired, or labored, or discovered the consecutive train of ideas,—whom one should pity rather than hate for such perversity.

But if one is curable, able to bear (like fire or steel) the outspokenness of the truth, which cuts away and burns their false opinions, let him lend the ears of the soul. And this will be the case, unless, through the propensity to sloth, they push truth away, or through the desire of fame, endeavor to invent novelties. For those are slothful who, having it in their power to provide themselves with proper proofs for the divine Scriptures from the Scriptures themselves, select only what contributes to their own pleasures. And those have a craving for glory who voluntarily evade, by arguments of a diverse sort, the things delivered by the blessed apostles and teachers, which are wedded to inspired words; opposing the divine tradition by human teachings, in order to establish the heresy. For, in truth, what remained to be said—in ecclesiastical knowledge I mean—by such men, Marcion, for example, or Prodicus, and such like, who did not walk in the right way? For they could not have surpassed their predecessors in wisdom, so as to discover anything in addition to what had been uttered by them; for they would have been satisfied had they been able to learn the things laid down before.

Our Gnostic then alone, having grown old in the Scriptures, and maintaining apostolic and ecclesiastic orthodoxy in doctrines, lives most correctly in accordance with the Gospel, and discovers the proofs, for which he may have made search (sent forth as he is by the Lord), from the law and the prophets. For the life of the Gnostic, in my view, is nothing but deeds and words corresponding to the tradition of the Lord. But "all have not knowledge. For I would not have you to be ignorant, brethren," says the apostle, "that all were under the cloud, and partook of spiritual meat and drink;" clearly affirming that all who heard the word did not take in the magnitude of knowledge in deed and word. Wherefore also he added: "But with all of them He was not well pleased." Who is this? He who said, "Why do you call Me Lord, and do not the will of My Father?" That is the Savior's teaching, which to us is spiritual food, and drink that knows no thirst, the water of gnostic life. Further it is said, knowledge is said "to puff up." To whom we say: Perchance seeming knowledge is said to puff up, if one suppose the expression means "to be swollen up." But if, as is rather the case, the expression of the apostle means, "to entertain great and true sentiments," the difficulty is solved. Following, then, the Scriptures, let us establish what has been said: "Wisdom," says Solomon, "has inflated her children." For the Lord did not work conceit by the particulars of His teaching; but He produces trust in the truth and expansion of mind, in the knowledge that is communicated by the Scriptures, and contempt for the things which drag into sin, which is the meaning of the expression "inflated." It teaches the magnificence of the wisdom implanted in her children by instruction. Now the apostle says, "I will know not the speech of those that are puffed up, but the power;" if ye understand the Scriptures magnanimously (which means truly; for nothing is greater than truth). For in that lies the power of the children of wisdom who are puffed up. He says, as it were, I shall know if ye rightly entertain great thoughts respecting knowledge. "For God," according to David, "is known in Judea," that is, those that are Israelites according to knowledge. For Judea is interpreted "Confession." It is, then, rightly said by the apostle, "This *Thou, shall not commit adultery, Thou shall not steal, Thou shalt not covet;* and if there be any other commandment, it is comprehended in this word, *Thou shalt love thy neighbor as thyself.*"

For we must never, as do those who follow the heresies, adulterate the truth, or steal the canon of the Church, by gratifying our own lusts and vanity, by defrauding our neighbors; whom above all it is our duty, in the exercise of love to them, to teach to adhere to the truth. It is accordingly expressly said, "Declare among the heathen His statutes," that they may not be judged, but that those who have previously given ear may be converted. But those who speak treacherously with their tongues have the penalties that are on record.

CHAPTER XVII.—THE TRADITION OF THE CHURCH PRIOR TO THAT OF THE HERESIES.

Those, then, that adhere to impious words, and dictate them to others, inasmuch as they do not make a right but a perverse use of the divine words, neither themselves enter into the kingdom of heaven, nor permit those whom they have deluded to attain the truth. But not having the key of entrance, but a false (and as the common phrase expresses it), a counterfeit key (ἀντικλεῖς), by which they do not enter in as we enter in, through the tradition of the Lord, by drawing aside the curtain; but bursting through the side-door, and digging clandestinely through the wall of the Church, and stepping over the truth, they constitute themselves the Mystagogues of the soul of the impious.

For that the human assemblies which they held were posterior to the Catholic Church requires not many words to show.

For the teaching of our Lord at His advent, beginning with Augustus and Tiberius, was completed in the middle of the times of Tiberius.

And that of the apostles, embracing the ministry of Paul, ends with Nero. It was later, in the times of Adrian the king, that those who invented the heresies arose; and they extended to the age of Antoninus the elder, as, for instance, Basilides, though he claims (as they boast) for his master, Glaucias, the interpreter of Peter.

Likewise they allege that Valentinus was a hearer of Theudas. And he was the pupil of Paul. For Marcion, who arose in the same age with them, lived as an old man with the younger [heretics]. And after him Simon heard for a little the preaching of Peter.

Such being the case, it is evident, from the high antiquity and perfect truth of the Church, that these later heresies, and those yet subsequent to them in time, were new inventions falsified [from the truth].

From what has been said, then, it is my opinion that the true Church, that which is really ancient, is one, and that in it those who according to God's purpose are just, are enrolled. For from the very reason that God is one, and the Lord one, that which is in the highest degree honorable is lauded in consequence of its singleness, being an imitation of the one first principle. In the nature of the One, then, is associated in a joint heritage the one Church, which they strive to cut asunder into many sects.

Therefore in substance and idea, in origin, in pre-eminence, we say that the ancient and Catholic Church is alone, collecting as it does into the unity of the one faith—which results from the peculiar Testaments, or rather the one Testament in different times by the will of the one God, through one Lord—those already ordained, whom God predestinated, knowing before the foundation of the world that they would be righteous.

But the pre-eminence of the Church, as the principle of union, is, in its oneness, in this surpassing all things else, and having nothing like or equal to itself. But of this afterwards.

Of the heresies, some receive their appellation from a [person's] name, as that which is called after Valentinus, and that after Marcion, and that after Basilides, although they boast of adducing the opinion of Matthew [without truth]; for as the teaching, so also the tradition of the apostles was one. Some take their designation from a place, as the Peratici; some from a nation, as the [heresy] of the Phrygians; some from an action, as that of the Encratites; and some from peculiar dogmas, as that of the Docetæ, and that of the Hærmatites; and some from suppositions, and from individuals they have honored, as those called Cainists, and the Ophians; and some from nefarious practices and enormities, as those of the Simonians called Entychites.

CHAPTER XVIII—THE DISTINCTION BETWEEN CLEAN AND UNCLEAN ANIMALS IN THE LAW SYMBOLICAL OF THE DISTINCTION BETWEEN THE CHURCH, AND JEWS, AND HERETICS.

After showing a little peep-hole to those who love to contemplate the Church from the law of sacrifices respecting clean and unclean animals (inasmuch as thus the common Jews and the heretics are distinguished mystically from the divine Church), let us bring the discourse to a close.

For such of the sacrifices as part the hoof, and ruminate, the Scripture represents as clean and acceptable to God; since the just obtain access to the Father and to the Son by faith. For this is the stability of those who part the hoof, those who study the oracles of God night and day, and ruminate them in the soul's receptacle for instructions; which Gnostic exercise the Law expresses under the figure of the rumination of the clean animal. But such as have neither the one nor the other of those qualities it separates as unclean.

Now those that ruminate, but do not part the hoof, indicate the majority of the Jews, who have indeed the oracles of God, but have not faith, and the step which, resting on the truth, conveys to the Father by the Son. Whence also this kind of cattle are apt to slip, not having a division in the foot, and not resting on the twofold support of faith. For "no man," it is said, "knows the Father, but he to whom the Son shall reveal Him."

And again, those also are likewise unclean that part the hoof, but do not ruminate. For these point out the heretics, who indeed go upon the name of the Father and the Son, but are incapable of triturating and grinding down the clear declaration of the oracles, and who, besides, perform the works of righteousness coarsely and not with precision, if they perform them at all. To such the Lord says, "Why will ye call me Lord, Lord, and do not the things which I say?"

And those that neither part the hoof nor chew the cud are entirely unclean.

"But ye Megareans," says Theognis, "are neither third, nor fourth,
Nor twelfth, neither in reckoning nor in number,"

"but as chaff which the wind drives away from the face of the earth," and as a drop from a vessel."

Clement of Alexandria

These points, then, having been formerly thoroughly treated, and the department of ethics having been sketched summarily in a fragmentary way, as we promised; and having here and there interspersed the dogmas which are the germs of true knowledge, so that the discovery of the sacred traditions may not be easy to any one of the uninitiated, let us proceed to what we promised.

Now the Miscellanies are not like parts laid out, planted in regular order for the delight of the eye, but rather like an umbrageous and shaggy hill, planted with laurel, and ivy, and apples, and olives, and figs; the planting being purposely a mixture of fruit-bearing and fruitless trees, since the composition aims at concealment, on account of those that have the daring to pilfer and steal the ripe fruits; from which, however, the husbandmen, transplanting shoots and plants, will adorn a beautiful park and a delightful grove.

The Miscellanies, then, study neither arrangement nor diction; since there are even cases in which the Greeks on purpose wish that ornate diction should be absent, and imperceptibly cast in the seed of dogmas, not according to the truth, rendering such as may read laborious and quick at discovery. For many and various are the baits for the various kinds of fishes.

And now, after this seventh Miscellany of ours, we shall give the account of what follows in order from another commencement.

Elucidations

I.
(Deception, cap. ix. p. 538.)

More and more, the casuistry exposed by Pascal in the *Provincial Letters* becomes an important subject for the investigation of Americans. Nobody who has any pretensions to scholarship can afford to be ignorant of these letters; for they belong to literature, and not merely to theology. But they belong in a sense to the past; not that "the Society of Jesus" has ceased to maintain all that Pascal has exposed, and to practice even worse, but that the Latin churches have, since the days of Pascal, been formally subjected to a system of casuistry, in some respects superficially reformed, but in all other respects radically bad, and corrosive to society. In Pascal's day this casuistry could only be charged upon individuals, and upon societies and communities: the Roman Church everywhere adopted it, but was not formally committed to it. But in the system of Liguori this corrupt morality has been made authoritative and *dogmatic;* so that in all the Latin churches it becomes the base of the confessional. For moral purposes, it is the Bible of the millions who resort to their confessors and "directors." These remarks, however, are here introduced merely with reference to the morals of Clement with regard to truth.

I have briefly indicated, in the footnotes, the points which are to be noted in forming an opinion of our author's conceptions of this vital principle. They seem to me conformed to the Gospel; to the teachings of Him who allows no hair-splittings, but says, "Let your yea be yea, and your nay, nay." But, as the text stood in the Edinburgh translation, it did injustice to Clement in one passage, which I have modified. It reads, "He (the Gnostic) both thinks and speaks the truth, unless, at any time, medicinally, as a physician for the safety of the sick, he may *lie,* or tell an untruth." To this, Clement adds significantly, "according to the Sophists." That is to say, our author tolerates the Christian who has not got beyond the *Sophists* with respect to benevolent deceptions. As *killing* is not always *murder,* so some, even among stern moralists, have maintained that *deception* by word of mouth is not always *lying.* This is the extent to which Clement tolerates sophistry, and he goes on to demand the practice of *truth* in Gospel terms.

Now, thank God, the English word "lie" is always infamous; and there is nothing like it, in this respect, in other languages. The Sophists themselves did not so understand the Greek word (ψεῦδος), when they apply it to the benevolent deception of a physician, or to the untruths used benevolently with the insane. Nothing infamous attaches to the French word *mensonge* when used for what are deemed "innocent deceptions." With this whole system of sophistry I have no patience at all; but, in justice to the Sophists, let us not make them worse than they were. They did not understand that such deceptions were *lies.* Hence, for "lie," I have used the word *deceive,* correcting a needless rendering of the text, and one to which Clement should not be made to extend even a contemptuous toleration.

In this respect, the holy Jeremy Taylor and Dr. Johnson go further than Clement, and seem to allow that benevolent deceptions may be innocent. Sanderson sustains a sterner morality, and is more generally accepted. Liguori's system is *verbally* as strong as the Gospel itself: lying is a mortal sin, and never justifiable. But, when he comes to the definition of a lie, it is made so feeble, that the worst liar that ever lived need never resort to it. He may practice all manner of subterfuge, and even perjury, without telling a lie. As, e.g., if he points up his sleeve, while he swears that he did not see the criminal *there,* he tells no lie: it is the business of the judge and jury to watch his fingers, etc.

II.
(True Gnostic, cap. x. p. 540, note 1.)

This unfortunate word *Gnostic* hides the force of Clement's teaching, throughout this work. Here he virtually expounds it, and we see that it refers even more to the heart than to the head. It carries with it *the conduct of life* by knowledge; i.e., by "the true Light which lighted every man that cometh into the world." (See p. 607, footnote.)

III.

(The Scriptures, cap. xvi. p. 550, note 3.)

The Primitive Fathers never dream of anything as *dogma* which cannot be proved by the Scriptures, save only that the apostolic traditions, *clearly proved to be such,* must be referred to in proving what is Holy Scripture. It is not possible to graft on this principle the slightest argument for any tradition not indisputably apostolic, so far as the *de fide* is concerned.
Quod semper is the touchstone, in their conceptions, of all orthodoxy. No matter who may teach this or that, *now* or in any post-apostolic age, their test is Holy Scripture, and the inquiry, Was it *always* so taught and understood?

BOOK VIII.

CHAPTER I.—THE OBJECT OF PHILOSOPHICAL AND THEOLOGICAL INQUIRY—THE DISCOVERY OF TRUTH.

But the most ancient of the philosophers were not carried away to disputing and doubting, much less are we, who are attached to the really true philosophy, on whom the Scripture enjoins examination and investigation. For it is the more recent of the Hellenic philosophers who, by empty and futile love of fame, are led into useless babbling in refuting and wrangling. But, on the contrary, the Barbarian philosophy, expelling all contention, said, "Seek, and ye shall find; knock, and it shall be opened unto you; ask, and it shall be given you."

Accordingly, by investigation, the point proposed for inquiry and answer knocks at the door of truth, according to what appears. And on an opening being made through the obstacle in the process of investigation, there results scientific contemplation. To those who thus knock, according to my view, the subject under investigation is opened.

And to those who thus ask questions, in the Scriptures, there is given from God (that at which they aim) the gift of the God-given knowledge, by way of comprehension, through the true illumination of logical investigation. For it is impossible to find, without having sought; or to have sought, without having examined; or to have examined, without having unfolded and opened up the question by interrogation, to produce distinctness; or again, to have gone through the whole investigation, without thereafter receiving as the prize the knowledge of the point in question.

But it belongs to him who has sought, to find; and to him to seek, who thinks previously that he does not know. Hence drawn by desire to the discovery of what is good, he seeks thoughtfully, without love of strife or glory, asking, answering, and besides considering the statements made. For it is incumbent, in applying ourselves not only to the divine Scriptures, but also to common notions, to institute investigations, the discovery ceasing at some useful end.

For another place and crowd await turbulent people, and forensic sophistries. But it is suitable for him, who is at once a lover and disciple of the truth, to be pacific even in investigations, advancing by scientific demonstration, without love of self, but with love of truth, to comprehensive knowledge.

CHAPTER II.—THE NECESSITY OF PERSPICUOUS DEFINITION.

What better or clearer method, for the commencement of instruction of this nature, can there be than discussion of the term advanced, so distinctly, that all who use the same language may follow it? Is the term for demonstration of such a kind as the word *Blityri*, which is a mere sound, signifying nothing? But how is it that neither does the philosopher, nor the orator,—no more does the judge,—adduce demonstration as a term that means nothing; nor is any of the contending parties ignorant of the fact, that the meaning does not exist?

Philosophers, in fact, present demonstration as having a substantial existence, one in one way, another in another. Therefore, if one would treat aright of each question, he cannot carry back the discourse to another more generally admitted fundamental principle than what is admitted to be signified by the term by all of the same nation and language.

Then, starting from this point, it is necessary to inquire if the proposition has this signification or not. And next, if it is demonstrated to have, it is necessary to investigate its nature accurately, of what kind it is, and whether it ever passes over the class assigned. And if it suffices not to say, absolutely, only that which one thinks (for one's opponent may equally allege, on the other side, what he likes); then what is stated must be confirmed. If the decision of it be carried back to what is likewise matter of dispute, and the decision of that likewise to another disputed point, it will go on *ad infinitum*, and will be incapable of demonstration. But if the belief of a point that is not admitted be carried back to one admitted by all, that is to be made the commencement of instruction. Every term, therefore, advanced for discussion is to be converted into an expression that is admitted by those that are parties in the discussion, to form the starting point for instruction, to lead the way to the discovery of the points under investigation. For example, let it be the term "sun" that is in question. Now the Stoics say that it is "an intellectual fire kindled from the waters of the sea." Is not the definition, consequently, obscurer than the term, requiring another demonstration to prove if it be true? It is therefore better to say, in the common and distinct form of speech, "that the brightest of the heavenly bodies is named the sun." For this expression is more credible and clearer, and is likewise admitted by all.

CHAPTER III.—DEMONSTRATION DEFINED.

Similarly, also, all men will admit that demonstration is discourse, agreeable to reason, producing belief in points disputed, from points admitted.

Now, not only demonstration and belief and knowledge, but foreknowledge also, are used in a twofold manner. There is that which is scientific and certain, and that which is merely based on hope.

In strict propriety, then, that is called demonstration which produces in the souls of learners scientific belief. The other kind is that which merely leads to opinion. As also, both he that is really a man, possessing common judgment, and he that is savage and brutal,—each is a man. Thus also the Comic poet said that "man is graceful, so long as he is man." The same holds with ox, horse, and dog, according to the goodness or badness of the animal. For by looking to the perfection of the genus, we come to those meanings that are strictly proper. For instance, we conceive of a physician who is deficient in no element of the power of healing, and a Gnostic who is defective in no element of scientific knowledge.

Now demonstration differs from syllogism; inasmuch as the point demonstrated is indicative of one thing, being one and identical; as we say that to be with child is the proof of being no longer a virgin. But what is apprehended by syllogism, though one thing, follows from several; as, for example, not one but several proofs are adduced of Pytho having betrayed the Byzantines, if such was the fact. And to draw a conclusion from what is admitted is to *syllogize;* while to draw a conclusion from what is true is to *demonstrate.*

So that there is a compound advantage of demonstration: from its assuming, for the proof of points in question, true premises, and from its drawing the conclusion that follows from them. If the first have no existence, but the second follow from the first, one has not demonstrated, but syllogized. For, to draw the proper conclusion from the premises, is merely to syllogize. But to have also each of the premises true, is not merely to have syllogized, but also to have demonstrated.

And to conclude, as is evident from the word, is to bring to the conclusion. And in every train of reasoning, the point sought to be determined is the end, which is also called the conclusion. But no simple and primary statement is termed a syllogism, although true; but it is compounded of three such, at the least,—of two as premises, and one as conclusion.

Now, either all things require demonstration, or some of them are self-evident. But if the first, by demanding the demonstration of each demonstration we shall go on *ad infinitum;* and so demonstration is subverted. But if the second, those things which are self-evident will become the starting points [and fundamental grounds] of demonstration.

In point of fact, the philosophers admit that the first principles of all things are indemonstrable. So that if there is demonstration at all, there is an absolute necessity that there be something that is self-evident, which is called primary and indemonstrable.

Consequently all demonstration is traced up to indemonstrable faith.

It will also turn out that there are other starting points for demonstrations, after the source which takes its rise in faith,—the things which appear clearly to sensation and understanding. For the phenomena of sensation are simple, and incapable of being decompounded; but those of understanding are simple, rational, and primary. But those produced from them are compound, but no less clear and reliable, and having more to do with the reasoning faculty than the first. For therefore the peculiar native power of reason, which we all have by nature, deals with agreement and disagreement. If, then, any argument be found to be of such a kind, as from points already believed to be capable of producing belief in what is not yet believed, we shall aver that this is the very essence of demonstration.

Now it is affirmed that the nature of demonstration, as that of belief, is twofold: that which produces in the souls of the hearers persuasion merely, and that which produces knowledge.

If, then, one begins with the things which are evident to sensation and understanding, and then draw the proper conclusion, he truly demonstrates. But if [he begin] with things which are only probable and not primary, that is evident neither to sense nor understanding, and if he draw the right conclusion, he will syllogize indeed, but not produce a scientific demonstration; but if [he draw] not the right conclusion, he will not syllogize at all.

Now demonstration differs from analysis. For each one of the points demonstrated, is demonstrated by means of points that are demonstrated; those having been previously demonstrated by others; till we get back to those which are self-evident, or to those evident to sense and to understanding; which is called Analysis. But demonstration is, when the point in question reaches us through all the intermediate steps. The man, then, who practices demonstration, ought to give great attention to the truth, while he disregards the terms of the premises, whether you call them axioms, or premises, or assumptions. Similarly, also, special attention must be paid to what suppositions a conclusion is based on; while he may be quite careless as to whether one choose to term it a conclusive or syllogistic proposition.

For I assert that these two things must be attended to by the man who would demonstrate—to assume true premises, and to draw from them the legitimate conclusion, which some also call "the inference," as being what is inferred from the premises.

Now in each proposition respecting a question there must be different premises, related, however, to the proposition laid down; and what is advanced must be reduced to definition. And this definition must be admitted by all. But when premises irrelevant to the proposition to be established are assumed, it is impossible to arrive at any right result; the entire proposition—which is also called the question of its nature—being ignored.

In all questions, then, there is something which is previously known,—that which being self-evident is believed without demonstration; which must be made the starting point in their investigation, and the criterion of apparent results.

CHAPTER IV.—TO PREVENT AMBIGUITY, WE MUST BEGIN WITH CLEAR DEFINITION.

For every question is solved from pre-existing knowledge. And the knowledge pre-existing of each object of investigation is sometimes merely of the essence, while its functions are unknown (as of stones, and plants, and animals, of whose operations we are ignorant), or [the knowledge] of the properties, or powers, or (so to speak) of the qualities inherent in the objects. And sometimes we may know some one or more of those powers or properties,— as, for example, the desires and affections of the soul,—and be ignorant of the essence, and make it the object of investigation. But in many instances, our understanding having assumed all these, the question is, in which of the essences do they thus inhere; for it is after forming conceptions of both—that is, both of essence and operation—in our mind, that we proceed to the question. And there are also some objects, whose operations, along with their essences, we know, but are ignorant of their modifications.

Such, then, is the method of the discovery [of truth]. For we must begin with the knowledge of the questions to be discussed. For often the form of the expression deceives and confuses and disturbs the mind, so that it is not easy to discover to what class the thing is to be referred; as, for example, whether the fetus be an animal. For, having a conception of an animal and a fetus, we inquire if it be the case that the fetus is an animal; that is, if the substance which is in the foetal state possesses the power of motion, and of sensation besides. So that the inquiry is regarding functions and sensations in a substance previously known. Consequently the man who proposes the question is to be first asked, what he calls an animal. Especially is this to be done whenever we find the same term applied to various purposes; and we must examine whether what is signified by the term is disputed, or admitted by all. For were one to say that he calls whatever grows and is fed an animal, we shall have again to ask further, whether he considered plants to be animals; and then, after declaring himself to this effect, he must show what it is which is in the foetal state, and is nourished.

For Plato calls plants animals, as partaking of the third species of life alone, that of appetency. But Aristotle, while he thinks that plants are possessed of a life of vegetation and nutrition, does not consider it proper to call them animals; for that alone, which possesses the other life—that of sensation—he considers warrantable to be called an animal. The Stoics do not call the power of vegetation, life.

Now, on the man who proposes the question denying that plants are animals, we shall show that he affirms what contradicts himself. For, having defined the animal by the fact of its nourishment and growth, but having asserted that a plant is not an animal, it appears that he says nothing else than that what is nourished and grows is both an animal and not an animal.

Let him, then, say what he wants to learn. Is it whether what is in the womb grows and is nourished, or is it whether it possesses any sensation or movement by impulse? For, according to Plato, the plant is animate, and an animal; but, according to Aristotle, not an animal, for it wants sensation, but is animate. Therefore, according to him, an animal is an animate sentient being. But according to the Stoics, a plant is neither animate nor an animal; for an animal is an animate being. If, then, an animal is animate, and life is sentient nature, it is plain that what is animate is sentient. If, then, he who has put the question, being again interrogated if he still calls the animal in the foetal state an animal on account of its being nourished and growing, he has got his answer.

But were he to say that the question he asks is, whether the fetus is already sentient, or capable of moving itself in consequence of any impulse, the investigation of the matter becomes clear, the fallacy in the name no longer remaining.

But if he do not reply to the interrogation, and will not say what he means, or in respect of what consideration it is that he applies the term "animal" in propounding the question, but bids us define it ourselves, let him be noted as disputatious.

But as there are two methods, one by question and answer, and the other the method of exposition, if he decline the former, let him listen to us, while we expound all that bears on the problem. Then when we have done, he may treat of each point in turn. But if he attempt to interrupt the investigation by putting questions, he plainly does not want to hear.

But if he choose to reply, let him first be asked, To what thing he applies the name, animal. And when he has answered this, let him be again asked, what, in his view, the fetus means, whether that which is in the womb, or things already formed and living; and again, if the fetus means the seed deposited, or if it is only when members and a shape are formed that the name of embryos is to be applied. And on his replying to this, it is proper that the point in hand be reasoned out to a conclusion, in due order, and taught.

But if he wishes us to speak without him answering, let him hear. Since you will not say in what sense you allege what you have propounded (for I would not have thus engaged in a discussion about meanings, but I would now have looked at the things themselves), know that you have done just as if you had propounded the question, Whether a dog were an animal?
For I might have rightly said, Of what dog do you speak? For I shall speak of the land dog and the sea dog, and the constellation in heaven, and of Diogenes too, and all the other dogs in order. For I could not divine whether you inquire about all or about someone. What you shall do subsequently is to learn now, and say distinctly what it is that your question is about. Now if you are shuffling about names, it is plain to everybody that the name *fetus* is neither an animal nor a plant, but a name, and a sound, and a body, and a being, and anything and everything rather than an animal. And if it is this that you have propounded, you are answered.

But neither is that which is denoted by the name *fetus* an animal. But that is incorporeal, and may be called a thing and a notion, and everything rather than an animal. The nature of an animal is different. For it was clearly shown respecting the very point in question, I mean the nature of the embryo, of what sort it is. The question respecting the meanings expressed by the name animal is different.

I say, then, if you affirm that an animal is what has the power of sensation and of moving itself from appetency, that an animal is not simply what moves through appetency and is possessed of sensation. For it is also capable of sleeping, or, when the objects of sensation are not present, of not exercising the power of sensation. But the natural power of appetency or of sensation is the mark of an animal. For something of this nature is indicated by these things. First, if the fetus is not capable of sensation or motion from appetency; which is the point proposed for consideration. Another point is; if the fetus is capable of ever exercising the power of sensation or moving through appetency. In which sense no one makes it a question, since it is evident.

But the question was, whether the embryo is already an animal, or still a plant. And then the name animal was reduced to definition, for the sake of perspicuity. But having discovered that it is distinguished from what is not an animal by sensation and motion from appetency; we again separated this from its adjuncts; asserting that it was one thing for that to be such *potentially,* which is not yet possessed of the power of sensation and motion, but will sometime be so, and another thing to be already so *actually;* and in the case of such, it is one thing to exert its powers, another to be able to exert them, but to be at rest or asleep. And this is the question.

For the embryo is not to be called an animal from the fact that it is nourished; which is the allegation of those who turn aside from the essence of the question, and apply their minds to what happens otherwise. But in the case of all conclusions alleged to be found out, demonstration is applied in common, which is discourse (λόγος), establishing one thing from others. But the grounds from which the point in question is to be established, must be admitted and known by the learner. And the foundation of all these is what is evident to sense and to intellect.

Accordingly the primary demonstration is composed of all these. But the demonstration which, from points already demonstrated thereby, concludes some other point, is no less reliable than the former. It cannot be termed primary, because the conclusion is not drawn from primary principles as premises.

The first species, then, of the different kinds of questions, which are three, has been exhibited—I mean that, in which the essence being known, some one of its powers or properties is unknown. The second variety of propositions was that in which we all know the powers and properties, but do not know the essence; as, for example, in what part of the body is the principal faculty of the soul.

CHAPTER V.—APPLICATION OF DEMONSTRATION TO SCEPTICAL SUSPENSE OF JUDGMENT.

Now the same treatment which applies to demonstration applies also to the following question.

Some, for instance, say that there cannot be several originating causes for one animal. It is impossible that there can be several homogeneous originating causes of an animal; but that there should be several heterogeneous, is not absurd.

Suppose the Pyrrhonian suspense of judgment, as they say, [the idea] that nothing is certain: it is plain that, beginning with itself, it first invalidates itself. It either grants that something is true, that you are not to suspend your judgment on all things; or it persists in saying that there is nothing true. And it is evident, that first it will not be true. For it either affirms what is true or it does not affirm what is true. But if it affirms what is true, it concedes, though unwillingly, that something is true. And if it does not affirm what is true, it leaves true what it wished to do away with. For, in so far as the skepticism which demolishes is proved false, in so far the positions which are being demolished, are proved true; like the dream which says that all dreams are false. For in confuting itself, it is confirmatory of the others.

And, in fine, if it is true, it will make a beginning with itself, and not be skepticism of anything else but of itself first. Then if [such a man] apprehends that he is a man, or that he is skeptical, it is evident that he is not skeptical. And how shall he reply to the interrogation? For he is evidently no sceptic in respect to this. Nay, he affirms even that he does doubt.

And if we must be persuaded to suspend our judgment in regard to everything, we shall first suspend our judgment in regard to our suspense of judgment itself, whether we are to credit it or not.

And if this position is true, that we do not know what is true, then absolutely nothing is allowed to be true by it. But if he will say that even this is questionable, whether we know what is true; by this very statement he grants that truth is knowable, in the very act of appearing to establish the doubt respecting it.

But if a philosophical sect is a leaning toward dogmas, or, according to some, a leaning to a number of dogmas which have consistency with one another and with phenomena, tending to a right life; and dogma is a logical conception, and conception is a state and assent of the mind: not merely sceptics, but everyone who dogmatizes is accustomed in certain things to suspend his judgment, either through want of strength of mind, or want of clearness in the things, or equal force in the reasons.

CHAPTER VI.—DEFINITIONS, GENERA, AND SPECIES.

The introductions and sources of questions are about these points and in them.

But before definitions, and demonstrations, and divisions, it must be propounded in what ways the question is stated; and equivocal terms are to be treated; and synonyms stated accurately according to their significations.

Then it is to be inquired whether the proposition belongs to those points, which are considered in relation to others, or is taken by itself. Further, If it is, what it is, what happens to it; or thus, also, if it is, what it is, why it is. And to the consideration of these points, the knowledge of Particulars and Universals, and the Antecedents and the Differences, and their divisions, contribute.

Now, Induction aims at generalization and definition; and the divisions are the species, and what a thing is, and the individual. The contemplation of the How adduces the assumption of what is peculiar; and doubts bring the particular differences and the demonstrations, and otherwise augment the speculation and its consequences; and the result of the whole is scientific knowledge and truth.

Again, the summation resulting from Division becomes Definition. For Definition is adopted before division and after: before, when it is admitted or stated; after, when it is demonstrated. And by Sensation the Universal is summed up from the Particular. For the starting point of Induction is Sensation; and the end is the Universal.

Induction, accordingly, shows not *what* a thing is, but *that* it is, or is not. Division shows what it is; and Definition similarly with Division teaches the essence and what a thing is, but not if it is; while Demonstration explains the three points, *if* it is, *what* it is, and *why* it is.

There are also Definitions which contain the Cause. And since it may be known when we see, when we see the Cause; and Causes are four—the matter, the moving power, the species, the end; Definition will be fourfold.

Accordingly we must first take the genus, in which are the points that are nearest those above; and after this the next difference. And the succession of differences, when cut and divided, completes the "What it is." There is no necessity for expressing all the differences of each thing, but those which form the species.

Geometrical analysis and synthesis are similar to logical division and definition; and by division we get back to what is simple and more elementary. We divide, therefore, the genus of what is proposed for consideration into the species contained in it; as, in the case of man, we divide animal, which is the genus, into the species that appear in it, the mortal, and the immortal. And thus, by continually dividing those genera that seem to be compound into the simpler species, we arrive at the point which is the subject of investigation, and which is incapable of further division.

For, after dividing "the animal" into mortal and immortal, then into terrestrial and aquatic; and the terrestrial again into those who fly and those who walk; and so dividing the species which is nearest to what is sought, which also contains what is sought, we arrive by division at the simplest species, which contains nothing else, but what is sought alone.

For again we divide that which walks into rational and irrational; and then selecting from the species, apprehended by division, those next to man, and combining them into one formula, we state the definition of a man, who is an animal, mortal, terrestrial, walking, rational.

Whence Division furnishes the class of matter, seeking for the definition the simplicity of the name; and the definition of the artisan and maker, by composition and construction, presents the knowledge of the thing as it is; not of those things of which we have general notions. To these notions we say that explanatory expressions belong. For to these notions, also, divisions are applicable.

Now one Division divides that which is divided into species, as a genus; and another into parts, as a whole; and another into accidents.

The division, then, of a whole into the parts, is, for the most part, conceived with reference to magnitude; that into the accidents can never be entirely explicated, if, necessarily, essence is inherent in each of the existences.

Whence both these divisions are to be rejected, and only the division of the genus into species is approved, by which both the identity that is in the genus is characterized, and the diversity which subsists in the specific differences.

The species is always contemplated in a part. On the other hand, however, if a thing is part of another, it will not be also a species. For the hand is a part of a man, but it is not a species. And the genus exists in the species. For [the genus] is both in man and the ox. But the whole is not in the parts. For the man is not in his feet. Wherefore also the species is more important than the part; and whatever things are predicated of the genus will be all predicated of the species.

It is best, then, to divide the genus into two, if not into three species. The species then being divided more generically, are characterized by sameness and difference. And then being divided, they are characterized by the points generically indicated.

For each of the species is either an essence; as when we say, Some substances are corporeal and some incorporeal; or how much, or what relation, or where, or when, or doing, or suffering.

One, therefore, will give the definition of whatever he possesses the knowledge of; as one can by no means be acquainted with that which he cannot embrace and define in speech. And in consequence of ignorance of the definition, the result is, that many disputes and deceptions arise. For if he that knows the thing has the knowledge of it in his mind, and can explain by words what he conceives; and if the explanation of the thought is definition; then he that knows the thing must of necessity be able also to give the definition.

Now in definitions, difference is assumed, which, in the definition, occupies the place of sign. The faculty of laughing, accordingly, being added to the definition of man, makes the whole—a rational, mortal, terrestrial, walking, laughing animal. For the things added by way of difference to the definition are the signs of the properties of things; but do not show the nature of the things themselves. Now they say that the difference is the assigning of what is peculiar; and as that which has the difference differs from all the rest, that which belongs to it alone, and is predicated conversely of the thing, must in definitions be assumed by the first genus as principal and fundamental.

Accordingly, in the larger definitions the number of the species that are discovered are in the ten Categories; and in the least, the principal points of the nearest species being taken, mark the essence and nature of the thing. But the least consists of three, the genus and two essentially necessary species. And this is done for the sake of brevity.

We say, then, Man is the laughing animal. And we must assume that which pre-eminently happens to what is defined, or its peculiar virtue, or its peculiar function, and the like.

Accordingly, while the definition is explanatory of the essence of the thing, it is incapable of accurately comprehending its nature. By means of the principal species, the definition makes an exposition of the essence, and almost has the essence in the quality.

CHAPTER VII.—ON THE CAUSES OF DOUBT OR ASSENT.

The causes productive of skepticism are two things principally. One is the changefulness and instability of the human mind, whose nature it is to generate dissent, either that of one with another, or that of people with themselves. And the second is the discrepancy which is in things; which, as to be expected, is calculated to be productive of skepticism.

For, being unable either to believe in all views, on account of their conflicting nature; or to disbelieve all, because that which says that all are untrustworthy is included in the number of those that are so; or to believe some and disbelieve others on account of the equipoise, we are led to skepticism.

But among the principal causes of skepticism is the instability of the mind, which is productive of dissent. And dissent is the proximate cause of doubt. Whence life is full of tribunals and councils; and, in fine, of selection in what is said to be good and bad; which are the signs of a mind in doubt, and halting through feebleness on account of conflicting matters. And there are libraries full of books, and compilations and treatises of those who differ in dogmas, and are confident that they themselves know the truth that there is in things.

CHAPTER VIII.—THE METHOD OF CLASSIFYING THINGS AND NAMES.

In language there are three things:—Names, which are primarily the symbols of conceptions, and by consequence also of subjects. Second, there are Conceptions, which are the likenesses and impressions of the subjects. Whence in all, the conceptions are the same; in consequence of the same impression being produced by the subjects in all. But the names are not so, on account of the difference of languages. And thirdly, the Subject-matters by which the Conceptions are impressed in us.

The names are reduced by grammar into the twenty-four general elements; for the elements must be determined. For of Particulars there is no scientific knowledge, seeing they are infinite. But it is the property of science to rest on general and defined principles. Whence also Particulars are resolved into Universals. And philosophic research is occupied with Conceptions and Real subjects. But since of these the Particulars are infinite, some elements have been found, under which every subject of investigation is brought; and if it be shown to enter into any one or more of the elements, we prove it to exist; but if it escape them all, that it does not exist.

Of things stated, some are stated without connection; as, for example, "man" and "runs," and whatever does not complete a sentence, which is either true or false. And of things stated in connection, some point out "essence," some "quality," some "quantity," some "relation," some "where," some "when," some "position," some "possession," some "action," some "suffering," which we call the elements of material things after the first principles. For these are capable of being contemplated by reason.

But immaterial things are capable of being apprehended by the mind alone, by primary application.

And of those things that are classed under the ten Categories, some are predicated by themselves (as the nine Categories), and others in relation to something.

And, again, of the things contained under these ten Categories, some are *Univocal,* as ox and man, as far as each is an animal. For those are Univocal terms, to both of which belongs the common name, animal; and the same principle, that is definition, that is animate essence. And Heteronyms are those which relate to the same subject under different names, as ascent or descent; for the way is the same whether upwards or downwards. And the other species of Heteronyms, as horse and black, are those which have a different name and definition from each other, and do not possess the same subject. But they are to be called different, not Heteronyms. And Polyonyms are those which have the same definition, but a different name, as, hanger, sword, scimitar. And Paronyms are those which are named from something different, as "manly" from "manliness."

Equivocal terms have the same name, but not the same definition, as man—both the animal and the picture. Of Equivocal terms, some receive their Equivocal name fortuitously, as Ajax, the Locrian, and the Salaminian; and some from intention; and of these, some from resemblance, as man both the living and the painted; and some from analogy, as the foot of Mount Ida, and our foot, because they are beneath; some from action, as the foot of a vessel, by which the vessel sails, and our foot, by which we move. Equivocal terms are designated from the same and to the same; as the book and scalpel are called surgical, both from the surgeon who uses them and with reference to the surgical matter itself.

The Stromata or Miscellanies

CHAPTER IX.—ON THE DIFFERENT KINDS OF CAUSE.

Of Causes, some are Procatarctic and some Synectic, some Co-operating, some Causes *sine quâ non*.

Those that afford the occasion of the origin of anything first, are Procatarctic; as beauty is the cause of love to the licentious; for when seen by them, it alone produces the amorous inclination, but not necessarily.

Causes are Synectic (which are also univocally perfect of themselves) whenever a cause is capable of producing the effect of itself, independently.

Now all the causes may be shown in order in the case of the learner. The father is the Procatarctic cause of learning, the teacher the Synectic, and the nature of the learner the cooperating cause, and time holds the relation of the Cause *sine quâ non*.

Now that is properly called a cause which is capable of effecting anything actively; since we say that steel is capable of cutting, not merely while cutting, but also while not cutting. Thus, then, the capability of causing (τὸ παρεκτικόν) signifies both; both that which is now acting, and that which is not yet acting, but which possesses the power of acting.

Some, then, say that causes are properties of bodies; and others of incorporeal substances; others say that the body is properly speaking cause, and that what is incorporeal is so only catachrestically, and a quasi-cause. Others, again, reverse matters, saying that corporeal substances are properly causes, and bodies are so improperly; as, for example, that cutting, which is an action, is incorporeal, and is the cause of cutting which is an action and incorporeal, and, in the case of bodies, of being cut,—as in the case of the sword and what is cut [by it].

The cause of things is predicated in a threefold manner. One, What the cause is, as the statuary; a second, Of what it is the cause of becoming, a statue; and a third, To what it is the cause, as, for example, the material: for he is the cause to the brass of becoming a statue. The being produced, and the being cut, which are causes to what they belong, being actions, are incorporeal.

According to which principle, causes belong to the class of predicates (κατηγορημάτων), or, as others say, of *dicta* (λεκτῶν) (for Cleanthes and Archedemus call predicates *dicta*); or rather, some causes will be assigned to the class of predicates, as that which is cut, whose case is to be cut; and some to that of axioms,—as, for example, that of a ship being made, whose case again is, that a ship is constructing. Now Aristotle denominates the name of such things as a house, a ship, burning, cutting, an appellative. But the case is allowed to be incorporeal. Therefore that sophism is solved thus: What you say passes through your mouth. Which is true. You name a house. Therefore a house passes through your mouth. Which is false. For we do not speak the house, which is a body, but the case, in which the house is, which is incorporeal.

And we say that the house-builder builds the house, in reference to that which is to be produced. So we say that the cloak is woven; for that which makes is the indication of the operation. That which makes is not the attribute of one, and the cause that of another, but of the same, both in the case of the cloak and of the house. For, in as far as one is the cause of anything being produced, in so far is he also the maker of it. Consequently, the cause, and that which makes, and that through which (δἰ ὅ), are the same. Now, if anything is "a cause" and "that which effects," it is certainly also "that through which." But if a thing is "that through which," it does not by any means follow that it is also "the cause." Many things, for instance, concur in one result, through which the end is reached; but all are not causes. For Medea would not have killed her children, had she not been enraged. Nor would she have been enraged, had she not been jealous. Nor would she have been this, if she had not loved. Nor would she have loved, had not Jason sailed to Colchi. Nor would this have taken place, had the Argo not been built. Nor would this have taken place, had not the timbers been cut from Pelion. For though in all these things there is the case of "that through which," they are not all "causes" of the murder of the children, but only Medea was the cause. Wherefore, that which does not hinder does not act. Wherefore, that which does not hinder is not a cause, but that which hinders is. For it is in acting and doing something that the cause is conceived.

Besides, what does not hinder is separated from what takes place; but the cause is related to the event. That, therefore, which does not hinder cannot be a cause. Wherefore, then, it is accomplished, because that which can hinder is not present. Causation is then predicated in four ways: The efficient cause, as the statuary; and the material, as the brass; and the form, as the character; and the end, as the honor of the Gymnasiarch.

The relation of the cause *sine quâ non* is held by the brass in reference to the production of the statue; and likewise it is a [true] cause. For everything without which the effect is incapable of being produced, is of necessity a cause; but a cause not absolutely. For the cause *sine quâ non* is not Synectic, but Co-operative. And everything that acts produces the effect, in conjunction with the aptitude of that which is acted on. For the cause disposes. But each thing is affected according to its natural constitution; the aptitude being causative, and occupying the place of causes *sine quâ non*. Accordingly, the cause is inefficacious without the aptitude; and is not a cause, but a co-efficient. For all causation is conceived in action. Now the earth could not make itself, so that it could not be the cause of itself. And it were ridiculous to say that the fire was not the cause of the burning, but the logs,—or the sword of the cutting, but the flesh,—or the strength of the antagonist the cause of the athlete being vanquished, but his own weakness.

The Synectic cause does not require time. For the cautery produces pain at the instant of its application to the flesh. Of Procatarctic causes, some require time till the effect be produced, and others do not require it, as the case of fracture.

Are not these called independent of time, not by way of privation, but of diminution, as that which is sudden, not that which has taken place without time?

Every cause, apprehended by the mind as a cause, is occupied with something, and is conceived in relation to something; that is, some effect, as the sword for cutting; and to some object, as possessing an aptitude, as the fire to the wood. For it will not burn steel. The cause belongs to the things which have relation to something. For it is conceived in its relation to another thing. So that we apply our minds to the two, that we may conceive the cause as a cause.

The same relation holds with the creator, and maker, and father. A thing is not the cause of itself. Nor is one his own father. For so the first would become the second. Now the cause acts and affects. That which is produced by the cause is acted on and is affected. But the same thing taken by itself cannot both act and be affected, nor can one be son and father. And otherwise the cause precedes in being what is done by it, as the sword, the cutting. And the same thing cannot precede at the same instant as to matter, as it is a cause, and at the same time, also, be after and posterior as the effect of a cause.

Now *being* differs from *becoming*, as the cause from the effect, the father from the son. For the same thing cannot both *be* and *become* at the same instant; and consequently it is not the cause of itself. Things are not causes of one another, but causes to each other. For the splenetic affection preceding is not the cause of fever, but of the occurrence of fever; and the fever which precedes is not the cause of spleen, but of the affection increasing.

Thus also the virtues are causes to each other, because on account of their mutual correspondence they cannot be separated. And the stones in the arch are causes of its continuing in this category, but are not the causes of one another. And the teacher and the learner are to one another causes of progressing as respects the predicate.

And mutual and reciprocal causes are predicated, some of the same things, as the merchant and the retailer are causes of gain; and sometimes one of one thing and others of another, as the sword and the flesh; for the one is the cause to the flesh of being cut, and the flesh to the sword of cutting. [It is well said,] "An eye for an eye, life for life." For he who has wounded another mortally, is the cause to him of death, or of the occurrence of death. But on being mortally wounded by him in turn, he has had him as a cause in turn, not in respect of being a cause to him, but in another respect. For he becomes the cause of death to him, not that it was death returned the mortal stroke, but the wounded man himself. So that he was the cause of one thing, and had another cause. And he who has done wrong becomes the cause to another, to him who has been wronged. But the law which enjoins punishment to be inflicted is the cause not of injury, but to the one of retribution, to the other of discipline. So that the things which are causes, are not causes to each other as causes.

It is still asked, if many things in conjunction become many causes of one thing. For the men who pull together are the causes of the ship being drawn down; but along with others, unless what is a joint cause be a cause.

Others say, if there are many causes, each by itself becomes the cause of one thing. For instance, the virtues, which are many, are causes of happiness, which is one; and of warmth and pain, similarly, the causes are many. Are not, then, the many virtues one in power, and the sources of warmth and of pain so, also? and does not the multitude of the virtues, being one in kind, become the cause of the one result, happiness?

But, in truth, Procatarctic causes are more than one both generically and specifically; as, for example, cold, weakness, fatigue, dyspepsia, drunkenness, generically, of any disease; and specifically, of fever. But Synectic causes are so, generically alone, and not also specifically.

For of pleasant odor, which is one thing genetically, there are many specific causes, as frankincense, rose, crocus, styrax, myrrh, ointment. For the rose has not the same kind of sweet fragrance as myrrh.

And the same thing becomes the cause of contrary effects; sometimes through the magnitude of the cause and its power, and sometimes in consequence of the susceptibility of that on which it acts. According to the nature of the force, the same string, according to its tension or relaxation, gives a shrill or deep sound. And honey is sweet to those who are well, and bitter to those who are in fever, according to the state of susceptibility of those who are affected. And one and the same wine inclines some to rage, and others to merriment.
And the same sun melts wax and hardens clay.

Further, of causes, some are apparent; others are grasped by a process of reasoning; others are occult; others are inferred analogically.

And of causes that are occult, some are occult temporarily, being hidden at one time, and at another again seen clearly; and some are occult by nature, and capable of becoming at no time visible. And of those who are so by nature, some are capable of being apprehended; and these some would not call occult, being apprehended by analogy, through the medium of signs, as, for example, the symmetry of the passages of the senses, which are contemplated by reason. And some are not capable of being apprehended; which cannot in any mode fall under apprehension; which are by their very definition occult.

Now some are Procatarctic, some Synectic, some Joint-causes, some Co-operating causes. And there are some according to nature, some beyond nature. And there are some of disease and by accident, some of sensations, some of the greatness of these, some of times and of seasons.

Procatarctic causes being removed, the effect remains. But a Synectic cause is that, which being present, the effect remains, and being removed, the effect is removed.

The Synectic is also called by the synonymous expression "perfect in itself." Since it is of itself sufficient to produce the effect.

And if the cause manifests an operation sufficient in itself, the co-operating cause indicates assistance and service along with the other. If, accordingly, it effects nothing, it will not be called even a co-operating cause; and if it does effect something, it is wholly the cause of this, that is, of what is produced by it. That is, then, a co-operating cause, which being present, the effect was produced—the visible visibly, and the occult invisibly.

The Joint-cause belongs also to the genus of causes, as a fellow-soldier is a soldier, and as a fellow-youth is a youth.

The Co-operating cause further aids the Synectic, in the way of intensifying what is produced by it. But the Joint-cause does not fall under the same notion. For a thing may be a Joint-cause, though it be not a Synectic cause. For the Joint-cause is conceived in conjunction with another, which is not capable of producing the effect by itself, being a cause along with a cause. And the Co-operating cause differs from the Joint-cause in this particular, that the Joint-cause produces the effect in that which by itself does not act. But the Co-operating cause, while effecting nothing by itself, yet by its accession to that which acts by itself, cooperates with it, in order to the production of the effect in the intensest degree. But especially is that which becomes co-operating from being Procatarctic, effective in intensifying the force of the cause.

Elucidations.

I.
(Scripture, cap. i. p. 558.)

On the 18th of July, 1870, Pius the Ninth, by the bull *Pastor Æternus* proclaiming himself *infallible,* and defining that every Roman bishop from the times of the apostles were equally so, placed himself in conflict, not merely with Holy Scripture (which repeatedly proves the fallibility of St. Peter himself, when speaking apart from his fellow-apostles), but with the torrent of all antiquity. Yes, and with the great divines of his own communion, such as Bossuet; including divers pontiffs, and the Gallicans generally. But note, here, what St. Clement says of the Holy Scripture, and of the search after truth. Is it conceivable, that he knew of any living infallible oracle, when he wrote this book, never once hinting the existence of any such source of absolute gnostic perfection? A like ignorance of such an oracle characterizes Vincent of Lerins, the great expounder of the rule of faith as understood by the four great councils of antiquity.

Clearly, Clement had never seen in Irenæus the meaning read into his words by the modern flatterers of the Roman See. The discovery of 1870 comes just eighteen centuries too late for practical purposes.

II.
(Of Book the Eighth, note 1, p. 567.)

In the place of this book, according to some mss., Photius found the tract τίς ὁ σωζόμενοςπλούσιος; in other mss., a book beginning as this does. He accused the *Stromata* of unsound opinions; but, this censure not being supported by anything we possess, some imagine that the eighth book is lost, and that it is no great loss after all. A rash judgment as to its value; but possibly this, which is *called* the eighth book, is from the lost *Hypotyposes*. Kaye's suggestion is, that, as the seventh book closed with a promise of something quite fresh, we may discover it in this contribution towards forming his Gnostic, to further knowledge.

It should be regarded as of great importance, that Christianity appears as the friend of all knowledge, and of human culture, from the very start. To our author's versatile genius, much credit is due for the elements out of which Christian universities took their rise.

www.ingramcontent.com/pod-product-compliance
Lightning Source LLC
Chambersburg PA
CBHW052005070526
44584CB00016B/1628